FOURTH EDITION

Cognitive Development

John H. Flavell
Stanford University

Patricia H. Miller
University of Florida

Scott A. Miller
University of Florida

Prentice
Hall

Upper Saddle River, New Jersey 07458

Library of Congress Cataloging-in-Publication Data

Flavell, John H.
    Cognitive development/John H. Flavell, Patricia H. Miller, Scott A. Miller.—4th ed.
      p. cm.
    Includes bibliographical references and index.
    ISBN 0-13-791575-6
     1. Cognition in children. I. Miller, Patricia H. II. Miller, Scott A. III. Title.

BF723.C5 F62 2002
155.4'13—dc21

00-051593

VP, Editorial Director: Laura Pearson
Senior Acquistions Editor: Jennifer Gilliland
Editorial Assistant: Nicole Girrbach
Managing Editor: Mary Rottino
Production Liaison: Fran Russello
Editorial/Production Supervision: Marianne Hutchinson (Pine Tree Composition, Inc.)
Prepress and Manufacturing Buyer: Tricia Kenny
Art Director: Jayne Conte
Cover Designer: Bruce Kenselaar
Director, Image Resource Center: Melinda Lee Reo
Manager, Right & Permissions: Kay Dellosa
Image Specialist: Beth Boyd
Photo Researcher Karen Pugliano
Senior Marketing Manager: Sharon Cosgrove

This book was set in 10/11 Times Roman by Pine Tree Composition, Inc.,
and was printed and bound by Courier Companies, Inc.
The cover was printed by Phoenix Color Corp.

 ©2002, 1993, 1985, 1977 by Pearson Education, Inc.
Upper Saddle River, New Jersey 07458

Reprinted with corrections June, 2002.

Printed in the United States of America
10 9 8 7 6 5

ISBN 0-13-791575-6

Prentice-Hall International (UK) Limited, *London*
Prentice-Hall of Australia Pty. Limited, *Sydney*
Prentice-Hall Canada Inc., *Toronto*
Prentice-Hall Hispanoamericana, S. A., *Mexico*
Prentice-Hall of India Private Limited, New Delhi
Prentice-Hall of Japan, Inc., *Tokyo*
Pearson Education Asia Pte. Ltd, *Singapore*
Editora Prentice-Hall do Brasil, Ltda., *Rio de Janeiro*

Contents

—⇒◆⇐—

Preface

⟫◈⟪

The intended audience for this book is anyone who has reason to read about human cognitive development. We hope and expect that it will be comprehensible and interesting to readers with a very wide range of backgrounds: people interested in the topic but with little or no background in psychology; undergraduate and graduate students in general, developmental, cognitive, educational, and perhaps social psychology, various fields of education, and possibly other social sciences; perhaps even postdoctoral professionals in these areas. It certainly should be suitable as a text for either an undergraduate or a graduate course.

We include several features to make the book useful to a wide variety of readers. We cite references in the text, especially secondary sources that would provide quick access to much of the primary research literature in an area. Some readers will find these quite useful; others obviously will not. On the other side, we have explained the meaning of most technical terms used, even those that people with only a little background in psychology might know. We try to give a sense of the issues in the field, which we hope conveys the big picture of cognitive development. We have also tried to make the exposition straightforward and readable, and perhaps a little lighter and less formal than textbooks sometimes are. Our goal is to tell the story of children's thinking and how it develops. We personally do not enjoy reading most textbooks and therefore would like this one to be, if not actually enjoyable, at least not wholly unenjoyable.

This edition of the book differs from the third edition in a number of ways. We have thoroughly updated the chapters. Because of the "baby boom" in research on infancy we have expanded that chapter into two—one on perception and one on cognition. This emphasis reflects the dramatic surge of interest in early competencies in recent years. We reorganized two previously chronological chapters on preschool and grade school/adolescence into two new chapters. We labeled one "Representation and Concepts" and the other "Reasoning and Problem Solving." All of the information on theory of mind now is in the (formerly) social cognition chapter. Thus, the new edition is completely topically organized, after the two chapters on infancy that set the stage for later development.

Other changes include additional theoretical frameworks in the introductory chapter. In keeping with recent trends in the field, the book has less emphasis on Piaget and his developmental-stages conception of cognitive growth, and more emphasis on information-processing (including connectionism), sociocultural, theory-change, neo-Piagetian, neuroscience, and constraint approaches. We give special attention to new or rejuvenated areas, such as toddlers' representational abilities, young children's theories of mind, autobiographical memory, suggestibility, variability in the use of strategies, and biological or other kinds of constraints on cognitive development.

More generally we hope to convey both the fascinating nature of children's thinking and the excitement and change in work in this area. Knowledge about cognitive development is very much a work in progress.

We wish to thank various people who offered suggestions for this edition or the previous one: Brian Ackerman, Joseph Beato, Susan Carey, Darlene DeMarie, M Jeffrey Farrar, Derek Montgomery, Marylynn Pfeiffer, James Probert, Carolyn Shantz, and Allison Suffield. We also thank Cynthia Hardin for her assistance with the preparation of this edition, as well as Jennifer Gilliland at Prentice Hall.

John H. Flavell
Patricia H. Miller
Scott A. Miller

1

Introduction

———◆———

A DEFINITION OF COGNITION

The really interesting concepts of this world have the nasty habit of avoiding our most determined attempts to pin them down, to make them say something definite and then make them stick to it. Their meanings perversely remain multiple, ambiguous, imprecise, and above all unstable and open—open to argument and disagreement, to sometimes drastic reformulation and redefinition, and to the introduction of new and often unsettling instances and examples of the concept. It is perhaps not a bad thing that our prize concepts have this kind of complexity and instability (some might call it richness and creativity). In any event, they do seem to have these properties, and therefore we would be wise not to expend too much of our time and energy trying to fix them in formal definition.

So it is with that concept called *cognition,* the development of which is the subject of this book. Obviously it is important here to communicate some ideas and images about the nature of cognition, but it is neither possible nor desirable to define it and limit its meaning in any precise or inflexible fashion.

The traditional image of cognition tends to restrict it to the fancier, more unequivocally "intelligent" processes and products of the human mind. This image in-

1

cludes such higher mental-processes types of psychological entities as knowledge, consciousness, intelligence, thinking, imagining, creating, generating plans and strategies, reasoning, inferring, problem solving, conceptualizing, classifying and relating, symbolizing, and perhaps fantasizing and dreaming. Although some of these activities would surely be credited to the psychological repertoires of other animals, they nonetheless have a decidedly human-mind ring to them.

Although no contemporary psychologists would want to exclude any of these traditional components from the cognitive domain, they would feel it necessary to add some others. Certain components would have a somewhat humble, less purely cerebral-intellectual cast to them. Organized motor movements (especially in infants) and perception are two such components. As described in Chapters 2 and 3, even infants exhibit intelligent-looking patterns of motor and perceptual behavior. It would seem arbitrary in the extreme to christen children "cognitive" only after they had achieved the ability to engage in the more exalted forms of cerebration. Imagery, memory, attention, and learning are other cases in point. Other components might look more social-psychological than the word cognition usually connotes. Instances here would include all varieties of social cognition (that is, cognition directed at the world of human rather than nonhuman objects) and the social-communicative versus private-cognitive uses of language.

Once embarked on this course of broadening and restructuring the domain beyond the classical *higher mental processes,* it is very difficult to decide where to stop. One is finally led to ask, what psychological processes can*not* be described as cognitive in some nontrivial sense, or do *not* implicate cognition to a significant degree? The answer is that mental processes habitually intrude themselves into virtually *all* human psychological processes and activities, and consequently there is no really principled, nonarbitrary place to stop. To be sure, this book says little about such noncognitive-sounding things as personality, aggression, sex-role development, and so on. There are many *practical* reasons for slighting these and other topics, such as space limitations, lack of an adequate database in some cases, consideration for teachers' and readers' expectations about what a book with this title should contain, and sheer personal preferences. The point to be underscored, however, is that there is no *principled* justification for excluding them. What you know and think (cognition) obviously interacts in a very substantial and significant way with the sort of person you are (personality), to take but one example. Depending only on the state of existing theory and empirical evidence, a longer or shorter cognitive story could be told about virtually any phenomenon mentioned in an introductory psychology textbook. We only have a single head, after all, and it is firmly attached to the rest of the body.

The need for a broad and complex conception of cognition also lies in the complex interweaving of the various aspects of cognition in the tapestry of actual, real-time cognitive functioning. Each process plays a vital role in the operation and development of each other process, affecting it and being affected by it. This idea of mutual, two-way interactions among cognitive processes is an exceedingly important one. What you know affects and is affected by how you perceive; how you conceptualize or classify things influences the way you reason about them, and vice versa; and so on and on. If we pretend for purposes of psychological analysis that the human mind is a machine or device that carries out a variety of mental operations to achieve a variety of mental products, the present argument would be that it is a very highly organized device, one whose numerous "parts" are richly interconnected to one another. It is not a collection or aggregate of unrelated cognitive components, but rather a complexly organized *system* of interacting components. And this system will not stay put; it is always developing. It would be tedious to keep pointing out these interactions and their development throughout the book, but it would be well to bear in mind that they are ubiquitous in cognitive functioning.

PERSPECTIVES ON THE DEVELOPMENT OF THE HUMAN COGNITIVE SYSTEM

At present there are a number of views of the nature and development of cognition. The great Swiss psychologist Jean Piaget set out the first major theory of cognitive development and formulated the questions that cognitive developmentalists have tried to answer ever since. In fact many of the other perspectives we discuss sprang from a dissatisfaction with some aspect of Piaget's theory. We discuss neo-Piagetian, information-processing, biological, theory theory, dynamic systems, and sociocultural approaches. We refer back to these perspectives in later chapters when findings associated with them appear. These views are by no means incompatible, and many contemporary psychologists favor some blend of them. Because it is beyond the scope of this book to provide a satisfactory account of these approaches, we can only point out several salient features and then direct readers to further reading. For general sources that cover several of the approaches see Miller (2001) and Lerner (1998).

Each approach addresses the two main questions of cognitive development. First, what does children's thinking look like at various points throughout development (the description question)? Second, how does this development come about (the explanation question)?

Piaget

Jean Piaget's contributions to our knowledge of cognitive development have been nothing short of stupendous, both quantitatively and qualitatively. Moreover his ideas about cognitive growth are often very complex and difficult to grasp, even when presented as an integrated whole, at length and in full detail. Piaget's ideas are particularly prone to distortion, oversimplification, and general misunderstanding when one tries to integrate brief summaries of them within a more general narrative about the field, such as this book aims to be. Thus we encourage readers to do some supplementary reading (e.g., Beilin, 1992; Beilin & Fireman, 2000; Chapman, 1988; Flavell, 1963, 1996; Lourenco & Machado, 1996; Miller, 2001; Montangero & Maurice-Naville, 1997; Piaget, 1970).

Piaget's intellectual passion was to discover the nature of knowledge—what it looks like, where it comes from, how it functions, and how and why it develops. We now look through Piaget's eyes at how children's intellectual structures change through a variety of forms (stages) and how they function (his assimilation-accommodation model).

Stages of Development. Piaget saw consistencies in children's behaviors across different areas at each point in development that led him to posit stages of development. These stages are summarized in Table 1.1, and are described more

---

TABLE 1.1   Piaget's Periods of Cognitive Development

PERIOD	APPROXIMATE AGES (YRS)	DESCRIPTION
Sensorimotor	0–2	Infants understand the world by overtly acting on it. Their motor actions reflect sensorimotor schemes—generalized action patterns for understanding the world, such as a sucking scheme. Schemes gradually become more differentiated and integrated, and at the end of the period infants can form mental representations of reality.
Preoperational	2–7	Children can use representations (mental images, drawings, words, gestures) rather than just motor actions to think about objects and events. Thinking now is faster, more flexible and efficient, and more socially shared. Thinking is limited by egocentrism, a focus on perceptual states, reliance on appearances rather than underlying realities, and rigidity (lack of reversibility).
Concrete-operational	7–11	Children acquire operations—systems of internal mental actions that underlie logical thinking. These reversible, organized operations allow children to overcome the limitations of preoperational thought. Conservation, class-inclusion, perspective taking, and other concepts are acquired. Operations can be applied only to concrete objects—present or mentally represented.
Formal-operational	11–15	Mental operations can be applied to the possible and hypothetical as well as the real, to the future as well as the present, and to purely verbal or logical statements. Adolescents acquire scientific thinking, with its hypothetico-deductive reasoning, and logical reasoning with its interpropositional reasoning. They can understand highly abstract concepts.

fully in later chapters. The four stages involve moving from knowing the world through overt actions on it (*sensorimotor*), to more or less static representations of it with symbols (*preoperational*), to mental operations (actions) on present objects (*concrete operational*), to mental operations on operations (*formal operational*). The sensorimotor stage of infancy centers on forming simple sensorimotor representations of motor behaviors directed toward objects, for example, reaching and sucking. During the age span of approximately 2 to 7, preoperational children elaborate symbolic representations to form simple notions of causality and physical reality. The concrete operational years (approximately 7 to 11) are marked by more flexible mental manipulations, such as mentally reversing an event in the real world. Piaget's idea that external actions *turn into* internal mental ones is an exciting one that shows how very different looking sorts of thinking can reflect an underlying continuity during development. Finally formal operational thought (ages 11 to 15) displays the abstract, flexible, logical, scientific thinking found in adults (on good days). Thus mental (operations) are applied first to concrete present objects and events and later to mental operations themselves, the thoughts about thoughts of formal operations. In Piaget's theory each of these stages emerges from the previous stage, incorporates and transforms that stage, and prepares for the next stage. We return to specific concepts studied by Piaget in each stage in future chapters.

Assimilation-Accommodation as a Model of Cognitive Functioning. Piaget viewed human cognition as a specific form of biological *adaptation* of a complex organism to a complex environment. The cognitive system he envisaged is, however, an extremely active one. That is, it actively selects and interprets environmental information as it constructs its own knowledge. It does not passively copy the information just as it is presented to the senses. While of course taking account of the structure of the environment during knowledge seeking, the Piagetian mind always reconstrues and reinterprets that environment to make it fit in with its own existing mental framework. Thus the mind neither copies the world, passively accepting it as a ready-made given, nor does it ignore the world, autistically creating a private mental conception of it out of whole cloth. Rather the mind builds its knowledge structures by taking external data and interpreting them, transforming them, and reorganizing them. It therefore does indeed meet the environment in the process of constructing its knowledge, and consequently that knowledge is to a degree "realistic" or adaptive for the organism. However, Piaget made much of the idea that the mind meets the environment in an extremely active, self-directed way—meets it more than half way, as it were.

Cognition, like other forms of biological adaptation, always exhibits two simultaneous and complementary aspects, which Piaget called *assimilation* and *accommodation*. Although it is convenient to talk about them as if they were distinct and separate cognitive activities, it must be kept in mind that they are two indissociable aspects of the same basic adaptational process—two sides of the same cognitive coin. Assimilation essentially means applying what you already know. You interpret or construe external objects and events in terms of your own presently available and favored ways of thinking about things. The young child who pretends that a chip of wood is a boat is, in Piaget's terms, "assimilating" the wood chip to his mental concept of boat. The child incorporates the object within the whole structure of his knowledge of boats. In contrast, accommodation roughly means adjusting your knowledge in response to the special characteristics of an object or event. You notice and take cognitive account of the various real properties and relationships among properties of external objects and events. You become aware of the structural attributes of environmental data.

Assimilation, therefore, refers to the process of adapting external stimuli to one's own internal mental structures whereas accommodation refers to the converse or complementary process of adapting these mental structures to the structure of these same stimuli. In the more obviously biological adaptation of ingestion—digestion of food—organisms simultaneously accommodate to the particular structure of the food (chew hard or easy, digest with the help of this enzyme or that, depending on what the food is) and assimilate the food to their own physical structures (transform its appearance, convert it into energy, etc.). Similarly, in cognitive adaptations we can say that individuals simultaneously accommodate to the particular structures of the objects of their cognitions and assimilate those objects to their own cognitive structures.

As another example, suppose someone shows you a symmetrical blot of ink on a piece of paper, asks you what it reminds you of, and hears you say that it resembles a bat. Piaget's theory would say that you had cognitively accommodated to certain physical features of the blot and had used these as the basis for assimilating the ambiguous blot to your internal concept of a bat. It is important to recognize that you did not just passively and mindlessly scan the blot and "discover" a bat "that was really there." Without a preexisting, well-elaborated conception of bat in your cognitive repertoire, you would not have detected and integrated into a whole perceptual structure the particular constellation of blot features that you did. If the perceiver were a 1-year-old baby, with a belfry as yet devoid of bats, the perceiver would not see the blot in the same way that you did because, in a manner of speaking, the perceiver's mind's eye would differ from yours. Thus the kinds of assimilation that can occur are constrained by what you know.

Similarly, in the opposite direction, the kinds of accommodations you can make are limited and constrained by what is there that could be assimilated. Obviously if there were no bat-compatible physical properties in the blot to be accommodated to, there would be no assimilation of the blot to "bat"—that is, no perception of the blot as resembling that animal. If the ink blot took the form of a thin, straight line, for instance, there would naturally be no temptation to construe it as a bat (except perhaps of the baseball type).

Both assimilation and accommodation operate in any cognitive encounter with the environment. What you know already will greatly shape and constrain what environmental information you can detect and process, just as what you can detect and process will provide essential grist for the activation of present knowledge and the generation of new knowledge. To return to our earlier example, the wood chip likely would never metamorphize into a boat if it could not float and were not vaguely boat shaped.

Assimilation-Accommodation as a Model of Cognitive Development. The description of the assimilation-accommodation process in its nondevelopmental side includes hints about its developmental side—how it gradually might bring about cognitive development. Let us reconsider the wood-chip example. In the situation we are imagining, a young boy is playing with his toy boats in the bathtub. He suddenly notices in the corner of the soap dish a tiny fragment of wood from the broken pencil of a professor parent who always keeps a pencil nearby to jot down brilliant ideas. He picks it up, and after some deliberation (he has sailed many a boat, but nary a wood chip), gingerly places it in the water. Upon discovering that it floats, he adds it to his armada and emerges from his bath some time later a wiser as well as a cleaner child. The question is, in what way wiser, and through what sorts of wisdom-building (cognitive-developmental) processes?

Let us credit him, at the beginning of the bath, with a certain organized body of knowledge and certain abilities concerning the concrete, functional properties of toy boats, small, nondescript objects, and water. He knows much about their characteristic look and feel and also something of their characteristic reactions to his actions upon them. We could say that he has already achieved a certain level of cognitive development with respect to this microdomain of his everyday world and, consequently, in Piaget's terms he assimilates it and accommodates to it in specific ways that faithfully reflect this cognitive-developmental level. As a result of the new things he did and observed during this particular bath, however, that level will have changed ever so slightly, and consequently his future assimilations and accommodations within that microdomain will also have changed ever so slightly.

Let us suppose he has discovered (accommodation) some things he did not know before about what little pieces of wood can and cannot do (float rather than sink, make only a tiny splash when dropped in water, fail to move a big toy boat when they bump into it) and about what one can and cannot do with them (sail them, make them bob to the surface by holding them under water and then letting go, give them rides on top of other toy boats). Additionally, during this process of "minidevelopment," the content and structure of his mind and its capacity to construe and interpret this microdomain (assimilation) has also altered slightly. For example his functional class of boatlike entities has now generalized to include at least certain small lightweight objects that do not closely resemble the more typical and familiar instances of this class (e.g., his toy boats). Subsequently this small change in conceptual structure may permit him to construe (assimilate) still other kinds of objects as novel candidates for boat play. Moreover, the category of boatlike things may now be functionally subclassified for him into big, strong ones and small, weak ones, whereas it may previously have been a more or less homogeneous, undifferentiated class.

Thus, in the course of trying to accommodate to some hitherto unknown functional properties of a relatively unfamiliar sort of object, and of trying to assimilate the object and its properties to existing concepts and skills (trying to interpret them, make sense out of them, test out his repertoire of actions upon them), the child's mind has stretched just a little. This stretching in turn broadens slightly his future assimilatory and accommodatory possibilities. By continually repeating this cycle, the dialectical process of development continues in this gradual, leg-over-leg fashion. Development is slow and gradual because each change is rooted in, constrained by, and free to deviate but slightly from its predecessor. However, many years of virtually continuous assimilation of milieu to mind and accommodation of mind to milieu lead to large changes and even stagelike changes.

Challenges to Piaget's Theory. Piaget, being an active, self-modifying cognitive creature himself, challenged his own theory in his later years (see Beilin & Fireman, 2000; Miller, 2001; and Montangero & Maurice-Naville, 1997 for descriptions). He gave less emphasis to stages and to his logical model, and more attention to developmental change and to models based on meaning more than logical structures. At the same time, other researchers were findings soft spots in the theory. We present many of these findings in later chapters, so we simply foreshadow them here, primarily as a bridge to the other theories below.

Two kinds of findings challenge the notion of dramatic across-the-child changes in Piagetian stages or anybody's stages for that matter. First, a child's cognitive performance is less consistent and stagelike than a Piagetian would expect. A child might, for example, seem to understand the concept of number with respect to small arrays but not large ones, or the child's number concept may be more advanced than related concepts that Piaget thought emerged at the same time. Second, it appears that infants and young children are more competent (as shown in most of the following chapters) and older children less competent than Piaget thought. Consequently the cognitive changes across childhood may be less stagelike and dramatic than Piaget imagined. Still, Piaget does seem to have captured important developmental *trends* that ring true. These should be thought of as rough age trends, not as sharp and clear contrasts among four entirely different and discontinuous mentalities.

For now let us look more closely at just one of these findings—Piaget's underestimation of young children's knowledge. The reasons for the underestimation are partly methodological. A child may perform an incorrect action or answer incorrectly on a particular task, but still have a partial understanding of the concept being assessed. As researchers probed the young child's mind with new and more sensitive diagnostic tasks, they turned up an impressive number of competencies—often fragile, to be sure, but genuine nonetheless. Some of these competencies are those previously believed by Piaget to develop later, whereas others are cognitive skills not studied by Piaget.

These studies of early competencies are important because they make us rethink our previous beliefs about childhood cognitive development. If young infants have concepts believed by Piaget to develop much later, might they be innate or at least have a strong biological push at birth (see modularity nativism below)? If preschoolers have at least the rudiments of abilities previously found only in older children, then are middle-childhood minds, and even adolescent and adult ones, as radically and qualitatively different from early childhood ones as Piaget believed? Thus our new knowledge presented us with some uncertainties and perplexities about childhood cognitive development that we were spared in the heyday of Piagetian developmental psychology. (Such are the joys of scientific progress!)

Finally, in the process of finding early competencies on Piagetian tasks, researchers discovered positive acquisitions during the preoperational period. In Piaget's theory the 1-year-old is "sensorimotor," the 10-year-old "concrete-operational," and the 15-year-old "formal-operational"—all good, positive-sounding designations. The poor 3-year-old, on the other hand, gets labeled "preoperational" (even at times "preconceptual"), and all too often a description of the child's thinking has been little more than a dreary litany of wrong answers to concrete-operational tests. Piaget saw this stage mainly as preparation for concrete operations, but the stage now seems to have its own set of "first appearances." These findings stimulated some of the new directions in which cognitive developmentalists went, as described below.

After Piaget: An Overview

Theories of cognitive development can be divided into B.P. (Before Piaget) and A. P. (After Piaget), because of the impact of his theory on the theorizing that came thereafter. He gave the field a new vision of the nature of children, and of the what, when, and how of their cognitive growth. Piaget had the "greenest thumb ever for unearthing fascinating and significant developmental progressions" (Flavell, 1996, p. 202). However, it becomes apparent throughout this book, and from the other approaches described in this chapter, that Piaget's model can be criticized. The question of how the process of cognitive growth is best described and explained is still unsettled, but Piaget's theory has provided a good start. After developmentalists found problems with Piaget's theory in the 1970s and 1980s, the field went in several very fruitful directions, which forms the story in the rest of this chapter. These approaches do not negate Piaget's theory, for the most part. Rather, they identify additional important aspects of development and provide a more specific account of Piagetianlike changes. In this way they give us a fuller view of cognitive development. The categories of post-Piaget directions described below provide a context for the rest of the chapter and give a sense of the issues and questions that cognitive developmentalists currently are addressing. These issues will start to look very familiar, for we return to them throughout the book.

1. *More limited structures.* Many developmentalists wanted to retain Piaget's idea that children's thinking is coherent and organized into a conceptual system, but it was becoming clear that children's thinking looks less like a single general cognitive system and more like a set of loosely connected systems, each for a single domain such as number or physical causality. Thus the neo-Piagetian and "theory theory" approaches arose.

2. *Performance.* Inconsistencies in children's performance across situations on Piagetian tasks led to an interest in children's *use* of their knowledge (competence) in "real time" in real situations (performance). Information-processing psychologists and neo-Piagetians looked at the role of attention, memory capacity, expertise, problem-solving strategies, and sometimes social supports, in influencing whether a child could apply a concept in a particular situation.

3. *Processes of change.* A desire for more specificity about change than that found in Piaget's notions, such as assimilation and accommodation, led to both information processing and theory theory accounts of change. The dynamic systems focus on self-organizing changes keeps the Piagetian focus on systemwide changes in an active child.

4. *Biological influences and processes.* The discovery of infant early competencies on Piagetian tasks increased developmentalists' attention to biological influences. Three threads are (a) modularity nativist and biological-constraints approaches that focus on innate aspects of humans' initial cognitive system at birth, (b) evolutionary accounts of species-specific cognitive skills that focus on how our cognition arose from adaptation during evolution, and (c) neuroscience, behavioral genetics, biopsychology, and related areas, that look at biological contributions.

5. *Social aspects of cognition.* In reaction to Piaget's focus on a child alone constructing concepts of the physical world, developmentalists were attracted to Vygotsky's theory and other accounts of the sociocultural context of thinking, and of concepts of the social world, including theory of mind (see Chapter 6).

Before looking at each approach, it is important to emphasize that although few current studies would be considered "classical Piaget," the field has assimilated his ideas so much that his contributions to current research often are invisible. We are in danger of underappreciating Piaget "for much the same reasons that fish are said to underappreciate the virtues of water" (Flavell, 1996, p. 202). Even developmentalists who do not consider themselves Piagetian see the need to look for some sort of structure to children's knowledge, whether in the form of rules, theories, central conceptual structures, scripts, patterns of neural connections, or something else. These new structures grow out of earlier ones, as in Piaget's theory, such that there is continuity in development. Moreover, nearly all see children as intrinsically motivated and cognitively active creatures who select from their experiences what is meaningful to them. In addition, most approaches posit some sort of change within constraints, along with reorganization, a process that looks very much like Piaget's processes of assimilation, accommodation, and equilibration. With respect to methods, researchers take for granted his notion that "the 'wrong' or 'cute' notions that preschool children have about the world are the symptom of a complex, probing intellectual system trying to understand reality" (Miller, 2001). Researchers also continue to study many of the content areas identified by Piaget:

> Piaget has systematically ploughed his way through most of the principal modes of human experience and knowledge—space, time, number, and the rest. And in each case he has laid bare a complex succession of preforms and precursors for the most mundane and obvious of cognitions, cognitions we had no reason to assume needed a prehistory, let alone such an involved one. (Flavell, 1963, p. 411)

We now examine each approach. We present the approaches in an order that seemed natural to us, given the historical and similarity relations among them.

Neo-Piagetian

The term *neo-Piagetian* refers to a group of researcher-theorists who generally share Piaget's view of development but address a problem with Piaget's theory mentioned earlier, his characterization of a child as being *in* a particular stage. The problem is that children often do not act as though they belong in that stage. "Conservers" do not always conserve; "formal operational" thinkers often think very concretely. The particular materials, task, social context, and instructions appear to influence the child's performance. Although Piaget never claimed that a child would automatically apply his cognitive structure to all contexts, he never worked out a systematic account of this variability in behavior.

From a neo-Piagetian perspective, this lack of consistency is not surprising if one considers the information-processing demands of a task, the problem-solving skills that the child has for that sort of task, and the degree of social support for obtaining experience with such tasks. Children express a concept through processes such as attention, memory, and strategies in a particular environment, and children's limited short-term memory capacity, or "working memory" constrains this expression. Both the unevenness of a child's expression of his knowledge and his progression to more mature thinking reflect processes such as increased capacity, more efficient strategies, more flexible attention, and cultural support for practicing the new skill. Thus neo-Piagetians draw on useful concepts from the information-processing and sociocultural perspectives.

We briefly describe the approach of one representative of this "school"—Robbie Case. We will focus on his view of cognitive change, but readers are referred to his writings (e.g., Case, 1992, 1998; Case & Okamoto, 1996) for details of other aspects of his theory. Although we have selected Case's work, we want to emphasize that other neo-Piagetians have made important contributions as well (e.g., Demetriou, Efklides, & Platsidou, 1993; Demetriou & Raftoupoulos, 1999; Fischer & Bidell, 1998; Halford, 1993, 1999; Pascual-Leone, 1970; Pascual-Leone & Johnson, 1999).

Case saw cognitive change as a process of dealing with more and more features of a problem, and eventually integrating them. Children appear to move through four phases: *predimensional, unidimensional, bidimensional,* and *integrated bidimensional.* For example, in a study of young children's understanding of intentionality (Case & Okamoto, 1996), when they are told to tell a story about a little child and an old horse, predimensional children make up a story with no mention of motives. Slightly older, unidimensional children create a story around the intentions of the central character. Later, bidimensional children create a chain of two or more event sequences in which the first sequence fails to obtain the character's goal, whereas the second one does. At the final, integrated bidimensional level, children integrate multiple attempts to obtain the goal into an overall, complex, organized plot. This coordination represents a qualitative shift to a new structure, much as combining oxygen and hydrogen produces a new product, water.

The same general sort of sequence (see Figure 1.1) can be seen in Chinese children's representations of spatial relations in their drawings. They show (a) no real concern with spatial relations, (b) placement of objects into a spatial dimension, (c) depiction of both foreground and background, and (d) creation of a coherent, unified picture.

Much more than Piaget, Case focused on the child's ability to handle more and more information, as seen in the earlier examples. The number of elements (goals, actions, and so on) a child can consider is determined by the size of his or her short-term storage for the particular set of operations involved in that task. During development this storage capacity increases in two ways. First, myelinization (insulation of neurons) in the nervous system increases the efficiency of conducting neural impulses. Second, practice with operations that are relevant to the task gradually makes an activity less effortful (automatization), thereby freeing capacity for other activities (see Chapter 7). Thus, at first all of short-term memory is needed for just one element, but later it can be spread between two elements, then three and four.

Case tested his model of cognitive change in a variety of content areas, such as manipulating other people's feelings, judging intelligence in others, telling time, understanding number, using money, following maps, and understanding a balance beam. He often tested children on several kinds of tasks to show that, when they have a similar task structure and capacity demands are the same, a child performs similarly on them. Thus, under certain circumstances children can show some cross-task consistency and look somewhat stagelike.

Case proposed a multilevel cognitive system, with levels ranging from the very general to the specific. To illustrate, cognitive change involves the following sequence. An increase in capacity (*general* systemwide change), along with the particular experiences offered by one's culture, leads to a change in the *central conceptual structures.* These structures are at an *intermediate* level of generality—less general than Piaget's overall structure for a stage, but more general than a structure for a single task, such as addition. Each structure is a representational system of a domain of knowledge such as number, space, or social interaction, which should permit a child to apply that knowledge to all tasks in that domain. These structures interpret specific tasks in that domain and assemble problem-solving procedures for these tasks (*specific*-level change). By including systems that vary in generality, Case accounted for both the evenness and unevenness of cognitive development across tasks or domains. Case found cross-domain generality when the requisite un-

FIGURE 1.1   Typical pictures drawn by children aged 4, 6, 8, and 10 (a-d, respectively) in Nanjing, China. They were told, "Draw a picture of a mother and a father holding hands in a park. A baby is in front of them and a tree is very far away behind them." Reprinted from "The Role of Central Conceptual Structures in the Development of Children's Thought," by R. Case and Y. Okamoto, 1996, *Monographs of the Society for Research in Child Development, 61* (1–2, Serial No. 246), p. 139. Copyright © 1996 by the Society for Research in Child Development. Reprinted by permission.

derlying cognitive skills and the capacity demands of the tasks are the same, and domain specificity when tasks differ in one or both of these respects.

If Case's theory of cognitive change has a metaphor, it is child-as-problem-solver. Cognitive development is a sequence of increasingly powerful procedures for solving problems. In an attempt to reach their subgoals and goals, children construct new strategies or draw on appropriate preexisting strategies. This arsenal of strategies for problem solving becomes more and more impressive as children grow older. Children experiment during attempts to solve problems, drawing on their internal and external resources: They explore objects, observe and imitate other people, and cooperate with other people in problem solving. If children have the necessary processing capacity, they can use these experiences to construct more advanced cognitive structures for problem solving.

In summary, Case kept the spirit of Piaget's theory, but drew heavily on the information processing approach, to which we now turn.

Information Processing

Basic Principles. Information-processing currently is a main approach for the study of cognitive development. Fuller descriptions can be found in Siegler (1998), Klahr and MacWhinney (1998), and Miller (2001). The information-processing approach focuses on cognitive change rather than stages of development. The approach conceives of the human mind as a complex cognitive system, analogous in some ways to the operations of a computer. Like a computer, the system manipulates or processes information coming in from the environment or already stored within the system. It processes the information in a variety of ways: encoding, recoding, or decoding it; comparing or combining it with other information; storing it in memory or retrieving it from memory; bringing it into or out of focal attention or conscious awareness, and so on. Thus, much more than Piaget, information-processing developmentalists focus on cognitive activities from one moment to the next. In addition they give much less attention to cognitive structures.

The information manipulated in the ways discussed is of different types and is organized into units of various sizes and levels of complexity or abstraction. As to types, some of the information that is processed is more "declarative" in nature, consisting of knowledge of word meanings, facts, and the like. Other information is more "procedural" in type, consisting of knowledge of how to do various things, such as solve a puzzle. As to sizes and levels, some units of information are small and elementary, such as an encoded perceptual distinctive feature that helps a child recognize a particular letter of the alphabet. Other units are organized wholes composed of elementary units and are at higher levels of abstraction, such as the meaning of the written sentence that contains the just-mentioned letter. More interesting higher order units include the representations or knowledge structures described in Chapter 4—event knowledge, scripts, concepts, categories, and so on—as well as plans, strategies, and rules used in thinking and problem solving. Thus an episode of information processing may involve retrieving or assembling a complex plan or strategy for constructing a toy village, attempting to execute that plan or strategy, revising it if it proves inadequate, and so forth. The mind is a well-populated and busy place indeed.

All this data-crunching has its limits, however, especially in the number of units of information that can be attended to and processed simultaneously. It is therefore possible for a task to overload the system—that is, to impose processing demands that exceed its processing capacity. For instance, if a task required a child to keep five units of information in mind at once and that particular child was only capable of keeping four in mind, we would have a case of information-processing overload, and the child would likely fail the task (as well as suffer from a tired brain).

Goals and Questions. Why does the information-processing approach bother with all these details? It tries to provide an explicit, testable, detailed understanding of what a child's cognitive system actually *does* when dealing with some task or problem, here and now or "on line" in "real time." It attempts to answer such questions as: What does the system do first, at the onset of the information-processing episode? What is the second thing it does, and the third? How much time does each step take? Are some of these processing steps carried out simultaneously (*parallel processing*) and others successively (*serial processing*)? An episode of information processing is thus conceived as a kind of odyssey of information flow from one destination and adventure to another. These questions are very different from the ones that Piaget asked.

Some information-processing psychologists construct computer programs to simulate the hypothesized operations of the human cognitive system; they use these *computer simulations* as a tool for testing and revising their models of thinking and even cognitive change (see Klahr & MacWhinney, 1998, and "Connectionism" below). They try to achieve a model of cognitive processing in real time that is so precisely specified, explicit, and detailed that it can actually be run successfully as a working program on a computer. The model should also make specific predictions about how the child (and computer) would behave under specific task conditions or constraints, and in response to specific inputs. Other information-processing psychologists use the computer as a metaphor rather than construct computer simulations, but still share the information-processing approach's paramount goal of producing an explicit, testable model of here-and-now cognitive functioning and change.

Information-processing work has reanalyzed various Piagetian concepts. For example, in Chapter 4 we describe Robert Siegler's (1996) work on the developmental sequence in which children acquire various rules of reasoning in Piaget's balance-scale task. In addition, the chapter on memory includes much information-processing work. Other work has examined numerous topics given little attention by Piaget, for example, reading and writing (Siegler, 1998) and individual differences (Bjorklund, 2000a; Sternberg, 1999). In fact humans have to process information in some way or another in nearly everything they do. As Simon (1995, p. 507) concludes, "if your goal is to understand human decision making, there are very few activities you cannot engage in on company time. Just keep the tape recorder handy." We now use one topic, strategies for adding, to represent current work from an information-processing point of view, as seen in Siegler's research (e.g., Siegler, 1996; Siegler & Jenkins, 1989). As in much of his work, there are important implications for formal instruction.

An Example of Research: Strategies.   One of the earliest mathematical operations that children acquire is adding. Children ingeniously come up with many ways to perform this simple operation. To add 3 and 5, a child could retrieve the previously memorized fact that the sum of these numbers is 8. The straight-memorization retrieval strategy is both fast and accurate. However, children have not memorized more difficult problems and thus on these problems must use strategies that are slower and more effortful, but have a high probability of giving the correct answer. One such strategy is to begin with 1 and count up to 8. Or a child could put up 3 fingers then 5 fingers and recognize them as "8" without counting. Or, in a long-honored tradition among school children, the child could simply guess. Finally an efficient strategy is to begin with the larger number and count up from there (5, 6, 7, 8)—a so-called *min strategy* which is illustrated in the following slice of laboratory life:

E: How much is 6 + 3?
L: (Long pause) Nine.

E: OK, how did you know that?

L: I think I said . . . I think I said . . . oops, um . . . I think he said . . . 8 was 1 and . . . um . . . I mean 7 was 1, 8 was 2, 9 was 3.

E: OK.

L: Six and three are nine.

E: How did you know to do that? Why didn't you count "1, 2, 3, 4, 5, 6, 7, 8, 9"? How come you did "6, 7, 8, 9"?

L: Cause then you have to count all those numbers.

E: OK, well how did you know you didn't have to count all of those numbers?

L: Why didn't . . . well I don't have to if I don't want to.

(Siegler & Jenkins, 1989, p. 66.

Children can be encouraged to use the efficient min strategy more often by giving them "challenge problems" such as 23 + 2 or 21 + 1, which are hard to solve in other ways.

When given a series of addition problems to solve, a child is likely to use most or all of the above strategies. Siegler describes cognitive change in both strategies and other cognitive skills as a series of overlapping waves, as depicted in Figure 1.2. As Siegler (1996, p. 239) comments, "a wave, like children's thinking, never stands still." At any point in time, a child typically uses several different strategies and may even use different strategies to solve exactly the same addition

FIGURE 1.2   Siegler's overlapping waves model of cognition development. Reprinted from R. S. Siegler, 1996, *Emerging Minds: The Process of Change in Children's Thinking* (p.89). New York: Oxford University Press. Copyright © 1996 by Oxford University Press. Reprinted by permission.

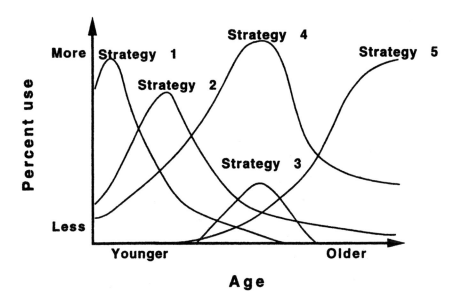

problem at different times, even a few minutes later. Strategies, like waves, overlap in that a child continues to use an old strategy even after a new one begins to develop. Many strategies look like waves because they gradually gather strength, peak, and then crash as the child discontinues them. During development several strategies vie for ascendancy, and the more efficient strategies very gradually become more frequent. Although children eventually replace poor strategies, they keep them for a surprisingly long time.

The overlapping-waves model of development, which emphasizes variability within a child and between children, obviously differs from Piaget's view of development as stagelike. For Siegler change and variability in children's behavior characterizes all of development, not just brief periods of transition from one way of thinking to another.

Children use multiple strategies not only on other kinds of math tasks, but also on diverse tasks such as scientific reasoning (Schauble, 1996), judging whether two arrays are the same or different (Miller & Aloise-Young, 1996), and infant locomotion (Adolph, 1997). We revisit strategy variability in Chapter 7, on memory. Siegler argues that it is adaptive for children to keep various strategies on hand because it permits them to approach a problem flexibly and to clarify which strategy is best in which situations.

Methods.   Siegler was able to discover strategy variability by paying less attention to the average behavior of the whole group of children and more attention to individual children's trial-by-trial behavior. He looked carefully at what each child did on each trial and how that was related to what the child did on the next trial. In this *microgenetic method,* a child works repeatedly and intensively within some problem domain—perhaps dozens of hours of observation spread across several weeks. The attempt is to condense naturally occurring development into a much shorter time frame and look for clues for the mechanisms of development in the trial-by-trial changes.

By using the microgenetic method, Siegler also uncovered some quirky behaviors in children. A commonsense view might be that a child would tend to continue to use a strategy that is successful and to drop a strategy that does not work. In contrast, Siegler found that children sometimes dropped a successful strategy soon after discovering it and returned to less successful strategies. For example, the child who eventually used the successful min strategy on the highest percentage of trials of any children in the group used it on only 7 of the 84 trials after discovering it. Strategy development seems to be driven less by success or failure than by considerations such as cognitive effort (little mental effort required) and even esthetic elegance ("My, what a lovely strategy") or novelty of a new strategy.

The microgenetic method's analysis of changes in behavior over a large number of trials suggests mechanisms of developmental change. For example, on the trial before the discovery of a new strategy and on the discovery trial, children sometimes exhibited odd behaviors. They took a long time to give the answer, or became inarticulate. These "hemming and hawing" behaviors at the point of discovery may reflect increased cognitive activity that signals cognitive change, a "cognitive moment," so to speak. Children even verbally contradicted their own behavior, as seen in a child who swore he never counted even though he clearly was heard counting.

Other typical information-processing methods include measures of how long it takes children to give their answer, which can provide evidence about how much time a processing step takes. Their verbal reports and the types of adding errors they make may reveal the plans and strategies they used. Children's eye movements or what they remember and forget of the information presented also provide clues about cognitive functioning.

Processes of Change. Researchers' strategy is to analytically decompose tasks into their components and try to infer what the cognitive system must do to deal adequately with each component. This approach has revealed developmental changes in the child's encoding of the problem, procedures for manipulating the numbers or other symbols, retrieval, capacity limitations, and the sequence of specific processing steps in real time. Children change in which perceptual aspects of the task they encode, for example, a change from encoding only the height of a container filled with a liquid to encoding both height and width when making a judgment of quantity. Cognitive change also can come from new combinations of the knowledge a child already has, as when children combine two strategies to solve a problem. Other very important processes of change are *automatization*—using mental processes or problem-solving strategies increasingly efficiently, with practice, so that mental resources are freed for other purposes—and related notions such as increased mental capacity, faster speed of processing a stimulus (e.g., identifying a written word), or applying a rule. Still other processes of change such as the acquisition of more complex rules are illustrated in Siegler's balance scale problem in a later chapter. Note that no stages are posited, though the change from one strategy to another or one rule to another is qualitative—a change in one's way of thinking about, or overall approach to, the task at hand.

Connectionist Models. As we mentioned earlier, some information-processing psychologists try to construct computer programs that mimic both the "output" of children of a particular age and the changes that real children seem to undergo. One version of these simulations—*connectionist* or *neural network* models—has drawn a great deal of attention recently, so it is described separately. One reason that connectionism is attractive is that it seems to some developmentalists to be a way to relate learning and development to the developing brain—hence the "neural" part of the term "neural networks." Although connectionist models vary in how closely the theorist relates them to what we know about the functioning of the brain, they at least have to be compatible with this functioning. And all models seem to draw on a neural analogy, as the following description shows. Still, it is important to keep in mind that connectionist models can focus on biological influences, experiences in particular sorts of environments, or, more commonly, an interaction of the two (e.g., Elman et al., 1996).

As can be seen in the very simplified version in Figure 1.3, similar to the brain a connectionist system consists of nodes connected by pathways, each with some degree of activation. Like the brain, the model has several layers, and activity in one level can excite other pathways in that same level or pathways to other levels. A unit "fires" if the amount of activation it receives from all of the other units connected to it exceeds a certain threshold. It may help to think of a map, with broader lines for the heavily traveled interstate highways and thinner lines for the less traveled minor highways. Similarly, in a connectionist brain "road trip," some pathways are stimulated more than others, and thus some connections are stronger than others. A connection between two nodes becomes stronger if the child often

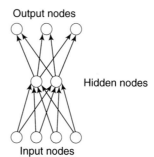

Output nodes

Hidden nodes

FIGURE 1.3 A simple connectionist model with nodes and pathways.

Input nodes

finds the two "items" associated in his or her experiences. One example is a connectionist model of the development of a grammatical rule (MacWhinney, Leinbach, Taraban, & McDonald, 1989). A German child notices that each particular version of the German article "the" occurs only with certain sorts of nouns, and thus these neural pathways become strong while others become weak. Thus a connectionist system learns by encountering examples and detecting the correlations or associations within them.

Connectionist models provide us with an interesting image of thinking—a pattern of activation distributed over many connections. It is a pattern of connections with various weights, or strengths. If Descartes had been a connectionist, he would have declared, "I have a pattern of activation in a neural-like network, therefore I am" (Miller, 2001). Learning or development is a change in this pattern. Each small developmental step brings a slight change in the pattern.

It remains to be seen whether connectionist models fulfill their potential to provide precise, testable models of cognitive development. At this point models have been developed for a wide range of behaviors, ranging from the concept of object permanence (Munakata, McClelland, Johnson, & Siegler, 1997) to mental disorders (Oliver, Johnson, Karmiloff-Smith, & Pennington, 2000) to causal reasoning (Shultz, Schmidt, Buckingham, & Mareschal, 1995). They will turn out to be quite useful if they succeed in tying brain development to thinking and behavior, particularly if they make new predictions about development. An example of the latter is one model (Mareschal, Plunkett, & Harris, 1999) that predicts, from infants' processing of visual information about objects, that babies should perform successfully on certain tasks that require them to integrate representations that are separated in the cortex later than on tasks that do not require this integration. For good accounts of connectionist models of development, see Elman et al. (1996) and Klahr and MacWhinney (1998). We will return to connectionist models of particular concepts, particularly the concept of object permanence (Chapter 3) and language acquisition (Chapter 8).

Biological Approaches

Developmental Cognitive Neuroscience. Although connectionism often is closely related to biological processes, and Piaget considered biology one important component of the formula for development, several other approaches more directly address biological and maturational contributions to the issue of nature versus nurture. A main "up-and comer" in developmental psychology today is *cognitive neuroscience*. This approach would be on most developmentalists' list of "hot" topics not only in developmental psychology but also in nearly all areas of psychology. It is both a set of techniques and a way of thinking about the development of cognition.

Recent technological advances in generating maps of brain activity partly account for the excitement about neuroscience research. One can, for example, compare these maps in children of different ages working on the same task, or in children of the same age working on different sorts of cognitive tasks. These comparisons can give us clues about brain maturation, the relations among various sorts of cognitive processes or domains, and changes in how knowledge is organized. Researchers examine, for example, whether certain areas of the brain or certain pathways become more specialized during development. They also are interested in whether different developmental timetables of specialization exist for different domains, different sorts of cognition, and different areas of the cortex.

It is important to emphasize that identifying brain-correlates of development does not necessarily mean that brain development determines behavioral development. Such evidence also indicates that behavior causes changes in the brain. The infant brain may have slight initial biases or constraints in that, for a particular situation and task, some neural pathways are more easily activated or more easily connected to certain outputs. However, infants in turn seek out appropriate stimuli that further specialize these pathways (Johnson, 2000). Thus nature and nurture are tightly interwoven, and changes in the brain reflect, as well as cause, behavior.

One example of the complex relations between biology and experience is that there is a biologically driven overproduction of synapses early in development, but certain ones are pruned as a result of experience. Most children, because they are physically normal and are raised in an environment typical for the species, have more or less the same sorts of experiences at about the usual time. Thus the pruning proceeds along similar lines for most children. However, what about atypical situations, such as children who are deaf or blind and thus do not receive auditory or visual stimulation? In deaf children certain areas of the brain that normally would be devoted to auditory processing if the brain received both auditory and visual stimulation instead gradually become devoted to visual processing (Neville, 1995). Conversely, in blind children areas normally devoted to visual processing when receiving both auditory and visual stimulation instead are devoted over time to auditory processing. Thus, when an area of the brain does not receive its normally expected input, it can be used for other purposes. The nature of experience, and consequently the nature of brain activity, determines which synapses are pruned and which survive. The brain is preset to rapidly guide children along certain developmental paths, but is also flexible enough to deal with adverse circumstances.

Stay tuned for further exciting findings in this area over the next few years. For good recent accounts, see M. H. Johnson (1998, 2000) and Diamond (2000). More generally there is current interest in a range of biological approaches to cognitive development, such as behavioral genetics (Plomin, 1999), psychobiological systems models of gene-environment interaction during development (Gottlieb, Wahlsten, & Lickliter, 1998), biological biases or constraints (Gelman & Williams, 1998; Spelke & Newport, 1998), and evolutionary developmental psychology (Geary & Bjorklund, 2000; Tomasello, 1999). Evidence about biological constraints appears in various chapters, particularly the ones on infancy and language.

Modularity Nativism.   A second main biologically oriented framework, of a very different sort, is sometimes labeled *modularity nativism* (Gopnik & Meltzoff, 1997). This term refers to a set of approaches that posit innate modules, structures, or constraints, each specialized for perception and cognition in a particular domain, such as language (e.g., Chomsky, 1988; Fodor, 1983; Pinker, 1997; Spelke & Newport, 1998). A module requires little experience in order to be triggered; experience simply requires appropriate content, such as adults talking, that activates the innate structure. Thus an infant is cognitively advanced in certain areas, such as language and primitive concepts of physics and mind. Moreover, each module is relatively independent of the others, such that advances in one area typically do not transfer to other areas.

Modularity nativism helps make sense of the fact that, contrary to Piaget's stage account, infants seem amazingly knowledgeable in certain areas and surprisingly ignorant in others. Evolved domain-specific aptitudes for certain concepts would give infants a cognitive edge on certain sorts of learning. Modularity nativism also holds some plausibility because of recent revelations of apparently advanced knowledge in young infants referred to earlier and discussed in Chapter 3. Other evidence comes from people with brain damage or disorders such as autism, who have very specific, rather than general, cognitive deficits. Neuroscience work on nonhuman primates also provides support. The various versions of modularity nativism differ in how strongly innate they consider the initial cognitive system, and, consequently, the role of experience.

Only some domain-specific approaches are modular nativistic. Other domain-specific approaches emphasize more equal interactions between biology and experience that produce knowledge about a specific domain. We discuss the issue of domain-specificity versus domain-generality more fully in Chapter 9. It is also the case that only some nativist approaches are modular nativistic. Many nativistic approaches posit other ways in which cognition is innate, such as a maturational unfolding of general processing abilities rather than specific modules. The notion of domain-specific concepts nicely provides a bridge to the "theory theory," another attempt to capture the nature of knowledge about a particular domain.

Theory Theory

In this attempt to characterize the apparent domain-specific nature of children's knowledge, which challenges Piaget's theory, the theory theory likens this knowledge to a scientific theory. A child's theory would differ from one domain to another, from physics to biology to the mind. Children's knowledge within a domain is organized into a set of interrelated concepts, consistent with Piaget's theory, but the knowledge structure is limited to a particular domain rather than applied to all domains. Throughout development children continually test these intuitive theories, like a scientist, in light of their experiences. Thus children are like little scientists (or scientists are like grown-up children?).

In infancy (see Chapter 2), these theories are very simple, such as the theory that the world consists of cohesive physical objects with boundaries, substance, and continuity over time and movement. A quick example is a baby with a theory that he can influence physical objects by contacting them physically. In the world of a 9-month-old, this theory works much of the time. Most things do move when push comes to shove. However, when he unsuccessfully tries to force a block into a bottle with a narrow neck, he must reconsider this theory, and eventually modifies it (Gopnik & Meltzoff, 1997). Older children's theories are more complex, as we discuss in later chapters. At any age development is a process of continually testing and modifying one's theories in a variety of domains.

Some members of the theory theory camp are modularity nativists and posit a strong initial theory (described by Gopnik & Meltzoff, 1997). Others prefer to attribute only an innate ability to construct and "test" theories to newborns, and expect to see at least some individual and cultural differences in what everyday theories are developed.

The important and compelling part of the theory theory perspective is that children very early on seem to be able to go beyond perceptual features and see the "essences" of objects, people, and events. For example, Carey (1985a) showed 4-year-olds a mechanical monkey that looked convincingly like a real monkey. She asked the children whether the mechanical monkey has bones and could eat, and have babies like a real monkey. Although the children believed that people and other animals have these properties, they denied that mechanical monkeys had them. Thus their monkey theories about the biological nature of real monkeys and the mechanical nature of toy monkeys include basic principles about the underlying nature of biological versus mechanical entities that overrode the perceptual similarity of these two categories. The children saw mechanical monkeys as more like hammers than real animals. The general point here is that two entities that are both similar and different can be assigned to the same category or different ones, depending on the child's intuitive theories about the world.

The theory theory proposes that children have a system of knowledge that relates various phenomena within the domain, such that a child's theory of mind includes connections between notions about beliefs, desires, and intentions. Thus the claim is that children's theories are abstract, coherent, and internally consistent. They provide a way for children to make the world coherent and to explain and predict events. We provide examples of the currently very influential theory theory in later chapters on infant cognition, the development of concepts during the preschool years, and social cognition (especially the theory of mind). For details see Wellman and Gelman (1998), Flavell and Miller (1998), and Carey (1999). As these chapters indicate, although developmentalists are impressed with infants' and young children's surprising degree of knowledge in certain areas, a main debate concerns how abstract and theorylike this knowledge actually is.

Dynamic Systems

The approach that comes closest to trying to keep a wholistic view of complex human behavior, which characterized Piaget's theory, is the dynamic systems approach. Because this model is very complex, it helps to start with an analogy of development as a mountain stream (Thelen & Smith, 1998). As it flows down the mountain, it is expressed as a fast stream, a small trickle, a waterfall, or a still pool, depending on many factors, such as how much it has rained, how steep the mountain is, and what obstacles are in the water's path. Much of the time, this pattern is about the same. However, after a drought or a heavy rain this pattern changes, though always in predictable ways. Moreover, to understand the current state of the stream we must consider many time frames, ranging from ancient geological history to the recent rainstorm. Similarly, many causes, ranging from the mountain and gravity to water molecules, affect the pattern of water flow.

Similarly, one can understand where a new behavior comes from (flows from?) only by looking at the overall pattern, at both previous and current events, and at many levels of causation. Proponents describe new behaviors as "falling out" of the current status of the system in its current context, just as a new stream falls out of a stream after a heavy rain. Given the current state of the overall system in its current setting, a certain outcome is inevitable. To say all of this more formally, children are active, self-organizing systems that tend to develop along certain paths but are continually adjusting to whatever they encounter. Thus children are both "dynamic" (active, always changing) and "systems" (organized and consisting of many interrelated levels).

A nice concrete human example is overdue. Consider the stepping reflex found in normal newborns. They appear to walk, much like a toddler does, when supported in an upright position with their feet touching the floor. Traditionally the disappearance of this reflex around two months of age was interpreted as showing that higher brain functions begin to control, and thus inhibit, these lower level reflexes. Dynamic systems researchers suggest another explanation (Thelen, Fisher, & Ridley-Johnson, 1984). They noted that babies continue to show this "walking" pattern when lying on their backs. Thus the reflex has not disappeared. Thelen and her colleagues proposed that as babies gain weight over the first few months their legs literally become too heavy to lift when babies are upright. They showed that babies who apparently had lost the walking reflex when upright demonstrate it when held in a waist-high tank of water which makes their legs lighter. Thus a child's behavior depends on the particular immediate set of physical capabilities and environmental circumstances in the system.

Another example is a toddler's walking. She has a preferred state of how she usually walks, but walks slightly differently on a water bed and a sidewalk, when walking fast and when walking slowly on the sidewalk. Children construct new behaviors on the spot out of whatever is available. Characteristic of a system, when you change one small part, such as the nature of the walking surface, you change the whole system.

The dynamic systems approach is most easily illustrated with motor behaviors, particularly during infancy. However, it now has been applied to a range of cognitive skills. For examples, see Thelen and Smith (1998) and Lewis (2000).

Sociocultural Approaches

Although the approaches discussed thus far assign some role to social and cultural influences on cognitive change, only the socioculturalists have focused on these influences. The approach goes back to the early part of this century, to the work of several Soviet researchers, most notably Lev Vygotsky (1896–1934). An interested reader could examine Vygotsky's works directly (e.g., 1978) or turn to more modern versions in approaches that examine the cultural or social context of behavior (e.g., Bronfenbrenner & Morris, 1998; Bruner, 1990; Cole, 1999; Nelson, 1996; Rogoff, 1998; Shweder et al., 1998).

These approaches view cognitive development as a process of active learning through the guidance and support of adults. We said earlier that a child only has a single head, and it is firmly attached to the rest of the body. We now add that this body-with-head has both feet firmly planted on sociocultural soil.

It is important to understand that the sociocultural approach is not simply proposing the interaction of two separate entities—the child and society. Rather the *child-in-social context* is a single unit of study; they cannot be separated. Although there are many sociocultural approaches, what they have in common is the belief that the social and cognitive realms are inextricably connected; thought is always social, even when the child is alone, because concepts are constructed and interpreted by the particular culture.

Levels of Sociocultural Context. Although many levels of the sociocultural context exist, they form two general levels. One is distal and molar—the social-cultural-historical moment in which the child exists. This sociocultural legacy includes "technologies such as literacy, number systems, and computers, as well as value systems and scripts and norms for the handling of situations" (Rogoff, 1990, p. 32). Thus a child who happens to be born into a society with computers and television may use these tools to develop his or her thinking in directions that differ from those of a child in a less technologically oriented society. Cognition is not necessarily more advanced in one society than the other; rather it is simply different. Cultures differ in the kinds of cognitive skills that are adaptive and valued, and consequently encouraged and developed. For example, a less technological society may nurture the narrative thinking involved in storytelling or the cognitive skills underlying pottery making rather than reading processes or computer skills. Events such as severe economic depressions, the invention of the printing press, wars, and a technological advance with political implications (such as the launching of Sputnik) can change the nature of children's experiences, and thus of their thinking. For example, as a society raises the level of literacy expected of its members, children in that society are given more schooling (Rogoff, 1990). In short, a culture's history and current configuration hand the newborn child a ready-made set of values, beliefs, rules, possibilities, and impossibilities.

The second sociocultural level lies closer to the child's head, that is, in the child's proximal social and physical setting. This level involves the moment-to-moment and day-to-day interactions with parents, siblings, peers, teachers, and other significant figures. Simple everyday parent-child interactions such as reading a book, building a tree house, conversing at mealtime, or feeding an infant have a social overlay of mediated-cultural and direct-parental influences. To some extent adults are simply "go-betweens"—mediators of the higher level social-cultural-historical forces described earlier. Parents, for example, encourage independent thinking or obedience to authority, depending on which is needed to succeed in that society—a democratic versus collectivist one. Thus in certain cultures children are discouraged from asking questions of adults (Rogoff, 1998). As another example, parents in different cultures vary in the value they place on mathematical and scientific studies and homework, as shown in research on Japanese and American children (e.g., Stevenson, Lee, & Stigler, 1986).

More specifically, adults guide, challenge, provide models of to-be-acquired behavior, and arrange and structure the child's participation in activities. In short, adults are "cognitive boosters," cheering children on and directing them so that they will be all that they can be. In this "guided participation," adults arrange the child's activities, regulate the difficulty of the task, direct the child's attention, and provide both explicit and implicit instruction. Parents' guidance can be very simple, as when a parent lightly holds onto a child as the child attempts to stand alone. Or it can be more complex and subtle, as when American adults ask preschoolers, "What are you drawing?" This question may encourage children to consider the possibility that their playful scribbles could represent something in the real world and to make up post hoc stories about their drawings (Cole & Cole, 1989).

The socioculturalists' metaphor for the process of cognitive change is "child as apprentice." A child develops by doing things with more advanced others, observing what they do, responding to their corrective feedback, listening to their instructions and explanations, and learning to use their tools and strategies to solve problems. This instruction can be formal, as in schooling or explicit instruction from parents, but more often is casually interwoven into the fabric of a child's home life. By learning from others how to carry out activities, a child learns how to think: "Apprenticeships provide the beginner with access to both the overt aspects of the skill and the more hidden inner processes of thought" (Rogoff, 1990, p. 40).

It should be noted that children are not passive in this interaction (Rogoff, 1998). They actively make use of the opportunities given them and try out their newly acquired strategies and other cognitive tools. As they become more competent, the division of responsibility for the activity shifts so that they have a greater share, and adults have a lesser share.

Zone of Proximal Development. A final process of cognitive change is perhaps the most important. Rogoff (1998) refers to the process of building bridges between what the child currently knows and new information. Cognitive change involves movement through the *zone of proximal development*, a concept of Vygotsky's. This zone is the area lying between where the child is now, cognitively speaking, and where the child could be with help. An adult or more advanced peer can guide the child through this zone. Just as the degree of change possible through assimilation and accommodation is constrained in Piaget's theory, so is the zone of proximal development limited. Children have to build on what they already understand and cannot skip over intermediate steps. Thus cognitive development necessarily proceeds gradually.

As an example of how the sociocultural approach can be applied to laboratory research, consider a study of the zone of proximal development (Freund, 1990) in which 3- and 5-year-olds helped a puppet move his furniture into his new house. This essentially was a sorting task in which dollhouse furniture was sorted into rooms. The children were told to put the things into the rooms where they belonged. For instance, a child could place the stove, refrigerator, kitchen sink, table, and chairs into one room and call it a kitchen. They created other rooms in a similar fashion. After the children performed the task on their own (current level of functioning), half of them interacted with their mothers on an easy and hard level of the task. These two versions differed in the number of rooms and items to be sorted. Mothers were told to help their children but not teach them. The other half of the children worked at the same tasks by themselves, but at the end of each task, the experimenter corrected any errors as the children watched. Finally, all children performed the task one more time on their own.

The children who had interacted with their mothers performed at a more advanced level on the final trial than those who had practiced on their own, even though the latter had been shown the correct solution at the end by the experimenter. More importantly, mothers adjusted their behavior to the cognitive level of the child. They gave more concrete specific content (e.g., "that stove goes in a kitchen") to the 3-year-olds than to the 5-year-olds. The latter received more general help, such as keeping the goal in mind and planning (e.g., "Let's make the bedroom and then the kitchen"). These general prompts were also more likely to be used in the easy version than the hard one, presumably because mothers thought that even 3-year-olds could use them in the easy version. Mothers also did more of the talking in the difficult version. Thus the results show that mothers gave their children as much responsibility as they thought they could handle, given their age and the task difficulty. Each mother, as a "cognitive guidance counselor," designed the nature of her child's participation in the activity so as to maximize his movement through the zone of proximal development. In addition the mothers sometimes drew on their shared history with their child, as seen in statements such as "Where do we keep our refrigerator at home?"

Themes and Issues

These various frameworks for studying cognitive development, which broaden and modify the view of development that Piaget gave us, should be kept in mind in the coming chapters. Although no one framework provides a satisfactory account of cognitive development, as a group they tell us where to look for clues to children's thinking. Because they focus on different aspects of cognitive development, they are complementary and portray the richness and complexity of the child's mind. They tell us that change comes about through assimilation-accommodation cycles (Piaget); improved procedures for problem solving and increased processing capacity, speed, and efficiency (information-processing and neo-Piagetian); and modifications of connections in a neural network (connectionism). Change also can come from neurological maturation or brain changes caused by experience (neuroscience); innate modules (modularity nativism); testing and modifying one's theories (theory theory); new emergent concepts arising from repeated self-organization (dynamic systems); and adult-guided or peer-guided improvement of existing competencies and engagement in progressively more complex tasks and activities (sociocultural). Our list of frameworks could have been much longer, of course. Readers are referred to accounts of frameworks concerning intelligence (Ceci, 1996; Sternberg, 1999), cognitive styles (Ferrari & Sternberg, 1998), and life span cognitive development (Baltes, Lindenberger, & Staudinger, 1998; Elder, 1998; Moshman, 1998).

One reason to begin a book on cognitive development by looking at various perspectives is that this account highlights the issues about cognitive development that will pop in and out throughout this book. We offer a short list here, and return to many of them in the final chapter. Here is our wish list of questions we wish we could answer: What causes X (some cognitive skill or concept) to emerge? When does X emerge? What are the various forms that X takes over time; that is, how are earlier, rudimentary versions related to later, fully mature versions? Are the changes from one version to the next quantitative (e.g., more, stronger) or qualitative (different in nature, type, or kind)? How does one version become the next version? Is

X domain-specific or domain-general? How does X relate to and contribute to other aspects of cognition? How does X relate to behavior; for example, does the child use the skill or concept when it would be useful to do so? What function does the skill or concept serve in the child's daily life? These questions show how a developmentalist thinks, and how you may think by the end of the book.

AN OVERVIEW OF THE BOOK

In Chapters 2 and 3, we describe the initial cognitive equipment found in the newborn and chronicle the major landmarks of general mental growth through infancy. Chapters 4 through 8 examine particular important content areas in more detail: representations and concepts, reasoning and problem solving, social cognition, memory, and language. Finally in Chapter 9, we discuss some major questions and problems concerning cognitive development, including those foreshadowed here.

In the spirit of "truth in packaging," we disclose that we could not possibly cover all aspects of cognitive development. We try to tell the essential story of how children's thinking evolves and refer the reader to more detailed sources for the trees in the forest. We hope the book conveys the fascinating, and often surprising, nature of children's perceptions, thoughts, and beliefs.

SUMMARY

The concept of cognition favored in this book is a broad and inclusive one, covering more than such traditional, more narrowly "intellectual" processes as reasoning and problem solving. The human mind is conceptualized as a complex *system* of interacting processes which generate, code, transform, and otherwise manipulate information of diverse sorts. The field is rich in useful frameworks for studying cognitive development. *Piaget*'s theory can be said to have started the field. He laid out the important issues that the other theories still address. He described qualitative changes through four stages—the *sensorimotor, preoperational, concrete operational,* and *formal operational stages.* A logic of actions becomes logical mental operations that are applied to increasingly abstract representations. During *assimilation* and *accommodation,* the cognitive system actively creates mental constructions of reality in the course of numerous experiences with its milieu. It does not simply make a mental copy of what is experienced. Assimilation essentially means interpreting or construing external data in terms of the individual's existing cognitive system. Accommodation means changing the cognitive system slightly in order to take account of the structure of the external data. By repeatedly attempting to accommodate to and assimilate novel, previously unassimilated environmental elements, cognitive development takes place.

After Piaget, and because of Piaget, cognitive developmentalists went in five main directions. New perspectives addressed (1) the possibility of cognitive structures more limited than stages, (2) the reasons why children's performance varies from task to task within a domain, or varies from one domain to another, (3) processes of change, (4) biological influences and processes, and (5) social aspects of cognition.

Neo-Piagetians combine the Piagetian, information-processing, and sometimes sociocultural approaches. Unlike Piaget, they address the domain-specificity of cognitive skills, developmental increases in mental capacity, and social supports for cognitive activities. For example, Robbie Case emphasized the roles of capacity and problem-solving strategies. Processing and coordinating more elements in a situation, differentiating information, and setting subgoals as means to a goal lead to cognitive development. A set of domain-specific *central conceptual structures* assembles activities such as exploring objects, observing and imitating other people, and cooperating with other people during problem solving in a particular area such as number or social cognition.

The *information-processing* approach takes as its starting point the flow of information through a computerlike system. Humans attend to information, transform it into a mental representation of some sort, compare it with information already in the system, assign meaning to it, and store it. An increase in children's speed of processing and thus an increase in capacity drive cognitive development. A growing flexibility and completeness in the child's encoding of stimuli and the acquisition of various strategies also appear to be important sources of change. However, limits on how much information can be processed put serious constraints on the child's development. Through either computer simulations or detailed, precise descriptions of behavior, researchers test hypothesized processes of cognitive development. Siegler's *overlapping-waves model* captures the variability of children's thinking and continual cognitive change. A recent focus within information processing, *connectionism*, involves computer simulations that "learn" from input, typically numerous examples. Changes in the pattern of connections of various strengths constitute cognitive change. Connectionists emphasize analogies with the brain.

Various *biological approaches* promise to reveal the functioning of the developing brain. Recent advances in neural imagining have spurred considerable interest in *developmental cognitive neuroscience*. Correlations between changes in the brain and in behavior suggest a two-way influence between the two, as the brain constrains and facilitates thinking at each developmental point, and behavior in turn determines the nature of the stimulation the brain receives. *Modularity nativism* takes the radical position that certain foundational concepts are innate. Each module is specific to a particular domain, such as language, face recognition, or physical objects, and is only very loosely connected to other modules. Other biological approaches include *behavioral genetics*, *psychobiological systems*, and *evolutionary psychology*.

The *theory theory* approach is very active at present, particularly in the area of theory of mind. Researchers study children's informal, intuitive "theories," or coherent causal-explanatory frameworks, about the world. Individual concepts are embedded in these larger theories. Later theories are more complex. Young children may only have a few theories, whereas older children may have theories for various domains. A theory includes a set of beliefs about the entities in a domain and about the relationships among these entities. In particular, theories differ from other types of mental representations in that they are explanatory; they can answer "why" questions. Theories differ from Piagetian conceptual structures in that they are specific to a particular domain, such as a theory of biology or physics or psychology.

The *dynamic systems* framework tries to incorporate the entire cognitive system. Because this system is self-organizing, it assembles a concept or behavior on the spot, given the current status of the system and the particular environment in which the system finds itself. A new behavior emerges or "falls out" of this matrix. The approach examines moment-to-moment changes in the system, which constitute cognitive change.

Sociocultural approaches, derived from Vygotsky, view the child-in-sociocultural context as the main unit of analysis. Global social-cultural-historical influences and proximal sociocultural influences, particularly parents, other significant adults, and older peers, are the main source of cognitive change. Adults and older peers guide, support, inspire, and correct children's active problem solving as they work their way through the *zone of proximal development*. By engaging them in guided participation, society helps children reach their maximal level of cognitive functioning. Children actively learn much as an apprentice does, by observing more competent others and trying out new skills under the direction of adults.

Together, the various approaches, all currently quite active, provide a fuller view of how children try to make sense of the world by constructing categories, rules, cognitive structures, skills, theories, and procedures. Biology and environment both stimulate and constrain this development. Children construct knowledge through assimilation, accommodation, encoding, and coconstruction with adults and peers. The chapters to follow describe the various "construction sites" of childhood.

2

Infant Perception

—⟫•◆•⟪—

As Eleanor Gibson (1969) defines it:

> Perception, functionally speaking, is the process through which we obtain firsthand information about the world around us. It has a phenomenal aspect, the awareness of events presently occurring in the organism's immediate surroundings. It also has a responsive aspect; it entails discriminative, selective response to the stimuli in the immediate environment. (p. 3)

It is to the origins of that "process," that "awareness," that "discriminative, selective response" that the present chapter is devoted. We begin our coverage of cognitive development with perception because perception is the necessary starting point for higher level, more clearly cognitive operations—reasoning, inferring, problem solving, and the like. Before infants and children can make sense of the world they perceive the world; and before we can ask what else infants and children do with their experiences, we must know what they are capable of perceiving—what "firsthand" information they can take in. We concentrate on perception

29

in infancy because this is when by far the most interesting and significant developments in perception occur—when, as Bornstein and Arterberry (1999, p. 244) put it,
"most of the 'action' . . . takes place." The nature of this "action"—and the ways in
which researchers have sought to understand it—makes for one of the most fascinating stories in contemporary child psychology.

In 1962 Hochberg said that it would be highly desirable to study young infants' visual abilities, but that "the human infant displays insufficient behavior coordination to permit its study to give us very much useful information" (p. 323).
Since that time Robert Fantz and other developmental psychologists have devised a
variety of ingenious methods for assessing the perceptual abilities and dispositions
of infants—even newborns. It is no exaggeration to say that we have witnessed the
emergence of a new field of study in the 40 years since Hochberg's pessimistic assessment. The most recent version of the *Handbook of Child Psychology* contains
four chapters devoted entirely or in good part to infant perception (Aslin, Juczyck &
Pisoni, 1998; Bertenthal & Clifton, 1998; Kellman & Banks, 1998; Spelke & Newport, 1998), and relevant material is scattered through a number of other chapters as
well. Clearly infant perception is one of the "hot" research areas in the field.

What has all this research taught us about infants' perceptual capabilities? A
brief answer is easy to give: The infant is a good deal more perceptually competent
than we used to think. The infant is, to be sure, not totally competent; recent years
have seen a swinging back from what Marshall Haith (1990, p. 9) dubs the "Gee-
whiz, look what baby can do" enthusiasm of the 1970s and 1980s to a more balanced picture of competencies and limitations. Nevertheless the conclusion
remains: There is more perceptual ability, present earlier in life, than psychologists
once believed.

Why did we underestimate the infant's perceptual competence? We believe
that there were two main reasons—one methodological, one theoretical.

Methodologically we made an unwarranted generalization from babies' motor
abilities to their perceptual abilities. Young infants have very poor motor skills.
They cannot control and coordinate well the movements of their heads, trunks, and,
especially, limbs. On the motor side, they fairly radiate behavioral incompetence.
What could be more natural, then, than to assume a similar level of incompetence
on the perceptual side?

Theoretically there has been a strong tradition in philosophy and psychology
to assume that we begin life with very minimal capabilities and only slowly and
gradually, through months and years of experience, construct these capabilities
(Gibson & Spelke, 1983). According to this view, we start with next to nothing (virtually a tabula rasa, or blank slate) and build all we have from the ground up, brick
by brick. This argument should sound familiar to you, for it represents one answer
to the most pervasive and long-standing question in developmental psychology: the
heredity-environment or nature-nurture issue. As applied to perception, the
heredity-environment debate concerns whether our mature perceptual abilities and
perceptual knowledge are provided by initial, inborn biological "nature" (the classic
nativist position) or subsequent, postnatal psychological "nurture" (the classic empiricist position). The general answer, as you doubtless realize, must be not one or
the other but *both*—recall the favorite cliché of introductory psychology texts: Development is always a matter of heredity *and* environment, never heredity *or* environment. Nevertheless the general acceptance of this truism has not prevented one
or the other position from dominating at particular times for particular topics, and

throughout much of the past century theorizing about perception had a decidedly empiricist cast to it. The assumption that the young infant is perceptually incompetent was a natural—indeed necessary—outgrowth of such thinking.

METHODS OF STUDYING INFANT PERCEPTION

Our view of the infant's perceptual abilities has changed as our methods of studying those abilities have changed. The great obstacle to such study, of course, is the fact that infants, unlike older participants, cannot verbally report on their perceptual activities and experiences. Nor, as we just noted, is the young infant capable of much in the way of skilled motor behavior. The key to studying infant perception has proved to be the clever exploitation of what infants *can* do—namely emit various nonverbal (and often minimally motoric) responses that can tell us something about what they are experiencing perceptually. Such nonverbal responses include both behavioral and physiological measures. Here we briefly describe some of the most important and broadly applicable of these measures; we add some further techniques later in the context of particular issues and studies.

Undoubtedly the most informative behavioral measure in the study of infant perception is looking behavior. It was, in fact, the invention of a looking-based procedure by Robert Fantz (1961) that is generally credited with initiating the revolution in the study of infant perception. In Fantz's "preference method," an experimenter displays two figures simultaneously and measures how long the baby looks at each. Let us suppose that over trials the baby looks systematically longer at one figure than the other—shows a "preference," to use the Fantz terminology. This finding tells us two important things about the infant's perceptual system. First it tells us that the system can distinguish or discriminate between these two stimuli. Preferences logically imply discriminability: An infant could not systematically attend to one thing rather than another unless she could somehow perceptually discriminate one from the other (note, however, that the reverse is definitely not the case—that is, the ability to discriminate does not imply that the infant will necessarily show a preference). Second preferences tell us about themselves—that is, what the infant is more or less disposed to attend to, and therefore something about the design of the infant's perceptual-attentional system. The comparison of specific stimuli tells us about specific preferences—that *this* stimulus is more interesting than *that.* More generally the very existence of preferences, from birth, tells us something very important about the human infant: Even the newborn is not completely at the mercy of the environment but rather is at least somewhat active and selective in what she attends to.

Other measures of looking can also be informative. With modern technology it is possible to measure not only which of two stimuli is being looked at but also exactly where the baby's eyes fixate and how they scan from one part of the stimulus to another. Such eye-movement recording can help to specify the information that the baby uses when she discriminates between stimuli. It can also tell us which aspects of a stimulus capture and which maintain the infant's attention.

Infants can do other things besides look. Another behavior that is present from birth is sucking. One way to utilize sucking in the study of perception is the following. The infant is given a pacifier nipple to suck on, and his baseline sucking rate is recorded. Then every time he increases his sucking rate above a certain predetermined level, he is reinforced by the presentation of a particular sound. This reinforcement leads to an increase in sucking rate. Even young babies seem happy to "work" in such ways (increased sucking, head turning, etc.) for purely auditory or visual wages—an important finding in itself, quite apart from its applicability to questions of perception. After repeated presentations of the same sound, however, interest in it begins to wane, as evidenced by a gradual decrease in sucking rate. The experimenter then presents a new and different sound. The infant may signal his recognition of the change and his heightened interest in the new sound by once again increasing his sucking rate. If he does so, then he has answered the question to which the paradigm is directed: He can hear a difference between the sounds.

In addition to overt behaviors such as looking and sucking, infants produce physiological responses that can give us clues as to what they are perceiving. Of the many physiological measures that have been used in the study of infant perception, the most informative and widely applicable is change in heart rate. Let us consider how the discrimination-of-sounds problem described in the preceding paragraph might be attacked with heart rate rather than sucking as the dependent variable. The experimenter produces the same sound as before, but this time measures changes in heart rate each time the sound appears. Initially heart rate slows down in response to the sound, a pattern that seems to reflect an orienting, attentional response. (In contrast heart-rate *acceleration* would mean startle, upset, etc.) Eventually, however, the sound loses its fascination, and heart rate no longer declines from baseline. At this point the experimenter switches to a new sound. Reappearance of the decelerative response would be clear evidence that the infant can perceive a difference between the two sounds.

The procedure just described illustrates a very general pair of phenomena known as *habituation* and *dishabituation*. Habituation is the first part of the process: a decline in interest as a repeated stimulus becomes familiar. Although our example concerned change in heart rate, other responses (including looking behavior) show the same pattern: an initial strong response when a stimulus is new, much less response when it has become old hat. Dishabituation is the second part of the process: the reemergence of interest when the stimulus is changed and thus becomes new again. Note that this procedure, like the Fantz preference method, tells us about both discrimination and preferences. The particular preference in this case is a preference for the relatively novel over the relatively familiar. And the fact that infants show such a preference allows us to conclude that they can discriminate between the stimuli in question. Note also that habituation of attention implies at least some sort of recognition-type memory capability. If the baby's cognitive system could not somehow code the fact that the repeated stimulus has been perceived before—could not "recognize" it, in some sense, as old or familiar—the system could not habituate to it (see Chapter 7). It is, after all, a physically identical stimulus from one trial to the next. Thus these research methods can actually give us information about three things rather than just two: (1) infant perceptual-discrimination abilities, (2) infant perceptual preferences, and (3) infant recognition-memory abilities.

Our brief description of current methods has made things sound more simple and straightforward than they really are. The recording and interpretation of looking, sucking, heart rate, and other response patterns are fraught with problems, problems that continue to be the focus of much attention, discussion, and debate among those who do such recording and interpretation for a living (Aslin et al.,

1998; Fox & Fitzgerald, 1990; Haith, 1990; Werker et al., 1998). Fortunately the topic of infant perception—perhaps precisely because it *is* so challenging—has attracted some of the field's most ingenious methodologists, and they have solved enough of the problems to give us some solid conclusions about what babies can do perceptually and when they can do it. In the following synopsis, we concentrate on vision and audition, the two most important sensory instruments of human learning and development.

VISION

Infant vision has received far more research attention than any other perceptual modality, and there is therefore no shortage of helpful summaries on the topic. Among the sources from which we draw are Hainline (1998), Kellman and Arterberry (1998), Kellman and Banks (1998), and Slater (1998).

We divide our coverage into three broad topics. We begin by addressing some basic questions having to do with how well infants of different ages can see. Can their eyes scan, fixate, and focus effectively? How good is their visual acuity or "eyesight"? Can they perceive the color in stimulation? We then move on to questions that have to do less with what infants *can* see than with what they *like* to see. What sorts of preferences do babies have with regard to their visual diet, and how do these preferences change as they develop? Finally—and most fully—we consider what meaningful information about the world infants of different ages can obtain by using their visual capacities. Can they perceive objects as such, for example, or is their perceptual experience instead one of individual parts (edges, angles, surfaces, etc.) independent of the whole? Can they perceive events that occur over time, or are they instead limited to discrete and noncontinuous snapshots? To what extent, in short, is their perceptual experience the same as yours or mine? And to the extent that it is not, when does it become so?

Basic Processes

A full account of infant vision would have to describe the anatomy and physiology of the various neural systems (retina, lateral geniculate nucleus, visual cortex, superior colliculus) that subserve human visual functioning. For our purposes it is sufficient to cite sources that provide such descriptions (Atkinson, 1998; Hickey & Peduzzi, 1987), along with some general conclusions about the physiological underpinnings for infant vision. First none of these relevant systems appears to be fully developed at birth; all seem to be immature to a greater or lesser degree. As a consequence very little if any of the neonate's visual functioning is of the quality it will be in later infancy. This is not to say that neonates cannot see, because they certainly can, but simply that their visual system has a good deal of developing to do. Second at least some of this developing appears to take place quite rapidly, for major changes occur across the early months of life. Thus by 6 months the visual system is a good deal more mature and adultlike than it was at birth. Finally many of the changes that can be observed in the infant's visual performance appear to reflect these biological-maturational changes in the underlying neural systems—perhaps especially changes in the visual cortex.

The neonate's visual system is immature in other ways as well. The quality of our vision depends not only on the functioning of the retina and relevant brain centers but also on various oculomotor mechanisms that serve to bring images into optimal focus on the retina (Aslin, 1988). Eye movements of various sorts are necessary to fixate a stimulus in the first place, to scan the parts of a complex field, and to pursue objects as they move through space. If we are to avoid double vision, we must be able to fixate both eyes on the same object simultaneously. Our pupils must be able to dilate and contract in response to changes in illumination. And we must be able to adjust the lens of the eye to bring objects of different distances into focus on the retina (a process labeled *accommodation*). Neonates and young infants are limited in their ability to do all of these things, and these limitations also affect the quality of their vision.

How well, then, does a newborn see, given these various physical limitations? One way to answer this question is in terms of visual acuity. Your visual acuity is defined technically as the highest spatial frequency you can detect. It can be measured, in infant or adult, by presenting patterns of alternating black and white stripes of equal width. The narrower the stripes (= higher the spatial frequency) that can be seen as stripes and not simply a gray field, the better the acuity. Acuity estimates for newborns fall in the range of 20/200 to 20/660 (Courage & Adams, 1990; Dobson & Teller, 1978). This is clearly not very good (at best only 1/10 as good as normal adult 20/20 vision); it does, however, indicate some ability to see patterning in stimulation, and it is probably quite sufficient for the visual needs of a young infant. As Hainline (1998, p. 8) puts it, "Young babies simply do not need to be good hunters or be able to read the fine print in a contract." By 6 months acuity has improved to about 20/70, and by 1 year it is fairly close to adult level.

Another important factor is contrast sensitivity. Your contrast sensitivity refers to your capacity for discriminating differences in light intensity (light-dark differences). Suppose that the stripes in the stimulus were broad rather than narrow, and therefore posed no visual acuity problem. The stimulus would obviously still become harder to see as striped rather than unpatterned as the intensity differences become smaller—that is, as the black and white stripes both change in intensity toward a common gray. Because intensity differences tend to be concentrated at the edges or contours of objects and object parts, they help to tell you where figure stops and ground begins, or where this object part ends and that one begins. Like acuity, therefore, contrast sensitivity is critical to your ability to perceive patterning. And like acuity, contrast sensitivity is poor at birth (again, perhaps only about 1/10 as good as adult functioning) but improves rapidly throughout infancy (Kellman & Arterberry, 1998).

So far we have talked only about the infant's ability to perceive an achromatic world—blacks, whites, and grays. What about color? Assessing infant color vision has long been extremely difficult to do (Teller & Bornstein, 1987). The biggest methodological problem has been to find ways to distinguish cleanly between infant discriminations based on wave length (what you are after) and infant discriminations based on brightness (a correlated, confounding variable that you want to control for). Although this problem has turned out to be solvable, the solutions all involve running a large number of trials, never an easy task with very young infants. Our knowledge of color perception in the first weeks of life therefore remains limited. What seems safest to conclude is that newborns can at least distinguish red from white; evidence for other color discriminations in the early weeks is less consistent and harder to interpret (Adams, 1995; Kellman & Banks, 1998). By 2 months, however, infants can make most of the discriminations that adults with normal color vision make, and by 4 months their color vision appears adultlike in every dimension that has been tested. Hence Teller and Bornstein's (1987) conclusion: "Color vision is in all probability an important component of the child's early mental machinery" (p. 231).

Preferences

How well babies see is one of the questions that we want to answer when we study infant vision. Another basic question is what infants *like* to see—that is, what preferences they have and why they have them. We have already noted that even newborns show some preferences in what they attend to; indeed the Fantz preference method is dependent on the fact that infants do not look indiscriminately but rather find some stimuli more interesting than others. The precise description, prediction, and theoretical explanation of infant preferences, however, has turned out to be an exceedingly difficult scientific task. Various possibilities have been proposed over the years: that infants prefer stimuli that are at an optimal level of complexity, or stimuli that are moderately discrepant from what they have experienced before, or stimuli with the right size and number of elements, or stimuli with a high level of contour density. The problem is that each of these models succeeds in explaining some infant preferences but fails to explain others; thus each gives at best a partial account of what infants find interesting.

A leading theory at the moment, at least with regard to preferences in the early weeks of life, is the "linear systems analysis" developed by Martin Banks and colleagues (Banks & Ginsburg, 1985; Banks & Salapatek, 1981). This model stresses limitations in the infant's visual capacities—in particular the young infant's relatively poor contrast-sensitivity capacity. This capacity allows only some of the pattern information present in the stimulus to reach "decision centers" in the baby's central nervous system. Banks and colleagues make their preference predictions on the basis of the information that reaches these centers—roughly speaking on the basis of what the baby actually sees rather than what the stimulus presents. The mathematical derivation of the predictions is both elegant and complex (see Banks and Ginsburg, 1985, for the details), but at some level the claim is a simple one: "Infants' visual preferences are governed simply by a tendency to look at highly visible patterns" (Banks & Ginsburg, 1985, p. 211). Thus far, the model's predictions of what should be highly visible in early infancy seem to accord well with what young babies tend to look at—edges, angles, areas of high contrast, exterior detail rather than interior, large detail rather than small.

Why do infants show the preferences that they do? More generally, why do infants, from birth, seem to have a positive *hunger* for visual stimulation—a desire to scan the environment and see whatever there is to see? Banks and Ginsburg (1985) suggest two explanations. One possibility (also proposed by Haith, 1980) is that visual stimulation is necessary for normal development of the visual cortex. Exposure to patterned information—not just light, but patterned stimuli—is known to facilitate the development of the cat visual cortex, and the same may be true in humans. By this use-it-or-lose-it view, the visual system grows through use, and infants' inborn tendency to exercise their visual abilities is therefore highly adaptive. As we discuss, the notion that various aspects of brain development are affected by experience has become increasingly popular in recent years (M. H. Johnson, 1998).

A second (not necessarily contradictory) possibility is that infants may be biased to attend to the information in the environment that is most important for them to learn about. Faces, for example, are clearly important to learn about, and characteristics of the face correspond nicely to infants' early preferences: a highly patterned stimulus, chock-full of contrast, presented at the optimal distance for babies to see it clearly. Similarly object movement is of clear ecological significance, and babies are also responsive to object movement from early in life. Obviously any tendency to attend to psychologically significant information would also be adaptive for the infant's development.

We noted that the linear systems approach works well for preferences in the early weeks of life. Preferences change with development, however, and the preferences shown by the older infant seem to have a different basis from that operative in early infancy. With development built-in processing biases become less important as determinants of visual preferences, and experience and memory and meaning become more important. Thus a 1-month-old may look at a face because the face presents a package of highly salient stimuli; a 4-month-old, however, looks at a face because of an interest in faces per se—both faces in general and mommy's face in particular. In general, as infants develop, their attention comes to be directed more and more to aspects of the environment that they are attempting to make sense of—to things that are new, things that are complex, things that are puzzling or surprising. Notice that all of these events are of interest only by virtue of their *relation* to the infant's cognitive system. Properties important in early development, like contrast or movement, can be specified in absolute terms, but a stimulus is never new or complex or surprising in itself; rather it is new or complex or surprising *to* someone. What infants find new or complex or surprising changes as their cognitive system changes, and thus the specific interests of an 18-month-old will differ from those of a 6-month-old. At both ages, however, it is the fit between new experience and current level that is critical. And at both ages the infant's preferences are, once again, highly adaptive. Indeed it is hard to imagine a more adaptive motivational system than the one that seems to govern infant attention: Pay most attention to the things that you still need to understand.

Perception of Objects

Our ability to make sense of our perceptual experience eventually extends well beyond the detection and discrimination of specific stimuli. Consider what we see when we gaze at the family cat stretched out before the fireplace. We see a single, solid, three-dimensional object, located in a particular region of space and separate from both the objects it touches (e.g., the rug on which it lies) and the objects it occludes (e.g., in the fireplace behind it). We see an object of a particular size, shape, and color, and do so regardless of the distance between us and cat, the angle of viewing, or the lighting in the room (all factors that change the image on our retina). If an object comes between cat and us, blocking all except head and tail, we do not perceive the cat as being bisected; rather our perception is still of a continuous, indivisible object. Should the cat meow we correctly perceive the sound as coming from the same object that we are viewing, and should the cat's wet fur emit a certain odor we are quite certain of its source also. If the cat stirs itself and strolls from the room, we do not expect its grin or any other part to remain behind; rather we realize that the parts of an animate object move together in predictable unison. If the movement takes the cat away from us, we correctly perceive that it is receding from us (but not changing size, despite changes in the size of the retinal image); on the other hand, if the cat suddenly makes a run for our lap, we perceive not only that it is approaching but also that its course guarantees contact within a very short time. (Of course, how we feel about such contact depends more on our attitude toward cats than on perception per se.)

The focus of the current section is on whether infants perceive objects and events in the adult-level fashion just described. Much of the work that we discuss was inspired by the theorizing of Eleanor Gibson and James Gibson (Gibson, 1969, 1988; Gibson & Pick, 2000). The Gibsonian emphasis has always been on complex, dynamic, ecologically significant forms of perception. The ability to perceive important invariances such as size and shape certainly fits this description, as does the realization that a visually "looming" stimulus (the cat in midair) signals an impending collision. Methodologically the Gibsonians stress the need to study perception in situations that approximate the richness and complexity of the natural environment, rather than only through presentation of isolated stimuli in stripped-down laboratory settings—in James Gibson's words, "perception outdoors under the sky instead of perception of points in a darkroom" (1979, p. xii). Theoretically their emphasis is precisely on the richness of information available in the natural environment—on the multitude of cues that specify properties such as size, shape, and movement, and on infants' gradually increasing sensitivity to these cues. Not all of the workers who have followed in this tradition accept all aspects of Gibsonian theory (a fate, as we shall see, that has also befallen Piaget in the realm of infant cognitive development). Nevertheless the Gibsons (like Piaget) have had a lasting impact on how we think about and study infancy.

Object Properties. Much of what we know about infants' perception of objects comes from the work of Elizabeth Spelke and colleagues (Spelke, 1982, 1985, 1988, 1990, 1998; Spelke & Van de Walle, 1993; Spelke, Vishton, & Hofsten, 1995). Their research has addressed several of the questions about object perception that were sketched in our vignette of the cat, including the infant's ability to perceive an object as distinct from the background surfaces behind it (the cat is not connected to the fireplace), as a separate entity from any surfaces that touch it (the cat and the rug are separate objects), and as continuing behind any surfaces that partly hide it from view (the cat remains a single and continuous object even if a footstool cuts off the view of its midsection). The general conclusion that Spelke et al. reach is that the young infant knows a lot but not everything about these characteristics of objects. This is, as we shall see, a fairly safe general conclusion for a number of aspects of perceptual development. The innovations of modern research have succeeded in demonstrating impressive levels of previously unsuspected competence at surprisingly early ages; very seldom, however, do we find adult-level ability from the start.

Consider first the realization that objects are distinct from their backgrounds—for example, that the cat is not connected to the fireplace. An adult can simply report that he perceives cat and fireplace as separate entities. How can we ever figure out what a nonverbal infant perceives? Spelke and Born (Spelke, 1982) decided to see whether infants were surprised when the usual rules of object unity were violated. Three-month-old infants first saw an orange cylinder suspended in front of a flat, blue surface. On some trials subsequently, they saw the cylinder as a whole move forward,

toward them, while the background surface remained still. On other trials the movement broke the object in half; half of the object moved forward in conjunction with an
adjacent portion of the background. The investigators "reasoned that if infants perceived the object as unitary and separate from the background, they would be surprised or puzzled when the object broke apart and moved together with part of the
background" (Spelke, 1982, p. 412). The infants did in fact exhibit more apparent surprise or puzzlement on the latter trials than on the former ones. Subsequent research
showed that infants of this age do not exhibit more surprise or puzzlement on trials of
the latter, abnormal-movement kind when object and background are both two-
dimensional and initially form part of the same surface, as in a picture, rather than
being separated in depth from each other. Spelke (1982) interprets these results as indicating that infants of this age probably do see as unified, bounded wholes objects
that are clearly separated in depth from their backgrounds.

Infants' tendency to reach for nearby objects can provide further evidence of
their ability to perceive object as separate from background. Hofsten and Spelke
(1985) presented 5-month-old infants with two blocklike objects of the same color
and texture but of different sizes, with the smaller object in front of the larger one. In
one condition the two objects touched, and in the other they were separated by a small
gap. Infants are known to reach for the closer of two clearly distinct objects (Yonas &
Granrud, 1985), and hence the expectation was that the babies would reach for the
smaller block if they perceived two blocks rather than one. On the other hand, infants
typically reach for single objects by grasping the lateral borders of the object; hence
any infant who perceived but one block was expected to reach for the edges of the
larger block (because it provided all the lateral borders in the display). When the objects were separated, infants reached for the smaller block, indicating that they correctly perceived two objects rather than one; when the objects touched, however, the
reach was for the larger block, suggesting that the perception was of a single block.
Further studies (Kestenbaum, Termine, & Spelke, 1987; Spelke, Hofsten, & Kestenbaum, 1989) demonstrated that infants perceive two back-to-back objects as one even
under conditions in which adults clearly see two distinct objects—for example, when
the objects differ in color and texture. On the other hand, infants are capable of disentangling the two objects if helpful motion cues are present—for example if the smaller
and larger blocks move at different rates. Motion is a quintessentially Gibsonian cue,
for in real-world environments objects or perceiver or both are often moving rather
than stationary. And motion, as we shall see, turns out to be a helpful cue with respect
to all sorts of aspects of perception.

Figure 2.1 shows a set of stimuli that were used to test for the realization that
partially hidden objects are continuous, unitary entities—that the cat, for example,
does not consist solely of head and tail even if these are the only parts that can be
seen. Shown in the top part of the figure is the original stimulus display: a straight
black rod positioned vertically behind a tan block. Adults looking at this array effortlessly and automatically perceive the rod as a single, continuous object located
behind another object. Kellman and Spelke (1983) used an habituation-of-looking
method to try to ascertain whether 4-month-olds would also perceive the rod as a
single object, or as two rods separated by a space, as the image of this stimulus on
one's retina would specify. The infants were first habituated to the sight of the original stimulus display and then saw the two test displays shown in the bottom part of
the figure. If the infants perceived the occluded rod in the original display as a single unitary entity, as adults do, they should look more at the two rods separated by a

HABITUATION DISPLAY

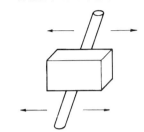

FIGURE 2.1 Habituation and test displays used to assess infants' understanding of partly occluded objects. Adapted from "Perception of Partly Occluded Objects in Infancy," by P. J. Kellman and E. S. Spelke, 1983, *Cognitive Psychology, 15,* p. 489. Copyright © 1983 by Academic Press. Adapted by permission.

TEST DISPLAYS

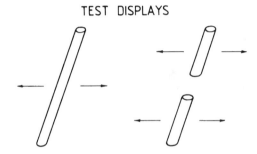

space than at the complete rod, because the two rods would be perceived as a novel stimulus and the complete rod as a familiar, previously seen one. If, instead, they perceived the occluded rod as two separate objects, they should look more at the complete rod, because that would constitute the novel stimulus for them. Much to the investigators' surprise, the babies did not look more at either test display. They acted as if they had no expectations one way or the other as to what was behind the block. Further studies revealed that this deficit is a general one across a variety of types of objects and methods of occlusion: Young infants often fail to perceive the unity of objects whose centers are invisible (Spelke, 1988).

On the other hand, the young infant's deficiencies are not absolute ones. Failure occurs when the object in question is stationary. If instead the object's visible parts are seen to move in unison—for example if the rod wiggles back and forth behind the block—then 4-month-olds, like adults, perceive one continuous object rather than two discontinuous ones. If further helpful cues are present, even 2-month-olds sometimes succeed in perceiving object unity (Johnson & Aslin, 1995). In contrast newborn babies fail to perceive the unity of occluded objects even when the parts move together (Slater, Johnson, Brown, & Badenoch, 1996; Slater, Morison, Somers, Mattock, Brown, & Taylor, 1990). Apparently, the ability to use movement as a cue to object unity emerges some time during the first few months of life. Even at 4 months, success is not total; only some kinds of movement are sufficient to produce a perception of unity (Eizenman & Bertenthal, 1998), and young infants cannot yet use all the cues available to older individuals (S. Johnson, 1998; Needham & Modi, 2000; Spelke & Newport, 1998). By 6 months infants no longer require movement cues to perceive the unity of occluded objects (Craton, 1996). We can see here a theme that we will encounter again: Many aspects of perceptual development are a matter of gradual and cumulative gains in competence—what Haith (1993) has labeled "partial accomplishments"—and not simply one-point-in-time achievements.

Faces.   One object that is found in every infant's environment is important enough to single out for special attention, and that is the human face. Babies are interested in faces from early in life. Exactly when they begin to respond to the face *as a face,* however, and not simply as a collection of interesting parts, has been difficult to determine. This question is part of a more general issue: When do infants become capable of perceiving patterns or wholes in stimulation, as opposed to the individual elements (edges, angles, contours, etc.) that are known to drive the very young infant's attention? Like many issues in infant perception, this question does not have a single "correct" answer; rather what we conclude about pattern perception depends on both the particular patterns in question and the ingenuity with which the experimenter has probed for infant competence. The best current evidence, however, suggests that infants begin to "put together" simple patterns between 1 and 3 months of age, with more complex forms of pattern perception emerging gradually across the first year (Cohen, 1998; Haith, 1990).

What, then, about faces? Here, too, the evidence for perception of patterning is clearest from about 2 to 3 months on. By 3 months infants look longer at a face than at a comparable nonface stimulus (Dannemiller & Stephens, 1988), and by about the same age, they show a preference for a familiar face (typically mommy's) over an unfamiliar one (Barrera & Maurer, 1981). By the second half of the first year, they are capable of all sorts of things with regard to face perception—recognizing a face as the same despite variations in expression or orientation (Cohen & Strauss, 1979), recognizing their own face as a familiar stimulus (Legerstee, Anderson, & Schaffer, 1998), classifying faces on the basis of sex (Fagan, 1976), differentiating various emotional expressions (de Haan & Nelson, 1998), even responding differentially to attractive faces compared to unattractive ones (Langlois, Ritter, Roggman, & Vaughn, 1991). As we discuss in the later section on Intermodal Perception, they also demonstrate an impressive ability to match the visual and auditory cues that emanate from a particular face.

What about newborns? As is true for many aspects of perception, conclusions about very early competence are still somewhat unclear. A preference for faces is sometimes found in the early weeks, but much less consistently so than in older babies. Furthermore, when the preference does occur it can often be explained on simpler bases—in particular, by the fact, revealed by the linear systems approach discussed earlier, that elements of the face tend to be especially visible to the newborn perceptual system. Several recent studies, however, have provided evidence for a preference for facelike stimuli in newborns even when the overall visibility of the stimuli is controlled for (Johnson, Dziurawiec, Ellis, & Morton, 1991; Mondloch et al., 1999; Simion, Valenza, & Umilta, 1998). This finding has been demonstrated with the Fantz preference method and also with a procedure that measures babies' tendency to track different stimuli as they move across the visual field. Figure 2.2 shows one of the sets of stimuli used with the latter procedure, along with an illustrative set of findings. The researchers who have identified such early preferences are careful to emphasize that they are not identical to the careful, selective processing of faces shown by older infants; indeed in Johnson and Morton's (1991) model, the early interest in faces is explicitly linked to different brain areas than the ones that will eventually mediate response. But these investigators also suggest that the early interest is adaptive, because it gets the baby started on the path toward more mature social perception.

Surprising though such early attention to faces may seem, a further finding from recent research is perhaps even more unexpected. Several investigators have reported that newborns show not simply an interest in faces but a preference for their own mother's face (Bushnell, Sai, & Mullin, 1989; Pascalis, de Schonen, Morton, & Deruelle, 1995; Walton, Bower, & Bower, 1992)—a preference that clearly must reflect postbirth learning. What is remarkable here is not only the rapidity of the learning (at most a few hours' worth of relevant experience) but also the fact that it is a accomplished with such a limited visual system—including, among other limitations, an acuity of about 20/200 at best. How could babies with such limited visual competence be learning the features of the mother's face? The study by Pascalis et al. (1995) suggests an explanation. After establishing that their 3-day-old participants showed an own-mother preference, they redid the experiment with one difference: Now the

FIGURE 2.2 Stimuli and results from the Johnson et al. (1991) study of newborns' tendency to track moving objects. The babies moved their eyes and heads more in response to the face than in response to the other two stimuli. Reprinted from "Newborns' Preferential Tracking of Facelike Stimuli and its Subsequent Decline," by M. H. Johnson, M. Dziurawiec, H. Ellis, & J. Morton, 1991, *Cognition, 40*, p. 6. Copyright © 1991 by Elsevier Science Publishers. Reprinted by permission.

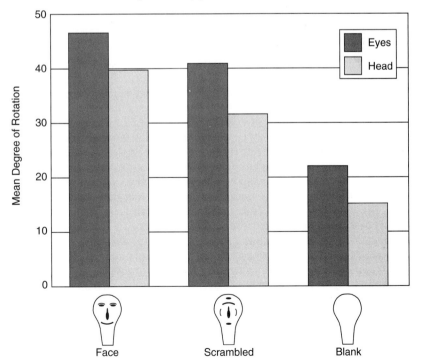

women wore scarves that covered their hair and part of their foreheads. With the scarves in place the babies no longer showed a preference for their own mothers. What this study seems to indicate, then, is that early recognition of the mother is not based on inner details of the face but rather on more gross and peripheral features, such as hairline and shape of head. Like the early interest in faces, therefore, early recognition of the mother is crude and limited in comparison to what it eventually will be. But like the general interest in faces, any early sensitivity to an especially important face seems clearly adaptive for eventual social development.

Constancy.   Objects maintain a constant size despite changes in distance from the perceiver (and hence changes in the size of the retinal image), and they maintain a constant shape despite changes in spatial orientation relative to the perceiver (and hence changes in the shape and the orientation of the retinal image). One of the classic questions of perceptual development concerns when and how an appreciation of perceptual constancy develops. Do young babies experience constancy from the start, or are they initially dependent on the retinal image, in which case they would inhabit a very different perceptual world? And how might we answer this question?

The most common method of studying constancy has been our old friend habituation (e.g., Slater, Mattock, & Brown, 1990). To investigate size constancy, for example, we might habituate the infant to an object of a particular size, then test for dishabituation to stimuli of two sorts: objects of the same size but presented at different distances, and objects that vary from the original in both size and distance but that maintain the same-sized retinal image (e.g., an object that is three times larger but also three times farther away). If infants dishabituate (i.e., notice a difference) more for the second sort of stimulus than the first, we would have evidence that they can perceive similarity of real size despite variations in distance and hence in size of the retinal image. Much the same logic underlies a second approach to studying constancy: operant conditioning followed by generalization. In this case we first condition the infant to respond to an object of a particular size, and then test for generalization of the response to objects of either the same size or the same retinal image (e.g., Bower, 1966).

Studies using these procedures have produced some remarkable findings in recent years. Even the newborn infant, it turns out, is not dependent on the immediate retinal image; rather some degree of both size and shape constancy is present at birth (Slater, Mattock, & Brown, 1990). Constancy is not full-blown at birth or for some time afterward, for like many aspects of perception its development is prolonged and gradual, and not an abrupt, absent-to-present transition. Nevertheless there is a fair amount of competence present fairly early—just as is true for other aspects of object perception.

Perceptual constancies fit into a larger developmental context that deserves brief mention. The growth of the human mind partly consists of the successive attainment or formation of cognitive *invariants*. As its name suggests, an invariant is something that remains the same while other things in the situation change. The identification of constant features or invariants in the midst of flux and change is an absolutely indispensable cognitive activity for an adaptive organism. Perceptual constancies represent one class of invariants: the realization that the perceivable characteristics of objects (size, shape, color, etc.) remain the same despite variations in viewing conditions and hence retinal image. As we go we will encounter more conceptual invariants that are mastered later in development, including two made famous by Piaget: the object concept of infancy and the conservations of middle childhood.

Depth Perception

Our mature perceptual capacities allow us to perceive and respond adaptively not only to objects but also to numerous aspects of the spatial environment within which objects appear—obstacles, openings, supporting surfaces and dropoffs, left-right and up-down relations, depths and distances. In this section we focus on the development of an especially important kind of spatial perception: the ability to perceive three dimensions or depth in stimulation. For more general treatments of spatial perception in infancy, see Kellman and Banks (1998) and Yonas and Owsley (1987).

The perception of depth has been of interest to psychologists for the same general reason that the perceptual constancies have been of interest: namely that our perception is better than it seems that it should be given the retinal image available to us. In the case of depth, we somehow perceive a world of three dimensions despite the fact that the retinal image is a flat two-dimensional one. The developmental question is how early infants are capable of such three-dimensional perception.

Looming and Reaching. How can we figure out whether babies are perceiving a two- or a three-dimensional world? Various kinds of evidence are available. In the present section we consider two sorts, both of which involve appropriate response to solid objects at some distance in space.

If you were to look up to see a basketball suddenly approaching your face, you would react in a predictable fashion: You would blink, your head would go back, your arms would fly up, and (time permitting) you would take some sort of evasive action. Although obviously not conscious, at a behavioral level such response to a "looming stimulus" signals an awareness that the ball is a three-dimensional object moving through space—and thus some ability to perceive depth. Tests of such awareness in infants typically make use of a shadow caster (to avoid the movement-of-air cues that a real object would produce) that creates the impression of a rapidly approaching solid object. Infants as young as 1 month blink in response to such a stimulus, and by 3 to 4 months, we see the full-blown defensive response just described (Yonas, 1981).

Looming studies measure response when a solid object approaches the infant. We can also examine infants' ability to approach solid objects—in particular to reach for things they want to feel or obtain. Reaching itself implies some perception of depth, and specific adjustments to the reach imply further sensitivity—for example, does the infant reach for near but not far objects, or perhaps shape his hand differently as a function of the object about to be grasped? Visually directed reaching is not present in the early weeks of life, although newborns do show "prereaching" behaviors (gross swipes in the direction of an object) that may be a precursor of later reaching (Bertenthal & Clifton, 1998). True reaching emerges by 3 to 4 months, and the various refinements sketched earlier follow soon thereafter. By 6 months babies can even use auditory cues to judge the distance of an object; they reach in response to nearby but not far away sounds (Clifton, Perris, & Bullinger, 1991). By this point they are also skilled at reaching for moving objects, directing the reach not toward the target's present location but toward its anticipated future locus (Hofsten, 1980; Wentworth, Benson, & Haith, 2000).

Drop-offs.   A particularly interesting form of depth perception—from both a theoretical and a pragmatic point of view—is the perception of drop-offs. As adult perceivers we are capable of making a number of closely related responses when we encounter deep drop-offs. First our depth-perception mechanisms enable us to see them instantly *as* deep drop-offs—as edges with slopes receding sharply downward to bottoms that are a considerable distance away. Second we experience fear if we do go off them, or perhaps even if we get too close to them. Third—and quite sensibly and adaptively—we avoid stepping off such fear-arousing drop-offs. Do infants show similar perceptual and behavioral responses to depth?

Eleanor Gibson and Richard Walk invented a device called a "visual cliff " to explore this developmental problem (1960). The visual cliff is a large glass-covered table divided by a center board (see Figure 2.3). On one side of the center board, the glass rests just above a patterned surface. On the other, deep or "cliff" side, the patterned surface lies a considerable distance beneath the covering glass. Gibson and Walk and other investigators have found that newborn animals of some species (goats, rhesus monkeys, chickens) would readily move from the center board onto the shallow side but would not venture onto the deep side. For these species, clearly, perceptual detection of a drop-off and avoidance of it is innate. On the other hand, the young of some other species (cats, rabbits) do not avoid the deep side initially; they only do so after a few weeks of visual experience (Campos, Hiatt, Ramsay, Henderson, & Svejda, 1978). For these animals perception and avoidance of drop-offs might be the product of postnatal biological maturation, experience, or some combination of the two.

Young human infants cannot be tested in the usual manner on the visual cliff because, unlike the very young of many other species, they are too immature motorically to be able to locomote. Once they are mature enough to crawl (typically somewhere around 7 months), the method usually used is something like the following: The baby is placed on the center platform facing his mother across the deep or the shallow side. The mother calls the baby to cross. (It seems vaguely immoral. . . .) If the baby does not cross within 2 minutes, the mother shows the baby a familiar toy and continues to coax for another 2 minutes. The same procedure is then repeated for the other side. Human infants also show some tendency to avoid the deep side under these testing conditions. Not all infants shun the drop-off (a point to which we return); most do, however, and the tendency to do so increases with age. Thus the ability to perceive and respond positively to drop-offs appears to be part of human competence by the last third of the first year.

Might the ability to perceive drop-offs be present earlier than can be demonstrated with a crawling-based methodology like the visual cliff? Quite possibly. There are many perceptual cues that help to specify depth, and the developmental literature on the ages at which infants first become responsive to these cues (Yonas & Granrud, 1985; Yonas & Owsley, 1987) makes the assumption of early competence seem reasonable. (We cannot resist quoting Yonas and Granrud, 1985, p. 45, on the multiplicity of cues for depth: "God must have loved depth cues, for He made so many of them.") There is also more direct evidence on the matter. Campos and his research colleagues have found that prelocomotor (2-month-old) infants show greater heart-rate deceleration when placed on the deep side of the visual cliff

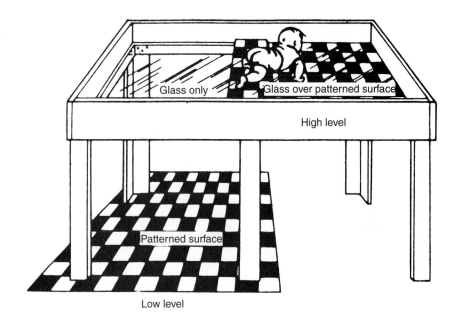

Low level

FIGURE 2.3 Visual-cliff apparatus for testing depth perception. From "A
Comparative and Analytic Study of Visual Depth Perception," by
R. D. Walk & E. J. Gibson, 1961, *Psychological Monographs, 75*
(No. 15, Whole No. 519), p. 8. Copyright © 1961 by the American
Psychological Association. Reprinted by permission of Dr. E. J.
Gibson.

than when placed on the shallow side, suggesting that they can perceptually discriminate between the two (Campos et al., 1978). More convincing yet, when
slowly lowered toward the glass on the shallow side, prelocomotor babies put their
hands out just prior to touchdown; they do not make this placing response just prior
to reaching the glass on the deep side, strongly suggesting that they perceive that
they still have some distance yet to go (Svejda & Schmid, 1979). Yet babies of this
age do not yet show fear in response to dropoffs. If placed over or on the deep side,
their faces appear calm, they do not cry, and—as just mentioned—they show heart-
rate *de*celeration, signifying attentiveness rather than fear. In contrast older, crawling infants have been found to show heart-rate *ac*celeration in this situation,
indicating fear (Campos et al., 1978; Richards & Rader, 1983).

The conclusion to this point is that some ability to perceive drop-offs is
probably present in the early months of life but that fear of drop-offs does not emerge
until the second half of the first year. The second half of the first year is also, as we
noted, the time during which babies begin to move around on their own. There is, then,
at least a rough temporal synchrony between self-produced locomotion and fear of
depth. Joseph Campos and Bennett Bertenthal have argued that there is also a causal
relation between the two developments (Bertenthal & Campos, 1990; Bertenthal,

Campos, & Kermoian, 1994; Campos, Bertenthal, & Kermoian, 1992). In their view moving about on one's own contributes to the perception of depth by providing the infant with new information about the spatial environment, as well as forcing increased attention toward and new uses of already available information.

Campos and Bertenthal cite a variety of kinds of evidence in support of this claim of a functional role for crawling. We noted earlier that not all babies who have begun to crawl succeed in avoiding the deep side of the visual cliff. The Campos/Bertenthal position predicts that there should be a positive relation between crawling experience and success on the cliff—that is, it should be those babies who have been crawling the longest who are most likely to avoid the drop-off. This, in fact, proves to be the case; even with age held constant, crawling experience relates to avoidance of the drop-off. The Campos/Bertenthal position also predicts that babies who have been crawling the longest should be most likely to show a fear response if they should happen to find themselves on the deep side of the cliff. This prediction, too, has been supported: Infants who have begun to crawl are more likely to show heart-rate acceleration to the deep side than are same-age infants who are not yet crawling. Finally the theory predicts that providing babies with increased locomotor experience should hasten the onset of the fear response. Bertenthal and Campos (1990) and Campos et al. (1992) summarize experiments in which groups of prelocomotor infants were given a minimum of 40 hours of experience using infant walkers to get around in the environment. These infants were subsequently more likely than matched controls to avoid the deep side of the cliff, and also more likely to show heart-rate acceleration when lowered over the deep side.

Fear of drop-offs is not the only form of spatial understanding that is affected by self-produced movement. Increased locomotor experience—again either naturally occurring or experimentally provided—has been found to help babies keep track of the locations of hidden objects when they themselves are moved subsequent to the hiding, a task that babies in the 7-to 9-month range find challenging (Bai & Bertenthal, 1992). It has also been shown to facilitate response to the sorts of search tasks that Piaget used to study object permanence, a topic that we take up in Chapter 3 (Kermoian & Campos, 1988). As Bertenthal et al. (1994) note, this sort of facilitative pattern may be common in development. As one behavioral system matures, the child is opened up to new experiences that then contribute to other sorts of development.

One more point about the visual cliff data is worth making. Whatever the interplay of maturation and experience may be that leads to fear of drop-offs, the timing of this accomplishment is highly adaptive. Babies begin to fear depth at just the time that they need such fear—namely when they begin to take control of their own movement.

AUDITION

This summary owes much to a recent review by Aslin et al. (1998). As do these authors, our discussion concentrates on an especially interesting and important form of auditory perception: namely, perception of human speech. Before turning to speech, however, we summarize some basic conclusions with respect to how well babies hear. We do so under three headings: detection (what sounds can the infant hear?), discrimination (what differences among sounds can the infant perceive?), and localization (how well can the infant localize sounds in space?).

Detection

Babies can hear at birth, a fact that has not always been apparent either to parents or to scientific professionals. They do not hear as well as they will eventually; estimates of newborn auditory threshold range from 10 to 20 decibels higher than the adult's at best to 40 to 50 decibels higher at worst. As this range of values suggests, thresholds are not easy to measure in very young babies. As infants grow older, their auditory sensitivity becomes both more easily measurable and more adultlike. Thresholds do vary with the frequency of the sound, however, and infants approach optimum-level hearing earlier for high-frequency sounds than for low-frequency ones (Trehub & Schneider, 1983).

Not only can babies hear at birth, but they also can hear before birth. Evidence from fetal recordings and prematurely born infants indicates that the auditory system begins to function at least several weeks prior to the normal term of birth. By the 25th week after conception, both physiological changes and motor movements (e.g., leg flexions) can be demonstrated in response to sound (Lecanuet, 1998). By the 28th week, fetuses clamp their eyelids (a component of the startle response) in response to a loud vibroacoustic stimulus presented near the mother's abdomen (Birnholz & Benacerraf, 1983). Interestingly all the fetuses that failed to respond were later born with hearing problems.

What sorts of things are fetuses likely to hear, given that the auditory system has started to operate? Recordings of the intrauterine environment provide a clue. Microphones implanted within the womb (in some cases literally swallowed by mothers!) reveal that some sounds from the outer environment do get through, including not only loud noises (as the work summarized in the previous paragraph demonstrates) but also speech from conversational partners near to the mother (Lecanuet, 1998). Such recordings also confirm what we would expect, however: namely, that it is the mother's speech that is transmitted most clearly to the fetus (Richards, Frentzen, Gerhardt, McCann, & Abrams, 1992). The mother, of course, is not only the clearest but also the most frequent source of auditory input prior to birth; we might predict, therefore, that if any prenatal auditory experience is going to have an effect it will be speech from the mother. Shortly we discuss some dramatic evidence in support of this conjecture.

Discrimination

Hearing requires not only the ability to detect sounds but also the ability to perceive differences among different sounds. Infants have been shown to discriminate differences along a variety of dimensions of auditory input: intensity, frequency, duration, and timing. In some cases they not only hear differences but also respond differentially; the soothing quality of low-frequency sounds is an example familiar to many a parent. Infants' discriminations, to be sure, are not as fine as those of adults, although in some cases they may come close; in one study, for example, 5- to 8-month-old infants discriminated frequency changes on the order of 2%, as compared with the 1% level achieved by adults (Olsho, Schoon, Sakai, Turpin, & Sperduto, 1982). And discrimination, like detection, becomes better as infants get older.

As Aslin (1987, p. 6) notes, "the most ubiquitous finding in developmental research is that infants show more adult-like performance as they grow older."

Localization

On the other hand, infants' ability to localize (i.e., turn toward the source of) sounds shows a surprising, albeit temporary, exception to Aslin's rule. Infants demonstrate a primitive ability to localize from birth—indeed, in one study, carried out in the delivery room, within 5 minutes of birth (Wertheimer, 1961)! By 2 or 3 months, however, this response has largely disappeared, only to reemerge again by 4 or 5 months (Muir & Clifton, 1985). Localization is one of several behavioral systems that show such a U-shaped developmental curve: a rudimentary form present very early, followed by disappearance of the response, followed by emergence of a more mature level of functioning (Bever, 1982). The usual explanation for such a nonlinear course of development is that early and later forms of response have different underlying bases. The argument in the case of localization (but see Kellman and Arterberry, 1998, for a dissenting view) is that the neonate's localization is a reflexive, subcortical affair, analogous to other reflexes that are present at birth. Like other reflexes, localization is automatically elicited by particular environmental stimuli, and like many such reflexes, it drops out with biological maturation. The localization of the older infant is different: cortical rather than subcortical, and considerably more exploratory, more skilled, and more attuned to environmental variation. And the localization of the older infant shows the developmental course that we would expect: greater and greater accuracy as the infant grows older (Morrongiello, 1988; Morrongiello, Fenwick, & Chance, 1990).

Perception of Speech Sounds

Studies of infants' perception of speech have addressed the same two general questions that have guided work on infant vision. One question concerns preferences: what infants like to listen to. The other question concerns abilities: what they hear when they so listen.

Preferences. A general answer to the first question is clear enough: Infants like to listen to speech. De Villiers and de Villiers (1979) summarize some of the evidence for this conclusion.

> Within a matter of days after birth, they are highly responsive to speech or other sounds of similar pitch to the human voice. In fact, speech seems to be rewarding to the infant in a way that other sounds are not. Newborns will learn to suck on an artificial nipple hooked to a switch that turns on a brief portion of recorded speech or vocal music, but they will not suck as readily in order to hear instrumental music or other rhythmical sound. In the first few months of life, speech elicits greater electrical activity in the left half of the child's brain and music elicits greater activity in the right half of the brain, as is the case with adults. This suggests that at a very early age the two hemispheres of the brain are already specialized for dealing with the different kinds of sound. So from the beginning of infancy children are able to discriminate speech from nonspeech, and they seem to pay particular attention to speech. (p. 16)

Infants' preferences extend beyond simply speech versus nonspeech. From early in life, they show a preference for the form of speech known as "motherese." Motherese (also referred to as "infant-directed speech" or "child-directed speech") is the label for the type of speech that not only mothers but adults in general typically direct to young children; among its features are a slow tempo, high pitch, and greatly exaggerated intonation (Fernald & Simon, 1984). It is, in short, the kind of speech that tells you that there must be a baby nearby. Among its attributes motherese has a strongly "up and down" quality that might be expected to attract an infant's attention. This, in fact, proves to be the case; from the first days of life, infants are more interested in and attentive to motherese than they are to adult-to-adult talk (Cooper & Aslin, 1990). Such preferences are evident even when the voice is that of a female stranger rather than the child's mother (Fernald, 1985). They are evident for male speakers as well as female speakers (Werker & McLeod, 1989). And they are evident even when the medium of communication is something other than the usual auditory one. Deaf mothers of deaf infants use a form of motherese in the sign language they direct to their babies, slowing down and exaggerating their gestures, and their babies are more attentive to such input than they are to adult-directed signs (Masataka, 1996). Indeed even 6-month-old *hearing* infants who have never been exposed to signs find the motherese form of sign language more interesting than the typical adult form (Masataka, 1998). There seems, then, to be something inherently compelling for babies about this kind of input, even in the absence of a history of specific experience with such messages.

Infants also prefer their own mother's voice over those of other speakers. Mehler, Bertoncini, Barriere, and Jassik-Gerschenfeld (1978) demonstrated such preferences as early as 1 month—only, however, when the speech was of the normal, mother-to-baby, motherese sort. When both voices took the form of nonintonated monotones, the infants showed no ability to discriminate mother and stranger. Early as it seems, 1 month is not the lower bound for such own-mother preferences. DeCasper and Fifer (1980) tape-recorded mothers as they read a Dr. Seuss children's story. These recordings served as the auditory stimuli for subsequent testing of the mothers' 3-day-old infants. In three experiments it was found that the newborns tended to suck in such a way as to produce the sounds of their own mothers' voices in preference to that of another mother. The authors concluded that "within the first 3 days of postnatal development, newborns prefer the human voice, discriminate between speakers, and demonstrate a preference for their mothers' voices with only limited maternal exposure" (DeCasper & Fifer, 1980, p. 1176).

How could infants so young have learned to recognize and prefer a specific voice? The exposure to the mother for the babies in DeCasper and Fifer's study was indeed "limited": a total of 12 or fewer hours of contact prior to the testing. These infants had, however, spent 9 months in close proximity to the mother prior to birth. Earlier we reviewed evidence indicating that the auditory system is functional for at least the last several weeks before birth. Perhaps, reasoned DeCasper and Fifer, it was the prenatal exposure to maternal speech that led to the postnatal preference for mother over stranger.

A subsequent experiment—often dubbed "The Cat in the Hat study"—was designed to test the hypothesis that infants could remember specific events that had been experienced only in utero. DeCasper and Spence (1986) asked pregnant women to read aloud twice a day for the last 6 weeks of pregnancy. Each mother was assigned one of three children's books (one of which was Dr. Seuss's *The Cat in the Hat*), and it was this story that she faithfully recited during the daily reading sessions with her fetus. Two days after birth, the infants were tested in the same sort of differential-sucking paradigm utilized by DeCasper and Fifer. In this case, however, the auditory stimuli being compared were not different voices but different stories: either the story that the mother had read during pregnancy or one of the other two stories. In each case the voice was that of a stranger—that is, one of the other mothers in the study (each mother had tape-recorded all three stories at the start of the study, and these tapes served as the test stimuli). The infants sucked more diligently to produce the story to which they had been exposed prenatally— and did so even though the voice reciting the story was unfamiliar to them. Thus the infants had clearly processed and remembered something specific about their prenatal auditory experience. Needless to say, no one thinks that this something has anything to do with the content of the story; presumably it was aspects of rhythm or pacing to which the infants were sensitive. Nevertheless the infants were somehow retaining much more about their prenatal experience than most of us would have thought possible prior to DeCasper and Spence's work.

The Cat in the Hat study suggests some remarkable conclusions about the young infant's response to speech, and it is worth taking a moment to spell out what these conclusions are. First the study adds another preference to the list of early preferences: a preference not just for a familiar voice but for a familiar, and complex, auditory stimulus. Furthermore the study suggests that a number of early preferences may have a common basis: namely, exposure to the mother's voice during the prenatal period. This early exposure may contribute to (but not necessarily fully account for) the preference for speech over nonspeech, for one's native language over another language, for the mother's voice over a stranger's voice, and for a familiar speech stimulus over an unfamiliar one (Cooper & Aslin, 1989; Moon, Cooper, & Fifer, 1993). All these preferences would seem adaptive not just for the task of learning language but for the equally important task of getting attached to the mother. Finally the study necessarily tells us something not only about preferences but also about our second general question: the infant's ability to process speech sounds. Earlier we reviewed evidence indicating that babies do perceive some sounds before they are born. The specific effects demonstrated by DeCasper and associates, however, go well beyond demonstrations that fetuses may kick in response to a loud noise. Rather babies can remember a specific prenatal speech input only if they possess sufficient perceptual ability to process particular aspects of that input and sufficient cognitive/mnemonic ability to store the processed information over time.

Basic Discriminations.   Interest in speech is an important part of language learning, but it is far from the whole story. To understand words the child must be able to perceive the phonological contrasts that make up words—must be able to tell the difference between a "pa" sound and a "ba" sound, for example. It is to this aspect of speech perception that much of the research of the last 30 years has been devoted, and the conclusions that it has produced can only be described as astonishing. Once again the young infant has proved to be much more competent than we used to believe.

It is necessary to say something about the nature of speech perception in adults before the infant findings can be understood and appreciated. The purely physical, acoustic difference between an auditory stimulus that sounds like "ba" and one that sounds like "pa" is a completely quantitative, continuous one. The acoustic dimension involved is a continuum, just like length or weight. Suppose we were to vary the auditory stimulus on that dimension. We start on the "ba" end of the dimension and gradually, continuously change the stimulus until we get to the "pa" end, much as we might gradually, continuously lengthen a line by slowly moving our pencils along a straightedge. What would we expect to happen perceptually? The "ba" should come to sound more and more "pa"-like, and there should be a broad zone in the middle of the dimension where the listener cannot easily say which of the two consonants the sound most resembles. He might be inconsistent in his choice from trial to trial within this broad zone, or report blends of "ba" and "pa."

A major discovery of speech-perception research is that adults do not perceive certain speech sounds in this expected, continuous fashion. What happens instead is that suddenly, abruptly—almost at a single point on that continuous dimension—the stimulus is heard as "pa" instead of "ba." As the stimulus continuously varies, the listener discontinuously reports "ba," "ba," "ba," "pa," "pa," "pa." Thus consonant perception tends to be discontinuous or "categorical" rather than continuous, in marked contrast to most other forms of perception. For instance our pencil line will not suddenly and thereafter be perceived as "long" rather than "short" when it reaches, say, 8.23 inches.

What the research of the last 30 years has shown (beginning with a study by Eimas, Siqueland, Jusczyk, & Vigorito, 1971) is that infants as young as 1 month also exhibit categorical perception of speech sounds. To illustrate the nature of the evidence, let us suppose that our "ba"-"pa" acoustic dimension was arbitrarily marked off into equal physical segments, like this: 1–2–3–4–5–6. Let us further suppose that adults hear stimuli 1, 2, and 3 as "ba" and stimuli 4, 5, and 6 as "pa," since the dimension's small transition zone lies between stimuli 3 and 4. Even though sounds 1 and 3 are no more different from each other from the physicist's standpoint than are 3 and 5, a listener hears the members of the first pair as the same sound ("ba"), and the members of the second pair as two different sounds ("ba" and "pa"). This is a clear instance of categorical speech perception. If a young infant is exposed to 1 until she habituates to it, she will continue to show habituation if 1 is replaced by 3. In contrast, if initially habituated to 3 and then presented with 5, she shows dishabituation. In other words the baby acts as if she does not hear the difference between 1 and 3, just as adults do not, but as if she does hear the difference between 3 and 5, just as adults do.

Could the early ability to make these discriminations possibly be the result of perceptual learning—that is, could it be acquired by infants through experience listening to the speech they hear around them? There are several reasons why that cannot be the case (Aslin et al., 1998; Werker & Tees, 1999). First, the ability to make many of the contrasts is evident by 1 month of age (the youngest age that is usually tested), and some of the contrasts have been demonstrated in newborns (Bertoncini, Bijeljac-Babic, Blumstein, & Mehler, 1987). Second, young babies who live in different speech communities and consequently hear different languages are nevertheless very similar to one another in the phonetic contrasts they can discriminate perceptually. They also tend to make discontinuous categorical discriminations at about the same points on the various acoustic continua. In the example given earlier, that is tantamount to saying that young babies would discriminate between sounds 3 and 5 but not between sounds 1 and 3, even if the language they heard did not make use of that particular contrast. If a language does not use a phonetic contrast, the adult speakers of that language may not be able to hear that contrast, at least not without some training and practice. We would expect, therefore, that young babies might be able to hear some speech contrasts that their parents could not easily hear. In fact the research evidence indicates that this is precisely what happens. To illustrate, Trehub (1976) tested the ability of young infants from English-speaking homes to discriminate a phonetic contrast that occurs in Czech but not in English. The infants showed clear evidence of being able to make the distinction. A group of English-speaking adults, on the other hand, had considerable difficulty hearing the contrast.

Findings such as Trehub's raise a natural next question: At what point in development is the facility at making certain discriminations lost? This question has been the focus of a concerted research effort in recent years, an effort that now encompasses a range of ages, languages, and specific phonetic contrasts. As Janet Werker (1989), one of the pioneers in this effort, notes, the initial assumption behind such research was that the decline would occur around puberty, a time when language flexibility in general was believed to decrease (Lenneberg, 1967). Werker's first study, however (Werker & Tees, 1983), found that 12-year-old English-speaking children were no better than English-speaking adults at discriminating Hindi contrasts; not only that, but 8- and even 4-year-olds were also no better. Subsequent studies therefore pushed younger, and they led to a clear conclusion: The decline in sensitivity occurs between 6 and 12 *months* of age— closer to the 6-month figure for vowels, closer to 12 months for consonants (Jusczyk, 1997, Werker & Tees, 1999). The decline, it is interesting to note, does not occur for all nonnative contrasts; infants in English-speaking homes, for example, do not lose their ability to perceive click contrasts that are necessary in Zulu but unused in English. What seems to be important is whether the nonnative contrast can be assimilated to some contrast in the native tongue; when it cannot (as in the Zulu-English example), it remains discriminable. Furthermore, even when declines do occur, they are a matter of degree and not absolute loss, for older participants *can* still make the distinctions. Without supportive experience, however, discriminations that were once made with ease become more and more effortful.

We began the chapter with a discussion of the nature and nurture issue. Note the particular sort of interplay of nature and nurture that seems to be at work in early speech perception. Experience is clearly important, but not in the sense of teaching infants the basic categories of speech sounds. Rather nature provides the initial pool of possibilities, and nurture then operates to winnow this pool down to those important in the language being learned. This is a pattern, it turns out, that is not unique to speech but applies also to at least one other form of auditory perception, namely, perception of music. Musical scales, like languages, show both some universal features and some variations across cultural settings. For example the Javanese pelog scale uses different intervals, and therefore has a distinctly different sound, than does the major Western scale. Six-month-old babies are equally good at detecting mistunings in the major Western and pelog scales; Western adults, however, find the former task easier than the latter (Lynch, Eilers, Oller, & Urbano, 1990). As with speech, experience seems to operate less in a teaching than a maintenance sense: Discriminations that are not regularly utilized become more and more difficult to make.

Categorical perception ensures that the infant will be able to hear the contrasts that are important in the language that she is learning (along, for a while, with many other contrasts as well). But categorical perception is not the only important component of speech perception; such skills must be complemented by the ability that Kuhl (1987) labels *equivalence classification*. Equivalence classification refers to the realization that acoustically distinct stimuli belong to the same phonological category—that all those various "pas," for example, are simply variants of the same basic sound. In part, of course, such equivalence is guaranteed by the limits of discrimination; as we have seen, we often have difficulty hearing the differences among various forms of "pa." In some cases, however, the differences are quite discriminable—most obviously, when "pa" come from different speakers. The infant who was unable to perceive a basic similarity between mommy's "pa" and daddy's (in some ways quite different) "pa" would have a difficult task indeed in learning language. Fortunately research indicates that some of the necessary abilities are in place by 2 months of age, and that by 6 months infants are quite skilled at identifying basic similarities in the face of irrelevant differences (Jusczyk, Houston, & Goodman, 1998; Kuhl, 1987). Note that such identification is central not only to perception of speech but also to the eventual ability to imitate speech. The 1-year-old whose goal was to match her daddy's "bye-bye" in every respect would be doomed to failure. Children, however, seem able from the start to recognize the equivalence of their sounds and those of their parents.

The impressive competencies that we have described have led to a quite natural hypothesis about the special nature of speech perception. This hypothesis is that we are equipped from birth with a highly specialized mode of perception, a so-called "speech mode," designed solely and specifically to help us acquire and use the phonological distinctions found in human natural languages. This hypothesis suggests two predictions: (1) Because only humans acquire human speech, only humans should show categorical, speech-mode–like auditory discriminations; and (2) because it is a "speech mode," humans should use this capacity only when perceiving speech sounds.

Experimental tests of these two quite reasonable-looking predictions yielded a very surprising outcome, however: The evidence ran counter to *both* predictions (Kuhl, 1987). The first prediction was initially disconfirmed in a particularly shocking fashion: *Chinchillas*, of all creatures, turn out to show categorical perception of human speech sounds (Kuhl & Miller, 1975). Subsequently macaque monkeys were also found to do the same (Kuhl & Padden, 1983). The second prediction was disconfirmed by the finding that certain nonspeechlike sounds are also perceived categorically rather than continuously, both by adults and by infants (Jusczyk, 1997). For that matter categorical perception turns out not even to be specific to the auditory realm, for it also occurs in the domain of color perception (Bornstein, 1981). Thus present evidence suggests that categorical auditory perception is—contrary to what many used to think—neither species-specific nor speech-specific.

If the capacity for categorical auditory perception is neither species-specific nor speech-specific, what are we to make of it? The best guess at present is that it is a general auditory capacity (thus, not restricted to speech perception) that other mammals also share (thus, not restricted to humans). Because other mammals also possess it, it may have been acquired quite early in our evolutionary history—earlier than the capacity for human oral speech. In humans the sound structure of language then evolved to fit the particular processing characteristics (e.g., proclivity for categorical perception) of this general auditory capacity; in other species evolution took different routes to different endpoints. To put it another way, it is at least conceivable that human speech sounds are as they are partly (probably *only* partly) because our mammalian auditory system is so constructed that it can easily discriminate and categorize them. If all this were true, we would expect that infants as well as adults would possess this capacity, because it will help them discriminate and eventually learn human speech sounds, and we should not be surprised to discover that other mammals also possess it, because it evolved so early, in the eons when we were mammalian but not yet human.

RELATING INFORMATION
FROM DIFFERENT SENSES

Objects and events commonly offer information to more than one of our sense modalities. People, for example, do not present themselves to babies as voiceless faces or faceless voices; there is simultaneously a face for the baby to look at and a voice to listen to. Moreover the face and the voice are unified in space and time: The voice and the face share the same spatial location, and the voice's sounds and the face's mouth movements are temporally synchronized. In addition certain specific faces always co-occur with certain specific voices; for example, the mother's face with her voice, the father's face with his voice. And, of course, there may be information for the sense of touch as well, both general cues common to humans as complex, three-dimensional objects and more specific cues that identify the particular human object in question (the caress of mommy's hands, the feel of her hair against the cheek). As adult perceivers we do not experience such sights, sounds, and touches as completely separate sensations; rather we experience them as related to one another. We can use information from one sense modality to guide our exploration of another—turn toward the source of a sound, reach out for what we see. Most basically we can recognize the equivalence or common source of our various sensations—recognize that sight, that sound, and that feel as all originating from one and the same object or event. We are, in short, capable of what is sometimes called *intermodal perception.*

Philosophers and psychologists have presented a variety of views over the centuries concerning the development of intermodal perception (Lewkowicz & Lickliter, 1994; Lickliter & Bahrick, 2000; Rose, 1990; Spelke, 1987). They have seldom disagreed about whether learning and experience play a role in this development. They clearly must play a role. For example it is obvious that only through experience could a child attain the ability to apprehend, from the sound alone, that the object he dimly sees off there in the fog is an ambulance rather than some other kind of vehicle (Spelke, 1987). Theorists have disagreed, however, on whether, or to what extent, or how, the senses might be related innately—prior to experience—versus being largely or wholly dependent on experience for their coordination. Many theorists, including Piaget, have believed that the major perceptual modalities are largely uncoordinated at birth and that the infant only gradually learns, through months of sensorimotor experience, to relate information from the different senses. Other theorists, including Gibsonians, believe that we are born with some intermodal perception abilities and/or with predispositions that greatly facilitate the early acquisition of such abilities through experience. Current evidence, as we will see, seems to favor some version of this second position. We discuss the evidence under three headings: infants' abilities to relate (1) sights and sounds, (2) sights and feels, and (3) sights and body movements that imitate what is seen.

Sights and Sounds

Much of the work on infants' perception of sight-sound relations uses a methodology devised by Elizabeth Spelke and illustrated in Figure 2.4. Two visible events are presented successively or simultaneously and a sound specific to one of them is played from a neutral (e.g., central) location. If infants perceive the sound as related to its sound-specified event, they should look more at that event than at the other one. We can then use the direction-of-looking data to draw inferences about the sorts of matches babies can make.

Infants as young as 3 or 4 months do in fact show the ability to link sights and sounds of a variety of sorts. We concentrate here on some findings related to the example with which we opened this section: the ability to match the sights and sounds that emanate from a particular face. Other examples of early visual-auditory coordination, spanning a variety of sight-sound relations, can be found in Spelke (1987).

Walker (1982) presented 5- to 7-month-old infants with two side-by-side films, one of which showed an adult stranger engaging in a "happy" monologue and the other of which showed an adult stranger engaging in an "angry" monologue. Infants looked longer at the film that corresponded to the sound track they were hearing, thus demonstrating an ability to detect the correspondence between visual expression of emotion (via facial expressions and gestures) and auditory expression of emotion (via tone of voice). A study by Walker-Andrews, Bahrick, Raglioni, and Diaz (1991) showed that 4-month-olds can also detect face-voice correspondences on the basis of sex. Infants looked longer at a male face when a male voice was played and longer at a female face when a female voice was played. Given this finding, it is not surprising to learn that infants as young as 3½ months can do the same thing when their own parents provide the faces and voices. Even when the faces are not in fact speaking, infants look longer at mother's face when they hear her voice and longer at father's face when they hear his (Spelke & Owsley, 1979). Finally, Bahrick, Netto, and Hernandez-Reif (1998) have shown that 4-month-olds can also match on the basis of age: They look longer at a child's face when they hear a child's voice and longer at an adult's face when they hear an adult's voice.

Impressive though the ability to match emotion or sex or age may seem, it is not the most impressive of the various feats of intermodal perception that young infants are capable of demonstrating. Spelke and Cortelyou (1981) presented 4-month-olds with the basic Spelke paradigm: two films shown side by side, with the sound track for one of the films played through a central speaker. In this case each film showed an adult female stranger talking to the baby in a normal, adult-to-baby manner. For only one of the two films, however, did the sounds coming out of the speaker match the movements of the adults' lips. You guessed it: Infants looked longer at the speaker whose mouth movements matched the voice on the sound track. This finding demonstrates the infant's ability to use temporal synchrony to link visual experience with auditory experience. But note how subtle the cues and synchronies are, that is, not just movement or nonmovement of the mouth (since both women were talking), but a particular pattern of mouth movements that is or is not compatible with a particular pattern of sounds.

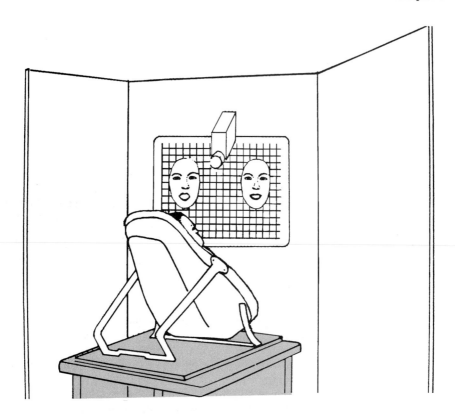

FIGURE 2.4   Experimental arrangement used to study intermodal perception in infants. In the example shown, both faces are talking, but the soundtrack corresponds to the lip movements of only one of the speakers. From "The Bimodal Perception of Speech in Infancy," by P. K. Kuhl and A. N. Meltzoff, 1982, *Science, 218,* p. 1139. Copyright © 1982 by the AAAS. Reprinted by permission.

A program of research by Kuhl and Meltzoff (1982, 1984, 1988) takes the story one step further. In their version of the Spelke paradigm, infants see two adults speakers repeatedly pronouncing the same two vowel sounds—for example /a/ (as in *pop*) in the case of one speaker, /i/ (as in *peep*) in the case of the other. By 4 months of age, infants look longer at the speaker whose mouth movements match the sounds they hear. Matching of this sort goes beyond the detection of global synchronies or asynchronies between sounds and movements shown by Spelke and Cortelyou (1981). Instead, Kuhl and Meltzoff's participants seem to be engaging in a kind of *lip-reading*—recognizing that /a/ sounds go with open mouths, /i/ sounds with retracted lips, /u/ sounds with lips that are protruded and pursed, and so forth. Finally, just in case such performance at 4 months does not seem impressive enough, a recent study demonstrates what appears to be comparable lip-reading competence in newborn babies (Aldridge, Braga, Walton, & Bower, 1999)!

Why might such a specialized-seeming skill be present so early? Probably because it serves a function. Research suggests that the ability to detect such visual clues to speech may aid listeners, infant or adult, in the task of accurately perceiving the sounds of speech (Werker & Tees, 1999). As Kuhl and Meltzoff (1988, p. 238) put it, "there is more to speech than meets the ear." And whatever the utility for speech perception, the ability to link specific sounds to specific lip movements is intermodal perception of a very high order indeed.

Sights and Feels

Some startling results have also been reported in the other two areas of intermodal perception mentioned: (2) sights and feels, and (3) sights and imitative bodily movements. The most dramatic evidence in the sights-feels category comes from Meltzoff and Borton (1979). They found in two experiments that 1-month-olds are apparently able to recognize which of two visually perceived shapes matches a shape they previously had explored tactually, in their mouths, but had not previously seen. The experimenter first put special pacifiers in the infants' mouths for 90 seconds: round, smooth ones for half of the infants; round ones with eight hard rubber nubs on them for the other half. The infants then saw two styrofoam spheres for 20 seconds, one visually resembling the smooth pacifier and the other resembling the nubbed pacifier. The infants tended to look more at whichever sphere resembled the pacifier they had previously felt in their mouths, thus apparently transferring purely tactile input to the visual realm.

Meltzoff and Borton's claims have met a mixed fate in follow-up research to date. Gibson and Walker (1984) obtained congruent results in a study with a similar design (in this case varying object rigidity or plasticity), and Pecheux, Lepecq, and Salzarulo (1988) also reported support; other investigators, however, have been unable to demonstrate such tactile-visual transfer in very young infants (Brown & Gottfried, 1986; Maurer, Stager, & Mondloch, 1999; Rose & Ruff, 1987). The title of the Maurer et al. report seems to sum the situation up well: "Cross-Modal Transfer of Shape Is Difficult to Demonstrate in One-Month-Olds." Note that they do not say "impossible"—any veteran researcher of infancy is aware of the danger of claiming that some competence is absolutely lacking at some age. But any very early ability here seems to be fragile and hard to elicit.

By later in infancy, however, it is clear that infants can bring together tactile and visual information in a number of adaptive ways. Here is one example; others can be found in Bushnell (1994), Rose (1994), and Streri and Spelke (1988, 1989). Bushnell (1982) presented her 8- to 11-month-old participants with objects that were distinctive in both shape and texture—for example, a fur-covered cylinder and a plastic "blob" with several protruding spikes. The babies were first shown the objects at a distance, and then they were encouraged to reach out and touch them. On control trials the touch corresponded to what they were seeing; on trick trials, however, they reached for one object and felt another—for example, felt a smooth furry surface while gazing at the spiky plastic (an outcome made possible by a clever arrangement of mirrors). The 8-month-olds showed no awareness of the mismatch, responding the same way to the trick outcomes as they did on the control trials. By 9½ months, however, the babies clearly realized that the tactile and visual information from a common source should coincide; they engaged in more double-checking and search behaviors on the trick trials, and they were rated as showing more facial expressions of surprise. If you have ever been the victim of a misleading joke object (e.g., the shiny red apple that turns out to be wooden), you probably can empathize with Bushnell's young participants.

Sights and Imitative Movements

We come finally to category (3): imitation of bodily movements. The kind of imitation that has been of greatest interest is the ability to imitate actions that one cannot see oneself perform. To illustrate this sort of imitation, suppose that someone makes a strange face, one that you yourself have never made, and asks you to make one exactly like it. You can probably produce a passable imitation of that face, despite its novelty for you and—especially important here—despite the fact that you cannot watch yourself making it or visually compare your facial appearance to the target's when you have finished. Presumably you accomplish this feat by somehow coordinating and uniting within a single, amodal representation the visual information your eyes provide and the proprioceptive (muscle-sensation) information your facial motor movements provide. In other words you engage in a form of intermodal perception to do this kind of imitation—namely, that of type (3) in our classification system.

One point that the preceding description is meant to convey is that your ability to imitate facial movements is actually a rather impressive cognitive achievement, requiring as it does the precise translation of purely visual input into the motoric commands necessary to produce a similar, unseen-by-you visual display. It is not the sort of achievement that one would expect to find in young infants. Piaget certainly did not think so—in his studies of infancy, this form of imitation was seen as emerging near the end of the first year, and thus only after months of sensorimotor experience and earlier, simpler imitative acts (Piaget, 1962). Yet Meltzoff and Moore (1977, 1983a, 1983b, 1989, 1994) have reported evidence from a series of studies which suggests that *newborns,* no less, are capable of this sort of imitation—and thus presumably of a very high level of intermodal coordination. As you might expect, the claim of such surprising early competence has sparked a firestorm of research and debate (Anisfeld, 1991, 1996; Jones, 1996; Poulson, Nunes, & Warren, 1989).

How can we test for imitation in neonates? Meltzoff and Moore (1983a) used the following method. The testing was done in a darkened room. The experimenter's face was illuminated by a spotlight to make it perceptually salient to the baby. The baby was seated semiupright in an infant's seat with his face positioned about 10 inches from the experimenter's. The experimenter would slowly open and close his mouth four times during a 20-second period, then adopt a passive face for 20 seconds, then slowly stick out and withdraw his tongue four times during a 20-second period, then adopt the passive face again for 20 seconds, and so on, for a total of 12 such alternating periods of mouth opening, passive face, and tongue protrusion. The baby's face was videotaped close up with an infrared-sensitive video camera during all these goings-on. The videotapes were later scored for mouth openings and tongue protrusions by an observer who was uninformed about which gesture had been shown to the infant in any given period. Meltzoff and Moore found that the neonates opened their mouths significantly more often in response to the experimenter's mouth openings than to his tongue protrusions, and also stuck out their tongues significantly more often in response to his tongue protrusions than to his mouth openings. Figure 2.5 shows some examples of the adult models and

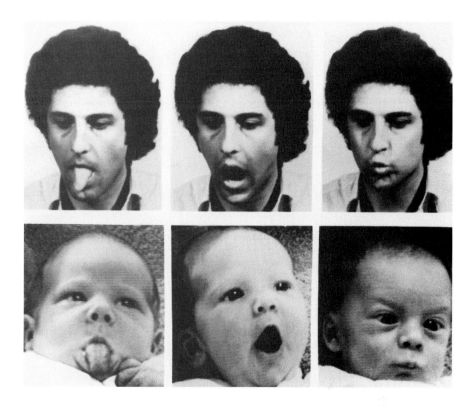

FIGURE 2.5 Adult model and infant response in Meltzoff and Moore's study of neonatal imitation. Even very young infants appear to imitate the adult's facial expressions. From "Imitation of Facial and Manual Gestures by Human Neonates," by A. N. Meltzoff and M. K. Moore, 1977, *Science, 198,* p. 75. Copyright © 1977 by the American Association for the Advancement of Science. Reprinted by permission. Photos from University of Washington CHDD.

corresponding infant responses. Quite reasonably the authors took these findings as evidence that the newborns had selectively imitated each of the two different facial movements. Other studies have reported evidence for newborn imitation of other adult gestures, including head rotation (Meltzoff & Moore, 1989) and lip pursing and widening (Reissland, 1988).

Critical objections to Meltzoff and Moore's claims have been of two sorts. One concerns replicability. Not all investigators who have searched for neonatal imitation have been able to find it. In two critical reviews, Anisfeld (1991, 1996) concluded that the only gesture for which there was solid, across-study evidence of infant-adult matching was tongue protrusion; data with respect to other gestures were too limited or too contradictory to permit conclusions. The second objection concerns the interpretation of positive results when they do appear. The point at issue here is whether matches between infant gesture and adult gesture really reflect genuine imitation or whether such matches might have some other, simpler basis. One alternative that has been proposed draws on the ethologists' concept of innate releasing mechanisms. Proponents of this position argue that certain adult gestures, such as mouth opening, automatically elicit similar-looking behaviors in neonates, much as a mark on the mother's beak might elicit pecking in baby birds. By this view the adult's behavior serves as a releaser rather than a model, the infant's behavior is a reflex rather than genuine imitation, and the early "imitations," like many other reflexes, simply wither away with age rather than developing into more mature forms of imitation. Not all critics of Meltzoff and Moore's conclusions favor the innate releasing mechanism interpretation; what the alternative proposals have in common, however, is that they all deny genuine imitation to the neonate (Anisfeld, 1991; Jones, 1996).

Having noted these criticisms, we should add that Meltzoff and Moore remain convinced of the validity of their conclusions, as indeed do many other students of infancy. We should add also a point that will become evident in Chapter 3: Perhaps *the* leading message from the last 2 decades of research in cognitive development is that young infants are a good deal more cognitively competent than we used to believe. When Meltzoff and Moore's claims first appeared they seemed wildly out of line with what we thought we knew about infant cognition. Now they could be argued to be part of the Zeitgeist.

SUMMARY

Are our adult perceptual abilities the result of inborn biological *nature* or postnatal experiential *nurture?* The answer is both.

The young infant—nonverbal and only minimally motoric—presents formidable obstacles to study. Advances in our understanding have occurred as investigators have devised increasingly sensitive techniques to probe for early competence. Thus babies cannot report their perceptual experiences, but researchers can make inferences about their perception from their nonverbal behaviors (sucking, head turning, blinking, reaching, and, especially, looking) and physiological responses (especially heart rate). For example researchers can measure which of two stimulus patterns an infant tends to look at more. They can also assess whether the infant's visual attention to a pattern *habituates* (wanes) after repeated presentation and recovers from habituation or *dishabituates* when a new pattern is presented. Such perceptual "preferences" tell us two important things about the infant's perceptual system: (1) what the system can discriminate perceptually, because a preference implies that a discrimination has been made; and (2) what the system is especially sensitive to or selectively attentive to in its perceptual processing.

The neural systems that subserve visual functioning are not fully developed at birth in humans. Consequently the newborn's visual functioning is of poorer quality than it will be in late infancy and early childhood, or even than it will be at 2 or 3 months of age. Newborns have some difficulty in executing the various oculomotor mechanisms necessary to bring images into optimal focus on the retina: fixating a stationary object and pursuing a moving one, converging both eyes on the same visual target, accommodating to objects of different distances. Visual acuity is surprisingly poor at birth—no better than 20/660 by some estimates. Contrast sensitivity (discrimination of light-dark differences) is also poor. Both acuity and contrast sensitivity improve rapidly in the early months of life, however. And recent evidence indicates that another important aspect of human visual competence—perception of colors—is present from very early in life.

The infant visual system is clearly more attracted or sensitive to some visual patterns than to others. It has proved very difficult to characterize and explain such visual preferences, however. The newborn and young infant's attention seems to be governed largely by physical characteristics of the visual surround (e.g., edges, contrast), characteristics that may reflect those aspects of the stimulation that the immature visual system sees most clearly. As infants learn more about specific objects and events in the environment (e.g., people and their actions), memory and meaning begin to supplant such inborn preferences as determinants of what they find interesting. Whatever their specific form and specific bases, the preferences that infants show constitute a highly adaptive motivational system for exploring and learning about the environment.

Researchers in the Gibsonian tradition study the development of higher order perceptual processing, including the infant's ability to perceive events, objects, and places. Research by Spelke and associates has shown that infants of 3 or 4 months are in many respects similar to adults in their ability to perceive an object as a continuous and unitary entity, distinct from other objects or surfaces that form its background, that touch it, or that partly occlude it. Young infants are more dependent than adults, however, on motion cues that specify object nature. As they develop, infants move beyond perception of individual elements to perception of patterns or wholes, including perception of a very important object in any infant's environment: the human face. Recent research indicates that the rudiments of face perception may be present at birth. Finally recent research also suggests that some degree of both shape and size constancy is present at birth. "Some degree," however, is not total competence; many perceptual attainments, including constancy, are gradual and multifaceted, and not one-point-in-time achievements.

A variety of kinds of evidence suggest that some ability to perceive three dimensions or depth is present in the early weeks of life. By about 3 or 4 months infants respond appropriately to a "looming stimulus," and by about the same age they also begin to reach appropriately for solid objects. Research using the visual cliff has shown that most infants exhibit behavioral avoidance of deep drop-offs by about the time that they begin to crawl (typically at around 7 months). Some ability to perceive drop-offs may well be present much earlier in development, but young infants do not yet show fear of drop-offs. The emergence of the fear response seems to be linked—at the least temporally and quite possibly causally—to the ability to locomote on one's own.

The auditory system is functional at least several weeks before birth, and fetuses are able to hear some external sounds. It is the mother's speech, however, that is transmitted most clearly through the intrauterine environment, and thus we might predict that maternal speech will be the most important prenatal auditory input—a conjecture that finds dramatic support in research demonstrating that newborns remember some aspects of the speech that they were exposed to as fetuses. Estimates of auditory threshold at birth range from close to adult-level (about 10 decibels worse) to 40 to 50 decibels higher than adult norms. With development improvements occur not only in the ability to detect sounds but also in the ability to discriminate among different sounds and the ability to localize (i.e., turn toward) the source of sounds.

An especially important form of auditory perception is the perception of speech sounds. Human infants appear to be biologically primed to respond to human speech. Babies are interested in and responsive to speech from early in life, especially speech from familiar speakers (such as the mother) and especially speech that takes the highly intonated form known as *motherese.* Infants are also skilled at making discriminations among different speech sounds. Unlike the perception of most things, perception of speech sounds in adults is discontinuous or *categorical* rather than continuous. Infants also show categorical perception of speech sounds, quite possibly from birth—an innately given ability that aids greatly in learning language. Experience also plays a role in speech perception but primarily in a maintenance sense, in that distinctions that are not present in one's native language become harder and harder to make.

Theorists have disagreed for centuries about whether the senses are related to one another *(intermodal perception)* innately—prior to experience—or whether they only become intercoordinated as a function of experience. Recent evidence seems to support the former position. By 3 or 4 months of age, babies tend to perceive sights and sounds as part of the same event if they are temporally synchronous. They can match particular voices to particular faces, for example; they can even detect the synchrony between particular lip movements and particular sounds. Infants are also capable of visual-tactual intermodal perception—that is, they can detect equivalences between what something looks like and how it feels. Finally, perhaps the most surprising evidence of early intermodal perception comes from demonstrations that newborns may be able to imitate facial movements that they cannot see themselves make. If valid (and this research area remains controversial), such findings would provide perhaps the strongest support for the nativist view of intermodal capacity.

3

Infant Cognition

———⟫◦⟪———

"The field of infant psychology is in crisis" (Meltzoff & Moore, 1998, p. 201). So begins a recent article by two long-standing researchers of infant cognitive development. The crisis, it soon becomes clear, does not stem from a lack of interesting questions to explore or of informative methods with which to explore them. Indeed, if anything the opposite is the case: Recent years have seen an explosion of new and surprising findings about young babies' cognitive capacities. These findings have shaken the traditional view that dominated thinking about infant cognition through much of the 20th century. At the same time, the interpretation of much of the recent work is controversial, and no new grand theory has arisen to replace the traditional model. Thus where there once was (at least by the standards of psychology) relative confidence and consensus, we now find a multitude of competing perspectives. It is an exciting, but also a confusing, time in which to be a student of infant cognition.

    The traditional view of infancy was that provided by the theorist with whom we opened the book: Jean Piaget. Piaget's studies of his own three infants (Piaget, 1952, 1954, 1962), carried out some 70 years ago, initiated the field of infant intelligence, and they have defined both the empirical phenomena and the theoretical issues that have most intrigued the field ever since. Piaget's account of infancy is by no means rendered irrelevant by the recent research. His theory remains our most comprehensive model of infant cognition, the descriptive accuracy of much of what he saw in his own babies has been amply confirmed by more rigorous follow-up studies, and the strongest challenges to his claims remain to varying degrees controversial and subject to alternative explanations. The Piagetian perspective thus remains part of the story of infant cognition. But it can no longer constitute all or even most of that story.

How has the research of the last dozen or so years changed how we think about infants' cognitive abilities? Much of the present chapter is devoted to this question, but we can provide a brief answer here. The recent research has revealed that infants are a good deal more cognitively competent than Piaget—and, until recently, most of the rest of us—believed. Moreover it suggests that infant cognition is not as qualitatively distinct from later cognition, not as much a world unto itself, as we used to think. Whereas once the very young infant (to quote the previous edition of this book) "scarcely seemed to belong to the same species," now the emphasis is on incipient competencies and unsuspected strengths and continuity across the developmental span. Thus Haith and Benson (1998), in the recent *Handbook of Child Psychology* chapter devoted to infant cognition, refer to "a connectedness between infants and adults not recognized earlier" (p. 199).

This is not to say, however, that there are no important cognitive differences between infants and adults, or even between infants and young children. One theme of the previous chapter was that earlier-than-expected competence does not mean total competence, and the same point applies at least as strongly to infant cognition as it does to infant perception. Infants may not be a separate species, but they are a good deal less cognitively mature than older members of their species, and their immaturities present both methodological challenges and theoretical complexities that make the study of infancy unique. Thus soon after their reference to "connectedness," Haith and Benson (1998, p. 199) go on to say, "However, infants are different." We hope in what follows to convey some appreciation of both the connectedness and the differences.

This chapter is divided into four sections. We begin by summarizing some central elements in the Piagetian approach to infant intelligence. The intent of this section is both to convey some of the legacies of Piaget's work and to identify some of the issues that continue to challenge students of infancy. We turn next to a development that both Piaget and later researchers have seen as especially important: the infant's mastery of the object concept. Because the object concept has been the most popular focus for follow-ups of Piaget, this discussion serves as a good transition to a broader consideration of contemporary, post-Piaget work. The third section provides such a consideration with a review of findings from several of the most active research topics in infant cognition. Finally the concluding section offers some general conclusions and some speculations about future directions.

THE PIAGETIAN APPROACH

Infant Cognition as Sensorimotor Intelligence

If the newborn or very young infant can be said to "think" and "know" at all, she certainly does not appear to do so in the usual sense of these terms. In what sense, then? What *does* the infant have or do that permits us to talk meaningfully about the nature and development of "infant cognition"?

According to Piaget, what she demonstrates, in an increasingly clear and unambiguous manner as she grows older, is the capacity for organized, "intelligent-looking" sensory and motor *actions*. That is, she exhibits a wholly practical, perceiving-and-doing, action-bound kind of intellectual functioning; she does not exhibit the more contemplative, reflective, symbol-manipulating kind we usually think of in connection with cognition. The infant "knows" in the sense of recognizing or anticipating familiar, recurring objects and happenings, and "thinks" in the sense of behaving toward them with mouth, hand, eye, and other sensorimotor instruments in predictable, organized, and often adaptive ways. Hers is an entirely unconscious and self-unaware, nonsymbolic and nonsymbolizable (by the infant) type of cognition. It is the kind of noncontemplative intelligence that your dog relies on to make its way in the world. It is also the kind that you yourself exhibit when performing many actions which are characteristically nonsymbolic and unthinking by virtue of being so overlearned and automatized—for example, brushing your teeth, starting the car, mowing the lawn, visually monitoring the grass in front of you for obstacles while doing so, and so on. It is, to repeat, intelligence as inherent and manifest in organized patterns of sensory and motor action, and hence Piaget's description of infant cognition as presymbolic, prerepresentational, and prereflective "sensorimotor intelligence."

Sensorimotor Schemes

In the opening chapter, we spoke of the child's assimilating external data to _____ and accommodating _____ to external data, with the blanks variously filled in with "internal mental structures," "favored ways of thinking about things," "conception," "internal concept," and similar expressions. All these terms refer to some sort of enduring cognitive organization or knowledge structure within a child's head that does the assimilating and accommodating. When talking specifically about infantile, sensorimotor assimilating and accommodating, as contrasted with developmentally more advanced, symbolic-representational forms, Piaget would fill in the blank with the word *scheme*.

The meaning of *scheme* is easier to convey by example than by formal definition. A scheme generally has to do with a specific, readily labelable class of sensorimotor action sequences that the infant repeatedly and habitually carries out, normally in response to particular classes of objects or situations. The scheme itself is generally thought of as referring to the inner, mental-structural basis for these overt action sequences; it is, in other words, the cognitive capacity that underlies and makes possible such organized behavior patterns. Thus the young infant who automatically sucks anything that finds its way into her mouth would be said to possess a "sucking scheme"—that is, she possesses an enduring ability and disposition to carry out a specific class of action sequences (organized sucking movements) in response to a particular class of happenings (the insertion of suckable objects). Similarly one can talk about sensorimotor schemes of looking, listening, grasping, hitting, pushing, kicking, and so on. A scheme is a kind of sensorimotor level counterpart of a symbolic-representational level concept. An older person *represents* (thinks of, verbally characterizes) a given object as an instance of the class, "nipple"; analogously the baby *acts* or *behaves* toward the same object as though it belonged to the (functional) class, "something to suck."

A very important property of schemes is that they may be combined or coordinated to form larger wholes or units of sensorimotor intelligence. For instance once she has achieved a certain level of cognitive development, the infant is capable of pushing aside ("pushing" being one motor scheme) an obstacle in order to seize (another motor scheme) a desired object. We see a similar integration of sucking and manual prehension schemes once the infant acquires the systematic tendency to bring to her mouth anything her hand chances to grasp. As elementary schemes gradually become generalized, differentiated, and above all intercoordinated and integrated with one another in diverse and complex ways, the infant's behavior begins to look more and more unambiguously "intelligent" and "cognitive."

Cognitive Motivation

Up to this point, we have described a cognitive system that is sensorimotor rather than symbolic-representational in type, and one that functions and gradually transforms itself developmentally by simultaneously assimilating data to schemes and accommodating schemes to data. We have said nothing, however, about why the cognitive system should ever operate in the first place, nor about the circumstances under which it would be most likely to operate with maximum intensity and persistence. What needs to be added is an account of cognitive motivation—that is, of the factors and forces that activate or intensify human cognitive processing.

Human beings obviously exercise their knowledge and cognitive skills for a wide variety of reasons, in order to attain a wide variety of goals. Some of these reasons and goals are basically noncognitive in character; they are *extrinsic* rather than *intrinsic* to the cognitive system itself. The infant who grasps and sucks his bottle simply to satisfy his hunger rather than to learn about the graspable and suckable potentialities of bottles is clearly activating his sensorimotor skills in the service of an extrinsic, noncognitive need or goal. The same is true of the 3-year-old who makes intelligent use of a pair of footstools to obtain an out-of-reach cookie, and of the high school student who studies hard solely for parental approval.

Most interesting, however, is the fact that a very great deal of human mentation, at all developmental levels, is intrinsically rather than extrinsically motivated. That is, the cognitive system is often turned on and kept running by purely cognitive factors, rather than by bodily needs or other motivational sources. Thus, what Piaget observed in his infants (and what, we can guarantee, you will observe should you have your own infants to watch) was that the babies were most cognitively active and receptive to new learning precisely when bodily needs were *not* pressing and the only reason to act was some interesting object or event in the environment. According to Piaget, it is simply in the nature of schemes to exercise themselves whenever possible, especially when first acquired. To ask, for example, why the child bangs when provided with a banging scheme and a compliant object to bang with is much like asking why she breathes when provided with lungs and air.

An intrinsic tendency to be active is part of the motivational story. The other part concerns the stimuli and events that are most likely to engage the infant's interest and activity. According to Piaget, the inputs that are most interesting are those that the infant can almost but not quite understand—that is, those events that are familiar enough to be assimilated by the current schemes but different enough to force some accommodative effort in order for the infant to make sense of them. More specifically, the kinds of events that engage the infant's activity are precisely those that we identified earlier as determinants of infant visual attention: events that—in relation to the infant's cognitive system—are in some way novel, complex, surprising, or puzzling. Because the earlier discussion concerned vision, it is important to note that such interest-arousing events are not limited to the visual realm; appropriate input to any sensory modality may activate the motivational system. It is important to note as well that response does not necessarily end with increased attention to the interesting event. Rather the infant will be motivated to continue to act toward the event until she has somehow made sense of it—until what was initially incomprehensible has been made once again comprehensible. And this, for Piaget, is the essence of cognitive motivation and cognitive change: The infant creates new experiences for herself through her own actions on the environment; some of these experiences prove to be especially interesting because they go optimally beyond what she currently understands; the infant then acts further toward these new experiences, varying her schemes in an effort to arrive at a new understanding; behaviors that serve to reduce uncertainty and lead to new knowledge are especially pleasureful and are likely to be repeated; and in this way—through countless instances of action, uncertainty, and further action—the cognitive system moves to new and better levels of understanding.

Piaget's Six Stages of Sensorimotor Development

The sensorimotor period is the first of four general periods into which Piaget's theory divides development. (We introduced the other periods in Chapter 1, and we consider them more fully in subsequent chapters.) The sensorimotor period is, in turn, divided into six stages. Table 3.1 provides a capsule description of the stages. We add several further points here.

A first point concerns what is and what is not important for a stage model. Age is not important. The age range designated for each of the six stages is meant to be only a very rough average. Individual infants might therefore pass through any of the stages more rapidly or more slowly than these crude age norms would suggest. The *sequence* of stages, however, is believed to be absolutely invariant for children the world over. Thus Piaget claimed that no earlier stage is ever skipped en route to any later one and no stages are ever navigated in a developmental order other than the one given.

A second point concerns Piaget's position on the nature-nurture issue. As Table 3.1 indicates, the Piagetian infant does not start life with much in the way of innately provided cognitive ability; the starting point, rather, is limited to a set of inborn reflexes. Some of these reflexes are of no cognitive-developmental interest because they are destined either to remain unchanged with age and never become cognitively relevant (e.g., the sneeze) or to actually disappear entirely (e.g., the Moro response, a specifically infantile type of startle pattern). Others, however (e.g., sucking, eye movements, movements of the hand and arm), are of very great importance because they constitute the initial, innately provided building blocks of human cognitive growth. They are, in other words, the infant's first sensorimotor schemes. Development occurs as the reflexes are applied to more and more objects and events in the environment (and thus as they assimilate new experiences), and as they slowly and gradually change in response to these new experiences (thus accommodate). Piaget's position on the nature-nurture issue is therefore definitely an interactionist one: Biological processes (innate reflexes, maturational changes, the

TABLE 3.1   Piaget's Six Stages of Sensorimotor Development

	AGES	DESCRIPTION
Stage 1	0 to 1 month	The infant begins life with a variety of inborn reflexes, and the first stage consists primarily of the exercise of these reflexes in fixed, preset ways whenever the environment presents an opportunity. With repeated experience, however, a subset of the reflexes (e.g., sucking, grasping) begin to show small but adaptive alterations. These reflexes constitute the infant's first schemes, and as such they are the building blocks for all that will follow.
Stage 2	1 to 4 months	With further experience, individual schemes become progressively more skilled and attuned to the environment. Schemes also become coordinated with each other to yield larger behavioral units. Among the important forms of coordination that begin to develop during this stage are vision-audition, sucking-prehension, and (especially) vision-prehension. Although these developments permit more effective forms of action upon the world, the infant's behavior still has a kind of self-centered, "objectless" quality, in that he seems to exercise his schemes for the pure pleasure of doing so, without a real interest in the object being acted on.
Stage 3	4 to 8 months	The infant's behavior is now more clearly externally oriented, more cognitively and socially "extroverted," than was true during the first two stages. This increased interest in the outer world, combined with increased facility at coordinating schemes, makes possible the major achievement of Stage 3: the ability to reproduce interesting outcomes by repeating the actions that led (initially accidentally) to these outcomes. Because of the after-the-fact nature of the causality, however, Piaget does not yet credit the infant with true intentionality.
Stage 4	8 to 12 months	This stage is characterized by the appearance of unmistakably intentional, goal-directed behavior. The essence of such behavior is the ability to separate means and end—the ability to use one scheme (e.g., pushing aside an obstacle) as a means en route to another scheme, the end or goal (e.g., playing with a toy). Piaget regarded such intentional sequences as an especially noteworthy development, characterizing them as "the first actually intelligent behavior patterns."
Stage 5	12 to 18 months	This stage differs from its predecessor along a dimension of familiar to novel or conservative to exploratory. It is characterized by active, trial-and-error exploration—either in response to some specific problem that needs to be solved or simply to see what happens if something new is tried. Such exploration often leads to the creation of new means of acting upon the world, and hence Piaget's name for the stage: "the discovery of new means through active experimentation."

TABLE 3.1 Piaget's Six Stages of Sensorimotor Development *(continued)*

	AGES	DESCRIPTION
Stage 6	18 to 24 months	The defining characteristic of Stage 6—and the development that brings the sensorimotor period to an end—is the emergence of symbolic/representational ability, or the ability to use one thing (e.g., a mental image, a word) to stand for something else. Whereas the Stage 5 child needed to try out all the possible solutions to a problem literally and overtly, now the child can do the trying out internally—through the mental combination of symbolically represented schemes. In addition to mental problem solving, the onset of symbolic ability makes possible a number of behaviors that are not seen earlier in infancy: deferred imitation, symbolic play, and the emergence of language.

biological tendencies to assimilate and accommodate) combine with experience to produce developmental change.

To a good extent, the movement through the six stages is defined by the ways in which the schemes change across infancy, and thus by the changing means that the infant possesses to act upon and make sense of the world. Change occurs partly through the continued evolution of individual schemes and partly through the gradual coordination or integration of one scheme with another. On the first point, individual schemes associated with such processes as sucking, looking, listening, vocalizing, and prehension (grasping objects) receive an enormous amount of spontaneous daily practice—recall our discussion of intrinsic cognitive motivation. As a consequence each of these schemes undergoes considerable developmental elaboration and refinement. More important, however, than this perfecting of individual, isolated schemes is the progressive coordination or coming-into-relation of one scheme with another. For example vision and audition begin to become functionally related. Hearing a sound leads the infant to turn his head and eyes in the direction of the sound source. Similarly the coordination of vision with prehension permits the infant to locate and grasp objects under visual guidance and, reciprocally, to bring before his eyes for visual inspection anything an out-of-sight hand may have touched and grasped. The evolution of vision-prehension coordination is an especially noteworthy development, because an ability to coordinate hand and eye will prove to be an extraordinarily powerful instrument for exploring and learning about the environment.

A further and particularly important type of coordination of schemes is the appearance, during Stage 4, of unmistakably intentional, means-ends behavior. This development builds upon the primary achievement of the preceding Stage 3: the capacity to reproduce interesting outcomes that are brought about by the exercise of one's schemes. The Stage 3 child, for instance, might grasp and shake a new toy, find that the toy produces an unexpected rattling sound, and then happily spend the next several minutes shaking and listening. Although such behavior would seem to signal a budding grasp of cause-and-effect relations, Piaget is unwilling to credit the Stage 3 child with a clear capacity for intentional, goal-directed action. The causality is too accidental and after the fact, and there is no clear separation of action and environmental result. The Stage 4 child's actions are more clearly purposeful and goal directed. In particular the child now demonstrates a clear means-end separation; he intentionally exercises one scheme, as means, in order to make possible the exercise of another scheme, as end or goal. He may push your hand (means) in order to get you to continue to produce some interesting sensory effect (end) you had been producing for his benefit. Similarly he may push aside (one motor scheme) an object in order to grasp (second motor scheme) another object.

The Stage 5 child takes this development one step further. Intelligent though it is, Stage 4 behavior is essentially conservative: The infant tends to carry out a small range of means-end behavior sequences in a more or less fixed, stereotyped way to produce a small range of effects. The essence of Stage 5, in contrast, is exploration and novelty—a very active, purposeful, trial-and-error exploration of the properties and potentialities of objects, largely through the relentless search for new and different ways to act upon them. Present the Stage 5 infant with a novel object, and he will actively try to lay bare its structural and functional properties by trying this, and that, and yet another action pattern on it, often making up new variations on old action patterns in the course of doing so. Faced with some means-end problem to solve, the Stage 5 child would be likely to vary the means scheme in a deliberate, let's-see-what-would-happen-if sort of attitude; he might, to refer back to a Stage 4 example, remove the offending obstacle this way, then that way, then still another way. With his strongly accommodative, exploratory bent, the Stage 5 child often discovers wholly new means to familiar ends. For instance Piaget describes his discovering that an out-of-reach object can be secured by pulling a string attached to it, or a small rug on which it rests. These particular examples are intriguing because they might be early precursors of tool use, an especially important type of human intelligent behavior.

The crowning achievement of the progression through the sensorimotor stages is the emergence of symbolic/representational capacity at Stage 6. Now for the first time, the child has the ability to represent the objects of cognition by means of symbols—that is, to realize that one thing (e.g., a word) can stand for some other thing (e.g., a class of objects). And now, for the first time, the child can act intelligently with respect to this inner, symbolized reality rather than simply, in sensorimotor fashion, with respect to the outer, unsymbolized reality. The Stage 5 child discovers new means to attain his behavioral objectives by overt, trial-and-error experimentation; he studiously varies his external behavior and, by doing so, may hit upon an effective procedure for achieving his goal. In contrast the Stage 6 symbolic child may try out alternative means *internally,* by imagining them or representing them to himself instead of actualizing them in overt behavior. If an effective procedure is found in this fashion, by taking thought rather than by taking overt action, we might think of it more as invention or insight than as trial-and-error discovery. Accordingly Piaget refers to this aspect of Stage 6 intelligence as "the invention of new means through mental combinations."

A celebrated example of the latter among Piaget readers was conveniently provided by his daughter Lucienne at the tender age of 16 months. Lucienne wanted to extract a small chain from one of those old-fashioned, sliding-drawer type matchboxes, but the drawer opening was too small for her to reach in and get it. After some unsuccessful, Stage 5 type fumblings, she paused, studied the box, slowly opened and closed her mouth a few times, then quickly widened the drawer opening and triumphantly retrieved the chain. It seems reasonable to interpret her mouth movements as a primitive, nonverbal, symbolic representation of a possible but as yet untried behavioral means to the desired end. To be sure her representational response was very similar to its referent physically and was also produced in the same immediate situation. Nonetheless it would take an unusually tough-minded and skeptical observer to find nothing of the genuinely symbolic and representational in this behavior. Certainly it is a type of behavior that we are unlikely to see in a younger infant but one that becomes increasingly common by the end of infancy, namely, problem solving based not on overt trial-and-error experimentation but on the generation and manipulation of mental symbols.

Mental problem solving is just one of the Stage 6 accomplishments that led Piaget to conclude that a general capacity for symbolic functioning has emerged. The child is now capable for the first time of *deferred imitation,* in which actions witnessed but not imitated on a given occasion are spontaneously reproduced in full detail at a later time. One of Piaget's children, for example, watched in mute fascination while another child threw a three-star temper tantrum. She then produced an excellent imitation of it the next day. Presumably she must have generated some sort of internal representation (possibly a visual image) of the tantrum as a guide for her imitative action, thus making possible her reproduction of a model that was no longer physically present. *Pretend* or *symbolic play* also makes its first appearance in Stage 6. At 18 months Piaget's daughter Jacqueline said "soap" while pretending to wash her hands by rubbing them together; at 20 months she pretended to eat bits of paper and other inedibles, saying "Very nice." Finally there is perhaps the most obvious example of symbolic capacity: the ability to generate a word to stand for an absent object. *Language* is an indubitably symbolic activity, and it is made possible, according to Piaget, by the general capacity for representational functioning that emerges as the culmination of sensorimotor development.

Sensorimotor intelligence does not disappear with the end of infancy; rather sensorimotor forms of functioning remain available to us throughout life. Once symbolic ability has emerged, however, the highest and most powerful forms of intelligence occur on a new plane. It is worth taking a moment to reflect on the momentous differences between symbolic-representational thought and sensorimotor intelligence. Sensorimotor actions must proceed slowly, step by step, one action at a time. Symbolic-representational thought can be much faster and more freely mobile in its operation; it can range over a whole series of past, present, and future events in one quick sweep of the mind. The former is by its very nature more oriented toward actions and concrete, practical results, whereas the latter can be more preoccupied with knowledge per se; one focuses more on acts and outcomes, the other more on information and truth. The former is ineluctably concrete and earthbound. The latter is potentially abstract and free to soar, and, in fact, becomes increasingly so as the child matures. Indeed it can eventually even take itself as its own cognitive object; that is, a relatively mature mind can think about its own thoughts. Finally the former is necessarily private, idiosyncratic, and uncommunicable to others; each baby is imprisoned in her own separate cognitive world. The latter comes to make fluent use of a socially shared symbolic system (natural language) and can thereby communicate with, and gradually become socialized by, other human beings.

As we will see when we turn to contemporary research, there are no disputes about either the power of representational thought or about the importance of the transition from being sensorimotor to being representational. What is very much a matter of dispute, however, is exactly when and how this transition comes about.

THE OBJECT CONCEPT

Piaget's *object concept,* or *concept of object permanence,* refers to a set of implicit, commonsensical beliefs we all share about the basic nature and behavior of objects, including ourselves. We tacitly believe, first of all, that we and all other objects coexist as physically distinct and independent entities within a common, all-enveloping space. We are objects in that space, so are you, and so is this book; we are all more or less equal-status "co-objects" together, each of us with our own individual quantum of space-filling bulk and our own individual potential for movement or displacement within our common spatial habitat. We also implicitly understand that the existence of our fellow objects, animate and inanimate alike, is fundamentally independent of our own interaction or noninteraction with these other objects. When an object disappears from our sight, for example, we do not assume that it has thereby gone out of existence. In other words we do not confuse our own actions toward another object—our seeing it, hearing, touching it, and so on—with the physical existence of that object, and hence we do not think it automatically becomes annihilated once we lose behavioral contact with it. Finally we believe that the object's behavior is also independent of our psychological contact with it, just as its existence is. We know that once gone from our sight, for instance, the object could perfectly well move or be moved from one location to another. It may or may not continue to await us at the place where we last saw it; we may or may not have to look elsewhere for it. In summary we all possess an implicit, unarticulated conception of objects which asserts that other physical objects and ourselves are equally real and "objective," volume-occupying inhabitants of a common spatial world, and that the existence and behavior of other objects is fundamentally independent of our perceptual and motor contact with them.

Piaget's Studies

Piaget made three rather startling claims about the object concept, again based upon observations of his own three infants' sensorimotor development. First he claimed that this utterly basic, "obvious" conception of objects is not inborn but needs to be acquired through experience. Second its acquisition is a surprisingly protracted one, spanning the entire sensorimotor period of infancy. Finally this process consists of a universal, fixed sequence of developmental stages or subacquisitions, the infant picking up different aspects or components of the full concept at different stages. Thus, there is a sense in which it could be said that a 1-year-old has "more of," or a "different level of," this concept than a 6-month-old, for instance, although the 1-year-old has not yet achieved the final, complete version of it.

It is inconceivable that anyone writing a textbook on cognitive development nowadays would fail to include something on the evolution of the Piagetian object concept. In the first place, the concept itself is so utterly basic and fundamental. If any concept could be regarded as indispensable to a coherent and rational mental life, this one certainly would be. Imagine what your life would be like if you did not believe that objects continued to exist when they left your field of vision. Worse yet, imagine how things would be if *nobody* believed it. It also happens that Piaget's developmental story here is just plain interesting to most people; it is simply one of the very best tales in the developmentalist's anthology. Moreover a massive research enterprise across the last 30 or so years has attempted to clarify our understanding of just how this development proceeds. Thus an account of the object concept is an account not only of Piaget's genius but also of much of modern infant cognitive psychology.

Piaget assumed that the development of the object concept is intimately linked to sensorimotor development as a whole. He therefore used the same six-stage framework to describe the developmental changes.

Stages 1 and 2 (Roughly 0 To 4 Months). During this early period, the infant characteristically will try to follow a moving object with his or her eyes until it disappears from view—for instance, until it goes behind a screen of some kind. Whereupon the infant will immediately lose interest and turn away or, at most, continue to stare for a short time at the place where it was last seen. There is as yet no behavior that could be interpreted as visual or manual search for the vanished object, and therefore, Piaget concludes, no positive evidence to suggest that the infant has any knowledge whatever of its continuing existence.

Stage 3 (Roughly 4 To 8 Months). The infant shows some progress during this stage in differentiating object-as-independent-entity from self's-action-toward-object, but it will become apparent that the differentiation process still has a long way to go. There are several positive accomplishments. By the end of Stage 2, the infant has become quite accomplished at tracking objects with his eyes, visually pursuing them when they move and visually fixating them when they stop moving. During Stage 3 he begins to anticipate their future positions by extrapolating from their present direction of movement—for example, begins to look to the right side of a screen after seeing an object disappear behind the left side (this behavior is not yet as consistent or skilled as it will eventually be, however). The Stage 3 child may also recognize and reach toward a familiar object even if only a part of it is visible, something he could not do earlier. For instance, he might recognize and grasp at his bottle even when all but the nipple end of it is covered by a washcloth.

If this very same bottle is totally covered, however, it is an astonishing fact that the infant will *not* manually search for it. The reaching hand can sometimes be seen even to drop in midflight once the desired object wholly disappears from view. Note that the infant is physically capable of reaching for objects—he will reach if a part of the target is visible, and he will reach if a transparent rather than opaque cover is placed over the object (Harris, 1983). Such manual search occurs, however, only if there is some visible evidence of continuing existence. Incredibly the Stage 3 infant will not retrieve an object *even when he has already grasped it,* if you quickly cover both object and grasping hand with a washcloth (Gratch, 1972; Gratch & Landers, 1971). Instead he is likely either to continue to hold onto the object and idly look around as if unaware that he has anything in his hand, or else to let go of it, remove his empty hand, and show no further search behavior. Piaget believed that in Stage 3 the object is not yet credited with an enduring life of its own, apart from and independent of the infant's perceptual—especially visual—contact with it.

Stage 4 (Roughly 8 to 12 Months).   The Stage 4 infant has overcome many of the limitations of Stage 3. In particular the child will now manually search for and retrieve hidden objects—even when the object is totally hidden and hence no visible clues signal its existence. There is, however, a most peculiar limitation on this newly developed ability to find hidden objects. The child watches you hide object X under cover A and he gleefully pulls off the cover and grabs it. You repeat the hiding a few times; he repeats the finding each time. Then you very slowly and conspicuously hide X under cover B, located to one side of cover A, making sure that the child watches you do it. Quite often the Stage 4 child will immediately search under A once again and then abandon the search when he fails to find anything there, thus making what has come to be called the $A\overline{B}$ (i.e., A not B) error. Why on earth would he do such an odd thing? What level of object-concept development might this bizarre-looking behavior reflect?

Piaget believed that the Stage 4 child does not yet have a clear and conscious mental image of X quietly abiding beneath a cover. He may instead have evolved in this situation a little sensorimotor habit or behavioral "rule" that says, in effect, "Search over there, under that, and you'll have an interesting visual-tactile-manipulative experience." The object of the interesting sensorimotor experience (i.e., X) is psychologically embedded in the experience itself and remains secondary to it. According to Piaget's interpretation, the differentiation between self's action and object is not yet complete; X is not yet the genuinely action-independent "object-of-contemplation" it will eventually become.

Stage 5 (Roughly 12 to 18 Months).   As Stage 4 draws to a close, Piaget believed that the balance begins to shift from previous motoric success to present perceptual evidence, and the Stage 5 child gradually learns to search at whatever place the object was most recently seen to disappear. In the $A\overline{B}$ setup described previously, this, of course, means going directly to B when X is hidden at B, even though X had previously been hidden and found at A. Piaget believed that the Stage 5 child has progressed further than the Stage 4 child in the crucial matter of differentiating the object per se from his actions toward it. The older infant can read the visual evidence of X's present location more or less objectively; he is no longer locked into a rigid dependence on previous patterns of successful action-toward-object.

There is, however, one final limitation to be overcome: The Stage 5 infant cannot imagine or represent any further changes of location the object might have undergone after it disappeared from his view. Let us suppose you put a small object in a felt-lined cup, turn the cup upside down, slide it under a large cloth, silently deposit the object underneath the cloth, and withdraw the empty cup. The prototypical Stage 5 child is incapable of searching for the object anywhere but in the cup, presumably because the cup rather than the cloth was the place where he saw it disappear. As yet, he cannot represent any unseen but readily (to us) inferable movement of the object when inside the cup. In Piaget's words, the child can cope with *visible displacements* but not yet with *invisible displacements*.

Stage 6 (Roughly 18 to 24 Months).   The just-mentioned limitation is overcome in this stage, with the child gradually acquiring the knack of using the visual evidence as a basis for imagining or representing X's unseen itineraries and hiding places. The really accomplished Stage 6-er can be very, very good at it. You put X inside your closed fist and move your fist first under cloth A, then under B, then under C, and then open it up, *sans* object (you have actually left it under cloth A). Many a 2-year-old will grin with anticipation and then systematically search each possible hiding place, sometimes in the reverse order from your hiding—that is, first under C, then under B, and finally under A. He may also spontaneously try the same game on you, with his doing the hiding and your doing the finding (and it would be a coldhearted experimenter indeed who would not let him do it). The full-fledged object concept is so clearly "there" in such a child that you feel you can virtually mind-read it. You are *sure* that he is somehow mentally representing that object during its invisible perambulations, and *sure* that he implicitly regards it as an external entity that exists and may move about in complete independence of his own perceptual or motor contact with it. But, of course, he is now in sensorimotor Stage 6, and the essential accomplishment of that stage is precisely that of being able to evoke internal symbolic representations of absent objects and events.

In our discussion of perceptual constancy, we noted that one important task for the cognitive system is to figure out what it is that stays the same—remains invariant—when other, usually more obvious, things are changing. The Piagetian object concept is the major such acquisition of infant cognition: the realization that the existence of objects remains invariant despite changes in our perceptual contact with them.

More Recent Research

Far more follow-up research has been done on object-concept development than on any other Piagetian infant acquisition. A variety of specific questions have been examined in this research, but two issues have motivated the greatest amount of study. One concerns the accuracy of Piaget's diagnosis of what infants know, the particular concern being that his techniques may result in an underestimation of infants' knowledge. The other involves an attempt to make sense of the most surprising of the many surprising findings from Piaget's account: the A not B error of Stage 4.

Did Piaget Underestimate Infants' Knowledge? We have already given the general answer to this question—yes, Piaget did underestimate babies' knowledge. Babies know more about objects—and indeed many other things—than Piaget believed. As we will see, there are disputes about how great the underestimation was and about how serious the implications are for Piaget's theory. But there is no dispute about the conclusion that infants are more competent than Piaget's descriptions indicate.

The primary reason for the underestimation is methodological. We noted earlier that the young infant is in some respects a rather limited creature, unable to speak, to locomote independently, or to perform much in the way of voluntary and controlled motoric behavior. The young infant just *looks* incompetent to the naked eye, and Piaget—working in the home and without the technological refinements of recent years—was very much dependent on overt behaviors that could be seen with the naked eye.

Consider the case of object permanence. Piaget's conclusions about the infant's knowledge of objects were based largely on the infant's ability to perform active motoric search behaviors—to reach out and remove covers, push aside or peer around screens, and the like. Later studies utilizing similar behaviors have confirmed the accuracy of Piaget's descriptive account: Very young infants tend not to search for objects at all, and when search behaviors do emerge they show the same initial limitations and the same gradual, sequential progress to full mastery reported by Piaget (Harris, 1983). But failure to search, in itself, tells us only that the infant is either not able or not disposed to organize an effective search routine. It does not prove that the infant has absolutely no knowledge of the continuing existence of the object.

What *could* a young infant do to demonstrate some knowledge of object permanence? Much of the research of the last 15 years has been based on the same general approach and rationale: See whether the infant somehow responds differently to possible events than to impossible ones—that is, events that in some way violate the rules of object permanence. See, in particular, whether the infant seems to find the latter, never-could-occur events especially interesting, surprising, or intriguing. The infant might signal such a reaction in a number of ways—through increased looking time, for example, or through a change in heart rate, or through a puzzled or perplexed expression. Any adult confronted with a violation of the object concept would certainly show such behaviors. Perhaps we can use similar responses to glean some evidence of understanding in the preverbal, largely premotoric young infant.

The violation-of-expectancy paradigm was first explored in the 1960s and 1970s in some pioneering studies by Thomas Bower and William Charlesworth (e.g., Bower, 1974; Charlesworth, 1966). Its most informative variant has come more recently, however, in an adaptation of the habituation-dishabituation procedure that has proved so valuable in the study of infants' perceptual abilities. A study by Renee Baillargeon (1987a) provides a good example of both the method and the kinds of findings that it yields. Baillargeon's participants first viewed the event shown in the top part of Figure 3.1, that is, a screen that rotated, like a drawbridge, though a 180° arc. After a series of such trials, the infants' looking times decreased, reflecting the fact that they were habituating to the repeated event. At this point a wooden box was placed directly in the path of the screen (see the bottom part of the figure). Note that the infant could see the box at the start of a trial, but that the box disappeared from view when the screen reached its full height. In one experimental condition, labeled the *Possible Event* in the figure, the screen rotated to the point at which it reached the box and then stopped—as of course it should, given the fact that a solid object was in its path. In the other condition, labeled the *Impossible Event,* the screen rotated to the point of contact with the box and then (thanks to a hidden platform that dropped the box out of the way) kept right on going through its full 180° arc! Note that in some respects this second event is less novel than the first: Infants in the Impossible Event condition see a 180° rotation, just as on the habituation trials, whereas infants in the Possible Event condition see only a truncated version of the familiar movement. To anyone with some knowledge of object permanence, however, the second event is decidedly more novel and less expectable, for in this case one solid object seems to pass magically through a second solid object.

Baillargeon found that infants as young as 4½ months (and even some as young as 3½ months) appeared to appreciate the impossibility of the impossible event. Looking times remained low when the screen stopped at the point of reaching the box; attention shot up, however, when the screen appeared to pass through the area occupied by the box. Baillargeon (1990, p. 6) concluded that the infants

(a) Habituation Event

(b) Impossible Event

(c) Possible Event

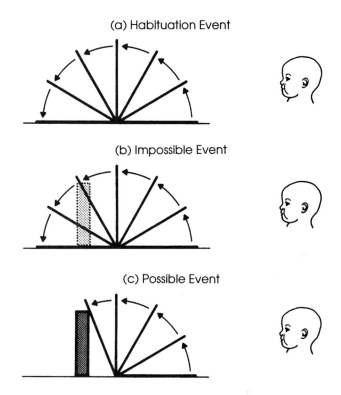

FIGURE 3.1   The Baillargeon test of object permanence. Infants were first
habituated to the event shown in part (a). Response was then
measured to either the possible event in part (c), in which the
screen rotates to point of contact with the box and stops, or the
impossible event in part (b), in which the screen continues to
move through the area occupied by the box. Adapted from
"Object Permanence in 3½-and 4½-Month-Old Infants," by R.
Baillargeon, 1987a, *Developmental Psychology, 23,* p. 656.
Copyright © 1987 by the American Psychological Association.
Adapted by permission of Dr. R. Baillargeon.

(a) believed that the box continued to exist, as a substantial entity, after it was
occluded by the screen; (b) realized that the screen could not rotate through the space
occupied by the box; and hence (c) expected the screen to stop and were surprised in
the impossible event that it did not.

In further studies Baillargeon has probed the extent of young infants' knowledge about hidden objects. Do infants understand not only that a hidden object still exists but also something about the object's enduring properties? Do they realize, for
example, that an occluded object retains its original size, and can they use this knowledge to reason about its possible effects when it is out of sight? The answer (at least by
6 months) is yes. Baillargeon (1987b) presented infants with a screen that rotated
through a 165° arc, in the course of which it occluded a box placed in its path. In one

condition the box was upright, as in Figure 3.1; in the other condition it was lying flat. The event in the lying-flat condition was therefore a possible one, since the screen stopped just when it should have, at the point of reaching the flattened box; the event in the upright condition, in contrast, was definitely not possible, since it involved the same magical movement of one solid through another as in the first Baillargeon study. Note, however, that to distinguish in this way between the events the infant must retain information about not only the existence but also the size and orientation of the hidden object. Infants looked longer at the first event than at the second, indicating that they were in fact able to remember and to use this information.

Infants know other things about the properties of hidden objects. They realize, for example, that only some kinds of objects hinder the movements of other objects. In another application of the rotating-screen procedure, Baillargeon (1987b) varied the nature of the hidden object: hard and rigid in half the cases, soft and compressible (e.g., a ball of gauze) in the other half. Infants were not surprised by the continued rotation of the screen in the soft-object case, indicating that they were able to retain and use information about the compressibility of the hidden object. Infants can also use information about the location of a hidden object. Baillargeon (1986) first habituated 6- and 8-month-old infants to the following event: A toy car rolled down an inclined ramp, passed behind one end of a screen, and exited at the other end. Following habituation, the infants saw a box placed behind the screen. In one condition (possible event) the box was placed behind the tracks on which the car ran; in the other condition (impossible event) the box was placed directly on the tracks. The screen was then set back in place, and the car again made its journey from one side to the other. Infants looked longer at the impossible event than at the possible one, indicating that they knew not only that the box still existed but also *where* it was—and that they drew different implications from the different locations.

Baillargeon and other researchers (most notably, Elizabeth Spelke and colleagues) have explored a variety of other forms of physical knowledge in addition to object permanence. Methodologically the general approach has been the same: compare response (usually looking behavior) to two events, one of which violates some physical principle and the other of which maintains the principle; what varies across studies is which particular principle is the focus of study. Among the physical principles that have been examined are gravity, inertia, solidity, continuity, containment, and support (Aguiar & Baillargeon, 1998, 1999; Baillargeon, 1994, 1995; Kim & Spelke, 1999; Spelke, 1998; Spelke, Breinlinger, Macomber, & Jacobson, 1992).

Figures 3.2 and 3.3 show some examples. The first assesses understanding of gravity and object movement (Spelke et al., 1992). Infants are first habituated to the event depicted in the top left panel of the figure—that is, a ball that drops behind a screen and then is revealed, once the screen is removed, to be resting on the floor. A table is then placed in the ball's path, the ball is again dropped, and the removal of the screen reveals either the ball on the table (the consistent event) or the ball on the floor (the inconsistent event). Infants as young as 4 months looked longer at the inconsistent event, suggesting that they were sensitive to the rules of object motion and were surprised when one solid object passed through another. The task in Figure 3.3 assesses understanding of gravity and support (Baillargeon, 1994). As the infant watches, a hand pushes a box across its supporting platform. In one case (possible event) the endpoint contact is sufficient to maintain support; in the other (impossible event) it is not. Infants as young as 6 months looked longer at the impossible outcome, suggesting that they understood the relation between contact and support.

Because we have stressed the successes demonstrated in this research, it is important to add that young infants do not know all that there is to know about objects. Many of the studies show age effects; some kinds of knowledge are evident by 3 or 4 months (the youngest ages that are usually tested), whereas others may not appear until later in infancy. The tasks in Figure 3.2 provide one example: Although 4-month-olds look longer at the inconsistent event shown in the top part of the figure, they are as yet unfazed by the violation of gravity shown in the bottom part. The work on support (Figure 3.3) provides another example: Although 6-month-olds respond to the impossible event, 3- and 4-month-olds do not—for them, *any* degree of contact is sufficient to provide support. More generally Baillargeon argues that quantitative reasoning about the exact physical properties of objects (just how much contact is necessary to produce support? just how tall or large must a hidden object be to produce an effect?) is more difficult than purely qualitative reasoning (knowing that support depends on some degree of contact, knowing that the object still exists and could affect another, without having to take into account precise quantities). In her view infants' starting-point knowledge across many domains is of a global and qualitative sort; experience then operates, under the guidance of

FIGURE 3.2 Consistent and inconsistent events in Spelke et al.'s study of infants' understanding of object movement and gravity. From "Origins of Knowledge," by E. Spelke, K. Breinlinger, J. Macomber, and K. Jacobson, 1992, *Psychological Review, 99*, pp. 611 and 621. Copyright © 1992 by the American Psychological Association. Reprinted by permission of Dr. E. Spelke.

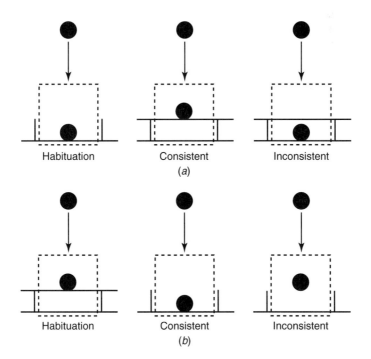

Possible Event

Impossible Event

FIGURE 3.3 Possible and impossible events in Baillargeon's study of infants' understanding of support. From "How Do Infants Learn About the Physical World?" by R. Baillargeon, 1994, *Current Directions in Psychological Science, 3,* p. 134. Copyright © 1994 by Cambridge University Press. Reprinted by permission.

biologically provided and highly constrained learning mechanisms, to produce progressively more refined degrees of understanding. Although the specifics of her argument are quite different from Piaget's, there is an interesting convergence on two points: Knowledge is not all or none but rather has multiple levels or degrees, and nurture combines with nature (a strong nature component in Baillargeon's case) to produce developmental change.

Our emphasis has been on the early-competence message that emerges from the Baillargeon and Spelke programs of research. We should therefore add that not all researchers of infancy have been persuaded by their data and interpretations. Criticisms of two sorts have been offered. The first concerns the possibility of methodological artifacts—that is, the possibility that the obtained results (typically longer looking times to some events than to others) might reflect unintended aspects of the methodology, and not the concept being measured. Several specific versions of this possibility have been proposed; we give one example here (see also Bogartz, Shinskey, & Speaker, 1997; Haith & Benson, 1998). It concerns the drawbridge procedure illustrated in Figure 3.1. Rivera, Wakeley, and Langer (1999) suggest— and provide data in support of their suggestion—that infants may look longer at the impossible 180° rotation than at the possible 120° rotation simply because they find the greater movement of the screen more interesting, and not because of any knowledge of object permanence. If generally valid this sort of criticism would obviously be very serious, because it would mean that the tasks are measuring something quite different from—and also less interesting than—the knowledge that they are intended to measure.

Baillargeon's (1999) response to this criticism seems reasonable to us. She does not deny the possibility of alternative explanations for particular outcomes; indeed she explicitly acknowledges that some artifactual alternative can probably be found for any apparent demonstration of early competence. She also points out, however, that many of the conclusions from her research program are based on converging evidence from several different procedures for studying the knowledge in question—for example various kinds of occlusion and containment events in the case of object permanence. To explain away the overall pattern of results, a different artifact might have to be evoked for each separate procedure—hardly a very plausible or parsimonious approach. It is hard to quarrel with this argument (converging evidence is always a good thing!). Still the possibility (perhaps inevitability) of alternative explanations in specific cases does illustrate just how hard it is to design experiments that can get into the mind of the very young infant.

The second kind of criticism is more conceptual than methodological. It assumes (contra the artifact criticism) that the positive results are genuine; the issue now is how to interpret the results. Baillargeon's interpretation is consistently a strong one. In the case of the object permanence research, the greater looking times to various kinds of violation are taken to indicate that the infant has represented the object in its absence and expects it to reappear when the cover is removed (thus, at the least, Piaget's Stage 4 knowledge). Here and in the other paradigms, infants are said to "reason," "expect," "infer," and "be surprised"—yet the only data reported are looking behaviors. Not all researchers are comfortable with such strong beyond-the-data inferences about mental constructs. The issue here is a general one in the study of children's cognition, especially at young ages when the response measures are limited—how much can we read into young children's limited behavior? We encounter this issue again in Chapter 8 in the debate between "rich" (credit lots of underlying knowledge) and "lean" (credit only what's absolutely necessary) interpretations of young children's early speech.

In addition to the general concern with rich interpretation, several investigators have proposed specific alternative, and more conservative, explanations for Baillargeon's object permanence results (Haith, 1998; Meltzoff & Moore, 1998, 1999; Munakata, 1998; Munakata et al., 1997; Rivera et al., 1999; Smith, Thelen, Titzer, & McLin, 1999). On our reading there is some similarity (along, of course, with some differences) across the various proposals; in the present section we present Meltzoff and Moore's model as an example of this kind of theorizing, and in the next section we add the analysis by Munakata and colleagues.

The starting point for the alternative proposals is a puzzle raised by Baillargeon's findings: If infants have a Stage 4 knowledge of object permanence by 3 or 4 months of age rather than at 8 to 12 months, why do they not search for hidden objects until many months later? Baillargeon's explanation—and also the explanation favored by a number of other researchers of the topic—is of the sort that Munakata et al. (1997) label the *ancillary deficit hypothesis*. By this view the knowledge of object permanence is indeed there; what babies lack is some ancillary skill or skills that must be added to the knowledge to make search possible. The particular skill that Baillargeon (1993) emphasizes is the capacity to organize means-end behavior sequences. Most object-concept searches require the coordination of at least two distinct actions into a means-end sequence—for example, reaching for and removing a cover (the means), in order to grasp and play with a hidden toy (the end). But recall that this sort of integration of separate schemes into intentional, means-end sequences is precisely what Piaget had shown infants cannot do prior to Stage 4, and hence prior to about 8 months of age. Thus it is not surprising that infants cannot act adaptively on their knowledge of object permanence prior to this point.

This analysis is plausible, it has some specific data to support it, and it may well prove to be correct. But it is not the only way to explain the seeming discrepancy between knowledge and behavior. The other way to explain why infants do not act upon their knowledge is to conclude that the knowledge is not really there. This, in somewhat different forms, is the gist of the various alternative models cited earlier in this section. As noted we present just one of these models here, and our presentation is a condensed one that does not do justice to the full theory. The point is simply to convey that it may be possible to make sense of Baillargeon's findings without crediting young infants with a mature understanding of object permanence.

The central element in Meltzoff and Moore's (1998, 1999; Moore & Meltzoff, 1999) explanation for Baillargeon's findings is a distinction between object permanence and what they label *representational persistence*. Representational persistence refers to a persisting representation of an object that is set up by a brief perceptual encounter with it. In tasks like Baillargeon's drawbridge experiment representational persistence is assumed to be operating: Having seen the box prior to its disappearance, infants maintain a mental image of a box sitting on the table throughout the brief time period during which it is no longer visible. Object permanence is a stronger notion; it refers to a belief that a once visible object continues to exist when it is no longer visible. In the drawbridge experiment this would mean that infants not only maintain an image of the box but that they also represent it as still existing behind the screen during the time that it is occluded. Although this distinction may seem subtle, a little thought should convince you that it is possible to have the first (a representation of a recently encountered object) without the second (a belief that that now invisible object still exists where last seen). Meltzoff and Moore argue that various considerations support the conclusion that young infants are working with only the first and not the second form of representation. To begin with, representational persistence is sufficient to explain the drawbridge data: Infants in the impossible event condition form a representation of a box on the table and expect to see it again when the table comes into view, this expectation is disconfirmed when the screen goes flush against the table and no box appears, and the infants therefore respond with increased interest—not because object permanence has been violated, but simply because an expectation has been disconfirmed. Furthermore the seeming discrepancy between knowledge and behavior disappears if we assume that young infants are limited to representational persistence. If infants do not represent the object as existing when it is out of sight, then there is no mystery in the fact that they do not search when it is out of sight. Finally Meltzoff and Moore argue that the notion of representational persistence is compatible with other evidence concerning early representational capacity—in, particular, their own work on early imitation (see Chapter 2).

Note that this analysis, like Baillargeon's, does credit the young infant with some capacity for adaptive, beyond-immediate-experience cognitive processing— just not as mature a level of processing as in her theory. Note also that the analysis is in some ways compatible with Piaget's theory and in some ways not compatible. It is compatible in denying a Stage 4 knowledge of object permanence to the

3-month-old child. It is definitely not compatible, however, in its claim that a capacity to represent absent objects is present from early in life. The issue of representation is a major way in which many modern theorists of infancy deviate from Piaget, and we therefore return to it in the General Conclusions section.

The A not B Error. The AB̄ phenomenon has been the most extensively researched aspect of object-concept development. Recall that the error consists of continuing to search for the hidden object X under cover A, where it has been hidden and found on previous trials, even though the infant clearly sees the experimenter put it under cover B. Of the many unexpected, hard-to-believe phenomena reported by Piaget, this bizarre search behavior of the Stage 4 infant has to rank among the most puzzling. It is important to note, therefore, that the phenomenon is not somehow idiosyncratic to Piaget's observations but has been replicated in later studies using larger samples and varied techniques of probing for the error (Harris, 1989b; Marcovitch & Zelazzo, 1999; Wellman, Cross, & Bartsch, 1986).

On the other hand, the specific results of these later studies do not always fit comfortably with Piaget's interpretation of the error—namely, that it reflects a kind of sensorimotor minihabit, in which the infant tries to re-create a pleasurable experience by repeating a previously successful action. If Piaget's theory is correct, then presumably the error should be likelier to occur if the infant is given more rather than fewer successful search trials at A prior to the hiding at B. It should also be likelier to occur if the infant does all the object finding at A, rather than just watching the experimenter repeatedly hide and find the object there. Neither of these predictions is consistently supported by follow-up research (Harris, 1983). Furthermore factors not considered in Piaget's analysis can affect whether the error occurs. The memory demand placed on the infant turns out to be an especially important variable. Infants seldom err when allowed to search immediately at B; confusion occurs when some delay is imposed between disappearance of the object and opportunity to search. Presumably the short-term memory for the object's disappearance at B is fragile and quickly overpowered by the more solidly established memory of the object being found at A. Diamond (1985) has shown, in fact, that the delay necessary to produce the AB̄ error increases at a rate of about 2 seconds a month across the age span of interest. At 7 months a delay of 2 seconds is sufficient to elicit the error, by 9 months the span has grown to 5 seconds, and by 12 months errors occur only with delays of 10 seconds or more. Indeed there is even evidence that *adults* with brain damage and consequent memory problems will make the AB̄ error (Schacter, Moscovitz, Tulving, McLachlan, & Freedman, 1986).

Are memory problems therefore a sufficient explanation for the AB̄ error? Various further findings tell us that memory cannot be the whole story. Infants may search at A rather than B even when transparent covers are used, and they therefore can see both that location A is empty and that X is waiting to be found at location B (Butterworth, 1977)! Whatever the explanation for this strange behavior may be, it must involve something more than memory problems. In addition infants may demonstrate memory for the object's location if they are freed from the task of manually searching for it. Correct response to the actual location is more likely when the criterion is simply to gaze in the right direction than when the criterion is to reach appropriately (Hofstadter & Reznick, 1996). Applications of the Baillargeon possible event/impossible event procedure are a further source of evidence. In one study, for example (Baillargeon , DeVos, & Graber, 1989; see also Ahmed & Ruffman, 1998; Baillargeon & Graber, 1988), infants watched as an object was placed on one of two identical placemats; screens then blocked the infant's view of the mats, and after a delay a hand reached behind one of the screens and removed the object. In one condition the reach was to where the object had actually been placed; in the other condition the reach was to the other location. Infants looked longer in the latter, impossible-event condition, indicating that they could remember the location of the object. And they did so across delays as long as 70 seconds.

The work on the $A\overline{B}$ error, then, provides another example of what appears to be a gap between knowledge and behavior. Infants seem to know that the object is in B before they are able to direct their search behavior consistently toward B. Again two general types of explanation for the gap have been proposed: explanations that posit some sort of ancillary deficit and explanations that posit limitations in the underlying knowledge.

Probably the most fully developed proposal in the first category has been provided by Adele Diamond. Diamond (1991a, 1991b; Diamond, Cruttenden, & Neiderman, 1994) argues that two abilities are central to successful $A\overline{B}$ performance. One, as we have seen, is memory: the ability to keep alive the information about X residing at B across whatever delay may occur before search is permitted. The other is the ability to inhibit the tendency to reach toward A. Diamond cites the evidence that we have reviewed indicating that infants often do seem to remember that the object is at B; she adds to it an observation from her own research that some infants even stare at B while reaching out to uncover A. These infants' problem seems to be that they simply cannot resist the pull toward making the prepotent response, which in this case is search at A. Diamond marshals evidence, moreover, to show that the difficulty in inhibiting dominant responses is not specific to the $A\overline{B}$ task but rather is a general characteristic of infant behavior during the first year of life. In many situations babies have difficulty not making the most natural, readily available response. Finally she makes a persuasive case for the proposition that these difficulties in inhibition stem from immaturities in brain development—specifically, from immaturities in the frontal lobe system. The case rests not just on parallels between infant behavior and the developmental course of brain maturation but on several further sources of evidence: the fact that infant monkeys show similar behavioral deficits that correspond to *their* level of frontal lobe development, the fact that experimentally induced lesions in the critical areas of monkeys' brains can produce deficits in behavioral inhibition, and the fact that injuries to the frontal lobes in adult humans are also associated with impaired ability to inhibit behavior.

Diamond's theory does quite well at explaining many aspects of $A\overline{B}$ performance; like all theories of the error, however, it runs up against some data that it cannot easily accommodate (Haith & Benson, 1998; Smith et al., 1999). A reasonable conclusion, therefore, is that the memory plus inhibition model provides a partial explanation of the phenomenon, but that it needs to be supplemented by other models with other emphases. The theory proposed by Munakata and colleagues (Munakata, 1998; Munakata et al., 1997) offers an alternative in the limited-knowledge rather than ancillary-deficit category. As with Meltzoff and Moore's theory, our presentation is brief, the intent being simply to convey the flavor of what seems likely to become an increasingly influential line of theorizing.

In Chapter 1 we introduced the connectionist approach as a recent emphasis within the overall information processing perspective. Munakata et al. (1997) offer a connectionist approach to object permanence. In their view object permanence is not best conceptualized as a principle that infants either "have" or "don't have." What infants have, rather, are innumerable experiences across the early months of life with objects that come into and go out of their perceptual field. Specific neurons in the brain are activated whenever the infant processes an object, and over time particular connections gradually become stronger and stronger. Eventually these connections become strong enough to support representations of absent objects, at first for brief periods and then across longer and longer delays. With experience connections are also formed between representations of objects and relevant behavior systems—in particular, looking and reaching. Reaching, however, requires a stronger level of object representation than does looking, which is why response to invisible objects occurs later for reaching measures than for looking measures. Similarly keeping track of multiple locations requires a stronger level of representation than does keeping track of a single location, which is why successful performance on the $\overline{\text{AB}}$ task lags behind success at finding objects in a single hiding place. These and other developmental changes, however, do not reflect either acquisition of new principles or shedding of ancillary deficits; rather they occur because of increases in the strength of object representations.

As noted we have offered a brief description of a complex theory, and there is a danger that the brevity may give the theory an arbitrary sound, as though its assumptions are being generated ad hoc simply to fit the object permanence data. We should add, therefore, that the general assumptions that underlie the model are grounded in a large body of theory and research in connectionist modeling of cognitive processes. In addition Munakata (1998; Munakata et al., 1997) reports both experiments with infants and computer simulations that provide support for particular aspects of the model. Whether the connectionist approach will prove to be the best way to explain object permanence remains to be seen. But the approach does illustrate how a levels-of-understanding model might be able to encompass the various phenomena that need explaining.

What conclusions can be taken away from all this recent work on the object concept? One conclusion, certainly, is that understanding this particular aspect of development is still—some 70 years after Piaget's pioneering studies—an ongoing enterprise. It does seem safe to conclude that young infants' knowledge of objects is greater than Piaget believed. It is possible that it is considerably greater—that infants have a basic realization that hidden objects still exist months earlier than Piaget's observations indicated, possibly even from birth. Such a conclusion is compatible with (although not, as we have seen, mandated by) the many ingenious studies by Baillargeon and coworkers. It is also compatible with other studies of early knowledge of objects, especially the Spelke research discussed in the previous chapter, and more generally with work on what has come to be called "naive physics" in infancy and early childhood (Wellman & Gelman, 1992). Evidence is accumulating that human infants are biologically endowed with a rich set of processing mechanisms that allow them to perceive and to make sense of the physical world. In Chapter 1 we introduced two relatively new theoretical positions inspired in part by such evidence: modular nativism and the theory theory approach. An early emergence of object permanence would be quite consistent with this work.

It is also possible that the early knowledge is somewhat less than the strongest reading of the evidence suggests. At the least the knowledge is initially not sufficient to support adaptive behavior; various further developments (in memory, attention, motivation, locomotor skills) need to be added to it before babies can act successfully toward objects. And it is possible, as we have seen, that developmental change occurs not just in these ancillary processes but in the knowledge itself. Piaget, of course, thought so (which is why his account has six stages rather than just two), and each of the contemporary theories that we cited earlier, despite differences in their specific formulations, shares Piaget's assumption that knowledge about objects is graduated rather than dichotomous. This also is our bias. But how to conceptualize different levels of understanding, and how to choose among different conceptualizations, are among the most challenging questions in the field. These questions are especially challenging when the target of the conceptualization is nonverbal, mostly nonmotoric, and so cognitively different (perhaps!) from those of us doing the conceptualizing. We are fairly confident, for example, that a 10-month-old who watches her mother walk out of the room can think about mom as still existing somewhere else in the house. Can a 3-month-old? Or is the younger infant limited to the Meltzoff and Moore notion of representational persistence—thus, an image of a no longer present mother, but no positive belief that she still exists elsewhere? If so, can she miss her mother? (What could "miss" mean for such a mind?) Can she form an attachment to her? We may eventually know the answer to questions such as these. At present, though, we're really all just guessing.

OTHER INFANT ACHIEVEMENTS

Object concept is just one of the foci for current research on cognitive development in infants. Here we consider three additional and very important aspects of human mental functioning that have their origins in infancy: causal reasoning, problem solving, and the formation of concepts or categories. We add some further infant accomplishments when we reach the appropriate context in coming chapters—in particular, work on early competencies with respect to number (Chapter 4), social cognition (Chapter 6), and memory (Chapter 7).

Causal Understanding

If young infants are required to demonstrate their understanding of causality through their own adaptive behaviors they do not perform very impressively, just as Piaget long ago observed. An alternative approach to assessing early understanding of cause-and-effect relations makes use, once again, of the habituation/dishabituation procedure. Leslie (1984; Leslie & Keeble, 1987) constructed an animated film in which a red brick moved from left to right across the screen until it made contact with a stationary green brick, at which point the red brick stopped and the green brick moved off to the right. Adults watching such a display have a strong experience of causality: The red brick appears to "launch" the green brick into motion (much as one billiard ball launches another). In contrast, events that lack the proper spatial and temporal relations between the elements do not elicit feelings of causality—for example, if the red brick stops short of the green one, or if the green brick moves off only a second or so after the contact is made.

To determine whether infants have a similar experience of causality, Leslie compared two groups of 6-month-olds. One group was habituated to the causal, red-launches-green event just described. The other group was habituated to a noncausal, delayed-launch event, in which the bricks made contact but the green brick moved off only after a delay. Both groups were then tested for dishabituation when their original film was run in reverse. Note that in most respects the dishabituation experience is the same for both groups: Both see a reversal in the spatial direction (right to left rather than the original left to right), and both see a reversal in the temporal order of movement (green moves first rather than red). We might expect, therefore, that the changes would be equally noticeable and the recovery of attention equally strong. There is, however, one difference between the conditions, and it concerns causality: Only the first group sees a causal event in the first film (red launches green) and thus a reversal of causal direction in the second (green launches red). The infants in this condition in fact showed significantly greater dishabituation than did their counterparts. The heightened interest in the case of causal reversal suggests that the infants were encoding not only the individual elements of the experience (particular colors, directions, speeds, etc.) but also the causal relation. What they saw, in other words, was red launching green, and they therefore were quite interested when things somehow changed and green began to launch red.

Some research by Cohen and colleagues (Cohen & Amsel, 1998; Cohen, Amsel, Redford, & Casasola, 1998; Oakes & Cohen, 1990) adds a qualifier to this demonstration of early causal competence. These investigators confirmed that 6-month-olds (although not younger infants) appear to perceive the causality in a launching event—only, however, when simple stimuli of the sort employed by Leslie were used. When toy cars and trucks replaced the geometric shapes, 6-month-olds no longer responded on the basis of causality, and success came only at 10 months. In the information-processing analysis offered by Cohen and colleagues, infants must first be able to discern that the moving stimuli are distinct objects before they can detect the causal relation between them. When simple shapes are the stimuli this first step is not a problem for 6-month-olds; with more complex, real objects, however, the information-processing demands at first overwhelm any chance of causal processing.

The ability to perceive the causal relations among complex stimuli is just one of the further developments that are not part of initial competence but that become evident by about 10 to 15 months. Here are several others. Infants become able not just to detect causality but to distinguish between different sorts of causal actions—for example, to tell the difference between pulling and pushing (Casasola & Cohen, 2000). They begin to move beyond a focus on events in isolation to make use of contextual cues to figure out the causal relations in what otherwise would be ambiguous situations (Woodward & Sommerville, 2000). They become able to reason about not only single actions (A impels B) but also causal chains (A impels B which then impels C—Cohen, Rundell, Spellman, & Cashon, 1999). Finally they become sensitive not just to the existence of a causal relation but also to the quantitative properties involved. They realize, for example, that the size of the force-instilling object is important, and they expect a large projectile to impart greater force and movement than a small one (Kotovsky & Baillargeon, 1994, 1998). There is some evidence, in fact, that this particular realization may emerge by about 6 months. And it would not be surprising, given the history of recent research on infant cognition, if the time period for some of the other accomplishments is eventually pushed earlier as well.

These examples of infant competence do not mean, of course, that understanding of causality is complete by 15 months of age—such is far from the case. But they do indicate a more mature, adultlike parsing of the causal flow than we formerly credited to the infant. The explanation that Leslie (1988, 1995) offers for such early causal competence is an example of the modular nativism approach introduced in Chapter 1. In his view (a position with which not all researchers agree—cf. Cohen et al., 1998; Haith & Benson, 1998), much of the early, adaptive response is made possible by a system of perceptual modules—that is, innately provided, highly specialized systems for rapidly analyzing and making sense of particular kinds of perceptual input (such as collisions and launches). These perceptual modules are not equated with a fully mature understanding of cause and effect; rather they are the starting point upon which a conceptual mastery of causality builds. Perhaps appropriately, Leslie (1986) uses a launching metaphor in speculating about the role of modules. In his words modules help to "get development off the ground."

Problem Solving

Our discussion to this point may have given the impression that infants know more than we used to think they know but that they still cannot act on this knowledge to get what they want to get. Thus they realize that hidden objects still exist but are unable to search for them; they appreciate basic cause-and-effect relations but are unable to organize intentional behavioral sequences; and so on. There is some truth to this picture—infants' ability to act adaptively *does* often lag behind their underlying knowledge. But the picture is not totally bleak. Here we consider several examples of important early achievements in problem solving.

Willatts (1989) presented 9-month-old infants with the task of retrieving an attractive toy. The toy was presented within view but beyond the infant's reach, thus preventing the infant from simply reaching out and grasping it. Fortunately for the infant, the toy was resting on an easily reachable cloth, and thus could be brought within range by a pull on the cloth. Unfortunately for the infant, a foam-block barrier prevented a direct reach to the cloth. Solution of the problem thus required several steps: push aside the barrier, and only then reach for and pull the cloth, and only then grasp and play with the toy. As Figure 3.4 illustrates, infants as young as 9 months readily executed this sequence of behaviors and thereby succeeded in retrieving the toy. Their behavior contrasted with that of a control group who were presented with toy, cloth, and barrier but with the toy sitting next to rather than on the cloth. As Figure 3.4 shows, the control participants did not bother to pull the cloth (why should they?); rather they played with the only object available to them, namely the barrier. What Willatts emphasizes is that both groups hit upon the most adaptive behavior in their particular circumstances immediately, on the first trial; they did not need to work through the steps one at a time before determining what the final outcome would be. They thus showed a capacity for the kind of insightful, planful behavior that Piaget saw as emerging only near the end of infancy.

Willatts's participants also demonstrated another precocious accomplishment: the Stage 5 ability to use one object (such as a supporting cloth) to obtain another object. As noted earlier such behavior can be seen as the earliest form of an extremely important type of intelligent activity: use of tools to achieve a goal. Tool use has been explored more fully in a number of research projects (Bates, Carlson-Luden, & Bretherton, 1980; Brown, 1989; Chen, Sanchez, & Campbell, 1997; Lockman, 2000; Schlesinger & Langer, 1999; Uzgiris & Hunt, 1975, 1987). These studies confirm both Piaget's claim that tool use is an emergent achievement of infancy and Willatts's

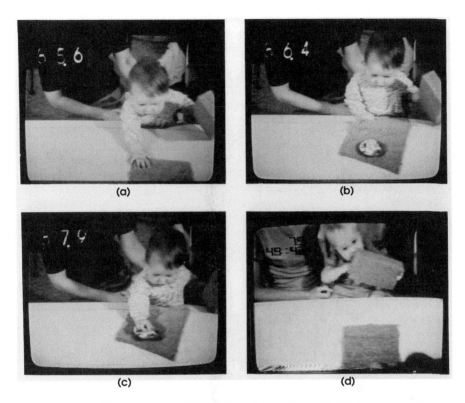

FIGURE 3.4 Problem solving at 9 months of age. The child (a) removes the block of foam, (b) pulls the cloth, and (c) grasps the toy. (d) In contrast an infant in the control condition ignores the cloth and plays with the block of foam. From "Development of Problem-Solving in Infancy," by P. Willatts. In A. Slater and G. Bremner (Eds.), *Infant Development* (p. 166), 1989, Hillsdale, NJ: Erlbaum. Copyright © by Taylor & Francis, Inc. Reprinted by permission. Photos from Charles Peters.

suggestion that simple forms of the skill may emerge earlier than Piaget believed. Success depends on a number of factors. The type of tool can be important. The ability to use a support (such as the cloth in Willatts's study) to retrieve a distant object seems to be mastered by most infants by the end of the first year; in contrast use of a stick to corral an out-of-reach goal (the other main behavior pattern studied by Piaget) is generally not seen until several months later. Perceptual factors can play a role. Infants are most likely to solve tool-use problems when the tool and the goal are clearly distinct perceptually—for example, different in color or texture. Presumably the perceptual separation of tool and goal helps the infant to realize that there are two distinct objects that must be brought together for problem solution (in the same way, perhaps, that the perceptual distinctiveness of the stimuli aids early detection of causality). Finally, with sufficient experience and support, infants can not only solve basic tool-use problems but also transfer their solutions adaptively to new situations. For example, in a study by Brown (1989), 20-month-old infants first learned to use a long, rounded, candy cane–painted hook to retrieve a desirable toy. When later tested on a similar task with other would-be tools, the babies ignored the instruments with the greatest perceptual similarity to the original tool (same candy cane color, same shape, etc.) and zeroed in on the one implement sufficient for the job at hand, namely, a rake with both sufficient length and the requisite pulling head. In simpler situations with more perceptual support, infants as young as 10 months have been shown to transfer solutions from one task to another (Chen, Sanchez, & Campbell 1997). The ability to move beyond immediate experience to apply cognitive gains more broadly is an absolutely essential step in adaptive problem solving. Studies such as these indicate that some such competence emerges very early.

Categorization

Haith and Benson (1998, p. 229) introduce the topic at issue now in the following way:

> Imagine an infant who must learn anew its parent's face for each perspective rotation, each expression, and each change of hair style. Or, consider the task of an infant who must acquire a new knowledge base for each separate cat that it encounters—that each eats, drinks, meows, and so on.

Another important way in which all of us move beyond immediate experience is by forming *categories* or *concepts* for the recurrent stimuli and events of our world—faces in general and familiar faces in particular, cats and other animals, raindrops and roses and all sorts of other favorite and not so favorite things. Categorization is a method of imposing order on what otherwise would be unmanageable diversity and change, and as such it is an absolutely indispensable cognitive activity. Indeed Thelen and Smith (1994, p. 143) go so far as to label categorization "the primitive in all behavior and mental functioning."

How can we determine whether infants have begun to organize their experiences into categories? The answer is that several kinds of evidence are informative, but they all rely on the same basic rationale: see whether the infant responds more similarly to the members of a category than to nonmembers, and thus seems in some way to be treating the category members as all instances of the same thing. Table 3.2 summarizes the specific forms of similar response that have been examined. Of these the most widely utilized technique, once again, has been habituation/dishabituation. The more active procedures (e.g., sequential touching), it is worth noting, have their roots in the Piagetian approach to categorization. As we saw earlier, in Piaget's sensorimotor theory of infant intelligence early concepts are defined in terms of the common action patterns that infants direct toward particular objects: the category of things to suck, the category of things to bang, and so on.

Categorization has been a fertile area for recent infant research, and we can only hit some of the highlights here (for fuller discussions, see Hayne, 1996; Langer, 1998; Madole & Oakes, 1999; Mandler, 2000; Oakes & Madole, 2000; Quinn, 1999). By 3 months of age (the youngest age examined in most research), infants have begun to form categories of a variety of sorts. By this age, for example, they can distinguish animals from furniture; if habituated to a series of animal pictures they remain bored when yet another animal appears but perk up when shown a table or chair (Behl-Chadha, 1996). They can also make various distinctions within

TABLE 3.2   Methods of Studying Infant Categorization

METHOD	DESCRIPTION	EVIDENCE FOR CATEGORIZATION
Habituation-Dishabituation (e.g., Behl-Chadha, 1996; Quinn & Eimas, 1996)	Present a series of pictures of different members of a category (e.g., different cats), then test for dishabituation to either new instances of the category (e.g., new cats) or to members of other categories (e.g., dogs, horses).	If dishabituation occurs more strongly when the category changes.
Operant Conditioning (e.g., Greco, Hayne, & Rovee-Collier, 1990; Hayne, Rovee Collier, & Perris, 1987)	Condition a response when a particular stimulus (e.g., a mobile) is present, then test for generalization of the response to new exemplars that vary in similarity to the trained stimulus.	If the conditioned response generalizes to the new exemplars.
Sequential Touching (e.g., Mandler & Bauer, 1988; Mandler, Bauer, & McDonough, 1991)	Present an array of objects from different categories (e.g., toy animals, toy vehicles, toy furniture), record the order in which the infant touches the objects.	If within-category sequential touches occur with greater than chance frequency.
Inductive Inference (e.g., Mandler & McDonough, 1996, 1998)	Teach responses appropriate for items from different categories (e.g., giving a dog a drink, putting a key in a car), then measure response to new exemplars of the categories.	If responses generalize to members of the same category.

these categories. They distinguish chairs from couches, beds, and tables, and cats from birds, dogs, and horses (not, however, from female lions—Quinn, 1999). Figure 3.5 shows some of the stimuli used in this research.

Various developmental advances are evident in the months following initial success. Most obviously infants form both more categories and progressively more subtle categories. By 9 months, for instance, they can distinguish birds from planes, even when both have outstretched wings and even when the planes are decorated with facelike markings (Mandler & McDonough, 1993). As they develop, infants also expand and enrich their initial somewhat crude categories. For example early distinction among animals seems to be based mainly on facial features; with development comes sensitivity to other important attributes, such as tail length and body shape (Quinn & Eimas, 1996). With development also comes a sensitivity to correlations among attributes—that is, to the fact that many features (e.g., wings and feathers) tend to occur

FIGURE 3.5 Examples of stimuli used to test infants' ability to form categories. From "Development of Recognition and Categorization of Objects and Their Spatial Relations in Young Infants," by P. C. Quinn. In L. Balter and C. S. Tamis-Monda (Eds.). *Child Psychology: A Handbook of Contemporary Issues* (p. 100), 1999, Philadelphia: Psychology Press. Copyright © 1999 by Psychology Press. Reprinted by permission.

together, a realization that enhances the probability of quick and accurate categorization (Younger & Cohen, 1986). Finally, as infants develop, the more active response measures listed in Table 3.2 become available, and these measures reveal forms of understanding that are not tapped by simply looking more or less in an habituation study. An especially important development is that infants begin to use knowledge of category membership to make inferences about new instances (Mandler & McDonough, 1998). In one study, for example, 14-month-olds first imitated various actions by an adult model, such as giving a dog a drink and turning a key in a car door, after which they were given a chance to reproduce the actions with new members of the animal and vehicle categories. Even when the new instances were both physically distinct from the modeled exemplars and unfamiliar (e.g., an armadillo as the animal and a forklift as the vehicle), the infants generalized appropriately; that is, they performed animal-appropriate activities only with animals and vehicle-appropriate activities only with vehicles (Mandler & McDonough, 1996).

The descriptive picture of infant categorization (which, again, is much fuller than we attempt to convey here) is not really a subject of much dispute among researchers of the topic. What is very much a matter of dispute is how to interpret what infants are doing. Here disagreements abound with regard to a number of specific issues (a point made graphically clear by the commentaries in response to the Mandler, 2000, article). We consider (but not necessarily resolve!) some of these theoretical issues when we return to children's concepts in Chapter 4. For now we note simply that whatever their ultimate explanation may be, infants' categorization abilities are both impressive and highly adaptive, and they clearly constitute another entry in modern psychology's ongoing documentation of infant cognitive competence.

SOME GENERAL CONCLUSIONS

We opened the chapter with a promise of complexity and controversy, and we assume that that promise has now been fulfilled. Infant cognition is not a topic for which clear and simple conclusions should be expected, and we do not pretend to offer any. What we do offer are what seem to us the *relatively* clear conclusions that emerge from recent research, along with our view of the most important unresolved issues and likely future directions.

Perhaps the clearest conclusion concerns early competence. That infants are more competent than Piaget believed is the theme that has run throughout our discussion. Piaget's emphasis on motor activity led him to underestimate infants' understanding of a number of aspects of their world. To be sure, there are disagreements about how serious the underestimation was. And even on the most positive reading of the evidence, earlier understanding does not mean complete understanding—there are limitations to be overcome and developmental advances to be made for all of the various topics that we have considered. In addition Piaget was correct in his assertion that infants often fail to act adaptively upon the world—to search for hidden objects, to organize means-end sequences, and the like. But he may well have been wrong about the reason why.

The astonishing precocity of many infant capabilities has pushed our conceptions of infant development in a more nativistic direction. Certain competencies emerge so early that it seems they must be largely innate rather than constructed through experience. It is at least roughly accurate to say that, whereas Piaget would think of these abilities as the gradually emerging products of infant development, many present-day infant researchers would instead construe them as the initial cognitive tools that make this development possible. Furthermore not just initial competence but developmental advances in competence are more likely these days to be seen as having biological-maturational and not solely experiential bases—recall Diamond's work on frontal lobe development and infant search behavior.

On the other hand, to say that biology is important leaves unanswered many questions about *how* biological processes affect cognitive development. Although our knowledge is growing, we are still in the early phases in the attempt to link specific biological mechanisms to specific cognitive processes, as well as the attempt to link the *changes* in biology that come with development to changes in children's cognition (we revisit this issue in Chapter 9). Even if we set aside the search for specific biological mechanisms, theorists who favor nativistic explanations face questions of how best to conceptualize the contribution of nature. For some theorists (e.g., Leslie, 1995; Spelke, 1991), biology provides important forms of inborn knowledge, although maturational limitations or ancillary deficits may delay the expression of the knowledge. In contrast Baillargeon, as we have seen, does not believe that infants are born with much in the way of specific knowledge; what biology provides are highly constrained learning mechanisms that guarantee the rapid acquisition of the knowledge in any expectable environment. This issue may eventually prove empirically resolvable, and Baillargeon (1995, 1998) provides some evidence in support of her position. At present, however, the question is far from resolved.

Questions also exist on the nurture side of the nature-nurture interaction. Experience plays some role in anyone's theory, but what sorts of experiences and exactly what role? Here our conceptions of the relative importance of different sorts of experience during infancy have definitely changed since the heyday of Piaget's theory. Not only does motor activity play a less important role than we used to believe, but perceptual activity almost certainly plays a greater role. Young infants may be limited in their ability to act motorically upon the world, but their perceptual systems have proved to be surprisingly powerful and mature. In various ways every modern theorist of infancy puts more emphasis on purely perceptual processing of experience than did Piaget. Attempts to formulate specific models of how perceptual processing results in knowledge are still works in progress, however; for some interesting ongoing efforts see Mandler (1992a, 1992b, 1998) and Meltzoff and Moore (1998, 1999).

Most modern theorists also put considerably less emphasis on stages of development than did Piaget. Piaget's model of infancy, as we have seen, is one of stages: All developments are seen as progressing through the same six-stage sequence, and at any given time all aspects of development are seen as falling within the same stage. There is undoubtedly some very general truth to such a conception. Later acquisitions often do build upon earlier, prerequisite ones; related competencies often do emerge at roughly the same time; and it is important for our theories to recognize and explain these facts. Piaget's theory, however, makes not just general but very strong and specific claims about the stage-tied nature of infant cognition, and these claims have not fared well in recent research. There are simply too many instances of earlier-than-expected competence, too many divergences in level of performance across different tasks, and too many aspects of development that do not seem to depend on the acting-upon-the world processes with which Piaget defined his stages. It may be that some modified version of a constructivist, stage model will prove viable; some interesting recent attempts in this direction have appeared (Langer, Rivera, Schlesinger, & Wakeley, in press; Muller & Overton, 1998; Muller, Sokol, & Overton, 1998). But the original model cannot survive unchanged.

Whatever the fate of Piaget's or other stage models may prove to be, such models do have the virtue of addressing one of the central questions that any theory of development must address. The question is how best to conceptualize different levels or degrees of knowledge—what Haith (1993), as we noted in the last chapter, has labeled "partial accomplishments." Many (perhaps most or even all) cognitive achievements of interest are not a matter of a simple absent to present transition; rather they are characterized by different degrees of knowledge—by various partial forms of "having" prior to the final, mature "has." Piaget's stage model provides one way to conceptualize degrees of knowledge. In the discussion of the object concept we saw several alternative ways to explain the prolonged course of development for one especially important form of knowledge. We also saw, however, that there is as yet insufficient evidence to choose with confidence among these alternatives. And still unclear as well is the breadth of the various explanatory models— that is, how well they speak not just to object concept but also to the many other aspects of infant cognitive development that need explaining.

We come finally to what is probably the most serious challenge to the Piagetian picture of infant intelligence. It concerns Piaget's claim that infancy consists of a prolonged period of purely sensorimotor—and thus nonsymbolic, prerepresentational—intelligence. We have seen that many competencies seem to be present earlier than Piaget believed. Could the same be true of symbolic-representational ability? A positive answer in this case would constitute more than simply an adjustment in age norms. It would mean that infant intelligence is, at least in part, basically different from what Piaget believed it to be.

Determining exactly when symbolic-representational competence emerges is an exceedingly difficult task (Mandler, 1988, 1998). Problems of definition and of interpretation abound—what exactly do we mean when we talk about this sort of competence, and what exactly could an infant do to demonstrate to us that he or she possesses it? Piaget's approach to these questions was a conservative one; he was reluctant to credit the infant with symbolic ability prior to the Stage 6 behaviors (deferred imitation, symbolic play, etc.) that announce its presence in unmistakably clear fashion. Other investigators have been more likely to see a representational underpinning to certain earlier appearing infant achievements. Many would contend, for example, that the basic Stage 4 knowledge that a hidden object still exists implies a capacity to form a mental representation of the object in its absence. If so, then representation is present by the last third of the first year—and possibly a good deal earlier, if successes in the Baillargeon research really do reflect knowledge of permanence.

Even if we accept Piaget's criteria for inferring representation, recent work suggests that he may have placed age of emergence considerably later than is in fact the case. One fascinating example comes from studies of infants learning American Sign Language (Bonvillian & Folven, 1993; Meier & Newport, 1990). Although their interpretation is controversial (see Petitto, 1992), such studies suggest that the first genuine symbolic signs may appear as early as 6 to 7 months of age—several months earlier than the typical first appearance of words for children learning a spoken language, and long before the expected age for such competence in Piaget's theory.

Work on deferred imitation provides another example. In a study by Meltzoff (1988), 9-month-old infants watched an adult model perform a series of actions on three novel objects (e.g., pushing a button on a box to produce a beeping sound). Twenty-four hours later the infants were given a chance to play with the same objects, and many reproduced the behaviors they had seen the model perform. Various control conditions served to verify that the babies had not hit upon these behaviors spontaneously but rather were imitating what they had seen a day before. It is important to note as well that the babies were not allowed to reproduce the behaviors immediately after seeing them; this control served to guarantee that their later reproductions were true imitations and not simply repetitions of their own earlier behaviors. Other research has shown some deferred imitation of simple motor actions in infants as young as 6 months (Barr, Dowden, & Hayne, 1996). If we agree with Piaget that such imitation requires representation—and it certainly seems reasonable to do so—then 6-month-olds are apparently capable of symbolic representation.

Is 6 months the lower bound for deferred imitation? It may be if the requirement is to imitate a motor behavior. Recall, though, that Meltzoff and Moore have reported evidence (still controversial, as our discussion in Chapter 2 indicated) that even newborn babies can imitate an adult model's facial expressions. Although the time period between model and imitation is brief in these studies, there is often a delay of several seconds before the infant's response; thus the imitations straddle the borderline between the immediate and deferred categories. Furthermore one study with 6-week-olds demonstrates imitation across a 24–hour delay period (Meltzoff & Moore, 1994). Although comparable effects have yet to be demonstrated with newborns, Meltzoff and Moore believe that the capacity to symbolically encode a model's behavior is present from birth and underlies the more short-term imitations that newborn babies do show. In their words: "In our view, the ability to act on the basis of stored representations is the starting point, not the crowning achievement, of psychological development in infancy" (Meltzoff & Moore, 1999, p. 57).

Is representational ability really present from the start? Such a conclusion would clearly be a radical departure from the Piagetian picture of the sensorimotor infant. Our impression is that most experts in infancy are not ready to reach this conclusion based on present evidence. But it is probably fair to say as well that no one is very confident anymore that representation is *not* part of infants' initial equipment. Representation is a long-standing topic in the field, and one on which considerable progress has been made, as Mandler's (1998) superb *Handbook of Child Psychology* chapter illustrates. Still perhaps the major challenge for the next generation of research and theory in infant cognition will be to wrestle still further with questions of representation: What exactly do we mean when we credit an infant with representational capacity? What are the more general cognitive underpinnings that make this capacity possible? When does the capacity emerge in development (almost certainly earlier than Piaget thought, but how much earlier?), and how does it relate to the nonrepresentational, sensorimotor forms of intelligence that clearly must remain part of the story of infant cognition? Answers to questions such as these would tell us something that all of us would like very much to know: What is it like to be a baby?

SUMMARY

The human cognitive system undergoes dramatic changes during the period from birth to the end of infancy. Yet research in recent years has also revealed that newborns and young infants are in some respects much more competent than we used to believe. Some of the most exciting contemporary research in developmental psychology is directed to uncovering exactly what competencies are available at what ages, and therefore exactly what it is that changes across infancy.

Historically Piaget's theory and research have dominated the study of infant cognition. Piaget saw the cognition of the infant as *sensorimotor* rather than *symbolic-representational* in nature—as an unreflective, practical, perceiving-and-doing sort of intelligence. Such cognition is expressed in the elaboration and inter-coordination of cognitive structures called *schemes:* classes of organized, repeat-edly exercised action patterns (e.g., sucking, listening, looking, grasping). External data (objects and events) are *assimilated* to the sensorimotor schemes, and schemes simultaneously *accommodate* to these data. The engine or driving force behind the exercise of schemes is a system of motivation intrinsic to the cognitive structures. This motivational system has exactly the properties that we would expect to be most adaptive for an organism that still has much to learn about the world: a tendency to exercise the schemes spontaneously and repeatedly; a disposition to focus attention and activity on events that are in some way novel or surprising and hence still in need of understanding; and a pleasureful sense of competence in achieving and re-peatedly reasserting its mastery over such previously unassimilated situations.

Piaget's description of sensorimotor development is divided into six stages. The starting point for infant intelligence consists of various inborn reflexes; the endpoint is the capacity for symbolic-representational thought—the capacity to rep-resent and act upon the world *internally,* through the use of mental symbols. The developmental sequence that links reflex and symbol is one of the progressive de-velopment, elaboration, and integration of various sensorimotor schemes. As infants assimilate new experiences and accommodate to them, they construct progressively more advanced and adaptive means for acting upon and understanding the world.

A particularly important achievement of infancy is mastery of the object con-cept: the realization that physical objects are distinct and independent entities whose existence does not depend on our actions or our perceptual contact with them. Piaget made the surprising claim that this fundamental and seemingly obvious piece of knowledge requires nearly the whole first 2 years of a person's life to become fully established. In the first two stages of his sensorimotor progression, he saw lit-tle evidence for understanding of object concept; at most the young infant might track a moving object until it disappears or stare briefly at the point of disappear-ance. By Stage 3 tracking has become more skilled and more clearly anticipatory, and the infant shows some ability to search for partially hidden objects. The ability to search for invisible objects emerges at Stage 4 and constitutes a major advance in the infant's mastery of object permanence. There is still a peculiar limitation, how-ever: After a few trials of finding an object under a given cover, the infant continues to search under the same cover even after watching the object disappear in a differ-ent place (the A not B error). This limitation is overcome at Stage 5, when the infant becomes capable of handling a series of visible displacements. This achievement, in turn, leads to the final step: the Stage 6, symbolically based ability to solve prob-lems involving *invisible* displacements.

Object concept has been a popular research topic for post-Piaget investiga-tors. Recent research, much of which has employed the habituation/dishabituation paradigm, has demonstrated that young infants know more about objects than Piaget believed. When freed from the demands of motoric search, infants as young as 3 or 4 months show evidence that they have knowledge of not only the existence but also some of the properties (e.g., size, location) of hidden objects. Exactly how much knowledge underlies these early responses, however, has been difficult to de-termine. In addition infants typically do not search for objects until the second half of the first year. Two kinds of explanation have been offered for the failure to search: Infants' initial knowledge about hidden objects may in fact be of a limited, pre-Stage 4 form that is insufficient to motivate a search, or young infants may lack the ancillary skills necessary for search, such as the ability to organize means-end behavioral sequences. Quite possibly both factors contribute. Multiple factors may also underlie infants' difficulties with the A not B task. Memory problems and difficulties in inhibiting dominant responses almost certainly contribute to the $A\overline{B}$ error; limitations in the underlying knowledge about objects may also play a role.

The conclusion that infants are more competent than Piaget believed is not limited to the object concept. Earlier (although not fully mature) competence has been demonstrated for a number of other aspects of infant development as well. Both problem solving and understanding of causality have proved, with modern methods of study, to be somewhat more advanced than Piaget's descriptions indicate. Infants' categorization abilities—that is, the capacity and propensity to group recurrent experiences into categories or concepts—are also operative from early in life and grow in power across infancy. In general contemporary research on infancy suggests several conclusions in addition to that of greater-than-expected competence: Development may be more strongly biologically-maturationally based than we used to believe; perceptual experience probably plays a greater role and motor experience a lesser role than was once thought; and attempts (à la Piaget) to characterize infant cognition in terms of general stages are at best only roughly accurate, for such attempts fail to explain the many inconsistencies and asynchronies in children's level of development.

Perhaps the broadest challenge to the Piagetian model comes from work (e.g., studies of deferred imitation) that suggests that symbolic-representational ability may emerge earlier than he believed, and thus that infant cognition does not consist only of sensorimotor forms of functioning. At the least some capacity to form representations seems to be present by the second half of the first year; some researchers believe that it is present from birth. The issue of when and how representation emerges is one of the central challenges still facing researchers and theorists of infant cognition.

4

Representation
and Concepts

———◆———

Chapter 3 described the making of the representational mind during infancy. Being able to mentally represent objects and events is one of the grandest achievements of the young thinker, for the child can now contemplate objects and events when they no longer are present. The subsequent growth of this new skill makes possible the developmental story of the rest of this book. Representations support concepts of the physical and social worlds, reasoning, problem solving, remembering, and language acquisition and use. In the present chapter, we first look at how infants' rudimentary representational ability blossoms into young children's emerging understanding of, and use of, a variety of symbols and other representations. Then we examine the use of representations to form basic concepts, including biology and number.

SYMBOLIC-REPRESENTATIONAL ABILITIES: PICTURES, MODELS, AND OTHER REPRESENTATIONS

Toddlers not only can form internal representations, but also are beginning to use external representations. They are surrounded by symbols and symbol systems—words, pictures, photos, numbers, videos, maps, miniatures, clocks, calendars, and so on. These symbols may be stationary, for example a printed word, or moving, as images in motion on a computer or television screen. What do all these symbols (to us) mean to young children? How do they interpret this profusion of images, large and small, of people and things? How do they "decipher the Rosetta Stones of their existence" (DeLoache & Smith, 1999, p. 64)? We focus on two important representational skills—understanding pictorial representations and using physical models to draw an inference.

Pictorial Representations

A 2-year-old points to a face in a family photograph and correctly says "Daddy" or looks at a cookie in a picture book then runs to the kitchen in hot pursuit of that goal. No observant parent would doubt that very young children understand that pictures represent real objects. Although 19-month-olds seem to have the concept of "picture," 9-month-olds pat and rub the pictures as if they are real objects and sometimes even try to pick them off the page (DeLoache, Pierroutsakos, Uttal, Rosengren, & Gottlieb, 1998).

When young children "understand" pictures, do they simply detect some similarity between the real object and a picture of it, or do they understand that pictures are representation because of people's intent for them to be representations? In one study (Bloom & Markson, 1998) 3- and 4-year-olds were asked to name pictures that were intended to be representations of real objects but did not clearly resemble these objects. For instance the children drew pictures of a lollipop and a balloon, and of the experimenter and themselves, that looked very similar (given their undeveloped artistic skills), as shown in Figure 4.1. They also viewed a drawing, by "a child with a broken arm," of "three pigs and a chicken," actually three vertical ovals and one horizontal oval. The children, like adults, were able to consider the representational intent of the picture and permit it to override perceptual similarity or difference between the picture and the real object. That is, they carefully differentiated between the lollipop and the balloon, even though each drawing looked equally like the real object. They vigorously corrected the experimenter if she described the intended balloon as a lollipop. By age 4 they said that the three horizontal ovals and one vertical oval were three pigs and a chicken rather than something that looked more like them, such as eggs. Thus preschoolers seem to understand that representations are not simply about physical similarities between the real and represented objects; rather, representations are mainly about people's *intent* to represent and communicate.

The concept of pictorial representations rapidly becomes more complicated once children get beyond the basic idea that a picture stands for, but differs from, a real object. For instance, people have representations of representations of representations, which must be confusing, as seen in the following episode witnessed by one

FIGURE 4.1 A child's drawings of a lollipop, a balloon, the experimenter, and herself. Children were told the four ovals were three pigs and a chicken drawn by a child with a broken arm. Adapted from "Intention and Analogy in Children's Naming of Pictorial Representations" by P. Bloom and L. Markson, 1998, *Psychological Science, 9,* pp. 201 and 202. Copyright © 1998 by American Psychological Society. Adapted by permission.

of us. A father and son, about age 3, were viewing a special exhibit of Remington paintings of the Old West at an art museum.

> Father: Look, Jason, this picture's in your book at home.
>
> Jason: I know, Dad. I was going to tell you that I don't have to look at it.
>
> Father: But this is the real thing.
>
> Jason: How can it be the real thing? It's a picture, and it's just like in my book.
>
> Father: (*Falteringly*) Well, um, it just is. It's, well, it's just the real picture.
>
> Jason: Well, I'm *not* going to look at it.

Here we have representations (in the father and son) of a representation (in the book) of a representation (painting) of an object (old-time cowboy) that no longer even exists. No wonder both father and son are struggling.

Young children's understanding of external representations is still limited. In particular they have trouble sorting out the *exact* nature of the relations between reality and its "nonreal" designators. A prime example is models, to which we now turn.

Models

Consider the following event. An adult shows a young child a dollhouse-size room, a tiny toy dog, and a larger stuffed toy dog. She points out to the child the correspondence between the model and a nearby real room, and between the two dogs: "This is Big Snoopy's big room, and this is Little Snoopy's little room. Look—their rooms are just alike; they both have all the same things in their rooms. . . . Look—this is Big Snoopy's big couch, and this is Little Snoopy's little couch. They're just the same." As the child watches, the adult places Little Snoopy behind the tiny couch in the model and asks the child to find Big Snoopy "in the same place" in the real room that is almost identical to the model in their furniture and their locations. DeLoache (1987; DeLoache & Smith, 1999) found that if this child is 36 months of age or older, she will immediately go to the couch and retrieve Big Snoopy. However, if she is only 6 months younger, she will have no idea where to look for Big Snoopy. She has not simply forgotten where Little Snoopy was hidden, for she can find him immediately when she returns to the model.

DeLoache concluded that 2½-year-olds understand the similarity between the two Snoopies and two rooms but have great difficulty in detecting the spatial correspondence between models and what they represent. They apparently do not understand that their initial knowledge has any relevance for the second room. They do not use the model to represent the real room. However, quite remarkably, they do much better if a photo, drawing, or videotape of the large room is used instead of the model! This is surprising because young children generally show more advanced knowledge on cognitive tasks when three-dimensional objects, rather than symbolic materials, such as drawings or photos, are used. DeLoache interprets this facilitation with a drawing as showing that the model's status as a real thing (i.e., a three-dimensional object) distracts young children from its symbolic role. The pull of the "is" overrides the "stands for" aspect. To solve the task, a child must be able to consider a model as two things at once: an object and a symbol of something else.

This is easier to do with a picture because its status as a real object is not so over-powering; it has no obvious function of its own.

If using a model as a model depends on detecting its representational aspect, then anything that decreases its thing-in-and-of-itself aspect should improve performance and anything that increases this aspect should undermine performance. The evidence supports these predictions. Placing the model behind a window in a puppet theater so that the child cannot touch it, which lessens its "objectness," improves performance. Conversely, encouraging 3-year-olds to play with the model before being given the standard model task causes poor performance. Presumably this interaction increases the objectness of the model.

DeLoache's hypothesis makes an interesting prediction: If a situation could be created in which the room *becomes* the model, then they are one and the same rather than in a symbolic relationship, and thus children should be able to transfer what they know about the room to the model. This prediction was tested by what DeLoache, Miller, and Rosengren (1997) call the "credible shrinking room": Each child saw big "Terry the troll" (with fuschia-colored hair) and "Terry's room." She then watched as the troll was placed in front of a "shrinking machine," which looked somewhat like an oscilloscope. The experimenter turned on the machine and waited with the child in an adjoining area, listening to the "sounds the shrinking machine makes while it's working." When they returned a miniature troll stood in the position of the orginal one (see Figure 4.2). The child then was shown that the machine worked in the opposite way, to make the troll unshrink, and could also shrink and unshrink Terry's room. The experimenters and the parents judged that all but one of the children completely accepted the notion of a shrinking room (not so amazing, given that, as DeLoache points out, children of this age also believe in the tooth fairy and Santa Claus).

FIGURE 4.2 DeLoache's "shrinking machine" with the troll before and after the shrinking. This photo was made available by Judy DeLoache.

Then came the crucial test. The child watched the experimenter hide the larger troll in the portable room, the machine shrank the room, and the child was asked to find the miniature troll. As in the standard procedure the child had to use her knowledge of where the toy was in one space to figure out where to search in the other. As predicted, performance was much better in this nonsymbolic task than in the standard one, even though children saw only "before" and "after" states as in the standard task. DeLoache concludes the following about "shrinking trolls and expanding minds" (1996): Children can see correspondences between two situations. What they have trouble with is the dual representation of an object as both an object and a symbol. In the shrinking room experiment, there is only one object, which simply changes size.

Given DeLoache's findings that the use of models is rare until 36 months, it might seem perplexing that a 2-year-old clearly uses a toy car to represent a real car or a doll to represent a baby but cannot grasp the relation between two rooms that are virtually identical except in size. One important difference is that toys refer to a general type of object, for example, cars in general rather than one specific car that exists in reality. It is this specific correspondence to a known referent required by scale models that causes part of the problem. The 2½-year-olds know that the miniature sofa in the model represents *a* sofa, but not that it represents *the* sofa in the real-life room next door. Another factor that makes using the model difficult for young children is that there is relational (spatial position) information in the model and the room that must be mapped on to each other in order to find the toy. This information may be more complex than that usually involved in play. Thus, 2½-year-olds understand external symbols; they just find it difficult to use them in certain ways.

DeLoache notes several implications of her research. First, giving plastic toy alphabet letters or mathematical "manipulatives" (e.g., blocks, beads) to young children actually can make it harder, rather than easier, to detect their symbolic aspect. That is, they become real entities rather than just squiggles on a page that stand for something else. Second, she finds that the anatomically correct dolls thought to facilitate young children's reporting of possible sexual abuse do not necessarily help children provide more information, because of the difficulty of simultaneously representing the doll as a doll and as themselves. For example, children aged 2½ to 3½ have difficulty placing a little sticker on a doll (described as similar to them) in the same place that a similar but larger sticker was placed on them (Smith, 1995). The difficulty comes in reasoning between two *different kinds* of entities, for example, self-to-doll, other child-to doll, and self-to-picture (DeLoache & Smith, 1999); they do much better between two people or between two dolls.

To sum up the DeLoache research, young children acquire three concepts about symbols (DeLoache & Smith, 1999). *Representational insight* involves realizing that something is a symbol that stands for something else. *Dual representation* refers to thinking about one thing in two ways at the same time—as both an object and a symbol. In Chapter 6 we return to this notion of dual representation when we discuss young children's difficulties with the distinction between appearance and reality, the concept of false belief, perspective taking, and other aspects of the understanding that an entity can have two "realities." *Representational specificity* is the realization that a symbol can represent a specific real entity. In order to use a symbol, a child must (a) detect the relation between a symbol and referent, (b) map their corresponding elements (for example, little toy = big toy; little room = big room), and (c) use knowledge about one to draw an inference about the other. It is surprising that representational insight on DeLoache's seemingly obvious situation is so difficult for 2½-year-olds. It also is surprising that developmental progress is so fast, consistently occurring between 30 and 36 months.

Other Representations

Young children use representations—both external and internal ones—in a variety of ways. We can only provide a brief sampling here in addition to the above (for others, see Sigel, 1999). The most obvious and important example is the explosive increase in language competence that occurs during this period (Chapter 8), and the use of language for thought (e.g., K. Nelson, 1999). The ability to use numbers to represent quantities is another example that is taken up later in this chapter. Children also begin to acquire skills in drawing and other forms of artistic representation and engage in pretense (e.g., Kavanaugh & Harris, 1999), including *pretend play* (see Chapter 6). Expressions of this latter symbolic-representational skill include such acts as pretending to drink out of an empty cup, pretending that a block is a car, and pretending that you are the mommy and your playmate is the baby.

One active area of research concerns children's representations of spatial relations, either mental ones such as mental maps of neighborhoods and spatial frames of reference such as features of the environment (e.g., Newcombe & Huttenlocher, 1998), or external ones, such as physical maps (e.g., Liben, 1999). Regarding the latter, preschoolers understand that maps stand for spaces and entities in the real world, and can use extremely simple maps, such as a dot in a rectangle that represents the location of a toy in a sandbox (Huttenlocher, Newcombe, & Vasilyeva, 1999). However, they do not yet fully understand the specific nature of maps. For example, they think that a red line on the map indicates a red road in the real world, or reject a line as showing a road because "it's not fat enough for two cars to go on" (Liben & Downs, 1991). Reading maps, like using models in the DeLoache research, requires dual representation. A line is both a line and a road.

Another active research area concerns discrepancies between different representational systems. In particular, young children sometimes reveal knowledge through their gestural representational system that they do not yet express verbally. Goldin-Meadow, Alibali, and Church (1993) refer to "using the hand to read the mind." For example, a 6-year-old given Piaget's conservation task may say that a short wide dish contains less water than did the taller thinner glass from which the water came, because "this one's tall and that one's short." However, as she says this she indicates with her hand shaped like a C the diameter of the glass which enlarges to become the diameter of the dish, indicating that on some level she is aware of the compensating difference in width (Goldin-Meadow, 1997). Thus she has a mismatch between her verbal and gestural representations of the situation. In our final chapter, we return to this finding, because it has significance for issues of cognitive assessment and cognitive change.

Finally, several of the theories in Chapter 1 focus on representations. Piaget thought that the representational ability emerged at the end of the sensorimotor period, and that the nature of representations changed in each subsequent stage. The neo-Piagetians and Karmiloff-Smith (1992) also address representational change. The theory theory approach examines not only how representational structures are theorylike, but also how children's eventual representation of representations transforms their thinking about the mind. Finally, Vygotsky's focus on language as a prime representational tool gives a cultural account of representation. Each of these theories stimulated a line of research on internal or external representations.

In summary, young children's representational skills show both positive acquisitions and important limitations in their thinking. Toddlers know that pictures stand for real things and that pretending stands for real things and events, but not until later do they fully sort out the differences between the representations (external objects and actions) and reality. Many of young children's representations seem rather simple minded. One thing stands for another thing. These representations do not stay simple for very long. During the preschool years, they become increasingly organized into structured systems of knowledge, such as scripts, to which we now turn.

EVENT KNOWLEDGE AND SCRIPTS

Life is eventful. People and objects in a young child's world do things, and she observes these events and enters into them, thus joining the flow of the world around her. She mentally represents these events (*event knowledge*). Some of these event representations are generalized and abstract (*scripts*). This event knowledge, including scripts, of everyday life is one of the most powerful mental tools for young children's understanding of the world.

As we describe in Chapter 7 on memory, even many 9-month-olds can reproduce some of a set of actions 5 weeks after seeing them (Carver & Bauer, 1999), though researchers debate the exact nature of infants' representations. During the second year of life, infants can reproduce an increasingly long string of events after an increasingly long delay (e.g., Bauer, 1997). Consider the following representative study.

Suppose you ask a 20-month-old to give a bath to "Teddy." You demonstrate by removing the teddy bear's pajamas, putting him in the bathtub, washing him, and drying him. Taking a bath is a familiar sequence to children of this age. Similarly you ask the child to imitate a sequence that also is causal, but unfamiliar—put a ball in a cup, cover it with another cup, and shake the cups to make a rattle. Finally the child must imitate an unfamiliar arbitrary sequence—bang a ring on a block, spin the ring on its side, and stack the ring on a stick. When Bauer and Shore (1987) conducted this study, they found that 17½- to 23-month-olds performed quite well in both causal conditions, but not the condition with arbitrary relations. Moreover they still recalled the causal sequences 6 weeks later. Thus even toddlers encode order information in their representations of events, even unfamiliar events, if the episode makes sense to them.

In addition to representing a one-time event, a young child also can construct a *script*—a generalized, temporally and spatially organized, sequence of events about some common routine with a goal. Repeated experience with taking a bath, for example, leads to a script representation of "how people usually take baths." There may be variations from one particular bath to another, such as whether you use "bubble bath," whether you get into the tub before or after you run the water, and whether you play with a rubber ducky or read a book, but certain elements stay the same. For example, normal people, unless very preoccupied, do not take baths without water. Moreover, certain causal relations are never violated. You do not dry off before the bath rather than after. In fact if you present familiar sequences out of order (dry off, wash, put bear in tub) to 20-month-olds, in their recall they sometimes "correct" the order to the real-life one (Bauer & Thal, 1990). Other common childhood scripts include "going to McDonald's" (ordering food, paying for it, getting it, sitting down, eating) or baking cookies (Nelson, 1986). Children rehearse scripts in pretend play, often deliberately manipulating and transforming scripts in imaginative ways, which may enhance this form of representation. For reviews of children's event representations, scripts, and related skills, see Fivush (1997), Hudson and Sheffield (1999), and K. Nelson (1996, 1999).

In addition to studying these naturally occurring scripts, it is possible to create scripts in children, thus condensing experience over months or years into a few hours. One example is Price and Goodman's (1990) novel event, visiting the wizard. A bearded man dressed in a colorful robe led the child through various events, such as a "magic chamber" and "magic goodbye" (a gesture and a slogan). Over a series of visits, children aged 2½ to 5 constructed a script for this recurring event—what you usually do when you visit a wizard. However, in some cases a script can be constructed after a single instance (Fivush & Slackman, 1986).

Scripts form general mental templates or molds that tell the child how things are "supposed to go" in such familiar routines. Scripts are adaptive because they help the child to predict the likelihood of future (frequently occurring) events and to anticipate and take part in human activities (Nelson, 1996). In this way, scripts provide stability to daily life by allowing children to predict what will happen next, for instance, in their dinner-bathtime-bedtime routine. Violations of this order can be perplexing to a young child. Hudson (1990) reports a 2-year-old who once was given a bath before dinner and became very upset because she thought she would not be fed that evening. Scripts also are important because they provide the foundation of shared social information that is necessary for successful social interaction in a particular culture. Anyone who has violated the "take a number and wait for your turn" script in our culture knows the social pressure against such sins.

Our final comments about scripts are, naturally, developmental ones. First, although even preschoolers produce well-organized, coherent accounts of familiar events, scripts increase in complexity during the preschool and grade-school years. Second, younger children have more trouble than older ones with representing the minor variations in events that typically occur in real life. In an experimental example of this, 4- and 7-year-olds experienced two arts and crafts projects (making a puppet and making a bird) four times (Kuebli & Fivush, 1994). The number of times that an action changed was systematically varied. The younger children seemed unable to represent the variations, and often even claimed that no change had occurred from one time to another. Third, developmental changes in scripts affect memory, which we describe in Chapter 7.

Closely related to event and script knowledge is narrative thinking (e.g., Uccelli, Hemphill, Pan, & Snow, 1999), or storytelling, for all involve a coherent set of occurrences over time and space. Even a simple, garden-variety story has a complex underlying structure that is relatively fixed (Mandler, 1983). A setting component introduces the protagonist and background information; then episodes construct the plot. Each episode has a beginning event to which a protagonist reacts, often by formulating a goal. The protagonist next attempts to attain the goal. The success or failure of that attempt draws the story to a close. The ending may refer to the long-range consequences of the episode, responses of the characters to the events, or simply "They lived happily ever after." Because young children have script representations they can use to assimilate these stories, they can comprehend stories at an early age. In fact they can infer important information that is not explicitly stated. They also can produce simple, but understandable, narratives about personally experienced events (see autobiographical memory in Chapter 7).

In summary, young children's representations of objects, events, and scenes incorporate temporal order and logical relations, and even permit them to tell coherent stories about real or make-believe other people or even about their own lives.

CONCEPTS AND CATEGORIES

Children develop representational knowledge structures of many sorts. Just as scripts serve to organize the events and scenes of the world, so do concepts serve to organize the types of entities that populate that world.

One of us once referred to the task of defining the term *concept* as "a lexicographer's nightmare" (Flavell, 1970a, p. 983). Despite numerous attempts to pin down what we mean when we speak of concepts, the notion continues to defy a single, agreed-upon, applicable-to-all instances definition. Rather than get bogged down in such definitional matters, we settle here for a rough characterization that will be sufficient to get our discussion started. A rough definition is that a concept is a mental grouping of different entities into a single category on the basis of some underlying similarity—some way in which all the entities are alike, some common core that makes them all, in some sense, the "same thing." All of us, for example, have a concept of *dog* that unites the numerous and diverse exemplars that share the properties of dogness; we also have a concept of animal that brings together the even more variegated members of this category. Concepts serve to cut the world into useful categories—to identify pockets of similarity in the midst of what would otherwise be unmanageable diversity. The interesting developmental questions then have to do with how children cut up their worlds. What bases do they use when they think about things as being similar—and how do these bases change as their cognitive abilities develop?

Natural Kinds and Other Kinds

A study by Susan Gelman and Ellen Markman (1986) is a good starting point, for it is typical—in issues examined, methods used, and results obtained—of much recent work in early concept development. Gelman and Markman first taught their 4-year-old participants some new information about pairs of pictured objects. The children were told, for example, that "This fish [experimenter presents a picture of a tropical fish] stays underwater to breathe," but that "This dolphin pops above the water to breathe." Similarly the children heard that "This bird's [picture of flamingo] legs get cold at night," whereas "This bat's legs stay warm at night." Following each pair the experimenter presented a third picture that closely resembled one member of the original pair but received the same label as the other member— thus in the first example a shark (quite perceptually similar to the dolphin) that was labeled a "fish," and in the second example a blackbird (close in looks to the bat) that was labeled a "bird." The child's task then was to infer which of the contrasting properties applied to the new object. Would the shark breathe like a fish or breathe like a dolphin? Would the blackbird's legs get cold at night or stay warm? The contrasting bases for response should be evident. Judgments on the basis of common label and category membership would result in one set of inferences; judgments on the basis of perceptual similarity would result in a quite different set of inferences.

A considerable body of theorizing and research prior to Gelman and Markman's study would lead us to predict that 4-year-olds' inferences will be governed by perceptual similarity. Young children have been quite widely characterized as perceptually oriented. Such a characterization is certainly part of the Piagetian notion of a preoperational period, and Piaget's research documented numerous situations in which young children tend to be misled by an overreliance on perceptual features. As we will see in Chapter 6, recent research has shown that young children often have difficulty in distinguishing appearance and reality—that is, in penetrating beyond immediate perceptual appearance to get at the true nature of things. Studies of so-called "concept formation," in which the child must discover some experimenter-defined criterion for correct response (e.g., pick the middle-size stimulus, or the one on the left, or the one not chosen last time), present a similar picture of the perception-bound young child. So too do studies of free-sorting behavior, in which children are asked to group objects on the basis of which ones "go together." Presented, for example, with a fire engine, car, and apple, most 3- and 4-year-olds group fire engine and apple—the two red things—rather than fire engine and car— the two vehicles (Tversky, 1985).

Given all this evidence of the perception-dominated 4-year-old, you have probably guessed by now that the interest of Gelman and Markman's results lies in the fact that their 4-year-olds did *not* respond perceptually. Faced with a choice between category membership and perceptual appearance, most children opted for the former as a determinant of the generalization of properties. They decided, therefore, that the shark would breathe like a tropical fish rather than a dolphin, despite its much greater resemblance to the dolphin, and that the blackbird would probably have cold legs at night, despite its resemblance to the warm-legged bat. A follow-up study demonstrated that these properties were not things that the children already knew about sharks or blackbirds; rather their choices were dependent on the inferences drawn from category membership. A further follow-up showed that the use of a common label (e.g., dubbing both tropical fish and shark as "fish") was not necessary for good performance; similar findings emerged when synonyms (e.g., "rockstone," "puppy-baby dog") were given rather than identical labels. Indeed, in a later publication, Gelman and Markman (1987) demonstrated that young children have some ability to recognize and to use category membership from pictures alone, in the absence of any labels. Finally yet another study showed that the children were properly selective in the inferences they drew. When attributes such as weight or visibility at night were at issue, the usual reliance on category membership gave way to judgments based on perceptual similarity. When told, for example, that a tropical fish weighs 20 pounds and a dolphin 100 pounds, children picked the latter as the more likely weight for a shark.

Whenever some sort of competence is demonstrated at a surprisingly early age, developmentalists tend to wonder whether age of emergence can be pushed even younger. Gelman and Markman (1986) showed that 4-year-olds are unexpectedly adultlike in their inference patterns. What about younger children?

Gelman and Markman (1987), using a somewhat simplified methodology, obtained similar results for 3-year-olds. Gelman and Coley (1990), using still simpler techniques, found that even 2½-year-olds have some ability to overlook perceptual appearance in favor of category membership when appropriate. At present 2½ is the youngest age at which the Gelman and Markman procedure has been attempted. Research with other methods, however, makes clear that categorization begins well before the preschool period. As we saw in Chapter 3, infants as young as 3 months have been shown to organize their experiences into simple categories. And by later in infancy, infants begin to use their knowledge of category membership to draw simple inferences that prefigure those produced by preschoolers—recall the Mandler and McDonough (1996) animals-vehicles study discussed in Chapter 3. Having learned that some animals drink, 14-month-olds assumed that others would also, just as they assumed that if keys opened some vehicles they would open others as well.

The message from the Gelman and Markman research—as well as from many similar studies in recent years (for reviews, see Gelman, 2000; Scholnick, Nelson, Gelman, & Miller, 1999; Wellman & Gelman, 1998)—is that young children's concepts are not simply collections of perceptual features. Rather children's concepts, like adults' concepts, emphasize basic, often nonobvious similarities among exemplars, similarities that permit powerful generalizations from one category member to another. Yet the older research literature cannot be totally in error; in many situations young children *do* respond on the basis of immediate perceptual appearance. Why, then, the more positive conclusions from the Gelman and Markman line of research? Wellman and Gelman (1988) point out two important differences between most earlier studies of children's concepts and the more recent work.

One difference concerns response measures. Much of the earlier work used the free-sorting ("which ones go together?") methodology. Although the ability to group members is certainly part of what is meant by having a concept, grouping alone cannot capture all of the knowledge that underlies concepts. *Why* do certain things belong together, and what functions do concepts serve? In contrast the *induction technique* utilized by Gelman and Markman speaks directly to the essential nature of concepts. One important role that concepts play is to permit inferences or inductions about category members, even those that have never been encountered before. If told, for example, that we are about to meet a new breed of dog called a malamute, we have some definite expectations about what we will encounter, even though we have never seen a malamute before. Furthermore the inductions that we make help to reveal the nature of our concept of dog. We are likely, for example, to draw inferences concerning such dog-defining matters as internal organs, diet, and general behavior patterns. In contrast we are unlikely to have any expectations with regard to such nonessential features as age, place of birth, or exact size.

The second difference identified by Wellman and Gelman (1988) concerns the nature of the concept. In some studies the concepts examined have been arbitrary ones created on the spot for the purposes of the research—for example, the category of blue circles in a study of sorting behavior. Naturally occurring concepts are not arbitrary, however; rather they reflect important commonalities among real-world entities, commonalities that children extract from their everyday experiences. Among the many concepts that children naturally form, a particularly interesting subset has to do with what philosophers call *natural kinds* (Schwartz, 1977). Natural kinds are categories that occur in nature—classes of things whose existence and nature are not dependent on human activity. Animals are natural kinds; so too are plants and minerals. The underlying structure of natural kinds makes them a particularly rich source for inductive inferences. The concentration on natural kinds in the Gelman and Markman research may well have contributed to the children's impressive performance.

Of course natural kinds are not the only sorts of concepts with which children or any of us must deal. Keil (1989) discusses two other general categories. *Nominal kinds* are categories defined more by human convention than by nature; examples cited by Keil include circle, odd number, island, uncle, and princess. Unlike natural kinds, nominal kinds tend to have clearly defining features and dictionarylike definitions—an island is a body of land surrounded by water, an uncle is your parent's brother, and so on. The third category is *artifacts:* objects created by humans. Examples here include cups, tables, chairs, cars, and computers.

All of us possess numerous specific concepts within each of these three general categories. But all of us also know quite a bit about differences among the categories. We know, for example, that cups are dependent on a human creator but that turtles, oaks, and grains of sand are not. We realize that a table can be transformed into a bookcase or a glass into a vase, but that neither science nor magic can turn lead into gold or a lion into a lamb. Do young children understand these basic differences among categories? The answer turns out to be "in part but not fully." Here we consider two lines of research, one initiated by Susan Gelman and the other by Frank Keil.

The Gelman and Markman (1986, 1987) studies demonstrated that even 4-year-olds use knowledge of category membership to draw a wide range of inferences. But not all categories are as conducive to inferences as are the natural kinds examined by Gelman and Markman. Children need to be able not only to make inferences but also to *constrain* their inferences—that is, avoid generalizing too broadly from one category member to another. If we learn, for example, that a particular rabbit has an omentum inside, we are likely to be quite confident that all rabbits have omentums (omenta?) inside and reasonably certain that all animals have them as well. Learning, however, that a particular chair has urethane inside gives us little basis for predicting to other chairs, let alone to furniture in general. Natural kinds typically have insides that are essential to their nature and common across category members; artifacts typically do not (though modern artifacts—the computer most notably—do blur the distinction). Gelman (1988) tested for this and related sorts of understanding and reported a developmental progression between ages 4 and 7, with the older children generally more likely than the younger ones to make appropriate, adultlike distinctions among categories. Young children, to be sure, are not totally lacking a natural kind-artifact distinction. Gelman found, for example, that even 4-year-olds can answer direct questions about which sorts of things are human-made and which are not, and other studies have elicited other sorts of evidence for some early appreciation of the distinction (Gelman & Kremer, 1991; Gelman & O'Reilly, 1988; Gelman & Wellman, 1991; Kalish, 1998). Nevertheless, one safe generalization in this area is that a full understanding of the differences among different sorts of concepts is a gradual developmental achievement.

This same conclusion emerges from Keil's research (Keil, 1979, 1989, 1991). Keil has devised a number of ingenious techniques to probe understanding of kinds and concepts; here we concentrate on his *transformations* procedure. Consider the vignettes in Table 4.1. As you can see, the idea of the transformations procedure is

TABLE 4.1 Examples of Keil's Transformation's Procedure

NATURAL KIND: RACCOON/SKUNK

The doctors took a raccoon (show picture of raccoon) and shaved away some of its fur. They dyed what was left all black. Then they bleached a single strip all white down the center of its back. Then, with surgery (explained to child in preamble), they put in its body a sac of super smelly odor, just like a skunk has (with younger children "odor" was replaced with "super smelly yucky stuff"). When they were all done, the animal looked like this (show picture of skunk). After the operation was this a skunk or a raccoon? (Both pictures were present at the time of the final question.)

ARTIFACT: COFFEEPOT/BIRDFEEDER

The doctors took a coffeepot that looked like this (show picture of coffeepot). They sawed off the handle, sealed the top, took off the top knob, sealed closed the spout, and sawed it off. They also sawed off the base and attached a flat piece of metal. They attached a little stick, cut a window in it, and filled the metal container with birdfood. When they were done it looked like this (show picture of birdfeeder). After the operation was this a coffeepot or a birdfeeder? (Both pictures were present at the time of the final question.)

Note: From *Concepts, Kinds, and Cognitive Development* (p. 184) by F. C. Keil, 1989, Cambridge, MA: MIT Press. Copyright 1989 by MIT Press. Reprinted by permission.

that an object starts out as indubitably one thing and ends up with the characteristic appearance (looks, smells, behaviors, functions) of something quite different. Some of the transformations involve natural kinds: tiger into lion, diamond into pearl, grapefruit into orange. Others involve artifacts: tire into boot, garbage into chair, tie into shoelace. The critical question in each case concerns what the transformed object really is—really a skunk, for example, or just a strange-looking, bad-smelling raccoon? Children at all ages accept the transformations of the artifacts, as indeed do most adults—if a former coffeepot looks like a bird feeder and functions as a birdfeeder, why not consider it a bird feeder? Four-year-olds, however, are also likely to believe that one natural kind can be turned into another. They do not, it is true, accept just any sort of transformation (putting a costume on is not sufficient), and they are reluctant to admit changes that cross fundamental category boundaries—in particular, any change from animate to inanimate or vice versa. Nevertheless their grasp of the natural kind-artifact distinction is still somewhat shaky, as the following protocol vividly illustrates.

> E: Well, which do you think the animal really is? Do you think it's really a raccoon or do you think it's really a skunk?
> C: A raccoon!
> E: Can it be a . . .
> C: (Interrupting) It's a skunk.
> E: Which do you really mean?
> C: A skunk.
> E: Can it be a skunk if its mommies and daddies were raccoons?
> C: Yes.

E: Can it be a skunk if its babies were raccoons?

C: Yes.

E: (Repeats entire story) Which do you think it really was?

C: A skunk. Because it looks like a skunk, it smells like a skunk, it acts like a skunk and it sounds like a skunk. (The child was not told this.)

E: So it can be a skunk even though its babies are raccoons?

C: Yes! (Keil, 1989, p. 188)

In the Keil studies, transformations operate to change surface appearance but leave basic nature (at least in the case of natural kinds) unchanged. A parallel line of research, labeled "brain transplant" studies, offers an interesting comparison case. These studies present stories in which the brain of one animal is transplanted into the head of another (e.g., child to pig, cow to horse, dog to cat); the transformation thus preserves surface appearance (the pig, for example, still looks like a pig) but changes something very fundamental beneath the surface (Gottfried, Gelman, & Shultz, 1999; Johnson, 1990). The question then is whether the transformed animal's thoughts and memories will be those typical for its species or those appropriate for its new brain. Presumably (although who really knows?) the latter alternative is the correct answer. It is, in any case, the answer that adults and children from about age 8 on tend to give. Not 4- and 5–year-olds, however; they expect a pig with a child's brain to continue to have the mental life of a pig. Once again, therefore, young children tend to weight surface appearance as more important than underlying essence.

Levels and Hierarchies

Concepts differ not only in the kinds of entities to which they are directed but also in the level of abstraction at which any particular entity is represented. A particular dog, for example, can be conceptualized not only as dog but also (among other possibilities) as animal and as poodle. In general almost any concept can be placed within a taxonomic hierarchy in which it stands simultaneously in a subordinate relation to the more general categories that contain it (as does dog to animal) and a superordinate relation to the more specific categories that it itself contains (as does dog to poodle). Much theorizing and research have been directed to the question of how children come to understand such taxonomic classification. With even more than our usual selectivity (these are large literatures!), we briefly discuss two kinds of research, one stemming from some theorizing by Eleanor Rosch and the other stemming from Piaget.

Rosch and colleagues (Mervis & Rosch, 1981; Rosch, Mervis, Gray, Johnson, & Boyes-Braem, 1976) have argued that there is a *basic-level* at which concepts are most naturally and readily represented. Basic-level representations are those that offer an optimal blend of within-category similarity and between-category dissimilarity; the members of the category are similar enough to permit easy mental grouping (less true at the superordinate level) but also distinct enough from nonmembers to permit ready separation of categories (less true at the subordinate level). "Dog" is thus basic-level, whereas "animal" and "poodle" are not. "Chair" is basic-level, whereas "furniture" and "rocking chair" are not. The main developmental prediction has been that basic-level categories, being most natural, should be the first ones that children form.

The evidence with regard to this prediction is mixed. Support comes from the finding (discussed more fully in Chapter 8) that children's first words tend to be at the basic-level (Anglin, 1977). Studies of sorting behavior are also supportive: Young children group objects more readily at the basic-level (e.g., all the dogs) than at the superordinate level (e.g., all the animals—(Rosch et al., 1976). On the other hand, tests of the supposed primacy of the basic-level have been complicated by difficulties in defining exactly what is basic, as well as by the possibility that there may be a "child-basic-level" (Mervis, 1987) that, at least for a while, is different from adult-basic-level. In addition research by Mandler and associates (see Mandler, 1998, for a review), some of which we summarized in Chapter 3, indicates that infants often distinguish and group objects more readily on the basis of global categories (e.g., animals vs. vehicles) than on the basis of basic-level distinctions within such categories. These researchers suggest that the primacy of the basic-level by age 3 (the lower age bound for most sorting studies) may mask an earlier reliance on more global categories.

Whether the basic-level is primary from the start or only becomes so with development, its ascendancy by age 3 has implications for how children draw inferences from their knowledge of category membership. Gelman (1988; Gelman & O'Reilly, 1988) has shown that children who are taught a new fact about an object are more likely to generalize to objects at the same basic-level than to objects that share only the same superordinate level with the original. This strategy makes sense: The basic-level, by definition, *is* more homogeneous and thus more conducive to inferences than is the superordinate level. Johnson, Scott, and Mervis (1997) add a parallel finding: Children are more likely to generalize from the basic-level to the subordinate level than the reverse. This, too makes sense: Anything that is true of birds in general must also be true of robins, but things that are true of robins do necessarily apply to all birds.

Piaget's interest in classes centered on children's understanding of the hierarchical structure of classes and the inclusion relation that holds between superordinate and subordinate. Because a subclass (such as dogs) is subsumed within a superordinate (such as animals), there can never be more members in the subclass than there are in the superordinate. Inhelder and Piaget (1964) demonstrated—and later studies (Winer, 1980) have confirmed—that even middle-childhood participants often have great difficulty correctly answering quantitative class-inclusion questions that probe for such knowledge. For example, after the experimenter establishes with an 8-year-old that, say, a bunch of 16 flowers consisting of 10 red ones and 6 blue ones are "all flowers," this child is asked "Are there more red flowers or more flowers?" A child of this age is likely to compare the red flowers with the blue flowers, rather than with the entire bunch, and incorrectly reply "More red flowers." Markman (1978) found that even children who pass this test may view the greater numbers of superordinate (e.g., flowers) than subordinate (e.g., red flowers) class members as an empirical fact rather than as a logically necessary truth. For example they may say "yes" when asked questions like, "Could you make it so that there will be more spoons than silverware on the table?" Similarly Miller (1986a) found that many children who passed the standard task were still quite willing to draw a picture that showed more cats than animals.

On the other hand, children's failures on some versions of the class-inclusion problem do not imply a total inability to construct taxonomic hierarchies or to reason about inclusion relations. Even more than is true for most Piagetian concepts, different forms of class inclusion vary greatly in difficulty, and the surprising failure of older children (and even college students—see Rabinowitz, Howe, & Lawrence, 1989) on some versions must be set against the precocious success of much younger children on other versions. A striking demonstration in the latter category has been reported by Smith (1979), who showed that 4-year-olds can sometimes make valid inferences based on class-inclusion representations. For instance most of her participants correctly said "yes" to questions like "A pug is a kind of dog, but not a German shepherd. Is a pug an animal?" and "no" to questions like "A yam is a kind of food, but not meat. Is a yam a hamburger?" Some children even justified their answers in ways that strongly suggest some class-inclusion knowledge: for the German shepherd question, for example, justifications like "Yes, you said it was a dog" and "Yes, dogs are animals."

The message from this discussion is that class inclusion is not the sort of knowledge that a child either "has" or "does not have." Rather there clearly are different senses and different degrees of "having," depending on the task and the response measure in question. Studies such as Smith's (1979) suggest that even young children possess some representations of class-inclusion relations that are, in most important respects, not qualitatively different from those of older people. That is, their basic conceptual organization is probably not radically different from that of adults. Other research on early concepts, both work already discussed and work still to be discussed, is certainly compatible with this conclusion of early competence. On the other hand, young children probably have less explicit and general or abstract knowledge about these representations, and consequently are less able to talk or reason about class hierarchies and class-inclusion relations than older people are. They solve a narrower range of experimental tasks, and they may not use their knowledge in everyday thinking as much or as fully as older children and adults. And their approach to class-inclusion problems may at first be primarily empirical, without a full appreciation of the logical necessity of the subclass-superordinate class relation.

Some General Conclusions

What conclusions can be taken away from recent work on how young children conceptualize the world? We offer four, each of which is further illustrated as we consider particular kinds of concepts later in the chapter.

1. One conclusion concerns the level of maturity of young children's concepts. It should be clear that research on conceptual development provides a prime example of a theme that runs throughout the book: Preschoolers are smarter than we used to think. Rather than being perceptually dominated, inconsistent, and illogical, the young child's concepts turn out, at least sometimes, to be surprisingly adultlike and powerful. Because our emphasis has been on this early competence, we should add that 4-year-olds' concepts are not fully equivalent to those of 8- or 10-year-olds, let alone adults. We have already noted some limitations and corresponding developmental improvements—in the ability to distinguish natural kinds and artifacts, for example. In studies of the Gelman and Markman (1986) genre, the preference for category membership over perceptual appearance, although sometimes found, is less solidly established in younger children than in older (Farrar, Raney, & Boyer, 1992). We see some further early limitations when we discuss biological and numerical understanding. The moral to be taken away here has to do with balance and the avoidance of overstatement in either

direction. At any age period, including adulthood, the cognitive system has both strengths and weaknesses. It is important that our models capture both.

2. Despite the cautions just expressed, a clear leitmotif of recent work on concepts is that young cognitive systems are not as qualitatively different from older ones as we used to believe. Young children often seem to be thinking in the same way as older children—just not as often, not as fully, or not as consistently. Often their problem seems to be that they simply do not know enough about the content area in question. The importance of content-specific knowledge has emerged as a major emphasis in recent research and thinking, both with regard to concepts in particular (Farrar et al., 1992; Kalish & Gelman, 1992) and with regard to cognitive functioning more generally (Bedard & Chi, 1992; Bransford, Brown, & Cocking, 1999). It is (as befits a pervasive emphasis) a notion that we will encounter again—in the discussion of problem solving, for example (Chapter 5), and in the treatment of memory and developmental changes therein (Chapter 7).

3. A third conclusion is related. If content-specific knowledge is an important component of children's concepts, then there is little reason to expect that all of a child's conceptual thinking will be at the same level of maturity and effectiveness. In fact children's concepts are not all at the same level. Keil (1979; Keil & Batterman, 1984) provides an example with regard to understanding of nominal kinds. He shows that there is a shift with development from an emphasis on characteristic features (e.g., an uncle is someone who gives presents) to an emphasis on defining features (e.g., an uncle is your parent's brother); the shift, however, is not across the board but rather occurs at different times for different concepts. Note that there *is* a general development change here: Less mature ways of thinking take one characteristic form, and more mature ways take a different characteristic form. Achievement of the mature form, however, requires not only general cognitive advance but also content-specific knowledge. The domain-specific nature of much of cognitive functioning and cognitive change will be another recurring theme in chapters to come.

4. We began our discussion by defining concept as "a mental grouping . . . on the basis of some underlying similarity." Thus far, however, we have mainly sidestepped the question of what sort of grouping and what sort of similarity. What, exactly, *are* concepts?

A first answer to this question is that there is no single answer. Children form concepts of a variety of kinds and they use concepts for a variety of purposes, and no single characterization can capture all the uses and all the kinds (Gelman & Diesendruck, 1999). We have argued, for example, that perceptual features often seem irrelevant to children's concepts. But clearly this cannot always be the case—some things *are* grouped together and responded to on the basis of their common appearance. Furthermore perceptual similarity is almost certainly the starting point for concept formation in infancy; how else could a 3-month-old respond differently to cats than to dogs? Indeed one of the debates that we passed over in our brief coverage of infant categorization concerns whether perceptually based categories eventually evolve into more cognitively based concepts, and if so when and how the transition comes about (compare, for example, Mandler, 2000, with Quinn & Eimas, 2000).

There is, then, no across-the-board answer to the question of what concepts are. Suppose that we focus on the kinds of concepts that we emphasize in this chapter—thus the natural kinds of the current section and the biological concepts that we consider next. How are concepts of this sort best characterized?

The most popular answer to this question at present is provided by the theory-based approach to knowledge introduced in Chapter 1. In this view (e.g., Gelman &

Diesendruck, 1999; Medin, 1989), concepts are theories that help us make sense of the world. No one believes, of course, that a concept has all the properties of a formal scientific theory. But concepts—perhaps especially those of the natural-kind ilk—do seem to function in some ways like minitheories ("theorettes," as Forguson, 1989, calls them) for particular aspects of reality. Consider our earlier example of the concept of dog. The set of beliefs that make up our concept of dog shares a number of features with scientific theories. Like a theory, a concept involves fundamental distinctions, such as natural-kind versus nonnatural, living versus nonliving, animal versus plant, and domesticated versus wild. As in a theory, the beliefs that make up a concept are not isolated but rather cohere into a tightly interconnected, mutually supportive system. Our beliefs concerning a dog's behavior patterns, for example, are related both to our general knowledge of its status as pet and more specific knowledge concerning what kind of dog it is (watchdog, hunting dog, etc.). Similarly our beliefs concerning behavior are in accord with beliefs concerning the physical attributes (e.g., teeth, claws, sense of smell) that make the behavior possible. As in a theory, causal relations among elements, such as the relation between behavior and requisite physical structure, play an especially important role in concepts. And like a theory, a concept serves to explain current experience and predict future experience. Such explanation and prediction, in fact, are at the core of the Gelman and Markman (1986) induction technique for studying concepts. It is our theory of what it means to be a dog that allows us to override perceptual factors in order to categorize Chihuahua and St. Bernard together and to use our knowledge of one to predict to the other. In the same way, children as young as 3 use their theories, incomplete or erroneous though they may sometimes be, to understand what they have already encountered and to make inferences about what is still to come.

As a number of commentators (e.g., Keil, 1989; Siegler, 1998) have noted, the term "theory" has been used with different degrees of breadth and scope by workers in the knowledge-as-theory camp. Its most specific use is the one just discussed: Every concept is a theory, and hence children develop many specific theories. At the other extreme, the term "theory" has been used to refer to broad domains of reality for which children eventually develop quite broad and multifaceted theories, theories that have a number of specific concepts, or minitheories, embedded within. In a recent review, Wellman and Gelman (1998) identify three grand theories of this sort that may subsume much of early cognitive development: a theory of the physical world, or naive physics; a theory of living things, or naive biology; and a theory of behavior and mental functioning, or naive psychology. Much of the work covered in Chapters 2 and 3 (e.g., Spelke's studies of knowledge of objects, Leslie's studies of causality) falls under the heading of naïve physics, as do several topics considered in Chapter 5. Work on naïve psychology has become important enough to merit a chapter in itself, and it is therefore the subject of Chapter 6. We turn next to Wellman and Gelman's third category: children's understanding of biology.

BIOLOGICAL CONCEPTS

The previous section said quite a bit about Concepts in general but little about concepts in particular—that is, important forms of knowledge that develop across the childhood years. Biological concepts certainly qualify as important forms of knowledge. Such concepts appear to develop—in part in similar ways—in every human culture, as recent work in so-called folkbiology demonstrates (Atran, 1998; Coley, 2000; Medin & Atran, 1999). They also are natural and frequent targets for children's cognitive efforts. Questions of life—of living versus nonliving, of animate versus inanimate, of origins and of growth—have fascinated children for as long as they have fascinated scientists. Such questions were among the topics that Piaget explored in his earliest work (Piaget, 1929), and they have recently reemerged, after a somewhat fallow period, as the focus of a good deal of exciting contemporary research. A consideration of some of this research both reinforces points already made and leads to some further conclusions about the nature of children's concepts.

We noted that biological categories fall under the general heading of natural kinds. Most research on natural kinds has in fact concentrated on animals and plants, and hence studies already reviewed have told us quite a bit about what children know about living things and how they use their knowledge to draw inferences. But biological categories are a subset of natural kinds in general, and they share certain properties that are not found either in other natural kinds or in human-produced artifacts. Furthermore animals share a further subset of properties that are not found in plants. Young children, it turns out, understand some but not all of the ways in which living things differ from nonliving and one kind of living thing differs from another. We consider research on biological understanding with regard to four properties that have received much recent research attention: growth, movement, inheritance, and illness.

Growth

The capacity for growth is one distinguishing characteristic of life. All living things grow, and only living things grow. Biological growth, moreover, is lawful and predictable. Organisms may increase in size as they get older but they do not decrease. They may change greatly in appearance but they do not change their basic identity; the wizened octogenarian is the same individual as the squirming newborn, just as the strapping tree is continuous with the tiny seedling. Although environmental factors (nutrition, sunlight) may be essential to growth, they do not provide its basic motor; the impetus, rather, is internal—something that organisms are born to do. None of these characteristics applies to the changes that occur in nonliving things. An artifact such as a car may change appearance over time as a result of human intervention (a new paint job) or environmental elements (sun and rain); such changes, however, do not constitute growth. Nor, despite our everyday use of the term "grow," do the increases in size that nonliving things (an expanding balloon, rising bread) may occasionally undergo.

Children as young as 3 or 4 have some appreciation of these distinctions. They are reasonably (although not perfectly) accurate in answering questions about which things grow and which do not (Inagaki & Hatano, 1996; Inagaki & Sugiyama, 1988); they also show some understanding of the inevitability of growth, indicating, for example, that a small and cute baby rabbit cannot be kept small and cute forever just because the owner wishes it so (Inagaki & Hatano, 1987). Even preschoolers recognize the directionality of growth, judging that living things but not artifacts grow larger as they grow older (Rosengren, Gelman, Kalish, & McCormick, 1991). This understanding is, to be sure, somewhat incomplete, for young children are less willing than older ones to accept the possibility of large increases in size or dramatic changes of the caterpillar-to-butterfly sort. They are also somewhat doubtful that really small things (butterflies, worms) can be said to grow (Gelman, 1990). Nevertheless the main message from this work is of fairly good understanding from fairly early on of which kinds of things grow and how they grow.

Living things not only grow; they often *re*grow—that is, they possess the capacity to heal or mend in response to certain kinds of injury or insult. Artifacts lack this capacity for spontaneous regeneration. Thus a cat with a scratch, given sufficient time, will eventually no longer be scratched; a car with a scratch, however, requires human intervention, and not merely time, to be made right again. By the preschool age, children have some understanding of this difference between living and nonliving. They appreciate the cat versus car contrast, for example. Similarly they realize that a plant may be able to regrow a cut rose or a dog its cut hair, but that a broken table is not going to regenerate its missing leg (Backscheider, Shatz, & Gelman, 1993).

As Wellman and Gelman (1998) note, there is an interesting contrast between the research on understanding of growth and Keil's (1989) studies of changes in natural kinds. Recall that Keil found that many young children were willing to believe that one animal could be so altered by surgical techniques or other interventions that it would actually become a different species. Keil's studies, however, involved distinctly nonnatural transformations that never in fact occur. Children's understanding of change is more impressive when the focus is on the natural changes that come with growth.

Movement

Movement is an ever present aspect of children's worlds from birth, but the very ubiquity of movement poses challenges to the child's understanding. People, leaves, and cars all move, but the underlying bases for the movements are quite different. Do children realize this? And do they realize that only animals are capable of *independent* movement?

That children are attentive to movement has been clear ever since Piaget's (1929) examinations of children's beliefs about what it means to be "alive." Piaget claimed that young children were often *animistic*—that is, attributed life to nonliving things—and that movement cues were one source of their confusion. Thus clouds, bikes, and watches might all be judged to be alive because they are seen to move. Later studies have verified that young children do sometimes have difficulty in drawing the border between living and nonliving; the confusion, however, is both less pervasive and less persistent than Piaget believed (Carey, 1985a; Gelman, Spelke, & Meck, 1983). In addition recent work has demonstrated that young children are surprisingly sensitive to the different types of movement that different sorts of objects can undergo. We consider just one example here; for other interesting demonstrations, see Gelman and Gottfried (1996); Gelman, Durgin, and Kaufman (1995); and Montgomery (1994).

Massey and Gelman (1988) presented their 3- and 4-year-old participants with photographs of the sort shown in Figure 4.3. The basic question with regard to each object was whether it could move up and down a hill by itself. The children proved quite good both at answering this question and at justifying their answers, despite the unfamiliarity of the objects and despite the limitation to pictorial cues. Note that we have here another example of the young child's ability to overlook on-

FIGURE 4.3   Stimuli used in the Massey and Gelman study of preschoolers' understanding of movement: echidna (top left), sloth (top right), and statue of quadruped (bottom). From "Preschooler's Ability to Decide Whether a Photographed Unfamiliar Object Can Move Itself," by C. M. Massey and R. Gelman, 1988, *Developmental Psychology, 24,* p. 309. Copyright © 1988 by the American Psychological Association. Reprinted by permission of Dr. C. M. Massey. The echidna photograph by A. L. Cooke is reprinted with permission of Oxford Scientific Films Ltd. (Picture No. 36991). It and the photograph of the sloth are from *Life on Earth* (p. 206 and 250, respectively) by David Attenborough (1979), Boston, MA: Little, Brown. The quadruped statue photograph is reproduced courtesy of the Freer Gallery of Art, Smithsonian Institute, Washington, DC (Acc. 40, 23).

the-surface perceptual appearance in favor of some deeper underlying essence. The statue certainly looks more like the self-propelling objects with which the child is familiar than does the echidna, yet only the latter is judged as capable of navigating a hill by itself. In Gelman's (1990) view, children's ability to make such distinctions is made possible by a set of innate processing mechanisms that direct attention, from very early in life, to the cues that differentiate self-propelled movements from externally generated ones (recall our discussion of movement and causality in Chapter 3). The child's understanding of animacy then builds upon this sensitivity to the causes of movement: Animate objects are things that can move themselves—things that have, in Gelman's phrase, "causal innards."

Inheritance

Living things are distinguished not only by growth but by origins. Living things come from other living things, and they inherit properties both of the species in general and of their own parents in particular. Recent research has shown that young children have some definite and at least partly correct ideas about inheritance (Springer, 1992, 1996; Springer & Keil, 1989, 1991; but see Solomon, Johnson, Zaitchik, & Carey, 1996, for some cautionary notes). Even preschoolers realize that like beget like—that dogs have baby dogs, and cats have baby cats. By age 4 children posit different mechanisms of transmission for biological properties than for nonbiological ones. The color of a flower or dog is assumed to be inherited from the parent through natural, lawful means (even though children may not yet understand the means); the color of a can, in contrast, is attributed to mechanical, human-engineered processes. Within biological kinds, some properties are assumed to be more heritable than others. Children are most likely to expect parent-to-child transmission when the property in question is one with functional consequences—for example a pink heart that is described as helping the animal stay healthy, as opposed to a pink heart that receives no further description. Interestingly the youngest children in these studies evidence a Lamarkian strain of reasoning, in that they do not differentiate between properties that are inborn and those that are acquired from experience. By age 6 or 7 a preference for inborn qualities as the stuff of inheritance has begun to emerge.

Beliefs about the power of inheritance are put to special test when biology and experience are placed in opposition to each other, which is what is done in so-called nature-nurture designs (Gelman, 2000). Suppose, for example, that a baby kangaroo is reared by goats from birth. Will the kangaroo still grow up to have a pouch and to hop? Suppose that a rabbit grows up in a family of monkeys. Will it prefer carrots or bananas when it reaches adulthood? Children presented with such scenarios tend to opt for nature over nurture as a determinant of ultimate outcome. Thus they judge, for example, that a kangaroo will end up with kangaroolike attributes however goatlike its rearing environment may be. Interestingly there is some evidence that the youngest children in such studies (typically 4-year-olds) may hold to the nature position more strongly for behavioral than for physical traits—just the opposite of the adult pattern of response (Gelman & Wellman, 1991).

Although children may be generally nativistic in their approach to questions of nature and nurture, they are not invariably so, and they typically become somewhat less so as they develop. This conclusion emerges from several studies of the nature/nurture sort that have focused on outcomes more important than kangaroo behavior or rabbit eating habits. For example Taylor (1996) examined beliefs about sex differences, presenting her 4- to 10-year-old participants with scenarios in which a boy was reared on an island with only females and a girl on an island with only males. The youngest children were indeed nativistic in their predictions of likely outcome, judging that stereotypically sex-typed attributes (e.g., likes to play with dolls, good at playing baseball) would be determined by biological sex rather than social experience. By 9 or 10, however, an awareness of social forces had begun to emerge, and children began to endorse a more balanced, interactionist explanation for the outcomes in question. Gelman and Heyman (1997) reached a similar conclusion with regard to beliefs about the origin of personality traits; in this case the contrast was between a baby born to nice parents but reared by mean ones, and a baby born to mean parents but reared by nice ones. Even 5-year-olds showed some awareness that experience would contribute to niceness versus meanness and other personality outcomes, although such awareness did increase with age. Finally Springer (1996) presented several stories in which the target character was born to one family but adopted early in life by another; the questions then concerned the extent to which the character would resemble the birth parents or the adoptive parents. Even preschoolers were properly differential in their responses, judging that physical outcomes (e.g., short vs. tall) would be determined by biology but that psychological/behavioral outcomes (e.g., likes cats more than dogs) would be determined primarily by experience.

The studies just discussed address an issue that we consider more fully in Chapter 6: How do children make sense of the differences they see among people? What these studies suggest is that with development children converge on two general beliefs that are also held by most psychologists: Both nature and nurture contribute to making people different, and the relative contribution of nature and nurture depends on what it is that we are trying to explain.

Illness

It should be clear by now that a central theme in the study of children's biological concepts concerns the understanding of nonobvious, beneath-the-surface features—thus the underlying bases for different sorts of movement, the genetic bases for parent-offspring resemblance, and so forth. Research directed to children's beliefs about illness continues this theme, because now the question is how readily children can reason about such unobservable entities as invisible germs and unseen contaminants.

The research literature directed to beliefs about disease is both older and larger than that for the other topics we consider in this section. Part of the reason for the long-standing interest is pragmatic: What children know or believe about the causes of illness has clear relevance for the socialization of health-promoting behaviors. Part of the interest, however, has always been theoretical—in particular Piaget's theory has long been seen as a source of predictions for how children will reason about illness. The most general expectation from Piagetian theory is that the understanding of young, preoperational children will be confused and incomplete. Preoperational children would be expected to focus on observable and tangible explanations for illness, with little ability to conceptualize unseen contributors such as germs. They would also be expected to reason inaccurately about cause and effect, perhaps inferring causation from the mere proximity of some event to the onset of illness. A more specific prediction concerns a concept from Piaget's studies of moral reasoning (Piaget, 1932) which he labeled *immanent justice*. Immanent justice is the belief that punishment automatically follows the occurrence of a misdeed. Young children who believe in immanent justice may think that illness is a punishment for being bad.

The older research literature provides some support for all of these expectations (Bibace & Walsh, 1981; Kister & Patterson, 1980). Young children's understanding of illness is indeed marked by gaps and confusions and preoperational-type errors, and there are clear advances in understanding as we move across the childhood years. This is not to say, however, that understanding is totally absent in young children. As we have seen already for several topics (and will see eventually for several more), recent studies with more sensitive assessment techniques often paint a more positive picture of young children's competencies than did earlier research. Such has proved to be the case for beliefs about illness. Here we give just a few examples.

Arguably the core knowledge with respect to illness concerns the role of germs and the conditions for contamination and contagion. Although they may be shaky about specifics and mechanisms, even preschoolers have some such knowledge. Most, for example, would refuse to drink a glass of milk with a cockroach in it; more impressively most would also refuse to drink milk from which a cockroach has been recently removed, and thus for which there is no visible evidence of contamination (Siegal & Share, 1990). On the other hand, the mere proximity of a contaminant is not sufficient, for a bug next to the glass is not seen as worrisome (Springer & Belk, 1994). Knowledge of a contaminant is not necessary for it to have an effect; preschoolers judge that someone who unknowingly eats contaminated food may become sick, but (in an impressive demonstration of their ability to separate physical and psychological) that only someone who knows about the contamination would feel disgusted (Kalish, 1997). Although germs and contagion are regarded as important, even preschoolers realize that not all maladies are caused by germs. They judge, for example, that someone with a headache because of illness may be contagious, but that someone with a headache from a blow to the head will not be (Kalish, 1996). Similarly children come to realize (although the developmental course here may be more protracted) that physical ailments can be transmitted by germs and contagion, but that mental ailments cannot (Keil, Levin, Richman, & Guthiel, 1999). Finally, despite their sensitivity to the physical bases for illness, preschoolers are also aware that behavior can play a role—in particular that certain behaviors (e.g., eating lots of vegetables, going to bed early) can help to ward off disease (Inagaki, 1997).

One more point is important to make. This quick sampling of findings may give the impression that development in this domain consists mainly of the accretion of isolated facts about illness. Such may be the case, but this is not the model that is guiding most contemporary work. Rather most such work falls within the theory theory approach discussed both in Chapter 1 and earlier in this chapter. This means that there is an emphasis not on beliefs in isolation but on the coherence and interrelatedness of the child's belief system—not just with respect to illness but with respect to biological understanding more generally. It means an emphasis on the functional role of concepts in the child's thinking about biological issues and on the causal-explanatory power of the various notions (germs, transmission, etc.) that are eventually developed. Finally it means a concern with identifying domains of development within which theories operate—in particular, of course, with determining whether and when biology becomes a distinct domain in children's thinking. There is, as yet, no agreement on the answer to these questions—or indeed, even on whether the theory theory perspective will prove the best approach within which to answer them (compare, for example, Keil, 1992, with Solomon & Cassimatis, 1999). But there is agreement that they are the right sort of questions to be asking.

BASIC NUMERICAL ABILITIES

The development of basic numerical abilities is an absorbing subject of study for several reasons. People spend years and years in school improving and building upon these basic skills, and years and years after they leave school putting them to practical use in everyday life. Numerical abilities are surely core, "ecologically significant" cognitive acquisitions if any abilities are. As a consequence they are of concern not only to psychologists but also to educators, parents, and others. Furthermore numerical abilities are of additional interest to the student of cognitive development because some of these concepts and skills are also informally picked up and extensively practiced on the child's own initiative prior to formal schooling, during the period of early childhood and possibly even (as we discuss shortly) in infancy. For these reasons numerical understanding has long been a popular topic for researchers of development, and some of our most informative forays into the developing mind have been attempts to determine what children do and do not know about number.

Much of the early, ground-breaking research on the development of basic numerical abilities was done by Piaget and his coworkers (Piaget & Szeminska, 1952; see also Flavell, 1963, pp. 309–316). This research was carried out within the framework of Piaget's general stage theory, and the youngest participants (children between about 3 and 6) were therefore seen as falling within the preoperational stage of development (see Table 1.1). Piaget painted a predominantly negative picture of preoperational competence, and the work on number was no exception. Most of what Piaget had to say about young children's dealings with numbers concerned confusions and deficits in understanding. Nowhere were the confusions more evident than with respect to the aspect of numerical understanding that Piaget regarded as most important: the ability to conserve number in the face of a perceptual change. As with conservation tasks in general, a conservation-of-number task pits immediate perceptual appearance against inferable conceptual reality. For example the experimenter might initially set two rows of 10 buttons each in visual one-to-one correspondence, with one of the two equal-length rows placed directly above the other. After the child agrees that the two rows contain the same number of buttons, the experimenter lengthens one of the rows. To conserve number the child must maintain that the two rows are still numerically equal despite the difference in appearance. And this, Piaget found, is precisely what children younger than about 5 or 6 cannot do. Instead the young child tends to be fooled by the misleading perceptual appearance, judging (usually) that the longer row now contains more.

That young children often fail not only conservation of number but other forms of the conservation task has been amply confirmed in hundreds (count them) of follow-up studies (Ginsburg & Opper, 1988; Modgil & Modgil, 1976). Yet the preschooler's understanding of number, although doubtless incomplete, is by no means as barren as the classic conservation literature suggests. Recent studies have convincingly demonstrated that preschoolers possess a good deal more knowledge and skill in the domain of number than we used to believe. The work of Rochel Gelman and her collaborators has been central in teaching us all about the competencies of young children, and we consequently begin with some of their findings.

What types of numerical knowledge and skills might be acquired during early childhood? Gelman and Gallistel (1978) have identified two major types: number-abstraction abilities and numerical-reasoning principles. Number-abstraction abilities refer to processes by which the child abstracts and represents the numerical value or numerosity of an array of objects. For instance the child could count the array and thereby achieve the representation that it contains "four" objects. Numerical-reasoning principles include those that allow the child to infer the numerical outcomes of operating on or transforming sets in various ways. For example these principles will allow the child to infer that the numerical value of a set of objects is not changed by merely spreading the objects out (the Piagetian conservation problem), but is changed—more specifically increased in value—by adding one or more objects to the set. Thus spreading out is a number-irrelevant transformation, whereas adding is a number-relevant transformation. In brief, the abstraction abilities help the child establish numerical values and the reasoning principles help the child make inferences about, and operate further upon, the numerical values thus established.

Counting Principles

Gelman has paid special attention to the number-abstraction process of counting. Her studies suggest that young children use counting as their principal method for obtaining representations of numerosity. She also shows that their counting activity comes to be governed and defined by five counting principles. The first three principles tell the child how to count properly, the fourth principle tells the child what can be counted, and the fifth principle involves a combination of features of the first four.

1. The one-one principle.   According to this principle, a counter must successively assign one and only one distinctive number name to each and every item to be counted. The first item attended to is ticked off as "one," the next as "two," and so on through the entire set of countables. The person counting should not skip any items that should be counted, should not count any item more than once, should not use the same number name more than once, and should stop the counting sequence precisely when the last item has been enumerated. Although preschoolers do make counting errors that violate the one-one principle, especially when trying to enumerate larger sets of items, there is good evidence that even 2½- to 3-year-olds are likely to have at least some implicit grasp of the one-one principle. For example Gelman (1982) reports that young children will notice and correct their own violations of the principle and also detect violations of it deliberately made by another (e.g., the experimenter's puppet). Thus their violations seem to reflect performance problems more than lack of tacit knowledge of the one-one principle.

2. The Stable-Order Principle.   When counting out a set of items, one should always recite the number names in the same order. For instance one should not count out a three-item set "one, two, three" sometimes and "three, one, two" other times. Gelman found that young children usually honor this principle, despite other—and often amusing—limitations in their counting abilities. For example a 2-year-old might enumerate a set of two objects by saying "two, six," or even "A, B," but would still use that same stable order of counting tags the next time he counted two objects.

3.   The Cardinal Principle.   This principle simply asserts that the final number name uttered at the end of a counting sequence gives the cardinal-number value of the set. For example we would use it this way in totaling up the number of counting principles described so far: "one, two, three—*three*." Gelman's research indicates that, as with the one-one principle: (a) Young children often do act as if they are following the cardinal principle when counting out sets of items, especially small sets, when they have good command of the relevant number words; (b) the information-processing demands of counting may sometimes interfere with the use of the principle, and thereby lead us to underestimate the young child's grasp of it. For example the child himself may not succeed in counting to n and then correctly indicating that there are n things there. On the other hand, he may well spot a puppet's mistake when the puppet counts up to n and then says there are $n + 1$ things there.

4.   The Abstraction Principle.   The three principles just discussed are how-to-count principles. This one is a what-to-count principle. It stipulates that anything is a potential countable; we may enumerate events, inanimate objects, animate objects, intangible and abstract objects (minds, Gelmanian counting principles)—any sort of entity whatever. Although no 4-year-old has yet been observed to enumerate the Gelmanian counting principles, children of this age do not seem to actively exclude any particular type of entity from the potentially countables. Likewise they are willing to try to count up all the objects in a room without worrying about their heterogeneity (e.g., animates lumped together with inanimates), treating them as if they were all identical, featureless "things" for purposes of counting.

5.   The Order-Irrelevance Principle.   This principle states that it does not matter in what order you enumerate the objects you are counting. For example in counting out a set consisting of a dog, a cat, and a mouse, you will end up with the same numerical value whether you begin with the dog and call it "one" or end with the dog and call it "three." Clever studies by Gelman and colleagues (Gelman, 1982; Gelman & Gallistel, 1978) have shown that 5-year-olds have fairly explicit knowledge of the order-irrelevance principle and that even 3-year-olds may well understand it implicitly. In one test, for example, the child was asked to repeatedly count a small set of objects, beginning sometimes with the left-most object, sometimes with the one second from the left, and so on. The children proved generally able to count successfully regardless of the starting point or order of counting; they were also unfazed by the fact that the same label (e.g., "one") might be applied at different times to different objects. In marked contrast they stoutly objected to moving around nonnumerical, *object* names in this fashion—for example calling a baby "baby" on one occasion and "doggie" on another. They clearly thought one should not play musical chairs with objects and object names but seemed to assume it was all right to do so with objects and number names.

The Gelman research program has inspired a number of related efforts in recent years (e.g., Briars & Siegler, 1984; Cowan, Dowker, Christakis, & Bailey, 1996;

Fuson, 1988; Rittle-Johnson & Siegler, 1998; Sophian, 1995, 1998; Wynn, 1990). In general outline these studies support two of Gelman's most important conclusions: that even quite young children use counting as a means of estimating number, and that even quite young children show some knowledge and some skill in their counting endeavors. At a more specific level, disagreements have arisen concerning just how early in development children should be credited with knowledge of the various counting principles. In Gelman's "principle-first" model, the principles are assumed to be available—albeit only in implicit, unverbalizable form—from quite early on and to guide even the 3-year-old's counting efforts. Gelman acknowledges, as we saw, that these early efforts sometimes go astray; the young child's problems, however, are attributed to various performance limitations that obscure the underlying knowledge about counting, not to a lack of knowledge per se.

Other investigators are less certain that it makes sense to credit children with knowledge of the counting principles when their performance is so variable and so error-prone. Siegler (1991b) has proposed a contrasting "skills-first" hypothesis: that children first develop some degree of skill at counting, prior to any knowledge of the general principles, and that experience in counting then leads to the gradual abstraction of the underlying principles. Children might come to realize, for example, that they always arrive at the same value no matter what order they count (the order-irrelevance principle), but that they get quite different values if they are not careful to count each item once and only once (the one-one principle). It may be, of course, that both positions have some truth to them: that the principles (or at least some subset of them) are indeed present in nascent form from early in life, but that they become more solidly established and more accessible with age and experience. In any case, however we conceptualize initial competence and developmental change, it is important not to lose track of the fact that improvements do occur across the preschool years. Three-year-olds may be more skilled at estimating numbers than we used to believe; they will be more skilled by age 4, however, and still more skilled at 5 or 6.

Numerical-Reasoning Principles

Children acquire numerical-reasoning principles as well as number-abstraction abilities during the early-childhood period. By the end of this period, they are likely to have learned that merely changing the color or identity of a set of items are not transformations that alter the number of items in the set. They are also likely to have learned that, contrariwise, adding items increases the set's numerical value, subtracting items decreases it, and first adding one item and then subtracting one item leaves the numerical value unchanged. They can also determine the numerical equality and inequality relations between two sets—that is, they can infer that set A and B contain the same number of items and that set C contains more items than set D. They are apt to rely heavily on counting to determine these relations and, as with number abstraction, are generally better at numerical reasoning when the sets involved are small, easily countable ones.

What about Piagetian conservation—the realization that changes in spatial arrangement do not alter number? We have already seen that preschoolers tend to fail the standard form of the conservation problem. Such failures, however, need not imply a total inability to reason about the invariance of number in the face of a perceptual change. In simpler, more child-friendly situations, even 3-year-olds show some ability to separate number from appearance. One of Gelman's so-called "magic" studies (Gelman, 1972) provides perhaps the most striking evidence for this conclusion.

Gelman's participants ranged in age from 3 to 6½ years. Each child saw two plates, each with a row of toy mice on it. There were three mice in one row and two in the other. For some children the lengths of the rows were identical, with the two-mouse row naturally being less dense than the three-mouse one. For others the densities or spaces between the mice were identical, with the three-mouse row consequently being longer than the two-mouse row. The child's initial task was simply to learn which plate was the "winner" (always the one containing three mice) and which the "loser" (always the two-mouse plate). Notice that the child could learn to identify winners and losers in this task without paying the slightest attention to number and number differences. In the first group, the winner row was denser as well as more numerous; in the second group, it was longer as well as more numerous. The child was reinforced for correctly identifying winner and loser plates but was never told why a given choice was correct.

After a series of such trials, the experimenter surreptitiously ("magically") made a change in the winner row before exposing the plates to the child. For some children in each group, she removed one mouse from the center or end of that row, thereby making the two rows numerically equal. For others she shortened or lengthened the winner row. Surprise reactions were noted, and the children were subsequently asked various questions about what happened. Even the youngest children conceptualized the winner and loser rows in terms of number rather than length or density. For example 29 out of 32 3-year-olds gave number descriptions of the rows at some point in the experimental proceedings, often using the terms "three" and "two"; in contrast not one ever referred to differences in length or density. Reactions following the experimenter's surreptitious change in the winner row also clearly showed that number, not length or density, was what the children were attending to. When length of row was changed, the children showed little surprise and continued to identify the three-mouse row as a winner, even when it had been made shorter than the two-mouse row. When a mouse was removed from the three-mouse row, on the other hand, they showed surprise, were uncertain as to which row was now the winner, asked where the missing mouse was or searched for it, and offered various explanations for the disappearance (our favorite: "Jesus took it"). In both situations, therefore, the children showed some ability to disentangle number from the countervailing cues of length or density.

Later Acquisitions

Children's numerical abilities continue to improve and expand during the middle-childhood and adolescent years, partly as a direct consequence of formal teaching in school and partly through a continuation of the spontaneous and informal learning about number that begins early in life. Skills that were rudimentary and situation-specific in early childhood become more powerful and more broadly applicable as children develop. Three-year-olds may recognize the invariance of number in certain simple situations, such as Gelman's magic task; 6- or 7-year-olds can handle any conservation-of-number task that might come along. Children's knowledge about how to abstract and reason about numbers also becomes more explicit with development. Whereas younger children can sometimes detect errors in counting or numerical reasoning, older children can go on to reflect on them and explicitly indicate why they are errors, what effects they have on the outcome, and the like. It is not hard to imagine carrying on a meaningful and articulate dialogue about Gelman's five counting principles with a child of 10, say. In contrast we surely could not do this with a child of 3, even though the 3-year-old might also abide by these principles when actually engaged in counting small sets.

Not surprisingly much of the work on understanding of number in the middle-childhood years has concentrated on numerical skills that are important in school—adding, subtracting, multiplying, dividing. We introduced one particularly informative example of such work in Chapter 1: Siegler's studies of the strategies that children use to solve simple arithmetic problems (Siegler, 1988, 1996; Siegler & Jenkins, 1989; Siegler & Shipley, 1995). As we saw there, Siegler's goal has been to move beyond simply documenting correct or incorrect answers to such problems to specify *how* children arrive at their solutions. Perhaps the main message from the research concerns the variety of methods of how—that is, the diversity of strategies that children develop to cope with the task of addition: counting up from one, counting up from the larger addend (the "min" strategy), relating the problem to similar problems, retrieving the answer from memory, guessing. Quite typically children use not just one but several strategies at any point in development. A main determinant of successful problem solving is the ability to select the most appropriate and efficient strategy for the task at hand. And a main determinant of developmental change is the gradual replacement, through a kind of survival of the fittest, of less efficient strategies by more efficient strategies. These conclusions apply, we should note, not just to addition but to other basic arithmetical operations that are mastered (at least in part!) during the middle-childhood years: subtraction, multiplication, division. More broadly, the emphasis on strategies and strategy change is one distinctive characteristic of the information-processing approach to children's thinking.

The various forms of arithmetic just discussed are not the only targets for children's mathematical efforts. Children also come to grips with fractions (e.g., Mack, 1990), proportions (e.g., Sophian, 2000), even notions of infinity (e.g., Hartnett & Gelman, 1998). For further discussion of these and other developments, see Geary (1994), Donlan (1998), and Ginsburg, Klein, and Starkey (1998).

Earlier Foundations

That 3- and 4-year-olds are as competent in dealing with numbers as they have proved to be came as a surprise to many of us. Even more surprising is recent evidence suggesting that *infants* are sensitive to the dimension of number and may even—more mind-boggling still—be capable of simple acts of arithmetic when presented with small sets of stimuli.

How might infants show a sensitivity to number? An experiment by Starkey, Spelke, and Gelman (1990) capitalized on the fact that even young infants are capable of showing habituation and dishabituation of attention—that is, of decreasing their attention to a repeatedly presented and therefore familiar stimulus and of increasing attention when they detect a change in the stimulus (see Chapter 2). Starkey et al. showed 6- to 9-month-old infants a series of slides of three-item displays until the infants habituated to them. The items shown were common household objects such as a memo pad, a comb, and a scraper. The three objects on any one slide were different from the three on any other slide and also differed in their spatial arrangement; it appears, therefore, that the only thing the object arrays had in common was their numerical value—their "threeness." After the infants had habituated to these slides, they were presented with an alternating sequence of three-item and two-item slides. These slides also contained new household objects in varying spatial configurations. Starkey et al. found that the infants looked longer at the slides that showed the new numerical value (the two-item slides) than at those showing the old one (the three-item slides). That is, they appeared to exhibit continued habituation of attention to displays of three things but dishabituation to displays of two things. This in turn suggests that they must have perceptually discriminated between the two types of displays. Other infants of the same age who were first presented with two-item slides and then with two- and three-item slides in alternation showed the same psychological pattern: They subsequently looked longer at the novel, three-item slides.

In view of the surprising and counterintuitive nature of these findings, it is important to note that similar studies with similar results have now been carried out in a number of laboratories (Antell & Keating, 1983; Cooper, 1984; Strauss & Curtis, 1981; Trehub, Thorpe, & Cohen, 1991; Treiber & Wilcox, 1984; van Loosbroek & Smitsman, 1990). There is nothing like successful independent replication to render hard-to-believe results believable. These further studies, moreover, have added in various ways to our picture of numerical sensitivity in infants. Some ability to discriminate very small-size sets has been shown even in neonates (Antell & Keating, 1983). By 4 months of age, infants can discriminate between sets as large as four and five elements (Treiber & Wilcox, 1984); no one, however, has yet shown successful performance on sets larger than this during the first 6 months of life. Infants' discriminatory abilities are not limited to static arrays; they can distinguish differences in number even when the objects are in constant motion (van Loosbroek & Smitsman, 1990). Discrimination of number is not limited to simultaneously present objects; infants can also perceive differences when the sets to be compared are presented sequentially (Canfield & Smith, 1996). For that matter discrimination is not limited to objects; infants can also differentiate number of actions—for example, two versus three jumps by a puppet (Wynn, 1996). Finally discrimination is not limited to the visual realm; comparable results have been obtained with auditory patterns that vary in the number of tones (Trehub et al., 1991).

We mention the variety of contexts in which success has been demonstrated because the breadth of the phenomenon is relevant to how we interpret infants' success. If apparent discriminations of number were limited to static arrays of objects, then it would always be logically possible that some aspect of the stimuli other than number (e.g., the length of the rows, the overall density) could be mediating response. The generality of the phenomenon, however, has convinced most researchers that number is indeed the dimension to which infants are responding (but see Clearfield & Mix, 1999, for a dissenting view).

Even if we agree that infants are sensitive to number, there are still disagreements about the bases for the sensitivity. Two possibilities exist. Some researchers (e.g., Gallistel & Gelman, 1992; Wynn, 1998b) believe that discrimination of number reflects the operation of a preverbal counting mechanism, a mechanism that is similar to the process that is believed to underlie numerical sensitivity in animals and that is continuous with later, symbolic competence in humans. Other researchers (e.g., Siegler, 1998) believe that the results can be accounted for by a simpler, and well-established, process known as *subitizing*. Subitizing is the term for the rapid apprehension of number in small sets (typically 4 or less) through perception alone, and thus without the use of counting. The fact that most demonstrations of infant success are limited to small set sizes is consistent with (although it does not prove) the subitizing position. On the other hand, recent research by Xu and Spelke (2000) seems to show that 6-month-olds can discriminate set sizes that are considerably larger than the previous 4 versus 5 upper limit, just so long as the contrast in number is sufficiently great (e.g., they can discriminate 8 vs. 16 but not 8 vs. 12). Clearly the question of what numbers infants can discriminate and how they do it is very much a story in progress.

Also unresolved at present is whether infants' numerical sensitivity extends beyond the ability to discriminate differences. In recent years a number of studies—most notably a program of research by Karen Wynn (1992, 1995, 1998b)—have suggested that it does. To return to the distinction from Gelman and Gallistel (1978) with which we began, Wynn believes that infants can not only abstract number; they can reason about number. Specifically, she believes that they are capable of simple forms of addition and subtraction.

How might an infant demonstrate an understanding of addition or subtraction? Wynn's evidence comes from the same violation-of-expectancy paradigm that has been utilized so effectively by Spelke and Baillargeon to study knowledge of the physical world. Figure 4.4 shows an example of both an addition and a subtraction problem. As you can see, the contrast is between two outcomes: a possible event $(1 + 1 = 2, 2 - 1 = 1)$ and an impossible event $(1 + 1 = 1, 2 - 1 = 2)$. If infants understand the arithmetic operations involved, they should expect to see a certain number of dolls when the screen is removed, they should be surprised when this expectation is violated, and they therefore should look longer at the impossible outcomes. And this is precisely what Wynn found: For both addition and subtraction, 5-month-old infants looked longer at the impossible than at the possible outcome.

This study seems to establish clearly that infants have some knowledge of what should happen when objects are either added to or subtracted from a set. It leaves unclear, however, just how precise the knowledge and consequent expectations are. One possibility is that it is quite precise: that infants expect two objects in the addition case and one object in the subtraction case. Another possibility, however, is that all that infants expect is that the number will have changed in some way following the operation; it is, after all, the reappearance of the original, unchanged number of dolls that seems to be surprising on both the addition and subtraction trials. A subsequent experiment was designed to pull apart these possibilities. In this case a $1 + 1$ manipulation resulted in either two dolls (possible) or three dolls (impossible). Here, therefore, both outcomes are different from the starting point; only one, however, is mathematically correct. Infants looked longer at the three-doll outcome, thus suggesting that they knew not only that addition increases number but also (at least in this simple case) how great the increase should be.

Wynn's studies are cleverly conceived and carefully executed; aspects of her results have now been replicated in other laboratories (Simon, Hespos, & Rochat, 1995; Uller, Carey, Huntley-Fenner, & Klatt, 1999), and her general conclusions seem compatible both with other work on infant numerical competence and with recent research in infant cognitive development more generally. In short it may well be that infants are capable of simple arithmetic. We must add, however (and by now you can probably guess what is coming), that not all researchers of infancy agree with her conclusions (see, for example, Haith & Benson, 1998; Simon, 1997; Wakely, Rivera, & Langer, 2001). Not all attempts to replicate have been success-

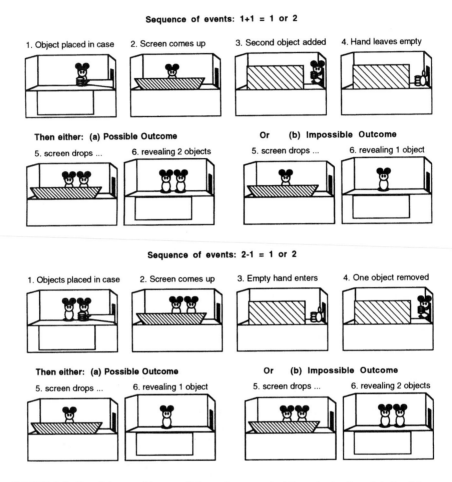

FIGURE 4.4 Possible and impossible outcomes in Wynn's study of infants' arithmetica l competence. From "Addition and Subtraction by Human Infants," by K. Wynn, 1992, *Nature, 358*, p. 749. Copyright © 1992 by Macmillan Magazines Ltd. Reprinted by permission.

ful. In addition the studies of infant arithmetic raise some of the same issues of interpretation, and are subject to some of the same criticisms, as the Spelke and Baillargeon work on knowledge of the physical world that we discussed in Chapter 3. At present, therefore, infant arithmetic must be considered another entry in our list of provocative but wait-for-further-developments topics.

Basic Numerical Skills: Natural Human Abilities?

The infant studies are taken by Gelman (1990, 1991; Gelman & Meck, 1992; Gelman & Williams, 1998; see also Wynn, 1998a) as evidence for her belief that basic numerical skills may constitute natural and universal abilities for members of our species. Number, she believes, is like language in this regard: a species-wide set of abilities that homo sapiens has evolved a special aptitude and disposition to acquire. It is, in Gelman's terms, a "core domain." As with objects (Chapter 2) and language (Chapter 8), the development of numerical competence builds upon a skeleton of innately given, domain-specific principles, principles that are not themselves learned but rather serve as the starting point that makes learning possible.

Various lines of argument support this position. First, as we have just seen, human beings appear to be both able and disposed to process numerical information from early in infancy—well before language, well before formal tuition, well before relevant experience of any obvious sort. Second young children show both high motivation and high aptitude to acquire basic numerical knowledge and skills on their own, without adult pressure or tutelage. In young children, Gelman's counting principles function very like a Piagetian scheme. Like a sucking or prehension scheme, they spontaneously and voraciously assimilate countable objects and new number words to their own structures. Young children seem to go around counting things and learning new numbers for the sheer pleasure of it. Furthermore some form of counting procedure seems to be found in every human culture, including those in which there is no formal schooling. Such universality is clearly compatible with the idea that numerical processing, like speech, is something that humans are born to do. Finally the plausibility of Gelman's position is bolstered by its congruence with the current Zeitgeist. As we discuss more fully in Chapter 9, the field is much more favorably disposed now than formerly to the notion that some degree of innate, domain-specific pretuning guides many aspects of development. Gelman's work on number both prefigured and contributed to these modern emphases.

Basic Numeral Skills: Social Contributors

Whatever the innate bases may be, no one, least of all Gelman, believes that numerical development results solely from the unfolding of biologically programmed abilities in the absence of any experience. Such is obviously not the case. Children, as we have seen, exercise their numerical skills frequently and spontaneously, and they clearly benefit from these experiences. Numerical concepts of various sorts are also the focus of thousands of hours of explicit tuition in school. The lives of both children and teachers would be much easier if all numerical knowledge were somehow programmed in from birth.

In recent years the development of numerical competence has also been a fruitful topic area for applications of the Vygotsky-inspired sociocultural approach to cognitive development. As we saw in Chapter 1, the emphasis of the sociocultural approach is on the social context within which cognitive development takes place, both the distal context provided by the general culture and the more proximal context of interactions with significant others, especially the child's parents. Cognition is assumed to be inextricably embedded within the social world and critically dependent on the kinds of information and assistance that social interaction provides. Researchers in this tradition who are interested in number therefore focus on the ways in which different cultures symbolize and transmit numerical knowledge, as well as the forms of guidance that more knowledgeable members of the culture provide to the growing child.

A monograph by Saxe, Guberman, and Gearhart (1987) provides an example. Participants for the research were 2- and 4-year-old children and their mothers.

Mother and child were videotaped as they worked together on several simple numerical tasks—counting the number of objects in a small array, for example, or matching the number of objects in one array with the number in a second array. Of interest were the kinds of help that the mothers provided to their children and the children's ability to benefit from the help. Saxe et al. found that mothers adjusted the level of their help to the level of the child; 2-year-olds received more explicit guidance than 4-year-olds, and less numerically competent children within an age group (as assessed by independent tests) received more guidance than more competent children. Mothers also showed an ability to make on-the-spot adjustments to the level of their child's performance. When a child succeeded at some step toward task solution, the mother's next instruction was typically at a less explicit, more on-your-own level; conversely when a child failed at some step, mothers tended to up the level of their help, spelling out procedures that had been only implicit before. This sort of flexible, child-sensitive method of teaching has come to be known as "scaffolding" in the Vygotskian literature (Wood, 1980), and it certainly appears to be a sensible way to help children learn. Finally Saxe et al. found that the children were often able to accomplish a task with maternal help that they had been unable to perform on their own. You may recall that such actualization of potential level of performance through appropriate assistance is the essence of the Vygotskian notion of the zone of proximal development.

Two more points can be made about the Saxe et al. (1987) research. The finding that maternal teaching is helpful on laboratory tasks would not mean much without evidence that mothers and children do in fact work together in situations involving number—naturally and spontaneously and not just when some experimenter sets them a task to complete. Through interviews with the mothers, Saxe et al. provide some evidence for such ecological validity (see also Blevins-Knabe & Musun-Miller, 1996). At least in their sample, the children dealt frequently with numbers, mothers and children engaged frequently in number games and activities of various sorts, and the complexity of the games and activities increased as the children developed. The second point is that the boost in performance in response to maternal help would be of limited significance if the gains did not transfer to the child's later, independent problem-solving efforts. Our interest, after all, is not just in what children can do with help but in what they take away from the help and make their own. Although Saxe et al. did not include such independent measures, other studies in the sociocultural tradition (e.g., the Freund, 1990, study discussed in Chapter 1) have, and they typically report improved independent performance following social interaction. We return to the issue of what children take away from interactions with more mature others, including possible differential effects across different sorts of development, in the concluding chapter.

Researchers in the sociocultural tradition have also provided some fascinating data with regard to the more distal level of cultural systems of number and cultural supports for numerical development. Here we briefly mention three findings. First, although basic principles of mathematics are of course universal ($1 + 1 = 2$ in every culture), the symbolic systems through which numbers are expressed and dealt with may vary greatly across cultures. In parts of New Guinea, for example, a body-parts system of counting is used (see Figure 4.5); the count begins with the thumb on one hand and progresses through 29 distinct locations before reaching the far side of the other hand (Saxe, 1981). Second, the ways in which a culture symbolizes numbers can affect the speed with which numerical operations are mastered during development and the ease with which they are executed in maturity. Saxe (1981, 1982) found, for example, that

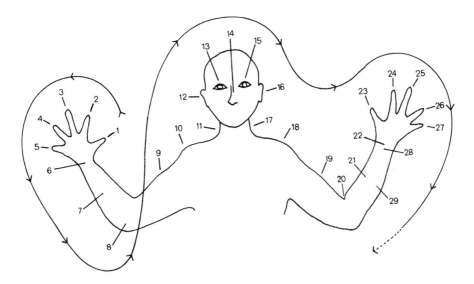

FIGURE 4.5 A body-parts system of counting used in parts of New Guinea. From "Body Parts as Numerals: A Developmental Analysis of Numeration among the Oksapmin in Papua New Guinea," by G. B. Saxe, 1981, *Child Development, 52,* p. 307. Copyright ©1981 by the Society for Research in Child Development. Reprinted by permission.

both number-abstraction and numerical-reasoning skills tended to be slower to develop among New Guinea children dependent on the body-parts method of counting than among Western children. Similarly Miller and Stigler (1987) reported that Chinese children were superior to American children in some aspects of counting, apparently because the Chinese language symbolizes the relevant terms in a more consistent, accessible fashion than does English (the "teen" numbers, like the "teen" years, are especially problematical). Finally, cultural experiences beyond simply the number system itself can either nurture or hinder the development of numerical skills. A striking example comes from studies of child candy vendors on the streets of Brazil (Nunes, Carraher, & Schliemann, 1993; Saxe, 1991, 1999). Faced with a multitude of numerical tasks, all of which must be performed quickly and accurately under highly competitive circumstances (purchasing the candy, setting the sale price, making change, adjusting for inflation), these children develop a mathematical facility that most of us, shorn of our pocket calculators, would be hard-put to match.

SUMMARY

Once children develop the ability to form mental representations during infancy, they then can acquire an impressive number of fragile but nonetheless genuine competencies. *Symbolic-representational skills* undergo a great deal of growth during early childhood. Because young children are beginning to understand the nature of these representations, they can understand pictorial representations and also grasp that what the person creating the representation *intended* to represent determines its referent, rather than simply what it looks like. Young children also can use models, engage in pretend play, follow simple narratives, form simple spatial frames of reference, and begin to understand maps, though they have important limitations in most of these domains that do not disappear until school age or later.

Young children have trouble sorting out certain relationships between representations and their real counterparts. For example, three-dimensional scale models cannot be used until about 36 months except under conditions in which the child is psychologically distanced from the model. At 36 months the majority of children can locate an object hidden in one physical layout based on a replica's hiding place in a larger or smaller layout. *Representational insight* involves realizing that something is a symbol that stands for something else. *Dual representation* refers to thinking about one thing in two ways at the same time—as both an object and a symbol. This understanding that an entity can be both itself and a representation of something else appears to be the main stumbling block for very young children. The model as an entity in its own right competes with children's perceiving it as a representation as well. A manipulation that removes the need for this dual representation, as shown in the "shrinking room" experiment, improves performance. *Representational specificity* is the realization that a symbol can represent a specific real entity. In order to use a symbol, a child must (a) detect the relation between a symbol and referent, (b) map their corresponding elements (for example, little toy = big toy; little room = big room), and (c) use knowledge about one to draw an inference about the other.

The simple representations of infancy become much more complex knowledge structures over the preschool years. These representations greatly assist children in predicting and making sense of their everyday worlds. For example, event representations, including *scripts*, can be thought of as mental forms, molds, or templates that help us assimilate and accommodate to environmental inputs. Children construct scripts for representing and anticipating the usual sequence of events in preschool, at bedtime, and during other familiar routines and have some understanding of their embedded causal relations. These scripts can be formed after even one instance, but typically are constructed over many instances. Scripts become more complex during development and can more easily incorporate minor variations among events. They also may help children construct early conceptual categories.

Preschoolers also form *concepts* that organize the world into meaningful categories. In contrast to traditional views of the perception-bound young child, these early concepts do not depend solely on perceptual appearance but often reflect deeper, less obvious relations among the members of a category. For example young children can use their knowledge that blackbird and dissimilar-looking flamingo belong to the same category, and that blackbird and similar-looking bat do not, to infer that the former pair are more likely to share fundamental properties than are the latter. Such inferences reflect a primary cognitive function that concepts serve: They help us to abstract basic similarities in the face of obvious dissimilarities, and to use our knowledge of familiar exemplars to predict to unfamiliar ones. Productive inferences based on underlying similarity are especially likely for the type of concept known as *natural kinds:* categories that occur in nature, such as animals and plants. Although their grasp of the distinction is somewhat shaky, even preschoolers show some appreciation of the ways in which natural kinds differ from other sorts of concepts such as nominal kinds and artifacts.

An important aspect of conceptual development involves understanding the hierarchically organized levels within which entities can be represented. Research inspired by Rosch has examined the prediction that representations at the *basic level* (e.g., dog, chair) are psychologically most natural and hence should emerge earlier in development than representations at either the superordinate (e.g., animal, furniture) or subordinate (e.g., poodle, rocker) levels. This prediction has received mixed support in research to date. Research inspired by Piaget has examined children's understanding of the hierarchical structure of classes, with a particular focus on the principle of *class inclusion:* the knowledge that a subclass cannot be larger than the superordinate class that contains it. The difficulty of class inclusion turns out to vary greatly across different forms of the problem and different response measures; even preschoolers show some understanding of the principle, but full mastery may not come until many years later.

We can make several generalizations about young children's concepts. Preschoolers' concepts are more advanced than we used to believe—a conclusion in keeping with much recent research on this age period. This understanding is not complete, however, and developmental improvements are evident for each of the concepts described in this chapter. Often differences between younger and older children seem to reflect differences in content-specific knowledge; young children have limited knowledge in many domains, and this lack of knowledge constrains the level of their concepts and reasoning. The importance of content-specific knowledge suggests that children's concepts will not all be at the same level of maturity, and research indicates that in fact they are not. Finally the most popular way at present to characterize the nature of concepts is to think of them as implicit *theories*. Like theories, concepts consist of a set of interrelated causal-explanatory principles, and, like theories, they help us to understand and predict experience.

Studies of children's understanding of biological phenomena (growth, movement, inheritance, illness) provide an interesting content area in which to examine particular childhood concepts. By age 3 or 4, children have some appreciation that living things differ from other sorts of entities in that they grow, regrow, and retain their identity despite physical alterations. They also know that only animals can move independently. Although they have a rudimentary notion of inheritance, they sometimes still confuse hereditary and environmental influences and have a nativistic bias. Finally preschoolers have some understanding of illness, germs, and contagion, though their understanding will continue to improve. Thus their biological concepts reveal a precocious ability to overlook on-the-surface aspects and reason about underlying essences.

The acquisition of basic numerical abilities is of compelling interest for several reasons, not the least of which is their great ecological significance. A great deal of exciting research on this topic has been carried out in recent years by Rochel Gelman and others. Gelman distinguished between *number-abstraction abilities* and *numerical-reasoning principles*. Prominent among the number-abstraction abilities is the preschooler's developing command of five *counting principles:* (1) assign one and only one number name to each and every item to be counted (*one-one principle*); (2) always recite the number names in the same order (*stable-order principle*); (3) the final number name uttered denotes the total number of items counted (*cardinal principle*); (4) any sort of entity may be counted (*abstraction principle*); and (5) the order in which the objects are enumerated does not matter (*order-irrelevance principle*). An important numerical-reasoning principle that children gradually acquire is the number-conservation rule first studied by Piaget: the knowledge that merely spreading a set of objects does not change the number of objects in the set.

It is not surprising to learn that children's numerical abilities continue to develop in various ways after early childhood; for example they acquire several addition strategies. Nor is it surprising to learn that aspects of the social context, such as parental teaching, can contribute to these developments. However, it certainly *is* surprising to learn that numerical abilities may begin their development *before* the early childhood period. Recent research suggests that infants, perhaps even neonates, are sensitive to the dimension of number in a variety of contexts. Furthermore, incredible though it sounds, infants may even engage spontaneously in some sort of nonverbal "counting," adding, and subtracting when presented with small-size sets. These astonishing findings, though interpreted in various ways, raise the possibility that basic numerical processes may—like walking and talking—be activities we humans are predisposed through evolution to learn and do.

The picture of conceptual development emerging from this chapter is that infants and preschoolers can and do make more inferences about the unobservable and the covert than developmental psychologists once thought. In particular preschoolers seem to prefer causal-explanatory representations that go beneath surface appearances to a deeper reality, though—like the rest of us—they sometimes are distracted by these perceptual features and have trouble integrating them with the underlying features. Much of their knowledge is acquired informally as they construct an intuitive understanding of natural domains—objects, events, and people. One issue is if, and when, domains become a distinct domain and theory in the child's thinking. Overall preschoolers have surprising cognitive strengths in their use of external representations, scripts, basic categories of reality, and intuitive grasp of number. At the same time, they still have much to learn about the more subtle aspects of representation, categories, and concepts.

5

Reasoning and Problem Solving

———⟫◆⟪———

Once children are able to represent their world, use external representations of the world, and form concepts and categories of the world, they are well equipped to reason about, and solve problems in, this world. A great deal of developmental change in reasoning and problem solving occurs from infancy through adolescence, and a main issue is how best to describe and explain the age differences. We first present Piaget's view of reasoning, and then look at more recent accounts of various sorts of reasoning, including scientific reasoning. Then we turn to problem solving in a variety of domains.

REASONING: PIAGET'S VIEW

Exactly how do the minds of older children, adolescents, and adults differ from those of young children? Much of the evidence on this question comes from work in the Piagetian tradition, both Piaget's original studies and the thousands of follow-ups they inspired.

As we saw in Chapter 1, Piaget's theory postulates marked changes in children's reasoning across the course of development. Specifically the theory identifies the following sequence of major stages or periods of cognitive development: (1) the sensorimotor period of infancy; (2) the preoperational period of early childhood, conceived as a period of preparation for concrete operations; (3) the concrete-operational period of middle childhood; and (4) the formal-operational period of adolescence (see Table 1.1). In this sequence the child moves from the physical actions that emanate from the sensorimotor schemes of infancy to symbolic, in-the-head mental processing during the preoperational period. These mental processes eventually evolve into systems of mental actions, or operations. The operations are applied first to concrete, present objects and events (concrete operations) and later to mental operations themselves, the thoughts about thoughts of formal operations.

Two kinds of findings, however, challenge the notion of dramatic across-the-child changes in Piagetian stages or anybody's stages for that matter. First, a child's cognitive performance is somewhat uneven across different domains (see Chapters 1, 4, and 9). Second, it appears that young children are more competent (see Chapters 3 and 4) and older children less competent than Piaget thought. Consequently the cognitive changes across childhood may be less stagelike and dramatic than Piaget imagined. Still Piaget does seem to have captured important developmental *trends* that ring true, and we organize our discussion in terms of some of the most important such trends. We divide these trends into two sets of contrasts: (1) contrasts between early-childhood and middle-childhood cognition; (2) contrasts between middle-childhood and adolescent-adult cognition. However, these should be thought of as rough age trends, not as sharp and clear contrasts among three entirely different and discontinuous mentalities. Note also that what follows is not a review of the vast research literature on concrete- and formal-operational thinking. Reviews of some of this literature can be found in Beilin and Pufall (1992), Braine and Rumain (1983), Byrnes (1988a), Chapman (1988), Flavell (1963, 1970a), Gelman and Baillargeon (1983), Ginsburg and Opper (1988), Gray (1990), Halford (1989), Keating (1990), and Moshman (1998).

Contrasts between Early-Childhood and Middle-Childhood Cognition

Perceived Appearances versus Inferred Reality. We illustrate the first several contrasts with Piaget's hallmark task, the conservation task. However, these trends also apply to other physical concepts and to social concepts such as role taking and person perception (see Chapter 6) as well.

We described the conservation of number task in Chapter 4. Conservation of liquid quantity is another basic and much studied form of conservation. In this task (1) the child first agrees that two identical glasses contain identical amounts of water; (2) the experimenter pours the water from one glass into a third, taller and thinner glass, with the child watching; (3) she then asks the child if the two amounts of water are still identical, or whether one glass now contains more water than the other. The typical preschool nonconserver is apt to conclude, after the liquid has been poured, that the taller and thinner glass now has more water in it than the other glass. Why? One reason is that it *looks* like it has more to her, and she is more given than the older child to make judgments about reality on the basis of the immediate, perceived *appearances* of things. More than her school-age counterpart, the preschool-age child is prone to accept things as they seem to be.

The middle-childhood conserver, on the other hand, may also think that the tall glass *looks* like it contains more water because the liquid column is higher, but she goes beyond mere appearances to *infer* from the available evidence that the two quantities *are really* still the same. That is, she makes an inference about underlying reality rather than merely translating perceived appearances into a quantity judgment. More generally the older child seems to be more sensitive to the basic distinction between what seems to be and what really is—between the phenomenal or apparent and the real or true (see the appearance-reality distinction in Chapter 6). Of course this is not to suggest that young children never make inferences about unperceived states of affairs or that older children never base conclusions on superficial appearances. Indeed some of young children's concepts discussed in Chapter 4, especially their "theories," clearly go beyond the perceptual information given. Still the tendency to do so (a) increases across this broad segment of childhood, and (b) becomes less limited to particular aspects of reality, for example, may include not only the identity and nature of an entity but also its quantity.

Centration versus Decentration.   The foregoing contrast emphasizes the younger child's heavy reliance on perceptual input when dealing with conceptual problems like Piaget's conservation-of-liquid-quantity task. But of course the older child also is carefully attending to the perceptual input throughout that task, even though he recognizes that the task ultimately calls for a conceptual rather than a perceptual judgment. Moreover he is apt to be distributing that attention in a more flexible, balanced, and generally task-adaptive way than the younger child. The preschooler is more prone to concentrate or *center* (hence, *centration*) his attention exclusively on some single feature or limited portion of the stimulus array that is particularly salient and interesting to him, thereby neglecting other task-relevant features. In the present example, the difference in the heights of the two liquid columns is what captures most of his attention (and "capture" often does seem the apposite word), with little note given to the compensatory difference in column widths.

In contrast the older child is likelier to achieve a more balanced, "decentered" (hence, *decentration*) perceptual analysis of the entire display. While, of course, attending to the conspicuous height differences, just as the younger child does, he also carefully notes the correlative differences in container width. He therefore attains a broader and more inclusive purview of the stimulus field. He is likelier to notice and take due account of *all* the relevant perceptual data—in this case the lesser width as well as the greater height of the new liquid column.

O'Bryan and Boersma (1971) have captured "live" ongoing patterns of centration and decentration by filming the eye movements of nonconservers and conservers. Nonconservers centrate on the dominant part of the visual display, such as the water level. Transitional conservers display a sort of dual centration, shifting occasionally between two dominant features such as water height and width. Conservers shift their gaze frequently over many parts of the display. Thus attention can be a window to the child's mind (as so much research on infant cognition, in particular, shows).

States versus Transformations.   The test of conservation of liquid quantity can be thought of as comprising two *states*, one initial and one final, plus a *transformation* or process of change that links these two states. In the initial state, two identical glasses of water contain identical amounts of water. In the final state, two dissimilar glasses contain identical amounts of water (identical in "reality," if not in "appearance"). The transformation that links them is, of course, the process of pouring water from one glass to another. The act of pouring is a dynamic event that changes, in the course of a brief time period, one static situation into another static situation; it is a transformational process that produces or creates a later state out of an earlier state.

Piaget made the profound observation that younger children, to a greater degree than older ones, tend to focus their attention and conceptual energies on states rather than on state-producing transformations, and also on present states more than on past or future ones. When solving problems of all sorts, they are less likely to call to mind or keep in mind relevant previous states of the problem, or to anticipate pertinent future or potential ones. In particular Piaget argued they are both undisposed and relatively unable to represent the actual, detailed processes of transition or transformation from one state to another. Thus they exhibit a kind of "temporal centration" analogous to the spatial one just discussed. They center their attention on the present spatial field or stimulus state to the exclusion of other relevant states and state-linking transformations in the "temporal field," which consists of the recent past, the immediate present, and the near future. They do this just as, within the present spatial field itself, they center their attention on a single, privileged segment of that field. In contrast the conserver is likely to make spontaneous reference to initial state and intervening transformation when asked to justify her conservation judgment. She might say that the two quantities had, after all, been identical at the outset (initial state), or that the experimenter had merely poured the water from one container to the other, and without spilling any or adding any (intervening transformation). The older child might even say that the continuing equality of amounts could be proved by pouring the liquid back into its original container (future or potential transformation, yielding new state equal to initial state). The conservation task is a conceptual problem rather than a perceptual one precisely *because* of the real or potential existence of such nonpresent states and transformations of states. The older child is more attuned to these background, not-now-perceptible factors and uses them in producing a conceptual solution to this and other, similar conceptual problems.

Irreversibility versus Reversibility. According to Piaget the middle-childhood subject possesses *reversible intellectual operations* (hence the term "concrete *operational* period"); his thought is said to exhibit the property of *reversibility*. Contrariwise the preschool child's mental operations are *irreversible*, and his thought is said to show *irreversibility*. In the particular conservation problem we have been using as an example, the older child can exhibit reversibility of thought or reversible mental operations in two distinct ways.

On the one hand, he may recognize that the effect of the initial pouring of the water into the tall thin glass can be exactly and completely undone or negated by the inverse action of pouring the water back into its original container. The older child readily senses the possible existence of such an inverse, wholly nullifying action that changes everything back to its original state, and he may cite this possibility as a justification for his conservation judgment. A middle-childhood mind is more sensitive than an early-childhood one to the fact that many mental and physical operations have opposites that exactly—in a rigorous, precise, quantitative way—negate them, and thereby reset the whole situation to zero, so to speak.

On the other hand, the older child similarly recognizes that something equivalent to situation zero can also be achieved by an action that compensates for or counterbalances the effects of another action, rather than one that literally undoes it in the manner of the inverse or opposite action just described. For example the child might justify his belief in conservation by pointing out that the increase in height of the liquid column which results from the pouring transformation is exactly offset or compensated for by the accompanying decrease in column width. According to this kind of reversible thinking, the column loses in width what it gains in height, and hence the quantity must remain the same. The width decrease obviously does not literally wipe out or annul the height increase, as actual repouring would. It has the same effect and cognitive significance (i.e., it provides a rational justification for a conservation verdict), but it does so by virtue of constituting an indirect compensation rather than a direct, literal negation. As with direct negation, the older child is more attuned than the younger one to the potential existence of such indirectly countervailing, compensation-type factors, and he better understands their utility in making rigorous quantitative inferences.

Other examples of these two forms of reversible thinking abound in Piagetiana. Conservation of length can be assessed by first placing two identical pencils (sticks, rods) side by side so that their ends exactly coincide and then, after the child agrees that they are equal in length, sliding one a bit to the right, so that its end leads or is ahead of the other's end on that side. The younger child focuses "irreversibly" on this "transformation"-produced, immediately perceptible "state" of the sticks ("temporal centration") and, within that state, equally irreversibly "centers" his attention on the right-hand portions of the sticks ("spatial centration"); mistaking "appearances" for "reality," he then concludes that the rightmost stick is now longer than its companion. (Whereby is it demonstrated that all four of the early-childhood–middle-childhood contrasts just discussed can be insinuated into a single sentence, although the use of the semicolon does admittedly represent a bit of fudging on our part.) In the same situation, the older conserver may exhibit reversible thinking, either by appealing to the results of the inverse, directly negating act of re-alignment of the pencils, or by suggesting that the length gained by the displaced stick at its right end is exactly compensated for by the length lost at its left end. These two types of concrete-operational reversibility are often referred to by Piagetians as *inversion* and *compensation*, respectively.

Qualitative versus Quantitative Thinking.   As we saw in Chapter 4, children do acquire some basic numerical skills during the preschool period. By 5 to 6 years of age, they also have mastered some simple measurement operations (Miller, 1989; Nunes & Bryant, 1996). Nevertheless most of what people come to know about mathematics and measurement is acquired after early childhood. A research example is Siegler's information-processing work on mathematical strategies described in Chapters 1 and 4. Older children have a more quantitative, measurement-oriented approach to many tasks and problems than younger children. The younger child's approach appears to have a more global, qualitative cast to it. The older child seems to understand better than the younger one that certain problems have precise, specific, potentially quantifiable solutions, and that these solutions may be attained by reasoning in conjunction with well-defined measurement operations.

The younger child often lacks the cognitive equipment to do other than guess or make simple perceptual estimates. In contrast the older child has come to understand that wholes are potentially divisible into unit parts of arbitrary size, and that these parts can serve as units of measurement in making a quantitative judgment about the whole.

Once again Piaget's conservation problems are useful in illustrating this difference between a qualitative, "guestimate"-minded approach and a quantitative, measurement-minded one. Six wooden matches are placed end-to-end but nonlinearly, so that they form a jagged, angular "road" on the table. An objectively shorter (e.g., only "five matches long") but perfectly straight stick representing a second road is placed directly above the first. Because it is straight, the crow's-flight distance between its endpoints is actually longer than the distance between the endpoints of the other, crooked road. Who makes the longest trip, the experimenter asks, the person who drives the entire length of the crooked road or the person who drives the entire length of the straight road? The second person, says the preschooler, centering only on the end points. The first person, says the fourth grader, carefully attending to what lies *between* the end points. Unlike the younger respondent, she recognizes that total lengths (distances, areas, volumes, etc.) are composed of, and are conceptually divisible into, subparts of any arbitrary desired magnitude. She understands that whole lengths are potentially fractionable into so-and-so many length segments of such-and-such size, or alternatively, into some different number of segments of any other, arbitrarily selected size. If asked to prove that the crooked road was actually longer than the straight road, appearances notwithstanding, she might, of course, simply straighten it out, align the two, and point to the difference. She might instead, however, use one of the matches as a convenient, preformed unit measure, and prove that the crooked road was "one match longer" than the straight one. Equivalently, she could use a ruler, or a meter stick, or a hairpin, or anything else that would allow her to arrive at a rigorous, exact, quantitative solution to the problem. Such a child, we would say, has a metric, genuinely quantitative conception of length. She has what Bearison (1969) has termed a "quantitative set," and it allows her to envision exact solutions to a variety of quantitative problems.

Quantification and measurement obviously do not apply only to one or a few specific knowledge domains. They are, as Carey (1985b) nicely puts it, "tools of wide application" to a range of situations. The ability to read is another such tool. The acquisition of these mental tools must indelibly color one's cognitive life (Flavell, 1982a).

Contrasts between Middle-Childhood and Adolescent-Adult Cognition

An experimenter and a subject face one another across a table strewn with poker chips of various solid colors (Osherson & Markman, 1975). The experimenter explains that he is going to say things about the chips and that the subject is to indicate whether what the experimenter *says* (i.e., his *statements*) is true, false, or uncertain ("can't tell"). He then conceals a chip in his hand and says, "Either the chip in my hand is green or it is not green," or, alternatively, "The chip in my hand is green and it is not green." On other trials he holds up either a green chip or a red chip so that the subject can see it and then makes exactly the same statements.

Middle-childhood participants are very likely to try to assess the truth value of these two assertions solely on the basis of the visual evidence. They focus on the concrete, empirical evidence concerning poker chips *themselves* rather than on the nonempirical, purely logical properties of the experimenter's *statements* about the poker chips. Consequently they say they "can't tell" on the trials in which the chip is hidden from view. When it is visible, both statements are judged to be true if the chip is green and false if it is red. In other words if the color (green) mentioned in the statement matches the color of the visible chip, the statement is said to be true; if there is a mismatch, it is judged false; and if the chip cannot be seen, its truth status is uncertain. What middle-childhood subjects fail to appreciate is that such "either-or" statements are always true and such "and" statements always false, regardless of the empirical evidence. Logicians call the former a *tautology* and the latter a *contradiction*, and they are true and false, respectively, solely by virtue of their formal properties as propositions.

Adolescent and adult subjects, on the other hand, are likelier to focus on the verbal assertions themselves, and to evaluate their internal validity as formal propositions. They appear to have a better intuition than do their younger counterparts of the distinction between abstract, purely logical relations and empirical relations. These more mature thinkers recognize that one can sometimes reason about propositions as such, instead of always "seeing right through them" to the entities and states of affairs to which they refer. Furthermore they realize that some propositions express *necessary* truths—things that not only are true but *have* to be true. "The chip in my hand is green" is a statement about empirical reality, and as such requires empirical evidence for its evaluation. "Either the chip in my hand is green or it is not green," however, is a logically necessary truth—no evidence is needed to confirm it, and no evidence could possibly disconfirm it.

An appreciation of the logical-empirical distinction and of the necessity of some forms of knowledge appears to be a gradual developmental achievement. Younger children are not totally lacking in such awareness, but the certainty and the breadth with which the distinction is drawn increase across the middle childhood and adolescent years. This conclusion applies to classically necessary logical truths of the sort studied by Osherson and Markman (Miller, Custer, & Nassau, in press; Morris & Sloutsky, 1998). It applies also to Piagetian tasks. Conservation and transitivity of weight, for example, are concrete-operational achievements within Piaget's stage framework. You are already familiar with the general form of the conservation task; when weight is the focus, a typical test presents two equal-weight clay balls, one of which is then transformed (rolled, flattened, etc.) so that they no longer look equal. Transitivity involves reasoning of the following sort: If A is shown to weigh the same as B and B is shown to weigh the same as C, then it follows that A and C also weigh the same. Similarly if A weighs more than B and B weighs more than C, then A must also weigh more than C. Miller and colleagues (Miller & Lipps, 1973; Miller, Schwartz, & Stewart, 1973) first verified that their participants had mastered these concepts by the usual measures and then put their understanding to a severe test: A rigged balance scale was used to present feedback that apparently violated the conservation or transitivity principle (an approach similar to the "impossible event" studies of infant cognition described in Chapter 3). Only a minority of elementary school participants continued to maintain their belief in conservation in the face of such disconfirming evidence; resistance was more impressive for transitivity, but even here some children succumbed to the false feedback. Older children and adults showed greater awareness that certain conclusions were primarily logical rather than empirical in origin, and thus could not be undone by empirical evidence. Recall from Chapter 4 that an appreciation of the necessity of class inclusion has also been shown to increase with development.

The studies of necessity provide further evidence for a point we have already seen: There often are developmental changes in particular competencies beyond the point when they first enter the system—that is, beyond the point when we can first talk of the child as "having" the knowledge in question. Thus both 8-year-olds and adults typically "have" conservation of weight, but the latter group's understanding may be more stable, more generalizable, and more imbued with feelings of necessity than is the former group's. We return to the issue of how to conceptualize levels or degrees of knowledge in the concluding chapter.

Real versus Possible.   Piaget argued that adolescents and adults tend to differ from children in the way they conceive of the relation between the real and the possible. The elementary school child's characteristic approach to many conceptual problems is to burrow right into the problem data as quickly as possible, using his various concrete-operational skills to order and interrelate whatever properties or features of the situation he can detect. His is an earthbound, concrete, practical-minded sort of problem-solving approach, one that persistently fixates on the perceptible and inferable reality right there in front of him. His conceptual approach is definitely not unintelligent, and it certainly generates solution attempts that are far more rational and task-relevant than anything the preoperational child is likely to produce. It does, however, hug the ground of detected empirical reality rather closely, and speculations about other possibilities—that is, about other potential, as yet undetected realities—occur only with difficulty and as a last resort. An ivory-tower theorist the elementary school child is not.

An adolescent or adult is likelier than an elementary school child to approach problems quite the other way around, at least when operating at the top of her capacity. The child usually begins with reality and moves reluctantly, if at all, to possibility; in contrast the adolescent or adult is more apt to begin with possibility and only subsequently proceed to reality. She may examine the problem situation carefully to try to determine what all the *possible* solutions or states of affairs might be, and then systematically try to discover which of these is, in fact, the *real* one in the present case. For the concrete-operational thinker, the realm of abstract possibility is seen as an uncertain and only occasional extension of the safer and surer realm of palpable reality. For the formal-operational thinker, on the other hand, reality is seen as that particular portion of the much wider world of possibility which happens to exist or hold true in a given problem situation. Possibility is subordinated to reality in the former case.

Empirico-Inductive versus Hypothetico-Deductive.   This subordination of the real to the possible expresses itself in a characteristic method of solving problems. The formal-operational thinker inspects the problem data, *hypothesizes* that such and such a theory or explanation might be the correct one, *deduces* from it that so and so empirical phenomena ought logically to occur or not occur in reality, and then tests her theory by seeing if these predicted phenomena do in fact occur. More informally put, she makes up a plausible story about what might be going on, figures out what would logically have to happen out there in reality if her story were the right one, checks or does experiments out there to see what does, in fact, happen, and then accepts, rejects, or revises her story accordingly. If you think you have just heard a description of textbook scientific reasoning, you are absolutely right. Because of its heavy trade in hypotheses and logical deductions from hypotheses, it is also called *hypothetico-deductive* reasoning, and it contrasts sharply with the much more nontheoretical and nonspeculative *empirico-inductive* reasoning of concrete-operational thinkers.

Notice that this kind of thinking begins with the possible rather than the real in two senses. First the thinker's initial theory is only one of a number of possible ones that she might have concocted. It is itself a possibility rather than a reality, and it is also only one possibility among many. Second the "empirical reality" predicted by or deduced from her initial theory is itself only a possibility, and also only one possibility among many. Actual, concrete reality only enters the scene when she tries to verify her theory by looking for the "reality" it has predicted. If it is not found, new theories and new theory-derived realities will be invented, and thus the sampling of possibilities continues.

What would really good, vintage hypothetico-deductive thinking sound like if it were verbalized aloud? Following are two made-up examples:

> Well, what I have just seen gives me the idea that W and *only W might* have the power to cause or produce Z, that the presence of X *might* prevent W from causing Z, and that Y *might* prove to be wholly irrelevant to the occurrence of Z. Now if this idea is right, then Z should occur *only* when W is present and X is absent, whether or not Y is also present. Let's see if these are, in fact, the only conditions under which Z does occur. . . . Oh no, that idea is shot down, because I've just found that Z also occurs sometimes when neither W nor X is present. I wonder why. Hey, I have another idea. . . .

> I am a college student of extremely modest means. Some crazy psychologist interested in something called "formal-operational thinking" has just promised to pay me $50 if I can make a coherent logical argument for the proposition that the federal government should under no circumstances ever give or loan money to impecunious college students. Now what could a nonperson who believed *that* possibly say by way of supporting argument? Well, I suppose he *could* offer this line of reasoning. . . .

Intrapropositional versus Interpropositional. The child of elementary school age can construct mental, symbolic representations of concrete reality and can also evaluate their empirical validity under many circumstances. He might, for example, quite explicitly formulate the proposition that there is still the same number of objects in the two rows after one has been spread out (number conservation test), and then he might prove it to you by counting the objects in each row. Thus middle-childhood subjects can produce, comprehend, and verify propositions. There is, nonetheless, an important difference between them and formal-operational subjects in the way they deal with propositions. The child considers them singly, in isolation from one another, testing each in its turn against the relevant empirical data. Because what is confirmed or inferred in each case is but a single claim about the external world, Piaget calls concrete-operational thinking *intrapropositional*— that is, thinking within the confines of a single proposition. Although a formal-operational thinker also naturally tests individual propositions against reality, she does something more that lends a very special quality to her reasoning. She reasons about the logical relations that hold *among* two or more propositions, a more subtle and abstract form of reasoning that Piaget terms *interpropositional*. The less mature mind looks only to the *factual* relation between one proposition and the empirical reality to which it refers; the more mature mind looks also or instead to the *logical* relation between one proposition and another.

The first of the two examples of hypothetico-deductive reasoning given in the previous section illustrates interpropositional reasoning particularly well. The individual's initial theory asserts ("proposes") that the logical relation called *conjunction* holds between three propositions: W is the sole cause of Z *and* (conjunction relation) X neutralizes W's causal effect *and* (conjunction relation) Y is not causally related to Z at all. Conjunction is also used to interconnect a set of hypothetical propositions or predictions about external reality: The conjunction of W present and X absent produces ("conjoins with") the presence of Z, and none of the other logically possible conjunctions involving the presence or absence of W and X will yield Z. Moreover the conjunction of Y's presence or absence with the foregoing changes nothing. There are other logical relations that our imaginary subject might also apply to various combinations of these propositions, although she would not necessarily use the logician's terminology in describing them. For instance, she would understand that, within her theory, the presence of Z (one proposition) *implies* (logical relation) the presence of W (another proposition), whereas the reverse implication, W implies Z, does not hold due to the *incompatibility* (logical relation) between X and Z. Above all the "if . . . then" phrasing in her second sentence shows that she knows that the entire complex of conjoined propositions which constitutes her theory logically *implies* the entire complex of conjoined propositions which constitutes her predicted reality. That is, she establishes a logical relation between two *sets* of propositions, the constituent propositions of each of which she has already knitted together by logical connectives. This is certainly "interpropositional" thinking in the fullest sense.

It should now be clear why this kind of reasoning is also called *formal*. To reason that one proposition "logically implies" ("contradicts," etc.) another is fundamentally to reason about the relation between a pair of *statements*, not about any *empirical phenomena* to which these statements might refer. The statements in question may not be factually correct assertions about the real objects and events to which they refer; they may not refer to real objects and events in the first place; or indeed they may not even refer to anything at all, real or imaginary. It is now apparent why the Osherson and Markman (1975) questions might differentiate a formal reasoner from a concrete one. The formal reasoner knows that the experimenter is asking about the logical truth or falsity of pairs of statements as a joint function of what they state (affirmation, negation) and how they are logically linked (conjunction, disjunction); she knows that the experimenter is not really asking anything about the color of chips. As Piaget put it, whereas concrete operations are "first-degree" operations that deal with real objects and events, formal operations are "second-degree" operations that deal with the propositions or statements produced by the first-degree, concrete ones (Inhelder & Piaget, 1958, p. 254).

The second of the two hypothetical hypothetico-deductive reasoners described in the previous section illustrates a closely related insight—namely that one does not have to believe something is either true or just in order to argue for it (although it sure helps). Formal-operational thinkers understand that logical arguments have a disembodied and passionless life of their own, at least in principle. Concrete-operational thinkers have enough trouble seeing what logically follows from credible premises, let alone from premises that actually contradict one's knowledge, beliefs, or values.

Researchers are still clarifying the nature of formal operational thinking. For useful discussions of various issues in this area, see Byrnes (1988a, 1988b), Keating (1988), Moshman (1998), and Overton (1990). Flieller (1999) provides an interesting recent examination of performance on formal-operational tasks—including the heartening finding that average performance has improved across the last 25 years.

REASONING: OTHER PERSPECTIVES

Although Piaget's work formed the foundation for the study of children's reasoning, and some researchers today continue within his framework, other work has broadened our thinking about how children reason about the world. Piaget compared children's thinking with formal operational hypothetico-deductive reasoning, characteristic of scientists, logicians, and many other adults on at least some tasks, some of the time. More recent approaches tend to look at the role of knowledge and context in reasoning much more than did Piaget (see DeLoache, Miller, & Pierrout-sakos, 1998; Moshman, 1998; and Scholnick, 1999). As in other chapters, we see that much of reasoning and problem solving is domain specific. In general, post-Piagetian research finds that adults often are less rational than Piaget believed and that children sometimes are more rational than he believed.

Reasoning typically involves inference—going beyond the information given to derive new information. This reasoning can be formal, as in the propositional logic studied by Piaget, or can be of the informal "everyday" sort. Whereas formal logic is devoid of content (if A = B, and B = C, then A = C), informal reasoning is full of content for it is imbedded in the everyday activities involved in just trying to get through the day. Formal reasoning tends to involve necessary truths; informal reasoning tends to involve probable or likely truths. We focus on informal reasoning to provide a contrast with Piaget's work on formal reasoning.

Similarity-Based Reasoning

We humans would be poor reasoners and problem solvers (as well as very tired ones) if we treated every situation as something completely new. If you had to make sense of something that is foreign to you, you probably would look for some similarity between this foreign something and that which you already understand, and reason about the novel situation on that basis. You might draw on perceptual similarity. Reasoning that "if B looks like A, it probably is somewhat like A" leads to an accurate conclusion much of the time. As DeLoache, Miller, et al. (1998, p. 806) comment, "Most dogs look and sound more like other dogs than they look and sound like cows, cats, or clarinets. A similarity heuristic thus gets one into the conceptual ballpark and usually to first base as well." Or, if the novel object has a familiar label, you probably would reason that, even though it does not look like objects you know that are given that label, it probably is like those objects in some important way. Do children also reason in this way? Consider the following "blicket detector" study by Gopnik and Sobel (2000).

A 3-year-old is shown 4 blocks—2 referred to as "blickets" and two as "not blickets." He watches as one of the "blickets" is placed on the machine, which immediately lights up and plays "You Are My Sunshine." He then is asked to show the experimenter another block that would set the machine off. On some trials the causal power conflicts with perceptual properties of the object; for example, two of the blocks look the same but one is a blicket and one is not. The 3-year-old, and in fact many 2-year-olds, predicts that only the blickets will make the machine light up, even when he has to choose a block that looks different from the demonstrated blicket over a block that looks like the blicket. Thus even very young children can make a simple inference that a novel object sharing a label with a known object will have a similar property. Chapter 4 provided other examples of how young children use conceptual similarity between a familiar and novel item to infer that they belong to the same category and thus have similar properties. What is particularly interesting about the blicket detector study is that even very young children were able to do inferential reasoning based on a causal relation. Causal power, what the object can do to something else, is a dynamic property that is not directly observable rather than a static perceptual property such as a similar color or shape.

Even young babies, however, detect certain perceptual and conceptual similarities and react to the novel but similar object as though it were somewhat like the familiar one (see Chapters 2 and 3). As the above study shows, after infancy these inferences become more complex.

DeLoache, Miller, et al. (1998) identify several other types of early similarity-based reasoning. For example, in the symbolic realm children learn to infer from a relation within a symbol to a relation within a real object or array. Chapter 4 provided several examples, such as reasoning from a map to a real town, or from a model room to a real room. Children learn that symbols and objects share some properties (e.g., spatial relations) but not others (e.g., a picture of a toy cannot be picked off the page). A final sort of similarity-based reasoning is analogical reasoning. Because this has been an active area of research in recent years, we look at it in more depth.

Analogical Reasoning

If we could not engage in analogical reasoning, we would not be able to understand and enjoy poetry; we could not see that a person choosing the road less traveled is like a person selecting the less popular "path" in life. Fortunately we are able to draw analogies between a familiar setting and a novel one. Research described in Chapter 3 showed that even infants can reason by analogy in very simple ways. For example (Chen et al., 1997), 10- to12-month-olds learned, from watching their parent, to remove a barrier (a box), pull a blue cloth to reach a black string on it, then pull the string to get a red car they wanted (see the third problem in Figure 5.1). They transferred this set of relations to problems that looked quite different from the original one, for example, a multicolored horse as the goal, a brown string, an orange-and-white striped cloth, and a blue box. To succeed they also had to ignore another cloth with a string that was not attached to the target object. Thus infants can apply their causal reasoning to a conceptually analogous situation (see Goswami, 1996, for additional experimental examples).

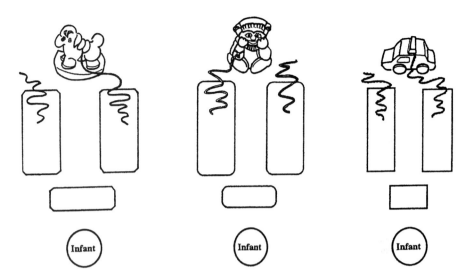

FIGURE 5.1   The configuration of the three problems involving analogical
thinking that 1-year-olds solved. From "From Beyond to Within
Their Grasp: The Rudiments of Analogical Problem Solving in 10-
and 13-month-olds," by Z. Chen, R. P. Sanchez, and T. Campbell,
1997, *Developmental Psychology, 33,* p. 792. Copyright © 1997
by American Psychological Association. Reprinted by permission.

Children's growing knowledge base after infancy greatly expands the relations that they can map analogically from one array to another. In a more classical
analogy format, 24-month-olds can map a "broken-to-fixed" relation (Freeman,
McKie, & Bauer, 1994). The experimenter first showed that a broken umbrella went
with an intact umbrella, and a broken piece of wood with a whole piece. Then children saw a broken eggshell and chose from the following array: the correct object
(whole eggshell), the correct transformation but wrong object (whole umbrella), or
the correct object but wrong transformation (broken eggshell strung on a string).
Importantly, the children were able to ignore perceptual similarity and choose the
whole eggshell. Later, preschoolers can use their knowledge of the *Goldilocks and
the Three Bears* story to solve a transitive inference analogy. They could use Daddy
Bear, Mommy Bear, and Baby Bear, with their "boiling hot," "hot," or "warm"
bowls of porridge, to represent big, middle-size, and little (Goswami, 1995; see also
Goswami, 1996). For example, if the experiment chose a middle-size plastic cup
("Mommy Bear") from his array of three cups, the child chose the middle-size cup
from her array of three cups. She could do this even though this required choosing a
cup of a different absolute size from the experimenter's middle cup, and she had to
ignore her smallest cup which was the same absolute size as the experimenter's
middle cup.

From these early competencies, it might seem that Piaget was wrong that children do not acquire analogical reasoning until the formal operational period of adolescence. As usual, though, this cognitive skill goes through a long period of

development from its first demonstration in a very simple setting in infancy to its final abstract, complex, stable, and verbally explained form in adolescence. Gentner, for instance, suggests that the ability to reason about perceptual similarity between objects such as a ball rolling on a table and a toy car rolling on the floor precedes the ability to reason about conceptual similarity. In the latter a relation such as an apple falling from a tree *permitting* a cow to reach it is analogous to a book falling from a table *permitting* a child to reach it (e.g., Gentner & Rattermann, 1991). Even smart adults sometimes fail analogies because they lack the requisite domain-specific knowledge. An example from DeLoache, Miller, et al. (1998) is the following analogy that few adults can solve: "beat" is to "45 degrees" as "reach" is to ——. We would not conclude from your silence that you cannot do analogical reasoning; instead we would assume that you do not know enough about sailing (nor do we) to give the answer—"90 degrees."

For various accounts of the development of analogical reasoning, see Gentner (Gentner, Rattermann, Markman, & Kotovsky, 1995), Goswami (1996), and Halford (1993). Together these reviews show both changes in analogical reasoning ability per se and its application due to growing knowledge, capacity, and metacognitive knowledge (see also DeLoache, Miller, et al., 1998). Clearly, there is a two-way street between the two developmentally. Knowledge supports the use of emerging analogical reasoning skills; analogical reasoning in turn makes possible new, and more abstract, knowledge as children detect increasingly abstract relations in the world.

Causal Reasoning

In one way or another, much of what we cover in this book involves causal reasoning. Chapter 3 described infants' rudimentary understanding of physical causality, as when they infer causality when one block makes contact with a second block, immediately followed by movement by the second block. In the "blickets" study described earlier, young preschoolers inferred causality from temporal and spatial contiguity when placing a blicket on a machine "caused" it to light up and play music. Chapters 4 and 6 describe how children's theories of biology and psychology involve causal relations, for example, "He is looking for a cookie because he wants it." Preschoolers also understand the causal relation among events in their everyday scripts. Casual reasoning continues to develop through adolescence and even adulthood (see Moshman, 1998, for a review). We now turn to a form of reasoning of great interest to developmentalists today—scientific thinking.

SCIENTIFIC THINKING

Piaget's pioneering work mapped out much of the cognitive change in reasoning—both as "pure logic" and as scientific concepts and reasoning. His work had enormous impact and his account of scientific concepts such as time, speed, distance, conservation, physical causality, density, and space is still being examined and refined today. More recent research by other investigators has identified additional developmental trends in scientific concepts and reasoning that must be incorporated into a satisfactory account of cognitive development. We look at both the nature of these concepts and how they change, as well as the process of scientific thinking.

Scientific Concepts

An 8-month-old infant looks longer at the impossible event of a toy car apparently rolling on tracks through a box placed on the tracks than at a possible event of the car rolling by a box placed by the tracks (Chapter 3). A 17-month-old intentionally varies the manner in which she drops a toy, and attends with interest to the outcome (Chapter 3). A 4-year-old knows that a rabbit raised by monkeys will still prefer carrots to bananas (Chapter 4). A 5-year-old claims that simply pouring a glass of juice into a taller, thinner glass can result in more juice, whereas a 7-year-old does not (discussed earlier in this chapter). All five children seem to have implicit, intuitive notions about the nature of objects and substances and how they typically behave. More generally, as discussed in Chapter 4, children appear to have naive theories in at least three areas—physics, biology, and psychology (Wellman & Gelman, 1998).

The metaphor of child-as-intuitive-scientist pervades the field of cognitive development. This view derives from Piaget's theory, the theory theory approach, and the information-processing approach (Chapter 1). According to this metaphor, cognitive development is a progression toward "better" thinking, with the "better" defined as "like a scientist." In this view children try to make sense of their physical environments by constructing mental models (some developmentalists would say causal-explanatory "theories") of some sort that account for the everyday physical events they observe. Like a scientist "wannabe," they revise these mental models as new evidence arises and substitute new theories for old ones.

Developmental change in scientific theories can be placed along a continuum from weak to strong restructuring (Carey, 1991, 1999). At the weak end, the child simply enriches his or her theory; the child may create new relations among its components or make new differentiations, but the theory maintains its core assumptions. For example, a 10-year-old sees more relations among processes such as growing, eating, dying, and having babies than does a 4-year-old (Carey, 1985a). At the other end of the continuum, in strong restructuring the child changes the core concepts or assumptions of the theory so that the old and new theories are *incommensurate* (i.e., incompatible). The new theory does not just revise the earlier theory but truly replaces it, similar to the historical change from phlogiston to oxygen theories of burning. In fact Carey (1985a) and others have argued that there are parallels between developmental changes in intuitive scientific theories and historical changes in the field of science. An example of strong theory change is elementary school-age children's models of the earth's shape and motion (Samarapungavan, Vosniadou, & Brewer, 1996; Vosniadou & Brewer, 1992). In an attempt to reconcile their daily experience of living on an apparently flat world and information from adults and books that the world is round, they come up with various theories. Examples are an earth shaped like a rectangle or a flattened disk or, remarkably, a dual-earth model in which the "world" is a flat surface and the "earth" is a spherical planetary body floating above us in space. Children holding this dual earth position point upward when asked to point to the earth!

We find children's naive intuitive scientific theories intriguing, especially in the realm of physics, in that infants are surprisingly knowledgeable and older children and adults are surprisingly unknowledgeable. Work by Spelke and others in Chapter 3 showed that infants know a great deal about the physical integrity and behavior of objects. Yet older children and adults hold many blatantly wrong theories of physics. Here are some examples:

1. The majority of sixth graders, and even many adults, think that when a person sees an object, energy or rays go out from the eyes a la Superman (Winer & Cottrell, 1991; Winer, Cottrell, Karefilaki, & Chronister, 1996).
2. Grade-school children often predict that a ball exiting from a curved tube will continue in a curved path based on a persistence-of-motion theory, whereas preschool children correctly predict a straight line (Kaiser, McCloskey, & Proffitt, 1986).
3. Children and even college students believe that when a race car travels around an oval track both car doors move at the same speed, ignoring the fact that the outer door is covering more distance in the same time (Levin, Siegler, & Druyan, 1990).
4. Both 11-year-olds and a sizeable minority of college students erroneously believe that an object dropped from a moving train falls straight downward from its release point, rather than in front of it (Kaiser, Proffitt, & McCloskey, 1985).

These intuitive scientists seem to overextend their everyday theories of physics. For example, in the third example children hold the "single-object/single-motion" theory that all parts of a single object must move at the same speed. This theory is accurate in many situations, such as movement in a straight line, but does not hold in certain other situations, such as the one described here.

It is important for educators to realize that students come to the classroom with *mis*conceptions of science, as opposed to *no* conceptions. These misconceptions can be remarkably resistant to instruction. Instruction often is not just a matter of teaching new information; it also involves correcting old beliefs—often by showing that the child's beliefs work in some situations but not others—or removing old beliefs and replacing them with new ones. The latter is an example of Carey's strong restructuring described earlier. An entire theoretical system of interconnected beliefs must be replaced.

Process of Scientific Thinking

Although it may be useful to use the metaphor of children and lay adults as intuitive scientists with "theories" of scientific phenomena, the metaphor may be misleading with respect to the *process* of scientific thinking because children and many lay adults do not appear to think like scientists (sometimes scientists don't either!). The essence of scientific thinking is the coordination of theories and evidence. There are two phases (Kuhn & Pearsall, 2000; see Klahr, 2000, for a related distinction). In the *investigative* phase, a person designs experiments to test a theory; in the *inferential* phase, a person interprets the resulting evidence as supporting or refuting the theory and, if necessary, considers alternative explanations.

Over both phases children and even lay adults appear to be flawed scientific thinkers in three main ways (Carey, 1999; DeLoache, Miller, et al., 1998; Klaczynski & Narasimhan, 1998; Klahr, 2000; Kuhn, Garcia-Mila, Zohar, & Andersen, 1995; Kuhn & Pearsall, 2000; Schauble, 1996). First, they tend to be *theory bound*. Unlike scientists, children and lay adults fail to distinguish conclusions based on observations from conclusions based on their prior beliefs or theories. That is, they often either ignore discrepant evidence, or attend to it in a selective, distorting way. They sometimes adjust evidence to fit their theories; the processing of evidence is biased toward a favored theory, especially if the evidence supports an explanation that seems implausible to them. This occurred in a study (Kuhn, Amsel, & O'Loughlin, 1988) in which adults were given evidence that there was no correlation between the kind of candy bar or the type of relish children eat and how likely they are to catch colds. Of adults who entered the study with the notion that kind of relish was causal and kind of candy bar was not, many interpreted the identical pattern of evidence (no correlation) as supporting their theories—correctly in the case of candy bars and incorrectly in the case of relish (e.g., they thought the evidence showed that mustard co-occurred with colds). These adults focused on the coincidental cases when mustard co-occurred with colds and ignored the cases in which mustard co-occurred with no colds.

Thus children and often even lay adults do not adequately differentiate evidence and a theory; they have trouble setting aside their own theory and viewing the evidence as separate from any theory. They have trouble understanding what it means to test an idea and even have trouble thinking of what kind of evidence would refute their theories. As a result, when they are asked to generate evidence to show that their theory is correct or incorrect, they simply restate their theory or give illustrations of the theory rather than refer to existing or potential evidence that stands alone from the theory and could test it. Relatedly, children misinterpret the task of hypothesis testing as generating an effect predicted by the theory rather than producing negative as well as positive evidence or testing alternative explanations. People must learn that data and theory are different before they can coordinate them. This poor differentiation of theory and evidence seems to occur mainly when the child or adult already has a favored theory and when several potential causes exist. Again we hear echoes from a recurring theme of this book that prior knowledge constrains thinking and learning.

When children have no preconceived notions, for instance, when they must decide whether a mouse in a house is large or small, even first and second graders can differentiate the evidence from a hypothesis (Sodian, Zaitchik, & Carey, 1991, but see Kuhn & Pearsall, 2000, and Ruffman, Perner, Olson, & Doherty, 1993). You do not have to be a Sherlock Holmes to draw the proper conclusion about whether a mouse is large or small when you use a mouse food box with a small hole (too small for a large mouse to enter) and note the disappearance of the food overnight. Other features of this study may have facilitated hypothesis testing as well. The children did not have to design their own experiments, which seems to be particularly difficult for them. In addition a single conclusive comparison, rather than a pattern of covariation, which entails greater complexity, could test the hypothesis. Although even infants, and certainly preschoolers, have some understanding of causality, they have trouble applying it in complex situations—and, the world being the way it is, situations typically are complex.

Another way that people are theory bound is that they hold their theories with certainty. In fact, of course, evidence can only make a theory probable because future evidence could disconfirm the theory. Half of the adolescents and adults in one study (Kuhn, 1990) believed that complex questions such as why prisoners become repeat offenders can be answered with complete certainty.

A second blatant flaw in scientific reasoning, in addition to being theory bound, is that children and many lay adults tend to be *data-bound*. Young children are able to draw an appropriate conclusion from the most recent result, but tend to ignore the entire earlier set of discrepant and congruent results. Older children and adults can consider more information. Third, children and adults appear to *need theories*, and perhaps even require them. When contradictory evidence mounts and can no longer be ignored, they will finally acknowledge the evidence, but only after they can generate an alternate theory to explain this contradictory evidence (e.g., some plausible way that certain types of relishes could increase resistance to cold germs). As argued earlier they do not seem to be able to deal with evidence independently of a theory. They need a plausible causal link between a factor and its results before they can accept the data.

A study by Schauble (1990) illustrates these three conclusions. She presented 9- to 11-year-olds with a computer microworld in which they were to determine the effect, if any, of five factors on the speed of racing cars. Initially children believed that a large engine, large wheels, and the presence of a muffler increase speed. They discounted tailfins or the color of the car. The microworld was set up so that a large engine and medium-size wheels increased speed, muffler and color were irrelevant, and absence of tailfins increased speed only when the engine was large. Over eight sessions the children could learn about the cars by putting whatever features they wished on different cars and seeing how fast they went. Pristine scientific procedure would dictate holding all variables constant except for one, and repeating this method for each factor. Not surprisingly given Piaget's work on concrete operational thinking, the children often failed to follow this procedure, frequently varying several factors at once. More interesting was the fact that even when children performed valid experiments they often drew conclusions from the results that were inconsistent with the results but consistent with their initial beliefs. Moreover, even after correctly predicting the effect of a factor and seeing the prediction confirmed, they were reluctant to abandon their previous beliefs until they could generate an alternative theory that could account for the unexpected observation. Finally, in their research journals not a single subject recorded covariation information (i.e., features and speed), the most essential information. Some recorded only features and others recorded only outcomes and some recorded neither. Thus the children did not even seem to know what they needed to know to solve the problem. On the more positive side, the children showed some improvement in their thinking over the sessions (see also Schauble, 1996).

Although these nonscientific ways of conducting experiments become less prevalent during the grade-school years, they show little change after about age 15 and are common even in adults. Still, it is important to point out that much of the problem lies in having to design appropriate experiments oneself. Children are considerably better at selecting an appropriately controlled scientific test from among those offered than at producing a controlled test themselves (Bullock & Ziegler, 1999). This finding shows that they *understand* the logic of experimental control but have trouble applying this knowledge in complex situations (see also Klahr, 2000).

In Kuhn's view (e.g., Kuhn & Pearsall, 2000), people must possess a metacognitive awareness of their own thought processes before they can gain control over the interaction between theory and evidence in their thinking. She argues that people must think *about* their theories rather than just *with* them (see also Moshman, 1998). If people are not aware that their theories are just theories, they are unlikely to monitor carefully how well they are supported by evidence. For scientific reasoning it is necessary to develop a metacognitive understanding of the nature of logic and its limits, and of why some mental strategies are better than others and what their range of application is (for additional empirical support, see Bullock & Ziegler, 1999). In other words, scientific thinkers understand, monitor, and direct their own higher order reasoning. Instruction based on these principles improves the scientific reasoning of children and adults (Kuhn et al., 1995; but see Chen & Klahr, 1999). Moreover, people sometimes can transfer what they learn from one type of problem to another, such as from determining what factors affect the speed of a boat moving through water to determining what factors affect student achievement in school.

Some of the most important developmental questions about scientific reasoning can be answered only by longitudinal studies, which are quite rare. In one such study (Bullock & Ziegler, 1999), children were followed from the third through sixth grades. They were asked to design a study to test a particular problem, for example, constructing an efficient airplane based on several dimensions (pointed versus rounded nose, placement of rudders, single versus double wings) that might make a difference. The content of the problems varied from one testing time to another, but all involved the need to hold all dimensions but one constant. The best predictors of understanding the logic of scientific testing (i.e., selecting a controlled experiment) in the younger children were general cognitive abilities—intelligence and memory span. The latter suggests that having adequate capacity to deal with a large amount of information may be critical, as we describe in a later section on problem solving. Later on, cognitive skills more specific to scientific reasoning, such as science metaconceptual knowledge, the understanding of indeterminacy, and combinatory reasoning, also became predictors of selecting and producing controlled experiments. Thus this longitudinal study makes the important point that when we look for influences on a cognitive skill we should keep in mind that different influences are critical at different developmental points. Until a child has certain basic cognitive resources, such as adequate capacity, more specific knowledge or skills may have little chance of being applied successfully. The longitudinal design also permitted a look at individual patterns of developmental change. It was interesting that "those who were already blessed received more" (p. 48). Those children whose scientific reasoning was better initially improved over the years at a faster rate and ended up at a higher level than those who were less skilled.

If we dare act as though we are scientists rather than lay adults, and thus claim immunity to the above pitfalls, we would use all the above facts to come to the following conclusions. The development of scientific reasoning involves basic cognitive resources (e.g., capacity), domain-specific content knowledge (e.g., beliefs about natural phenomena), and domain-general reasoning—designing useful experiments and drawing evidence-based conclusions (Klahr, 2000; Schauble, 1996). Domain-general scientific reasoning is quite difficult, for adults as well as for children. This reasoning process is most difficult when people have preexisting theories about the phenomenon and the evidence contradicts these theories, when the theory that the evidence supports is implausible, when they must design their own experiments, and when they must test several possible causes.

It appears that thinking about a phenomenon in one way often precludes thinking about it in any other way. This begins to sound like the sort of thinking that is involved in children's theory of mind (Chapter 6). Just as 3-year-olds have trouble understanding false beliefs because they would have to entertain two different representations of the same reality, so do they and much older children (and adults in many situations) have trouble constructing or even entertaining two contradictory theories of the same set of data. Relatedly they have trouble seeing that their pet theory might actually be a false belief. Although 4- to-6-year-olds have some understanding that theories differ from evidence, they "exhibit an epistemological category mistake regarding the source of knowledge. They confuse a theory making it plausible that an event occurred (based on their preexisting beliefs) and evidence indicating that the event did occur (based on observed data), as the source of their knowing that the event occurred" (Kuhn & Pearsall, 2000, p. 113). Children must understand that theory and evidence come from distinct epistemological categories before they can be said to be doing scientific reasoning. For other accounts of scientific reasoning see Klahr (2000—e.g., discovery in a microworld of how to make a BigTrak device in dragon costume "breathe fire") and Koslowski (1996).

PROBLEM SOLVING

Sometimes we seek problems, just for the joy of solving a crossword puzzle or for the sense of achievement of meeting a challenge in our jobs. More often in life, problems seek us. Because children have less experience than do adults, they often cannot automatically understand a situation because it is new to them. Thus they must often engage in problem solving; they bring their knowledge and skills to a particular problem and attempt to solve it. Reasoning on both Piagetian and other scientific tasks obviously involves problem solving. In addition researchers have studied the ability to detect and solve problems more broadly in recent years. We provide a sampling of these research programs (see Ellis & Siegler, 1994, and DeLoache, Miller, et al., 1998, for other examples).

Problem solving is a goal-directed cognitive activity. The goal can be general, such as understanding something, or can be quite specific, such as solving a maze. Some approaches to problem solving are very general and can be applied in a number of situations. Examples are trial and error, and trying to figure out which of various possible means lead to the goal and, if necessary, creating subgoals.

Problem Solving of Infants and Toddlers

If problem solving involves trying to reach some goal, then infants obviously cannot be said to try to solve problems until they have the notion of cause and effect, cognitively separate means from ends, and learn to engage in goal-directed behavior. Both Piagetian work and contemporary work on infants' problem solving described in Chapter 3 show that these skills are acquired, in a rudimentary way, in the first year of life. For example, recall that Willatts (1989) showed that 9-month-olds could push aside a foam-block barrier in order to pull a cloth on which an out-of-reach toy rested. They hit on this insight immediately; no trial and error was necessary. Note that this almost looks like planning, which we discuss later. Because not everything we want in life is conveniently placed on cloths that we can pull toward us, problem solving soon gets much more complicated.

Recent evidence suggests that there is not a "great divide" between the problem solving of the infant-toddler years and later years (Chen & Siegler, 2000). Specifically, on a task solved by using a hooked tool to pull a toy toward oneself, similar to that used by Brown (1989) and described in Chapter 3, toddlers aged 18 months or 30 months show the same sorts of processes of problem solving as do older children on very different sorts of tasks. That is, at all ages children acquire new strategies, strengthen them so they are used consistently, and transfer them to novel problems. They also gradually refine their choices among variants of the strategies (increasingly pick the best tool) and improve their execution of the strategies. Siegler's overlapping waves model described for older children in Chapter 1 also characterizes toddlers' problem solving (overlapping wavelets?). Toddlers use several problem solving strategies from the beginning, including not only various tools but also leaning forward and reaching for the toy, asking their parent for help, or the less industrious approach of just sitting and staring at the toy in the hope that it will be given to them. Also like older children, they continue to use less useful strategies even after they have learned a better one.

Although people of all ages rely on external, sensorimotor sorts of problem solving, during development children become increasingly able to engage in more complex, purely mental sorts of problem solving. Children solve problems ranging from solving a math problem to finding the shortest route to a friend's house to figuring out how to get an older sibling away from a new computer game. Next we look at some of the resources that permit more advanced problem solving after infancy and toddlerhood.

Resources and Skills for the Development of Problem Solving

One important resource, particularly from the perspective of the information-processing approach described in Chapter 1, is an increase in information-processing capacity. Because this capacity is closely related to short-term memory, we save our discussion of it for Chapter 7. At this point we just note that because effective problem solving requires keeping in mind the goal and sometimes several subgoals, accessing several possible means to the goal and selecting one or several of these means, and monitoring progress toward the goal, it obviously is helpful to possess a cognitive system that does not "crash" under all of these demands. Similarly the discussion of strategies in Chapter 7 also pertains here, for nearly all attempts to achieve some goal during problem solving involve using several strategies, sometimes in concert. Other developing skills, already discussed, also contribute to problem solving: mental representation of the problem "space" (as information-processing inclined researchers say), use of external representations such as sketches or models to plan out possible approaches, culturally given cognitive tools such as language and a writing system, and analogical or scientific reasoning to generate or test possible solutions. These resources help children apply their knowledge and skills already discussed to solve problems. We now look at some other resources that we have only mentioned in passing in this book thus far.

Domain-Specific Knowledge (Expertise). One obvious source of help for problem solving is that various knowledge structures (e.g., naïve theories of physics, biology, and mind) and concepts (e.g., of number) continue to develop. Consequently they become increasingly accessible for problem solving. We have seen that the period of time between first budding and final blooming of a cognitive acquisition, between first fragile emergence and final stable form, can be surprisingly long. Moreover competencies may become linked with other competencies to form larger systems of interrelated knowledge and skills. Competencies may also become more accessible to conscious reflection and verbal expression (Karmiloff-Smith, 1992), so that children can explain how they solved the problem. Such changes may constitute or engender further development of these competencies. For example, once we become able to reflect on and deliberate about the distinction between natural kinds and other kinds (see Chapter 4), we may become capable of generating new ideas about the distinction and of identifying new and more subtle instances of it. All these changes enrich problem solving.

A recurring theme of this book has been that much of children's growing knowledge seems to be specific to a certain domain rather than available for all domains. This is true for problem solving as well. Much of the improvement in problem solving comes from knowing more and more about specific problem domains. Researchers are painstakingly trying to build up, through careful research, a precise and detailed picture of exactly what the acquisition of expertise in a domain does to and for our heads (e.g., Johnson & Mervis, 1994, 1998).

Chi and Glaser (1980; Glaser & Chi, 1988) make a rough distinction between two components of human information processing relevant to expertise: (1) a knowledge structure or content component that can be conceptualized as a network of concepts and relations—"what you know"; and (2) a set of processes or strategies for performing a sequence of cognitive actions on the content—"what you do." Chi and Glaser identify several novice-expert differences within the knowledge structure or content component in the domain of elementary physics, a richly structured area of knowledge. First and most obvious, the physics expert simply knows more different domain-specific concepts than does the novice. Whereas the novice might be able to define and recognize a few concepts such as mass, density, and acceleration, the expert also commands many others (e.g., force, momentum, coefficient of friction). Moreover a physics expert can represent physics problems at a deeper, more abstract, and causal level. The expert may, for example, categorize together problems on the basis of a physics principle, such as the conservation of energy, rather than a surface similarity, such as the presence of coiled springs.

In addition the expert's stored representation of each concept is apt to be richer than the novice's, in that it contains more conceptual relations and features. For the novice mass may only be represented as related to the concepts of weight and density. In contrast, the expert's mental representation of mass may additionally include acceleration, force, and other related concepts. This means that each of the expert's concepts is closely connected in long-term memory with many other concepts. As a consequence there are multiple routes from each concept to each other concept in the expert's stored conceptual network; we might say that each concept is multiply cross-referenced in the expert's mental dictionary of physics concepts. These multiple interconnections make it likely that thinking of any one concept will cue the retrieval from memory of related concepts and concept features. Consistent with this claim is Larkin's (1979) finding that an expert in physics is more likely than a novice to recall small groups of conceptually related equations in rapid bursts, with pauses in between groups, as if related equations were stored together as chunks in the expert's long-term memory.

We turn now to the second component—differences between novices and experts in the cognitive processes or strategies they use in solving problems. For example, experts are apt to be more planful. They are more likely to analyze and categorize a problem before attempting to solve it. This initial processing may then provide the expert with an effective plan of action to execute in the actual solution of the problem. Here also the expert's vast and richly organized memory store of knowledge gives her many advantages over the novice. For instance a very effective way to solve a new problem is to notice its similarity to some other problem that one already knows how to solve. The noticing is partly a matter of memory (recognition memory) and so is the knowing how to solve it (stored procedural knowledge). Obviously this "memory method" of solving problems can be used much more often by the expert than by the novice because the expert has, over many years, gradually acquired the ability to recognize and respond adaptively to a surprisingly large number of domain-relevant problem patterns. For example, the work of Herbert Simon and his colleagues suggests that chess experts have learned to recognize and react appropriately to some 50,000 chessboard patterns (Anderson, 1980).

We usually think of the expert as more able to reason—to engage in extended chains of complex inferences or judgments (within his area of expertise) and fancy computation—than the novice. However, it also is true that experts often solve problems rather automatically. They quickly and easily remember solutions that novices must try to solve by slow and laborious reasoning. In such instances the expert appears more cognitively mature and sophisticated than the novice because the expert's mental processing is so fast, effortless, and effective. In reality, however, the expert's processing may have been more "mnemonic" than "rational" in nature. And, of course, the expert's processing was not fast, effortless, and effective *despite* the fact that it involved "mere remembering" rather than "sophisticated ratiocination." Rather it had these qualities precisely *because* of this fact—that is, because it involves the relatively automatic processes of detecting familiar problem patterns and executing overlearned solution procedures. Thus, if one benefit of expertise is the ability to think better in the area of one's expertise, another is the ability to solve many problems in that area without having to think much at all. Even in the social realm, a vast store of organized social knowledge allows us to recognize and respond appropriately to a very large number of specific patterns of input from our everyday "social chessboard." This memory-based pattern-recognition process often allows us to behave reasonably in many complex social situations without benefit of much, if any, complex social reasoning.

Expert knowledge appears to facilitate problem solving not only by supplying ready-made solutions or strategies but also by freeing mental capacity. When concepts, technical terms, problem patterns, and other domain-specific data are highly familiar, they require less time and mental energy to process. This in turn means that more of them can be attended to or held in working memory at one time, effectively increasing the person's attentional or short-term memory capacity. This increase in capacity has at least two beneficial effects. First, because more units of information can be held in focal attention or working memory at the same time, more of them can be compared and related to one another. Complex tasks often demand the active interrelating of a number of dimensions or other pieces of information. Second, this functional increase in information-processing capacity creates some unused mental work space or mental energy that can be devoted to higher level "executive" or "metacognitive" processing. The person has some capacity left over for selecting problem-solving strategies, for regulating their activity, for monitoring their effectiveness, and for other vital managerial activities.

Chi and Glaser's depiction of adult domain-specific expertise works for children as well. Much of this book is about the domains in which children and adolescents build up complex knowledge structures through years of experience and learning. Children do better on a task when they know something about it, when they are familiar with the content. We make this point at length in our later chapter on memory (Chapter 7), for example, the fact that child experts in some domain, such as chess, remember better than adult novices in that domain. That is, expertise overrides age. Similarly 4-year-old experts on dinosaurs (Gobbo & Chi, 1986) and 10- to 13-year old tennis experts (McPherson & Thomas, 1989) exhibit the characteristics of adult experts. Children also build up elaborate knowledge structures through countless hours of experience and practice with various sports, games, hobbies, all sorts of cultural artifacts and institutions, and numerous forms of social interaction and exchange. The outcome for problem solving is that children solve a problem quite well in one setting in which they have expertise but not another in which they have little experience. An example from the previous chapter was the child candy vendors on the streets of Brazil (Saxe, 1999). When these children are asked to solve similar math problems but without the vending context, they perform much more poorly; nonvendors show the opposite pattern (Carraher, Carraher, & Schliemann, 1985). The take-home message from such findings is that although older children and adults generally are more cognitively advanced than younger children, at any age children can perform more like an older child or adult in domains in which they are experts.

Current accounts of children's expertise emphasize children's rich theories in domains such as physics, biology, and psychology (see Chapters 3, 4, and 6). In these areas children seem like experts in that they detect the nonobvious underlying structures or essences in those domains. In the social cognitive realm, for example, young children appear to be experts at using deception, teasing, pretense, and language to manipulate and cooperate with others within the familiar domain of family—siblings and parents (Dunn, 1999).

Children's theorylike expertise allows them to generate causal explanations about that domain. These causal explanations in turn constrain the inferences they generate about novel instances. For example, 4- to 7-year-old experts on dinosaurs used their causal understanding of categories of dinosaurs to constrain their inferences about novel dinosaurs: "It's a meat-eater because it has sharp teeth" (Chi, Hutchinson, & Robin, 1989). Novices had to use animals in general as a source for inferences, so often drew on information about the novel dinosaur that was irrelevant to assigning it to a family of dinosaurs: "Could walk real fast 'cause he has giant legs." In other words, the experts sought out critical features in the novel dinosaur that allowed them to assign it to a category of dinosaurs, then generated additional inferences on the basis of this initial classification (e.g., "he's pretty dangerous"). Thus the experts were reasoning deductively in this domain at an age not known for rampant use of such a skill.

The evidence is beginning to suggest, then, that having a great deal of knowledge and experience in an area has all sorts of positive, beneficial effects on the quality of children's problem solving in that area. Unlike the novice the expert attends to and keeps in mind all the right features of the problem situation, selects the right problem strategies and uses them in the right ways, and generally engages in sustained feats of reasoning that appear highly logical in quality. In short the expert looks very, very smart—very, very "cognitively mature"—when functioning in his or her area of expertise.

What does work on expertise in problem solving tell us more generally about cognitive development? Expertise can make younger children look much like older children or adults, and adults even resort to sensorimotorlike thinking when encountering a highly novel robot whose movements they try to control (Granott, 1991). Thus we do not seem to be dealing with two very different sorts of cognitive machines. If the cognitive differences between young children and their elders prove to be largely due to differences in knowledge, we would hesitate to speak of large qualitative differences between the two. The recent trend in the field has been to highlight the cognitive competencies of infants and young children (see particularly Chapters 3 and 4), the cognitive shortcomings of adults, and the cognitive inconsistencies of both, effectively pushing from both ends of childhood toward the middle and blurring the difference between the two groups.

Of course the view of development as a number of novice-to-expert shifts is not the whole story of development. As Markman (1979) points out, when adults are in a novel situation they know a great deal more than do children about how to quickly move from novice to expert status. They are experts at becoming experts. They quickly detect what it is they do not understand, have more potential solutions in their cognitive bank from which to draw, and more easily see similarities between the current situations and other previously encountered situations. Experts know how to acquire new relevant information, and to hone their new skills.

The demonstrations that a person's cognitive functioning varies considerably from domain to domain, depending on the level of expertise in those domains, are compelling evidence against the view that cognitive development involves broad-based stages that spread across all domains. Thus a related question is whether the child's mind is simply "a collection of different and unrelated mindlets" (Flavell, 1992a). Are there no systemwide cognitive frameworks? There are many views on this issue; contrast, for example, the modularity nativists and Piaget in Chapter 1. The truth probably lies in between the two extremes—some independence, some connection and integration. Rather than debate the two positions, it is more useful to try to identify in what ways representation and processing are domain-general and in what ways they are domain-specific, and how the two types of knowledge develop together during childhood and interact during problem solving. For example, Siegler (1989) suggests that children tend to use backup strategies (strategies other than simply retrieving the answer) during problem solving in all domains when they are unsure of the correct answer. However, the particular backup strategies they choose (e.g., counting on the fingers), and the efficiency with which they use them, are specific to each domain (reading, addition, subtraction). Moreover, during development concepts that are restricted in their domains of application may become more linked with each other, and thus more domain-general (Case, 1998). For example, a child's theory of biology can integrate several domains within biology, and the theory may become broader and more integrated during development. We return to this question of domain-specificity versus generality in Chapter 9.

Metacognition.   Underlining key points in a textbook on cognitive development, taking notes while listening to a lecture, writing a shopping list before leaving for the supermarket, feeling puzzled after reading the instructions for a tax form, and rereading a particularly difficult paragraph in this book are all examples of your metacognition. *Metacognition* has usually been broadly and rather loosely defined as any knowledge or cognitive activity that takes as its object, or regulates, any aspect of any cognitive enterprise (e.g., Flavell, 1981a). It is called *meta*cognition because its core meaning is "cognition about cognition." Children not only think when solving a problem, but they also learn to think about thinking and about tasks, strategies, and the process of solving a problem. Metacognitive territory includes both what you know about cognition and how you manage your own cognition. In Chapter 7 we discuss metacognition with respect to what has been its main application—to memory (metamemory). In the current chapter, we focus on metacognition more broadly and its role in problem solving.

Metacognitive skills are believed to play an important role in many types of cognitive activity that are related to problem solving. Examples are oral communication of information, oral persuasion, oral comprehension, reading comprehension, writing, language acquisition, perception, attention, memory, logical reasoning, social cognition, and various forms of self-instruction and self-control. It also could be argued that Piagetian formal-operational thinking is metacognitive in nature because it involves thinking about propositions, hypotheses, and imagined possibilities—cognitive objects all. The "sense of the game" described in the next section is also clearly a form of metacognition; it is given a section of its own only because we want to highlight it. Metacognition has also seen service in the fields of cognitive psychology, artificial intelligence, intelligence, human abilities, social-learning theory, cognitive behavior modification, personality development, gerontology, and education. For example, metacomponents, a close cousin of metacognition, play a central role in Sternberg's (1985) theory of intelligence.

Metacognition refers to metacognitive knowledge and to metacognitive monitoring and self-regulation. For an excellent theoretical analysis of more subtle distinctions among various aspects of metacognition, see Kuhn (1999). *Metacognitive knowledge* refers to the segment of your acquired world knowledge that has to do with cognitive matters. You have knowledge and beliefs not only about politics, football, electronics, needlepoint, or some other domain, but also the human mind and its doings. Metacognitive knowledge can be roughly subdivided into knowledge about *persons*, *tasks*, and *strategies*.

The person category includes any knowledge and beliefs you might acquire concerning what human beings are like as cognitive processors. It includes cognitive differences within people, cognitive differences between people, and cognitive similarities among all people—that is, about universal properties of human cognition. Examples of the within-people subcategory might be your knowledge that you are better at psychology than physics or your belief that your friend learns better by reading than by listening. An example of the between-people category could be your belief that your parents are more sensitive to the needs and feelings of others than many of their neighbors are (a belief about others' social-cognitive skills). The cognitive-universals subcategory is the most interesting of the three. It refers to what you have come to know or believe about what the human mind in general is like—any person's mind, from Shakespeare to Hitler to your next door neighbor to your own. For instance you did not have to read this book to sense that everybody's short-term memory is of limited capacity and highly fallible. Similarly you are aware of the important fact that sometimes people understand, sometimes they do not understand, and sometimes they understand incorrectly, or *mis*understand. More generally you have learned that the human mind is a somewhat unpredictable and unreliable cognitive device, although still a remarkable one. Try this thought experiment to convince yourself of the usefulness of metacognition: Imagine how well you would fare as an adult in any human society if you were incorrigibly ignorant of the fact that you and other people sometimes misunderstand or forget things.

The task category has two subcategories, both of which are relevant for problem solving. One subcategory has to do with the nature of the information you encounter and deal with in any cognitive task. You have learned that the nature of this information has important effects on how you will manage it. For example, you know from experience that complex and unfamiliar information is liable to be difficult and time-consuming for you to comprehend and remember. You have also learned that having only skimpy and unreliable information at your disposal implies that judgments and conclusions based on this information are apt to be wrong. The other subcategory concerns the nature of the task demands. Even given the exact same information to work with, you have learned that some tasks are more difficult and demanding than others. For example you know that it is easier to recall the gist of a story than its exact wording.

As for the strategy category, there is much you might have learned about what means or strategies are likely to succeed in achieving what cognitive goals—in comprehending X, remembering Y, solving problem Z, and so on. For instance you know the strategy of spending more time studying important or less well-learned material than less important or better learned material. Knowledge about persons, tasks, and strategies interact during problem solving. For example, if you are a metacognitively "intelligent novice" (Brown & Palinscar, 1985), you know you do not have the background knowledge needed in some domain about which you are reading, such as twelfth-century Japanese poetry, but you know how to go about getting that knowledge by stopping occasionally to summarize or to rehearse important points. You know that such activities are not necessary in your area of expertise.

The mind is a rich and varied instrument. It comprises different, but related, mental activities such as comprehending, remembering, attending, and inferring. Do children appreciate the differentiation and integration of the mind? For example do they know that they might have *memorized* the Pledge of Allegiance but not *understand* it? Children sometimes even distort the words of a memorized song because of their lack of comprehension, and encode "Gladly, the Cross-Eyed Bear" instead of "Gladly the Cross I'd Bear." Are they aware of such discrepancies between memorizing and comprehending? These two mental activities of memorizing and comprehending are an interesting case in point, for they are highly interconnected in many cognitive tasks, yet differ in important ways. For example, some strategies that help us remember (e.g., rehearsal) provide little help in understanding. And the amount of material typically affects memorization much more than comprehension. Failure to realize that rotely memorizing material does not ensure understanding can cause serious processing errors during problem solving.

To examine this issue, Lovett and Flavell (1990) showed first graders, third graders, and undergraduates three tasks—a list of words to be rotely memorized (memorization but not necessarily comprehension), a list of words to match up to a picture (comprehension but not necessarily memorization), and a list of words to both memorize and match. The experimenter asked them to decide which of three strategies was the best way to prepare for each task. The strategies, uniquely suited to the above three tasks respectively, were rehearsal; word definition, which provided a verbal description of unfamiliar words; and a combination of the two. Lovett and Flavell also tested for knowledge about how different task variables differentially affect comprehension and memory tasks. They asked which of two lists of words would be easier to learn for a memory test and which would be easier to learn for a comprehension test. The lists differed with respect to length, length and word familiarity (i.e., a short list of unfamiliar words versus a long list of familiar words), and whether they formed a category (e.g., kinds of fruit).

Only the third graders and undergraduates showed some understanding that rehearsal would help memorization and word definitions would help comprehension, but that each strategy would not help the other task appreciably. The variables task proved to be even more difficult. Only the undergraduates understood their differential effects. The pattern of errors suggests that the children understood memory better than they understood comprehension. In fact they seemed to treat comprehension tasks as if they were memory tasks, as when they chose a rehearsal strategy for the comprehension task (see also Lovett & Pillow, 1995, 1996). In other research children rate the similarity of how the mind is used in various common activities (Fabricius et al., 1989; Schwanenflugel, Henderson, & Fabricius, 1998). During development children become increasingly aware that the mind engages in a variety of activities, for example, memory, comprehension, attention, and inference.

Its exotic and high-sounding name may suggest to you that "metacognitive knowledge" must be qualitatively different from other kinds—perhaps a different species of knowledge altogether. However, there is no good reason to think it actually is fundamentally different. Like much other knowledge, metacognitive knowledge is acquired gradually and is somewhat domain-specific (though we will *not* further metastasize "metas" by labeling it a "metadomain"). It also appears to become more theorylike—differentiated, integrated, and causal.

Let us turn now to *metacognitive monitoring and self-regulation*—one's management of one's cognitive activities during problem solving. A high school student settles down at her desk to do her homework. She may plan in what order to do the assignments, test herself on a few of the vocabulary items on tomorrow's test to see how much she has to study, check whether the vocabulary flash cards actually are helping her, and switch to a strategy of using each word in a sentence. These monitoring and self-regulation activities develop hand in hand with metacognitive knowledge. Her metacognitive knowledge that she often makes careless adding errors leads her to double check her solutions to some problem or, more likely, look for her electronic calculator. In the opposite direction, her metacognitive monitoring and self-regulation can lead to new metacognitive knowledge, as when she learns that her own memory for word meanings is helped more by a meaning-based strategy than rote memorization.

If you look carefully at toddlers, you can see a rudimentary ability to monitor their problem solving. Even 18-month-olds will self-correct their errors when they try to find a route that will take them around a barrier (Fabricius & Schick, 1995).

Children's metacognitive control of their problem-solving activities often determines whether they use, in a particular setting, the various concepts and skills we describe throughout this book. In the other direction, learning, from feedback during problem solving, which strategies work and which do not, contributes to cognitive development itself. Kuhn (2000) argues that metacognitive activities help to explain how and why cognitive development both occurs and fails to occur. A new competency may seem to float (to keep Siegler's overlapping-waves metaphor going) in and out of children's problem-solving activities; children go back and forth between old competencies and new ones for an extended period of time. In Kuhn's view a good new strategy gradually appears more frequently if a child has the metacognitive self-regulatory skills to detect whether the strategy is useful for the task at hand. Metastrategic knowing provides you with information about the enterprise or your progress in it.

Metacognition has many practical applications. It is a "tool of wide application" for solving many sorts of problems. It serves us well when we play chess, or solve physics problems, or engage in mental activity in any other knowledge domain. For example double-checking one's cognitive procedures and products is useful for almost any problem. Because of its central role in problem solving and learning, metacognition has important applications in the field of education (e.g., Brown & Campione, 1990; Garner, 1990; Paris, 1988; Rosenshine & Meister, 1994; Schneider & Pressley, 1997, Chapters 7 and 8). Consider the cognitive activity of reading, for example. Younger/poorer readers seem to show metacognitive or metacognitivelike deficits in no fewer than ten areas (Baker, 1982; Garner, 1990): (1) understanding the purposes of reading; (2) modifying reading strategies for different purposes; (3) identifying the important information in a passage; (4) recognizing the logical structure inherent in a passage; (5) considering how new information relates to what is already known; (6) attending to syntactic and semantic constraints—for example, spontaneously correcting errors in the text; (7) evaluating text for clarity, completeness, and consistency; (8) dealing with failures to understand; (9) deciding how well the material has been understood; and (10) attributing successful comprehension to their strategies. As an example of one of these components (2), there is some evidence that older/better readers are more likely than younger/poorer ones to expend additional effort on more demanding reading assignments, such as the assignment to study a text versus that of only skimming through it to find one specific piece of information (Forest & Waller, 1979).

Thus a good teacher has many avenues for intervention. A review of attempts to teach metacognitive skills to children as an integral part of the school curriculum (Rosenshine & Meister, 1994) gives us reason to be optimistic, particularly regarding *reciprocal instruction* (Palincsar & Brown, 1984). In such instruction an adult and a small group of students take turns in activities such as summarizing a passage, clarifying it, asking questions about it, and anticipating future questions. It appears that these metacognitive skills can be successfully taught, perhaps because of the child's active participation. There is evidence that gains in reading comprehension can be maintained for a year or longer (Palincsar, Brown, & Campione, 1993).

A Sense of the Game. One important resource for problem solving closely related to metacognition is a vague one and thus hard for us to put into words; we settle on the phrase "a sense of the game." As children develop they gradually learn more and more about what "the game of thinking" is like and about how it is supposed to be played (Flavell, 1977, 1982a). We have seen (Chapter 4) that young children acquire schemas and scripts for "how things are supposed to go" in stories, daily routines, and the like. It seems likely that as they grow older they also build knowledge structures concerning "how things are supposed to go" in cognitive enterprises, especially problem solving.

They might learn the following things, and doubtless many more (see also Moshman, 1998). Tasks and problems usually have solutions. One normally has to engage in some sort of cognitive activity in order to solve them—that is, cognitive activity is the usual means to achieving ("scoring") goals in cognitive games. Some cognitive outcomes or end products are of better quality than others. They are likely to be of better quality (more true, more adaptive, more in accordance with the rules of the cognitive game) if they were arrived at by plausible or logically valid reasoning, if they can be justified or explained by appeal to sound evidence or compelling arguments, if they are not incoherent or self-contradictory, and the like. It helps to think of what you know about other similar problems that you have solved before. One is not playing by the rules of the cognitive game if one just picks an answer or solution at random, reasons illogically, ignores crucial evidence, tolerates contradictions or inconsistencies, and so on.

It helps to be able to explicitly express the sort of cognitive game that is being played. For example being able to explicitly describe the difference between the logical validity of an inference and empirically demonstrated truths is associated with advanced logical reasoning (Markovits & Bouffard-Bouchard, 1992).

The fact that one has acquired a sense of the cognitive game does not imply that one will play it well. Although older children, adolescents, and adults usually do engage in higher quality cognitive play than young children do, it is nevertheless true that the quality of their play is often not very high. Even very bright and well-educated adults often fail to process information adequately and reason intelligently. In fact adult cognition is frequently of poor quality—sometimes of surprisingly, even shockingly poor quality. Examples include the use of false analogies, preference for positive instances, neglect of alternative hypotheses, overreliance on familiar content, and the tendency to delete, change, or add premises (e.g., Nisbett & Ross, 1980; see also the scientific reasoning section earlier). Yet the fact that most of us can understand and appreciate the force of these claims—namely, that we often play the thinking game quite poorly—suggests to us that we *have* acquired a fair sense of what the game is about and how it *should* be played. We do not think that preschool children possess this sense. They have little sense of explanation, justification, evidence, hypotheses, proof, logical necessity, contradiction, and other intellectual creatures that figure importantly in the game.

Social Supports. Children do not have to solve all of their problems by themselves. As Vygotsky and the socioculturalists (see Chapter 1) have shown, parents, teachers, or older peers often support poorly developed problem-solving skills with prompts and encouragement until children can use these skills on their own. One example is the study described in Chapter 1 (Freund, 1990) in which mothers helped their preschoolers solve the problem of having a puppet move his furniture into his new house. In many cultures, however, children learn how to solve problems mainly by watching adults go about their daily activities and sometimes participating in these naturally occurring activities, rather than learn by direct instruction in special learning situations (Rogoff, Mistry, Goncu, & Mosier, 1993). In addition, in some cultures, such as Dhol-Ki-Patti in India and the Guatemalan Mayan town of San Pedro, instruction often is nonverbal, such as putting the child's hands in the correct position for a jumping jack toy. The constant across cultures is that adults and older children teach younger ones how to solve problems; what varies is how they do it and what cultural values are being transmitted in the process. For example, encouraging children to learn by watching others implies that this is how one should learn to solve problems and that the community is an important resource for this problem solving (it takes a village to raise a child?).

In a related study (Chavajay & Rogoff, 1999), toddlers and their caregivers from a Guatemalan Mayan community were more likely than those in U.S. families of European descent to attend simultaneously to two or more competing events in the environment. The U.S. dyads instead tended to alternate their attention between these events. Thus even attention management is culturally formed. These examples show that when children attempt to solve problems by themselves, they are not really "by themselves" because they have internalized those ways of gathering information and approaching problems that are encouraged by their culture.

Children are not passive in these collaborations. They learn very early on to request this help from others when trying to solve problems that are beyond them. For example 6-month-olds use gestures, often accompanied by attention-getting grunts, to try to get their mothers to obtain desired objects (Mosier & Rogoff, 1994).

Another social resource is peers, a case of two heads being better than one, though it turns out that sometimes one head is better (see Rogoff, 1998, for a review). What contributes to successful collaborative problem solving? In one study of child dyads solving decimal problems (Ellis, Klahr, & Siegler, 1993), the most successful ones were those in which one child reacted with interest and enthusiasm to the other child's correct explanation. Thus a child who generates a correct strategy may abandon it if the other child does not respond positively. In addition, dyads who generated the correct solution together, rather than one after the other or one child not at all, gave the clearest explanations.

When one peer is older, and thus more expert, the social dynamics change, and affect the process of problem solving—often for the better, but not always. Consider the following exchange in which a 9-year-old "teacher" refuses to relinquish control of the task of building a model from geometric shapes and connectors, thus preventing the 7-year-old learner from acquiring independent problem-solving skills (Azmitia & Hesser, 1993, p. 438):

Teacher: Now a little tube.
Learner: Where does it go?
Teacher: Here you gotta look.
Learner: OK, let me try. Another little tube . . .
Teacher: I'm supposed to tell you what to do.
Learner: But I'm looking. Let me.
Teacher: No. She *[the experimenter]* put me in charge.
Learner: You think you know everything.
Teacher: I do cause I did this before. Get a little tube.
Learner: *(Complies).*

Processes of Problem Solving

How do all these resources together help children's problem solving? They increase the chances that children actually will access and use their existing knowledge and skill to solve problems. In fact much of development seems to involve learning to use what you already have, rather than acquiring new "haves." For example, when a competency first emerges it may be activated and properly used on one presentation of a task but not on the next presentation of that very same task, as Siegler (1996) found for children's emerging strategies. Embryonic competencies tend to have this unreliable, "now-you-see-them-now-you-don't" quality. Children may not be able to produce them consistently, or, as we discuss in Chapter 7, a good strategy may not at first pay off, perhaps because it is so effortful to produce.

A closely related notion is that new competencies tend to be highly restricted and limited in their range of application, often seeming tightly bound or "welded" (Brown et al., 1983) to a few specific task situations and not generally available for solving problems. Here are two examples: (1) Ten-year-olds were asked to predict where, on a computer screen, an object would land. They had to try to figure out a rule for an abstract set of features (size, color, shape) of objects and their movement (e.g., large objects move diagonally from lower left to upper right, whereas small objects move in the opposite direction). Children could solve this problem after only 6 or 7 trials when told to use the joystick to place the "butterfly net" in order to "capture the prey" on each trial (Ceci, 1996). Solution time was much longer for children not given this game context, which gives a rationale for the task and a meaningful framework. Thus, although the task was the same for the two groups, and both groups possessed the ability to figure out the solution rule, this ability at first could be applied only in a meaningful context. (2) Preschoolers may be able to apply some of their number knowledge (see Chapter 4) only to small sets—for example, sets of two to four objects. Older children can apply this knowledge to larger sets. In addition to this extension of range, or generalization, there may also be some restriction of range, or differentiation. For example children may initially apply a strategy to some problems for which it should not be employed and then later restrict its use to appropriate situations only.

Researchers currently are interested in how children of various ages actually use their various resources in their moment-to-moment problem solving (Kuhn, 2000; Siegler, 1996). A child's problem solving might be likened to *bricolage,* or, in the closest English translation from French, *tinkering* (DeLoache, Miller, et al., 1998; Levi-Strauss, 1967). A bricoleur has a number of general-purpose tools that can be used on a variety of tasks; he is a handyman, or a jack-of-all-trades. Similarly children have a cognitive toolbox, mostly containing general-purpose tools. They make do with what they have to try to solve a wide variety of problems about which they often have little expert knowledge or experience. Through experience they gradually learn to select the concepts and skills that are most effective for a particular task. Because child bricoleurs often do not have all the information they need, they must search for information and decide which of that information is useful.

There is a great deal of current interest in thinking about problem-solving processes as *executive functions*, particularly *planning, inhibition of prepotent responses, keeping information alive in working memory*, and *representational flexibility* (e.g., Hughes, 1998; Zelazo, 1999). Good problem solvers nearly always have a plan. Simple planning starts early in life. By age 5 children show some planning in their daily activities, such as laying out clothes the night before to put on the next morning (Kreitler & Kreitler, 1987). An older child is more apt than a younger one to search for information in a planful, systematic fashion. An example is deciding to open doors to look at analogous parts of two rows of objects, from one end of the rows to the other, when asked to decide whether the two arrays are the same or different (e.g., Miller & Aloise-Young, 1996).

Children (and even adults) fail to plan for many reasons (Ellis & Siegler, 1997). For example, planning requires effort and delay or suppression of easier or more automatic behaviors (e.g., just jumping into the task). Furthermore, planning typically is difficult and time-consuming, and is not guaranteed to pay off. Also it often is downright boring. So why bother? For discussions about the development of planning, see Friedman and Scholnick (1997) and Ellis and Siegler (1997).

Regarding the other executive functions, inhibiting prepotent responses such as long-standing but inferior strategies is as important as acquiring superior ones (Kuhn, 2000; Siegler, 1996). The contributions of working memory were discussed in the section on capacity and in Chapter 7. Finally an example of the lack of representational flexibility is that once a 3-year-old has sorted items in a certain way, such as color, while ignoring shape, the child has great difficulty switching to sorting them by shape and ignoring color (Zelazo, 1999). These executive functions describe basic processes for problem solving on a variety of tasks, though currently the greatest interest is in their contributions to performance on theory of mind tasks (e.g., Frye, 1999; Hughes, 1998; Perner, Stummer, & Lang, 1999). This work is also connected to neuroscience research because executive functions are thought to be associated with the prefrontal cortex (Duncan, 1986).

An Example of Problem Solving: Siegler's Rule-Assessment Approach

Many problems in real life are solved by detecting regularities and abstracting a rule, or "if-then" statement. A simple one discussed earlier is "if it's called a 'blicket' it can make the machine light up." More complex problems call for more complex rules. To illustrate how one might examine age differences in problem solving, we now offer an extended description of one classic program of research in this area. Siegler (1998), an information-processing researcher (see Chapter 1), has used *rule assessment* to study problem solving. He begins by drawing on work by Piaget and others to predict the different problem-solving rules that children of different developmental levels might use in one domain. Siegler's next step is to administer a special, very carefully selected set of problems in that domain to children of different ages. A child's pattern of responses across this set of problems may then help to determine which of Siegler's hypothesized rules, if any, he is using. One response pattern might suggest that rule *A* had been used, another that rule *B* had been used, and so on.

In one series of investigations, Siegler (1978) presented children of different ages with a simple balance scale that had four equally spaced pegs on each side of the fulcrum (see Figure 5.2). The arm of the scale could fall down to the left or right, or remain horizontal and balanced, depending on the number of equal-sized weights that were placed on the pegs and their distance from the fulcrum. Weights were never placed on more than one peg on a side on each trial, to simplify the problem. The child's task was to predict which, if either, of the two sides would go down if a lever that kept the scale from moving were released.

Siegler hypothesized that the knowledge children of different ages would have about the balance scale could be represented as four developmentally ordered, increasingly complex rules. The simplest and earliest-acquired rule, Rule I, takes into account only the number of weights (thus the total weight) on each side of the fulcrum. If the number of weights is the same on both sides, Rule I users always

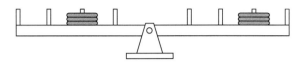

FIGURE 5.2   One problem on Siegler's balance scale task.

predict that the scale will balance; and if the number of weights is greater on one side, that side is always predicted to go down. Rule I children completely ignore the distances the weights are from the fulcrum on each side. Thus they would be correct on some problems, for example, when three weights are on the third peg from the center on both sides and the children say they will balance. But they would be incorrect on other problems, for example, the one in the figure. Children who follow Rule II also predict solely on the basis of which side has the greater number of weights, except when the number is equal on both sides. When that happens, and only then, the distances from the fulcrum are correctly taken into account. That is, Rule II children predict balance if the two distances are equal. If they are not equal, as in the figure, they correctly predict the descent of whichever arm has its weight located farther from the fulcrum. However, they incorrectly predict that the side with more weights will go down when three weights close to the fulcrum are pitted against two weights far from the fulcrum.

In contrast, children who follow Rule III always try to consider both weight and distance equally in making their decisions. If both dimensions are equal on both sides, balance is predicted. If one dimension is equal and the other not, the decision is based on that other dimension. For instance, if the weights are equal but the distances are not, the child predicts that the side with the weights farther out will go down. And, of course, if both are unequal and favor the descent of the same side, that side will be predicted to go down; thus, if one side both has more weights than the other and also has them placed on a peg that is farther from the fulcrum, that side will be judged to go down. However, if both dimensions are unequal but favor the descent of different sides, Rule III children have no recourse but to guess— "muddle through," as Siegler puts it. For example, Rule III children do not know what to predict if the left side has three weights situated two pegs out from the fulcrum and the right side has two weights situated four pegs out.

Finally, Rule IV children know how to compute specifically the downward force on each side. That is, they multiply the distance (expressed as the number of pegs out from fulcrum) by the number of weights placed at that distance, and correctly predict that the side with greater product will tip down. In the problem just mentioned, for instance, they would correctly predict that the right side would go down ($2 \times 4 = 8$) and the left side would go up ($3 \times 2 = 6$).

Note that inferences about rule use are based on the child's *pattern* of responding over the entire *set* of problem types, rather than on how any single problem is handled, because it is only the pattern as a whole that discriminates among the four rules. All children would be correct when only the number of weights on the two sides differs; only some of the children would be correct when, for example, weight and distance conflict. Notice also that Siegler's model predicts that more cognitively advanced (Rule III) children will actually do worse than less advanced (Rules I and II) children on certain problems—not the usual "older-children-do-better" developmental prediction. Specifically, when the left side has three weights three pegs out and the right side has two weights four pegs out, Rule III children have to guess whereas Rule I children will encode only weight and thus be correct, though for the wrong reason.

How well does the rule model fit children's response patterns across a set of various scale-balance problems? Very well indeed, it turns out. Of the 120 children aged 5, 9, 13, and 17 years, fully 107 (89 percent) consistently responded in accord with one of the four rules: 29 used Rule I; 22, Rule II; 48, Rule III; and 8, Rule IV (Siegler, 1976). Children's verbal descriptions of how they solved the problems were also highly consistent with their response patterns, and thus provided additional corroborating evidence that the children were using Siegler's rules. All the 5-year-olds who could be classified as rule users employed Rule I. Most of the older children used one of the other three rules; among these older subjects, there was also a slight increase with age in the tendency to use more advanced Rules III and IV. Studies with other problem-solving tasks successfully predict a similar sequence of rules (e.g., Case, Marini, McKeough, Dennis, & Goldberg, 1986; Siegler, 1978, 1981; Zelazo & Shultz, 1989).

Can children learn a more advanced rule? Siegler (1976) has shown that children who use the same rule in a problem area may still differ cognitively from one another in ways that affect their subsequent learning and development in that area. For example, he found that groups of 5-year-olds and 8-year-olds, both of whom consistently used Rule I at the beginning of the experiment, nevertheless differed in how much they profited from additional experience with problems in which distance and number of weights conflict. The 8-year-olds advanced to the use of Rules II or III following this additional experience, whereas the 5-year-olds continued to use Rule I. Subsequent research suggested an explanation for this age difference in responsiveness to a learning opportunity: The younger children were encoding the distance dimension less adequately than were the older ones; the younger ones were not attending to it and storing it in memory as well. For instance Siegler showed that the younger children were less likely than the older ones to notice and remember how far out on each side the weights were placed on any given problem. Once 5-year-olds had been trained to encode the distance dimension adequately, they too advanced in rule use following additional experience with conflict problems—that is, once their encoding problems were remedied, they benefited from the same learning experience that had previously benefited only 8-year-olds. This strongly suggests that inadequate encoding had been at least the proximate cause of their inability to learn to solve the problem.

Some of the resources and processes described earlier probably contribute to the development of Siegler's rules. An increasing information-processing capacity may make it easier for older children than younger ones to think about both weight and distance information. Also, a sense-of-the-game understanding that you are supposed to look for rulelike regularities that work for all the problems may be important as well. Moreover, during training, older children likely have a greater metacognitive ability to monitor their progress and change their strategy if necessary. Finally 5-year-olds, when faced with a task with which they have little domain-specific knowledge, may tend to behave on the basis of the most salient or important-seeming dimension present—in this case the weight dimension. They may in fact find it quite difficult to inhibit this response. Children of this age also tend to respond in a similarly "unidimensional" manner in other conceptual areas where they lack sufficient knowledge, such as Piagetian conservation tasks (Siegler, 1981, 1983).

Although on these tasks Siegler finds a developmental sequence of rules and much intrachild consistency in the use of these rules, he more recently (Siegler, 1996) has emphasized tasks on which children show more variability, particularly in the strategies that they bring to problem-solving situations. We discuss these findings in Chapters 1 and 7.

Many of the issues about reasoning and problem solving are similar to those about others topics in this book. Under what circumstances do children express their full competencies and why? How do earlier forms of reasoning relate to later forms? What processes are involved in this developmental change? How do children transfer their knowledge to other situations? How should we depict children's scientific concepts? As theories? As isolated facts? In what ways is cognitive development more than just increased expertise? How do children learn to orchestrate their various problem-solving skills for a particular task? What do they actually do from moment to moment when trying to solve a problem? In the next three chapters, we continue to look at these issues and examine how reasoning and problem-solving skills contribute to, and benefit from, social cognition, memory, and language.

SUMMARY

Much of the cognitive activity to which children apply their growing representational abilities might be called reasoning and problem solving. Piaget believed that the forms of reasoning shown by early-childhood (*preoperational*), middle-childhood (*concrete-operational*), and adolescent-adult (*formal-operational*) thinkers are qualitatively different from one another. However, there is growing doubt in the field that these differences are that radical and stagelike. Specifically, a child's cognitive performance is somewhat uneven across different domains. Moreover, young children are more competent and older children less competent than Piaget thought, thus making age differences less dramatic. Still, many of the developmental trends Piaget described seem very insightful and largely on the mark even today. Development from early to middle childhood exhibits the following closely related trends. In conservation and other tasks, younger children often base their judgments on *perceived appearances*, older ones on *inferences* that go beyond surface appearances to the underlying *reality*. Younger children are prone to *center* their attention on a single, highly salient task element (*centration*), older ones to *decenter* their attention and distribute it more equitably across all important task elements (*decentration*). Younger children focus on problem *states*, especially the current state, whereas older ones also take note of the *transformations* that link one state with another. Younger children's thinking tends to be *irreversible*; older children's thinking is more *reversible*, showing an understanding of *inversion* and *compensation*. Finally, younger children are more likely to approach problems in a *qualitative* way, older children in a more *quantitative* measurement-oriented way.

Piagetian work on development from middle childhood to adolescence and adulthood also shows a set of trends that are closely linked to one another. In scientific reasoning problems, especially, the elementary school child begins with the *real* and moves reluctantly, if at all, to the *possible*; the adolescent may begin by trying to imagine all that is possible in the present situation and then try to find out which of these possibilities actually obtains in this situation. Therefore the child's approach is more *empirico-inductive* in nature, whereas the adolescent's is more *hypothetico-deductive*. The child considers propositions singly, in isolation from one another (*intrapropositional* thinking); the adolescent reasons, in addition, about the logical relations (e.g., logical implication) that hold among two or more propositions (*interpropositional* thinking).

Other perspectives on reasoning focus on more informal sorts of everyday reasoning, such as seeing similarities between something you already know and something new you are encountering. Analogical reasoning is a particularly powerful example. Although even infants show inklings of this reasoning, it becomes much more abstract and complex throughout childhood and adolescence.

One important sort of reasoning in our culture—scientific thinking—illustrates both similarities and differences between child and adult reasoning. Children of all ages and adults appear to possess intuitive concepts, perhaps informal theories, about natural phenomena. During development these concepts may undergo either weak restructuring—an elaboration of the same "theory"—or strong restructuring—the replacement of one theory by another. Although many of these concepts are accurate, a startling number are not—even in adults. These misconceptions can interfere with scientific instruction at school.

Children and many lay adults are surprisingly deficient at designing tests of a theory and evaluating the theory in light of resulting evidence. They apparently do not clearly understand the difference between a hypothesis and evidence and their respective roles. This is especially true when they already have a theory that they try to apply to the problem at hand. Several problems result. First, they tend to be theory bound; they often ignore evidence that does not support their theory or distort it so that it does. Second, children and lay adults tend to be data bound; they focus on the most recent result, ignoring earlier results. Third, they find it difficult to deal with evidence independently of a theory; they are reluctant to abandon a failed theory until they have a plausible new theory to explain the discrepant result. Metacognition about one's own thinking processes may be essential in overcoming these problems.

Problem solving is evident event in infants, in their use of means-end behaviors. Child bricoleur problem solvers have many resources on which they can draw for their problem solving. Their increasing *domain-specific knowledge (expertise)* makes for better cognitive performance in these domains. Experts possess a more abstract, complex, causal knowledge structure for a particular domain and are more planful and cognitively efficient during problem solving. In addition they can solve many problems more by automatic-looking memory processes than by complex reasoning processes. Both child and adult minds can vary considerably over domains and occasions in the quality of their cognitive performance. Domain-specific knowledge appears to account for some, but not all, of cognitive development.

Another resource, *metacognition* ("cognition about cognition"), includes any knowledge or cognitive activity that takes as its object, or regulates, any aspect of any cognitive enterprise. A distinction can be made between *metacognitive knowledge* and *metacognitive monitoring and self-regulation*. The former refers to your accumulated knowledge concerning cognitive matters, and can be divided into three categories: *person, task,* and *strategy*. The person category includes your knowledge and beliefs about people as cognitive processors. The task category refers to your knowledge about the cognitive-processing implications of task information and task demands. The strategy category includes your knowledge about various strategies. Children gradually understand the differences among various mental activities, such as memorizing and comprehension. Metacognitive monitoring and self-regulation involve activities driven by metacognitive knowledge that provide information about one's progress in some cognitive enterprise. Metacognitive knowledge and monitoring and self-regulation are assumed to interact with one another as they influence our cognitive activities. There is reason to believe that metacognitive skills play important roles in reading and other areas of school learning, and therefore reason to try teaching them directly to children.

Closely related to metacognition is a *sense of the game* of thinking. Children learn, for example, that problems usually have solutions and that problem solvers are supposed to seriously engage in cognitive activities. Other people are *social supports* for children's emerging problem solving skills, but we are just beginning to understand how social relations among the participants affect their interactions during problem solving.

All these resources help children strengthen and appropriately access for problem solving the competencies they already possess. During actual problem solving, we see the operation of *executive functions* such as *planning, inhibition of prepotent responses, keeping information alive in working memory*, and *representational flexibility*.

Robert Siegler's *rule-assessment approach* provides a good example of the study of children's problem solving. Siegler argues that during development children acquire increasingly powerful rules for solving problems. He gives children of different ages a set of problems that is carefully designed so that a child's overall pattern of answers reveals the particular rule that the child is using to solve the problem. Siegler has successfully predicted a developmental sequence of rules in several problem areas, for example on a balance scale problem.

6

Social Cognition

Stephanie (7 months) developed a very shrill shriek which her parents saw her as using primarily in situations when she was getting no attention; for example in a supermarket her mother would hear the shriek and turn around in a hurry with some alarm, to find Stephanie sitting in her trolley grinning at her. (Reddy, 1991, p. 145)

Matt (11 years) wanted to go to a hobby store on Memorial Day. Mother, doubting it was open, told him to call. Matt went off to the phone, returned, and said, "Let's go."

They arrived to find the store closed. The frustrated mother inquired: "I thought you called." Matt: "I did, but they didn't answer, so I figured they were too busy to come to the phone." (DeLoache, Miller, & Pierroutsakos, 1998, p. 801)

Up to this point, our story of cognitive development might appear to have the plot of "child-in-the-physical world." The child seems headed toward becoming a scientist. But even scientists, whether age 4 or 40, are feeling people with social needs and goals who think about the world of people. As the above observations show, from infancy to late childhood the young of our species have concepts about other people and their behavior and engage in behaviors with other people based on these concepts. Hints of this second story plot of cognitive development emerged in previous chapters—sociocultural theory (Chapter 1), attention to faces (Chapter 2), infants' deferred imitation of adults (Chapter 3), social script knowledge and concepts of living things (Chapter 4), and metacognition (Chapter 5). We now flesh out the story of "the other cognitive development."

Social cognition takes humans and human affairs as its subjects; it means cognition about people and their doings. Social cognition deals with the strictly social world, not the physical and logical-mathematical ones, even though all three worlds obviously have people's fingerprints all over them. The scientific investigation of this kind of cognition currently is of great interest to psychologists, but its actual practice has undoubtedly been of even greater interest to practically everybody since the dawn of the species. Numerous motives, ranging from self-preservation to idle curiosity, must continually impel people the world over to try to make sense out of themselves, other people, interpersonal relations, social customs and institutions, and other interesting objects of thought within the social world.

Social-cognitive development has received a good deal of scientific study, especially in recent years. Recent general sources on this topic include Flavell and Miller (1998), Hala (1997), and Rochat (1999). The early work came directly or indirectly from Piaget's work. His work on taking the physical or psychological perspective of other people (or more often not), misattributing mental characteristics to physical objects (animism) and physical characteristics to mental events (realism), moral reasoning, and concepts about the mind such as memory, thoughts, and dreams, laid the foundation for most of what we have studied since in the social domain. Work on social cognition today includes a variety of topics. We focus on theory of mind, the understanding of mind, because that is where most of the scientific action is at present. In fact it is one of the most active current arenas for research and theorizing in all of cognitive development. Although we discuss metacognition in other chapters, it could have appeared here as well, because most psychologists would consider the terms "metacognition" and "theory of mind" as more or less synonymous.

We first present some ways to think about what happens during the development of social cognition. Next we describe the general nature of social cognition and compare and contrast it with nonsocial cognition. Our central story starts with the beginnings of social cognition in infancy. We next turn to children's understanding of the mind, the main topic of this chapter. Subsequent sections discuss children's understanding, and use, of traits and other psychological bases of behavior, their knowledge about self, and the understanding of social relationships. A final section looks at the uses of social cognition for social behavior. Except under unfortunate circumstances, this developmental story has a happy ending: by constructing concepts of other people, ourself, and our relationships, we both connect with other people and differentiate ourself from them.

THE NATURE OF SOCIAL COGNITION

One way to think about what happens during an act of social cognition is illustrated in Figure 6.1. S means the self and O means another person or group of persons. The dashed arrows represent acts and products of social cognition. They mainly include a person's inferences, beliefs, theories, or conceptions about the inner psychological processes, mental states, or attributes of human beings, and are therefore represented in the figure as penetrating into the interior of their targets. The solid arrows represent overt social acts rather than covert mental ones, and consequently they cannot "penetrate" their objects in quite this sense. For instance, a person may be able to infer what is going on inside your head if given enough clues (social cognition), but can affectionately pat only the outside of it (social act). The top part of Figure 6.1 shows that the self can have all manner of cognitions about the self, as well as about another person or group of persons. The bottom part shows that social cognition can also encompass various relationships and interactions among individuals or groups. It further shows that the self can be one of the interacting individuals the self is mentally representing, and that the interactions represented can themselves include covert social cognitions, as well as overt social acts. Thus, a person may think about himself in isolation, about you in isolation, and also about the social acts and social cognitions each may carry out with respect to the other.

Successful social cognition requires three conditions: *existence, need,* and *inference* (Flavell, 1974; Flavell, Botkin, Fry, Wright, & Jarvis, 1968/1975). *Existence* refers to the person's basic knowledge that a particular fact or phenomenon of the social world exists as one of life's possibilities. The point is a most unprofound one: If an infant has not yet become aware that people even *have* such psychological goings on as percepts, thoughts, beliefs, and motives, for instance, she manifestly cannot try to infer their presence and detailed characteristics in particular people on particular occasions. Later in this chapter we show that young children, and arguably even infants and toddlers, have some awareness of the existence of mental activity or states.

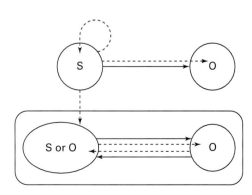

FIGURE 6.1 A representation of social cognition.

Need refers to the disposition or sensed need to attempt an act of social cognition. A person may know perfectly well that she and other people have experiences called feelings (Existence), and yet she may not even try to diagnose them when opportunities arise (Need). She may not think to, may not want to, or may not see any point to making such an effort. One of the great truths about child cognition is that children often do not make use of the knowledge and cognitive skills they possess.

Inference concerns the skill or capacity to carry off a given form of social thinking successfully. The thinking need not involve "inference" strictly defined—any social-cognitive process qualifies. Someone may know of the existence of the type of thought or feeling you are currently having (Existence), and may badly want to figure out what you are presently experiencing (Need), and yet may simply not have the ability to identify it on the basis of the evidence provided (Inference). The person can infer, perhaps, that you are feeling something unpleasant, and knowing even that much, of course, requires some Inference ability. However, lack of sufficient evidence, general inadequacies as a people reader, or both, may prevent a more detailed and precise understanding of exactly what sort of unpleasant affect you are experiencing. Another example is that a young child may know that your view of a toy village is different from his on the opposite side of it, but not be able to calculate *exactly* what your view is.

Thus, social-cognitive development is the developing awareness and general knowledge (Existence) of the enormous variety of possible mental states and activities. It is also a developing awareness (Need) of when and why one might or should try to take readings of such objects. Finally, it is the development of a wide variety of cognitive skills (Inference) with which to take these readings. It is a useful exercise to think about each of the areas of social cognition we discuss in terms of these models.

SIMILARITIES AND DIFFERENCES BETWEEN SOCIAL AND NONSOCIAL COGNITION

Children's social and nonsocial cognition are both similar and different in their nature and in their course of development (e.g., Damon, 1981; Flavell & Ross, 1981; Hoffman, 1981; Shantz, 1983). We look at similarities first.

Similarities

There obviously have to be many similarities between social and nonsocial cognition. In the first place, the head that thinks about the social world is the selfsame head that thinks about the nonsocial world. All the basic mental tools described in previous chapters (knowledge structures, symbolic abilities, information-processing capacities, etc.) can be used to categorize, remember, reason about, and otherwise manipulate social data as well as nonsocial data. Thanks to these tools, both the social and nonsocial world come to be experienced as "structured, stable, and meaningful" (Schneider, Hastorf, & Ellsworth, 1979, p. 10). In addition, as with nonsocial cognition, some of our social cognition involves complex reasoning (e.g., elaborate perspective taking), and some of it involves only the recognition of familiar input patterns and the automatic running off of overlearned responses to these patterns.

Social and nonsocial inputs are similar in certain fundamental respects. Things are physical objects in space and so are people. Things participate in events that take place over time and so do people. Things relate to and interact with one another in numerous ways and so do people. Nonsocial concepts can be concrete ("ball") or abstract ("entropy") and so can social ones ("girl," "friendship"). Not surprisingly, therefore, many of the trends in the development of nonsocial cognition described in previous chapters can also be seen in the area of social-cognitive development. Following are the most salient examples.

Surface to Depth.   Both social and nonsocial cognitive development tend to proceed from surface appearances to the construction of an inferred underlying reality. In both realms, recent research suggests that this understanding of various sorts of underlying realities or essences of objects starts earlier than we used to think, probably during infancy and certainly by early childhood. Still, the most external, immediately perceptible attributes of the self, other people, social interactions, and other social-cognitive objects remain quite salient. The covert-social-psychological processes, meanings, and causes that underlie them gradually become more accessible. For example, young children can read the big, obvious signs of gaiety in another, but will require additional social-cognitive growth before they can also pick up the little, nonobvious signs that indicate that this individual's gaiety is forced and false. Seeing through social facades is not the long suit of young children, any more than is seeing through Piagetian-task nonconservation facades. The dashed arrows in Figure 6.1 initially stop at the boundaries of those circles and ellipses, and only gradually penetrate into the interior. Development involves going deeper and deeper into the depths of mind.

The Pull of the Present.   As in nonsocial cognition, the social cognition of young children also shows vulnerability to salient features of the here-and-now. They are likely to hew closely to the immediately present social situation. It is only later that they will spontaneously infer its likely past antecedents and future consequences—for example, what prior social experiences, motives, intentions, and so on, led the people to act as they are now acting, and what will be the likely next steps in the episode. Although infants can predict the next behavior, they only gradually learn to integrate over time and events, to interlink states and transformations, and this is as true in the social domain as in the nonsocial one.

Construction of Invariants.   Children gradually come to think of themselves and others as stable human beings who conserve, over time and circumstances, their personhoods, personalities, social and sexual roles and identities, and many other attributes. Day to day changes in one's own or another's mood and behavior come to be construed as variations on an enduring theme, rather than as a succession of unrelated melodies. The cognitive construction of personal continuities that persist over time can reflect a breaking away from the pull of the salient present.

Abstract and Hypothetical Thinking.   The person becomes capable of thinking about groups, institutions, and people in general (concepts of "human nature," etc.), as well as about specific individuals. Moreover, specific individuals, both self and others, become endowed with more general, enduring traits and dispositions, as well as more specific and transient processes. Likewise the mature thinker may think about all manner of abstract ideas and ideals in such areas as morality, religion, and politics. Finally, the hypotheses the thinker makes in a science experiment have their social-cognitive counterparts in the speculations she makes about her personal future.

Cognitive Shortcomings.   As in areas such as scientific reasoning, our inferences about ourselves and other people are subject to numerous biases and distortions. For example, adults tend to overestimate the degree to which behavior is governed by stable and general internal traits and dispositions rather than variable, external circumstances (e.g., Mischel & Peake, 1982). This is especially true when trying to explain another's behavior rather than our own (Jones, 1990): You tripped because you are clumsy (a stable trait) whereas I tripped because it was dark (a variable circumstance). Children also show biases such as overestimations of their abilities and knowledge, and over- and underestimations of the occurrence of mental activities, as we discuss later.

An ailment that particularly bedevils social cognition, however, is what Piaget called *egocentrism*—the failure to differentiate or distinguish clearly between one's own point of view and another's. For instance, a person's assessment of your opinions and feelings about something is egocentric to the degree that that person has unwittingly misattributed his or her own opinions and feelings to you. Although we now know that even young children have some awareness that others' desires and beliefs can differ from theirs, and egocentrism declines throughout childhood, most people are "at risk" (almost in the medical sense) for egocentric thinking all of their lives, just as they are for certain logical errors. The reason lies in our psychological designs in relation to the jobs to be done. Our own points of view are usually more cognitively "available" to us than another person's (Tversky & Kahneman, 1973). Furthermore, we are usually unable to turn our own viewpoints off completely when trying to infer another's. Our own perspectives produce clear signals that are much louder to us than the other's, and they usually continue to ring in our ears while we try to decode the other's. For example, the fact that you thoroughly understand calculus constitutes an obstacle to your continuously keeping in mind a friend's ignorance of it while trying to explain it to him; you may momentarily realize how hard it is for him, but that realization may quietly slip away once you get immersed in your explanation.

Interestingly, the "other" can be oneself in another time and condition, rather than a different person (Flavell, 1981b). For example, it can be hard to imagine yourself feeling well and happy next week if you feel terribly ill or unhappy today. Taking the perspective of yourself, when that perspective is different from your current one, can sometimes be as hard as taking the perspective of another person.

A Sense of the Game.   Although infants have a glimmer of the nature of the game of predicting and influencing other people, and preschoolers learn that mental life is about representations, only a more mature thinker has developed a full "sense of the game" of people reading, just as he has in the case of impersonal thinking games. Older children and adults know that others may intentionally hide their mental life, that their own prior knowledge may bias their representation of others' knowledge and beliefs, that people try to influence other people's minds, and other Existence-type truths about social cognition.

Differences

People are different from most other objects in a number of ways; otherwise this chapter would not be necessary. These differences lead to differences in our relations with people versus other objects, and thus how we think about these two categories. As Shweder put it, "What one thinks about has some influence on how one thinks" (1980, p. 270).

Unlike nonsocial objects, people objects are conscious, with a continual stream of mental activity. They can psychologically connect to objects as they perceive, represent, know, believe, think, mean, intend, want, emote, and learn. They are causal agents who can, within limits, spontaneously, freely, and intentionally generate their own mental and physical acts and hence can be held responsible for these acts. They can be influenced; we can use words or behaviors to make them attend to us or change their minds. Their behavior is often difficult to predict because they respond to internal as well as external events, and also to their own representations and interpretations of external stimuli rather than to the "raw stimuli" themselves. They can deliberately reveal and conceal critical information about themselves, and this adds to their unpredictability.

Our relations with people are typically very different from our relations with other objects. We are very similar to the objects of our social cognition (indeed we *are* those objects in the case of social cognition about the self). We often use the self as a point of reference; we assume that others feel about things the same way that we do, or note our diverse desires and beliefs. This similarity makes possible the use of cognitive processes that are distinctively social cognitive. In contrast, toys are not us. There are also the dynamic relations that include all the special ways we respond to social objects and they to us. Our interactions with other people are often intricately coordinated, mutual, reciprocal affairs, interactions quite unlike those we have with nonsocial objects. Our thoughts and behaviors concerning another person are apt to be importantly guided by our cognitive representations of the social roles, relations, and behaviors in play between us. Our thoughts and behaviors may also be guided by our representations of the other person's representations (beliefs, desires, thoughts, and intentions) concerning us, even including the other person's possible representations of these representations of ours (e.g., "I think she knows I like her ideas"). Thus, the social cognitions of two people can overlap and include one another in complex and changing ways over the course of a social interaction between them (see Figure 6.1).

In addition to these differences in type of cognitive object and in self-object relations are differences in content. Examples of distinctively social-cognitive content include our mental representations of (1) other people's thoughts, desires, beliefs, and attitudes about us and our behavior; and (2) their and our own moral or social-conventional obligations and responsibilities. Obviously, when trying to solve a problem in, say, mechanics, our mental contents do not include inferences about the attitudes and moral responsibilities of the various masses and forces involved.

In conclusion, social cognition is both similar to and different from other sorts of cognition. There do seem to be some distinctive, "domain-specific" cognitive tools for gaining information about social objects. In fact it would not be surprising if it turned out that our species has evolved some innate modules for this task (Leslie, 1994), just as it probably has for acquiring natural language (Chapter 8). Still, we should also remember that it is the same human mind that does the thinking, and most of the basic processes and operations used in social cognition are probably also used in nonsocial cognition.

We now turn to the beginnings of the understanding of people and their behavior. We first look at infant social cognition before moving to research more commonly associated with a theory of mind. We then turn to other domains of social cognition and finally to the uses of all of this knowledge.

SOCIAL-COGNITIVE DEVELOPMENT DURING INFANCY

The observation of Stephanie that began this chapter shows that even babies are beginning to develop notions about other people, themselves, and the relation between the self and others. It should not be surprising that babies possess the ability to forge these social cognitions early in life, for they are members of a species that is dependent on other people for survival during infancy. Fortunately, human infants, like the young of many other species, are well equipped cognitively by evolution to begin the developmental process of interacting with and understanding conspecifics. Cognitive equipment that helps infants attract the attention of adults, keep them nearby, and predict and control their behavior clearly boosts their social cognitive development. For good recent accounts of infant social cognition, see Meltzoff, Gopnik, and Repacholi (1999), Rochat (1999), and Tomasello (1999).

Early Social Cognitive Understanding

The social utility of infants' abilities described in Chapters 2 and 3 will now become apparent. Early preferences for attending to voices and faces; intermodal perception (for example, matching mouth movements with speech patterns, or a happy voice with a happy face); imitation of facial expressions and other human behavior; and the concept of object permanence are put to good use as the baby becomes a social thinker.

Consider first their visual abilities and preferences. As indicated in Chapter 2, babies tend to be especially visually attentive to large objects that move, have edges and contours that exhibit high light-dark contrast, and are brightly colored or shiny. And what objects in the baby's environment have those properties in spades? You guessed it—looming and animated human faces displaying high-contrast hairlines and prominent, shining eyes. People are goods with flashy packaging for the infant consumer. Better yet these animated faces also make noise. As described in other chapters, babies seem to be pretuned to process human speech sounds, and may even be able to learn about their mother's voice prenatally. Infants prefer human voices, particularly infant-directed speech, over other stimuli. They also appreciate the synchrony of a voice and its proper face, and take on the emotion in their mother's face.

Young infants perceive people as having a constant size and shape; by the second half of the first year, they can even recognize their own face as a familiar stimulus (Legerstee, Anderson, & Schaffer, 1998) and classify faces on the basis of sex (Fagan, 1976). Thus infants clearly are well on their way to learning about the social world.

Imitation is a prime social tool for an infant. As discussed in Chapter 2, probably even newborns can imitate some facial expressions. Moreover, infants apparently somehow know when they are being imitated and prefer to attend to adults who do so. Meltzoff (1990) showed this in an experiment in which a 14-month-old baby faced two adults across a table. All three had the same toy. Whenever the baby moved or otherwise manipulated the toy, both adults responded immediately. One imitated the baby's actions, while the other performed some other action with the toy (i.e., those of the previous subject). The baby smiled and looked longer at the imitating adult. We would not conclude that babies, like adults, know that imitation is the sincerest form of flattery, but we would conclude that they detected behaviors that matched their own and were interested in adults (usually parents in real life) who tend to imitate them.

Parent and child shared attention to some object or event is still another critical social cognitive skill (Moore, 1999). This *sharing* of attention progresses to *following* another person's gaze and later *directing* others' attention and behavior (Carpenter, Nagell, & Tomasello, 1998). By 9 months, babies reliably and easily follow their mother's line of sight (Scaife & Bruner, 1975) and begin to follow her pointing gestures (Murphy & Messer, 1977). Babies care deeply about what their mothers are attending to (i.e., look at me!), as illustrated in one mother's report about her 8-month-old:

> He likes the curtains—to try and close them, he doesn't like to be told off for that; he usually waits to go for the curtains when I'm in the kitchen, when I'm around here he doesn't tend to go that much because he knows he's not really allowed to do it, because if I just go into the kitchen and get something, he thinks I'm not looking and makes a beeline for the curtain. Makes a dash for it, you can see him looking over his shoulder to see if I'm watching him, and if I tell him from the kitchen "no"—he stops and looks at you and grins for a while and if I sort of say no really loudly—not loudly it's actually more deep—he lets go and gives a start and whimpers a bit. As soon as I've turned my back he makes another move for it—tends not to do it if I'm actually watching. (Reddy, 1991, p. 146)

Joint attention to some object or event of mutual interest often scaffolds infants' intentional nonverbal (for example, pointing) and verbal communications, described in Chapter 8. In this way infants both initiate connections with another person and speed along their language development.

Infants not only express a variety of emotions themselves—often long and loud—but also gradually become responsive to other people's facial and gestural expressions of emotion. They eventually even learn to use these expressions as guides to prudent actions, a behavior called *social referencing* (Saarni, Mumme, & Campos, 1998; Thompson, 1998). For example, when a 12- or 18-month-old is introduced to a novel and somewhat frightening toy in the company of his mother, he is likely to consult her facial expression before making his next move. If her expression is happy, he will approach the toy; if it is fearful, he will approach her instead. Imagine, if you can, an infant's "consulting" a nonsocial object in this way.

Babies show that they distinguish human from nonhuman objects because their behavior shows that they know that humans can do things (with them) that other objects cannot. By age 5 to 8 weeks, babies imitate mouth openings and tongue protrusions produced by an adult but not similar-looking behaviors produced by an object (Legerstee, 1991). Infants also are more surprised when an inanimate object seems to move entirely on its own, with nothing pushing it, than when a person does (e.g., Spelke, Phillips, & Woodward, 1995). Or, consider the following study (Poulin-Dubois & Shultz, 1988): Infants saw a ball "spontaneously" roll and hit a second ball, which struck a wobbling doll. The 13-month-olds did not significantly decrease their attention (habituate) to this ball-as-agent condition over the 10 trials. In contrast they did habituate to a person-as-agent condition, a person pushing a ball, which is a less interesting event if you believe that people but not objects are agentic. A final example is that infants try to retrieve a just-disappeared object by reaching toward its place of disappearance, but try to retrieve a just-disappeared person merely by vocalizing to the person (Legerstee, 1992).

Thus, early on, an infant seems to know that people, unlike most other objects, will spontaneously interact and communicate with her and are responsive to her signals. She learns that when she wants a ball, no matter how much she shouts at it or smiles at it, the ball does not roll to her. Through these experiences a baby becomes aware that other people's behavior is predictable and can even be contingent on her own behavior.

With all of these tools and skills, infants are ready to begin to construct concepts of people, mind, and society. In particular, they learn to monitor, control, and predict the behavior of others. One important product is the child's first major social connection—attachment to her caregivers.

Internal Working Models

Early social relationships would be impossible without the skills described earlier. The predisposition to look at faces ensures that babies attend often and long to the people they see most often—usually the parents. Even newborns may prefer their mother's face, and they proceed to discriminate other specific people with whom they will become attached. As infants learn to discriminate one looming face with a silly grin from another (no mean achievement, when you think about it), they recognize or identify particular faces as special, recurrent, and familiar; and thus form social-emotional bonds to particular individuals. More generally, the parent constitutes a complex bundle of sights, sounds, feelings, and smells, and this bundle must become quickly and easily distinguishable from other, quite similar bundles before the infant can become differentially attached to it. In addition, the concept of object permanence seems implicated in social attachment. So long as "out of sight, out of mind" applies to the infant's mother as well as to other objects, one could hardly say that a baby's attachment to her had progressed very far.

A currently "hot" area of research on cognition and attachment concerns infants' *internal working models* (Bowlby, 1969; Bretherton, 1993; Bretherton & Munholland, 1999) of this relationship (see Thompson, 1998, for a review). As an infant becomes attached to her caretaker, she constructs a mental model or "representation" of the caretaker, of herself, and of their interactions. This mental model includes expectations about self and other, such as whether the parent will be responsive to her needs, and whether she herself is worthy of attention. That is, infants generalize similar routine interaction sequences with a caretaker into generalized episodes, much like the scripts described in Chapter 4. Infants use these internal working models to interpret events and predict what will happen in the future. For example, if a mother has consistently responded to the baby's signals, the baby will develop the expectation that the mother will do so in the future.

These models affect subsequent relationships, for the models serve as "interpretive filters through which new relationships and other experiences are construed, providing implicit decision rules for relating to others that may, for better or worse, help to confirm and perpetuate intuitive expectations about oneself and others" (Thompson, 1998, p. 36). These cognitions concerning relationships with others are believed to continue into adulthood (Main & Goldwyn, 1998) and spill over into romantic relationships and to relationships with one's own children (Bretherton, 1993; Steele, Steele, & Fonagy, 1996). Currently there is great interest in how disordered parent-infant relationships due to disturbances in the parent or the physically at-risk nature of the infant lead to disordered internal working models (Thompson, 1998). For example, clinically depressed mothers, who may not synchronize well with their infants' behaviors, present such an environment (e.g., Field, Healy, Goldstein, & Guthertz, 1990).

In summary, some grasp of the person-nonperson distinction and the unique features of human beings is achieved by the end of infancy. Infants' social cognitive skills help them win the biggest prize of all—one or more caretakers with whom they have cognitive and emotional bonds. Moreover, as a baby succeeds in making other people treat him like a person, this may thereby help him become one. Other people's imbuing him with a mind may cause them to give him even more exposure to the psychological world in the form of conversations, turn-taking games, and mental verbs.

Young infants' understanding of other people leads naturally to the next section on theory of mind. After a brief description of what is meant by theory of mind, we revisit infancy to look for early evidence of understanding of the mind in the early competencies previously described.

CHILDREN'S KNOWLEDGE ABOUT THE MIND

An experimenter shows a 5-year-old a candy box with pictures of candy on it and asks her what she thinks is in it. She of course replies "candy," as would any adult (at least those not suspicious of psychological researchers). Then the child looks inside the box and discovers to her surprise that it actually contains not candy but crayons. The experimenter then asks her what another child who has not yet seen inside the box would think is inside it. The child says "candy," amused at the deception. Things go a bit differently with a 3-year-old, however. His response to the initial question is the same—"candy"—but his response to the second question is surprising—an unamused "crayons." It may surprise you even more to know that in response to further questioning he also claims that he had initially thought there were crayons in the box and had even said that there were! This difference between

3- and 5-year-olds illustrates a critical difference in their conceptions of mind. That is, 3-year-olds do not yet realize that people have representations of the world that may be true or false and that people act on the basis of these mental representations rather than the way the world actually is. In contrast, 5-year-olds understand the nature of such "false beliefs." This now-classic set of findings (Gopnik & Astington, 1988) illustrates what is called children's "theory of mind."

A child cannot make much progress toward understanding everyday events involving people until she has some understanding of the mind. For example she makes sense of her friend's behavior of purposefully rummaging through his toy box by assuming that he *wants* a particular toy, *believes* it can be found there (is *looking* for it), *intends* to play with it, will *feel* sad if he does not find it, and so on. This commonsense understanding, or "folk psychology" (Churchland, 1984), about how the mind works brings order to the social events around her. It provides explanations of others' behavior and allows her to predict others' actions by referring to their beliefs, desires, perceptions, thoughts, emotions, and intentions. Researchers have dubbed these implicit notions about the psychological realm children's *theory of mind* (Bretherton & Beeghly, 1982; Premack & Woodruff, 1978; Wellman, 1979).

Investigators use the term "theory of mind" in both a loose and a restricted way. It can refer loosely to any knowledge about the mind—any naive psychology—the beginnings of which can be seen in infants. Or the term can be used more strictly, as it is in the "theory theory" approach described in Chapters 1 and 4 and later in this chapter. This more restricted definition refers to an everyday, informal "framework" for understanding the mental world. This "theory" consists of an abstract, coherent, causal-explanatory system that allows the child to explain and predict behavior by referring to unobservable mental states such as beliefs and desires. In this view children do not merely have a set of unconnected facts about the mind and behavior. Rather, by age 5 or so their concepts of emotions, desires, beliefs, and perceptions are all interrelated, as shown in the toy box example. And minds are clearly distinguished from nonminds. Researchers disagree regarding the extent to which young children have a theory of mind in this stricter sense, however. We discuss theory of mind in the broader sense but return to the more restricted theory theory in the section on theoretical accounts of the development of the understanding of the mind.

It is hard to imagine what the world of people would seem like without knowledge about the mental world. When lecturing on theory of mind, Alison Gopnik makes this point with the following imagery (see Flavell, 2000). Imagine what it would be like for you to give a lecture to an audience if you had no conception of mental states. The audience might appear to you as bags of meat with two small holes at the top. You would see these bags and the shiny things in their holes shift around unpredictably in a way that perplexes and terrifies you, although of course you do not realize that you are perplexed and terrified. Perhaps people seem a bit like this to people with autism, who apparently are deficient in knowledge about the mind.

We first present the beginnings of understanding the mind during infancy and then look at later developments as children become better "mind readers." Final sections address differences in theory of mind and then theories of mental understanding. Just to give a quick overview, we could say that children appear to learn that the mind exists, and is separate from but has connections to the physical world.

Children also learn that the mind can represent objects and events accurately or in-accurately, and, rather than function like a camera, actively mediates the interpretation of reality and the emotion experienced.

The following account of the developing knowledge of the mind is our view of this phenomenon. Although there is general agreement among theorists of theory of mind about the general pattern of development, there is disagreement as to the details, for example, the age of attainment of a particular concept and the causes of development. For reviews of a variety of views on theory of mind, and recent findings in this area, see Astington (1993, 2000), Bartsch and Wellman (1995), Carpenter, Nagell, and Tomasello (1998), Flavell (1999), Flavell and Miller (1998), Hala (1997), Mitchell (1997), Moore (1996), Perner (1999), Taylor (1996), Wellman and Gelman (1998), and Zelazo, Astington, and Olson (1999).

Infants' and Toddlers' Understanding of Mind

Researchers recently have shown considerable interest in the infant beginnings of understanding of mind (Baldwin & Moses, 1994; Moore, 1996; Rochat, 1999). A main issue in theory of mind research today is how much and what kind of knowledge about the mind we should attribute to infants.

Our earlier discussion of social cognition in infancy describes advances that set the stage for acquiring knowledge about minds by creating a social situation that would encourage such learning. An infant tends to look at his parent's face and listen to her voice, imitate it, note where she is looking, use her facial expression to interpret a potentially fearful event, and predict what she will do if he does such and such. Other precursors or early forms of knowledge about minds might include responding differently to people versus things and intentionally trying to communicate with others and influence them to approach, comfort, and entertain. These rudimentary skills lead to two social skills of infancy that form the beginnings of a theory of mind. One skill is *reciprocity*—back and forth behaviors between an infant and another person. The other is the *matching* between infant and another person of mental states, behaviors, or emotions; infants first physically match through imitation of actions and later match psychologically. We now look at both reciprocity and matching.

Reciprocity with an Agentic Other. A prime way for babies to learn about other people's behavior and their relation to themselves is to interact with them. They know that human beings are very special objects with which they can interact in very special ways (Poulin-Dubois, 1999). A baby becomes aware that other people's behavior is predictable and can even be contingent on her own behavior. She acts, and the other person reacts appropriately. If her action is a request, the other person will function as a means to her goal without her making physical contact with him—that is, the other person will behave as an active, communicative agent in the service of her needs and wants (her personal slave) rather than as a passive, uncommunicative tool or instrument that she must physically manipulate. The baby senses both her personal active initiatives, or *agency* (e.g., "I can make Mommy come by crying"), and the agency inherent in others (e.g., "Mommy can feed me"). Thus infants come to see other people as "compliant agents" who are influencable at a distance and who honor requests for help in obtaining goals. That is, other agents can be influenced by the infant's intentional communications and consequently can make good things happen. Babies learn that contingency proceeds in the opposite direction as well. The other person acts and the baby reacts appropriately. Eventually the baby expands her awareness to extended reciprocal contingencies. She learns how to manage an alternating sequence of reciprocal actions with another person by taking a turn in a simple social game such as peek-a-boo or in a baby-style "conversation" of prelinguistic utterances, then she waits for the other person to take a turn, then she takes another turn, and so on (see Chapter 8, on language). Babies expect these routines to form a particular pattern. For example, by four months of age, babies differentiate between a stranger performing the usual peek-a-boo sequence (lean forward, make eye contact, cover face, drop hand, say "peekaboo!" lean back, nod, and smile) and one performing a randomly scrambled one (Rochat, Querido, & Striano, 1999). That is, they tend to smile at the former and stare solemnly at the latter.

These parent-child interactions can become quite elaborate. Consider the following example of a sequence of contingent social interchanges between an infant and her father (F):

> Shamini (9 months) within a chatting session following some showing-off with eye-crinkling, etc., and following a few pleasant give and take exchanges, offers objects to F saying "ta" and waving her fingers with it as an additional call, looking at F's face intently; F stretches hand out to take it, as F's hand comes closer, Shamini with eyes intently on F's face begins to smile, then withdraws object with smile broadening and turns away, then looks back, F laughs, and says in a voice acknowledging being teased "You, gimme, gimme, gimme" stretching his hand closer to her face; Shamini makes briefly as if to run, but is caught by the high chair she is in, then turns around again, by which time F has withdrawn his hand. She repeats offer saying "ta, ta" with her face this time less intent and with a slight smile, F holds out hand again, Shamini repeats withdrawal with smile broadening as F's hand approaches and as she turns rapidly away. (Reddy, 1991, p. 146)

One cannot imagine a baby trying to engage in such behavior with her blocks or blanket.

Do reciprocal interactions such as these indicate some understanding that people have something mindlike? Infants do seem to understand that people possess "something"—perhaps agency (self-initiated movement) and influenceability at a distance by communicative signals (compliance)—that non-people entities do not. Later, older infants seem to infer not only human agency (self-initiated movement) but also intentionality. For example, they recognize what a person is trying to do (e.g., detach one object from another one) even if the person does not succeed in doing it and therefore never actually demonstrates the intended action (Meltzoff, 1995).

Matching of Experiences.   Reciprocity surely encourages a sense of "us," of shared experiences such as internal feelings, affects, and public expressions of feelings—an "intersubjectivity," "mirroring," or "echoing" between adult and child (Rochat & Striano, 1999). This notion seems to involve matching, the second skill mentioned earlier. Through interactions infants have the opportunity to match their feelings and actions with those of adults. This "like me" stance may begin to emerge as early as two months of age (Rochat & Striano, 1999).

Infants may dimly perceive that others, and perhaps the self, are experiencers. Their behaviors toward others described earlier suggest that by the end of the first year they at least dimly realize that inner experiences, which adults would call desires, emotions, and intentions, exist (the Existence category). Furthermore, these inner states can be shared with another person, a "meeting of minds," through signals (Bretherton, 1990). An infant points to her open toy box and says "ga!" Her "compliant agent" mother picks up a toy and says "You want this one?" (Typically, of course, the mother has to repeat the question for a dozen toys, under a barrage of progressively louder "ga"s, before guessing the desired toy.)

The way that this "connecting" of minds transforms the infant's earlier social skills can be seen in a study comparing early and advanced social referencing (Striano & Rochat, in press). Babies observed a remote-controlled toy dog that barked every 30 seconds. Seven-month-olds looked at the experimenter's face after the barking events (in astonishment, no doubt) regardless of whether the experimenter was attending to them. In contrast, 10-month-olds looked at the experimenter only if the experimenter was attending to them. Striano and Rochat interpreted this as showing that only the older infants could detect the adult's intentional stance, or connecting, toward them.

Aboutness. Reciprocity and matching of experiences are related to a third quality of the human mind—aboutness. Early in the first year, infants begin to learn how people *differ* from objects. Late in the first year, they begin to learn how people *relate* to objects psychologically. This special way that people relate to objects might be called "aboutness." That is, people relate to objects psychologically; they connect with objects and experience something about an object. A father's behavior with a toy is "about" the toy if he looks at it, smiles at it, calls it a "panda," thinks about handing it to the baby, tries to reach it, or relates to it in some other psychological way.

Infants certainly seem to do certain things that make us infer this dawning awareness of aboutness. An infant can infer that his father is looking at the panda and looks at it himself. He looks back and forth between his father and the panda. He tries to get his father to get the panda through vocalizing or pointing or just bouncing up and down. That is, he is trying to bring about new "aboutnesses" in others. By 12 months infants expect a person to reach for an object that the person is looking at with positive affect rather than for an unattended object (Spelke, Vishton, & Hofsten, 1995). This facial expression is "about" a particular object, as is the adult's spoken label "about" the object (Moses, Baldwin, Rosicky, & Tidball, in press). By 18 months, infants know to give an adult a food that the adult had reacted to positively rather than one reacted to negatively (Repacholi & Gopnik, 1997). By 19–20 months, an infant recognizes that when the father says "panda," he is referring to the black and white object that father is looking at rather than the toy airplane that he himself is attending to (Baldwin, 1993; Baldwin & Moses, 1994). This understanding is particularly intriguing because it suggests that the infant knows that it is the adult's attentional focus rather than his own that indicates the adult's referential intent. We return to the role of joint attention in word learning in Chapter 8. These behaviors taken together suggest that during the second year of life babies have a remarkably nonegocentric sense about other people's intentions and desires—their aboutness with respect to objects and events.

Infants' growing ability to infer an adult's aboutness with respect to objects and predict the adult's behavior lays the foundation for later, more advanced inferences about "dispositions to behave." The awareness of these dispositions may be central to what is called a desire psychology in 2- and 3-year-olds—their belief that a person's desires lead to certain behaviors that satisfy that desire.

Advances During Toddlerhood.   During the second year of life, one sort of evidence for an awareness that others have inner experiences is that infants comfort younger siblings in distress by hugging, patting, or kissing them, and may even bring a security blanket to an adult expressing pain (Zahn-Waxler, Radke-Yarrow, Wagner, & Chapman, 1992). Their attempts to cheer up others sometimes take unexpected forms. Dunn and Kendrick (1982a) describe a plump 15-month-old who often amused his parents by pulling up his shirt to reveal an impressive stomach. One day, upon observing his 3-year-old brother crying after a fall, he approached him, pulled up his shirt to show off his stomach, and looked expectantly at him! This new power to change emotions, however, is a force for evil as well as good. As parents stretched to the limits of their patience know, young children sometimes tease or otherwise annoy siblings, hoping to elicit frustration and anger. These episodes usually involve destroying a favorite possession or taunting, but occasionally are more subtle, as when one 24-month-old child teased her sister by pretending to be her imaginary friend (Dunn & Munn, 1985). Such behaviors, positive or negative, are revealing, for they suggest that children understand that mental states can be manipulated and are beginning to identify the conditions that elicit or change these emotional states.

Toddlers more clearly show some understanding of mental states by spontaneously referring to these states, for example, "those ladies scare me" (Wellman, 1993). Two-year-olds mention emotional states and even participate with a sibling in pretend games in which they take on a pretend internal state themselves, assign it to the sibling, or share it with the sibling (Dunn, Bretherton, & Munn, 1987). They also discuss the causes of the feeling states, and sometimes use these states to try to influence behavior, as illustrated in the following exchange between a mother and a 24-month-old who spots a chocolate cake (Dunn, Bretherton, & Munn, 1987, p. 136).

> *Child sees chocolate cake on table.*
> Child: Bibby on.
> Mother: You don't want your bibby on. You're not eating.
> Child: Chocolate cake. Chocolate cake.
> Mother: You're not having any more chocolate cake either.
> Child: Why? [*whines*] Tired.
> Mother: You tired? Ooh!
> Child: Chocolate cake.
> Mother: No chance.

By age 2 or so, children more clearly refer to needs, emotions, and other mental states: "My baby needs me," "Don't feel bad, Bob," and "I forgot my pacifier" (Bretherton & Beeghly, 1982). They also use intentional action or desire words, for example, "wants to" (Bartsch, 1990; Huttenlocher & Smiley, 1990). Cognitive terms such as know, remember, and think generally come after perceptual and emotional terms, but are in place before age 3. Later, children will make finer distinctions in their language among mental phenomena, such as guessing versus knowing, believing versus fantasizing, and intending versus "not on purpose."

Issues of Interpretation. Of course, it is not clear whether children actually have mental states in mind when they use these mental state words. Instead, children may be referring to behaviors or internal physical states or perhaps a more rudimentary "aboutness" toward objects and events in the situation. A 3-year-old and a 9-year-old who say "think" and "want" undoubtedly have different degrees of sophistication in their concepts.

More generally researchers disagree as to whether to give a "rich" or "lean" interpretation to the early theory of mind competencies (rich) or precursors (lean) described in this section (Baldwin & Moses, 1994; Moore & Corkum, 1994). Do infants actually represent people as having inner mental states, or do they simply detect regularities in people's overt behaviors? For example, in social referencing perhaps an infant simply associates his or her parent's fearful face with "this object is dangerous," with no understanding of a mental state of fear and negative valence (Perner, 1991). The latter understanding is nice to have, but arguably not necessary for responding appropriately. This argument for a conservative interpretation is appropriately scientifically parsimonious. Still, to both professionally trained researchers and experientially trained parents, older infants convey the strong sense that they are indeed doing some kind of mind reading. Particularly convincing is the fact that infants show these behaviors in a variety of ways: "For example, around this age important developments take place in areas as diverse as pretence . . . , self-recognition . . . , imitation . . . , empathy . . . , and internal state language . . . , suggesting that infants may have already achieved some general conceptual insight into the minds of others" (Baldwin & Moses, 1994, p. 150). The jury is still out as we await further empirical evidence, particularly from the discovery of better methods for peering into the infant mind.

Later Developments in Knowledge about the Mind

Regardless of whether one gives a rich or lean interpretation to infant behaviors, it is clear that a detailed and penetrating knowledge of the psychological characteristics of personhood (e.g., that people have false beliefs or may not mean what they say) is still a thing of the distant future. A now-vast literature from the last 20 years has much to say about theory of mind after infancy. To give a sense of where we are headed, we provide Figure 6.2, which presents one influential view of what a mature theory mind might look like. It shows, for example, that people believe that what they perceive influences what they think about and believe; that what they believe may bias what they perceive; and that various mental and physiological states lead to desires. It also indicates that beliefs and desires can lead to intentions, which in turn may lead to goal-directed actions, and that people will react emotionally to the success or failure of these actions. Thus what is developing is a system of understanding of the nature and operations of the entire structure and content of the mind. We now examine children's understanding of various aspects of mind—visual perception, attention, desires, emotions, intentions, beliefs and related mental representations, pretense, and thinking.

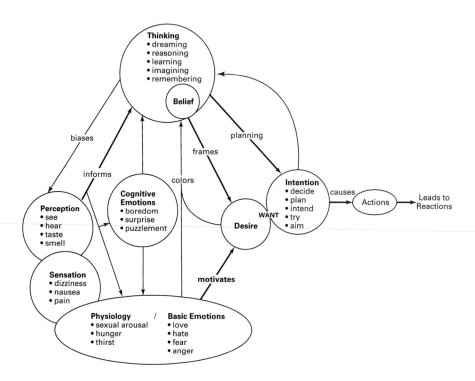

FIGURE 6.2   A belief-desire theory of mind. From *The Child's Theory of Mind* (p. 109), by H. M. Wellman, 1999, Cambridge, MA: MIT Press. Copyright © 1990 by MIT Press. Reprinted by permission.

Visual Perception.   Understanding percepts is important, because knowing what goes into the mind through the senses (e.g., "She sees a candy bar") affects inferences about what another person desires ("She wants it") and believes ("She thinks she can reach it if she stands on her tiptoes on a chair"), other aspects of theory of mind. We saw earlier that young infants can follow an adult's gaze and try to direct the adult's gaze. By the end of infancy, if not earlier, children have some understanding that people see things and that looking at them psychologically connects people to ("is about") these objects. Even 18-month-olds, when asked to show a picture to someone who has covered her eyes with her hands, will move the hands or try to put the picture between the hands and eyes (Lempers, Flavell, & Flavell, 1977). They try to show pictures to another person in such a way that they too can continue to see them, whereas a slightly older child turns the pictures away from himself and faces them toward the other. Similarly, when asked to show a small picture glued to the inside bottom of an opaque cup, 18-month-olds try to hold the cup low and tilt its opening back and forth so that both they and the other person can get alternating glimpses of it! Toddlers rejoice in their newfound knowledge by not only creating such percepts in others but also preventing them by hiding objects.

During the preschool years, children go through two levels of understanding of percepts. In Level 1, 2- and 3-year olds understand that a person sees an object only if the person's eyes are open and directed toward the object and if there are no obstacles blocking his view (Flavell, 1992). This understanding permits them to do some simple visual perspective-taking. For example, they can infer that they and another person might see different objects, or only one of them might see a particular object. In an impressive show of nonegocentrism, they can deny that another person sees something that is compellingly visible to them. They know that they can see what is on their side of a vertically held card, whereas another person, seated opposite, cannot.

Level 1 understanding concerns *whether* something is seen, whereas Level 2 understanding concerns exactly *how* that something looks to another person. Level 2 knowledge is that even though both self and other can see the same object, it looks different to people viewing it from different positions. A 4- or 5-year-old knows that a drawing of a turtle placed between him and someone across from him can appear "right side up" to him and "upside down" to the other person (Masangkay et al., 1974). Thus the Level 1 child thinks about *viewing objects*, but not yet about *views of objects*.

Attention. Another psychological connection ("aboutness") between mind and the external world is a mind attending to something in the world. Infants' understanding of what a person is looking at and attending to, from the person's direction of gaze (Baron-Cohen, 1995), becomes more complex later on. Children acquire at least four facts about attention (Fabricius & Schwanenflugel, 1994; Flavell, Green, & Flavell, 1995a; Miller, 1985; Pillow, 1995). First, people attend selectively rather than to everything in their surroundings. Four-year-olds may conceive of the mind as more like a lamp than a flashlight; they do not understand, for example, that when one is busy trying to recognize the people in a group photograph, one will not at the same time pay any significant amount of attention to the photo's visible but unremarkable picture frame (Flavell et al., 1995a). Second, different people may mentally represent in different ways the same attended-to information; the mind is constructive. Third, attention involves a limited capacity; only a certain amount of information can be processed. Fourth, people process stimuli at various levels of attention or awareness. For example, older children and adults watching a videotaped sleeping person stir but not wake up in response to a light touch tend to say that the sleeper "sort of" felt the touch but did not consciously know that she had been touched. Most kindergartners, however, do not yet make this distinction; they usually say that the person has both the conscious thought and the low-level feeling (Flavell, Green, Flavell, & Lin, 1999).

Children become increasingly aware of the psychological processes underlying attention, particularly the distracting aspects of noise and the failure to attend to verbal messages. Miller and Bigi (1979) found that when talking about attention, young children usually assert that unless the situation is noisy, a person will hear and comprehend what someone says. The disruptive effect of noise was vividly described by an 8-year-old: "When it's noisy, I can't read; it seems as though everything around me is moving around and dropping on the floor and breaking or something, so when I'm reading I just can't stand it." By about age 8, children begin to realize that the mind controls the attentional process to some extent. This shows some awareness of the active, interpretive nature of mind that we discuss later. They know, for example, that a lack of interest in what someone is saying (usually a teacher!) makes a person shut out the message, even if the room is quiet. Similarly, strong interest in an activity reduces attention to other sounds. One child thought that she would not hear her mother calling her if she were engrossed in reading because "when I'm really getting into something everything just stops and I can't hear anything except what I'm doing." As usual, less verbally demanding methods suggest that some of this knowledge emerges earlier (e.g., Miller & Shannon, 1984; Miller & Zalenski, 1982; Pillow, 1988, 1989).

Desires. Infants' rudimentary grasp of desires, described earlier, and toddlers' use of "wants" and "tries" leads to the 2-year-old's "desire psychology." This theory includes simple causal relations among desires, perceptions, emotions, actions, and outcomes (see Bartsch & Wellman, 1995). Young children understand that if Joey wants hot oatmeal for breakfast he will be happy if that desire (goal) is satisfied and sad if he gets cold spaghetti instead (Banerjee & Wellman, 1990). Similarly they know that people stop searching if they find the desired object they have been seeking but keep searching if they do not. They also grasp the possibility that different people can have different desires and attitudes about the same thing, for example, that they themselves do not like coffee but an adult might (Flavell, Mumme, Green, & Flavell, 1992).

Emotions. Children must understand emotions in order to do effective "social work," such as identifying the feelings of other people toward them, anticipating whether their parents will be angry or pleased about their behavior, and hiding their socially inappropriate feelings. Such knowledge surely promotes positive (or negative) relationships with others, effective self-presentation, and the attainment of rewards or interpersonal advantage. The early understanding of emotions clearly is linked to other aspects of theory of mind, for example, in the understanding that a person who does not like chocolate (hard to imagine) would not be happy upon receiving it and would not be sad if he does not. For useful reviews of the literature, see Banerjee (1997) and Saarni, Mumme, and Campos (1998).

Earlier we mentioned infants' social referencing, which may indicate some understanding of emotions. Then, by 20 months, they may use the words "happy," "sad," "mad," and "scared" (Bretherton, McNew, & Beeghly-Smith, 1981) and, by 28 months, "have fun" and "love" (Bretherton & Beeghly, 1982). By 2½ they even talk about such theory-of-mind-like topics as the causes and consequences of these emotions in themselves and others (Beeghly, Bretherton, & Mervis, 1986). For example, "Santa will be happy if I pee in the potty" and "Bees everywhere. Scared me" (Bretherton & Beeghly, 1982). Note that these causal statements can refer to the past or the future, and imagined circumstances, as well as the present. Concepts of emotion evolve from a global "feels good" and "feels bad" to a range of differentiated emotions, for example, "mean," "excited," "proud," "worried," and "disappointed." Although, as we noted earlier, the level of understanding of mental states involved in the early utterances is still an open question, children clearly are distinguishing "something" inside and unseen from the overt facial expressions and behaviors such as hitting and hugging that are caused by emotions.

Children also come to understand an even more complex relation between emotions and behavior in *display rules*—for example that someone can look happy but hide sadness, as when a boy wants a computer game for his birthday, receives socks instead, but smiles nevertheless. Parents may socialize display rules by prompts such as, "Tell Aunt Grace how much you like the nice shirt she gave you." Preschools do not understand display rules very well (Gnepp & Hess, 1986; Harris, Donnelly, Guz, & Pitt-Watson, 1986), for it requires understanding that a single reality can lead to two contradictory mental representations—the felt emotion and the socially appropriate one.

The concept of facial display is an important one, permitting new and adaptive ways of interacting with others—ways that prevent negative reactions from others. A child learns very quickly that expressing certain emotions leads to taunts of "scaredy-cat," "party-pooper," "wimp," or "crybaby" from peers or censure from adults. One grade school child who suddenly felt like giggling at a funeral said, "I'd walk over away from Mom, like walk over to a tree, turn away, and then giggle if I really had to" (Saarni, 1989). Children learn many ways to put Satan behind them! Older children also believe, however, that it is maladaptive to go to the extreme of always hiding disapproved emotions. As one psychodynamically oriented 13-year-old girl expressed it, if a girl "kept everything inside her all the time, she'd consume all her anger, jealousy, whatever, and then one day she'd explode, commit suicide, and get emotionally disturbed" (Saarni, 1988, p. 289). Finally, understanding facial displays is "an important element in children's understanding of the potential privacy of their mental world" (Meerum Terwogt & Harris, 1993, p. 760).

Another complex notion is that people can experience two conflicting emotions at the same time, for example, feeling happy about going on a long summer vacation while feeling sad about leaving friends. Young children explain that it is impossible to feel happy and sad at the same time because, for example, "You can't make your mouth go up and down at the same time" (Harter & Buddin, 1987) and "You haven't got two heads—you haven't got enough brains" (Harris, 1989a). Before 6 or 7 years of age, children generally are limited to describing situations eliciting two successive emotions: "If you were in a haunted house you'd be scared but then you'd be happy after you got out of it" (Harter, 1982, but see Kestenbaum and Gelman, 1995, for earlier competencies in this area). Not until approximately age 10 do children understand that two opposite-valenced emotions, such as happy and sad, can be experienced simultaneously: "I was mad at my brother for hitting me but at the same time, I was really happy that my father gave me permission to hit him back" (Harter & Buddin, 1987; but see Stein & Trabasso, 1989, for evidence of earlier competence). Thus, children have problems with these dual, conflicting representations.

Intentions. Tomasello (1999) argues that infants' understanding that others are intentional beings makes the transmission of culture from one generation to another possible. When an infant sees an agentic adult using language or tools, she knows that he has intentions, as she does, and intends to achieve some goal, as when he uses a knife *in order to* cut bread or reaches for an object because he *desires* it. Once this social-cognitive skill evolved, humans could "imagine themselves 'in the mental shoes' of some other person, so that they can learn not just *from* the other but *through* the other" (p. 6). In this way each generation can build on the knowledge of the previous generation so that culture accumulates over generations rather than starts anew with each generation. Tomasello argues that other primate do not have the concept of intentions and thus cannot understand events from others' point of view.

Knowledge about intentions also is indispensable for understanding responsibility and morality. Children must learn that people deserve to be praised or credited, blamed, or judged to be blameless, depending in part on whether what they did was intentional or unintentional. Good sources on the childhood development of knowledge about intentions include Moses (1993) and Zelazo, Astington, and Olson (1999).

We saw that infants have some notion of humans as "free agents" that can move on their own accord. This early notion of agency may serve as a building block for the more mature concept of intentions. The mature concept of intentions goes beyond that of agency by clearly inferring an internal mental state that guides behavior. People not only *can* act, they deliberately *plan* to and *try* to act.

In 2-year-olds, their "desire theory of mind" may cause them to confuse desire and intent, possibly because each is either fulfilled or not fulfilled by an outcome. Three-year-olds may have some rudimentary ability to distinguish intended actions from such nonintentional behaviors as mistakes and reflexes. For example, when 3-year-olds were asked to repeat tongue twisters (e.g., "She sells sea shells by the sea shore"), and inevitably made mistakes, they knew that they did not mean to say the sentence wrong (Shultz, 1991). By age 4 or 5, children can discriminate intentions from desires or preferences and from the outcomes of intentional behaviors (Astington, 1993; Moses, 1993). For example, they know that a person who tried to get object A but instead obtained the more desirable object B nevertheless originally intended to get A rather than B (Feinfield, Lee, Flavell, Green, & Flavell, 1999). What children understand by age 4 or 5, in a true concept of intention, is that intent is a mental state that exists regardless of the outcome. Intention is a prior state, a mental representation, that plays a mediating causal role between desires and actions.

Beliefs and Related Mental Representations. Older infants have mental representations, toddlers can create mental and external representations in their pretend play, and many 3-year-olds know that a mental representation is not the real thing. However, 3-year-olds probably do not reflect on mental representations—have representations of representations. That is, they do not engage in metarepresentation—both representing the belief and representing it as a belief. In perhaps the most major shift in children's knowledge about the mind, by age 4 or 5 they understand that a specific real-world thing can be mentally represented in different ways, some of which may be false. Younger children, who believe that an object or event can be represented mentally in only one way, have a theory of mind that is qualitatively very different from that of 4- and 5-year-olds. Stated differently, the earlier stimulus-mind-behavior connections are transformed to a higher level in that a 4-year-old now knows these connections may be inaccurate; the world (stimulus)-representation link may be false—*a false belief.*

It would be an understatement to say that the false belief task has "attracted the attention" of cognitive developmentalists in recent years. A recent meta-analysis of false belief studies included 77 research articles that included 178 separate studies and 591 false-belief conditions (Wellman, Cross, & Watson, in press), and the numbers are still growing rapidly. For reviews see Bartsch and Wellman (1995),

Flavell and Miller (1998), Lewis and Mitchell (1994), S. Miller (2000), and Wellman et al. (in press).

The example of the crayons in the candy box, with which we began this section on theory of mind, illustrates this understanding of false belief. Four-year-olds, but not 3-year-olds, understood that representations can be wrong and can change, as theirs did, even when the reality that the representation is about did not change.

Similarly, consider the following story acted out for children with dolls. A boy puts some chocolate in a blue cupboard and goes out to play. In his absence his mother moves the chocolate to a green cupboard. When the boy returns and wants his chocolate, children are asked where the boy will look for it. Three-year-olds generally say "the green cupboard," where the chocolate actually is, even though the boy had no way of knowing that the chocolate was moved (Wimmer & Perner, 1983). Thus, 3-year-olds do not understand that a person acts on the basis of what that person believes to be true, which can differ from what actually is true in reality. Part of the problem is not fully understanding that a person's access to information determines that person's knowledge and beliefs. The boy's absence during the moving of the chocolate prevents his knowledge of the new hiding place.

In contrast 4- and 5-year-olds usually understand this false belief. They know why a belief can be false (i.e., it is only one of many possible representations) and know that one's belief, rather than reality, guides one's behavior. The false belief test has been called the "litmus test" (Wellman, 1985) of the child's *belief-desire psychology* because it assesses the understanding that representations are just that—representations—and therefore may be true or false but still affect behavior.

This belief-desire psychology is preceded by a *desire psychology,* around age 2, and a *desire-belief psychology* around age 3 (Bartsch & Wellman, 1995). In a desire psychology, children link the mental states of simple desires, emotions, and percepts to external objects through wanting, fearing, and seeing them. However, the child does not yet understand that people have mental representations of these things, accurately or inaccurately, as being a certain way. In a desire-belief psychology, beliefs and thoughts are added to desires, and children seem to understand that beliefs are mental representations that can be false as well as true and can differ from one person to another. However, children continue to explain behavior in terms of desires rather than beliefs. For example, if Sam wants to find his rabbit but does not find it in one location, children predict that he would be sad and would look for it somewhere else. But they do not know that Sam's *beliefs* about possible locations influence where he will look. A desire is an internal experience or disposition (longing, leaning) toward an object or state; a desire can be satisfied or not satisfied. In contrast a belief is a conviction about reality; it is true or false.

Some findings on false belief tasks are particularly compelling. One study (Russell, Mauthner, Sharpe, & Tidswell, 1991) was an attempt to teach children a competitive game in which they were supposed to point deceptively to a box that does not contain candy rather than one that does so that they could keep the candy themselves rather than lose it to their opponent. Although 4-year-olds quickly caught on, 3-year-olds continued trial after trial to point to the box containing the candy rather than the empty box. They did this despite their desire to win the candy and their obvious frustration as they inexplicably kept losing the candy to their opponent. Remarkably, in another study, when 3-year-olds knew there was a blue cup behind a barrier, even when a confederate *said* that she thought there was a white cup behind the barrier, they said that she thought there was a blue cup there (Flavell, Flavell, Green, & Moses, 1990).

Despite these compelling demonstrations, several clever studies have shown that there are some circumstances in which even 3-year-olds may possess at least a shaky understanding of false beliefs. For instance, 3-year-olds can create a false belief in another person in a simple situation involving deception (Chandler, Fritz, & Hala, 1989; Hala, Chandler, & Fritz, 1991). Children used a puppet, who left washable purple footprints as she walked, to hide a treasure in one of several table-top containers. They were told to hide the treasure so the seeker, momentarily absent, would not be able to find it. Most of the 2-year-olds and 3-year-olds erased the footprints to the real hiding place, made small footprints to the wrong box, or lied about the treasure's location, in an attempt to deceive the seeker, which suggests some understanding of false belief (but see Sodian, Taylor, Harris, & Perner, 1991).

Given the occasional demonstration of understanding false beliefs in 3-year-olds, it probably would not surprise you to know that a main point of disagreement among theory-of-mind researchers is whether the understanding of false beliefs emerges at age 3 or at age 4 and, if it does emerge at age 3, the critical conditions for eliciting it. Some ideas about these "critical conditions" include the following. First, children may have an "excessive reality orientation" (Mitchell, 1994, p. 25)—they are more oriented to what actually is the case than to what someone might think is the case. Second, young children know that people try to satisfy their desires and thus may find it natural to say, incorrectly, that the child who wanted the chocolate would search where it really is. Third, they may have limited executive, linguistic, or memory abilities that prevent them from understanding task questions, keeping track of everything, and translating this information into the correct response (e.g., Hughes, 1998; Lewis, 1994; Perner, Stummer, & Lang, 1999; Russell, Jarrold, & Potel, 1994). Fourth, executive functioning skills (see later under Theories), such as self-regulation and inhibition of responses, may be critical. Children may, for example, have trouble inhibiting a dominant response (e.g., pointing to where the chocolate really is).

In light of these proposals, two recent large-scale analyses have tried to identify the important factors that affect children's performance on false belief tasks. One is a recent meta-analysis (Wellman et al., in press) of 178 studies and more than 4,000 children. It identified four task factors that increased the likelihood of passing false belief tasks: (1) the target object was out of sight, and thus reality was less salient, at the time the false belief question was asked; (2) the motive for the transformation (e.g., moving the object) was clear (e.g., to trick the protagonist); (3) the child participated in the transformation; and (4) the protagonist's mental state during the transformation was salient (e.g., "Maxi is gone and can't see"). Although these assessment factors affect performance, children younger than 3½ did not perform above chance levels even under optimal conditions. Thus, some competency has to be in place before performance factors that affect the expression of a competency can matter.

Most of the studies in this meta-analysis created a temporary belief for the testing situation, for example, a person's belief that the chocolate is in a particular location. But consider very different sorts of scenarios (S. Miller, 2000). A 5-year-old who has the concept of conservation of number tries to make sense of the judgments of a peer who consistently expresses a belief in nonconservation. Or a schoolage child tries to decide whether an older brother or father would be more knowledgeable for helping with difficult homework. Unlike in most experiments, these differences in beliefs and knowledge are *brought to* the situation and reflect naturally occurring, preexisting beliefs and knowledge. Thus a second large review (S. Miller, 2000) examined whether children realize that such differences in beliefs exist and what they understand about them. That is, do young children understand that specific real people bring different beliefs and knowledge to the situation and are they able to infer these preexisting differences? Some conclusions confirm, for these preexisting differences, the developmental changes found for understanding temporary situationally created beliefs. Others add to our picture of children's understanding of beliefs. For example, 3- and 4-year-olds realize that adults or older children know more and can do more than younger children. Still, young children are prone to overestimations of the abilities of both adults and children. Thus, the development of understanding of false beliefs becomes even more complex when one adds real-life beliefs and knowledge to the formula.

The most revealing (and remarkable) behaviors may be the transitional ones one occasionally observes, such as the following. Clements and Perner (1994) presented a cardboard mouse who did not know that his cheese had been moved to another box and asked: "I wonder where he is going to look?" followed by "Which box will he open?" They observed some young 3-year-olds look at the location that would indicate that they understand false belief after the first question, but then, when asked the second question, usually used on such tasks, indicated the other box! What would you conclude that these children know? Clearly there are many levels in the acquisition of false belief, from its fragile beginnings to its robust, accessible version much later.

The main issue about false belief is exactly what gets acquired, and when and how it is acquired. For example, exactly what does the false-belief task measure? Some researchers (including us) believe it assesses children's nascent understanding of mental representation, but others would attribute less cognition to children of this age. The various positions here can be inferred from the discussion of theories later in the chapter—children's theories of mind in the strict sense of theory, innate modules, and learning information about mind from experience (including perhaps extrapolating from one own's mind to that of others). See discussions in Flavell and Miller (1998), Leslie (1994; Leslie & Roth, 1993), Harris (1992), Hobson (1991), and Wimmer and Weichbold (1994).

This awareness of the possible discrepancy between the mental and physical, or a belief and the true state, revealed on the false belief task, may be related to four other distinctions that emerge at about the same time. First, consider perceptual perspective taking, described earlier. Just as two different people can have different, even conflicting, beliefs about reality, so can they have different visual perceptions of an array. Second, the domain of emotions, especially the facial displays discussed earlier, also illustrates the discrepancy between two representations. When a child sees a friend smile after falling off his bike and cutting his knee, she is faced with two conflicting representations of the friend's emotion: happy because the child is smiling, sad because of the physical evidence of pain. Only a child who understands the representational process will not be confused by these conflicting representations. Knowing that a single reality can be represented in two conflicting ways also is relevant for understanding that a single situation may elicit different emotions in different people. For instance, whereas one child may feel happy when a peer gives him a snake, another could feel apprehensive.

Third, the notion that an experience can be ambiguous implies that two conflicting knowledge representations can be imagined—a true one and a false one. Four-year-olds are beginning to understand, for example, that the identity of an animal cannot be inferred from seeing only its color through a small hole in a box if two kinds of animals are the same color (Ruffman, Olson, & Astington, 1991). For instance, seeing gray through the hole could lead to a representation of either a gray elephant or a gray rabbit.

A fourth related acquisition is the *appearance-reality distinction,* which we now describe. Just as a child knows that a wax apple that looks remarkably like (appearance) a real apple is not a real apple (reality), so may the child know that someone might falsely believe that it is a real apple. And just as two different people can have different representations (beliefs about or perspectives) of the world, so can a single person represent an object in two different ways—the way it appears at the present moment and the way it really is. Similarly, just as someone can feel sad but appear to be happy, an object can appear one way but really be another way.

Adults continually detect misleading appearances. What we take to be a star turns out to be a plane flying toward us; what we think to be a Picasso proves to be a forgery; what looks like an innocent conversation from a distance is actually a robbery in progress. Finally, all theory and research in all fields of scholarship amount to an effort to find new realities hidden beneath new and old appearances (Carey, 1985a). The need for erasers in this world has no limits.

Typically, 3-year-olds perform poorly on appearance-reality tasks, even when the distinction is made clear to them during pretraining. For example, if 3-year-olds see a red filter wrapped around a glass of white milk, they say that the milk looks red and it "really and truly" is red (Flavell, Green, & Flavell, 1986). Remarkably there are informal observations that they say the same about their own hands under a filter. They apparently do not understand that something can look different from what it really is. Because they do not realize that their perception of the object's appearance is *just* a representation that can be changed, they find this perception a very compelling characterization of what that object *is* right now. Older children, in contrast, can "mentally tag each representation for the cognitive perspective or stance that gave rise to it, for its epistemic credentials, so to speak" (Flavell, 1988, p. 247). Thus they tag one representation as "what it looks like it is" and the other as "what it really is."

Children sometimes make the opposite appearance-reality error as well; they let their knowledge of what something is override their perceptual judgments. For instance, Flavell, Flavell, and Green (1983) presented preschoolers with an extremely realistic fake egg. After the children found out that it actually was a painted stone, many then claimed that it looked like a stone! It is an eerie experience to see a 3-year-old peer at an imitation egg that would fool the most discerning hen and solemnly indicate that it *looks* like a stone to his eyes right now.

Everyday observations also attest to this confusion of appearance and reality, as when one unsuccessfully tries to convince a 3-year-old that a scary, cackling Halloween witch actually is a benign neighbor. Still, 2- and 3-year-olds have some inkling of the true nature of an object. When asked, for example, to choose something to keep a piece of paper from blowing away in the wind, they choose a real rock over a realistic sponge rock (Gauvain & Greene, 1994).

Knowing that what you see may not be what you get has adaptive significance. Young children need to know not to eat plastic food or walk through glass patio doors that appear to be an open passage. The bias toward believing appearances suggests that it might be difficult for parents to instill in their 3-year-olds a healthy wariness of pleasant-appearing adults who might want to harm them.

We can point to still other possible instantiations of a representational concept of mind: understanding the nature of lies or other false statements, jokes, metaphors, sarcasm, and ambiguous statements. People, like fake eggs, present positive external impressions that may differ from their underlying realities. In displaced aggression (e.g., Miller & DeMarie-Dreblow, 1990), Person A is angry at Person B but aggresses against Person C. In all of these realms, things are not always as they seem.

As we describe in other chapters, children younger than age 4 have trouble understanding dual representation in other contexts as well. In early word learning, children often are reluctant to accept a second name for an object; if they know an animal as "kitty," they may reject "cat" (Clark, 1987; Markman, 1989). They also have trouble with hypothetical statements that refer to how things might have been at some other time (Kuczaj, 1981). Finally, younger children have trouble coding a small scale model of a room as both a real three-dimensional toy array and a representation of a real room, as we saw in Chapter 4.

The take-home message is that by age 4 or 5 children have a *representational theory of mind* that understands that reality can be represented in different ways. Thus a representation can be false with respect to a real object or event (in false beliefs and ambiguous visual displays), behavior can be false with respect to a mental state (as when a sad person smiles), physical appearance can be false with respect to an object's identity or property (appearance-reality distinction), and two people's perceptual views or beliefs can differ (perspective taking). These concepts appear to emerge in a child at about the same time and are positively correlated with one another within children (e.g., Flavell et al., 1986; Friend & Davis, 1993; Gopnik & Astington, 1988; but see also Slaughter & Gopnik, 1996).

Knowledge. Several reviews (Bartsch & Wellman, 1995; Montgomery, 1992; O'Neill, 1996; and Taylor, 1996) point to the following sequence of development. Even very young children seem to understand that seeing leads to knowing, and not seeing leads to not knowing. As we described earlier, a 2-year-old can manipulate stimuli to bring about a certain perceptual state when she hides objects so that another person cannot see them (Flavell, Shipstead, & Croft, 1978) or ensures perception by bringing a small picture on the bottom of a box near a person's eyes (Lempers, Flavell, & Flavell, 1977). By age 3, children more clearly are aware of the influence of perception on knowledge. For example, they know that if an object is hidden in a container, someone who has looked in the container knows what is in there, whereas someone who has not looked does not know. However, 3-year-olds will attribute knowledge on the basis of something like desire or engagement rather than perceptual access alone (Montgomery & Miller, 1997). Moreover, preschoolers seem to have little notion of what it means for someone to know something and how that knowledge is acquired (Taylor, 1996). Not until early elementary school age do children know how and when they came to know some recently acquired fact, for example, by seeing it themselves rather than by hearing it from someone else. In addition, 4- and 5-year-olds will without shame claim that they have always known information that they have just learned a few moments ago (Taylor, Esbensen, & Bennett, 1994).

Knowing that access to information is a prerequisite for knowing something becomes more differentiated during the school years. For example, 3- and 4-year-olds have a very limited understanding of the modality-specific nature of knowledge. In one study they were likely to claim that they needed to feel an out-of-view football to find out what color it is and even proceeded to feel it (O'Neill, Astington, & Flavell, 1992). One 3-year-old felt the football, looked at the experimenter with a blank expression, was silent for a few seconds, then said, emphatically, "Red! I can tell it's red," and (lucky guess) triumphantly pulled the red football into view! Thus, young children appear to overestimate what can be learned from one modality. Three-year-olds have a great deal of difficulty with the concept that specific aspects of knowledge, such as shape and color, are the products of specific sensory experiences.

More generally, preschoolers have a lot of trouble tracking the flow of information—from the world to the mind (e.g., perceptual access), within the mind (e.g., inferences), and from one mind to another mind (e.g., communication). They will sometimes wrongly deny knowledge to a person with perceptual access, as well as wrongly attribute knowledge to a person without access, suggesting that they are often unclear about the perceptual conditions that lead to knowledge (Montgomery, 1992; Taylor, 1996). They have difficulty sorting out the contributions of reality and the mind in this process. Although a 3-year-old knows that knowledge comes from being exposed to something in reality, not until age 4 or 5 does the child know that information leads to a representation, that different kinds of information lead to different kinds of representations, and that knowing should not be confused with successful behaviors or outcomes such as a lucky guess. Moreover, he now is beginning to understand how he knows what he knows, for example, from seeing, feeling, or being told something (O'Neill & Gopnik, 1991).

By the beginning of the elementary school years, children seem to know several other important truths about the mental state of knowing (Flavell & Miller, 1998; Montgomery, 1992; Perner, 1991; Taylor, 1996). They understand that in order for perceptually acquired knowledge to be accurate, it must be presented adequately. For example, unlike younger children they know that one often cannot be certain of an object's identity when only a small part is visible. They also realize that the word *know* indicates more speaker certainty than *think* or *guess* and is more likely to be an accurate depiction of the way things really are. In short, although 3-year-olds know that information comes from the world, they do not appreciate the complexity of this process.

At least one more qualitative change of major proportions happens in theory of mind during childhood (and there probably are many more that we still will discover—see Moshman, 1998). Consider the cognitive situation of a 6-year-old. She has understood for a while that the mind mediates the experience of reality, through representations. If it mediates then it potentially could select, organize, or transform information from the environment and therefore distort, correct, or enrich reality. Thus, this next mental leap, during middle childhood and later, is the understanding that the mind actively interprets percepts, emotions, intentions, beliefs, knowledge, and thinking in light of preexisting expectations, knowledge, and other biases (e.g., Chandler & Lalonde, 1996; Fabricius & Schwanenflugel, 1994; Pillow & Henrichon, 1996; Wellman & Hinkling, 1994). Consequently, an advanced understanding of knowledge includes the understanding that the mind shapes knowledge.

An example of understanding that the mind is interpretive is awareness of biases in the processing of social information (Pillow, 1991). Suppose that a child is told a story in which Mike dislikes Tom because he thinks he is mean, starts fights, and gets into trouble a lot. One day Tom bumps into Mike's desk at school, knocking Mike's special airplane he built onto the floor where it breaks into pieces. Second graders realized that Mike, because of his negative beliefs about Tom, would interpret this ambiguous event as showing that Tom knocked off the plane on purpose. Social processing biases show the workings of an active, interpretive mind.

This insight about the essence of human thought—its active, constructive nature—contrasts sharply with the 3-year-old's copy theory of the mind. Children's understanding of mind moves from a Lockeian mind that passively takes in information to a Piagetian mind that actively constructs and interprets, from an entity notion of mind to a process one (Wellman, 1990). In the early years, as Chandler and Boyes (1982, p. 391) colorfully describe it:

> Children seem to proceed as though they believe objects to transmit, in a direct-line-of-sight fashion, faint copies of themselves, which actively assault and impress themselves upon anyone who happens in the path of such "objective" knowledge. Within such a view, projectile firings from things themselves bombard and actively victimize individuals who function as passive recorders and simply bear the scars of information which has been embossed upon them.

This "copy-container" mind is considered a passive receptacle that takes in information automatically, accurately, and without modification. For example, in the perceptual realm, preschoolers tend not to understand that what information a person acquires through perception is influenced by what that person already knows. Suppose you show a child a picture of a giraffe, then place a card with a small hole on top of it and show that to another person who can see so little of the giraffe through the hole that it cannot be identified. Preschoolers believe that the person can see that it is a giraffe, but 6-year-olds are beginning to understand that whether you know it is a giraffe beforehand influences whether you see it as one (Taylor, 1988). Young children fail to comprehend that prior knowledge can bias current knowledge or perception.

Finally, children have difficulty comprehending the fact that the capabilities of the mind affect what you can know through verbal messages. Montgomery (1993), for example, found that even 8-year-olds think that a preverbal baby will understand a verbal message that would be understood by an adult (e.g., "The poster is in the bottom drawer"). They make this claim even though they understand that babies cannot talk and do not even know the meaning of the words in the message.

These studies suggest a new interpretation of Piaget's notion of *egocentrism*—a young child's assumption that others think, feel, perceive, and know the same as the child does. Instead of indicating a lack of differentiation between self and other, egocentric behaviors may indicate a lack of understanding that people know, understand, and interpret on the basis of their experiences or, in the case of visual perspective taking, their visual perspective. Moreover, some of this understanding of knowing may be in place much earlier than Piaget thought. O'Neill (1996) found that 2-year-olds will sometimes communicate about a situation more fully to a parent who had not shared that situation with them just previously and thus needed more information about it than to a parent who had.

Thus far, we have focused on the understanding of exactly how the mind connects with the physical world. In pretense, the mental state is not intended to correspond to reality; we now turn to children's understanding in this domain.

Pretense.

Karen: I'm hungry. Wa-a-ah!

Charlotte: Lie down, baby.

Karen: I'm a baby that sits up.

Charlotte: First you lie down and sister covers you and then I make your cereal and *then* you sit up. (Paley, 1984, p. 1)

In pretend play, children turn props (even living sisterly ones) into representations, in this case a baby. They act as if these props were their real referents, but can tell you that they are not: "That's *real* money, but that's not; those are *playing* money" (Woolley & Wellman, 1990). They know that they are pretending. If a child understands that, when pretending that a banana is a telephone, the banana differs from, but represents, a telephone, this would seem to be quite similar to the knowledge necessary for understanding false beliefs. "Pretending that" and "believing that" would appear to involve the same sort of knowledge about mind, and in fact Leslie (1987, 1994) makes such an argument. However, researchers disagree as to whether understanding pretense, like understanding false beliefs, requires the ability to understand representations (for a review of this debate, see Lillard, 1998b; Flavell & Miller, 1998; Gopnik, 1998; and Joseph, 1998; for discussions of pretense more generally see Kavanaugh and Harris, 1999; Lillard, 1994; Nichols & Stich, 2000; Perner, Baker & Hutton, 1994; and Taylor, 1996).

One problem with putting the understanding of pretense in the same category as false belief is that pretense is understood by age 2, but children demonstrate an understanding of false belief, appearance-reality, and related phenomena only around age 4 or so. Leslie and others argue that performance obstacles such as language limitations and limited memory capacity account for the apparent later emergence of false belief, but most developmentalists have trouble believing that 2-year-olds actually do understand false belief.

Another possible problem for Leslie's position is that 2-year-olds and even older children may in fact lack a fully mentalistic conception of pretense (Harris, 1994; Lillard, 1996, 1998b; Perner, 1991). What do young children think goes on in people's minds when they pretend? Young children *possess* a mental representation of a telephone when they pretend that a banana is a telephone, but it is not clear whether they *understand* this representational process. To examine this question, Lillard (1993) posed situations of the following sort. She showed a troll doll and told the children:

> This is Moe. He's from the land of the trolls. Moe's hopping around, kind of like a rabbit hops. Moe doesn't know that rabbits hop like that; he doesn't know anything about rabbits. But he is hopping like a rabbit. Does he know that rabbits hop like that? Is he hopping like a rabbit? Would you say he is pretending to be a rabbit, or he's not pretending to be a rabbit?

Most of the 4-year-olds and many of the 5-year-olds claimed that Moe was indeed pretending to be a rabbit. They ignored the fact that he could not possibly have a representation of a rabbit, never having seen one. Thus, young children apparently think he can "pretend" even without a mental representation; he merely needs to act like the referent. In further support of this conclusion, many preschoolers classify pretense with physical activities, such as clapping their hands, rather than with mental activities, such as thinking (Lillard, 1996). However, although pretense usually involves action, it does not always. A child could pretend to be a banana by remaining still and simply thinking bananalike thoughts (the jungle? ripening? banana splits?) without also acting in bananalike ways, such as forming a curve or hanging from a tree.

It is surprising that in Lillard's research 4-year-olds appear not to understand the representational nature of pretense. First of all, they have engaged in pretend play for several years. Secondly, they understand that people have representations such as beliefs, preferences, and perceptions. Subsequent research has uncovered a more mentalistic understanding of pretense in 3- and 4-year-olds (Custer, 1996; Hickling, Wellman, & Gottfried, 1997). And even Lillard (Lillard & Sobel, 1999) finds better understanding when she uses a fantasy character, such as the Lion King. Thus, the debate about this important issue continues.

Closely related to children's understanding of pretense is their understanding of imagining and dreaming (Harris, 2000; Lillard, 1994; Woolley, 1995). Understanding of pretense, imagining, and dreams is part of the more general topic of children's differentiation of real from the not-real, the physical from the mental. Wellman and Estes (1986) report that even very young children know that mental representations are not physical things. They know that the mind is different from rocks, roller skates, and even the head. As one example a 3-year-old who is told that one boy has a cookie and another boy is thinking about a cookie knows which cookie can be seen by others, touched, eaten, shared, and saved for later. Moreover, young children spontaneously make explicit contrasts between mental states and reality: "The people thought Dracula was mean, but he was nice" (Shatz, Wellman, & Silber, 1983).

Young children also know that because thoughts are not external entities, they are not public. Other people cannot directly know our thoughts. Children's explanations for these judgments give the flavor of their understanding (Wellman, 1990): You cannot see an image because "People can't see my imagination." You cannot touch an image, for "How can you reach inside your head; besides it's not even there," and "Imaginations is imaginations." You also can mentally transform an image: "I have dream-hands" and "Your mind is for moving things and looking at things when there's not a movie or a TV around." The children know that, in contrast, you cannot transform a real cup hidden in a box just by thinking.

What about fantasizing about things that do not even exist, such as martians, ghosts, dragons, or a spoon that sings? Even 3-year-olds know that they can fantasize these things (Wellman & Estes, 1986). Thus children know that the mind can soar, can transcend reality, can have flights of fantasy. If young children know that monsters and things that go bump in the night are not real, does this mean that they do not really fear them? Obviously they do fear them. DiLalla and Watson (1988) observed a young child pretend to be a monster in order to frighten other children, then burst into tears himself when his pretense seemed too real. For a more experimental analysis, we can consult a series of studies (Harris, Brown, Marriott, Whittall, & Harmer, 1991) in which 4- and 6-year-olds asserted that an imagined monster was not real, even when they imagined it chasing after them. Yet they showed signs that they were not totally convinced that an imaginary creature could never wander across the barrier between fantasy and reality. When they pretended that an empty box contained a monster, although they said it was not real, they avoided that box in favor of a box with an imaginary puppy and preferred to poke a finger into the puppy box and a stick into the monster box, rather than the reverse! These behaviors did not appear to be mere pretend play; almost half of the 4-year-olds spontaneously suggested that the monster had disappeared before they had a chance to see it, perhaps escaping, as one child suggested, "to that University place where they put the skeletons" (the museum?). In addition, when the experimenter said he needed to leave the room to get something, several of the 4-year-olds in the condition with the monster box asked the experimenter not to leave, even after they had checked that the box was empty. It appears that something scary can be not real, and yet, in a sense, very real. And, of course, even adults have been known to scream at horror movies.

One interesting line of research has looked at children who have imaginary companions (e.g., Gleason, Sebanc, & Hartup, 2000; Taylor, 1999). Some examples of these companions appear in Table 6.1. Interestingly, contrary to what one might expect, these children are not inferior to their peers in their ability to distinguish between fantasy and reality.

Thinking. Thus far we have examined mental states. But the mind is an active entity; it does things. Preschoolers understand some of the most basic and important facts about thinking (Flavell, Green, & Flavell, 1995b, and Flavell & O'Donnell, in press). They seem to know that thinking is an activity that only people and perhaps some other animate objects do. Second, they also realize that

TABLE 6.1 *Examples of Children's Imaginary Companions,* as Reported by Their Mothers

NAME	DESCRIPTION
	Invisible Friends
Star Friends and Heart Fan Club	Groups of preschool-aged human friends with whom the child had birthdays, went to the fair, and spoke a language called Hobotchi.
Goofy & company	Disney character Goofy and invented relatives including Goofy Jr. (son), Max (cousin), and The Doctor, who tended Goofy's asthma (child had asthma as well).
Herd of cows	Cows of many colors and varying sizes who were often fed or diapered like infants. Discovered when the child's father accidentally stepped on one.
Danny	An imaginary version of the child's best friend from preschool.
Maybe	A human of varying gender whom the child routinely summoned by shouting out the front door of the family's house.

Note: Adapted from "Imaginary Companions of Preschool Children" by T. R. Gleason, A. M. Sebanc, and W. W. Hartup, 2000, *Developmental Psychology, 36,* p. 422. Copyright © 2000 by the American Psychological Association. Adapted by permission.

mental entities like thoughts and images are internal, in-the-head affairs that differ from physical actions or other external objects and events. They see the mind and brain as necessary for mental actions. Third, they know that thinking, like desires and other mental entities, has content and refers to objects and events, even nonpresent and nonreal ones. Fourth, young children are at least beginning to understand that mental experiences may cause other mental experiences. Older preschoolers understand a story about a girl who sees a dog chase her pet rabbit away and then many days later feels sad again upon seeing the same or similar dog. That is, they explain her sadness by saying that seeing the dog made her think about her lost rabbit, which caused the sad feeling.

However, preschoolers lack other important knowledge and skills concerning thinking. They have trouble determining *when* a person is thinking (unless the cues are very strong and clear) and *what* the person is and is not thinking about, even in situations where this is obvious to an older child or adult. They greatly underestimate how much mental activity goes on in people. For example, they do not realize that people have what William James (1890) referred to as the "stream of consciousness"—a continual flow of mental content and experiences. If they see a person just sitting quietly, "waiting," they do not attribute mental activity to the person. Even when the person is reading or talking, they do not assume that the person's mind is "doing something." In fact in one study (Flavell, Green, & Flavell, 1998), half of the 5-year-olds thought that it was possible to go for several days without thinking if one tried very hard. Even when they do attribute mental activity, they have little inkling of what the person might be thinking even when it seems obvious.

Particularly surprising is evidence that preschoolers seem to be remarkably unaware of when and what they themselves think, even when the testing situation is stacked toward making this quite easy (Flavell et al., 1995b). For example, 5-year-olds who had been caused to think silently about which room in their house they keep their toothbrush often denied that they had just been thinking!

In addition to these underestimations of thinking, preschoolers show overestimations. For example, they think that an unconscious person ("sound asleep and not dreaming") has some self-awareness and decision-making abilities (Flavell et al., 1998). For instance over half of the 5-year-olds thought that the people knew they were asleep. Thus children attribute too little thought to a conscious person and too much thought to an unconscious one.

Older children are much more aware of their own thinking. They not only have a much better idea of when people are thinking and their degree of awareness, but also know that often it is very hard, and even impossible, *not* to think. When told to sit in a chair labeled "Do Not Think," close their eyes, and try to keep their mind blank, few 5-year-olds, but the majority of the 8-year-olds, reported that they had had thoughts anyway. We like one 8-year-old's report:

> Well, for a bit of time I thought about black, how black it was, and then I thought about, oh, a nice big splash of magenta, and then I thought, "Oh, it's impossible not to think" [giggles] and then I thought, "Ooh, a nice orange," and then I saw a clay face that sort of looked like the face I saw before only it didn't have ears, and then I think I saw a little bit of black and then you asked me to open my eyes. (Flavell, Green, & Flavell, 2000, p. 106)

Younger children may be less disposed to notice their thoughts or perhaps do not think of them as "thoughts."

Differences in Development

Thus far we have focused on the big picture—developmental trends in the development of understanding the mind. Equally important, however, are differences in this development. Differences are important for two reasons. First, they are important because they are there. If we ignore them, our own interpretive minds would construct an erroneous view of development as universal and unvarying. Second, differences are important because they provide clues about the causes of change from a less advanced to a more advanced theory of mind. If children of the same age vary in their theory of mind, the causes of these differences might also contribute to developmental differences. Researchers recently have given a great deal of attention to three types of differences in development: intracultural, intercultural, and interspecies (Flavell & Miller, 1998).

Intracultural Differences. Certain social experiences within the family appear to foster theory-of-mind development (Bartsch & Estes, 1996; Dunn, 1999). For example, preschoolers who have more siblings to interact with (with the usual quarrels, appeals, tricks, and so on) perform better on false-belief tasks than those who have fewer or no siblings (Jenkins & Astington, 1996; Perner, Ruffman, & Leekam, 1994). Moreover, conversations about emotions and their causes and consequences with parents and siblings at 3 years of age predict the ability to infer and explain the feelings of others at 6 years (Dunn, Brown, & Beardsall, 1991), and early family conversations about desire predict later understanding of false belief (Bartsch & Wellman, 1995). In addition, deaf children with hearing parents who are not fluent in sign language (most are not) perform more poorly on a false belief task than deaf children with deaf parents who can sign fluently (Peterson & Siegal, 1997; Remmel, Bettger, & Weinberg, in press). These studies suggest that social-communicative experiences facilitate theory of mind development.

An interesting gender difference has emerged in several studies. Parents discuss more of the emotional aspects of past experiences with daughters than with sons (Adams, Kuebli, Boyle, & Fivush, 1995), and this difference is paralleled in their children's language (Dunn, Bretherton, & Munn, 1987). Overall, mothers discuss anger more often with their sons than their daughters, and sadness or positive emotions more often with daughters than sons (Fivush, 1990). Importantly mothers cognize about anger differently to their sons and daughters, as seen in the following two conversations (Fivush, 1990, pp. 13 and 17):

> Mother: Does it make you sad when mommy and daddy tell you that you can't do something?
> Son: No.
> Mother: No?
> Son: No, you make me mad.
> Mother: I make you mad? Oh, ok.

> *(Mother and daughter are discussing a time when a sister took the child's crayon)*
> Mother: How did you feel?
> Daughter: ummmm, FINE.

Mother: You cried?

Daughter: NO! FINE!

Mother: Oh, fine (*laughs*). You felt fine. Were you upset when Catherine took your crayon?

Daughter: Yeah.

Mother: Umm-hmmm. What did you say to her?

Daughter: To not take it!

Mother: Right. Don't you take it. That's my crayon. Do you love Catherine?

Daughter: Ummm, let's see . . . YEAH!

Mother: Good, I'm glad you said that. Good answer.

The first mother accepts anger in her son. In contrast the second mother, even in a situation in which anger in her daughter would be a reasonable response, directs the conversation toward keeping the relationship with the sister intact, despite the sister's inappropriate behavior toward the child. Given these experiences it is not surprising that both girls and women are poorer than males at identifying anger (or more reluctant to identify anger) in characters in videotaped episodes (Riess & Cunningham, 1989). They performed equivalently for other emotions. As Fivush (1990, p. 2) concludes, these findings suggest "that the way in which emotions are talked about early in development has an impact on the individual's developing understanding of emotions and the way in which emotions are integrated into one's self-concept, gender-concept and interpersonal behavior."

Intracultural differences arise not only in how early a child acquires a particular component of theory of mind, but also in the very nature of their beliefs about certain human attributes. Children (and adults) vary, for example, in their views of the nature of intelligence (Dweck, 1999). Some people think of intelligence as fixed and uncontrollable (*entity theory*), and others think of it as a malleable and controllable ability that can be improved with effort and training (*incremental theory*). In general, when a boy performs poorly, such as when receiving a poor grade on a test, he tends to attribute it to not trying hard (i.e., not studying much for the test), an incremental view (e.g., Dweck, 1991; Dweck & Repucci, 1973). In contrast, girls tend to attribute failure to poor ability ("I'm just not good at math"), an entity view. You can see the cause for concern here if you predict their behavior before the next exam or when they must choose courses for the next year. A boy would assume that he could do better if he studies more, whereas a girl might assume that this would have little payoff, given her limited ability. She also might not be likely to select advanced math courses. Fortunately intervention can change these attributions, with the expected changes in behavior (Dweck, 1975). For a good account of other individual differences in social cognition that affect motivation to succeed in school, see Eccles, Wigfield, and Schiefele (1998). Finally, because we would categorize psychologists as people as well, their varying explicit theories of human cognition are another form of intracultural differences in theory of mind.

Another sort of intracultural difference suggests biological rather than experiential contributions to theory of mind. Children and adults with autism have striking deficits in theory of mind, compared with normal children or even children of the same mental age with mental retardation (Baron-Cohen, 1995). Autism is believed to involve an inborn neurological deficit. Individuals with autism are deficient in social relations. The deficit seems to be specific to processing social information, for the afflicted can perform much better on tasks requiring an understanding of physical causality. The specificity of this deficit supports Leslie's (1994) proposed innate theory-of-mind module described later. Because low-IQ children of the same or lower mental age do not show this deficit, general retardation does not seem to account for these results with autistic children. In fact some autistic children are rather intelligent but still have great difficulty with social interaction.

Intercultural Differences.   We know less about these differences. The issue here is how universal are the developments described in this chapter. There is evidence for both similarities and differences across cultures such as Africa, China, Japan, and Peru (Avis & Harris, 1991; Flavell, Zhang, Zou, Dong, & Qi, 1983; Gauvain, 1998; Joshi & MacLean, 1994; Lillard, 1998a, 1998b; Vinden, 1996; Wellman, 1998; Wellman et al., in press). Here are some differences: Japanese and American children and Japanese mothers believe that a child lost in a store would experience sadness, whereas American mothers believe the emotion would be fear (Lewis, 1989). Samoans do not verbally distinguish between hate and disgust (Gerber, 1975), and the Utku of Canada distinguish fear of physical calamity, *ighi,* from fear of being treated unkindly, *ilira* (Briggs, 1970). When a child experiences an emotion and the parent gives it a label, this naming makes the emotion salient and influences how a child interprets the feeling. For example, Ifaluk parents sensitize their children to the emotion *metagu,* roughly translated as "social fear and anxiety," by frequently, and approvingly, labeling children's reactions as *metagu* in the presence of strangers, in large groups, and in other appropriate settings (Lutz, 1983). The important point here is that to some extent emotion concepts are social constructs. The culture teaches the child how to define, categorize, and label emotions differently in different cultures.

Thus, cultural differences are undeniable, and would be predicted by sociocultural theorists (see Chapter 1). The culture's value system concerning emotions leads to parental socialization practices that teach children how to interpret their emotions in such a way that they can stay safe in their particular culture. What is not yet clear is whether these beliefs form a "theory" in the strict sense or simply reflect a set of social and cultural practices and conventions. In this latter view, "children would learn how to psychologize appropriately in the way that they learn how to dress properly or eat politely" (Astington & Gopnik, 1991, pp. 19–20).

Interspecies Differences.   Are we the only species having anything like a theory of mind? After all, there is about a 98 percent overlap in the genes of humans and chimps. Considerable controversy surrounds this issue. Chimpanzees appear to engage in both pretense and elementary mind-reading activities. They have been seen to pull an imaginary pull toy, carefully disentangling the imaginary string (Hayes, 1951), and to pretend to eat imaginary food, even spitting out a bad bite and communicating "bad" on keyboard symbols (Savage-Rumbaugh & McDonald, 1988). Judge for yourself whether mind-reading activities are displayed in the following episode reported by Byrne and Whiten (1988): A chimp observed a second chimp acting as if no food were available at a feeding hopper. There in fact was food. The first chimp appeared to depart, but actually hid behind a nearby tree and watched until the other chimp took the food. At this point the first chimp emerged and snatched the food! Although such observations seem rather persuasive, most recent experimental work with chimps suggests much less knowledge about the mental world (Call & Tomasello, 1999; Povinelli & Eddy, 1996; Reaux, Theall, & Povinelli, 1999). Chimps may have a behavioristic rather than mentalistic conception of seeing, for example. They can follow a person's gaze, but may not understand that this behavior causes seeing and knowing.

Conclusions about Differences and Their Causes. The above intracultural, intercultural, and interspecies differences lead to the conclusion that, as in most developmental matters, both experience and biology appear to contribute. Biology is most apparent in intracultural differences due to specific neurological deficits and in interspecies differences. Experience appears to contribute to at least some intracultural and intercultural differences.

Still, the many similarities in children's lives everywhere push toward more similarities than differences. Children everywhere have environments providing experiences that would stimulate the awareness of cognitive connections, and of the mental world in general. These experiences often would reflect the independence of different mental connections, as when a child simultaneously hears and sees an object, then closes his eyes and discovers that he continues to hear it but no longer to see it. Also, subjective experiences and objective reality sometimes do not match: A flower in a vase turns out to be plastic, and a favorite toy is not where a child thinks it was left. In addition, parents often point out their children's false beliefs to them—"You think it's not bedtime, but it really is." Moreover, cooperative interactions with siblings apparently encourage an understanding of representations (Dunn, Brown, & Beardsall, 1991). Another apparently universal experience is pretend play, which could help sensitize children to the distinction between the way things are and the way they are made to seem. Given these universal experiences, it is not surprising that intact human minds seem to be *basically* the same everywhere.

Theories of Children's Knowledge about the Mind

Theory Theory. You already know, from Chapters 1 and 4, how theory theory theorists theorize (!) about children's understanding of natural kinds, biology, physics, and so on. They believe that children have an informal everyday theory or framework about a domain. The mind is one such domain. This theory has three properties. First, it specifies a set of entities or processes (philosophers call it an ontology) that are found in the domain of mind and not in other domains. Entities or processes such as beliefs, desires, thinking, and so forth, are found only in the domain of the mental. Second, the theory includes causal principles that are unique to mind—what affects the mind and what the mind affects. Many of the distinctions between physical and social objects that we made in the introduction to this chapter would be included here. Psychological causality (wants, intends.) is found only in the domain of the psychological; such mental events do not cause physical objects to move. Third, a theory of mind sees the mind as an organized set of interconnected mental states that are connected to input from reality and the output in the form of behavior. Going back to an earlier example, a child wants a toy and believes that it can be found in a toy box and thus looks for it there. Or, more formally, Figure 6.2 shows that beliefs and desires may lead to intentions which in turn may lead to goal-directed actions, and that what we believe may bias what we perceive.

Theories that meet these criteria appeared in earlier sections, such as a desire psychology in 2-year-olds, a desire-belief psychology in 3-year-olds, and a belief-desire psychology in 4-year-olds (Bartsch & Wellman, 1995). Figure 6.2 showed a belief-desire theory of mind. As children use their current theory of mind, they find that, in light of their experience, they must revise it into a new theory. Thus desire psychologists become desire-belief psychologists because they repeatedly see people behave in ways that cannot be explained by a notion of desire alone.

Although most cognitive developmentalists would agree that children's understanding of the mind has some coherence, and is not just a list of isolated facts or pieces of knowledge, there is considerable disagreement as to how theorylike children's knowledge is. That is, there is disagreement as to how well it meets the three criteria.

Modularity Theory.   Modularity theorists regarding knowledge about mind fall within the modularity nativism approach discussed in Chapter 1. According to modularity theory (e.g., Leslie, 1994; Leslie & Roth, 1993), neurological maturation, rather than theory revision from experience, directs the development of theory of mind. Experience does little more than serve as a trigger for several theories of mind during physical maturation. Most developmentalists agree that infants and toddlers are biologically predisposed to process a great deal of information about the social objects in their world. And neuroscience research is identifying the neural foundations of theory of mind (e.g., Sabbagh & Taylor, 2000; Stone, Baron-Cohen, & Knight, 1998). However, there is great disagreement as to the relative roles of biological maturation versus experience. A theory squarely on the side of experience is the next one.

Simulation Theory.   In this view, children use their awareness of their own mental states to simulate, or infer, the mental states of others. To take the false-belief task as an example, when asked what a naïve other child would think was in the candy box, children would imagine what they themselves would think if they were that person and had not seen inside the box. Practice in role taking, then, is the aspect of experience that is important for developing increasingly advanced theories of mind.

Harris (1992), for instance, has proposed that children's understanding of others' mental states arises in part from their pretend play. Between ages 2 and 2½, children begin to use their imagination to endow dolls with desires, emotions, and sensations. They say that a doll wants to eat, feels happy, and feels cold. This capacity for make believe allows them to conjure up possible mental states in both dolls and people, based perhaps on their awareness of their own mental states and their ability to imagine being in various mental states. Because a child can imagine herself wanting a pizza and also imagine being happy if a pizza is obtained, she may be able to simulate these mental states in others. Once a child can construct the other person's desires, then she can anticipate that person's behavior intended to achieve the goal and then the emotion that results from satisfaction, or lack of satisfaction, of the desire. Thus, through a sort of "phenomenological bootstrapping," a young child could use her awareness of her own feelings, desires, and other mental states to infer others' mental states and to construct during development more general theorylike concepts of mind.

There is little evidence that understanding of self mental contents develops in advance of those of others (S. A. Miller, 2000; Wellman et al., in press). However, the relations between the two sorts of knowledge are still very much a matter of debate in the field.

Other Perspectives.   A variety of other views have identified other important developments that contribute to theory of mind. One explanation focuses on more domain-general limitations in executive functioning: planning, response inhibiton, self-regulation, and cognitive flexibility or complexity (e.g., Carlson, Moses, & Hix, 1998; Hughes, 1998; Perner & Lang, 1999). For example, even a child with some understanding of false belief might nevertheless be unable to inhibit his tendency to blurt out the perceptually salient current position of the chocolate rather than the position that a naïve other child would select. It may feel unnatural to point to where an object is not. Carlson and Moses (in press) provide supporting evidence: Preschoolers who could, for example, inhibit their tendency to do what both the dragon and bear said to do, and instead do only what the bear said to do, performed better than other children on theory of mind tasks. Other abilities related to information processing, such as limited memory capacity and skills, may turn out to contribute to wrong answers as well. Also, with improved language skills, children may be better able to express their developing theory of mind (Flavell & Miller, 1998). Finally, some positions emphasis experience with others, particularly interactions with parents and siblings (e.g., Dunn, 1999), as a way to learn about mental states.

Conclusions about Theories.   Each approach is supported by a set of evidence, and an adequate theory will include elements from all of these approaches. Children's understanding of the mind does seem to involve some sort of informal "theory, " though it is not yet clear how large the quotation marks should be. This account need not preclude building on some innate or early maturing people-reading capacities and drawing on our knowledge about our own mental states and a variety of other experiences when changing these theories. In addition, as in the development of other concepts, improved information processing is surely part of the story.

Current Status of Knowledge about Children's Understanding of Mind

Thanks to the explosion of research on understanding of mind in the last decade or so, we now have a reasonably good description of this understanding, though more so for the preschool years than for infancy and older childhood and adolescence, and much more so for false beliefs than for any other topic. We also have some sense of where to look for influences on this development and for consequences of this knowledge for behavior. It is not always clear how to interpret these findings, though research over the next few years will help us sort this out. A richer developmental story will emerge in all these areas.

We see the need to explore both the vertical and horizontal ties of a theory of mind. Vertical ties refer to connections between the sequence of theories of mind during development. What is missing is a specific account of exactly how early understandings of mind gradually are transformed into later understandings of mind.

One strategy is to look at transition points at first and last developmental points for each acquisition. For example, for false beliefs, understanding at the early end includes the finding that young 3-year-olds who respond incorrectly to standard false-belief questions nonetheless show by their eye movements that they may have some sort of rudimentary, implicit understanding of false beliefs (Clements & Perner, 1994). How is this "partial accomplishment" (Haith & Benson, 1998, p. 245) related to later levels of understanding? Similarly, at the upper end, the understanding of false belief continues to develop further even after age 4 or 5, the age of first clear emergence (Carpendale & Chandler, 1996; Fabricius & Imbens-Bailey, 2000). What are the mechanisms of development from one level to another? That is, how do children revise their theories?

Regarding horizontal ties, we know little about how theory of mind relates to other skills and concepts developing at the same time such as langue, emotional development, play, and collaborative problem solving. We mentioned some ties in the Differences section and describe others in a final section, Connections with Social Behavior. Also, research on ties to the neurological level is important and is likely to continue.

We know even less about how theory of mind knowledge relates to traditional cognitive tasks such as memory, attention, and problem solving. For example preschoolers who understand that the quality of information affects quality of knowledge are more likely to use a strategy that involves selecting items to view that are relevant to the problem solving task (i.e., high-quality information—Welch-Ross & Miller, 2000). The former was assessed by a task mentioned earlier in which the viewer could see only a small ambiguous part of an animal and had to judge what the viewer knew (Taylor, 1988). In addition, children who could deceive another player on the strategy task by reversing the cues indicating relevant and irrelevant information were more likely to select relevant information themselves during problem solving.

Finally, we know little about the on-line, moment by moment use of theory of mind in real time. How do children detect the need to attempt an act of mind reading, encode and interpret information indicating mental states, resolve discrepancies among representations, access prior social knowledge, and finally select a behavior? We expect that work on the role of executive functioning in this process will likely be a particularly active area (Flavell, 2000).

UNDERSTANDING TRAITS AND OTHER PSYCHOLOGICAL BASES OF BEHAVIOR

Theory of mind research shows that the "person-on-the-street" (or "child-on-the-playground") constructs plausible "folk theories" about why people do the things they do. It is clear that even young children are beginning to explain behavior by appealing to desires, beliefs, emotions, and percepts. We now describe children's mind-reading skills in the broader context of their understanding of other people's personalities and social behaviors (see also Taylor, 1996).

Suppose a 3-year-old sees a friend walking down the street holding his mother's hand as a Great Dane approaches them. He could encode this event as

"He's holding his mommy's hand" or "He's scared of the dog"—a more informative and satisfying account for someone trying to understand human behavior. We know that preschoolers tend to prefer to describe and explain behaviors in terms of psychological attributes when psychological and physical choices are presented (Lillard & Flavell, 1990; Miller & Aloise, 1989). For example they choose interest or effort over external reward or conducive surroundings (Miller, 1985). Moreover, most of children's early causal utterances in natural settings refer to the social world (their own or others' desires, emotions, and intentions) rather than the physical world (Bloom & Capatides, 1987; Hood & Bloom, 1979). For example a 4-year-old refers to mental causes of an action to explain that he has paint on his hands "because I thought my hands were paper" (Wellman, 1985c), giving new meaning to the phrase "finger painting." Still, much remains for children to learn about the psychological basis of behavior. Two trends are salient. First, concepts of personal attributes become more differentiated and subtle. For example, not until middle or late childhood do children fully differentiate closely related psychological attributes, such as ability and effort (e.g., Skinner, 1990; Stipek & MacIver, 1989), and become aware of more subtle psychological causes. Second, children become aware of traits, to which we now turn.

As we noted earlier, adults tend to explain other peoples' behavior in terms of their traits. An example of their use of traits that is quite relevant to child development is parents' perceptions of their children's attributes and abilities (e.g., Bugental & Johnston, 2000; Goodnow & Collins, 1990; Miller, 1986b, 1988; Miller & Davis, 1992). Research shows that these perceptions that parents form can influence their behavior toward their children and hence the children's development.

It is important for children to become aware of traits because they help them predict others' likely behaviors in different times and places. A "mean" peer can be counted on to steal the candy bar from your school lunch, distract you in the middle of an intense video game, and push you down in the park. If he did these things last month, last week, and today, you can sadly assume he will do them, or something equally mean, tomorrow.

From a theory of mind perspective, one would ask when children conceive of a trait as an organized, enduring tendency to have certain mental states. Understanding traits involves knowing that these mental states can be used to explain behavior, perhaps drawing on their belief-desire theory of mind (Heyman & Gelman, 1999; Wellman, 1990; Yuill, 1997). Children may see traits as stable states of mind that generate desires and beliefs (Yuill, 1992), as when helpfulness generates a desire to help others and a belief that a person needs help. As Yuill (1997, p. 284) explains it, "Traits provide a rationale for why differences in desires occur, so the perceived need to use traits as explanatory devices will not arise until children understand that such differences in desire exist." Although 2-year-olds have some understanding of desire, the more advanced understanding that comes several years later may be needed for seeing the link with traits. A fuller understanding of traits may be related to understanding that two different constructive, interpretive minds (two people with different traits) would react to the same situation differently.

How early in life do children explain and predict behaviors on the basis that "he is just that kind of person"? Much of the debate centers on the age at which children can be said to understand traits as a stable, *psychological* phenomenon that the person expresses in various situations over time rather than simply as consistent *behaviors* (Ruble & Dweck, 1995). That is, when does a child see another person as a helpful person with a motive to be helpful rather than simply someone who usually does helpful things (which might or might not be based on a helpful motive)?

If preschoolers do not have to generate the traits themselves, they show some understanding of traits (Eder, 1989). For example, 4-year-olds can use trait labels to make inferences about mental states and the reaction of people with these traits-states to an event (Heyman & Gelman, 1999). For example, a "shy" person is less likely than a "not shy" person to be pleased about encountering a lot of people. Still, some children seem to use their own or normative responses as guides in making their prediction, for example, in a clue to modern-day childhood happiness, "everyone is happy when there are a lot of people at the mall" (p. 614).

Age 5 to 7 seems to be the transitional period for conceiving of traits as a stable *psychological* phenomenon (e.g., Cain, Heyman, & Walker, 1997; Heyman & Gelman, 1998; Rholes, Newman, & Ruble, 1990) that can be used to predict behavior. But there are limitations. For example, children of this age overpredict that a person with a positive trait would do well in unrelated domains, for example, predicting that a "nice" classmate would jump over higher hurdles than classmates labeled not nice (Stipek & Daniels, 1990). On the other hand, they underpredict in that they often have only a shaky understanding that a trait can be expressed in different, but related, behavior (Rholes & Ruble, 1984). Thus, young children detect behavioral regularities, give them a trait label, and sometimes treat them as causes, but may not see the trait as a stable, abiding, differentiated internal cause until the elementary school years. For good reviews of this research, see Rholes et al. (1990), Ruble and Dweck (1995), and Yuill (1997).

Although young elementary school children have the Existence knowledge that we described earlier, they are still weak in the Need and Inference skill areas. In particular they rarely use traits to describe others (e.g., Livesley & Bromley, 1973; Shantz, 1983). When asked to describe what particular other people are like, they show a developmental trend from using physical descriptors to using more psychological descriptors, including, eventually, traits. Children aged 6 to 7 years or younger are very prone to describe the other person's general identity, appearance, family, possessions, environment, and so on (Livesley & Bromley, 1973). Thus, although their theory of mind includes an understanding that people have desires and beliefs, they rarely spontaneously mention these in their descriptions of others. If any personal traits do get mentioned they are apt to be global, stereotyped, and highly evaluative ("He is very bad"), or else somewhat self focused ("She gives me things"). For example, "She is very nice because she gives my friends and me toffee. She lives by the main road. She has fair hair and glasses. . . . She sometimes gives us flowers" (Livesley & Bromley, 1973, p. 214).

During middle childhood children cognitively penetrate beneath the skin (as discussed for Figure 6.1), and their descriptions become more focused on traits, including a range of less global ones ("nice" gives way to "considerate," "helpful," etc.). They often endow the other person with attitudes, interests, abilities, and other psychological qualities seldom found in younger children's descriptions. The middle-childhood subject's character sketch is still likely to be rather poorly organized, however, with different attributions just strung together in a more or less random sequence, and little integration or explanation. This 10-year-old's description illustrates these points:

He smells very much and is very nasty. He has no sense of humour and is very dull. He is always fighting and he is cruel. He does silly things and is very stupid. He has brown hair and cruel eyes. He is sulky and 11 years old and has lots of sisters. I think he is the most horrible boy in the class. He has a croaky voice and always chews his pencil and picks his teeth and I think he is disgusting. (Livesley & Bromley, 1973, p. 217)

An adolescent carefully shapes attributes into an organized, integrated portrait of the other. He knows that his impression of the person is only *his* impression, and may therefore be inaccurate or different from other people's. An adolescent, unlike a younger child, is sensitive to the presence of seemingly contradictory traits and of different levels of depths within the individual's personality. Drawing on his theory of mind knowledge about appearance versus reality, he notes that the individual may appear to be this and really be that "underneath." For example, a 13-year-old acquaintance of one of us began his written character sketch of a friend this way (it was an English class assignment, and was therefore judged to require fancy vocabulary—this too represents a bit of social cognition): "He may appear a joker in class because of his unique style of eloquence, but in reality he feels a deep responsibility towards the advancement of his own personal knowledge." Perhaps because of his understanding of the interpretive, constructive nature of mind, he knows that one must appeal to dispositions, motives, personal history, environmental factors and forces, or other internal and external causes to explain and reconcile apparent discrepancies in behavior. The best examples of these higher forms of personality description are, of course, to be found in great literature, not in psychology articles. Nonetheless the latter include some fairly impressive specimens from lesser mortals: "She is curious about people but naive, and this leads her to ask too many questions so that people become irritated with her and withhold information, although she is not sensitive enough to notice it" (Livesley & Bromley, 1973, p. 225).

Thus, if one were to think of the "child as a psychologist" who subscribes to certain positions or theories, prior to 7 or 8 years of age children's descriptions are those of a demographer and behaviorist. They tend to describe people in terms of their environmental circumstances and observable behavior. Some behaviorists, such as B. F. Skinner, might argue that social cognitive development should stop right there! Later the child becomes a trait-personality theorist and, by adolescence, takes an interactionist position, in which personal characteristics and situational factors interact to produce behavior (Shantz, 1983).

Evidence for cultural influences, emphasized by socioculturalists, comes from comparisons of individualist North American and more collectivist cultures. One such comparison is the types of causes used by children (ages 8, 11, and 15) and adults in the United States and in traditional Hindu cultures in India, all from the middle class (J. Miller, 1986, 1987). Participants had to explain why a person performed a particular prosocial or deviant behavior that was described. With increasing age, Americans tended to increase their references to traits, whereas Hindus increased their references to contextual causes. That is, Hindus referred to the duties of one's social position, mutual interdependence between people, sensitivity to the needs of society, and one's social relationships with other people. Thus, social cognitions are influenced by cultural beliefs that people are individualistic and autonomous entities with rights and desires that may conflict with the social system versus the belief that people are an inherent part of that system. The latter focus on relationships more than personal traits.

KNOWLEDGE ABOUT SELF

Cognition about the self is an active area of research with many complexities and connections to other aspects of development that are too numerous to cover or even refer to adequately in this chapter. Thus, we direct readers to good sources (Harter, 1998, 1999; Lewis, 1999; Ruble & Dweck, 1995). To illustrate just one complexity, we now know that there are many aspects of knowledge of self. Neisser (1993), for example, refers to five types: ecological (self-acting-in-physical environment), private, interpersonal, conceptual ("self-concept"), and extended (self over time). And studies of children (e.g., Harter, 1999) typically find separate domains such as the cognitive self ("I am smart") versus the social self ("I am popular").

In the introduction we stated that a central task for the child is to acquire the sense that he or she is a distinct and separate entity, clearly differentiated from all others, but also socially and emotionally connected to others. The reciprocal interactions with others, described earlier, serve as a training ground for an infant's primitive sense of self—the "mind's I." She learns that she is a physical object that occupies a particular location in space, is physically detached and separate from other objects, and has her own distinctive physical properties (physical appearance, voice quality, etc.). She sees herself as an agent in relation to other agents with whom she interacts and can influence. In addition, she begins to see herself as a psychological being (a person, a self) as well as a physical one, again to be distinguished from all of her fellow psychological beings; she has her own unique selfhood and they all have theirs. Her theory of mind includes not only other people's minds, but also her own desires, emotions, intentions, beliefs, and knowledge. This self eventually will be conceived as somehow retaining its own singular, unique identity ("me-ness") over time and the physical and psychological changes that time brings. Later, she may make further differentiations between her own conception of herself and the various conceptions of her that she thinks various other people have.

Many other self-other and within–self-differentiations also will follow this development. She will learn that she is a female rather than a male, a differentiation that will have profound implications for her conception of what and who she is, and will engender many other differentiations. Within the self, but achieved through comparisons with others, she will distinguish between attributes (personality traits, intellectual competencies, moral qualities, etc.) she thinks she has and those she thinks she lacks. She will build up a differentiated psychological profile of herself. These differentiations will in time lead to a greater or lesser differentiation between the self she thinks she is stuck with (actual self) and the one she wishes she owned instead (ideal self). Thinking of the development of self-conceptions as an extended process of making many differentiations will not take us the whole way in understanding this development, but it definitely helps.

Our story of the development of the self-concept began earlier with our discussion of infant social cognition. Reciprocal behaviors between parent and infant clarify for the infant the sort of being she is. Infants' internal working models of the self-other relationships described earlier lead to a working model of the self, as well as of the caregiver (e.g., Bretherton, 1991). Later, toddlers refer to their own mental states in simple ways, as we saw earlier.

One of the most basic aspects of knowledge about self is simply to recognize one's own image. Years ago Gallup (1977) observed chimps using a mirror to groom parts of their bodies that they could not see, for example, pick bits of food out of their teeth. Instead of treating the image in the mirror as if it were another creature, they seemed to construe it as a *self* image. He developed a procedure to test this, which has been adapted for use with toddlers as follows (Lewis & Brooks-Gunn, 1979). Infants aged 9 to 24 months were first observed, unmarked, in front of a large mirror to get baseline data. Their mothers surreptitiously applied rouge to their noses with a cloth, under the pretense of wiping dirt off their noses, after which they were again placed in front of the mirror. Only 2 infants touched their noses during the baseline period, whereas 30 did after the rouge was applied. No child younger than 15 months of age showed this mark-directed behavior, and the number increased from ages 15 to 24 months (see also Bullock & Lütkenhaus, 1990, and Hart & Fegley, 1994, for reviews).

In addition to touching their noses, toddlers will also say "nose," show clear nonverbal signs of recognizing themselves in videotape replay and still photographs as well as in mirrors, and use their own names to refer to the external image of themselves that they see. This behavior before mirrors does not depend on having experience with mirrors; infants from a nomadic desert culture in Israel, who had no prior experience with mirrors or other reflective surfaces, showed the same self-recognition behavior as infants in a nearby city (Priel & de Schonen, 1986). The understanding of the physical self may be necessary before a child can feel self-conscious. Infants who act embarrassed in the mirror test nearly always touch their noses (Lewis, Sullivan, Stanger, & Weiss, 1989).

The onset of language gives us more information about self-concepts. If you were to ask a preschooler to describe himself, as did Harter (1988), he might, if un-usually articulate, give you something like the following:

> I am a boy, my name is Jason. I live with my mother and father in a big house. I have a kitty that's orange and a sister named Lisa and a television that's in my *own* room. I'm four years old and I know all my A,B,C's. Listen to me say them, A, B, C, D, E, F, G, H, J, L, K, O, M, P, R, Q, X, Z. I can run faster than anyone. I like pizza and I have a nice teacher. I can count up to 100, want to hear me? I love my dog, Skipper. I can climb to the top of the jungle gym. I have brown hair and I go to preschool. I'm really strong. I can lift this chair, watch me! (Harter, 1988, p. 47)

Jason's self-portrait, besides leaving us breathless, illustrates the developmental trend from external to internal descriptors, and from specific attributes to psychological traits, reported earlier with respect to concepts of other people. Also, his knowledge of the alphabet makes us question the accuracy of his self-assessment, though not his pride in his achievement!

Young children's overly rosy view of their abilities pervades the literature (for example, their overestimations of their memory abilities described in Chapter 7). Perhaps children are confusing the *wish* to be competent with reality—being competent (Harter, 1988). Or they may overestimate the power of effort or do not yet use the performance of other children to determine how hard a task is and how much ability they have if they succeed on the task (Stipek & MacIver, 1989). This

Pollyanna view actually may be beneficial, and help young humans adapt to their environments, for it may encourage children to try tasks that they would be discouraged from trying if they had a more realistic self-appraisal (Bjorklund & Green, 1992). Indeed, by age 11 or 12 when children fully differentiate ability and effort, their enthusiasm and optimism is dampened, for they now realize that they have inherent limitations in certain areas that cannot be overcome simply by trying harder (Skinner, 1991). It is interesting that a slightly overly positive perception of one's competence is associated with mental well-being in adults (Taylor, 1989).

By middle childhood these self-descriptions become the opposite of those of preschoolers: general dispositions (often bolstered with examples) that are fairly accurate. Moreover, now that children do more comparing of themselves with other children, they include comparative information: "I'd like to be an actress when I grow up but nobody thinks I am pretty enough. Jennifer, my older sister, is really pretty, but I'm smarter than she is" (Harter, 1988, p. 49). Also, as children approach preadolescence, their self-descriptions become increasingly based on their relationships with others: "I'm pretty popular. That's because I'm nice and helpful, the other girls in my class say that I am. I have two girlfriends who are really close friends, and I'm good at keeping their secrets. Most of the boys are pretty yucky" (Harter, 1988, p. 49). At this age children also refer to how they feel about what they are like. The expression of shame and pride are particularly revealing of the child's *evaluation* of his or her perceived self (see Harter, 1998, for a discussion of developmental changes regarding self-esteem).

An adolescent's descriptions of self are more advanced in that she knows that she behaves differently in different situations and that these varying characteristics of self can be contradictory. Figure 6.3 illustrates this in Harter's (1999) work.

As for descriptions of others, descriptions of self underestimate what children know in this domain. What we know about 4- and 5-year-olds' understanding of their false beliefs is a main source of evidence for this. In addition, we know that preschoolers have at least a rudimentary notion about what they usually are like or usually do, because similar notions appear in their scripted knowledge (see Chapter 4)—abstract concepts of what they usually do in certain events. Tapping into more awareness of traits with less verbally demanding assessments is another source of evidence. For example, Eder (1990) used pairs of puppets to present dispositional statements such as "I get mad a lot" and "I don't usually get mad." Three-year-olds were asked to choose the puppet who was more like them. Their choices of dispositional self-descriptions formed psychologically meaningful groups, and were somewhat stable over one month. For example, if a child chose the high end of the bipolar dimension for one "aggression" item, he tended to do the same for other aggression items. He also tended to be low on a "self-control" factor: He would say he feels like hitting people when he is angry, tries to push in front of people in line, gets grouchy a lot, thinks it would be fun to hang upside down on a jungle-gym, and disobeys his mother or teachers. Thus, even preschoolers seem to possess general, organized knowledge about the self, rather than just a set of concrete, independent descriptions of specific behaviors. These traitlike descriptions of the self may be an early version of young children's "theory of self," in the sense that we used "theory" earlier in this chapter—an organized, coherent set of concepts.

Harter (1998) recently concluded her review of the literature on self with three main developmental changes, which serve as a nice summary for us. First, isolated representations of self become more coordinated and organized. Eventually

What I Am Like With Different People

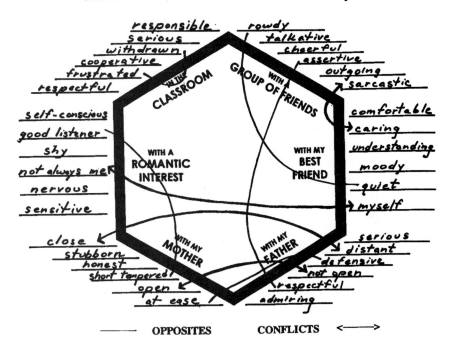

responsible
serious
withdrawn
cooperative
frustrated
respectful

self-conscious
good listener
shy
not always me
nervous
sensitive

close
stubborn
honest
short tempered
open
at ease

rowdy
talkative
cheerful
assertive
outgoing
sarcastic

comfortable
caring
understanding
moody
quiet
myself

serious
distant
defensive
not open
respectful
admiring

IN THE CLASSROOM
GROUP OF FRIENDS
WITH A ROMANTIC INTEREST
WITH MY BEST FRIEND
WITH MY MOTHER
WITH MY FATHER

——— OPPOSITES   CONFLICTS   <———>

FIGURE 6.3   The multiple selves of a prototypical 15-year-old girl. From
S. Harter, *The Construction of the Self: A Developmental
Perspective* (p. 70), 1999, New York: The Guilford Press. Copyright
© 1999 by The Guilford Press. Reprinted by permission.

inconsistencies are resolved by a higher order concept. Second, characterizations of
the self become more abstract, comparative (with peers), and differentiated according to different role and social contexts. Third, evaluations of self become more realistic, and negative as well as positive.

Children's theory of self influences what information they seek about themselves and how they interpret this information in light of their beliefs about themselves (Ruble, 1987). For example, at around age 7, children begin to seek
information about others' levels of performance to adjust their self-conceptions.
These conceptions then organize future cognitions; for example once children have
labeled themselves as incompetent, they may interpret feedback in a way that per-
petuates that belief, such as attributing failure to lack of ability.

Another area of current interest is the construal of self in cultures that value
autonomy versus those that value connectedness (e.g., Shweder et al., 1998).
Markus and Kitayama (1991) contrast the American view of the autonomous self
with the Japanese emphasis on an interdependent self that attends to others and fits
in with others in a harmonious, connected relationship. They liken the two concepts
to the beliefs that "the squeaky wheel gets the grease" versus "the nail that stands

out gets pounded down." Moreover, Japanese and Chinese parents encourage their children to engage in self-reflection and self-criticism to facilitate self-improvement and mastery, unlike the Western tendency to praise and worry about self-esteem (Lewis, 1995; Miller, Fung, & Mintz, 1996). Chinese parents view shaming as a way to keep children from disgracing themselves or family or from losing their important connection to others.

Another issue concerns relations between autobiographical memory (discussed in Chapter 7) and the self. Autobiographical memories and narratives help construct the self (e.g., Fivush, 1997)—"the story of me," and some knowledge of self may be necessary before autobiographical memory is possible (Howe & Courage, 1997). One unanswered question concerns the developmental relation between theory of mind regarding others and the self, as discussed earlier in sections on false belief and simulation theories. Do they both tap into the same cognitive competency and operate at the same level? Does one pull the other along, as might be predicted by simulation theory mentioned earlier? Do they pull each other along?

UNDERSTANDING SOCIAL RELATIONSHIPS

Much of a postinfancy child's social cognition discussed thus far has to do with his distancing himself from other people by treating them as objects of his cognition, albeit interesting objects full of psychological equipment. What of the complementary component of understanding connections between the self and others and between other people? As the socioculturalists remind us, a thinking child is always part of a social network, and we dare not ignore the child's concepts about this network. An understanding of this network begins early, as seen in our earlier discussion of infants' working models of attachment and their reciprocal interactions with others.

Preschoolers' theory of mind provides a solid foundation for the many social-cognitive abilities that school age children need in order to make their way among peers, parents, siblings, and strangers. Their knowledge about the mind allows them to operate much like a research psychologist: They observe stimuli and behavior, make attributions about behavioral tendencies, mental states, or psychological traits, and predict future behavior. The social world around them becomes somewhat predictable and they can make intelligent guesses as to what ripples their own behavior will make in the world. Their awareness of conflicting mental representations gives meaning to the concepts of opinion, prejudice, belief, deception, dispute, impression, irony, sarcasm, illusion, and interpretation. They know that people hold different representations of reality and that they themselves may hold false beliefs, and so are open to the possibility that they might be wrong about something. Their understanding of the appearance-reality distinction may be applied to relationships, as in the inference that "they act like they like each other, but they really don't." Developmentalists are interested in how this increasing knowledge impacts a child's cognitions about social relationships.

One important theory of mind concept is that minds bear particular relations to each other; that is, children take the "influenceability" of people that they understood during infancy to a new level. In social relationships minds influence each other; they persuade, agree, disagree, empathize, collaborate, coconstruct, and share knowledge. A child cannot easily think about human relationships until she realizes that people can think about each others' thoughts.

Understanding Recursive Thinking

One of the most intriguing and distinctive properties of thought or mental representation is its potentially *recursive* nature. That is, it can repeatedly (i.e., recursively) operate upon itself or its own output, thereby creating increasingly longer and more complex self-embedded structures: "I'm thinking that she's thinking that he's thinking. . . ." To see these mental wheels within wheels in action, consider a study (Flavell et al., 1968) in which children ages 7 to 17 years played a game involving two cups placed upside down on a table. One had a nickel glued to its upturned bottom to show that it concealed a nickel inside; the other was similarly marked to show that it contained two nickels. The child was told that another person would shortly enter the room, select one or the other of the two cups, and get to keep any money that might be hidden under it (two nickels had not yet inflated to the status of play money when this study was done). The child's task was to fool the person by taking the money out of one cup, whichever one she thought the person would select. She was also told that the person knew full well that she was going to try to fool him in this way. She was encouraged to think hard, pick a cup, and explain why she thought the person would choose that one.

A few of the older children showed some bravura displays of social cognition on this task. For example, one child first reasoned that the other person would probably select the one-nickel cup because he (the other person) would anticipate that the child would think he would choose the two-nickel cup (because it contained more money), and hence he would try to fool the child by selecting the one-nickel cup. (Clear so far?) However, the child then went on to reason that the other person would anticipate this whole line of reasoning on the child's part and therefore would switch back to the two-nickel cup in a master stroke of double duplicity. We experimenters could empathize with the subject's struggle to put all this complex thinking about thinking about thinking into words:

> . . . he might feel that we, that we know that he thinks that we're going to pick this cup so therefore I think we should pick the dime cup, because I think he thinks, he thinks that we're going to pick the nickel cup, but then he knows that we, that we'll assume that he knows that we, that we'll assume that he knows that, so we should pick the opposite cup. (Flavell et al., 1968, p. 47)

Complex, wheels-within-wheels social cognition of this genre really occurs in life and literature as well as in the laboratory. Here is our favorite example from literature:

> "Does he know I know?" I asked. "No, he doesn't. Does he know you know? Who can tell?"
> "Does he know I know you know they know she knows you know?" Steven asked. (Francis, 1978, p. 206).

These mind-boggling displays of social cognition illustrate not only an awareness of the active (overactive?) nature of mind, but also a highly sophisticated understanding of representation. This thinking seems to require "an ability to create and manipulate a mental model of two individuals' belief states about each other" (Bretherton, 1991, p. 29). In fact, understanding recursive thought would be a good candidate for a theory of mind during early adolescence to follow the active-interpretive theory of mind of middle childhood. Although there is evidence for some understanding of recursive thinking by middle childhood, this understanding continues to improve during adolescence (e.g., Landry & Lyons-Ruth, 1980; Miller, Kessel, & Flavell, 1970; Perner & Wimmer, 1985).

Understanding Peer Relationships and Interactions

Understanding that people think about each other recursively opens up the possibility of understanding a variety of peer relationships and interactions. These may be positive, as in friendship, or negative, as in aggression and peer rejection. It seems likely that children's cognitive and social skills in this area would be related, though not all studies find this relation, and even those that do often report modest effects. Our account draws on good reviews of this area, such as Asher and Coie (1990), Berndt and Perry (1990), Coie and Dodge (1998), and Rubin, Bukowski, and Parker (1998).

The "surface to depth" developmental trend described earlier for other domains is clearly evident in the case of friendship. During the late preschool and early school years, children tend to conceive of friends as peers who are nice and are fun to be with, and with whom one plays and shares material goods. They tend to regard friendships as transient affairs, quickly and easily formed and quickly and easily terminated. There is no sense of either liking or disliking particular stable and distinctive personal traits in the other children. During middle and late childhood, friendship is seen as a psychological relationship; friends are people who help and trust one another. Friends are individual persons who have specific traits and dispositions that one likes. Finally, during adolescence, intimacy and disclosing feelings are part of the concept.

Researchers also have looked at cognitive aspects of negative relationships, as seen in peer aggression. Some have used the information-processing approach described in Chapter 1 to analyze the step-by-step processing of social information during social interaction (e.g., Dodge, 1986, 1991). Imagine a playground episode in which a child is hit with a ball from behind. Most children would see this as an ambiguous event; the act could have been an intentional act of aggression or an accident. However, only highly aggressive boys interpret such an act against them as intentional (Dodge, Murphy, & Buchsbaum, 1984). Highly aggressive and normal children process the same event differently because of differences in their database of remembered similar past experiences. During encoding and representation, the children attend to, and interpret, certain cues: A nonaggressive child may notice that the children's ball throws are not very accurate, so conclude that the "aggressor" may actually have unintentionally overthrown the ball, but an aggressive child may not look for such information. If a child thinks he has been the victim of an intentional aggressive act, he is likely to retaliate, and not consider more pacifist solutions. A highly aggressive child may, for example, conduct a biased search for a response and consider only deviant responses.

Several programs that teach social cognitive skills relevant to friendship in children without these skills have succeeded in enhancing social behavior. For example, a group of adolescents incarcerated for aggression offenses were trained to attend to relevant nonhostile cues, seek additional information, and generate nonviolent responses (Guerra & Slaby, 1990). They showed increased social problem solving, decreased endorsement of beliefs supporting aggression, and decreased aggression. Such programs also may be effective because they change peer interaction, which then increases the understanding of peer relations, which in turn enhances peer interaction, and so on in a continual back-and-forth process. One wishes that schools would provide "friendship coaches" to increase the peer acceptance of unpopular and aggressive children, just as they provide athletic coaches.

Peers are important in another way, namely, as sources of developmental change. Piaget (1932) and Kohlberg (1969) were aware of this in their accounts of how cooperation, and conflict, with peers force a child to consider different perspectives and thus progress to a higher, more relativistic level of moral reasoning. A more recent example is peer tutoring, in which children teach other children in a school setting, or peer collaborations (e.g., Rogoff, 1998).

Connections with Social Behavior

What do children actually do with their social cognition, particularly their understanding of belief and other mental states? We know much less about this than about the acquisition of this understanding, but it is a topic of great current interest. A certain general level of social cognitive development does not *ensure* the occurrence of a particular kind of social behavior but it makes it *possible*. For example, a person cannot cooperate with another person in some common endeavor (social behavior) unless he has the wherewithal upstairs (cognitive processes) to integrate and coordinate his responses with that person's in such a way as to merit the term *cooperative behavior* (see also Tomasello et al., 1993). At the same time, the mere possession of the necessary penthouse equipment obviously does not *oblige* him to be cooperative. For want of sufficient cognitive skill, young babies *cannot* cooperate; for want of sufficient motivation rather than sufficient cognitive skill, old misanthropes *can* cooperate but *will not*.

We already have discussed some ways that social cognition and behavior are interwoven throughout development; each constrains and facilitates the other. For example, the internal working models of attachment mentioned earlier serve as a nice example of the mutual coconstruction of a social relationship and cognitions about this relationship. Dunn's (e.g., 1999) research on young children's interactions with family members has provided a rich picture of young children's use of their understanding of other minds—in teasing others, in deception in order to try to get out of trouble, in pretend play, and in their narratives constructed with others. Each skill may contribute to the development of the other. For example, 2- and 3-year-olds' joint pretend play predicts later understanding of mind (Youngblade & Dunn, 1995), and 3- and 4-year-olds' understanding of mind also predicts later pretend play (Maguire & Dunn, 1997). Thus social cognition is both developed and applied within an emotional-social world of family and peers. Each sort of social relationship has unique emotional dynamics and thus makes a unique contribution to cognitive development: A child's relationship with his or her parents is quite different from the child's relationship with siblings. Dunn (1999, p. 65) describes the latter as a conversational partner "who does not make the 'allowances' of a parent or teacher who is motivated to respond sensitively to a relatively inexperienced conversationalist, but who may share interests and fantasies more closely than an adult partner."

Examples of other evidence of social cognition-behavior links include empathy-related cognitions and prosocial behavior (Eisenberg, Losoya, & Guthrie, 1997), self-evaluations and social behavior (Harter, 1999), and various sorts of social cognition and popularity and rejection by peers (Rubin et al, 1998). Examples of studies focused on theory of mind in particular include those looking at correlations between understanding false belief and social skills with peers (Lalonde & Chandler, 1995; Watson, Nixon, Wilson, & Capage, 1999), including joint proposals (e.g., "Pretend you're squirting me again") and role assignment during play (e.g.,"Let's be firegirls now"—Jenkins & Astington, 2000). Other interesting studies address links between understanding of others' mental states (e.g., Jeff's mother thinks a pet bird would be noisy) and construction or selection of persuasive arguments (e.g., telling the mother that the bird is quiet—Bartsch & London, 2000) and conversations with mothers about the past (Welch-Ross, 1997).

We expect that future research on theory of mind will follow up these correlations with more specific questions such as the following: Does awareness of the possibility of false belief cause a child to communicate more clearly with others in anticipation of their lack of access to relevant knowledge? Does the awareness that different people represent a situation differently facilitate peer collaborations? Does the lack of awareness of the active nature of the mind lead to intolerance of the opposing views of another person with a different cultural heritage?

Moral Judgments

The development of moral reasoning is a fascinating and important area of research, but unfortunately too large and complex to be covered adequately in a book of this size. We simply will briefly describe Piaget's (1932) seminal work on this topic, note that it still is an active research area today, and refer the reader to good recent accounts (Turiel, 1998; Walker & Hennig, 1997). One of Piaget's many findings was that there is an increasing tendency to judge blame on the basis of intentions rather than amount of damage done. For example, children were asked which child is naughtier—a child who clumsily breaks one cup in the course of doing something he should not or one who, through a completely unavoidable accident, breaks fifteen cups in the course of doing what his mother told him to. Children of 6 to 7 years of age were apt to say that the second child was naughtier because his action resulted in more damage. In contrast, children of 9 to 10 years were likelier to assert that the first child was naughtier because of his bad intentions. Research using different methods suggested that this shift comes earlier (e.g., Shultz, 1980), which is consistent with our earlier discussion of preschoolers' understanding of intentionality.

SUMMARY

Social cognition is cognition about people and what they do and ought to do. It includes thinking and knowledge about the self and others as individuals, about social relations between people, and about social customs, groups, and institutions. Figure 6.1 is one representation of what social cognition entails. Another emphasizes three preconditions for successfully identifying any social-cognition object (e.g., another person's feeling state): knowing that such states can exist in people (*Existence*); being motivated or disposed to identify them (*Need*); being able actually to identify them on the basis of the available evidence (*Inference*).

There are both similarities and differences between social and nonsocial cognition. There are inevitable similarities stemming from the fact that it is the self-same head that does both social and nonsocial cognition and from the fact that social objects and concepts are similar in some respects to nonsocial ones. As a consequence of these similarities, many of the developmental trends in nonsocial cognition described in previous chapters can also be seen in social cognition. Like its nonsocial counterparts, social-cognitive growth tends to become increasingly sensitive to inner mental states as opposed to external appearances, and to past events as well as the here-and-now. Both worlds consist of invariant objects, and both move from concrete to abstract and hypothetical thinking. Children show cognitive shortcomings (e.g., *egocentrism*) in both realms, but gradually develop a *sense of the game* of people reading.

People differ from most other objects in several ways. Unlike other objects they are sentient beings who can intentionally behave and reveal/conceal information about themselves. Our relations with people usually differ from our relations with other objects. As examples, we are similar to other people and our relations with them entail mutual and reciprocal coordination of actions, communication, and perspective taking. There are also some distinctively social-cognitive processes, such as empathy and using information about ourselves to make inferences about others.

Babies are born with or soon develop precisely the sorts of perceptual skills and preferences (e.g., for faces) that predispose them toward social cognitive development. An infant forms a "working model" of herself, her caretaker, and their relationship. By the end of infancy, a child seems to have a fragile sense of an autonomous agentic self that is physically and psychologically separate from other autonomous agentic creatures. At the same time, she knows that she connects with these separate social objects in many ways, such as shared imitations, the turn-taking of games and vocalizations, and the satisfaction of her desires by compliant others. Reciprocal interactions and the matching of mental states are believed to contribute to, and reflect, an early theory of mind. The child knows that people have an "aboutness" with respect to objects. Babies sometimes seem to detect that others possess unseen internal states (e.g. dispositions to behave, desires). Researchers disagree as to whether to give a "rich" or "lean" interpretation, regarding understanding of mind, to infant competencies such as reciprocity with an agentic other and matching mental states with another person.

The theory theory approach is clearly illustrated in recent research on young children's *theory of mind*. Such a theory helps a child explain and predict others' behaviors by referring to their desires, beliefs, emotions, and so on. Many developmental psychologists consider knowledge about the mind to be one of the most significant aspects of all human cognitive development. Shortly before age 2, children's spontaneous speech refers to mental states, suggesting a rudimentary awareness of other people's minds.

By age 3, children more clearly understand that they and others have internal experiences (mental states) that connect humans cognitively to external objects and events. Later, when they understand mental representations, they develop the understanding that the same object or event can be seriously mentally represented in different ways.

A developing theory of mind includes visual perception, attention, desires, emotions, intentions, beliefs and related mental representations, pretense, and thinking. At least two developmental levels of cognition concerning visual percepts exist: At Level 1, 2- and 3-year-olds represent *whether* another person sees a given object; at Level 2, 4- and 5-year-olds also represents *how* an object that the person sees looks to that person from his particular spatial perspective. Young children have trouble understanding attention, but readily understand desires. In fact, 2-year-olds can be said to have a *desire psychology*, a causal-explanatory theory of mind which attributes desires to other people and predicts their behavior based on these desires. Young children spontaneously refer to emotions. Not until later do they understand complexities such as display rules (e.g., look happy but feel sad) and conflicting emotions. Infants' understanding of agency may become refined into a clearer understanding of intentions.

The most studied concept in theory of mind is 4- or 5-year-olds' acquisition of *false beliefs.* In a *belief psychology,* children have representations about representations. In this understanding, beliefs (a) are representations, (b) can differ among people and change within a person, (c) may be accurate or inaccurate, depending on one's experience, and (d) cause behavior. Younger children may understand mental states, but they generally fail to understand representational mental states. However, under some circumstances 3-year-olds show glimmerings of understanding of false beliefs. The understanding of conflicting representations of reality may be expressed in a variety of other skills such as perspective taking, understanding that one's facial expression may mask one's real emotion, understanding ambiguity, and distinguishing between appearance and reality. The guileless, trusting preschooler becomes the more suspicious, "street smart" older child and adolescent.

With respect to the understanding of knowledge, children come to understand that a particular experience provides access to certain information, which causes a particular representation and even a particular interpretation, which in turn causes a particular behavior. But young children still have trouble tracking of the specific sources of information. Finally, children acquire an active-interpretive theory of mind. During the grade school years, children increasingly understand that the mind actively contributes to what is known. Prior knowledge, expectations, and psychological limitations can distort or embellish reality. The mind does not simply copy reality.

Pretense poses an intriguing challenge to theory-of-mind researchers because toddlers engage in it but even 5-year-olds do not seem to have much understanding of it. Relatedly, they have trouble fully sorting out what is imaginary (a scary monster) and what is real.

Minds are continually active, or at least conscious. Preschoolers attribute too little thought to a conscious person and too much thought to an unconscious one. They think that people are not thinking even when they clearly (to us) are, and seem to have little idea about what they themselves or someone else might be thinking. At the same time, however, they overestimate the self awareness and decision-making abilities of a sleeping person.

Research reveals three sorts of differences in the understanding of mind. Important *intracultural differences* include opportunities for sibling interaction, conversations about mental states with parents, and biological irregularities that result in autism and its associated deficits in social interaction and the understanding of mind. *Intercultural differences* in views about the mind exist, though the similarities are more striking. A lively area of debate concerns *interspecies differences.*

Theories have interpreted children's understanding of mind in various ways. The *theory theo*ry posits a causal-explanatory system that links beliefs and other representational states to behavior. *Modularity theory* proposes an innate module that is triggered by experience. *Simulation theory* focuses on social experience, particularly the use of knowledge about one's own mind to infer attributes of others' minds. These and other perspectives all seem to explain certain aspects of the findings.

Children not only learn about mental states but also *understand traits and other psychological bases of behavior.* Preschoolers have a rudimentary understanding of traits, and even often prefer psychological descriptions and explanations over nonpsychological ones that are presented to them. Still, they do not clearly see a psychological attribute as a stable psychological phenomenon until later. And not until still later do they freely use traits to describe others. That is, there is a trend from "surface" to "depth" descriptions. Children also begin to produce a more differentiated and organized set of trait-descriptive terms. The development of knowledge and cognition concerning the self closely parallels and overlaps the development of knowledge about other people. Both apes and older human infants recognize their images in a mirror as images of their own bodies, suggesting that they possess at least a rudimentary form of *self-concept* or *self-awareness.* Later knowledge about self is more abstract.

Social-cognitive growth includes the development of children's knowledge about between-person *social relations.* School age children are beginning to understand that thought is potentially *recursive*—that is, one thought can subsume or take as its object another thought, which in turn can simultaneously include yet another, and so on, to create complex and extended chains of inference: "I think that you think that he thinks . . ." Children increasingly come to conceive of friendship as a subjective, "psychological" affair entailing mutual assistance, trust, and intimate communication. It appears possible to increase the popularity of unpopular children simply by coaching them in social skills that are useful in making friends. Children's *moral judgments* change from a focus on amount of damage to a focus on intent. Finally, the new frontier concerns links between social cognition, especially understanding of the mind, and social interaction.

7

Memory

In *The Man Who Mistook His Wife for a Hat*, Oliver Sacks describes a man with a neurological impairment that left him with almost no memory for recent events:

> He is . . . isolated in a single moment of being, with a moat or lacuna of forgetting all round him. . . . He is man without past (or future), stuck in a constantly changing, meaningless moment. . . . a man without roots, or rooted only in the remote past. (1985, p. 29).

This tragic situation illustrates how central memory is to our sense of self and to our ability to conceptualize constancy and change in the world around us. For children, memory does all of this and more. Children could not develop even basic concepts of reality without somehow representing the past in order to interpret the present.

Children have a mixed reputation regarding their memory ability. They recall poorly, compared with adults, with lists of words or pictures presented in laboratory studies or on IQ tests. On the other hand, the accuracy of their recall of certain everyday events, such as a story or television show or a salient event that happened to them, may be startling.

Children's memory is one of the oldest and most studied areas of research on cognitive development—"more an enduring chapter title than a passing fancy" (Kuhn, 2000, p.21). Most of the work falls within the information-processing approach described in Chapter 1. This research shows that if we feed younger and older memory machines the same amount of information, the older machines can usually give more of it back to us than the younger ones can. But *why* can they? The older ones presumably were thinking and doing something different or better than the younger ones were in the period between the beginning of our input to them and the conclusion of their memory output to us. Other memory research, particularly autobiographical memory, falls more within the sociocultural framework discussed in Chapter 1. We discuss work from both approaches in this chapter. Good secondary sources on memory development include Cowan (1997), Schneider and Bjorklund (1998), and Schneider and Pressley (1997).

In a very broad sense, everything we have told you about cognition so far is memory, in that children store their acquired knowledge about the world. They "remember" that hairy four-legged creatures that bark are called dogs, that there are many kinds of dogs, and that these creatures continue to exist even when they are out of sight. However, most research examines memory in a narrower sense, such as remembering a list of items or remembering a specific event occurring at a particular time and place. A child may remember that yesterday she tried to give her own hairy, barking, four-legged creature a bath and he ran away. Memory in the broad and narrow sense do, of course, heavily influence each other. Also, the distinction sometimes is blurry, as when "I remember that my dog usually runs away when I try to give him a bath."

SOME CONCEPTS AND DISTINCTIONS

Let us begin with some concepts and distinctions that are useful for thinking about memory and its development. Students of memory distinguish between *encoding, storage,* and *retrieval* activities. Encoding happens while the event is occurring. The child either forms a verbatim representation of the event, such as the exact words said or another person's exact actions, or extracts the "gist" or essence of the event, such as the basic plot of a story someone is telling (Brainerd & Reyna, in press). As their names suggest, storage activities put information into memory while retrieval activities recover information from memory. When you store a set of definitions in preparation for an exam, you attend to, encode, study, and memorize them: "Learning" is sometimes a good synonym. Your retrieving means recognizing, recalling, and reconstructing them—the "remembering" of what had previously been stored.

These storage and retrieval activities not only occur between your ears but also take place in the external world when you take notes, use a tape recorder, type your thoughts into a computer, or (among the lazy members of the species) ask others to remind you later to do something. In real life most retrieval scenarios involve a sequential, back-and-forth movement between internal and external memory stores. For example, you remember (internal) that you made a note on your calendar and so you go look at it; it explicitly spells out (external) certain information, which in turn reminds you (internal) of yet other information not contained in the note. Storage and retrieval also are closely interdependent in practice. For instance, how information is organized when initially stored in memory determines in what manner (e.g., via what retrieval cues) and how successfully it will be retrieved subsequently. Organizing items into categories may provide little help if you are asked to recall the order in which you encountered the items.

There are a few other concepts to mention on the retrieval side of memory. Two kinds of retrieval are commonly distinguished: *recognition* and *recall*. You may recognize as familiar something that is presently perceived or thought about— that is, you may identify it as identical to, similar to, or reminiscent of something previously experienced. After studying a list of words, you could pick them out of a larger list of words because you have created some sort of enduring representation of the earlier words in memory that is somehow contacted in the course of your experiencing the present words. This contact somehow gives rise to the feeling of recognition. For recall, on the other hand, the words you studied are not in front of you; the familiar something is not initially present in conscious thought or perception. Rather, *recall* is the term we use for the very process of retrieving a representation of it from memory. In recognition, the thing that is recognized is already there to serve as its own "cue" for retrieval. In recall, people have to do more of the retrieval job on their own (but not all of it, because it is usually assumed that there must be some sort of retrieval cue present to lend a hand).

Recall-like processes are often involved in recognition activities and recognition-like processes are often involved in recall activities. For example, after recognizing something as familiar, we commonly go on to recall additional information about it, such as where we were and who we were with when we first encountered it. Similarly, when trying to recall someone's name, for instance, we will test for recognition any name that comes to mind—that is, we see if we can recognize it as being the name we are after.

Models of memory often make a distinction between a *sensory register*, *short-term memory* (also called "working memory"), and *long-term memory* (e.g., Atkinson & Shiffrin, 1968). Stimulation exists very briefly in the sensory register before moving on to short-term memory, a system of limited capacity. Unless a person does something quickly to the information, such as rehearse it, the information is lost forever. If the material is kept alive in short-term memory and transferred to long-term memory, it joins the person's permanent memory and knowledge. Long-term memory possesses a large capacity and includes memory in both the broad and narrow sense.

A final distinction is between *explicit* and *implicit* memory. Explicit memory occurs when you consciously retrieve information from long-term memory, whereas in implicit memory you remember something without being consciously aware that you are remembering. Most forms of infant memory would be one example of implicit memory. An example in older children is that even when 9- and 10-year-olds do not on a conscious level recognize photos of classmates from several years earlier, there are greater changes in skin conductance for these photos than for photos of unfamiliar children (Newcombe & Fox, 1994). Thus the children implicitly, with no awareness, remembered their classmates. Implicit memory shows little change with age.

With these distinctions in mind, we turn to the research on children's memory. Our discussion is divided into two parts: an initial section on memory in infancy, followed by a longer section on memory in childhood and adolescence.

INFANT MEMORY

The first question to ask about infant memory is whether babies have any sort of memory capability. Both logical considerations and a great deal of research evidence clearly indicate that they do (Rovee-Collier & Gerhardstein, 1997; Schneider & Bjorklund, 1998). Infants do many things that logically imply the existence of a memory system. The following are a few examples. As indicated in Chapter 2, habituation of attention presupposes some sort of recognition-type memory ability. If the baby could not somehow retain the fact that the repeatedly presented stimulus has been experienced previously, the baby could not habituate to it—that is, treat it as "old" or familiar. Infants also come to recognize familiar people, objects, and events (e.g., daily routines). Imitation and search for hidden objects (object permanence) likewise require memory for previous events. So too do classical and operant conditioning, both of which can be demonstrated from very early in infancy.

Not only does memory exist from early in life, but experiments have shown that infants have quite good information-retention abilities. In an experiment by Fagan (1973), 5-month-olds exposed to a photograph of a face for only a couple of minutes gave evidence of recognizing it as long as 2 weeks later. With a more dynamic, moving stimulus, recognition has been demonstrated across a 3-month-delay for infants who were only 3 months old at the time of initial exposure (Bahrick & Pickens, 1995).

The findings just discussed came from habituation studies. Figure 7.1 shows another influential paradigm in the study of infant memory. In the research by Rovee-Collier and colleagues (Rovee-Collier & Hayne, 1987; Rovee-Collier, 1999), infants are operantly conditioned to kick their feet when they see a mobile. Infants as young as 2 months can learn this association and can also retain it for at least a day or two, as shown by the fact that kicking immediately resumes when the mobile is reintroduced after a delay. With age the span across which the association can be remembered steadily increases, growing to at least 2 weeks by 6 months of age. Memory is even more durable if the infant is given a reminder of the association in the interim between initial learning and memory test—for example, if the experimenter jiggles the mobile in a familiar way (Rovee-Collier, Sullivan, Enright, Lucas, & Fagen, 1980). Rovee-Collier and Hayne (1987) argue that naturally occurring instances of such *reactivation*—that is, reencounters with at least some aspect of the to-be-remembered situation—may act to ensure that many memories remain intact for considerable periods of time. And certainly there can be little doubt, for

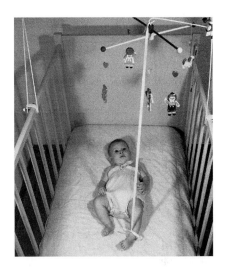

FIGURE 7.1 An experimental arrangement for studying infants' ability to learn and remember. When the ribbon is attached to the baby's ankle, kicking the leg makes the mobile above the crib move. These photos were made available by Dr. C. K. Rovee-Collier.

this and for other reasons, that memory for often-presented and important stimuli, such as mom's face, must extend for considerably longer than a few weeks.

Although memory may be operative and effective from early in life, it is not at full strength from the start. Various improvements occur across the span of infancy. Older babies can typically retain information for longer periods of time than can younger babies. They also require less initial exposure, or less "study time," in order to place some stimulus or event into memory. With development, infants come to encode more and more of the information from any particular experience; they also, as their cognitive abilities grow, become sensitive to, and thus likelier to remember, increasingly subtle and increasingly complex aspects of the world around them. Furthermore, an act of recognition in an older infant or young child undoubtedly includes processes not found in the young baby. Older individuals are likely to be conscious and explicitly aware of the fact that the object or event they have recognized is familiar and has been experienced before. Furthermore, recognizing it may stimulate additional retrieval activity. This activity could even include, in older children, deliberate and effortful attempts to recall further information concerning the recognized stimulus. In contrast, recognition in the neonate and young infant is probably of the unelaborated, "bare-bones" variety that we associate with recognition processes in lower organisms. The very young infant may respond differently to familiar stimuli than to unfamiliar stimuli, but probably has no "I-have-seen-that-before" type feelings or cognitions. To evoke a distinction made in the previous section, the memory is probably of the implicit rather than explicit sort.

Recognition, then, changes across infancy. What about recall? Are there developmental changes here as well? Piaget certainly thought so. As we saw in Chapter 3, in Piaget's view the infant is capable of recognition memory but not of recall memory, because recall requires symbolic-representational abilities that the infant lacks. Like many aspects of Piagetian theory, the claim that recall is impossible prior to about 18 months has come under attack in recent years. Two kinds of evidence furnish the main challenge.

The infant's response to vanished objects provides one possible index of early recall. In Chapter 3 we saw that babies begin to search reliably for hidden objects by about 8 to 9 months of age. Whether such search requires a capacity for conscious, explicit recall—given the behaviors and the time spans involved—is debatable, but some researchers (e.g., Mandler, 1990) believe that it does. Indeed, some researchers, as we saw, believe that the capacity to represent hidden objects, and thus to recall them in their absence, is presently considerably earlier than the first successful searches—recall our discussion of Baillargeon's research program.

Recall is perhaps more clearly implicated in the infant's ability to remember the typical locations for familiar objects across more extended periods of time than those at issue in the typical object permanence task. An example would be the child who crawls to the cupboard where a favorite cereal is kept, even though she has not seen the cereal for several days. Most babies show such long-term memory for familiar locations by the end of the first year (Ashmead & Perlmutter, 1980). Indeed, the heroine of the following vignette was only 7 months old:

> Trying to change Anne's diaper and dress in a.m. on changing table. She immediately turns over and crawls to top edge of table and reaches over edge several times. Today I had picked up the pink lotion so it wasn't where she expected it to be. Anne paused, looked back and forth and looked at me puzzled. Her eyes brightened when she saw the bottle—immediately took it from me. (Ashmead & Perlmutter, 1980, p. 11)

Work on deferred imitation provides the second piece of evidence that recall memory is probably present well before 18 months. Recall from Chapter 3 that Meltzoff (1988) has demonstrated that infants as young as 9 months can imitate a model that was viewed 24 hours earlier, a behavior that would seem to require recall of previous experience and not merely recognition of something that is perceptually present. A study by Carver and Bauer (1999) offers even more impressive evidence: A subset of their 9-month-old participants were able to reproduce some, although typically not all, of a set of target actions 5 weeks after seeing them modeled.

Infants can remember not only individual actions but also sequences of related actions. We saw in Chapter 4 that toddlers and preschoolers form event representations, or scripts, for meaningful sequences of actions (e.g., giving a teddy bear a bath). A series of studies by Mandler, Bauer, and associates (Bauer & Mandler, 1989, 1990; Bauer, Wenner, Dropik, & Wewerka, 2000; Mandler, 1990; Mandler & McDonough, 1995) has probed for the possible emergence of such representations in infancy, using the infant's ability to imitate a sequence of modeled actions as evidence. By 13 months babies can reproduce simple, three-act sequences; by 24 months they can remember sequences of five steps; and by 30 months the retention span has increased to sequences of eight distinct actions (Bauer, 1997). A number of these studies, moreover, demonstrate not just immediate but more long-term memory. In a study by Bauer, Hertsgaard, and Dow (1994), for example, infants ranging in age from 21 to 29 months showed some success in reproducing three-act sequences that they had learned 8 months earlier. The 23-month-old participants in a study by McDonough and Mandler (1994) were able to reproduce some individual actions that they had seen modeled a full year earlier, and thus at the tender age of 11 months. Finally, even longer term memory has been demonstrated in research by Perris, Myers, and Clifton (1990). In their study 6½-month-old infants learned to reach in the dark for a sounding object. Some of the children showed memory for this one-time experience when placed in the same setting a full 2 years later!

The studies of infant recall are relevant to one of the classic puzzles in child psychology: the phenomenon of *infantile amnesia*, or the inability to remember events from the first 2 or 3 years of life. The unavailability of early memories would be easy to explain if no such memories ever exist—that is, if infants are incapable of forming enduring representations of their experiences. But the studies just reviewed make clear that this is not the case; infants can recall earlier experiences, and they can do so across considerable periods within the span of infancy. Why, then, have all such memories disappeared by later in childhood? The earliest explanation was Freud's (1905/1953) proposal that the unavailability of early memories results from repression of forbidden thoughts into the unconscious. Although few contemporary workers accept the Freudian position, there is no consensus on what a better explanation might be, beyond a general agreement that the explanation is likely to involve multiple contributors rather than a single factor (Harley & Reese, 1999; Howe, 2000; Newcombe, Drummey, Fox, Lie, & Ottinger-Alberts, 2000). Among the contributors that have been proposed are immaturity of the prefrontal cortex, the absence of a sense of self within which to embed early memories, qualitative differences between early and later memory systems (e.g., nonverbal vs. verbal), and the absence of a social system within which to share and rehearse memories. We consider this final contributor more fully in the next section, when we discuss the emergence of autobiographical memory. As we will see, autobiographical memory is in a sense the converse of infantile amnesia, in that the term refers to memory for specific events involving the self. The onset of autobiographical memory therefore marks the end of the period of infantile amnesia.

One more finding from infancy research is worth mentioning before we turn to older children. Studies of recognition memory, as we saw, have often used the habituation paradigm, in which infants' recognition of a stimulus is inferred from their decreased interest as the stimulus is repeatedly presented. In such studies some infants habituate more quickly than do others. Some investigators of infant habituation have followed their participants up in later childhood to see whether rapid or slow habituation in infancy is predictive of any aspect of later intellectual functioning. It turns out that infant habituation *is* predictive, and of a kind of intellectual performance that has received considerable attention, namely, scores on IQ tests. On the average, children who were relatively rapid habituators as infants do well on childhood IQ tests; so too do children who showed an especially strong interest in novelty when tested in a Fantz-type paired-comparison paradigm as infants (Bornstein & Sigman, 1986; Slater, 1995). This was a surprising finding, because previously psychologists could find no infant predictors of later cognitive ability. We hasten to add that the infant measures are far from perfectly predictive of later IQ— and that IQ, in any case, is a far from complete measure of cognitive development. Still, this research does provide tantalizing evidence for some continuity in intellectual functioning from infancy to childhood, continuity previously thought to be lacking. And the fact that an early interest in novelty is predictive of later intelligence fits with the model of cognitive motivation that we presented in Chapter 3:

Infants who make sense of events quickly and seek out new experiences are most likely to benefit from their experiences and to make cognitive progress.

We turn now to memory in older children. As noted, our concern is not just in documenting the memory improvements that come with age but in explaining *why* these improvements occur. We first examine young children's memory for events, because this clearly is an elaboration of event memory during infancy. We then turn to memory strategies, the most studied topic in children's memory. Next we examine other causes of developmental changes in memory—increased knowledge, metamemory, and capacity. A final section describes current issues in children's remembering.

REMEMBERING EVENTS

We already have seen that infants can remember simple events and, in Chapter 4, that preschoolers develop a variety of representational systems that take their memory for events even further. With the help of language, they can better encode single events in which they participate and also develop script representations of generalized event sequences, such as going to the grocery store. We examine two important topics in event memory that are among the most active areas of memory research on children today—autobiographical memory and eyewitness testimony.

Autobiographical Memory

Emily, at age 2½, reminisces about her day to herself just before falling asleep: We *bought* a baby, cause, the well because, when she, well, we *thought* it was for Christmas, but *when* we went to the s-s-store we didn't have our jacket on, but I saw some dolly, and I *yelled* at my mother and said I want one of those dolly. So after we were finished with the store, we went over to the dolly and she *bought* me one. So I have one. (Nelson, 1996, p. 163)

Infants' ability to remember simple events develops into preschoolers' ability to remember more complex events, such as those in Emily's presleep monologue. This *autobiographical memory* involves remembering a specific event that happened to you, often from some time earlier. How good is preschoolers' autobiographical memory? How do they represent and recall these events and how does this change with age? What contributes to the ability to form these memories? Do these memories contribute to other aspects of development? Good accounts can be found in Fivush (1997) and Nelson (1996).

Children's autobiographical memory for novel events often is quite good. Children who visited Disney World at age 3 or 4 recalled a great deal about the trip even 18 months later (Hamond & Fivush, 1991). In general, younger children need more prompts or directed questions than do older children, but with this help they often can recall as much as older children. In contrast, adults have difficulty recalling events occurring before age 3 or 4 (Pillemer & White, 1989)—the infantile amnesia mentioned earlier.

Children learn, in adult-guided conversations, how to remember and to recount in a coherent narrative form personally experienced events in the distant past

(Fivush, 1997). Adults implicitly teach children how to conduct a memory search with their prompts and questions: "What did you do at school today?" "Do you remember how scared you were when you saw a big black stretch limo like that the first time you went to the city?" A reply often is followed by "And what did you do next?" In this way adults provide a narrative structure, with temporal and causal relations and contextual information that is lacking in the child, then gradually withdraw it as it no longer is needed. They build on toddlers' rudimentary ability to keep a sequence of events in mind. Such conversations also help young children understand previous events—or at least they learn how their parents interpret them, right or wrong. In the other direction, children are active participants in their own memory development through their interest in engaging in memory conversations with their mothers (Farrant & Reese, 2000).

As evidence that this adult scaffolding helps recall, families that talked about a trip to Disney World more frequently than other families had children who recalled more information about it 18 months later (Hamond & Fivush, 1991). The facilitating effect of these memory conversations may show the need to rehearse an event in order to keep it accessible. This may partially account for adults' infantile amnesia (Fivush, 1997). Refreshing a memory by means of reminders such as photos, videos, and verbal conversations can serve to "innoculate against forgetting" (Hudson & Sheffield, 1999, p. 193) and sustain memories over long intervals. With increasing age, young children require less and less information in order to access and refresh the memory, perhaps because their representations become more specific (Hudson & Sheffield, 1999).

It should be emphasized that remembering in young children often is a jointly constructed activity. These findings should remind you of the sociocultural approach, particularly Vygotsky's theory, described in Chapter 1. Note the parent's guidance and coconstruction activities in the following episode:

P: Did we see any big fishes? What kind of fishes?

C: Big, big, big.

P: And what's their names?

C: I don't know.

P: You remember the names of the fishes. What we called them. Michael's favorite kind of fish. Big mean ugly fish.

C: Yeah.

P: What kind is it?

C: Um, ba.

P: A ssshark?

C: Yeah.

P: Remember the sharks?

C: Yeah.

P: Do you? What else did we see in the big tank at the aquarium?

C: I don't know.

P: Remember when we first came in, remember when we first came in the aquarium? And we looked down and there were a whole bunch of birdies in the water? Remember the names of the birdies?

C: Ducks!

P: Nooo! They weren't ducks. They had on little suits. Penguins. Remember, what did the penguins do?

C: I don't know.

P: You don't remember?

C: No.

P: Remember them jumping off the rocks and swimming in the water?

C: Yeah.

P: Real fast. You were watching them jump in the water, hm. (Reese & Fivush, 1993, p. 606)

Such activities also communicate cultural values about memory to children—what events are important to remember and which people they should remember. Parent-child conversations about the past also teach children how to have a conversation. They communicate that one should share one's experiences with other people and talk together about experiences that both participants had. This may seem trivial and obvious, but there are cultural and individual differences in the extent to which parents encourage children's autobiographical remembering and full engagement in conversations with adults. For example, mothers in the U.S. talk about past events with their 3-year-olds almost three times as much as do Korean mothers, and also focus more on the child's perspective (Mullen & Yi, 1995), and U.S. children talk about past events more than do Korean children (Han, Leichtman, & Wang, 1998). Gender also matters, especially in some cultures. Mothers with sons talk more to them about learning interactions at school whereas mothers with daughters talk more about social interactions. This is truer in Hispanic than Anglo families (Flannagan, Baker-Ward, & Graham, 1995). If we may be philosophically postmodern for a moment, and deconstruct these conversations, we note that it is important not only what parents say but also what they do *not* say.

A main difference among parent-child conversations other than amount is that some mothers are *elaborative* whereas others are *repetitive*. The earlier conversation about ugly fish and penguins shows the elaborative style in which the mother elaborates on the child's partial recall, asks further questions to flush out the child's memory, and corrects the child's memory if necessary. Repetitive mothers tend to ask the same questions repeatedly, switch topics frequently, and fail to elaborate on the child's contribution.

M: And where did we eat breakfast? Where did we go for breakfast?

C: What?

M: Where did we go for breakfast? Remember we went out, Daddy, you and I? What restaurant did we go to?

C: Gasoline.

M: Gasoline? No, what restaurant did we go have breakfast at?

C: Ummm . . .

M: Do you remember? It was Burger . . . ?

C: King!

Children of repetitive mothers tend to recall less and have less organized memories 18 or 32 months later than do children of elaborative mothers (Reese, Haden, & Fivush, 1993). Thus, the mother's style is "passed on" to the child. (We're still curious about the gasoline in the above example!)

A recent finding of interest is that the nature of the relationship between the parent and child affects the nature of their conversations (Farrar, Fasig, & Welch-Ross, 1997). Mothers were asked to discuss four events that elicit positive and negative emotional themes with their children, aged 3½ to 4½. The mother-daughter dyads with insecurely attached girls engaged in more talk about negative emotions than did dyads with securely attached girls. In addition, once a negative topic was introduced, the secure dyads were more open to exploring the negative topics. (Results for boys were inconsistent.) Thus, in summary, both the content and structure of memory activities are embedded in a larger social matrix that includes culture, gender, maternal characteristics, and mother-child relationship. For a different perspective on contributors to the development of autobiographical memory, see Howe (2000).

These studies of children's memory for real-world events in meaningful familiar contexts reveal better memory than appeared to be the case in laboratory studies with materials, such as lists of words, as described later in this chapter. Research on autobiographical memory also is important because it shows how children actually use memory in their daily lives. As Fivush (1997, p. 157) concludes, "Memory is not something children have, but something that children use, in their everyday world, to anticipate and predict their environment and to share their experiences with others."

In the list of questions that started this section, the final one concerned what the development of autobiographical memory does for development more generally. One answer is that memory for past events helps children predict and anticipate future events (Nelson, 1996). Memory for personally experienced events also provides a sense of continuity through time, and thus may be closely related to the emergence of a sense of self (e.g., Howe & Courage, 1997). We see connections between our past selves and our current selves.

Eyewitness Testimony

A very active research area right now concerns the accuracy of children's eyewitness testimony. The increase in crimes, particularly sexual abuse, involving children, has raised important questions concerning children's competence to testify about events they have experienced or witnessed. Often the child is the only witness to the crime. More than 100,000 children testify in court cases in the United States each year (Ceci & Bruck, 1995), and among criminal trials most involve sexual abuse (13,000 children). In our society "a child who reports a sexual assault may be seen as an innocent, truthful victim or a creature of uncontrolled sexual fantasy" (Goodman, 1984, p. 11). The difficulty of this issue is illustrated in a case in which young children described sexual abuse from their baby-sitter and her husband—later corroborated by the sitter's confession—but also fantasized that they later were eaten for dinner by the couple (Goodman, Aman, & Hirschman, 1987).

The main questions are the following: How good is the memory for witnessed events among children of various ages? Are children susceptible to misinformation or misleading information given during repeated questioning, so that they "remember" the false postevent information given to them by others rather than what they actually experienced? Do children's emotional states at the time of the event affect their recall of the event? Is retrieval affected by the types of questions asked during interrogation? In the typical case in which at least 6 months elapse between the initial event and the trial, can a 3- or 4-year-old be counted on to maintain the original memory trace? For in-depth discussions of research on these questions, see Bjork-lund (2000b), Bruck and Ceci (1999), Ceci and Bruck (1998), and Qin, Quas, Redlich, and Goodman (1997).

Basic research addresses some of these questions. As described above, infants' and young children's memory for events often is quite good over rather long periods of time, especially if the event is salient. Four-year-olds accurately report events oc-curring before age 2½ (Fivush & Hamond, 1990), and by age 5, children can store an event for up to 6 years later (Hudson & Fivush, 1991). And when a young child sim-ply has to reenact events of several weeks ago rather than describe them, even 2-year-olds give good evidence of remembering (Fivush & Hamond, 1989).

On the negative side, as we describe later in this chapter, children, like adults, have a constructive memory that embellishes encoded events in a schema-consistent way. Accurately reporting one abusive event when many similar abusive events have occurred over time, as in a "child abuse script," should be difficult for young children. But this problem of constructive memory exists with adult eyewitness tes-timony as well. In fact, adults may be more likely to make errors of plausible infer-ence than are children (Goodman et al., 1987).

When asked open-ended questions, children typically report less information than adults. However, what they report may be equally accurate, at least from age 5 on (Poole & White, 1995). Importantly, at least some studies find that children al-most never make up sexual incidents, even when anatomically correct dolls are used (Goodman & Aman, 1990) or an adult touches the child's body, for example, when lifting her onto a table (Goodman, Rudy, Bottoms, & Aman, 1990; Rudy & Good-man, 1991). Leading questions, such as "He touched you on your arm, didn't he?" show more evidence of confusion and bias, and children may succumb to the adult's implied suggestion (Bruck & Ceci, 1999).

Basic research has shown young children's suggestibility to misinformation (e.g., Ceci, Ross, & Toglia, 1987). Children 3- to 12-years-old were told a story about a little girl named Loren who, on the first day of school, ate her eggs too quickly and got a stomachache. The next day, half of the children were given misin-formation, namely, that Loren ate her cereal too fast and got a headache. The other half received neutral information—that Loren ate her breakfast too fast and got sick. Two days later the children had to choose between eggs and cereal for what Loren ate and between stomachache and headache for how she felt. The youngest children were most susceptible to the misinformation, a commonly reported developmental finding (Qin et al., 1997). Not all assessments, however, reveal such suggestibility in children (Zaragoza & Wilson, 1989). It also should be noted that suggestibility also occurs in adults (see Zaragoza, 1987, for a review).

In addition to basic research, some studies more directly examine elements of abusive situations. A crime differs from nearly all experiences in laboratory studies of memory in that the former usually involves intense fear and sometimes pain, whereas the latter never do, for ethical reasons. One way around this ethical dilemma is to create experimental settings that reproduce some elements of the abuse situation in an ethical way. An example is children's memory for events dur-ing a Simon Says game in which the child and the experimenter touch parts of each other's bodies (see Bruck & Ceci, 1999, for a review). Another strategy is to study children's memories for a personally significant, painful, and fear-arousing experi-ence, though not involving abuse, that they had to endure in their daily lives. Exam-ples are a visit to the dentist or doctor, which may involve a physical examination (sometimes including a genital exam, having blood drawn, or receiving shots), or a hospital stay (Goodman & Quas, 1997; Ornstein et al., 1998).

Drawing on this analog, Goodman et al. (1987) examined 3- to 6-year-olds' memory, several days later, for receiving inoculations. Children's recall generally was quite good. They were more willing to accept erroneous information about peripheral details, such as characteristics of the room, than central information, such as the actions that took place or the physical characteristics of the "criminal" (the nurse giving the shot). Moreover older children resisted misleading information more than did the younger. However, the children never made up false stories of abuse even when asked questions that might encourage such reports. In fact, children often seem reluctant to mention sexual content. Even when the physical exam involved a genital exam, 5- and 7-year-old girls tended not to report that information unless asked specific questions, such as "Did the doctor touch you here?" (Saywitz, Goodman, Nichols, & Moan, 1991). Other studies, however, suggest that preschool children sometimes give in to suggestions about some sorts of bodily touching (Bruck & Ceci, 1999).

Still other studies of laboratory or medical events are particularly helpful to attorneys and judges because they focus on the sorts of questioning that child victims must undergo, specifically, repeated questioning by officials, parents, and attorneys over weeks and even months. Experimental simulations of this include repeated questioning, leading questions, insisting that the child "keep a secret" about what happened to her, and so on (Ceci & Bruck, 1998). When asked the same or similar questions repeatedly in a single session, young children sometimes are more likely to change their answers than are older children (e.g., Cassel, Roebers, & Bjorklund, 1996), perhaps because they think that the interviewer considers their first answer wrong. Such an effect of repeated questioning is worrisome, because the average child witness is officially questioned 12 times during the course of an investigation (Whitcomb, 1992), not including additional unofficial questioning by parents, friends, and mental health professionals (Ceci & Bruck, 1998). Certain interviewing procedures facilitate children's later recall (Qin et al., 1997). For instance interviewing children immediately after an event, such as a staged minor crime episode in which a male intruder entered the room and stole a box, can help their recall two weeks later (Ricci & Beal, 1998).

Researchers continue to look for the best way to conduct legal interviews. For example interviewers sometimes have used anatomically correct dolls (dolls with genitalia). The results, however, are mixed on whether this procedure elicits more accurate reports or reenactments (Qin et al., 1997).

Although research on children's eyewitness memory cannot yet provide definitive answers about the accuracy of children's testimony, it does identify the sensitive spots where children's memories are particularly vulnerable. For example, adults who question children need to be careful to separate a specific event from general scripted knowledge and to provide retrieval cues that can trigger recall, but do not mislead the child. Adults also need to establish good rapport, use a neutral tone, and avoid social demand characteristics—making children feel that they must agree with answers suggested by the adults' questioning. Preschoolers may not recall as much when asked open-ended questions, so may need to be asked more specific questions very carefully so as not to suggest a particular answer. In some situations preschool children are particularly vulnerable to misinformation, so officials need to be very careful about repeated or leading questioning of them.

Researchers have offered several possible reasons for susceptibility to misinformation (see Qin et al., 1997, for a discussion): The more recent misleading information may be stronger in memory than the earlier memory trace, or the two memories may blend together, or the more recent memory may overwrite the earlier one. Or it has been proposed that young children are especially susceptible to suggestion because they tend to rely more on verbatim memory traces than do older children who tend to extract the gist of an event (Brainerd & Poole, 1997). Verbatim traces tend to deteriorate rapidly so may be weak or nonexistent when suggestive questions are asked. Young children's limited knowledge and reasoning seems implicated as well. For example, young children may have difficulty with *source monitoring*. That is, they often have trouble differentiating between what, at an earlier time, they actually did, what someone else did, what someone else said, and what they imagined doing (e.g., Ackil & Zaragoza, 1995; Mazzoni, 1998). Thus they may confuse their own experience and what someone else told them.

Recent work suggests that children's theory of mind may contribute to suggestibility effects as well. As we discussed in the earlier chapter on theory of mind, young children often have trouble reasoning about mental states, especially counterfactual and conflicting representations. In particular, they have a limited understanding of the source of knowledge in another person and themselves, and thus may have trouble judging the accuracy of the knowledge of an adult who suggests false or misleading information (Welch-Ross, 2000). Consider the evidence in the following studies.

In one study (Welch-Ross, Diecidue, & Miller, 1997), the experimenter read a story, accompanied by pictures, to 3-, 4-, and 5-year-olds. Four minutes later a second researcher entered the room and asked "straightforward" questions about half of the story details (e.g., "Did Sally feed a pet fish?"). Half of these questions contained accurate information and half contained inaccurate information. In addition to asking these straightforward questions, the experimenter asked misleading tag questions about the remaining target details that contradicted the original story (e.g., "Sally ate cereal for breakfast, didn't she?"). One week later a third researcher asked the children straightforward questions ("Did Sally feed her pet fish?" "Did Sally eat cereal for breakfast?"). Then children were given a set of theory of mind tasks, such as false-belief and appearance-reality tasks, that involve conflicting and counterfactual mental representations. A suggestibility score was calculated from the number of questions children answered incorrectly at the second session concerning episodes about which they had been misled in the first session. The outcome was that children with higher theory-of-mind scores were less likely to be misled by the misleading questions (i.e., children confirmed the original information and rejected the suggested information). This finding was independent of age.

These findings suggest that children with more advanced theory of mind knowledge, because they are better able to consider the knowledge state of the person asking the misleading questions than are other children, are less likely to be misled. They may be able to think about two conflicting mental representations—their own and the other person's—including one that is counterfactual. Other evidence for this argument is that when children with good theory of mind knowledge have reason to think that the interviewer giving misleading information could have some knowledge about the situation, they are more likely to go along with that suggested information than when they know the interviewer to be naïve (Welch-Ross, 1999). Children with poorer theory of mind did not make this distinction. Finally, children who could reason about conflicting and counterfactual mental representations (on theory of mind tasks) took longer to answer questions about a story for which they had accurate and inaccurate information than did children with lower scores (Welch-Ross, 1997). This outcome suggests that they were considering representations of both original and suggested information. As this research program shows, we "need to look beyond the variable of age to determine the specific cognitive and social processes that underlie misinformation effects in preschoolers" (Welch-Ross et al., 1997, p. 47).

In summary, although young children sometimes report events incorrectly, they rarely appear to make up memories about abuse that would wrongfully condemn a defendant in a child abuse case. In general, they are much more likely to make errors of omission rather than of commission. A good conclusion may be that of a recent review by Bruck and Ceci (1999). They emphasize that even young preschoolers can provide highly accurate memory reports unless adults use suggestive questioning techniques.

We now turn to the main area that has most preoccupied memory researchers—memory for objects and symbolic materials such as words, sentences, and numbers. We focus on four main contributors of development—strategies, knowledge, metamemory, and capacity.

STRATEGIES

Suppose an experimenter showed you a card with these 12 words printed on it, arranged as shown here:

apple	bicycle	house	bear
cheese	lion	apartment	tiger
carrot	car	hotel	bus

Your task is to memorize them well enough to be able to recall them all, in any order, when the card is removed. You, as a sophisticated memorizer, probably would think of preparing yourself for this free-recall test with one or more of the following activities: Rehearsing the list by saying the words over and over to yourself. Organizing the list by studying together words that are closely related semantically. This means mentally rearranging it so that, for instance, "lion" is moved over with the other two animals and "bus" with the other two vehicles. Elaborating the list by creating meaningful connections among the words; for instance, by making up a story or imaging a silly scene that includes these objects. Testing yourself for readiness to recall all the words before you are tested, and when you are tested, checking to be sure you have recalled all three objects from each of the four categories (food, vehicles, dwellings, animals) before you say you are finished. All these activities are memory strategies that keep the words alive in short-term memory and encourage transfer to long-term memory. The goal is to overcome the limited human information-processing capacity.

The category of memory strategies encompasses the large and diverse range of potentially conscious activities a person may voluntarily carry out in an attempt to remember something. Verbally rehearsing a telephone number during the brief interval between looking it up in the phone book and going to the phone to dial it is an everyday, nonlaboratory example of a mnemonic strategy. Others include (1) taking notes in class; (2) underlining key expressions in a textbook; (3) noting tomorrow's dentist appointment on your calendar; (4) trying to reconstruct your day's events step-by-step in hopes of recalling where you may have left that missing watch; and (5) attempting to remember someone's name by trying to recall people and events associated with that person.

The distinction between strategies and other aspects of memory may be more apparent if we consider memory in animals (Flavell & Wellman, 1977). An adult horse surely has basic memory processes—for example, mechanisms of recognition memory. It has also certainly acquired much practical knowledge of its world from years of experience that enormously influences what it will learn and remember. And it has enough memory capacity for simple horselike memories of greener pastures. We doubt, however, if many psychologists would want to argue for the existence of intentional and planful equine memory strategies, let alone equine metamemory—knowledge about memory.

The childhood acquisition of memory strategies has been the subject of a great deal of research. In fact it was mainly the discovery of memory strategies as fruitful objects of developmental investigation in the 1960s that launched memory development as a popular area of scientific inquiry. You know from other chapters in this book that there currently is great interest in unearthing the earliest possible competencies or "protocompetencies" in all areas of cognitive development. The recent surge of interest in infant memory, described earlier, is one symptom. The search for evidence of memory strategies in the postinfancy years is another.

Strategic Behaviors in Very Young Children

Toddlers and preschoolers do very poorly with lists of the type presented to you, and show little evidence of any strategies. However, strategic-looking behaviors arise in the recall of the locations of objects fairly early in life. In one study (DeLoache, Cassidy, & Brown, 1985), children aged 18 to 24 months watched the experimenter hide a toy, such as a Big Bird stuffed animal, under a pillow (or some other location) in a living room or laboratory playroom. The children were told that they should remember Big Bird's location so they could find him later. Although they then were distracted with attractive toys for 4 minutes, they frequently interrupted their activities to talk about Big Bird or his hiding place ("Big Bird chair"), point at the hiding place, look at it, hover near the hiding place, or attempt to retrieve the toy. These seemed to be attempts to keep the information about location alive in short-term memory rather than just incidental comments about Big Bird. To ensure that these behaviors actually were mnemonic strategies, two control conditions were included: Big Bird was simply put on top of the pillow ("get Big Bird after he's taken a nap"), so that no memory was required for retrieval, or the experimenter rather than the child was to retrieve the toy. In these conditions the above activities occurred much less frequently.

In general, preschoolers do not spontaneously and deliberately use the strategies mentioned earlier, such as grouping items into categories when trying to memorize them. However, such grouping occurs in simple tasks, especially when the categories are spatial rather than meaning based, such as "animals" or "transportation." DeLoache and Todd (1988) had preschoolers watch an experimenter hide either candies or small wooden pegs inside a variety of small opaque containers. The experimenter told the children that they should remember which of the 12 containers held the candies. The children took each container as it was handed to them, and placed it on the table. By age 5 children spontaneously placed the containers into two groups—the containers holding candies versus small wooden pegs. This behavior appears to be strategic because they did not do this grouping in a control condition in which no recall was required. Informal observations also suggested the intentional use of a strategy. One child who put the containers with the candies together close to her and the containers with the pegs far away gleefully announced: "I know how to keep the pegs out!"

In a subsequent study, when the two categories of containers were made perceptually distinctive (e.g., paper clip boxes held candies and film canisters held pegs), children aged 2 to 4 were also able to use the spatial categorization used by the 5-year-olds in the first study. DeLoache and Todd concluded that the younger children used the perceptual differentiation already present in the two sets to form categories, but 5-year-olds in addition could construct categories based on an internal representation. The overall lesson here is that when young children are given the chance to organize materials in a manner consistent with their knowledge base, in this case spatial rather than meaning-based categories, they can be strategic. These behaviors most likely are precursors of the more complex, generalizable, and effective strategies of older children, to which we now turn.

Rehearsal

We use a commonly studied strategy, verbal rehearsal, as a vehicle within which to present some general conclusions about the development of memory strategies in children. Numerous studies have shown that spontaneous rehearsal becomes more common throughout the grade school years (e.g., Flavell, Beach, & Chinsky, 1966). What causes this increased strategic competence? Keeney, Cannizzo, and Flavell (1967) administered the following task to first graders, a transitional age at which some children would be expected to have developed a tendency to rehearse and some would not. On each of several trials, seven pictures of common objects were displayed and an experimenter slowly pointed in turn to, say, three of them. The child understood that his task subsequently would be to point, after a 15-second delay, to those same three pictures in exactly the same serial order. The child wore a toy space helmet with a translucent visor. The visor was pulled down over the child's eyes during the delay interval, so the child could see neither pictures nor experimenters. One of the experimenters had been trained to lip-read semicovert verbalization of these particular object names and carefully recorded whatever spontaneous verbal rehearsal he could detect.

There were four major findings. First, children who spontaneously rehearsed the picture names, according to the lip-reading evidence, recalled the sequences of pictures better than those who did not. Second, the nonrehearsers were quite capable of rehearsing and could be gotten to do so with only minimal instruction and demonstration by the experimenter. Third, once induced to rehearse, their recall rose to the level of that of the spontaneous rehearsers. Fourth, when subsequently given the option on later trials of rehearsing or not rehearsing, more than half of them abandoned the strategy, thereby reverting to their original, preexperimental status as nonrehearsers.

These studies and the many that followed led to the current view of the development of memory strategies presented in Table 7.1. Initially (left column), the component skills and skill integrations that make up an act of verbal rehearsal are largely or wholly absent from the child's repertoire. These components might include the ability to recognize and subvocalize stimulus names quickly and accurately; the ability to repeat (rehearse) words or word sequences to yourself in a fluent, rapid, well-controlled fashion; and the ability to keep constant track of where you have been and where you are going in the execution of your rehearsal plan. When you stop to think about it, it is apparent that verbal rehearsal entails a rather complex coordination and integration of skills. Needless to say, if children are unable to rehearse at all, it follows that they will show no spontaneous rehearsal in a memory-task context. We also assume, to simplify matters, that no significant amount of mnemonically useful rehearsal can be elicited from children in this earliest period, even with strenuous efforts at rehearsal training.

The second period in Table 7.1 (second column) is much more interesting because it is a transitional period. Recall that some of the first-graders in the above study did little or no spontaneous, deliberate rehearsing in that particular memory-task setting. Nevertheless, these children proved to have good ability to rehearse, rehearsal was easily elicited by the experimenter, and its elicitation did help their subsequent retrieval. A distinction made in the trade is between a *production deficiency* and a *mediational deficiency* (Flavell, 1970b). A child is said to have a production deficiency for a particular strategy if he fails to produce it on his own for reasons other than the sheer lack of ability or skill to enact it properly. A child is said to have a mediational deficiency if he cannot use a strategy to help his recall. There is much evidence for production deficiencies, but little for mediational deficiencies (Flavell, 1970b; Schneider & Pressley, 1997).

Why would a child exhibit a production deficiency? If he is equipped with the strategy and if its production would benefit his memory performance, why on earth would he fail to produce it spontaneously? To say that he does not produce it because it does not occur to him to produce it sounds like a gross evasion of the question. Nevertheless, thinking about production deficiencies this way may point us toward some deeper explanations.

TABLE 7.1 Typical Course of Development of a Memory Strategy

| | MAJOR PERIODS IN STRATEGY DEVELOPMENT | | | |
	Strategy Not Available	Production Deficiency	Utilization Deficiency	Mature Strategy
Basic ability to execute strategy	Absent to poor	Fair to good	Good	Good to excellent
Spontaneous strategy use	Absent	Absent	Present	Present
Attempts to elicit strategy use	Ineffective	Effective	Unnecessary or mild	Unnecessary
Effects of strategy use on retrieval	—	Positive	Absent or minimal	Positive

There are several possible reasons why it might not occur to the child to produce it. One possibility is that it may not be as obvious to him as it would be to you that he ought to do *something* special with those pictures now in order to enhance his memory of them later. The child may not achieve or maintain, at storage time, a clear image of what is going to happen later, at retrieval time. In short, he may be insufficiently planful, foresighted, or goal oriented, at least in this particular memory-task situation.

Another possibility is that, although the child can produce certain strategies, he cannot spontaneously invoke and use this particular strategy—for example, verbal rehearsal specifically—again, either in this particular task situation or more generally. An easier strategy might win out over rehearsal because it has been in the child's repertoire longer, is less difficult and effortful to execute, or for some other psychologically sensible reason. Examples from the Keeney et al. (1967) task might be simple one-time naming, or careful visual inspection of each object as the experimenter points to it, but without any appreciable cognitive processing of the items during the 15-second delay period that follows.

There may be yet other reasons why it "happens not to be rehearsal," however. A rather banal one is that this child simply has not yet learned that rehearsal can benefit recall, and indeed, there are circumstances in which some kinds of rehearsal do not (Skeen & Rogoff, 1987). In fact, many studies have shown that young children are likelier to use a memory strategy spontaneously once they have learned that using it aids their recall (e.g., Fabricius & Cavalier, 1989).

A less banal reason is that a skill must be fairly well developed in its own right before it can be effectively deployed as a strategic means to a memory goal. A behavior pattern such as verbal rehearsal is still rather effortful, challenging, and attention demanding as an act in itself for a young child (e.g., Guttentag, 1997). Thus, the child may have trouble incorporating it as a subroutine within a larger cognitive program such as a memorization problem. Needless to say, such problems are likely to be more severe as we move leftward in Table 7.1—that is, as the child we are considering has a fair rather than good or a poor rather than fair ability to execute the strategy. The child's production deficiency may be then coupled with a marked *production inefficiency*—that is, an actual inability to carry out the strategy skillfully and efficiently (Flavell, 1970b). This large effort required to execute the strategy increases the probability of a production deficiency. In summary, then, there are many reasons why a child might exhibit a production deficiency for a given strategy.

The third column describes a curious transitional phase preceding mature strategy use, a so-called *utilization deficiency* (Bjorklund, Miller, Coyle, & Slawinski, 1997; Coyle & Bjorklund, 1996; P. Miller, 2000; Miller & Seier, 1994). This deficiency refers to a developmental phase when children first begin to spontaneously produce the appropriate strategy completely but accrue no benefit, little benefit, or less benefit than do older children. For instance, when a younger and older child are executing the strategy to the same extent, their recall is not equivalent (DeMarie-Dreblow & Miller, 1988). Older children somehow can more fully exploit the strategy. A utilization deficiency differs from a mediational deficiency in that in a utilization deficiency a child is unable to profit from the strategy only under certain conditions, such as when the strategy requires a great deal of effort to execute. Also, a utilization deficiency refers only to *spontaneously* produced strategies, mildly prompted strategies, or trained strategies that children spontaneously produce during the transfer phase when no longer instructed to produce them. That is, the term refers only to cases when children's strategy production shows some degree of spontaneity. Children show utilization deficiencies on a wide range of strategies and tasks, over a wide age range (Bjorklund et al., 1997; Miller & Seier, 1994).

Two questions arise about utilization deficiencies. First, why does a good strategy provide little or no help for the younger children? Second, why would a child continue to use a strategy that does not help? One plausible candidate for answering the first question is that strategy production is very effortful for novice strategy producers (Bjorklund & Harnishfeger, 1987; Miller, Seier, Probert, & Aloise, 1991). If producing and executing the strategy require most of the young child's information-processing capacity, then little remains for mnemonic processing per se. Older children, who can rather automatically execute the strategy, do not have this problem. As evidence, young children recall more when the capacity required for a strategy is decreased (Miller, Woody-Ramsey, & Aloise, 1991) and when they possess greater than average capacity (Pressley, Cariglia-Bull, Deane, & Schneider, 1987; Woody-Dorning & Miller, in press). Being able to fit the strategy into some meaningful context, such as a story about an event at preschool for preschoolers, also decreases children's utilization deficiency (Miller, Seier, Baron, & Probert, 1994). The existence of utilization deficiencies shows that (a) there are costs as well as benefits to spontaneously producing a strategy, and (b) we need to have a better understanding of the various degrees of "spontaneous" so that we might better understand the psychological side effects of producing a strategy only with prompts and contextual support versus producing it partly or completely on one's own (P. Miller, 2000).

We have less of an answer for the second question—why children continue to use a strategy that does not help. The answer may be mundane—for example they do not notice that it is not helping. Or it may be more interesting, for example, a sense that they are on the right track and the strategy will pay off in the long run (*next* time, for the ever-optimistic young child), or that the strategy is aesthetically pleasing (Siegler, 1996).

The right-most column of Table 7.1 is almost self-explanatory. Production of the strategy can now occur spontaneously, without the experimenter's assistance, and it helps recall. As already suggested, this spontaneity may be explainable partly by the child's increased ease and fluency in executing the strategy. There may now be enough space in his cognitive operating room to rehearse efficiently, *and* to monitor the progress of his memorization, *and* to keep the upcoming retrieval task firmly in mind—*and* perhaps even to worry about how well he will perform on it.

One cannot speak of *the* age when the child changes from being production deficient to spontaneously producing and utilizing a particular strategy because that age is likely to vary considerably within a single individual as a function of the exact task conditions in which strategy use-nonuse is assessed. These conditions include the various factors that we discuss later in this chapter, such as knowledge about the task materials and the capacity demands of the task. As children become older and more experienced, they become more active in initiating strategy use in a variety of situations, including those that do not so strongly encourage optimal processing or strategy use—that is, children show strategy generalization to even nonsupportive contexts.

Children use many memory strategies besides rehearsal, which after all is only a form of imitation or mimicry in which the child adds little or nothing conceptual to the process. We now turn briefly to these other strategies (for a fuller description see

Schneider & Bjorklund, 1998, and Schneider & Pressley, 1997). They tell basically the same developmental story as does rehearsal, however—gradual development of the strategy per se, and gradual increase in accessibility and utilization.

Other Strategies

Some of the most frequently studied strategies are *organizational* ones—meaning-based strategies involving organizing items into categories. Here children do go beyond the bare bones of the input by adding relationships. In your list earlier in the chapter, you probably automatically noticed that there were a few animals and some things to eat and perhaps rehearsed them by category. During the retrieval you would use *clustering*, and recall the animals together, foods together, and so on. In children, clustering can be an intentional strategy but can also simply reflect associations among words that cause them to drag each other along automatically, so to speak (Bjorklund, 1987).

Another, closely related type of strategy is called *elaboration*. Children identify or construct some sort of shared meaning or other link between two or more things to be remembered. Elaboration strategies are usually studied in the context of a paired-associate learning task. In such tasks the child has to learn pairs of items so that when one word (e.g., "elephant") is presented, she can recall the other (e.g., "pin"). You would be using an elaboration strategy here if you deliberately generated an absurd or otherwise memorable visual image linking the two members of the pair. You might, for example, create an image of an elephant delicately balanced on the head of a pin, demurely acknowledging the applause of the audience. A lot of research shows that elaboration can be a very effective method of cementing items together in memory. Just try forgetting what object was paired with "elephant" in the preceding example. As a real-world application, the use of elaboration techniques can be helpful in learning the meaning of words in a foreign language (Pressley, Levin, & Bryant, 1983). Both organizational strategies and elaboration are later-developing strategies than at least the simpler forms of rehearsal (Schneider & Pressley, 1997).

In the experiments described thus far, the experimenter presents the material to be recalled. However, in many or even most natural settings, the child must select certain material to process and commit to memory. It is appropriate to remember only a subset of the material when only part of it is relevant or when the child has only enough capacity to remember the most important material. Thus, an important memory strategy is the *allocation of cognitive resources*. Miller (e.g., Miller, 1990; Miller & Weiss, 1981) devised a procedure for directly observing the child's choice of information to process. The 12 items that can be selected for viewing are behind a 2×6 matrix of small doors (see Figure 7.2). Only six items are relevant—for example, the child might be told to remember where each of six drawings of animals is hidden. The other doors conceal household items. The type of item concealed is indicated by a drawing of a cage or a house on each door. Children have a study period, typically 30 seconds, for opening whichever doors they wish, as many times as they wish. The most efficient strategy is to be selective, that is, to open only the relevant doors.

Are young children efficient "information hunters and gatherers"? School-age children tend to use the selective strategy and open only relevant doors. Preschoolers, however, tend to simply follow the spatial layout of the apparatus, usually opening first one row (some animals and some household objects) and then the

FIGURE 7.2   Apparatus used to assess children's strategies for selecting
information. Opening only the doors with animals, when the goal
is to remember locations of only animals, would be a selective
strategy. This photo was made available by Patricia H. Miller.

other. During a transitional period, children are selective part of the time. Older
children also are more flexible in the allocation of their attention, adjusting their
pattern of door-openings to the goal of the task so that they look at all the information (when all is relevant), at up-down pairs (when making same-different judgments), or at some of the materials (when only those are relevant—Miller, Haynes,
DeMarie-Dreblow, & Woody-Ramsey, 1986). Thus, as children develop they become more flexible and efficient in how they invest their resources.

Still another strategy category might be called *strategies for learning and remembering complex material.* Learning to study effectively in school settings is a
familiar and very important example of developing planful strategies for comprehending and retaining complex, meaningful information, rather than the simpler
materials typically used in laboratory studies. Just idly reading a passage about the
complex and interrelated causes of World War II probably will yield some understanding and memory. But reading it very actively and "intelligently," taking really
good notes, using a yellow highlighter on important passages, deliberately searching for relationships that are only implicit in the text, summarizing each section,
asking oneself examlike questions—these are strategies that can yield much better
understanding and memory. For this kind of material, the best memory strategy is,
ultimately, to strive for a really rich and deep understanding. For an account of
research-based learning techniques that work well in classroom settings, see Renninger (1998).

The strategies discussed thus far focus on storage—getting the right information in correctly, keeping it alive, and ensuring its safe arrival in long term store.
The other side of the coin is *retrieval strategies*—getting the information out when
you need it. Children's attempts at retrieval have been likened to finding a particular book in a badly organized library (Sechenov, 1935). Like storage strategies, retrieval strategies vary greatly in complexity and sophistication. A less sophisticated
one is not to give up your memory search immediately just because the sought-for
item does not come to mind immediately (Flavell, 1978). Sticking with the problem
a little longer does not always pay off, of course, but it certainly qualifies as an

elementary retrieval strategy. More sophisticated, later developing strategies often involve knowledge about what retrieval cues are and how to use them effectively, knowledge noticeably lacking in young children.

With age and experience, children gradually learn that it is useful to take a stroll down memory lane—a systematic, exhaustive mental walk through a relevant section of the internal world. They acquire the ability and propensity to search the internal world intelligently: efficiently, flexibly, systematically, exhaustively, selectively, in-directly—whatever the retrieval problem at hand demands. Older children, who have the metacognitive knowledge that one thing can remind us of another, know that when the entire potential set is not known, it is useful to use an indirect, circumlocutious retrieval strategy in which nontarget items may trigger other items, some of which may be target items (Gordon & Flavell, 1977). Advanced retrieval strategies may involve a complex interplay between specific memory fragments, general knowledge of the world, and reasoning or inference: "I remember hearing the sound of waves outside (memory fragment), so it probably happened near an ocean (inference, general knowl-edge); but I've only been to the ocean once, in 1969 (memory fragment), so it must have been that summer, during vacation (inference)."

Contemporary Models of Strategic Behavior

Strategy development appears to be messier, but consequently even more inter-esting, than it did at first. Four themes are on center stage. First, strategy development is not linear. Rather, development seems to sputter and almost stall at certain points, during production deficiencies, utilization deficiencies, and failure to transfer trained strategies when they no longer are prompted. Children sometimes even regress when showing a utilization deficiency, as when their initial spontaneous production of a strategy may actually hurt their recall briefly (DeMarie-Dreblow & Miller, 1988).

Second, both the overlapping waves model presented in Chapter 1 (Siegler, 1996) and utilization deficiency work show that a good strategy continues to de-velop well beyond the point of its first, full emergence. Months or years can go by between the first emergence of the best strategy and its exclusive and effective use. A third, closely related, theme is that children show considerable variability in strategies, perhaps because this increases their flexibility during problem solving (Siegler, 1996). Children show at least three sorts of variability: in the number of different strategies used on a single trial or during the testing session, in the number of trial-by-trial changes in the set of strategies used (Coyle, in press), and in the oc-currence of strategy utilization deficiencies. Children may generate as many as three or four strategies on a single trial and change the particular set of strategies from one trial to the next (Coyle & Bjorklund, 1997). A child may, for example, re-hearse the words to be remembered, but also mentally organize the words into cate-gories and perhaps even use some imagery. On the next trial, the child may replace one or more of these with another strategy. Children typically go back and forth among various better and poorer strategies in their strategy tool kit even after they have acquired the most efficient strategy, and it has worked well for them. In the third form of variability from trial to trial, children sometimes show strategy effec-tiveness on one trial and a utilization deficiency on the next (Blöte, Resing, Mazer, & Van Noort, 1999; Miller & Aloise-Young, 1996).

The fact that children use multiple strategies raises the question of how chil-dren select a strategy or set of strategies. Both the overlapping waves model and the utilization deficiency show that children do not always choose a strategy on the basis of what leads to immediate success.

A fourth theme is: How do children integrate these strategies? We draw on one recent study for a good example of how researchers study this question (Hock, Park, & Bjorklund, 1998). Second and fourth graders were given five study-recall trials. A careful analysis of the temporal pairing of strategies revealed that children tended to start a trial with sorting, often paired with naming the category, and follow it up with rehearsal later in the trial. This was especially true for the children with good recall. Thus, in ending this section, we offer our own mental image of a cognitively mature information processor—that of a conductor who directs an ensemble of musicians (memory processes and resources)—now calling forth one instrument, now another, now a blended combination of several or all, depending on the effect desired. We think we do not so much "have strategies" as "play our cognitive system"—that is, we intentionally exploit and deploy strategies and other mnemonic skills in a flexible, situation-contingent, adaptive fashion. The acme of strategy development is the ability to select the most effective strategy or strategies for the memory problem at hand, organize them temporally in the most efficient way, and then to modify or replace those strategies appropriately as the mnemonic situation changes. It is clear that the story of strategy development is a full-length book rather than a short story.

KNOWLEDGE

The research on the influence of knowledge on memory development has taken two main directions. One examines how a person's content knowledge, particularly the semantic knowledge about relations between words or concepts, influences her memory in a particular domain (see Bjorklund, 2000a). This approach focuses on the organization of knowledge, and is closely associated with the work on organizational strategies discussed earlier. The second area, constructive memory, illustrates our tendency to both improve and distort our memories by making our experiences richer and more coherent by filling in with what we know or believe about that input.

Content Knowledge

An expert chess player looks at a chess board with chess pieces arranged as if in the middle of a game and can easily reconstruct the array later, showing that he remembered it well (Chi, 1978). A novice chess player recalls much more poorly. Thus people's acquired knowledge powerfully influences what they store and what they retrieve from storage. You already know another good example—using one's knowledge of categories to form subgroups of items to be recalled. Also, as a living example, consider yourself as an experiment in the making. If we have done our job, by the time you finish reading this book, we will have filled your head with concepts and associations, transforming you into a memory expert regarding cognitive development.

Returning to the chess study, what makes it particularly interesting is that the chess experts were children and the novices were adults. Impressively, knowledge overrides age. The effect of knowledge on memory is domain-specific; the child experts' general memory capacity, as assessed on a digit span test, was not larger than that of the adult novices. And knowledge about chess affects memory for chessboards but not memory for the names of contemporary rock bands. Still, except for these occasional age reversals, adults generally know more than children and consequently tend to remember better. Children are "universal novices" (Brown & DeLoache, 1978). Thus much information does not fit readily into their acquired knowledge structure and cannot easily be assimilated into their existing cognitive schemes, and consequently tends to be hard to store and retrieve. This fact is consistent with the domain-specific nature of our knowledge structures, as discussed in Chapters 4 and 5.

After this initial demonstration with chess experts, research on expertise went in three directions. First, the findings with chess experts were found to apply as well to other domains such as soccer (Schneider, Korkel, & Weinert, 1989), dinosaurs (Chi & Koeske, 1983), and names of classmates (Bjorklund & Zeman, 1982). Second, knowledge can override not only age, but also general learning ability, which has important educational implications. For example, children in grades 3, 5, and 7 who were poor learners, but were experienced soccer players, recalled a soccer story better and made more story-consistent inferences than did soccer novices who were good learners (Schneider et al., 1989).

Third, and most importantly, studies showed that the structure, or organization, of the knowledge is critical for memory. That is, the quality of your knowledge in a domain is as important as the quantity. One piece of evidence is that the child experts described earlier assimilated the items to be remembered into meaningful units—for example, an attack strategy in which a subset of chess pieces was engaged, and categories of giant plant eaters and armored protection, in the case of dinosaurs.

In addition to this research on expertise, studies have looked at children's semantic knowledge—a sort of mental dictionary of objects and the relations among these objects (Bjorklund, 1987; Chi, 1985). The organization sometimes is taxonomic—a hierarchical arrangement of superordinate (e.g., animal) and subordinate (e.g., house, farm, and jungle animals) classes. Each item has associations not only with other items but also with features that characterize it (e.g., has stripes, eats other animals).

Such content knowledge can help a child's recall during development in three main ways (Bjorklund, 1987). First, it can make specific items more accessible, perhaps because they are more richly represented (e.g., have more features) and therefore are more vivid. For example, for most children "pizza" is a more elaborated representation than "casserole." An experimental example is that when the meaningfulness of words on a list is equated for younger and older children, age differences in recall are eliminated (Ghatala, 1984). Second, a well-developed knowledge system facilitates recall by activating relations (associations) among sets of items in a relatively effortless, automatic way. These associations contribute to the clustering described earlier. The nature of the associations changes during development. Seeing Mickey Mouse may cause a child to look for Donald Duck at age 4, but not age 2. The older child's more elaborate semantic knowledge has more associations and stronger associations among items. Thus the child is more likely to be able to access items because they can be triggered by more stimuli; there are alternate retrieval routes.

Third, well-developed content knowledge can support strategies, metacognitive processes, and the processing of material at a more abstract categorical level, which in turn help recall. Bjorklund (1987; Bjorklund & Harnishfeger, 1990) hypothesizes that capacity is freed for these activities in older children because familiar items with many associations are processed with little effort. Content knowledge can also facilitate strategies by providing the conceptual foundation for an organizational strategy. Children obviously cannot organize items to be recalled into categories until they possess the relevant categorical structure. Simply increasing children's knowledge about a domain through instruction does not necessarily increase their recall in that domain (DeMarie-Dreblow, 1991). Children have to develop their knowledge to the point that it becomes well structured before they can use it to help their recall. Child experts would have this structure in a particular domain but other children might not. In sum, not only what you know, but also the form in which you know it, affects your recall.

Constructive Memory

We now turn from content memory to the second general way that knowledge affects memory. Students of constructive memory share with the Piagetians the view that memory is "applied cognition" (Flavell, 1971b, p. 273)—that is, the application to mnemonic problems of whatever intellectual weaponry the individual has so far developed. Most of this book describes how children use their cognitive system to actively construct an understanding of the world rather than to passively copy reality. Thus, applying cognition to memory means that during storage a child disregards some features of the input, highlights others, integrates or reorganizes still others, and even adds information not actually present in the input. Similarly, retrieval is an active and assimilatory process of *reconstruction*, rather than a passive, unedited copying out of what is stored in memory. It is somewhat akin to the archaeological reconstruction of an ancient civilization based upon building fragments, bits of pottery, and other artifacts, plus a lot of logical inference, conceptual integration, and just plain guessing on the archaeologist's part. The point is that the memory machine is nothing at all like a tape recorder or camera. We most emphatically do *not* simply take mental photographs of inputs at storage and then simply develop them at retrieval.

It is time for an example. The following story certainly qualifies as a meaningful input to memory:

> Linda was playing with her new doll in front of her big red house. Suddenly she heard a strange sound coming from under the porch. It was the flapping of wings. Linda wanted to help so much, but she did not know what to do. She ran inside the house and grabbed a shoe box from the closet. Then Linda looked inside her desk until she found eight sheets of yellow paper. She cut up the paper into little pieces and put them in the bottom of the box. Linda gently picked up the helpless creature and took it with her. Her teacher knew what to do. (Paris, 1975)

A person could not really understand Linda's adventure, let alone recall it, without doing a lot more than simply copying its constituent sentences into memory. Consider the eight memory questions Paris (1975) asked his subjects after reading them the story.

1. Was Linda's doll new?
2. Did Linda grab a match box?

3. Was the strange sound coming from under the porch?
4. Was Linda playing behind her house?
5. Did Linda like to take care of animals?
6. Did Linda take what she found to the police station?
7. Did Linda find a frog?
8. Did Linda use a pair of scissors?

You may have noticed a difference between questions 1 to 4 and questions 5 to 8. The first four could be answered by a tape recorder–type of memory machine, because the answers are literally "there" in the surface structure of the story. In sharp contrast, questions 5 to 8 can only be answered by a human type of memory machine, because they require the subject to draw inferences from what is on the surface. The ability to make those inferences clearly depends, in turn, on stored knowledge about the world (e.g., that birds have wings but frogs do not) and reasoning abilities (e.g., a person who would do what Linda did probably likes to take care of animals).

The constructivists' argument is that we are constantly making spontaneous inferences and interpretations of this sort in processing, storing, and retrieving information. Such additions and elaborations are the rule rather than the exception, and they are believed to be of the very essence of cognition and memory. The argument is buttressed by the fact that we may not even be able to distinguish on a later memory test what we have constructed or elaborated from what had actually been initially presented. For instance, after hearing sentences like "The box is to the right of the tree" and "The chair is on top of the box," a person may falsely believe that "The chair is to the right of the tree" was one of the presented sentences, because it is semantically consistent with the mental representation of the input the person has constructed (Paris & Mahoney, 1974). A similar but nonconsistent sentence like "The chair is to the left of the tree" will likely be identified as nonpresented, on the other hand. Under some circumstances the person actually may be even *more* confident that he or she remembers hearing a semantically consistent but never-presented proposition than one that was presented (e.g., Bransford & Franks, 1971).

Grade school children show the sorts of constructive-memory phenomena just described (Paris, 1975). They are apt to believe that Linda found a bird, used scissors, and so on. Similarly, they are likely to think they previously had heard semantically consistent but not presented sentences, while correctly denying that they heard nonpresented sentences that were not consistent with their semantic integration of the input. They also seem to extract the "gist" of the material—the essence of a story, for example—rather than recall the material verbatim, especially after the preschool years (Brainerd & Reyna, 1993). As Hagen, Jongeward, and Kail (1975) point out, children could scarcely carry on everyday conversations if they could not make the kinds of spontaneous inference, integrations, elaborations, and reorganizations we have been talking about. A great deal has to be assumed, presupposed, or otherwise added by a listener in understanding and remembering what a speaker says; a surprising amount of what gets said in an ordinary conversation is implicit and elliptical. As children grow older, they generally seem more prone and able to make the sorts of inferences that allow for a full, integrated, and meaningful memory representation of what they experience.

Finally scripts are a knowledge structure that seems to be a particularly potent organizer of memory for preschool children. As described in Chapter 4, a script refers to knowledge about real-life routine events, such as attending a day care center, baking cookies, or going to a fast food restaurant. It involves a causal-temporal sequence of events that is constant across its occurrences. In general, scripts perform good memory work. Just as the semantic memory structure facilitates grouping and then recall, so does a script, scene, or story schema facilitate the storage of material that can easily be assimilated into it. However, scripts sometimes hinder recall because an episode that fits a script may be quickly fused with it, causing any one episodic event to lose its distinctiveness. An example of confusion between a single episode (i.e., the autobiographical memories discussed earlier) and other episodes or a general script is a 5-year-old, trying to remember a particular trip to the zoo after several visits: "I remember only a time that I went to the Israel one. There was a wolf there. I think. . . . No, that was another zoo. There was no wolf. . . . There was a duck. There wasn't no zebras. . . . I think there was zebras, but I'm not sure" (Hudson, 1986, p. 114).

Children as young as 2½ years tend to recall the mundane, scriptlike features, rather than any one specific episode or distinctive features of events (Fivush & Hamond, 1990). They usually can recall atypical actions quite well on immediate recall, but after a delay the script information intrudes; the specific episode becomes "normalized" to the script (Fivush, 1997). For example, when presented with stories about scripted events, but with the acts out of sequence, children's recall will repair the stories. That is, they will state that children took presents (party favors) home at the end of a birthday party story in place of the misordered act at the end, "children brought presents" (Nelson & Hudson, 1988).

Farrar and Goodman (1990) argue that such confusions are especially true for young children when they are faced with a complex event that is difficult to organize. Their explanation of this developmental phenomenon assumes that schema-based processing of information involves two phases. In a schema-confirmation phase, children attempt to use a schema (e.g., a going-to-the-zoo script) to understand an event. If they have a well-developed schema, they focus cognitive resources on information expected by the schema (e.g., zebras, tigers), thereby confirming the schema. If the schema is confirmed, the second phase can begin.

In the schema-deployment phase, children process script-inconsistent information (e.g., a magic show at the zoo). The latter process forms an episodic memory for a single event, distinct from the scripted memory. Older children and adults, because of their large repertoire of strong scripts that permit rapid processing, quickly process schema-consistent information and then concentrate on processing schema inconsistent information unless they face a situation not covered by a strong script. In contrast, young children may remember only the script-consistent information or confuse the episodic and script memories because the first phase, schema confirmation, was so effortful for them that they have no remaining capacity for the second phase. They may not recall the magic show. In support of this model, Farrar and Goodman (1992) found that when given equal amounts of experience with events 4-year-olds have more difficulty than 7-year-olds with keeping separate, in memory, script-consistent and script-deviant events. This outcome suggests that the younger children are still forming the script, so cannot both confirm it and encode unexpected events separately from the script (see also Farrar & Boyer-Pennington, 1999).

A final example of how cognition can distort, as well as facilitate, memory comes from children's stereotyped beliefs. For example, school-age children with the most stereotyped views of gender roles recalled more pictures of traditional (e.g., female secretary) than nontraditional (e.g., male secretary) activities (Signorella & Liben, 1984). They sometimes even reconstructed the pictures, for example, recalling that a secretary was female when in fact the person was a male. Children who held rigid, traditional gender stereotypes were more likely than children with less rigid stereotypes to distort their recall of items in these ways. Similarly, racial stereotypes biased Euro-American children's recall of the personal characteristics of African-American and Euro-American children in stories (Bigler & Liben, 1993), especially among children with more stereotyped attitudes and those who spontaneously sorted people by race rather than age. These results carry the rather sobering message that simply presenting instances that are counter to gender and racial stereotyped concepts may not change these stereotypes. More intensive cognitive training, however, increases memory for counterstereotypic information (Bigler & Liben, 1992).

We conclude this section on knowledge by noting that what the head knows has an enormous effect on what the head learns and remembers. But what the head knows changes enormously in the course of development, and these changes consequently make for changes in memory behavior.

METAMEMORY

We now look at knowledge in a different way. Metamemory is one aspect of metacognition, which was discussed in an earlier chapter. Metamemory refers to children's knowledge about what memory is, how it works, and what factors influence its functioning. These beliefs obviously are closely related to children's theory of mind. One example of metamemory is the following item in an interview study of children (Kreutzer et al., 1975, p. 8):

> Jim and Bill are in grade _____ (S's own grade). The teacher wanted them to learn the names of all the kinds of birds they might find in their city. Jim had learned them last year and then forgot them. Bill had never learned them before. Do you think one of these boys would find it easier to learn the names of all the birds? Which one? Why?

This task probes the child's intuitions about a specific fact about memory—namely, the advantage or "savings" involved in relearning something previously learned.

Many of the children, even at the kindergarten and first-grade levels, did, in fact, believe that the relearner would have the advantage. Moreover a number of them gave reasonable justifications for their choice—for example, "Because as soon as he heard the names, they would probably all come back to him" (an allusion to the process of recognition memory). That answer clearly testifies to some metamemory. This third grader's answer clearly testifies to even more: The new learner would actually do better than the relearner, the child said, "because the kid who learned them might think he knew them, and then he would get them wrong, but the kid who didn't learn them last year might study more than the kid who *thought* he knew them" (Kreutzer et al., 1975, p. 9).

Following the conceptualization given in Chapter 5, we can roughly distinguish between *metacognitive knowledge concerning memory* and *metacognitive self-monitoring and regulation*, with the former further divisible into knowledge about mnemonic *persons, tasks,* and *strategies.* Useful reviews and critiques of work on both include Joyner and Kurtz-Costes (1997), Kuhn (1999), Schneider (1999), Schneider and Bjorklund (1998), and Schneider and Pressley (1997). Before discussing metamemory development, however, a quick test of *your* metamemory: Do you think you can recall everything said about metacognition in Chapter 5? If you cannot (and our own knowledge about memory assures us that you couldn't possibly), we suggest that you review it before reading on.

Metacognitive Knowledge Concerning Memory

Persons.   This category refers to what children could come to know about themselves and others as mnemonic beings in all their capacities, limitations, and idiosyncrasies. Children learn to recognize and identify experiences of remembering and forgetting when they occur, conceptually differentiating these experiences from such others as thinking, dreaming, and perceiving. Preschoolers begin to form primitive concepts of remembering and forgetting during the early preschool years, as part of the development of their implicit "theory of mind" discussed in Chapter 6. Then children work their way through the various "facts" about human memory described throughout this chapter. For example, children might "induce from experience the related, sad fact that one cannot always count on retrieving later what was stored earlier, plus the happy fact that what cannot be remembered right now will often be remembered eventually" (Flavell & Wellman, 1977, p. 11).

Older children tend to have a more realistic and accurate picture of their own memory abilities and limitations than younger ones do (Flavell & Wellman, 1977; Schneider, 1985). In one study (Flavell, Friedrichs, & Hoyt, 1970), the experimenter briefly exposed a strip of pictures of common objects, with the number increasing on each trial until the child said the series had gotten too long to remember the objects in order. The kindergarteners greatly overestimated their memory span. In fact, over half of the kindergarteners thought they would remember all ten items, when they actually could remember only about four! Such wild inaccuracies might seem maladaptive. However, Bjorklund and Green (1992) suggest that overestimations actually may be beneficial because they keep children optimistic and eager to try tasks that in reality are beyond their current abilities. If young children were more realistic about their abilities, and their reach did not exceed their grasp, they might make less cognitive progress. With increasing age, children's estimations become more accurate.

Tasks.   Children gradually learn that task difficulty depends on two things: the amount and kind of information that has to be stored and the nature of subsequent retrieval demands. As an example of storage, even young children know that increasing the sheer number of individual items to be remembered makes a memory task harder (Kreutzer et al., 1975; Yussen & Bird, 1979). Children also learn that items become easier to remember if the learner discovers or creates meaningful connections among them (Flavell, 1978). For example, when asked to think of three words that would be very easy to remember along with the word "blue," older elementary school children are much likelier than younger ones to think of three more color words (Tenney, 1975). As an example of the retrieval side of metamemory about tasks, older grade-school aged children know that is easier to retell a story in your own words than in the exact words it was told to you (Kreutzer et al., 1975).

Strategies. Preschoolers have only rudimentary concepts regarding strategies. For example, when asked to choose between two strategies demonstrated on videotapes, 4-year-olds know that they can better help themselves remember where Cookie Monster is hidden by marking his hiding place with a colored chip rather than by looking away when the stimulus array is rotated (Justice, 1989). By age 5 they also know that touching the hiding place or looking at it is better than looking away. In contrast they know little about the value of organizational strategies for recall compared to older children (Best & Ornstein, 1986). Consider, for example, *cognitive cueing*, the fact that thinking about one thing can lead you to think about another thing—that one mental event tends to trigger or cue others. The strategy of placing a police car in front of a police officer's house is a better cue than a lamp when remembering in which of the identical houses the officer lives (Schneider & Sodian, 1988). However, many young children do not understand the basic notion that reminders should be placed where they will be seen, before they are needed. In a study by Beal (1985), children were to remember the location of a penny hidden inside one of four identical opaque cups with lids. Almost 40 percent of the 4- and 5-year-olds thought that hiding a paper clip marker inside the cup with the penny would be an effective reminder!

Kreutzer et al. (1975) asked children how many things they could think of to do to make sure they would not forget to take their ice skates to school with them the next morning. Children tended to think of strategies involving external reminders, rather than internal ones such as verbal rehearsal. They would, for example, put their skates where they would be sure to see them the next morning. One child wanted to guarantee retrieval by sleeping with his skates on—a heroic but exceptionally powerful retrieval cue! Other external strategies included asking their mothers to remind them and writing themselves a note. The fact that they could not write failed to deter a number of the subjects from proposing the note-writing strategy.

Some of Kreutzer et al.'s (1975) subjects gave strategy descriptions that attested to some unexpectedly sophisticated intuitions about the nature of memory. The following is our favorite example. The question was: "What do you do when you want to remember a phone number?" A third-grade girl replied:

Say the number is 633–8854. Then what I'd do is—say that my number is 633, so I won't have to remember that, really. And then I would think now I've got to remember 88. Now I'm 8 years old, so I can remember, say, my age two times. Then I say how old my brother is, and how old he was last year. And that's how I'd usually remember that phone number. [Is that how you would most often remember a phone number?] Well, usually I write it down (Kreutzer et al., 1975, p. 11.)

Self-Monitoring and Self-Regulation

A good way to see metamemory in action is to look at how children use this knowledge to monitor their own memory status and regulate their mnemonic activities. Self-monitoring involves knowing where you are with respect to your goal of understanding and remembering the material. Self-regulation includes planning, directing, and evaluating your mnemonic activities. Metacognitively sophisticated children or adults are like busy executives, analyzing new problems, judging how far they are from the goal, allocating attention, selecting a strategy, attempting a solution, monitoring the success or failure of current performance, and deciding whether to change to a different strategy.

Self-monitoring sometimes involves "metacognitive experiences." An example of an illusory, misleading metacognitive experience is when a college student, perplexed at a low grade on a test, exclaims, "But I felt really confident that I knew the material." A more accurate and useful metacognitive experience would be correctly perceiving that someone's name is on the threshold of recall (that tantalizing "tip of the tongue" feeling) and feeling optimistic about retrieving the name with a little more effort. Finally, as you skim through next week's reading assignment, you may get the buoyant feeling that the material will be very easy to remember—or the sinking feeling that it will be almost impossible to remember (e.g., because you just cannot understand it). You then react accordingly: Study lightly in the former case, study hard, get help from others, or give up in despair in the latter case.

Through years of experience as a rememberer (and forgetter!), you have learned to recognize and respond adaptively to your metacognitive experiences. Preschoolers show some minimal competencies regarding metacognitive experiences. DeLoache and Brown (1984) found "feelings of knowing" in 2-year-olds in a vanishing toy situation. Children saw a toy hidden, then searched at that spot after the experimenter had surreptitiously removed the toy. The children kept researching the hiding spot or nearby or related areas as if they felt sure the toy had been hidden there. One child exclaimed, "Darn! Somebody taked him!" By age 4 children are aware of tip-of-the tongue states (Cultice, Somerville, & Wellman, 1983). Still, most developmental changes are yet to come: for example, elementary school age children are better able than preschoolers to sense when a set of items has been memorized sufficiently to ensure perfect recall (Flavell et al., 1970).

Metamemory-Memory Relations

Metamemory is of interest in its own right as one aspect of children's cognitions about the world. In addition, however, metamemory is important because it should help children become effective rememberers. For example, we suggested earlier that a child might have a production deficiency because she does not know that she needs to "do something special," such as use a strategy, in order to remember well. The evidence overall is that children often, but not always, use their knowledge in this way. In a way this failure to use existing knowledge is not surprising. Certainly one of the lessons from many areas of cognition that we already have discussed is that children often do not use their available knowledge (true also of adults, alas). Thus in general only a moderate-to-good correlation between metamemory and memory performance would be expected. And this is what is generally found. An analysis of 60 studies (with 7,097 subjects) produced an average correlation of .41 (Schneider & Pressley, 1997, p. 220). The size of the correlation appears to depend on several factors such as the type of task (e.g., memory monitoring or organizational strategies), age of the children, task difficulty, and presentation of the metamemory assessment before or after the memory task. For example, the relation appears to be stronger among older children than younger, and after experience with a memory task rather than before.

The causal relation between metamemory and recall is also complex in that metamemory sometimes has an indirect effect on recall, as when knowledge about organizational strategies leads to grouping during study, which produces good recall (e.g., Hasselhorn, 1995; Weinert, Schneider, & Knopf, 1988). Moreover, influence seems to be bidirectional. Metamemory can influence memory behavior, which in turn leads to enhanced metamemory (Schneider & Bjorklund, 1998).

It is not enough for psychologists to know that strategies help recall. Children need to know this too. Children who are aware that strategic behavior is related to recall tend to recall more than do children who do not have this awareness (Justice, Baker-Ward, Gupta, & Jannings, 1997). It is better yet if children, like good developmental psychologists, understand the nature of this causal relation. For example, children aged 4 to 6 who attributed their good recall to their use of a labeling strategy were more likely to spontaneously use the strategy at a later time if they understood the psychological basis for the effect of the strategy (Fabricius & Cavalier, 1989). These children said that labeling worked because it kept them thinking about the pictures after they said the names, gave them pictures in their mind, or made them say the words in their minds. Most of these child amateur cognitive psychologists also were aware that their thinking was disrupted on a trial in which they had to count rather than label. As one 6-year-old expressed it, "I couldn't say the names in my mind when I said the number. It disturbed my mind" (p. 303). Unlike these psychological explanations, explanations that referred to perceptual or behavioral activities such as looking longer at the pictures were not associated with later spontaneous labeling. Thus it is not enough to know that a particular strategy helps recall; children are more likely to use a strategy if they have plausible psychological explanations of how it works.

Contemporary Models of Children's Use of Their Metamemory

The traditional way of thinking about the relations between metamemory and memory is based on an obsolete model (Kuhn, 1999). That model addressed how metamemory affects the emergence of a single strategy, which then replaces any earlier, less mature strategies. As was apparent in the introductory and problem-solving chapters, children actually have a number of strategies at any one time. What we need to explain, then, is what causes shifts in the relative frequencies of use of these strategies. That is, we need to focus less on whether or how metamemory affects the emergence of a single strategy and more on how metamemory affects strategy *choice*. Contemporary models address this issue and depict metamemory as a number of interacting components involved in complex relations with multiple strategy development.

One recent model (Kuhn, 1999; Kuhn & Pearsall, 1998) focuses on how children select strategies for a particular task and change their selection microgenetically (across several sessions) and developmentally. One component of metamemory is understanding the nature and goal of the task. Another component is knowing what strategies one has in one's repertoire. During development children learn to use their metamemory to coordinate strategies with goals so that they select an appropriate strategy or strategies. They receive feedback about how well that strategy worked. This feedback in turn enhances their metamemory as they learn about each strategy's power and limitations. This new and improved metamemory then is applied to tasks and affects later strategy selection, and the cycle continues so that metamemory and task performance improve throughout development. Thus metamemory both affects, and is affected by, memory performance.

As an example, a child might try to memorize the locations of rooms at her new school by rehearsing their names in the order in which she entered them. However, after she discovers that this is not helpful if she enters by another door she may draw a map to help her find the right rooms. This experience increases her knowledge about the limitations of a rehearsal strategy. This model of metacognition as an activity over time captures the dynamic relations among metamemory, strategies, and memory.

Contemporary memory strategy training programs usually include some metamemory component (see Schneider and Pressley, 1997, Chapter 7, for a description). The Good Strategy User Model illustrates the numerous skills and knowledge that must be considered in any satisfactory program of this sort (e.g., Borkowski & Turner, 1990; Pressley, Borkowski, & Schneider, 1987). Not surprisingly, good strategy users possess strategies. In addition, they also possess the various sorts of knowledge about strategies and their monitoring and regulation that we have already discussed. Children sometimes can learn on their own how, when, and where to use a particular strategy. Alternatively, another person—a teacher, parent, or peer—can directly or indirectly convey this information. At Disney World's immense parking lot a father may say, "Now I want someone in this family to write down that we're in the Goofy lot or we'll never find our car again."

Various strategy self-monitoring training programs for normal, hyperactive, learning disabled, and low-IQ children teach children to assess their performance when using different types of strategies and to attribute their relative performance to these various strategies. Training often involves group discussion and modeling of strategies. The following is an example of what a trainer might say:

> Today we're going to talk about some ways that we can use our minds better. There are two parts to remembering things. First, we have to fasten things in our minds, then we have to take out the things we put in. Today we're going to talk about things we can do to help us both put things in our minds and take them out. (Kurtz & Borkowski, 1984, p. 341)

CAPACITY

The most straightforward explanation of memory development might be that you remember more simply because your mind can hold more, perhaps because of neurological maturation. In this container model, children have small boxes in their heads and adults have bigger boxes (Schneider & Weinert, 1989). Yet this chapter is filled with talk of knowledge, strategies, and metamemory. What about memory capacity per se? This section addresses the important issue of memory capacity and shows how it interacts with these other aspects of the cognitive system.

Suppose someone were to read aloud to you a random sequence of numbers at the rate of one per second. Your task is to reproduce the sequence exactly, right after you hear it. The experimenter might begin, for instance, with "3–6–5–9," and you immediately respond "3659." She then tries a five-digit series, then a six-digit one, and continues making them longer and longer until you reach your limit, sometimes referred to as your *memory span* for this kind of input. Your memory span provides an estimate of your processing capacity. A main legacy from the information-processing approach (Chapter 1) is evidence that the human cognitive system has significant limitations on its information-processing capacity: Each processing step requires a certain amount of time and cognitive resources for its execution; only a small number of units or "chunks" of information can be kept active in working memory at once. These limitations are more severe in children than adults. For example, digit, letter, and word spans increase from 4 or 5 for 5-year-olds, to 6 for 9-year-olds, to 7 for adults (Dempster, 1981, but see Halford, Maybery, and Bain, 1988, for lower estimates).

The gradual increase with age in capacity makes possible more complex and higher order forms of cognition as well as greater recall (see discussions by Cowan, 1997; Guttentag, 1997). The general idea is that below a certain age children may find it difficult or impossible to engage in certain types of mental activity, acquire concepts of a certain level of complexity, and engage in strategies because doing so would require them to attend to and cognitively interrelate more pieces of information than their working-memory capacities can handle. As capacity gradually increases with increasing age, such interrelating of information becomes possible and cognitive growth can occur. The neo-Piagetian approaches described in Chapter 1 provide many examples of this argument, particularly the idea that increases in capacity are necessary, along with relevant experience and knowledge, for children to move to the next stage. Moreover, children do better on tasks requiring less capacity than those requiring more capacity, which can make cognition appear domain specific rather than domain general.

What is it, exactly, that determines a person's capacity? Speed of processing seems to be the main contributor. How fast a child can identify a number, read a word aloud, or decide if a toy standing upside down is identical to a toy standing right side up influences his capacity (Hitch & Towse, 1995; Kail, 1997). The faster the processing, the greater the amount of information that can be kept "alive" or "on stage" at once in active, working memory. Kail's (1991) analysis of 72 studies involving a wide age range suggests a general developmental increase in processing speed. This age difference seems to be consistent across tasks, which suggests a strong role for maturational, "hard wired," neurological change. As evidence, 9- and 10-year-olds who are early maturers can process information faster than children of the same age who are later maturers, and thus physically less mature (Eaton & Ritchot, 1995). It should be noted, however, that theorists disagree as to whether children have a single pool of resources or several somewhat independent resource pools specific to particular sensory modalities, representational codes, and types of response (e.g., motor versus verbal—Guttentag, 1997).

Does experience play any role? Consider a rough analogy to physical capacity, such as muscular strength. Obviously, two people could differ in "raw muscle power" as evidenced, for example, by how hard they could push or squeeze something. We could say that the person with more raw muscular strength had more physical-strength capacity than the other. More specifically this person's absolute quantity of resources is greater. However, two people with identical structural physical-strength capacities might nevertheless differ considerably in their functional (usable, actual, effective) capacities in specific physical tasks. That is, they would differ in how well they can do with what they have despite the quantitative similarity of their physical, maturation-based resources. Experts at karate, boxing, shotputting, weightlifting, golf, and the like can deploy and exploit their structural, raw-muscle-power capacities far more fully and effectively in their areas of skill than can physically identical nonexperts. They know how to deliver the maximum force possible at precisely the right moment and place and can thereby get consider-able more mileage (total functional capacity) than nonexperts can out of a fixed and limited physical potential (the structural contribution to functional capacity).

Turning this analogy to mental activity, during development "raw mental muscle power" or structural processing capacity increases because of both neuro-logical maturation which permits faster processing and various experience-based changes which improve efficiency in the use of resources. As an example of the lat-ter, older children and adults may be more likely than younger children to use their world knowledge and activities such as rehearsal or organizational strategies. In the digit span task described earlier, older children may be able to remember 149217761918 because it can be chunked into 1492, 1776, and 1918, important dates in history (Lachman, Lachman, & Butterfield, 1979). Similarly helpful are ex-ternal aids, or "mental prostheses," such as pencil and paper, libraries, computers, and other people's minds. There is a physical-capacity analogue here also, although it is a bit absurd: An athlete could lift much heavier weights than his structural ca-pacity permits by enlisting the aid of his friends or, better still, by using a crane. As another example, even the language system that children acquire can matter. Chi-nese speakers have longer digit spans than do English speakers, which has been at-tributed to the fact that Chinese number words are shorter and thus can be spoken more quickly (Geary, Fan, Bow-Thomas, & Siegler, 1993).

Another type of experience-based difference in efficiency is that people of var-ious ages use similar mental activities, such as a memory strategy, but these activities are more difficult, and therefore take more effort, for younger children. Consequently, younger children use up more of their capacity when performing these activities, leav-ing little capacity for other activities. Strategies undoubtedly become faster or other-wise less capacity-consuming in the course of years of practice, experience, and accumulation of knowledge. Highly practiced strategies can be performed more auto-matically and thus less effortfully. Indeed, the ever present possibility that these fac-tors may be at work in any task situation makes it difficult to assess the contribution of maturation-based structural capacity to total functional capacity. On any given task in which older children behave as if they command more information-processing capac-ity than younger children, it is hard to be sure that experientially-based factors like highly practiced strategies are not the sole causes. Both global speed of processing and experientially based, domain-specific processing skills are believed to contribute to increases in capacity (Kail & Salthouse, 1994).

Let us look more carefully at age differences in how effortful a strategy is. The "dual task" paradigm is based on the notion that if performing one task uses most of one's capacity, then performing a capacity-demanding second task will draw capacity away from the first task. If you foolishly volunteered for this study, you first would be asked to push a button (or perhaps tap a key) rapidly, certainly a familiar activity for a generation that is growing up with computer games. The experimenter then would compare this baseline rate of the number of finger taps per second on this task alone with the rate when you were told to perform simultaneously a second task, such as cu-mulatively rehearsing a set of items to be recalled. Your decrease in finger tapping from the one-task to the two-task situation provides a rough measure of the capacity you need to execute the rehearsal strategy. When testing children, instructing all ages to use the strategy of cumulative rehearsal ensures that strategy performance on that task is equated across ages. Seven- and 8-year-olds slow their finger tapping more than do 11-year-olds (Guttentag, 1984), indicating that the strategy is more capacity-demanding for the younger children. In addition, an easy strategy (rehearsing one word at a time) is less effortful than a more difficult strategy (cumulative rehearsal) for the younger children. Finally, when older and younger children use an equal amount of capacity for the strategy, older children rehearse more and recall more than do the younger ones. All these outcomes indicate that a strategy "costs more" in capacity for younger children than older (see also Guttentag, 1997 for a review). As children acquire experience with using a strategy during development, this strategy becomes more automatic and demands less capacity (but for a different interpretation, see Brainerd & Reyna, 1989, and Howe & Rabinowitz, 1989).

Young children may exhibit a production deficiency in part because they are reluctant to try to produce an effortful strategy (Guttentag, 1997). Moreover, even when children spontaneously produce the strategy, if they must devote most of their capacity to executing it, they may have little capacity remaining to perform other mnemonic activities such as metamemory or other strategies that would help recall. Thus, they may show a utilization deficiency, described earlier, in which a strategy provides little or no help for recall. This deficiency, then, would disappear in older children for whom strategy production is less effortful. As evidence, dual-task studies that increase demands on capacity increase the utilization deficiency (Miller, Woody-Ramsey, & Aloise, 1991) and studies that have an adult execute the strategy, which eliminates the capacity demands of the strategy on the child, decrease the utilization deficiency (DeMarie-Dreblow & Miller, 1988; Miller, Woody-Ramsey, & Aloise, 1991).

In summary, although the child memory machine has wondrous memory aids such as knowledge, strategies, and metamemory, capacity constrains their use. Only a limited number of mental items (to-be-recalled items, knowledge about strategies, factual knowledge, concepts, etc.) can be activated at any one time and kept alive. Thus, a child may be unable to make full use of these memory-relevant abilities because of capacity limitations. As both capacity and these other abilities improve, they help each other develop.

CURRENT ISSUES IN MEMORY DEVELOPMENT

What issues, questions, and research problems most preoccupy students of memory development these days? Various issues surrounding eyewitness testimony and autobiographical memory, described earlier, continue to be of great interest. For other content areas, the following issues are at the forefront.

Variability

One main issue concerns strategy variability versus stability and consistency. Variability seems to have the upper hand right now. We described (e.g., Siegler, 1996) findings of considerable variability within a child and between children over the time scale of minutes and days. A recent longitudinal study suggests that variability also characterizes children's strategies over months and years (Weinert & Schneider, 1999). For example, children who are most strategic in their group at Time 1 may not be among the most strategic one year later. Children show more stability on tasks such as word span and story recall that are less dependent on strategies.

Intrachild variability in the nature and degree of strategic behavior over minutes, days, months, and years has shifted from being a nuisance for developmentalists looking for regularities and universal developmental milestones to holding considerable interest in its own right. Is there any particular advantage or disadvantage to using strategies inconsistently or even shifting the particular set of strategies that one is using together on each trial? Does strategy variability in a young child mean the same thing as strategy variability in an older one? Why are some children more variable than are others? Researchers currently are trying to solve this puzzle (e.g., Coyle & Bjorklund, 1997).

Domain Specific Memory Skills

A related issue is whether memory is a domain-general ability or a set of domain-specific abilities. That is, can we characterize a particular child as a "good rememberer" or does it depend on whether we are talking about the child's memory for the route to the movie theater or for the names of countries in Africa? The current thinking is that similar memory skills "hang together," so that a child who does well on one span task tends to do well on another sort of span task, but there is little consistency across types of memory tasks (Kurtz-Costes, Schneider, & Rupp, 1995; Schneider & Weinert, 1995). This conclusion, though tentative, is somehow satisfying because it fits with conclusions about other cognitive abilities in other chapters.

Acquiring New Strategies: Sociocultural Influences

Another issue concerns the role of experience in the development of strategies or procedures for remembering. Where do strategies come from? Do children discover them on their own? Do parents, siblings, peers, and teachers provide models or direct instruction in strategy use or other procedures for remembering? Consistent with the sociocultural theories of Vygotsky and others discussed in Chapter 1, cultures or subcultures vary in the extent to which they encourage and support particular types of memory or particular mnemonic activities (e.g., Kurtz, 1990; Mistry, 1997). For example, schooled Western children recall better on list-learning tasks, which require rehearsal or organizational strategies, than do unschooled children in less industrialized societies (e.g., Cole & Scribner, 1977). In contrast this superiority does not appear in memory for stories or visual scenes. Kearins (1981) found that Australian aboriginal children are better at remembering locations of objects in an array than are Anglo-Australian children. Similarly Dube (1982) reported better recall of stories in African junior high or unschooled adolescents than American junior high students. Children in all cultures have considerable exposure to oral stories and spatial arrays, and may even excel in memory on these tasks if their culture has a strong tradition of oral storytelling or requires strong visual-spatial skills for survival. An example of the latter is an ability to orient oneself spatially in a relatively unvaried terrain.

Cultural differences exist even within Western culture. Compared with American parents, German parents and teachers give children more direct strategy training than their American counterparts. German parents also buy their children more games requiring strategic thinking and more frequently check their homework (Carr, Kurtz, Schneider, Turner, & Borkowski, 1989; Kurtz, Schneider, Carr, Borkowski, & Rellinger, 1990). It should come as no surprise, then, that German children spontaneously use strategies moreso than do American children. Thus, different sociocultural contexts create different memory-relevant learning environments and consequently enhance different skills (Rogoff, 1998). Remembering is a socially situated activity. It is something that children do in social settings when they are trying to achieve some goal.

Schooling appears to underlie some of the cultural influences on memory (Cole, 1996; Rogoff, 1998). Using a clever design, Morrison and his colleagues (Morrison, Griffith, & Alberts, 1997; Morrison, Smith, & Dow-Ehrensberger, 1995; Varnhagen, Morrison, & Everall, 1994) have compared two groups of similarly aged children whose birthdays clustered around the cut-off date used for permitting entry into school. That is, the "old kindergarteners" just missed the cut-off date for the first grade and the "young first graders" barely made that date. The latter group, which had an extra year of school but was only a few days older, was superior in recall and strategy use, as well as various other cognitive tasks. Thus, the experience of schooling appears to be powerful.

Multiple Causes

It no longer is an issue whether strategies, knowledge, metamemory, and capacity influence recall. They clearly do, along with other variables such as IQ and age. Memory researchers now would like to put these single variables together into a meaningful package. What is the relative impact of these various factors? How do they interact? We were tempted to end this chapter with a section titled "Putting it all together." Though our hubris failed, we do think that memory research is on the verge of revealing the interplay among the various influences on memory development. Advances in statistical techniques for testing causal models of relations among several variables have helped this research along (see, for example, Alexander & Schwanenflugel, 1994; DeMarie-Dreblow, Miller, Cunningham, & Wielgos, 1999; Hasselhorn, 1992; Schneider, Korkel, & Weinert, 1987). Thus far, content knowledge and metamemory appear to be the major players in these models. Many effects are indirect, and involve complex interactions. For example, whether strategy training leads to improved recall may depend on the child's metamemory, particularly the child's attributions about the mechanisms by which a strategy has its effect (Fabricius & Hagen, 1984). Another example is that good metamemory affects the recall of child soccer experts but not novices (Schneider, Schlagmüller, & Vise, 1998). Many loose ends obviously still remain to be tied. In particular, the mechanisms underlying some of the observed relations are frustratingly unclear. Also, it must be kept in mind that the relative impact of the influences may vary from age to age and task to task. There is much to do.

Cognitive Neuroscience

Finally, researchers are assessing the importance of several new areas of research. Striking progress in neuroscience is providing another level of explanation for memory development (C. A. Nelson, 1997; 1999). Imaging techniques are beginning to suggest not only the areas of the brain that are most involved in various aspects of memory but also the nature of the links between brain and behavior. Both neuroscience and behavioral research point to the important role of the development of the ability to inhibit thoughts and responses. Just as important as the acquisition of new memory skills is the inhibition of earlier strategies, rules, associations, and memories (e.g., Harnishfeger, 1995). We return to the neuroscience approach in the concluding chapter.

SUMMARY

The importance of memory can be summed up by a comment from an adult who was asked in an experiment to rate the relative importance of various cognitive processes in everyday mental activities. He looked at the experimenter and said, "Memory is part of everything" (Fabricius, 1997). This fact makes memory both easy and difficult to study. Several concepts are useful in analyzing memory development. *Encoding* an item or event gets it into *storage;* getting it out again is called *retrieval.* Retrieval may consist of *recognition* of something that is already present in perception or thought; *recall* of something that is not present (often with the help of reminders or *retrieval cues*); and blends and mixtures of the two. This memory flow is typically "through" a *sensory register, short-term memory,* and *long-term memory.* Memory can be *explicit* or *implicit,* depending on whether the person is aware of trying to remember.

Recent research on infant memory shows some startling competencies. In particular, habituation and conditioning studies demonstrate recognition memory—the realization that a present object or event has been seen before—even in newborns. Over the next few weeks and months, infants can retain more material, and more complex material, over a longer span of time. Recall memory—the retrieval of some past object or event that no longer is present—seems to exist in some rudimentary form by the end of the first year of life, though researchers disagree as to how rich an interpretation to make of these studies. One-year-olds can, for example, search for vanished objects and imitate models from the past, which indicates some kind of mental representation of the past object or event. However, we still have much to learn about the exact nature of these changes during infancy. *Infantile amnesia,* the inability of adults to recall very early events, is a particularly intriguing puzzle.

Memory does not operate in isolation. It can be understood only within a broader context that includes *sociocultural context, strategies, knowledge, metamemory,* and *capacity.* Researchers have studied the sociocultural context of memory mainly with respect to *autobiographical memory,* memory for personally experienced events. Remembering is a social activity the young child engages in with adults, as they talk about their shared experiences. It appears that children learn how to have a remembering experience; they eventually can use it on their own. These memories often are quite good.

Another sort of memory for events is related to *eyewitness testimony.* Like adults, children have vulnerabilities in their reporting of events that happened to them or others. Older children tend to recall more than younger children when asked open-ended questions ("What happened?"), but what young children do say typically is accurate. Asking more directed questions pulls out more information from young children but also introduces the danger of altering their memory. The observed *suggestibility* of young children is worrisome from a legal perspective, though researchers disagree as to how suggestible they are. There is agreement, however, that certain questioning procedures reduce this risk.

Strategies are potentially conscious activities that a person may use to facilitate memory. Rudimentary versions of many memory strategies emerge in the post-infancy period. Looking, pointing, naming, and talking about items to be re-membered keep the information alive over a period of time. We used *rehearsal* to describe the typical course of development of memory strategies. Initially the child is unable to execute the potentially strategic activity at all, even under experimenter instruction or tuition. Subsequently the child is likely to exhibit a pattern of *produc-tion deficiency* with respect to the strategy. That is, she can and will use it if explic-itly directed to do so, and using it benefits her memory in the expected fashion, but she does not use the strategy spontaneously, on her own initiative.

Several factors make this simple picture of strategy development more com-plex. First, strategies become increasingly effective during development, as chil-dren overcome a *utilization deficiency* and accrue greater "payoff" for recall. Second, many contextual variables influence whether children produce a strategy already in their repertoire. Older children need less contextual support than do younger ones. The focus has shifted from simply identifying production deficient children to identifying task and situational factors that influence strategy produc-tion and recall. Third, strategies become more complex, flexible, and tailored to the task at hand.

There are other storage strategies that are more sophisticated and sometimes more mnemonically effective than rehearsal. Examples are an *organizational* strat-egy (studying conceptually related items together), *elaboration* strategies (e.g., con-struction of a vivid visual image linking two normally unrelated objects that are supposed to be remembered together), and strategies for the efficient *allocation of cognitive resources* and for *learning and remembering complex material.* The onto-genetic pattern shown in Table 7.1 also appears to apply to these types of strategies. The developing child acquires *retrieval strategies* as well as *storage strategies.* De-velopment here consists largely of an increasing ability and propensity to search memory intelligently: efficiently, flexibly, systematically, exhaustively, selectively, indirectly—in whatever manner the specific retrieval problem at hand requires.

Contemporary models of strategic behavior focus on four themes. First, de-velopment is not always linear; it includes regression, spurts, and advances that do not immediately pay off. Second, strategies continue to develop long after their first emergence, as shown by the overlapping waves and utilization deficiency models. Third, children show considerable variability in the number of different strategies used during a session and the particular set of strategies selected for a particular trial. Fourth, children acquire important skills for integrating these strategies so that they work well together.

The *Knowledge* section showed that memory operates in the context of a larger cognitive system. The argument was made that what people know greatly in-fluences what they learn and remember. The power of knowledge is illustrated when child chess experts can remember chessboard arrangements better than adults who are less knowledgeable about chess. Developmental changes in the knowledge structures should lead to developmental changes in what is stored and retrieved. Well-developed *content* knowledge helps recall in at least three ways. First, its vivid, rich representations can be accessed quickly. Second, the organized connec-tions automatically activate the associations among items. Third, it supports the use of strategies, perhaps by freeing capacity for that purpose.

Memory is *constructive.* We do not simply make a copy of information pre-sented at storage and then simply reprint that copy when we retrieve. Rather, we fill in the gaps and make inferences, as we try to achieve a meaningful representation of the information. Scripts, in particular, appear to be a powerful shaper of young children's memories, towards both increased and decreased accuracy.

Metamemory means knowledge or cognitive activity bearing on anything mnemonic; it is, therefore, metacognition (Chapter 5) that takes memory enterprises as its object. Two major categories of metamemory were distinguished: *metacognitive knowledge concerning memory* and *self-monitoring and regulation*. The former is further divisible into knowledge about mnemonic *persons, tasks*, and *strategies*. In the *person* case, children learn, among other things, to recognize the capacities, limitations, and idiosyncrasies of the human memory system. Regarding *tasks*, children discover that a set of items will be easier to recall if the items are few in number, familiar, and meaningfully related to one another—for example, categorizable. Children also become better able to think of and articulate plausible storage and retrieval *strategies* in response to hypothetical memory problems.

The other major category of metamemory, *self-monitoring and regulation*, can be considered applied metacognitive knowledge concerning memory. Children learn to assess their current memory state, select a strategy, evaluate their progress toward their goal, and so on. Some of the most successful programs to train strategies in laboratory or academic settings involve teaching knowledge about strategies and self monitoring and regulation. An important component of self monitoring is *metacognitive experiences* concerning memory, which include judgments or feelings ("mnemonic sensations") about how difficult or time-consuming something will likely be to store or retrieve, about whether the present situation is one that tacitly calls for storage or retrieval efforts, and the like. The relationship between metamemory and strategic behavior or recall is far from clear, but in general there is a moderately positive correlation. We discussed several promising new models that deal with the two-way developmental street between metamemory and memory, as well as other complexities among memory-related skills.

Memory capacity refers to the total mental workspace available for basic mental processes during encoding, retrieval or strategy use. As basic mental processes, such as identifying words, become more practiced they become faster and less effortful. The freed capacity can be devoted to strategies or to storing more items. Similarly executing a strategy becomes less effortful with increasing age, thus freeing capacity for other mnemonic activities.

A number of issues currently preoccupy students of memory development. What is the significance, for development, of intrachild and between-child variability in strategic behaviors? Are memory skills domain-specific or domain-general? What is the role of social experience in the development of strategies? Which individual differences are the most powerful predictors of memory? How do strategies, knowledge, metamemory, and capacity interact and affect recall? What can we learn about memory from neuroscience research?

8

Language

Father, making up a story to help his little girl settle down for the night: ". . . and then Trina (the canine heroine of his impromptu narrative) was chased by another dog. I wonder what happened next." Girl: "I know—the dog catched her!"

What tacit knowledge about language can we reasonably attribute to this little girl on the basis of this brief interchange? First she has clearly acquired a lot of expertise in both producing and understanding the speech sounds of English. Thanks to her considerable *phonological* development, she effortless segmented and interpreted her father's rapid and unbroken burst of sound ("anthentrinawuz . . . ," roughly) as the English word string ". . . and then Trina was . . ." Imagine what it would have sounded like to a person who knew no English; he would likely not even be able to make out the individual vowels and consonants, let alone know where one word ended and the next began. Similarly the "accentless," native-speaker–like word pronunciation and intonation pattern of her reply would be the envy and despair of most adults trying to learn English as a second language. A little probing would undoubtedly also show that her knowledge of English phonology is a productive, generative, rule-governed affair, like the rest of her linguistic knowledge. For instance, "Trina" undoubtedly sounds like a proper word to her, although she has never heard it before. In contrast "Zdrina"—which does not follow English phonological rules for word construction—would probably just not sound right.

Second there is also evidence of substantial *semantic* development, or acquisition of linguistic meaning. She knows how a great many concepts and relationships among concepts can be expressed in English words and word combination (phrases, sentences). She probably knows by now which creatures are called "dogs" and which are not almost as well as her father does. She has also acquired more subtle semantic knowledge: She knows that "chase" implies more than just "run" but is not synonymous with "catch." And she knows that the "I" her father utters does not refer to the same person as the "I" she utters. She also knows how semantic relations like agent-action-object (e.g., one animal chasing another) can be expressed in English—that is, by the left-to-right order of words.

Third her tacit knowledge of English *grammar* is likewise noteworthy. She knows how word order and word formation, such as the addition of inflections, are used as clues to sentence meaning. For instance she tacitly knows that "another dog" is the logical subject and "Trina" is the logical object of the verb "chase" in her father's passive sentence. A younger, less grammatically advanced child would not have learned to interpret sequences like "was-verb-ed-by" as clues that the normal subject-object order is reversed; in fact the younger child would undoubtedly interpret the sentence as a declarative and think that it was Trina rather than the other dog that did the chasing. Even the childish expression "catched" attests to an important grammatical attainment. Her addition of the inflection or grammatical morpheme "-ed" to "catch" proves that she has productive, generative command of the grammatical rule for forming the simple past tense in English. What she has not yet learned is the much more trivial fact that the past tense of a few common verbs (irregular verbs like "catch") is not generated by this rule.

Finally the little girl has learned much about the *pragmatic* or *communicative* side of language. She knows how to produce and comprehend *speech acts*, such as assertions, requests, and questions, and to engage in linguistic discourse with others. For example she knows that her father's second utterance is not the simple assertion a purely grammatical analysis of it would indicate. Rather it is really an indirect question or request that invites the child to participate in the story-construction process. That is the kind of speech act the father intended to produce and that is the kind of speech act the child interpreted it to be. Similarly the child seems to have acquired the rule of discourse according to which (roughly stated) one first refers to something by an indefinite article (*a* dog, *a*nother dog) and only subsequently by the definite article (*the* dog). It is a good bet that she would have used "a" rather than "the" if the unnamed chaser of Trina had not already been introduced into the story when she referred to it.

This interchange hints at the many and diverse sorts of accomplishments that mark the miraculous-seeming accomplishment that is human language acquisition.

The field of language development has undergone a striking metamorphosis in the past 30 or so years. The study of children's language used to be, arguably, a rather dull enterprise. What facts we had seemed colorless and pedestrian. The main reason they seemed so was that there were no interesting theoretical perspectives to organize and enliven them. We lacked an adequate, theoretically informed conception of all the many and marvelous things a person knows and can do when she has acquired a native language. Because we had an impoverished vision of what people end up having inside their heads when language has been fully acquired, we had a correspondingly impoverished vision of the developmental steps, sequences, and processes or mechanisms that describe and explain the course of that acquisition.

Thanks to the work of Noam Chomsky, George Miller, Roger Brown, and many other scientists, both visions are far richer now. As a consequence language development has become one of the most stimulating and challenging areas in all of developmental psychology. It also has the frustrating property of being more stimulating and challenging the more one knows about it. Frustrating, because that means an introductory chapter like this just cannot communicate all the excitement that is really there. For instance it may be necessary to know a fair amount of linguistic theory to fully appreciate the staggering amount of complexly organized grammatical knowledge a native speaker of any language tacitly has. The excitement comes from trying to imagine how on earth she could possibly have acquired all that as a young child.

PREVERBAL DEVELOPMENTS

Important developments in infancy help prepare the child to acquire her first words. Phonological skills, both innate and acquired, help her discriminate and produce the speech sounds that compose these words. Communicative skills allow her to exchange meanings and intentions with other people even before the onset of words. Furthermore these early, preverbal interchanges provide the framework within which words and the first genuinely linguistic communications eventually emerge.

Phonological Development in Infancy

Perception of Speech Sounds. We discussed research on infant speech perception in Chapter 2, in the context of a general consideration of infants' auditory abilities. As we saw then, their facility at perceiving the sounds of human speech is perhaps the most impressive of the many perceptual competencies that young infants have been demonstrated to possess. From early in life, possibly from birth, infants have an astonishing ability to hear the differences between sounds that are physically and acoustically almost identical but that fall in different phonemic categories (Aslin et al., 1998). This remarkable skill, called *categorical speech perception*, gives them an invaluable start toward the task of "cracking the phonological code" of the language they are learning.

Infants' skills at discriminating the sounds of speech are complemented by another highly adaptive quality: an interest in listening to speech. Speech is babies' favorite auditory input from early in life, again quite possibly from birth. Recall also that babies are especially interested in speech that takes the slowed down, highly intonated form known as *motherese*, or *infant-directed speech*. Motherese not only heightens attention; it helps babies to make various discriminations that are important for language. Infants discriminate the sound contrasts in multisyllable ut- terances (e.g., "marana" vs. "malana") more readily when the speech is in moth- erese than when it takes the normal adult-to-adult form (Karzon, 1985). Similarly they are most successful at segmenting speech at the boundaries between clauses— an important skill with respect to the acquisition of grammar—when the speech is in motherese (Kemler Nelson, Hirsh-Pasek, Jusczyk, & Cassidy, 1989). We con- sider some other possible benefits of this kind of speech input later in the chapter.

Production of Speech Sounds. Language involves production as well as reception, and the productive side of the enterprise also gets started in infancy, well before the appearance of the first words. Between 4 and 6 months of age, roughly, infants begin to *babble*—that is, to make vocalizations that sound quite speechlike. Vintage babbling, complete with complex intonation patterns, sounds for all the world like fluent speech in a language you do not happen to know. Infants will usu- ally continue to do some babbling even after they start producing words, at about 1 to 1½ years.

There are good reasons to believe that at least the onset and early course of babbling are largely controlled by maturational factors rather than inputs from the external environment (Locke, 1983). First babies the world over begin to babble at about the same age, and their initial babbling sounds much alike from one speech community to another. Second there seems to be no evidence that one can change the kinds of sounds young babblers produce by modeling or selective reinforcement (de Villiers & de Villiers, 1978). Finally Lenneberg, Rebelsky, and Nichols (1965) have shown that infants doggedly begin to make the usual babbling sounds even if those around them cannot hear and respond (deaf parents), and even if they cannot hear themselves babble (deaf infants). And Petitto (1993; Petitto & Marantette, 1991) has shown that deaf infants who are exposed to sign language produce a ges- tural form of babbling, shaping their hands and fingers in speechlike ways—cer- tainly compelling evidence that there is something natural about this early phase of language development.

On the other hand, the course of babbling is not entirely maturational, for ex- perience can also exert effects. Deaf infants may babble, but their productions begin later, end sooner, and are less varied in form than those of hearing infants (Oller & Eilers, 1988). Experiences of a different sort can be examined in the case of tra- cheostomized infants, that is, infants who have been prevented from uttering any sounds because respiratory problems have forced them to undergo tracheostomies (insertion of a breathing tube in the throat). In one particularly detailed case study, Locke and Pearson (1990) examined the first vocalizations of a 20-month-old girl in the weeks following the removal of the tube. They found that her vocalizations were markedly restricted in both quantity and variety, showing closer resemblance to those of very young infants or deaf infants than to those typical for her age. These data suggest that neither maturation nor the experience of hearing others' speech is sufficient to ensure normal babbling; rather the infant must have an opportunity to practice and to hear her own sounds. Finally studies of babbling across different languages suggest that the initial equivalence of babbles ("all babies sound the same") has disappeared by about 10 months; French babies babble somewhat differ- ently from Chinese babies who in turn babble somewhat differently from Arabic babies (Boysson-Bardies, 1999; Boysson-Bardies, Halle, Sargart, & Durand, 1989). As Boysson-Bardies et al. note, there is an interesting temporal convergence between their findings and those of Werker (1989): Infants' babbling begins to show effects of the surrounding speech environment at about the same time that their perception of speech becomes less sensitive for sounds not represented in that environment. We should add, however, that the cross-language differences in babbling are not large: Babies around the world still sound much more alike than different.

Much of the interest in babbling—for both psychologist and parent—lies in possible links to first words and to language. Is babbling a preparatory period for language, a phase during which infants practice and perfect the sounds that they will need when they begin to produce words? Such a speculation seems reasonable, and it has in fact been embraced, in somewhat different forms, by theorists of a variety of stripes. Finding clear evidence in support of such a "continuity hypothesis," however, has proved surprisingly difficult. We know, for example, that babbling of the normal sort cannot be *necessary* for language acquisition, because children who are unable to babble can nevertheless learn language (Locke and Pearson's tracheostomized child, for example, eventually developed excellent language). We know also that babbling of specific sounds is not necessary for those sounds to appear later in language. Infants do not (in contrast to what was once believed) babble all or even close to all of the world's speech sounds. This naturally implies that there will be sounds in the language they learn that they have never practiced during the babbling period, yet they master these sounds when words require them.

Despite these caveats, most contemporary opinion seems to favor some form of continuity hypothesis (Jusczyk, 1997; Locke, 1997; Vihman, 1996). It is simply hard to believe that there could exist a universal and extended period of babbling if it did not serve *some* role in the development of language. Continuity does in fact seem to hold with respect to phonological form: For the most part, the sounds that make up children's first words are the same sounds that occur in their contemporaneous babbles. As Locke (1983, p. 83) puts it, the beginning talker "reaches—as it were—into his collection of readily available articulations. The available articulations, at this point, are the segments of his babbling repertoire." Continuity may also hold with respect to the functions served by babbling and by first words. Many of the important functions of language—requesting, asserting, negating—emerge first in infancy, prior to the appearance of language. Infants recruit a number of their available behaviors, both vocal and nonvocal, to achieve these functions, and babbling is among the behaviors so recruited. We consider such preverbal communications more fully in the next section.

Communicative Development in Infancy

Children have already acquired some communicative skills by the time they start learning to talk, and these skills continue to serve them when their interchanges with others become linguistic (Reddy, 1999; Sachs, 1997). It has been argued, in fact, that preverbal communicative experiences may play an important role in the child's mastery of the grammatical and semantic rules of the language (Bruner, 1975; Zukow, Reilly, & Greenfield, 1982). We consider this claim in the later Explaining Language Development section.

Preverbal infants can send and receive messages in a variety of ways. They can engage and direct other people's attention by vocal and manual actions, such as crying or pointing or simply staring at an object of interest. Conversely they become able to respond to other people's attention-directing actions—for example, to look where someone else is looking or pointing. They can initiate and maintain interactions with others by making eye contact with them—a behavior of enormous reinforcement value to parents. They can also terminate interactions by averting their gaze from the other person.

At first infants' message-bearing behaviors do not constitute intentional communications—that is, the behaviors are not produced with the goal of instilling a particular understanding in another or eliciting a particular response from the other. The cry of the hungry newborn sends a message, but this message is not an intentional communication. The question of when and how intentional communication emerges has been a topic of much interest among researchers of infancy (e.g., Harding, 1984; Wetherby & Prizant, 1989). Decisions at the extremes are clear enough—the cry of the hungry newborn, the determined pointing of the 18-month-old—but there is a long in-between period during which interpretation may be doubtful. Did the infant point at the out-of-reach toy in an attempt to elicit help from her mother, or simply because of general interest and excitement? As we will see, the same problem of how much meaning and knowledge to read into the child's behavior arises at all levels of language acquisition: Should our interpretations of the child's language competence be "lean" or "rich" (Brown, 1973)? For example, should we interpret the young child's one-word utterances as having the force and meaning of full sentences? Similarly are we justified in reading grammatical structure into the child's two-word utterances? There is always the danger of reading more into the child's communicative act than is there, or even of misreading it entirely.

With this caution in mind, we can note that most researchers of the topic agree that children are capable of intentional communication by 1 year of age, and possibly even a few months earlier (Bretherton, 1988; Sachs, 1997). By this age parents begin to see behaviors that seem to cry out for such an interpretation. Bates (1976), for example, describes the following sequence of behaviors from a thirsty 13-month-old:

> C. is seated in a corridor in front of the kitchen door. She looks toward her mother and calls with an acute sound *ha*. Mother comes over to her, and C. looks toward the kitchen, twisting her shoulders and upper body to do so. Mother carries her into the kitchen, and C. points toward the sink. Mother gives her a glass of water, and C. drinks it eagerly. (p. 55)

This sequence illustrates many of the characteristics that have been proposed as criteria for intentionality, including the use of multiple means to achieve the goal (vocalizing, gazing, pointing) and the persistence when the first signals proved insufficient. Indeed the ability to correct "failed messages" has been argued to be both a clear indication of intentionality and a major developmental achievement of infancy (Golinkoff, 1983).

Infants' preverbal communications embody early forms of two basic speech acts: *requesting* and *asserting* (Bates, 1976). Requests for objects that are out of reach may be made by urgent and insistent open-handed reaching out toward the objects, often accompanied by heart-rending calls or whines and beseeching looks at the would-be adult "tools." If you have ever been the recipient of this communicative package you know that it has "REQUEST!" written all over it. The example from Bates clearly falls in this category. The nonverbal precursors of verbal assertions look quite different. Infants see objects that interest them, and they touch them, hold them up and show them, or point to them. In addition the manual gestures are accompanied by looks at the other people, perhaps to make sure that they also see the interesting objects.

In addition to learning how to send and receive specific messages, infants learn something about how to behave in a continuing nonverbal dialogue, involving an alternating sequence of communicative sending and receiving. For example they are likely to have learned how to take turns in peek-a-boo games or other ritualized interactional routines (Rochat et al., 1999). This skill will serve them well later, when they begin to engage in verbal conversations.

We can note finally that the various communicative competencies that we have described do not arise in a vacuum; rather such competencies clearly relate to other skills that the infant is in the process of mastering. The question of when intentional communication emerges is part of the more general question of when infants become capable of intentional behavior of any sort (see Chapter 3). The emergence of symbolic forms of communication during the second year, including nonverbal symbols such as ritualized gestures, can be linked to a more general capacity for representational functioning (Acredolo & Goodwyn, 1990). Finally the core element of communication, the attempt either to convey or to receive information from others, could be argued to depend on a basic realization that others are psychological beings who possess mental states—that is, upon some primitive theory-of-mind understanding (see Chapter 6). The contribution of theory of mind is emphasized in recent theorizing about language acquisition, and we consequently return to possible theory-of-mind underpinnings for language later in the chapter.

METHODS OF STUDY

Before beginning the description of language development, we should say a little about where the findings come from. How do researchers study child language?

The most influential method of study is—at least on the surface—a simple one. Most of what we know about child language has come from listening to how children talk—that is, by recording samples of children's spontaneously occurring speech. We will have occasion at various points to refer to one of the pioneering studies of this sort, Roger Brown's (1973) examination of the early language of three children whom he labeled Adam, Eve, and Sarah. Brown's study was longitudinal—that is, he observed the children repeatedly across an extended period—and such longitudinal data collection is characteristic of every major study of this sort. Typically researchers begin their observations at some point early in the language-learning process and follow the child for at least several months and sometimes several years thereafter, the goal being to identify the major changes and successive phases in the development of language. A fairly high proportion of this research has been done by parents studying their own children's development, in which case the continuity and density of the observations are typically greater than when researchers must make periodic visits to the home to collect their data.

The studies of spontaneous speech have been of enormous value, but they do have their limitations. One obvious limitation is sample size. The modal sample for studies of this sort is somewhere between 1 and 3 children—which is not surprising, given how difficult and time-consuming an enterprise it is to collect, and then analyze, a reasonable speech sample from even a single child. Given this limitation, an important contribution in recent years has been the development of a computerized data-sharing system labeled CHILDES (for Child Language Data Exchange System—MacWhinney, 1995, 1999a). CHILDES brings together, and makes available to the interested researcher, the original data from dozens of studies of child language spanning the last 30 or so years. It also provides a standardized system for coding transcripts, as well as automatized procedures for tabulating numerous specific aspects of the speech stream (e.g., frequency of particular types of words, occurrence of particular grammatical constructions). The existence of such a resource means that many issues can be examined through analysis of archival data rather than the collection of new data. It also means that conclusions can be based on dozens of children rather than just one or two.

Another limitation of the spontaneous speech studies is their focus on just the productive side of language use. Language, of course, involves not only producing speech but also comprehending the speech of others. Furthermore there is a common belief—a belief with a good deal of validity, as we will see—that children often understand more than they can produce. Because comprehension is difficult to study in the natural setting, researchers have devised various experimental procedures to explore what children understand when exposed to different sorts of linguistic input (McDaniel, McKee, & Cairns, 1996). One possibility, for example, is to have children choose between pairs of pictures that pose some grammatical contrast—"Show me *the boy runs*." "Show me *the boys run*." Or children may be given dolls with which to act out the events depicted in simple sentences—"Show me *the cat kisses the dog*." "Show me *the cat is kissed by the dog*." With sufficient ingenuity, it is possible to probe for understanding of a variety of linguistic contrasts in this way.

The techniques just described are intended for children who have already developed some language and thus can respond to the verbal directions. Suppose that we want to determine whether infants or toddlers, who may be producing little or no speech themselves, can nevertheless understand certain aspects of language. Figure 8.1 shows a procedure that has proved informative in this regard. The general setup may look familiar to you, since it is a version of the Spelke approach to studying intermodal perception that we discussed in Chapter 2 (see Figure 2.4). As in Spelke's research, conclusions are based on the fact that infants tend to look at events that correspond to what they are hearing. In this case what they see are two simple ongoing events and what they hear is a sentence that describes one of those events. If infants look consistently at the event being described, the conclusion is that they understand the particular linguistic forms being used.

Experimental techniques are not limited to the study of comprehension. Another limitation of an exclusive focus on spontaneous speech is that a child may be capable of producing a form but simply happens not to during the time period that she is being recorded. Another category of experimental procedures, therefore, is directed to children's ability to produce particular linguistic forms when given the appropriate context. Figure 8.2 shows an example from the most famous such study, Jean Berko Gleason's "wug" experiment (Berko, 1958). The item depicted tests the

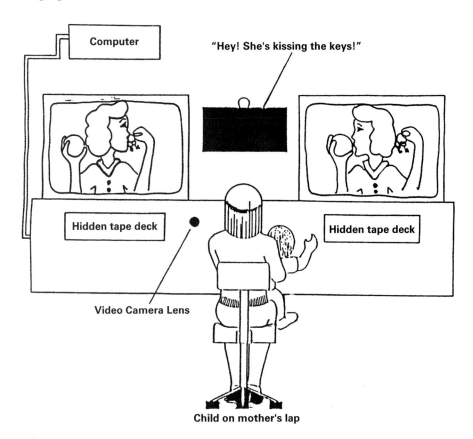

Computer

"Hey! She's kissing the keys!"

Hidden tape deck

Hidden tape deck

Video Camera Lens

Child on mother's lap

FIGURE 8.1   Experimental arrangement used to test language
comprehension in infants and toddlers. From *The Origins of
Grammar* (p. 60) by K. Hirsh-Pasek and R. M. Golinkoff, 1996,
Cambridge, MA: MIT Press. Copyright © 1996 by MIT Press.
Reprinted by permission.

child's knowledge of the "s" ending for plurality, and comparable items with other
nonsense words served to elicit knowledge of other morphological forms (e.g., past
tense, progressive tense, possessives). Berko's study was the forerunner of a number of similar experimental techniques for probing children's ability to produce particular grammatical constructions (Menn & Ratner, 2000).

The methods that we have described so far reflect two of the general ways in
which psychologists gather their data: namely observing behavior in the natural setting and devising experimental procedures to elicit the behavior of interest. A third
general approach is to collect reports of the behavior from some informed source, and
this approach is also represented in the child language literature. The MacArthur
Communicative Development Inventories (Fenson et al., 1993; Fenson et al., 1994)
are based on reports from the most informed of all possible sources: the child's parents. Rather than rely on the parents' ability to recall specific details of their child's
language, the measure taps into the parent's recognition memory. For example, to
measure the number of words that the child produces at 16 to 30 months of age, the

THIS IS A WUG.

NOW THERE IS ANOTHER ONE.

THERE ARE TWO OF THEM.

THERE ARE TWO _____.

FIGURE 8.2   An example of a stimulus used to test children's ability to produce inflectional endings. From "The Child's Learning of English Morphology," by J. Berko, 1958, *Word, 14,* p. 155. Copyright © 1958 by the International Linguistic Association. Reprinted by permission.

parent is given a list of the 680 words that appear most often in children's early vocabularies, and she checks off those that she has heard her child say. In addition to productive vocabulary, other aspects of language tapped by the Inventories include early use of gestures, number of words understood, use of word endings, and production of simple sentence forms. We consider some findings from this measure shortly.

ONE-WORD UTTERANCES

Children usually begin to produce their first words sometime around 10 to 13 months of age. They typically understand at least a few words prior to the first productions of their own, and most children continue to understand more words than they can say (Ingram, 1989). This pattern, in fact, is a general one that holds for an extended period and across a variety of aspects of language: Children often comprehend more than they produce.

Vocabulary growth proceeds slowly at first for most children. At roughly 18 months, however, many children show a spurt in word learning that is variously referred to as either the *naming explosion* or the *vocabulary spurt* (Bloom, 1993; Woodward & Markman, 1998—but see P. Bloom, 2000, for an alternative position). The naming explosion is a phenomenon that may be all too familiar to the parents of a toddler. The child has discovered that things have names, and now—tirelessly, incessantly—demands to know what the names are. In one well-documented case, a 16-month-old learned 44 words in a single week (Dromi, 1987)!

The Nature and Meaning of Children's First Words

What sorts of words are children learning during the one-word stage? Not surprisingly children's first words often refer to things that the children themselves can act on, and more generally, to objects and events that are salient, familiar, and important to them (Nelson, 1973). In our society, at least, first words often denote family members (e.g., "Mama"), animals ("dog"), vehicles ("car"), toys ("ball"), edibles ("juice"), salient body parts ("eye"), items of clothing ("hat"), and household implements ("cup"). Although names are common in most early vocabularies, children also learn greetings ("hi"), actions words ("up"), relational words ("more"), and locational terms ("there") (Gopnik & Meltzoff, 1986).

Both the words that make up children's early vocabularies and the meanings assigned to those words may differ from the words and meanings of the adult lexicon. When children first learn names for objects or events, they tend to learn labels that are at an intermediate level of abstraction or generality—labels that correspond to what is called the "basic-level" of categorization (see Chapter 4).This means, for example, that "dog" will be learned before "spaniel" (less general) and "animal" (more general), just as "flower" will be learned before either "rose" or "plant." Presumably intermediate-level labels are learned first because they reflect the level of abstraction that is functionally most useful for children in their early dealings with the world (Brown, 1958). It is more important, for example, for the child to distinguish dogs from other animals than spaniels from other dogs. The early labels that children learn also clearly relate to parents' labeling practices, which in turn may reflect parental beliefs about the distinctions that the child needs to make (Adams & Bullock, 1986). A mother of a 1-year-old is unlikely to point down the street and say "There goes the spaniel."

When first learning a new word, the child may not use it to refer to exactly the same objects or events an adult would (e.g., Clark, 1983; de Villiers & de Villiers, 1999). A common and easily observed referential error is *overextension*. For example a child might initially overextend "cat" by applying it not only to cats, but to dogs and squirrels as well. Words are often overextended to objects that are perceptually similar to the words' correct referents, and sometimes also to objects that are functionally similar—for example those that can be acted on in the same way. One examination of the first 75 words learned by a sample of 1-year-olds found that 33 percent of the words were overextended (Rescorla, 1980).

Children's early meanings for words may show other deviations from the adult language. Sometimes children *underextend* word meanings instead of overextending them. For instance a child may initially apply "cat" only to the family pet, or only to cats seen out the window, rather than to cats in general. Underextensions are harder to detect than overextensions, because they involve absence of a correct response (e.g., failing to call a particular cat "cat") rather than production of an incorrect response (e.g., calling a dog "cat"); careful studies reveal, however, that they too occur frequently (Kay & Anglin, 1982). Whereas the child who overextends must eventually narrow the scope of reference (attaching "cat" to cats only and not all small animals), the child who underextends must broaden the scope to encompass all the exemplars (small cats, large cats, striped cats, fat cats, etc.) that adult usage entails. Some children initially go too far in this broadening and for a while overextend a word that they had initially underextended (de Villiers & de Villiers, 1999).

The meanings that children are attempting to convey with their one-word utterances may also be less stable and consistent than the meanings that the words hold in the adult language. With *complexive* meanings the child seems to shift from one feature or set of features to another when using the same word in different situations, with there being no single feature that all objects named by that word have in common (Bowerman, 1978). As a striking example (de Villiers & de Villiers, 1979), the de Villiers's son Nicholas successively applied the family dog's name to other dogs, to all animals and birds, to various other furry or cuddly objects, and even to a salad with black and shiny pitted olives reminiscent of the dog's nose! With *holophrases* the child uses the single word not simply as a label but rather to convey a meaning akin to an entire sentence, with the particular meaning varying from one context to another. Thus "ball" might mean not simply "That's a ball" but "I want the ball," "I threw the ball," or "The ball hit me." We should add, however, that this sort of "rich" interpretation of one-word speech is controversial. It is in fact very difficult to know how much sentencelike meaning to credit children with when they are limited to producing one word at a time (Barrett, 1982).

Children's deviations from adult usage are not limited to words from the adult lexicon. Many children invent words of their own when faced with the challenge of talking about something for which they do not yet know an adult word. Clark (1995) and Becker (1994b) document a number of charming instances: "fix-man" for mechanic, "scale it" for weigh something, "nose-beard" for mustache, "many talls" for height. This phenomenon is not limited, by the way, to children learning oral language; creative coinages are even more striking in the gestures that many deaf children invent in order to communicate (Goldin-Meadow, 1979).

So far we have concentrated on the child's production of words. Language requires comprehension as well as production, and it is therefore important to ask whether children make the same sorts of errors in understanding others as they do when speaking. For instance does the child whose own use of "cat" extends to all small, furry animals have a similarly broad interpretation when she hears others use the word? Studies of comprehension reveal that overextensions *do* occur in comprehension, but that they are far less frequent than in the child's own speech (Hoek, Ingram, & Gibson, 1986; Thompson & Chapman, 1977). Thus the same child who calls all small, furry animals "cat" may have no trouble at all correctly picking out the cat from an array of similar-looking animals when told to "find the cat." If the child knows the word as well as this comprehension test suggests, why does she overextend it in production? There are various possible explanations (Bloom, 2000; Clark, 1983; Smith, 1988). She may have learned that the small animal that climbs trees in the back yard is called "squirrel" but, unable to recall that word on a particular occasion, she produces a word that she *is* able to recall: "cat." Alternatively she may not yet have learned "squirrel" at all; however, trying to find some name to apply to this interesting object, she comes up with the most appropriate name she can think of: again, "cat." Yet a third possibility is that she is perfectly aware that squirrels are not cats but is commenting, metaphorically, on the similarity—saying, in effect, that the squirrel is like a cat. Each of these explanations suggests that overextensions, at least sometimes, should be thought of less as errors than as the child's attempt to fill gaps in the lexicon or to comment upon the world. And each also suggests—as studies of comprehension often do—that children know more about language than their own speech reveals.

Differences among Children

For years (and to some extent still today), the study of language development was dominated by a concern with identifying commonalities or universalities in development—a focus on the striking ways in which all children seem to be alike as they go about the task of learning language. In recent years, however, there has been a growing appreciation that the commonalities are accompanied by some important individual differences and that these differences also deserve description and explanation (Goldfield & Snow, 1997; Shore, 1995). Some differences are evident even at the one-word stage.

One obvious difference is in the size of children's early vocabularies. A primary source of evidence here are the MacArthur Communicative Development Inventories, one of the measures that we described in the Methods of Study section. As we noted then, the MacArthur Inventories use parental reports to assess a number of aspects of early language development. One of the aspects assessed is the number of words in the child's productive vocabulary. In the Fenson et al. (1994) study, the range for the number of words produced at 16 months was from 0 to 347; at 24 months the range was from 7 to 668. That young children differ in how many words they know is, of course, not surprising. We include these specific values in an attempt to convey just how striking the differences can be.

Another difference concerns the types of words that make up children's early lexicons. The nouns-first pattern we described earlier is not an inevitable starting point; rather, children vary in the sorts of early vocabularies they construct (McCabe, 1989; Nelson, 1981). Some children, dubbed "referential," do begin with a preponderance of object names that allow them to talk about the inanimate world ("milk," "blocks," "shoes," etc.); other children, dubbed "expressive," concentrate less on names than on personal-social terms that can be used in social interaction ("want," "please," "yes," "no," "stop it"). The two groups seem to have somewhat different ideas about the purpose of language, with referential children focusing on its informational aspect and expressive children more concerned with interpersonal uses. As Pinker (1994, p. 267) puts it, "Babies are people, only smaller. Some are interested in objects, others like to shmooze." Such differences, however, are matters of degree rather than of absolute kind, for all children learn words of both sorts (Goldfield & Snow, 1997).

Early language development also shows some on-the-average sex differences. Girls are faster, on the average, to acquire first words than are boys, and they tend to have larger vocabularies than do boys. Girls are also more likely than boys to fall in the referential rather than expressive category. We should add, however, that the differences here are small and there are many exceptions. Girls and boys are much more alike than they are different—in language and in every other aspect of cognitive development.

Finally there also are some cross-language differences. The nouns-first pattern is more marked in children learning English than it is in several other languages whose early acquisition has been studied. Children learning Japanese, for example, are slower to acquire object names than are children learning English, and the same is true of children learning Korean; conversely Korean children are faster to learn verbs of action (Choi, 1997, 2000; Choi & Gopnik, 1995; Fernald & Morikawa, 1993). These differences among children correspond, in turn, to differences in the kinds of inputs that parents in different cultures tend to provide. American mothers tend to talk about objects and to provide many object names; Japanese and Korean mothers focus more on ongoing actions and on engaging the child in social routines. Indeed, even within a language, variations among children in aspects of early language are related, not surprisingly, to variations in the ways in which different parents talk (Goldfield, 1987; Pine, 1994).

TWO-WORD UTTERANCES

Around 18 months of age, children's single-word utterances begin to be joined by two-word and sometimes even longer expressions. Parents start to hear the likes of "put book," "mommy sock," and "more milk." Just before genuine two-word utterances appear, parents may hear two one-word utterances produced close together—for instance, "more" (pause) "milk" (Bloom, 1973). Both the intonation pattern and the evident semantic link between the words suggest that the child is struggling to produce a longer utterance but is not quite able to get all the parts together. This situation is in fact a common one throughout language development: parts in isolation first, and only later in larger combinations (Scollon, 1976).

The utterances of young children the world over have a "telegraphic speech" quality (Brown, 1973). Much like telegrams, they tend to omit the small and communicatively less essential words, such as articles (e.g., "the"), conjunctions ("and"), auxiliary verbs ("can," "will"), and prepositions ("on"). Two-word utterances, at least in English, also seldom contain any morphological inflections (e.g., progressive "ing," as in "going," past tense "-ed"). Gleitman and Wanner (1988) suggest one contributor to this early selectivity: Children tend to reproduce those aspects of speech that receive the strongest intonational stress (typically nouns, verbs, and adjectives) and leave out those that are less heavily stressed.

Despite the commonalities just noted, not all children go about forming their initial sentences in the same way. The individual differences that we discussed at the one-word level have parallels in children's earliest word combinations. Some children, for example, build sentences primarily from combinations of content words ("mommy sock," "daddy sit," etc.), a natural continuation of the early referential style; others show higher proportions of pronouns, function words, and person-oriented expressive forms (Bates, Bretherton, & Snyder, 1988). As you might expect, differences are even more marked when we move beyond the bounds of a single language to compare different languages (Slobin, 1985). Such variations do not negate the simultaneous presence of important similarities among children, a point to which we return later. Researchers of early language are much more aware than they used to be, however, that children do not follow a single, invariant path to language mastery.

A striking and important characteristic of children's speech even at the two-word phase is its creativity. From the start of their sentence-generating careers, children produce utterances that could not possibly be imitations of the adult models around them. Examples of such creative constructions abound; two of our favorites are "More up" (produced by a child who wants his daddy to continue tossing him in the air) and "Allgone sticky" (produced, triumphantly, by a child who has just succeeded in washing his hands). The originality of children's utterances tells us that they are not simply mimicking what they have heard but rather are generating sentences based on some sort of rule system. Exactly what these early rules are, however, has been the subject of much debate.

Semantics

One possibility is that the child's early language is organized in terms of semantics or meanings. There do appear, in fact, to be characteristic meanings that young children try to express in their two-word utterances. Brown (1973) carefully reviewed developmental data from a number of languages and suggested that the majority of two-word utterances seem to express any of eight semantic relations: *agent-action* (e.g., "mommy kiss"); *action-object* ("hit ball"); *agent-object* ("mommy doll," when the child wants her mother to do something with the doll); *action-locative* ("sit chair"); *entity-locative* ("cup table"); *possessor-possession* ("daddy car"); *entity-attribute* ("big car"); and *demonstrative-entity* ("that car"). Two-word utterances also seem to express meanings like *recurrence* ("more milk") and *nonexistence* ("allgone milk"). These meanings, moreover, are likely to be very similar in different languages the world over. "If you ignore word order and read through transcriptions of two word utterances in the various languages we have studied, the utterances read like direct translations of one another" (Slobin, 1970, p. 177).

That children are expressing meaning relations in their speech is therefore much clearer than was the case during the one-word utterance period. What is still not clear is whether this is *all* they are doing at this phase, or whether some knowledge of grammar must also be assumed. It is this issue to which we turn next.

Grammar

What sort of evidence would indicate that there is a grammatical and not only semantic basis to children's two-word utterances? The most obvious possibility is word order. If a child consistently said "pat daddy" when she was patting her father and "daddy pat" when he was doing the patting, and did the same for all other action-object and agent-action expressions, we might credit her with some grammatical knowledge: She would be exploiting the purely grammatical device of differential word ordering (syntax) to signal differences in intended meaning. The words are the same in both utterances; only the word order discriminates them. Most young children do seem to make use of word order in their two-word utterances. Likewise, during this period children can often use word order as a clue to meaning when listening to the speech of others (Tager-Flusberg, 1997). Indeed children as young as 17 months, whose own productions are still at the one-word level, show some ability to infer meaning from word order—a conclusion derived from the differential-looking procedure illustrated in Figure 8.1 (Hirsh-Pasek & Golinkoff, 1996).

Should we conclude, then, that some knowledge of grammar underlies early child language? The matter is still not resolved. The problem is that the systematicity that is evident in early speech might be accounted for solely on semantic and not grammatical grounds—by the tendency for agents to come before actions, actions before objects, and so forth. A purely grammatical category such as *noun* is defined not by semantic criteria (dog, lightning, and truth are all nouns) but by the way in which nouns work within sentences and interact with other units (e.g., all can be preceded by "the"). Similarly, the grammatical *subject* of a sentence may but need not be the actor or agent; subjects can also be the object of the action ("The door was opened") or the instrument with which the action was performed ("The key opened the door"). Early child language does not provide clear evidence for such abstract grammatical categories that transcend specific semantic relations. It is possible, with a sufficiently rich interpretation, to read such knowledge into the child's early utterances. But it is also possible to remain skeptical.

LATER DEVELOPMENTS

Grammar

As the child's sentences grow longer, the evidence for grammatical knowledge becomes clearer. The use of word order becomes more definitely syntactic, as links are established between grammatical and not merely meaning-based classes. Morphological inflections begin to be added to words—the "-s" for plural, the "-ed" for past tense, and so forth. The child's sentences also begin to exhibit the hierarchical grammatical structure so characteristic of human language. In the four-word child sentence "Big dog run home," for instance, "Big dog" is one main sentence constituent (called a *noun phrase*), "run home" is another (*verb phrase*), and the syntax of English demands that the two be produced in that order. However, each of these main constituents also has lower-level constituents nested within it (hence, "hierarchical") that must also be produced in the order given: "Big" before "dog," "run" before "home." As in the passage from one-word utterances to two-word ones, transitional forms are sometimes seen. For instance the child might say "Go nursery" and then immediately afterward crank it up to "Lucy go nursery" (Maratsos, 1976).

The Ordered Development of Grammatical Morphemes. The acquisition of what Brown (1973) calls "grammatical morphemes" makes an interesting and informative developmental story. These morphemes consist of the little function words and inflections that "tune" or "modulate" the meanings associated with the major content words like nouns, verbs, and adjectives. For example adding the grammatical morpheme "-ed" on the end of "push" to make "pushed" modulates or qualifies the verb's meaning by indicating that the pushing action (the main meaning expressed) occurred in the past (modulation of that main meaning). The presence of these morphemes in the child's sentence makes the sentences seem more adultlike, less telegraphic.

Brown (1973) made an intensive developmental study of 14 grammatical morphemes. They included three "-s" inflections: the plural ("dogs"), the possessive ("dog's"), and the third-person singular verb ending ("runs"). They also included the present progressive ("-ing") and past ("-ed") inflections, the prepositions "in" and "on," the articles "the" and "a," various forms of "be," both when used as an auxiliary verb ("I *was* going home") and as a main verb ("I *was* home"), plus several other morphemes. The reason the developmental story here is interesting is the remarkable finding (Brown, 1973; de Villiers & de Villiers, 1973) that young English-speaking children tend to master these 14 morphemes in the same fixed sequence. For example, although the three "-s" inflections are identical phonologically, children almost always acquire the plural earliest, the possessive later, and the verb inflection later still.

Why a constant order of development, and why the particular constant order found? Perhaps how often children hear these morphemes in the parents' speech explains the order of their acquisition. Morphemes frequently modeled by parents offer more learning opportunities for the child and therefore might be acquired first. Although this explanation seems reasonable, the available evidence suggests that it is wrong: The frequency of occurrence of these morphemes in parental speech to children and their order of appearance in children's speech seem to be essentially uncorrelated (Brown, 1973). As Maratsos (1998) points out, this finding does not mean that experience is unimportant; clearly, children must hear the forms in order to learn them. All of the forms studied by Brown, however, occur with high frequency in the child's early speech environment, and it is the further differences in *relative* frequency that apparently do not matter.

Rather than frequency per se, what seems to be important is the semantic or grammatical complexity of the form. An example involving semantic complexity shows how this explanation works (de Villiers & de Villiers, 1978). To use "was" correctly the child has to take into account the person of the subject ("I" and "he/she" can precede "was" but "you" cannot), the number of the subject (e.g., singular "I" but not plural "we"), and when the event happened (in the past rather than in the present or future). In contrast, to use the verb ending "-ed" correctly, the child has to take into account only one of these three factors—when the event happened. The correct use of "was" can therefore be interpreted as a more complex cognitive achievement than the correct use of "-ed," because the user must keep track not only of time of occurrence, but also person and number. Accordingly "-ed" should be mastered before "was" and other forms of "be," and it is.

The clearest evidence that grammatical as well as semantic complexity can contribute comes from cross-language comparisons. Johnston and Slobin (1979) studied the acquisition of the morphology used to express location (such as the prepositions "in" and "on") in four languages: English, Italian, Turkish, and Serbo-Croatian. In this case the semantic complexity is held constant, because the relevant concepts are the same whatever the language. The languages differ, however, in the grammatical complexity with which these concepts are encoded. And there were in fact differences in order of acquisition that corresponded to the differences in grammatical complexity.

The Acquisition of Inflections. Imagine for a moment that you are a participant in the Berko (1958) "wug" study that we introduced in the Methods of Study section. The experimenter shows you a picture of a man swinging an object and informs you, "This is a man who knows how to rick. He is ricking. He did the same thing yesterday. What did he do yesterday? Yesterday he _____." You confidently finish the sentence: "Yesterday he ricked." In similar fashion you are able to indicate that a man who knows how to spow must have spowed yesterday and that one who likes to naz every day probably nazzed yesterday as well. You could supply these forms despite the fact that you had never heard the words "rick," "spow," or "naz" before. You could do so because your knowledge of English past tense is based not on rote memorization but on rule: Form the past tense by adding "-ed" to the end of the verb.

It is a striking fact about human languages that they are strongly rule governed. To master the grammatical structure of one's native language is to acquire a rich network of implicit, functional rules. What is even more striking is that young children seem to expect language to be strongly rule governed. They are constantly on the qui vive for rules and regularities in every corner of language—in grammar, phonology, semantics, and pragmatics or communication. They act as if they are constantly forming and testing hypotheses about the lawful and systematic properties of their language. They learn by rote when they must, but learn by rule when they can. More than that, they often resist learning by rote when they must—that is, they try to apply rules to irregular, nonrule-governed forms in the language.

Young children's deep-seated and abiding penchant for finding order in language—even when there is not any—is nowhere more striking than in the acquisition of inflections (e.g., Ervin, 1964; Kuczaj, 1977). For instance the child may begin by using the irregular plural form "feet" as a rote-learned vocabulary item. Then, having discovered the plural "-s" rule and using it to make "dogs," "boys," and so on, she may start alternating "foots" or even "feets" with "feet." Later, having learned the likes of "kisses" and "horses," she may even try "footses" for a while before finally reinstating "feet" as the only plural of "foot." Another developmental sequence that makes the same point is first "went," then "goed," and finally "went" again. Such errors, in which the child applies a regular form too broadly, are referred to as *overregularizations*.

Overregularizations do disappear eventually, of course, and even at their height they occur on a minority of the possible instances. Children are right more often than they are wrong in their attempts to form plurals and past tenses (Marcus et al., 1992). Still overregularizations are informative, because they provide further testimony to the creativity of children's language. It is obvious that these strange forms could not possibly be rote parrotings of adult utterances. What adult ever said "footses" to his child? Rather, they are reasonable, albeit incorrect, applications of grammatical rules that the child is in the process of mastering. Such overregularizations are not limited to young learners of English. Children the world over exhibit the same predilection for hypothesis testing and rule discovery in their grammatical acquisition. Indeed overregularizations may be even more common in languages that are more highly inflected than English (Slobin, 1985). Overregularizations are not limited to children learning an oral language; children acquiring sign language make the same sorts of errors (Meier, 1981). Finally the search for systematicity is not limited to grammar. In the area of semantic development, for instance, children may invent "tomorrow day" and "yesternight" in analogy with "tomorrow night" and "yesterday" (Maratsos, 1976).

Negation and Questions.   Other grammatical acquisitions may also proceed according to a fixed and sensible-looking sequence of developmental steps (Tager-Flusberg, 1997). For example children usually begin to express negation by simply attaching "no" or "not" to whatever utterance they want to negate—"No mitten," "No I go," and so forth. This primitive grammatical rule of merely attaching a negative marker to an entire sentence is also an initial developmental step in languages in which the full negation system differs appreciably from that of English. Perhaps it is a common first step because its cognitive processing demands are so low. It is not a very satisfactory system, however, because of its imprecision and potential ambiguity. As Bloom (1970) pointed out, the "No" in "No mitten" can convey any of three meanings: nonexistence ("There's no mitten"), rejection ("No, I won't wear a mitten"), and denial ("That's not a mitten"). Progress toward a better system occurs when the child begins to insert the negative word inside the sentence, in front of the word it negates. "No I go" now gives way to "I no go" or "I not go." Finally, as the child gradually learns how to use auxiliary verbs correctly (a complicated enterprise in English), grammatically correct negative sentences like "I won't go" and "Mary isn't coming" become more frequent. However, the more subtle and tricky aspects of negation in English may continue to give children trouble for some time, resulting in sentences like "No one didn't come in" and "I didn't see something."

The mastery of the syntax of questions shows a somewhat similar developmental sequence. Again children the world over hit upon a simple starting point: a rise in intonation at the end of the sentence to convey that a question is being asked. Thus "No more milk?" from a thirsty toddler staring at an empty container carries a different message than "No more milk!" from an inveterate milk-hater. As with negations, the eventual mastery of the adult system is a gradual process. The parallels are well illustrated in the development of so-called *wh* questions—those beginning with "where," "what," "why," and so on. At first the question word is simply tacked onto the front end of an unmodified affirmative, as in early negations. One hears "What Mommy doing?" and later, when auxiliary verbs are used, "What Mommy is doing?" Still later the child correctly inverts subject and auxiliary verb to produce "What is Mommy doing?" "Where are we going?" and so on. However, more complicated interrogatives still present difficulties. When asking negative questions, for instance, the child may fail to invert subject and auxiliary and thus produce questions like "Why you aren't going?"

Other Grammatical Acquisitions. Needless to say children acquire a functional command of many other grammatical rules during the early- and middle-childhood years. For example they learn how to relate sentences and clauses to one another to form more intricate sentences, just as they earlier learned how to relate individual words to one another to make simple sentences. They become able to co-ordinate two sentences or sentence parts and embed one within another. Following are some examples, with one of the two related sentence parts italicized: "Billy ran *and so did I.*" "If you hit me *I'll hit you back.*" "The man *who fixed the fence* went home." "I don't want *you to use my bike.*" and "I asked him *what to do.*" If you tried

Frank and Ernest by Bob Thaves. Reprinted by permission of United Media/ United Feature Syndicate, Inc.

to write a system of rules of sentence production that would always generate grammatically correct English sentences of these complicated types and never generate any grammatically incorrect ones, you would better appreciate what a prodigious, almost unbelievable cognitive accomplishment the child's acquisition of grammar is. Those who try to do it for their living tend to be downright awestruck when they contemplate human grammatical development.

Semantics

Children's semantic development proceeds along two general fronts as they move beyond the two-word phase. One sort of development, labeled *propositional semantics* by Ingram (1989), has to do with the ability to convey meaning by combining words in sentences. The various semantic relations identified by Brown (1973)—agent-action, action-object, and so on—become more unequivocally evident in the child's speech. Rather than occurring only in isolation, these relations begin to be combined into larger units; "Mommy drive the big car," for example, encompasses agent-action, action-object, and entity-attribute. Meanings that were not evident at the two-word stage emerge—the indirect object, for example ("Give me the book"), and the instrumental ("Sweep with the broom"). Finally the child's mastery of inflections permits the encoding of a range of new meanings, such as plurality and present or past tense.

The second sort of development concerns the acquisition of word meanings, or what Ingram (1989) labels *lexical semantics*. Children learn an amazing number of words amazingly quickly (one estimate puts the average 6-year-old's vocabulary size at 10,000—Anglin, 1993); they also adjust and refine the meanings of words that are already part of their vocabularies. The goal of research on this aspect of semantics has been to uncover general principles that might account for what children do and do not understand about word meanings. We consider one small part of this very large literature here; we pick up some further aspects of it in our later Explaining section.

Much research attention has focused on children's understanding of *relational words*—that is, words that do not carry an absolute meaning but whose meaning depends on some sort of comparison or relation. Some examples are quantifying adjectives such as "big"-"little," "tall"-"short," and "more"-"less," and spatial or temporal prepositions such as "before"-"after" and "in front of"-"in back of." Such terms have been of interest for several reasons. One reason is precisely that they *are* relational and hence would seem to pose problems of understanding not found with words (e.g., "red," "cat," "run") whose meanings are more fixed and point-at-able. The same quantity that is "big" in one context (e.g., when pouring a drink of water) may be "little" in another (e.g., when filling a bathtub). Such words also embody a number of linguistic and conceptual distinctions that might be expected to affect their difficulty. "Big" and "little," for example, are maximally general quantitative terms, and as such might be expected to emerge earlier than more precise designations such as "tall"-"short" and "wide"-"narrow." Furthermore, within such contrasting pairs one member is the positive or "unmarked" term, in the sense that it is the label for the entire dimension. Thus we ask how big, tall, or wide something is but not (under ordinary circumstances) how small, short, or narrow it is. This distinction has led to the prediction that unmarked terms should be learned earlier than marked ones. Finally relational words would seem to have obvious ties to the child's cognitive development, and hence the learning of such words has been seen as a prime area in which to look for links between cognition and language. Piaget's work, in particular, offers a host of claims about children's mastery of relevant quantitative, temporal, and spatial knowledge.

Studies of children's understanding of relational words indicate that all of these proposed contributors can in fact be important (Blewitt, 1982; Ingram, 1989; Kuczaj, 1999). At the same time, there are exceptions and qualifications to any conclusion that might be offered—precisely because many factors can play a role, no single factor consistently accounts for how children interpret relational words. In general, however, children do seem to learn general terms, such as "big"-"little," before more specific terms, such as "tall"-"short" (Bartlett, 1976). Children also usually (although here there are definitely exceptions) find the unmarked or positive member of a pair easier than the marked member—thus "tall" before "short," "deep" before "shallow," and so on (Donaldson & Wales, 1970). It used to be believed that children's difficulty with the unmarked term extended to confusing it with its opposite (believing, for example, that "less" means the same thing as "more"); this idea, however, has not held up well (Carey, 1977).

The child's grasp of the relevant cognitive distinctions can clearly affect when words are acquired and how they are understood. Children's mastery of spatial prepositions, for example ("in," "on," "over," "under," etc.), shows a fairly good fit with the Piagetian account of when various kinds of spatial understanding develop (Johnston, 1985). More prosaic, real-world knowledge can also be important; an example here is the fact that children's knowledge of the sizes of things contributes to their ability to use adjectives such as "big" and "little" appropriately (Sera & Connolly, 1990).

On the other hand, comparisons of development in different languages make clear that cognitive factors are not the only contributor to the learning of spatial terms. Consider the terms "in," "on," and "together." In English these terms encode (roughly) the notions of containment, support, and proximity or contact, and as speakers of English we tend to assume that these distinctions reflect the natural, perhaps inevitable, way of cutting up the spatial world. In Korean, however, the comparable terms in the spatial lexicon carve the world up quite differently. In Korean, tightness of fit is the central spatial dimension, and different spatial terms encode various kinds of bringing together and taking apart. If our "in" and "on" really represent a universal way of cognizing the spatial world that underlies language learning, then Korean children should struggle to learn their "less natural" system. But they do not—Korean children master their spatial lexicon at the same rate at which English-learning children master theirs (Bowerman, 1989, 1996).

The general message that emerges from this work is that children utilize a variety of cues and recruit a variety of kinds of knowledge for the task of making sense of relational words, and that no single process provides a complete explanation of how such words are learned. We will see shortly that this is a conclusion that can hold for word learning in general.

Communicative Development

Communication Skills. As their cognitive and linguistic development progress, children acquire a wealth of knowledge and skill in the social-communicative uses of language (e.g., Harris, 1999; Ninio & Snow, 1999; Pan & Snow, 1999; Warren & McCloskey, 1997). They learn how to converse as well as to talk—that is, how to maintain focus on a single topic during an extended verbal interchange with another person. They gradually become able to go beyond the here, the now, and the real in what they converse about. They gain command of new and cognitively more advanced types of speech acts. For instance they eventually find out that language can be used not only to assert, request, and question, but also to express psychological states ("I'm sorry"), to commit oneself to future actions ("I promise I'll come"), and even to bring about new states of affairs by verbal declarations ("I quit").

Children learn that what is really meant by an utterance often goes beyond or even differs from what is literally said. They become able to infer what is implied and presupposed but not stated explicitly, an absolutely essential skill for comprehending ordinary discourse. For example they learn that a statement such as "That's not a cat" does more than explicitly deny that some creature is a feline; it also implicitly presupposes that someone thought or said it *was* a cat. One does not normally deny what nobody has asserted. Similarly they discover that an utterance that sounds like one kind of speech act may really be another in disguise. For instance children early on discover that the assertion "My, it is noisy in here" and the question "Why are we so noisy today?" are really adult euphemisms for the request "Please be quieter."

Children also learn to adapt their speech production and comprehension to numerous properties of the speakers, the listeners, and the social settings in which the speech occurs. Lakoff (1977) has suggested that such adaptations by adult speakers are in the service of two general goals: be polite and be clear. Children become progressively more skilled both at producing polite utterances and at recognizing politeness (or its absence) in others (Baroni & Axia, 1989; Becker, 1986, 1994a; Garton & Pratt, 1990). They learn, for example, how to produce requests of different forms, and how to alter their speech as a function of the familiarity or the status (e.g., adult vs. peer) of the listener. For many children injunctions from parents ("What do you say?" "What's the magic word?") are a definite part of this learning process (Becker, 1988). We will see shortly that there is little evidence that parents intentionally teach grammar to their children. Instruction in etiquette, in contrast, is a common occurrence in many households.

For years thinking about children's ability to achieve the second of the general goals—be clear—was dominated by Piaget's assertions about the young child's egocentrism. Young children were believed to communicate in an egocentric fashion, without adapting or tailoring their speech to the communication-relevant properties of the listener. There is certainly some truth to this Piagetian picture; young children *are* more "at risk" for egocentric speech than are older children or adults (see Chapter 6). Nevertheless, more recent developmental research in this and other areas of cognitive functioning indicates that we had underestimated the young child's capacity for nonegocentric thinking. In the communication area, there have been a number of impressive demonstrations of nonegocentric-looking adaptations of young children's speech to listener characteristics and needs. Here we offer just a sampling.

When a 4-year-old tells a 2-year-old rather than a peer or an adult about a toy, he is likely to "talk down" to his young listener—for example, use shorter utterances (Shatz & Gelman, 1973). Similarly, when the listener indicates comprehension failure, preschoolers adjust their message in one way for an adult listener and in a different, simpler way for a child listener (Warren-Leubecker & Bohannon, 1983). Even

2-year-olds show some ability to adjust to different listeners; they talk differently to an infant sibling than to a parent (Dunn & Kendrick, 1982b) and differently to a doll than to an adult (Sachs & Devin, 1976). Two-year-olds also can converse quite effectively with each other, assuming that the referents are simple and the context familiar (Wellman & Lempers, 1977). Familiarity is also an important variable for older children; preschoolers show better adjustments to the listener in natural settings than on laboratory tasks (Warren & McCloskey, 1997), and their conversations are most successful when the content is scripted knowledge familiar to both children, such as grocery shopping or eating at McDonald's (Furman & Walden, 1990).

Preschoolers can adjust not only to general status differences among listeners (e.g., younger versus older) but also to momentary variations in what the listener does or does not know. A study by Menig-Peterson (1975) provides a nice example (see also Perner & Leekam, 1986). Adult A and a preschooler are in room X. Adult A "accidentally" spills a cup of juice on a tablecloth. The two discuss how best to clean it up and eventually do so. A week later the preschooler returns to room X with either adult A or supposedly naive adult B. The empty cup is present and the adult asks, "I wonder what that cup is doing there" and similar queries (if adult B), or "Look at that cup. Do you remember what happened when we were here before?" (if adult A). Menig-Peterson (1975) found that her preschool participants appropriately—and nonegocentrically—varied their recounting of the spilling incident as a function of which adult was the listener. Working with a much shorter delay between relevant experience and communication (a minute or so rather than a week), O'Neill (1996) showed that even 2-year-olds have some sensitivity to their listener's knowledge state: Requests to mom for help in obtaining an out of reach object were fuller and more informative when the mother had been absent during the object's placement than when she was present and hence already knew where the object was.

Finally even quite young children show some ability to adjust their messages in response to on-the-spot cues and feedback from a listener (Marcos & Bernicot, 1997; Wilcox & Webster, 1980). In a study by Shwe and Markman (1997), for example, an adult listener responded to 2-year-olds' requests with either comprehension or noncomprehension and by either granting or not granting the request. The children were more likely to persist in and attempt to clarify their communicative attempts when the adult had failed to understand the initial message—and they did so even when they had obtained the object they wanted and thus had no material reason to continue to communicate.

Metacommunication. The successes that we have just documented, however, are not the whole story of communicative development. A number of studies have turned up some unexpected, even startling shortcomings in young children's thought and behavior in communication situations (e.g., Asher, 1979; Dickson, 1981; Flavell, 1981a; Flavell, Speer, Green, & August, 1981; Lloyd, Camaioni, & Ercolani, 1995; Lloyd, Mann, & Peers, 1998; Robinson & Robinson, 1981). Most of these studies bear on the child's knowledge and cognitive actions concerning communications—thus, on a type of metacognition or cognition-about-cognition sometimes referred to as *metacommunication* (Flavell, 1976).

The researchers have frequently used variations of the referential-communication task developed by Glucksberg and Krauss (Glucksberg, Krauss, & Higgins, 1975). In one version of this task, the speaker and the listener cannot see one another but both know they have identical sets of objects in front of them (see Figure 8.3). The speaker's task is to describe one of his objects specifically enough for his listener to identify its duplicate in her own set. Many of the young child's metacommunicative problems can be illustrated using this simple task situation.

Suppose the speaker's message is referentially ambiguous. For instance suppose he says "Pick the red block" but there are two red blocks, one square and one round, in each person's set of objects. The research evidence suggests that a young child listener—age 5, say—would be less likely than an older one to show even minimal signs of detecting the ambiguity. She would be more apt than an older child to listen to the message, focus her attention on only one of the red blocks in front of her, and unhesitatingly pick that block. She should feel that she does not know which red block he means, one would think, but she does not appear to. Instead young children turn out to be surprisingly poor monitors of their own comprehension. They do not understand something but are often not aware that they do not understand it.

Other metacommunicative immaturities may become apparent even if the young child does notice that two objects fit the speaker's description. If she does notice it, we may see her look properly uncertain and hesitant before settling on one of the two red blocks. However, this feeling of uncertainty is likely not to have the same meaning, importance, and implications for her that it would for an older child or adult. Thus she probably will not ask the speaker to be more specific, even though she knows she may ask him questions at any time. Also, if asked if she is sure the block she chose is identical to the one the speaker had in mind, she is apt to say that she is sure it is. If asked whether the speaker's message did a good or a

FIGURE 8.3   Experimental arrangement for one version of the Glucksberg and Krauss communication task. From "The Development of Communication: Competence as a Function of Age," by R. M. Krauss and S. Glucksberg, 1969, *Child Development, 40,* p. 259. Copyright © 1969 by the Society for Research in Child Development. Reprinted by permission.

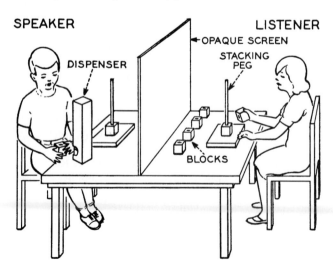

poor job of telling her exactly which block to pick, she is very likely to say that it did a good job. Finally, if asked who is responsible should the outcome prove to be a communication failure, she is likely to blame herself (or whoever the listener may be) and her incorrect block selection, and not the speaker and his inadequate message (Beal & Flavell, 1982; Flavell et al., 1981; Robinson & Robinson, 1981).

We should add some qualifications to this bleak picture of the young child's metacommunicative abilities. As is true for performance in the speaker's role, children's ability to function as effective listeners does vary across settings and across different types of message. Once again performance tends to be more impressive in natural settings than on somewhat artificial laboratory tasks, such as the Glucksburg and Krauss paradigm (McDevitt & Ford, 1987; Revelle, Wellman, & Karabenick, 1985). Listener skills are also more evident when the focus is on children's ability to respond appropriately in an ongoing dialogue, as opposed to making an abstract judgment of message adequacy (Revelle et al., 1985). These findings make sense: If children's performance as listeners were always as poor as the preceding paragraphs suggest, they could hardly have the success as conversationalists that we have seen they have. Aspects of the speaker or message can also affect children's apparent metacommunicative competence. Children are more likely to believe a message from an informed speaker than an uninformed one (Robinson, Champion, & Mitchell, 1999). They are more likely to spot message inadequacy from a dishonest speaker than from a merely incompetent one (Bonitatibus, 1988b). And they are more likely to recognize the inadequacy of a message that is incorrect or impossible to follow (e.g., "Pick the red one" when there are no red ones present) than of a message that is ambiguous (e.g., "Pick the red one" when there are two red ones present—Flavell et al., 1981). Unlike the patently incorrect message, the ambiguous message at least offers the child a basis, albeit an insufficient one, for making a response.

Despite their occasional successes, children do often show the various metacommunicative deficits and confusions that we have described. Why do they respond in these curious ways? Here are some possible reasons (see also Beal, 1988; Flavell, 1992b; Flavell et al., 1981; Mitchell, Munno, & Russell, 1991; Robinson, 1981). The most general reason may be that they are just not much given to thinking about and critically analyzing such intangible mental products as spoken messages. In this area as in others, the development of metacognitive dispositions and skills is simply not very far advanced (recall our discussion in Chapter 5). As a corollary, they tend not to understand as clearly as older children the seemingly obvious fact that the quality of a message affects communicative success. The listener's incorrect choice is a salient and recent event that the child may easily interpret as the cause of a communication failure; in contrast the speaker's inadequate message may be generally less salient for young children, and is also more temporally distant from the outcome. As noted, ambiguous, insufficiently specific messages may be particularly hard for young children to evaluate accurately. They may have learned that a speaker's message should refer to whatever the speaker has in mind, but may not have also learned that the message should refer to that *alone*—in other words, that it should not be referentially ambiguous. In general young children seem to have difficulty focusing on the literal words of a message—on what was actually said—as opposed to whatever they may already know or believe on other bases. They have special difficulty, therefore, in detecting message inadequacy in cases in which they already know the speaker's intended referent (Beal & Belgrad, 1990; Beal & Flavell, 1984). And they tend to equate performance with intention, judging a message and its likely effects in terms of what they believe the speaker meant to convey, rather than what his words actually do convey (Bonitatibus, 1988a, 1988b; Montgomery & Miller, 1997).

As we noted earlier, communication involves an attempt to create mental states in others, and children's beliefs about communication are therefore necessarily linked to their more general theory of mind—in particular, their beliefs about the sources of knowledge. By age 4 children have acquired the important understanding that communication, and not just direct perception, can be a source of knowledge (Wimmer, Hogrefe, & Perner, 1988). They may also understand that a false communication can be the source of a false belief (Perner & Davies, 1991). For the most part, however, young children seem to operate on a one-to-one principle, in which access to information of any sort is assumed to lead automatically to knowledge. Thus unclear or ambiguous messages are assumed to produce knowledge in their listeners, just as an unclear perceptual experience is assumed to be interpretable and informative (Chandler & Helm, 1984; Taylor, 1988). And a potentially adequate message is assumed to produce knowledge in recipients of any sort—recall Montgomery's (1993) demonstration that even 6-year-olds believe that babies can acquire information from a verbal message. It is only gradually that children come to the realization—a very important realization for their performance as both speakers and listeners—that the informativeness of a message depends simultaneously on two factors: the quality of the message and the cognitive level of the person who receives it (S. Miller, 2000; Mitchell, Robinson, Nye, & Issacs, 1997; Sodian, 1988).

EXPLAINING LANGUAGE DEVELOPMENT: SEMANTICS

Describing the interesting phenomena of development is one of the tasks for the developmental psychologist; explaining how those phenomena come about is the other task. We have seen throughout this book that our ability to describe often outstrips our ability to explain, and such is certainly the case in the study of children's language. Nevertheless some intriguing and no doubt partially correct explanations have been proposed, and these are the subject of the next two sections. We begin with semantics.

At first glance learning the meanings of new words might seem a simple task, at least in comparison to the obvious complexities involved in mastering the grammar of the language. Presumably what the young word learner must do is to come to associate particular sounds with particular concepts—thus "milk" means that good-tasting liquid I like when I'm thirsty, "cat" means those small, furry, pet-able animals, and so forth. In fact, the task is enormously more complicated than this simple description suggests. The following passage from Markman (1989), based on an argument by the philosopher Quine (1960), summarizes some of the complexities. The example concerns a young child, ignorant as yet of the word "rabbit," who sees a rabbit nearby.

> Someone points in some direction and utters a word. On what grounds is the child to conclude that a new unfamiliar word—say, "rabbit"—refers to rabbits? What is to prevent the child from concluding that "Rabbit" is a proper name for that particular

rabbit, or that "rabbit" means "furry" or "white" or any number of other characteristics that rabbits have? Finally, what prevents the child from concluding that "rabbit" means something like "the rabbit and its carrot" or "the rabbit next to the tree" or "mother petting the rabbit"? (Markman, 1989, p. 20)

The point that both Quine and Markman make is that there are always an indefinite number of logically possible meanings for any word—that is, meanings that are compatible with the evidence available to the child. Some possibilities, to be sure, can be ruled out as more evidence becomes available ("the rabbit and its carrot" can be rejected if "rabbit" is used in the absence of a carrot), but others will always remain (the rabbit's ears plus its tail, the rabbit that is not floating in space, etc.). How, out of this wealth of possibilities, does the child ever figure out that "rabbit" means rabbit? And note that we have not even mentioned a prior problem: How does the child hear "rabbit" in the first place—that is, how does she parse the continuous speech stream ("Lookattheprettyrabbitnearthetree") into the individual words?

Fast-Mapping

Perhaps the most obvious implication of the Quinean argument is that word learning should be a slow, laborious process, as the child encounters a particular word in enough different contexts to rule out many possible meanings and to zero in on the correct meaning. Yet if there is one thing that we know about word learning it is that the process often appears far from slow; it has been estimated that children acquire an average of nine new words a day in the years between 2 and 6 (Carey, 1978). Any theory of word learning must somehow account for the rapidity with which at least some words are acquired.

An often-cited experiment by Carey and Bartlett (1978) attempted to identify some of the conditions under which rapid learning occurs. These investigators presented 3- and 4-year-olds with a new color term, "chromium," which was used to refer to the color olive. The term was introduced in a natural, nondidactic manner: In the course of the nursery-school day, the teacher told the child, "Bring me the chromium tray, not the blue one, the chromium one." Note that this instruction contains some potentially quite useful information; "chromium" does not mean blue, and it probably does mean some other color. Carey and Bartlett found that most of their young participants did learn, from this single exposure, that "chromium" was the label for a color, and some of them learned something about the particular color as well. The learning, to be sure, was partial, for most did not come, even with further exposures, to associate "chromium" solely with the color olive. Nevertheless the children had learned a fair amount about a new word from a single, naturally presented instance. Such a rapid acquisition of at least part of a word's meaning from one or a few exposures is referred to as *fast mapping*.

Since the Carey and Bartlett (1978) report, a number of other studies have verified that fast mapping occurs (e.g., Au & Markman, 1987; Heilbeck & Markman, 1987; Rice & Woodsmall, 1988). Fast mapping has been demonstrated in children as young as 2 and as old as 11. It has been shown for nouns as well as for adjectives, and for terms having to do with shape or texture as well as for color terms. It has been shown when a number of new words are introduced at the same time, as opposed to the one-word-at-a-time method of Carey and Bartlett. And it has even been shown for words presented on TV. Whether fast mapping is present from the start of word learning is not clear; some researchers (Schafer & Plunkett, 1998) believe that it is, whereas others have argued that it emerges only after the vocabulary spurt, and therefore only at about 18 months or so (Mervis & Bertrand, 1994). Furthermore even when fast mapping does occur, the learning that it produces is often rough and partial; children may still need an extended period to work out the exact meanings of words they are in the process of mastering (Carey, 1978). Nevertheless children seem to be able to hit upon the basic, core nature of a word—this is a color term, this is the name of an animal, and so on—amazingly quickly and accurately.

How do children do this? In what follows, we summarize three kinds of explanations that have been offered. Before doing so, however, we will state the general conclusion toward which we are moving, and that is that all of the processes discussed—and quite possibly some further ones as well—contribute to the task of word learning. The grounds for this conclusion are both empirical—there is evidence in support of each of the processes—and logical—word learning is too complex a task to be explained by a single process. The conclusion that word learning is a multiply determined achievement is in fact embraced by every recent expert summary of the evidence (Bloom, 2000; Deak, 2000; Hollich, Hirsh-Pasek, & Golinkoff, 2000; Woodward & Markman, 1998).

Constraints

The first explanation we consider stems directly from the Quinean puzzle with which we began the discussion: How does the child ever narrow down the innumerable logically possible meanings of a word to the one actual meaning? In recent years a number of researchers have suggested that such narrowing down is possible only if children's word learning is guided by a set of *constraints* concerning the possible meanings that words might have.

Waxman (1989) provides a capsule summary of what is meant by the notion of constraints: "The essential idea in a constraints approach is that the child brings to the task of learning and development tacit biases or tendencies that lead her to favor some interpretations of events and objects over others" (p. 13). As applied to the task of word learning, the central claim of the constraints approach is that the child encountering a new word is constrained to consider only a small number of the many logically possible interpretations of what that word might mean. In the case of "rabbit," for example, it simply never occurs to the child that the reference might be to some subset of the animal's parts, or to the animal and some nearby object, or to the animal in some particular spatial location. Because all these possibilities are ruled out from the start, the task of figuring out what the word actually does mean is enormously simplified.

What sorts of constraints might guide children's word learning? A variety have been proposed (Clark, 1987, 1993; Hollich, et al., 2000; Markman, 1991; Waxman, 1994; Woodward & Markman, 1998). Here we concentrate on three (drawing on Woodward and Markman's, 1998, overview—terminology and distinctions vary some across authors).

One very basic constraint is the Whole Object constraint: the assumption that words label whole objects and not the parts or attributes of objects. This constraint implies that a child who hears "rabbit" in the presence of a furry, hopping animal should assume that the label applies to the animal as a whole, and not to a part such as the tail or an attribute such as the color.

A second, closely related, constraint is the Taxonomic Assumption. The Whole Object constraint provides a good start toward word learning, but this principle alone leaves unclear how a word is to be extended—to what other objects, besides the specific labeled example, should "rabbit" apply? Conceivably the other objects could be ones that enter into some sort of thematic relationship with the rabbit—the rabbit's food, the rabbit's dwelling place, and so on. In fact children's extensions seem to follow the Taxonomic Assumption: the belief that words label categories of like objects—objects from the same taxonomic category. Thus "rabbit" will be extended not to carrots but to other furry, hopping animals. Note that the extensions need not be at first correct—the child may call a squirrel "rabbit"— but at least they will be to the right *kind* of thing.

Finally the constraint of Mutual Exclusivity refers to the belief that each object has only one label—that the referents for different words are mutually exclusive. This constraint applies most obviously to situations in which the child already knows some of the relevant words. Suppose that the child hears "rabbit" while watching a dog chase a rabbit. Because the child already knows the label "dog," he will reject the possibility that "rabbit" refers to dogs, thus increasing his chances of attaching the word to the correct referent.

As the "rabbit" example suggests, various constraints may often work together. Indeed constraints *have* to work together for mature word learning to be possible. Consider the Whole Object constraint. This constraint may be very useful for early word learning, but eventually it must be overcome; after all, not all words refer to whole objects. Markman (1991) has argued that Mutual Exclusivity may help children to overcome the limits of the Whole Object constraint. Suppose that mother says "Feel the soft fur" while petting a rabbit. The child who already knows the label "rabbit" should, following Mutual Exclusivity, reject the possibility that "fur" is also a label for rabbit. Once the whole object has been ruled out, the child can concentrate on the particular aspect on which the mother is concentrating. It is in this way that children learn that words can apply to parts and attributes and not simply whole objects. They also may learn that a particular object can be labeled at several levels of abstraction: basic (e.g., "dog," "car"), superordinate (e.g., "animal," "vehicle"), and subordinate (e.g., "collie," "Chevy"). The child who hears either "animal" or "collie" applied to an object that he knows to be "dog" should assume, following Mutual Exclusivity (and also Clark's Principle of Contrast—see Clark, 1987, 1988), that some difference in meaning is being signalled—that "animal" is not simply another label for "dog." Waxman (1990) has shown that the particular alternative labels that are supplied can help children to form both superordinate and subordinate categories.

Both logical arguments and a fair amount of empirical data provide support for the notion of constraints. Such arguments have not won over every student of early word learning, however (Bloom, 1998; Deak, 2000; Kuczaj, 1999; Nelson, 1988, 1990). Critics of constraints theorizing point to both weaknesses in the evidence offered in support of constraints and a certain fuzziness in the theories themselves. Empirically, both naturalistic and experimental studies verify that children often do honor all of the various constraints that have been proposed (Merriman & Bowman, 1989; Woodward & Markman, 1998). Such studies also make clear, however, that constraints are sometimes more honored in the breach than in the observance, for exceptions and violations are not hard to find. It is true, of course, that we would expect the child eventually to violate constraints, since no constraint is invariably applicable (recall our discussion of the Whole Object constraint). Nevertheless children's adherence to such principles as Whole Object or Mutual Exclusivity does not have the predictability and uniformity that the term "constraints" would seem to imply. Some softer term—"bias," "tendency," "strategy"—may be a more accurate depiction of what is going on.

The origin of such biases or tendencies is also an unresolved issue at present. Another common implication of "constraint" is that of a biological basis—that development is constrained by biological forces to follow a certain course. Such a nativistic emphasis is evident in discussions of constraints for cognitive development in general (e.g., Keil, 1981), as well as in the use of constraints to explain aspects of grammatical development (e.g., Chomsky, 1981)—indeed the application of the notion of constraints to grammar predated and has clearly influenced the recent work in semantics. Various features of semantic development, however, have been cited as evidence against a really strong biological determination of semantic constraints—the fact that constraints can be so readily violated, for example, or the fact that some seem to emerge with development rather than being always present (Nelson, 1988). It is true, as constraints theorists have replied, that such characteristics need not rule out an important biological contribution (innate need not mean present at birth, for example); it is also true that most such theorists have not committed themselves to a nativistic position but rather have remained open on the innate vs. acquired issue (Woodward & Markman, 1991). Nevertheless there may be something to Nelson's (1988) point about the consequent blurring between description and explanation: "Labelling certain behaviors . . . 'constrained' adds nothing to the description of those behaviors themselves. . . . The term constraint only appears to be explanatory because it appears to invoke an innate mechanism" (p. 239).

A final (and related) issue with regard to constraints concerns their generality. Are constraints such as Whole Object or Mutual Exclusivity limited to the task of learning words, or do they reflect something more general about the child's cognitive system? There have been some intriguing suggestions for more general links (Bloom, 2000; Markman, 1991). The Whole Object constraint, for example, may relate to the special status that objects seem to have for children from early in life; recall Spelke's (1990) demonstrations of the infant's interest in and ability to apprehend whole objects (Chapter 2). Mutual Exclusivity may relate to the difficulty that young children have in realizing that the same object can be represented in more than one way (Flavell, 1988); recall our discussion of representations and theory of mind in Chapter 6. The specific difficulty in the case of Mutual Exclusivity would lie in realizing that the same object can receive more than one label.

The question of the generality of constraints is a particular instance of a more general question that cuts across all aspects of language: To what extent are the capacities that underlie language learning specific to language and to what extent do they reflect more general properties of the cognitive system? This issue has been considered most fully with respect to grammar, and we consequently return to it when we discuss the acquisition of grammar.

Syntactic Bootstrapping

Imagine that you hear the sentence "The duck is gorping the bunny." Even though you have never heard the word "gorping" before you could infer various things about its likely meaning. Its placement between "is" and "ing" strongly suggests that it is a verb. These same cues suggest as well that it refers to some on-going action—to something that is happening in the present. Finally the three-part, A-B-C construction suggests that it is a transitive verb and that the duck is the one doing the gorping and the bunny is the one being gorped. (Of course you would need more information before deciding whether you would enjoy being gorped yourself.)

The term "bootstrapping" is computerese for using one system to "boot" or guide another into operation, and thus *syntactic bootstrapping* refers to the use of syntax to guide learning about semantics. The idea is that once children have mastered some aspects of grammar they can use this knowledge as they attempt to make sense of new words. There are, in fact, numerous grammatical cues to word meaning, in English or in any language. Table 8.1 presents some of the most important examples in English.

Can children use such cues? The usual way to answer this question is to do experimental studies in which children have a chance to learn a new word from the grammatical cues in the sentences they hear. Such studies demonstrate that children can exploit a variety of cues, including all of those in Table 8.1 (Bloom, 1996, 2000; Woodward & Markman, 1998). If told, for example, that something is "a zax" they tend to assume that "zax" is a count noun that labels multiple exemplars; in contrast, they are likely to interpret "this is Zax" as the name of a particular individual and "some zax" as the label for a continuous substance. Grammatical cues are seldom sufficient to determine the exact meaning of a word (e.g., what kind of substance zax is); rather they need to be supplemented by other sorts of information. But they do help to narrow down the possibilities.

Obviously children have to know some grammar before they can use knowledge of grammar to aid other kinds of learning. We would expect, therefore, both that the utility of syntactic bootstrapping would increase with age and that there will be a lower bound below which it does not occur, and both of these predictions have been confirmed. The lower bound, however, is not necessarily very low. The "gorping" example with which we opened was taken from a study with 2-year-olds (Naigles, 1990). The method used was the Hirsh-Pasek and Golinkoff (1996) differential-looking procedure (Figure 8.1). Children first heard "gorping" in one of two contexts: either the "The duck is gorping the bunny" sentence given earlier or

TABLE 8.1 Syntactic Cues to Word Meaning

SYNTACTIC CUE	USUAL TYPE OF MEANING	EXAMPLES
"This is a *fep*/the *fep*"	Individual members of a category	*cat, forest*
"These are *feps.*"	Multiple members of a category	*cats, forests*
"This is *fep.*"	Specific individual	*Fido, John*
"This is some *fep.*"	Nonindividuated stuff	*water, sand*
"John *feps.*"	Action with one participant	*sleeps, stands*
"John *feps* Bill."	Action with two participants	*hits, kisses*
"This thing is *feppy.*"	Property	*big, good*
"The dog is *fep* the table."	Spatial relationship	*on, near*

Note. From *How Children Learn the Meanings of Words* (p. 205) by P. Bloom, 2000, Cambridge, MA: The MIT Press. Copyright 2000 by the MIT Press. Reprinted by permission.

the nontransitive "The duck and the bunny are gorping." When later told to "find gorping," they looked at the event that was consistent with the grammatical structure that they had heard—thus, an actor-action-recipient event in the first case and a two actors-one action event in the second.

Another point of interest in the "gorping" example is the focus on verb learning. Learning the meanings of verbs poses some special challenges for the young word learner (Bloom, 2000; Gleitman & Gillette, 1999). Constraints positions, for example, have been skewed toward the learning of nouns, and it is questionable how well they work for verbs (but see Golinkoff, Hirsh-Pasek, Mervis, & Frawley, 1995, for one application). Also parents may label objects for their children, thus aiding in the learning of nouns, but they seldom label ongoing actions. Verbs, however, are inherently relational—that is, they specify relations among the elements in a sentence—and this means that the grammatical structure of a sentence can convey a good deal of information about the nature of a verb. It has therefore been argued—with some supporting evidence—that grammatical cues may be especially helpful in the learning of verbs (Fisher, 2000; Gleitman 1990).

Social-Cognitive Contributions

It may have occurred to you that there has been a strangely nonsocial quality thus far to the discussion of an ability whose function is mainly social. Children are described as hearing sentences and utilizing the information contained therein, possibly guided by constraints about the likely meanings that words can have. But who is producing these sentences, and what is the context in which they occur?

The answer, of course—at least for most young children most of the time—is the child's parents. That parents contribute to word learning has never been in doubt. Children must hear words in order to learn them, and parents are a major source of the necessary models. Parents also do some explicit teaching of words to their children, engaging in what Roger Brown (1958) labeled the Original Word Game. And, as we saw earlier, there are relations between the kinds of words children learn and the kinds of input that parents provide.

Despite this unquestioned contribution of parents, attempts to ground word learning in parental tuition have always run up against the Quinean dilemma: How does the child figure out what the parent is talking about? Recent work on early developments under the theory-of-mind heading provides a possible answer to this question. It is really a two-part answer.

Part of the answer is that parents seem to be very good at discerning what their children are attending to and interested in learning about. Parents tend to talk about objects and events to which their children are already attending, and children are most successful at learning new words when parents have accurately judged their focus of attention (Harris, Jones, & Grant, 1983; Tomasello & Farrar, 1986). As Nelson (1988, pp. 240–241) puts it, "Children do not try to guess what the adult intends to refer to . . . it is the adult who guesses what the child is focused on." In the rabbit example, the argument is that the parent would not have said "rabbit" if the child's attention were focused on the rabbit's ears or the background trees or the pursuing dog. Rather, the parent labels what the child is attending to, and the child is thus in a good position to link label and referent.

Parents, however, are not the only important participants in early parent-child interactions. An exclusive reliance on parents' mind-reading prowess would be a risky strategy, because even the most sensitive parent is going to misread his or her child's attentional focus occasionally (indeed, up to 50 percent of the time in the studies that provide evidence on this point—Baldwin, 1991). The other part of the answer, therefore, is that children are very good, from quite early in life, at discerning what their parents are attending to. By some time near the end of the first year (with the exact age of emergence depending on how generously one reads the available evidence—see Chapter 6), infants develop the critical realization that other people are intentional agents with various sorts of psychological connections to the world around them. Among the manifestations of this realization is the emergence of joint attention—that is, both the ability and the strong inclination to follow the gaze of another and thereby to enter into and share the other's attentional focus. To the extent that the child can achieve joint attention with a parent, one of the main challenges of word learning has been solved: Both child and parent are thinking about the same thing.

Of course children, just like parents, are not always going to be successful in figuring out their conversational partner's attentional focus. But they can be surprisingly skilled at doing so, as a number of ingenious studies demonstrate (Akhtar & Tomasello, 1996, 1998; Baldwin, 1991, 1993; Tomasello & Barton, 1994). For example children can link an adult's object label with its intended referent even if they themselves are focused on or interacting with another object at the time the label is produced. They can link label and referent even when there is a temporal delay between the two, just so long as the initial focus of attention was clear. They can even use affective cues from the adult to decipher what otherwise might be ambiguous word-referent pairings. For instance, if an adult searching for a "toma" frowns upon uncovering a particular object they do not associate "toma" with that object; similarly, if an adult says "Whoops!" while attempting to "meek," they do not assume that "meek" refers to the action actually performed. Figuring out what others intend by their speech may be the most important use to which 2-year-olds put their theory-of-mind knowledge. Fortunately it may also be the aspect of theory of mind at which they are most skilled.

EXPLAINING LANGUAGE DEVELOPMENT: GRAMMAR

The concerted interest in word learning is a relatively recent development; indeed, just about all the positions that we just discussed have emerged in just the last dozen or so years. In contrast the question of how to explain the acquisition of grammar has been an intensely debated topic for at least 35 years now—or ever since Chomsky's writings changed how both linguists and psychologists think about the nature of language. What Chomsky (e.g., 1972) argued is that to "know" a language as an adult native speaker does is to have a functional command of an exceedingly rich and intricate system of grammatical categories and rules. If our grammatical knowledge were a very simple, impoverished system, clearly evident in the speech we hear, then explaining its acquisition would not present much of a problem. However, most in the field today agree with Chomsky's claim that the system is in fact incredibly vast and complex. Most also agree that clues to the underlying grammatical structure of sentences are often not present in the surface structure or external form of these sentences. These facts make the task of explaining grammatical development more intriguing—and much more difficult. Useful further sources on this topic include Bohannon and Bonvillian (1997), de Villiers and de Villiers (1999), Hirsh-Pasek and Golinkoff (1996), Maratsos (1998), MacWhinney (1999b), and Ritchie and Bhatia (1999). For a recent and in some respects quite different approach to both the nature of language and the task of language acquisition (an approach which, unfortunately, is beyond both our space and our expertise to present), see Tomasello (1998, 2000) and Tomasello and Brooks (1999).

The Role of the Environment

Let us first examine possible roles of the external environment, especially of what other people do and say. We can immediately reject the extreme—and absurd—possibility that the external environment plays no role whatever. For example, although all normal children are obviously capable of acquiring as a native language any human language to which they are exposed—witness the many, many different languages in the world—they just as obviously have to be exposed to that one to learn it. But what sorts of experiences, beyond mere exposure, might play a role in this learning?

Imitation and Reinforcement. A traditional view emphasizes the processes of imitation and reinforcement. By this view a child learns to speak like adults because his caregivers model grammatically correct sentences in their speech, he imitates these sentences, and his caregivers selectively reinforce both these imitations and the child's spontaneous utterances, responding more positively to grammatical than to ungrammatical productions. Plausible though this account may seem—and helpful though such a state of affairs would no doubt be—the available evidence goes strongly against it.

First the evidence clearly shows that a great deal of learning can and does go on without benefit of sentence imitation. Some children hardly ever imitate adult sentences. Most children rarely imitate adult sentences after the early phases of grammatical acquisition, although of course they still continue to acquire new rules. When children do imitate, their imitations are typically no more advanced than their spontaneous productions, a finding that suggests that imitations reflect already acquired knowledge rather than mediate the acquisition of new knowledge. Children typically comprehend new grammatical forms before they produce them in their own speech—again, grammatical acquisition without benefit of imitation. Finally whatever contribution imitation may sometimes make, children quickly transcend any dependence on literal imitation, for their sentences are creative constructions from early in life. We gave some examples of such creative, clearly not imitated productions earlier; here are a few more: "I'm magic, amn't I?" "Why not me can't dance?" "Did I didn't mean to?" "He was disingappeared."

What about reinforcement? The available evidence (more limited than in the case of imitation) suggests that selective reinforcement of grammatical versus ungrammatical utterances is not a necessary or even an important shaper of grammatical development. Parents tend to reinforce and explicitly correct on the basis of the truth value rather than the grammatical quality of their children's utterances. A mother who is curling her child's hair responds "That's right" to the child's ungrammatical "Her curling my hair" rather than saying "No—say *she* is curling my

hair." However, the grammatical but factually incorrect sentence "There's the animal farmhouse" gets a "No, that's *not* the animal farmhouse" (Brown & Hanlon,
1970). Note Brown, Cazden, and Bellugi's (1969) wry comment on this rather surprising finding: "Which renders mildly paradoxical the fact that the usual product of
such a training schedule is an adult whose speech is highly grammatical but not notably truthful" (p. 71).

Imitation and reinforcement, then, do not seem to do the job. What other sorts of
assistance might the environment in general, and parents in particular, provide? In recent years attention has focused on three potentially helpful practices in which at least
some parents engage while interacting and conversing with their young children.

Preverbal Interchanges. Some researchers have stressed the fact that the
process of language learning gets started well before the first words appear at a year
or so of age (Bruner, 1975; Messer, 1983; Ninio & Snow, 1996). We saw earlier
that communications on the infant's part are certainly evident long before the first
words are heard. Our focus now is on the parent's part in these early interchanges.
Parents have been observed to do a variety of things that might help their infants
begin to learn about the nature of language. Most generally they engage in "dialogues" with their babies, producing some appropriately babyish utterance, waiting
for a response from the baby (a smile, coo, babble, or whatever), responding in turn
to this infant response, waiting for the baby to behave again, and so on. As the infant grows older, parents "up the ante": Their own messages become more complex
and languagelike, and their criteria for accepting an infant response as appropriate
also grow more stringent—where once mere eye contact would do, now a vocalization is required, and where once a burp or gurgle would suffice, now a babble or
even a word may be demanded. In this way parents help their infants learn how to
engage in conversational interchanges (the necessity of turn taking, the appropriate-
ness of certain responses) well before the infants are capable of genuine language.
They also help the baby learn how to perform basic speech acts, such as questioning
and requesting.

Preverbal interchanges of the sort just described seem a sensible way to initiate the process of language learning. At best, however, such experiences are a start,
and much still remains to be explained. There is, clearly, an enormous leap from an
exchange of babbles in infancy to the complex syntax of a passive sentence or negative question. Furthermore it seems clear that not all infants experience these sorts
of interchanges with their parents, yet all infants eventually learn language. The
verdict with respect to the role of preverbal interchanges must therefore be a cau-
tious one: probably helpful, but very probably not necessary, and in any case far
from sufficient. This is a conclusion that we will see applies to other parental practices as well.

Motherese. Speech directed to young children tends to differ in various
ways from speech directed to adults. As we discussed earlier, such speech is simplified phonologically, with slow pacing and exaggerated intonation and stress. It also
is simplified grammatically and semantically: Sentences tend to be short, simple,
and grammatical, and the focus is on present objects and events. Although "motherese" is the usual label for such speech, mothers are not its only practitioners; fathers and adults in general also simplify their speech to young children (hence the
alternative label: *infant- or child-directed speech*). Children do too: As indicated

earlier, even 4-year-olds will "talk down" when speaking to 2-year-olds (Shatz & Gelman, 1973). In fact—and happily—it seems virtually impossible to talk to a young child without some such adaptation.

Are such adaptations helpful? We noted two benefits earlier in the chapter: Motherese enhances infants' interest in speech (Fernald, 1985), and motherese helps infants to make phonological distinctions (Karzon, 1985; Kemler Nelson et al., 1995). There also is some correlational evidence in support of the benefits of motherese. A relatively high use of motherese by mothers during infancy and toddlerhood has been found to relate to relatively rapid language gains during early childhood (Furrow, Nelson, & Benedict, 1979).

Just how beneficial motherese is, however, remains controversial (Warren & McCloskey, 1997; Valian, 1999). The reasons for caution are both empirical and logical. Empirically, the data from correlational studies turn out to be only partially supportive; not all studies report positive relations between motherese and language gains, and when relations do emerge they are generally small. Furthermore cross-cultural work suggests that motherese may not be universal (Schieffelin & Ochs, 1983), yet all children (to repeat a point made earlier) somehow learn language. Theoretically, some linguists have questioned whether motherese is really simplified syntactically; questions and imperatives, for example, are common in motherese, yet in most syntactic analyses such forms are more complex than active declarative sentences (Newport, Gleitman, & Gleitman, 1977). And even if motherese *is* simplified, it is debatable how much such input should really aid language learning; after all, the restriction of forms means that the child is receiving less rather than more information about the structure of language (Wexler, 1982). We therefore repeat our earlier conclusion: probably helpful, but neither necessary nor sufficient.

Response to Child Speech. The work of Brown and Hanlon (1970) demonstrated that parents do not typically provide explicit corrections of their children's grammar. Perhaps, however, parents furnish more subtle cues about the structure of language. Parents sometimes expand their children's incomplete utterances into some fully formed adult equivalent. For example the child's "Throw Daddy" might be reworked into "Throw it to Daddy." Parents also recast their children's utterances into semantically similar expressions that add new information. Thus "He's going home" might be recast as "He is going home, isn't he?" or "Is that where he's going?" Parents do other things as well, such as prompts, follow-up questions ("You're going where?"), and full or partial repetitions of their own or their children's utterances. There is some evidence, moreover, that parents do these things differentially—that is, that they respond differently to utterances containing grammatical errors than they do to correct utterances (Bohannon & Stanowicz, 1988). For example, when parents repeat their children's utterances, they tend to leave grammatically correct sentences unchanged but to expand or recast sentences with grammatical flaws (Clark & Chouinard, in press). Thus children may receive information both about what is incorrect in their speech and about how to correct it. There is also evidence that children can benefit from such parental practices (Farrar, 1990, 1992).

The data on how parents respond to child speech are relevant to the issue of whether children receive "negative evidence" about the nature of language (Bohannon, Padgett, Nelson, & Mark, 1996; Bohannon & Stanowicz, 1988; Farrar, 1992;

Pinker, 1989; Saxton, 1997; Sokoloff & Snow, 1994; Valian, 1999). Children clearly receive "positive evidence" about language—that is, examples (many thousands of examples) of correct linguistic forms. Negative evidence would consist of information about what is *not* correct, about what is *not* a part of language. Parental correction of grammatical errors would fall under the heading of negative evidence. The point of the debate about negative evidence is that how readily language can be learned—and in particular how much innate knowledge must be assumed to make learning possible—depends on whether children have negative as well as positive evidence to work with as they try to make sense of language (Gold, 1967; Wexler & Culicover, 1980). Our own position on the issue of available evidence is somewhere in between the extremes in either direction. The research of recent years makes clear that children (or, again, *some* children) do receive helpful-looking input—certainly more helpful-looking than nativistically oriented theorists used to claim. Helpful is merely helpful, however, and it is still up to the child to perform the task—a very large task by anyone's theory—of transforming this input into knowledge about language. The remainder of our Explaining section considers two somewhat different approaches to accounting for the child's contribution to language learning.

The Role of Cognition

Some researchers have attempted to embed language learning within cognitive development in general. By such views language is but one of many aspects of the world that children come to understand, and the principles that account for cognitive mastery in other domains should therefore be useful when we attempt to explain the mastery of language. The first two positions that we consider are examples of this general-cognitive approach. The third, as we will see, starts with cognition but also adds some important language-specific elements.

Piaget and Language. Piaget's theory offers a number of claims about the cognitive bases for language acquisition (Bates & Snyder, 1985; Piatelli-Palmarini, 1980). Two of these claims are relatively uncontroversial. One concerns the most general cognitive prerequisite for language: the symbolic function, that is, the ability to use one thing to refer to something else. As we saw in Chapter 3, Piaget argued that the capacity for representation is not inborn but rather is a developmental achievement of infancy, and that its emergence makes possible not only the use of words but a number of other phenomena of late infancy (object permanence, deferred imitation, symbolic play). We also saw that there are disputes about how early representation emerges; no one, however, doubts that representational capacity is a necessary prerequisite for language.

The other claim concerns the cognitive bases for the semantics of children's early language. The argument is a straightforward one: Children talk about what they know about, and what they know is what they have mastered during 2 years of sensorimotor development. Gopnik and Meltzoff (1986; Gopnik, 1984, 1988) have demonstrated a number of such cognitive-linguistic links during the one-word stage of language production. They have shown, for example, that words referring to disappearance, such as "gone," emerge at the time that the child is in the process of mastering the most advanced forms of object permanence. Similarly words denoting the success or failure of actions, such as "there" and "uh-oh," are related to means-ends sorts of achievements in the more general cognitive realm. Brown (1973) has offered a similar analysis with regard to the set of core meanings (agent-action, action-object, etc.) that we saw characterize children's earliest sentences. He argues that these characteristic early meanings reflect the cognitive achievements of the sensorimotor period—knowledge about objects and the effects of actions on objects, about spatial and causal relations, about self and world.

The Piagetian approach is strongest with respect to the questions of how children can use words at all (symbolic ability makes it possible) and why they use the particular words and convey the particular meanings that they do. It is weakest with respect to the specific topic of the current section: how children master grammatical rules. Despite efforts by workers in the Piagetian tradition (see, in particular, Bates & Snyder, 1985), no plausible Piagetian account of the acquisition of grammar has ever been forthcoming. A major obstacle to constructing such an account has always been that the prime period for language growth—the years between 2 and 4—is characterized in such negative, can't-yet-do terms in Piagetian theory. As earlier chapters make clear, our views of the "preoperational" child have grown progressively more positive in recent years, and it may be that newer models of preschoolers' abilities can provide a better explanation for language than does Piaget. Thus far, however, there still seems to be a gap: Nothing that 2- or 3-year-olds have been shown to do in the general cognitive realm seems very close to their extraordinary facility at learning language.

Information Processing.   The major attempt to explain language development from the point of view of information-processing theory is the MacWhinney and Bates Competition Model (Bates & MacWhinney, 1987; MacWhinney, 1987, 1989). The Competition Model is one of a number of recent connectionist approaches to language acquisition (Plunkett, 1998); consideration of the model will therefore give us another example of the connectionist approach.

Several emphases characterize the Competition Model. One is an emphasis on the functional aspect of language. Language evolved to serve a variety of pragmatic purposes, and the structure that it eventually attained (e.g., the different kinds of sentences that are found) is assumed to reflect these functional origins. Similarly children's language serves a variety of pragmatic goals (asserting, denying, requesting, sharing information, bonding with others, etc.) from the start, and children learn forms that help them to achieve these goals. An emphasis on the functional nature of language is decidedly *not* a characteristic of the more nativistic approaches that we consider in the final section of the chapter.

A second emphasis of the Competition Model is on the variety of kinds of information that must be simultaneously processed and represented for language to perform the functions that it does. Even to produce a simple sentence like "Doggie runned," the child must deal simultaneously with lexical information that governs the choice of words to convey actor and action, phonological information that determines how these words will be pronounced, and grammatical information that determines the way in which the words will be ordered and the selection of the past-tense ending. An emphasis on the multiplicity of processes that underlie cognitive activity, as well as the simultaneous execution ("parallel processing") of many of these processes, is a general characteristic of the information-processing approach.

A further emphasis concerns the "competition" part of the Competition Model. The execution of the numerous processes that underlie language use is complicated by the fact that there are always multiple alternatives at every point in the decision process. "Doggie," for example, may have to compete with "kitty" and other labels for similar-appearing animals, and the "ed" ending on "run" may have to compete with the frequently heard "ran." The child's past experience will have given these different possibilities different activation strengths in any particular context, and the alternative selected will be the one with the greatest immediate strength. Development occurs as the child's experience in hearing and producing language leads to changes in activation strength. Eventually, for example, "kitty" will become a very low-probability response in the presence of a dog; at the same time, the childish "doggie" will be supplanted by "dog," and more specific labels ("spaniel," "Spot," etc.) will come to the fore in particular contexts. A variety of aspects of the speech input can be important in directing such change, including the availability of a cue (frequently available cues, such as the "ed" ending, will be more influential than less frequent cues), the detectability of the cue (the more detectable, the more influential), and the reliability of the cue in signalling the linguistic form of interest (the more reliable, the more influential).

A final point about the Competition model concerns what it is that is being learned as the child acquires language. What is *not* being learned is a system of rules. In eschewing the concept of rules, the approach departs radically from the traditional view of language and language acquisition that has long dominated the field (and also, obviously, from the approach that we take throughout this chapter). Learning, rather, consists of strengthening or weakening particular connections and thus making particular responses more or less likely. In the traditional view, developmental change is qualitative and discrete; children initially do not possess some rule (e.g., the "ed" ending for past tense) and eventually they acquire it. In the connectionist approach, developmental change is quantitative and gradual, and performance is always probabilistic; what changes with experience is not an underlying rule system but rather the probability of producing correct linguistic forms.

Connectionist approaches to language acquisition are still a relatively new enterprise, and even proponents of the approach admit that there are limitations in the existing implementations (Klahr & MacWhinney, 1998). In addition there is good reason, as we will see in the concluding section of the chapter, to believe that very strong and specific forms of biological pretuning underlie the development of language. Although there is no in-principle reason that connectionist approaches could not incorporate such specialized, built-in knowledge, specific models to date have taken a more empiricist, general-learning-mechanisms approach. Still the connectionist approach does have a number of clear strengths: a solid grounding in work on cognition in general, a grounding as well in knowledge about the neural bases for intelligent behavior, and powerful methodologies (including computer simulations) to test specific models. Thus connectionist theorists seem to be doing all the right things to test the limits of their approach.

Semantic Bootstrapping. Earlier we discussed the notion of syntactic bootstrapping, or the use of grammatical knowledge to figure out aspects of semantics. Semantic bootstrapping, as you might guess, is the converse process: use of knowledge of semantics to learn aspects of grammar.

Pinker (1984, 1987) is the theorist who has developed this position most fully. A simplified version of his argument is the following. Children can learn the meanings of individual words prior to mastering much if any of the grammatical system of their language. They can then use these meanings, along with contextual information, to arrive at a semantic interpretation of many sentences, again without knowing much if any grammar. Once certain basic semantic categories and relations have been worked out, the child can exploit the correlations that exist in every language between semantic concepts and grammatical concepts. Names of objects or people, for example, are universally nouns; thus the child who has noted how names are used in sentences can use this information to begin to figure out how nouns in general are used. Similarly agents of transitive action verbs are invariably the subjects of sentences; thus the young child who has mastered agent-action-object relations can begin to identify the grammatical subject. It is through noting such associations that children gradually extract grammatical knowledge from their previously developed conceptual and semantic knowledge.

The gist of the bootstrapping approach is that semantics provides a starting point for grammar. It is important to add, however, that semantics is only a starting point. As we noted earlier, the correlation between semantics and grammar is an imperfect one; not all nouns are names of objects, for example, just as not all subjects are agents. To master fully an abstract category such as noun, the child must go beyond the initial dependence on meaning and begin to utilize purely grammatical-distributional information (he might note, for example, that "truth" and "beauty" can appear in the same slots within sentences as "dog" and "car"). Furthermore, there is no assumption in such an approach that the combination of linguistic input and general cognitive development is sufficient to explain the acquisition of grammar. Just the opposite, in fact. Semantic bootstrapping is assumed to work in conjunction with powerful innate constraints concerning the form that grammar can take (knowledge that there is such a category as nouns, for example) and the ways in which semantics and grammar can relate. Semantics may "boot" the grammatical system into operation, but grammar is by no means reducible to semantics. Our final section deals more generally with the idea that grammatical development simply cannot be explained without the assumption of a strong innate contribution.

The Role of Biology

Evidence and arguments of a variety of sorts converge on the conclusion that language acquisition has a strong biological-maturational component (Newport, 1990; Pinker, 1994; Ritchie & Bhatia, 1999; Spelke & Newport, 1998—but see Elman et al., 1996, for a different interpretation of the evidence we present here). Such arguments do not deny a role for experience or for cognitive abilities, but they do maintain that such explanations are far from sufficient.

Biological Pretuning. We seem to be biologically constructed to learn and use oral language of the human type. The human brain and articulatory apparatus are specialized for producing rapid and extended streams of human speech sounds. There is also some left-hemisphere specialization in the brain for the analysis of language-like input, specialization that may be evident as early as birth (Molfese & Molfese, 1979). We are also biologically programmed to attend to and analyze the speech sounds we hear. We seem biologically prepared for language learning in rather the same way we are biologically prepared for perceptual and motor-skill learning. We are strongly disposed to do all three and are born with powerful, specialized tools for doing them (recall the discussion of modularity nativism in Chapter 1).

Maturation. Language development has properties that suggest the workings of an endogenous, maturationlike process. Children the world over go through roughly the same major stages of language acquisition, in the same order, and at approximately the same ages. They do not, to be sure, do so in completely identical fashion, as our earlier discussions of individual differences indicated (and some contemporary workers would emphasize these differences more than we have done). Nevertheless there appears to be a core of fundamental similarity within which the variations occur.

Evidence for such maturationally given predispositions comes as well from studies of the optimal age period for learning language. Most things, of course, are learned better by older children than by younger, and better by adults than by children. Not so language. Johnson and Newport (1989) examined the English facility of 46 Chinese and Korean speakers who had emigrated to the United States and learned English as a second language. Age of arrival in the United States, and thus time of first exposure to English, ranged from 3 to 39. Johnson and Newport found a strong linear relation between age of exposure and mastery of grammar—that is, the earlier the learning of English began, the fuller the eventual mastery proved to be. This relation held even when other potentially important factors, such as total amount of exposure, were controlled. It held, however, only up until puberty; the limited learning shown by adult emigrants was unrelated to age. Johnson and Newport summarize this surprising pattern of results as follows: "It appears as if language learning ability slowly declines as the human matures, and plateaus at a low level after puberty" (p. 90). It is important to add that greater childhood facility is not limited to second language learning but applies to first language acquisition as well. It has been shown, for example, for deaf individuals who are first exposed to American Sign language at varying points in life; that is, those who learn it earliest learn it best (Newport, 1988).

Why should the younger, less mature brain be better at learning language than the older and generally more powerful brain? No one knows for sure, but Newport (1988, 1990) suggests an intriguing hypothesis. The gist of her proposal is that developmental improvements in cognitive ability actually work *against* language learning. They work against language learning because the mature cognitive system, in effect, takes in and retains too much information. Acquisition of grammar requires the ability to analyze the speech stream into the components (morphemes, inflections, clauses, etc.) that convey meaning—requires the ability to deal with pieces and not just unanalyzed wholes. Children—or so Newport argues—are in a favorable position to identify components because pieces are often all they can take in; their limited information-processing abilities save them from the overly inclusive, unanalyzed-wholes sorts of processing that impede language learning in adults. This provocative explanation for childhood superiority is aptly named the "Less is More" hypothesis.

Independence of Language and General Intelligence. If language is a reflection of cognition in general, then we would expect to find a close relation between linguistic ability and general intellectual ability. In particular we would expect to find that problems in one domain are paralleled by problems in the other—for example, that general mental retardation is accompanied by lowered linguistic abilities. Such, to be sure, is often the case. But it is by no means always the case—language development sometimes proceeds remarkably well in the face of severe intellectual problems; conversely, in some clinical syndromes language is greatly impaired yet general intelligence remains intact. Either sort of disassociation provides evidence that language is not reducible to cognition in general but rather has its own special, perhaps modular, status.

Work on Williams syndrome provides an example (Pinker, 1991; Reilly, Klima, & Bellugi, 1990—but see Karmiloff-Smith et al., 1997, for an opposing position). Williams syndrome is a rare metabolic neurodevelopmental disorder that results in mental retardation. Individuals with Williams syndrome typically perform poorly on a wide range of cognitive tasks, including measures of linguistic competence that appear dependent on general intellectual ability (e.g., memorization of irregular past tense verbs). Yet their mastery of other aspects of language, including basic grammatical rules, is typically at normal or close-to-normal levels, as is their ability to use language for communicative and affective purposes. In this respect they show an interesting divergence not only from other categories of retardation (e.g., Down syndrome) but also from children with autism. As we saw in the discussion of theory of mind in Chapter 6, autism is characterized by a very specific, almost certainly biologically based, deficit in certain areas of social understanding and social interaction. With Williams syndrome, social/affective and linguistic processes remain relatively intact, yet many other aspects of cognitive functioning are impaired. In both cases the pattern of outcomes suggests a mind composed of many separate, biologically prepared abilities, rather than a single, all-purpose cognitive automaton.

Universality.   Just as there are similarities among children the world over as they go about the task of learning language, so are there similarities among the many different languages that are so learned. The most basic similarity is the existence of a rich, grammatically complex language in every human society. Human language is specieswide or universal. Human language is also species-specific; although other species have systems of communication, some quite intricate, none of them closely resembles human language. Of particular relevance to the present argument is the fact that none has a rule-governed, productive grammar of the type found in all human natural languages. There are, moreover, important properties that all of the world's many languages have in common (Clark & Clark, 1977; Slobin, 1985). All, for example, draw from the same pool of possible sounds when forming words, and all show similar restrictions with respect to which types of grammatical rules are or are not possible. The existence of such common properties, or "linguistic universals," is, in fact, a necessary prediction of any biologically oriented account of language development. No one believes that children are prepared by evolution to learn English or Japanese; whatever biological pretuning there may be must work for any language that the child happens to encounter—which means that all languages must be alike in certain fundamental ways. The evidence suggests that all languages *are* alike in fundamental ways.

Nativistic Theory.   The general theoretical tradition within which biologically oriented approaches fall is labeled *nativism*, and the theorist most associated with the nativistic view of language is Noam Chomsky (e.g., 1972, 1981, 1988). A rough and simplified version of Chomsky's argument is the following:

1. The grammatical structure of any human language is extremely complex.

2. Clear clues to this complex structure are surprisingly lacking in the utterances children hear. In consequence an infinite number of different grammars could be induced or inferred from these utterances by a grammar-learning device that was not specifically designed by nature to look for only certain kinds—namely, those found in human languages.

3. Because children do succeed in acquiring the correct grammar in a few short years, they must have such specific design features. They must bring to their learning task the functional equivalent of specific, innately given ideas and expectations about the general kinds of grammatical rules and structures they will find.

The idea that evolution has provided us with language-learning equipment *that* powerful and specific seemed highly implausible to most of us when Chomsky first proposed it, and still seems farfetched to many. Various alternative positions, however, also tend to seem implausible, or at least incomplete, when examined carefully. Certainly no one has yet demonstrated that language acquisition can be explained without positing an important biological contribution.

In any case it is one thing to favor Chomsky's or some other general stance on the issue and quite another to formulate a detailed and specific theory of language acquisition. One criticism of the nativistic approach has always concerned its lack of specificity: No theorist has explained how—through what experiences and what processes—children transform their innately given knowledge about the universal features of language into specific knowledge about the particular language they are acquiring. Fortunately such efforts are beginning to appear. The work on semantic bootstrapping, for example, represents one attempt to capture the interplay of innate knowledge about the possible forms that language can take and more language-specific experiences and acquisitions. The contributions in the Ritchie and Bhatia (1999) volume include several distinct formulations of how an innately given universal grammar might combine with experience to yield the known facts of grammatical development. The chapter by Spelke and Newport (1998), in addition to summarizing available evidence, provides an excellent discussion of the issues that must be addressed by nativistic theories and the kinds of explanations that might be offered.

Efforts such as these represent a promising start. They are, however, just a start, and much remains to be learned. How little children acquire language is still, to borrow from Winston Churchill, "a riddle wrapped in a mystery inside an enigma."

SUMMARY

Thanks to the work of Chomsky and others, we now recognize that the native speaker of any human language commands astonishingly rich systems of knowledge and skills. Our picture of the childhood acquisition of these systems is also becoming correspondingly rich, and the field of language development is currently one of the most exciting areas in developmental psychology.

The developmental story begins before the advent of language. Phonological and communicative acquisitions during infancy precede and prepare the way for the acquisition of language. Human babies appear to be biologically primed to respond to human speech; they are interested in and responsive to speech from early in life, and they are skilled at making discriminations among different speech sounds (categorical speech perception). Biological-maturational factors also contribute to the infant's ability to produce speech sounds—in particular, to the onset and developmental course of prelinguistic *babbling*. Although the issue is still not resolved, recent evidence suggests that babbling may play a functional role with respect to later language development. Continuity has been more clearly established in the realm of communication, where various acquisitions of infancy prefigure eventual linguistic communication. Such prelinguistic communication achievements include the ability to direct and "read" another person's attention, to produce preverbal forms of *speech acts* such as requests and assertions, and to take turns in nonverbal "conversations."

Children usually begin to produce recognizable words sometime around their first birthdays. Children's first words typically refer to salient and familiar objects and events, and they tend to be at an intermediate, so-called "basic," level of generality (e.g., "dog" rather than "spaniel" or "animal"). There are, however, both individual and cultural differences in the sorts of early lexicons that children construct, differences that relate to variations in the kinds of linguistic input that different parents provide.

When first learning a new word, children may attach a somewhat different meaning to it than do adults. *Overextensions* (e.g., "dog" used to refer to all animals) are common, although less so in comprehension (which is generally more advanced) than in production. *Underextensions* (e.g., "dog" refers only to the family dog) and *complexive* (unstable, shifting) word meanings are also found, as are original coinages, in which the child invents a word to fill a lexical gap. At least sometimes the child in this period may be trying to express a meaning akin to an entire sentence with her single-word utterances (thus producing so-called *holophrases*); such a "rich" interpretation of early language remains controversial, however.

Two-word utterances often begin to appear around 18 months of age. These telegramlike expressions ("more milk," "Mommy kiss," etc.) are remarkably similar in form and meaning the world over. The occurrence of novel utterances (e.g., "Allgone sticky") tells us that even children's earliest sentences are creative, rule-based constructions. Nonetheless questions remain as to how much and what kind of *semantic* (linguistic meaning) and *grammatical* (sentence structure) knowledge we should attribute to the child in this period.

Important advances in both grammar and semantics are made subsequent to this period. The child develops *grammatical morphemes* (function words like "in," *inflections* like the past-tense "-ed" ending on verb stems) in a systematic order that is jointly determined by the forms' cognitive and grammatical complexity. The *overregularization* errors that the child produces as she masters the inflectional system (resulting in words such as "foots" and "goed") illustrate her active propensity for testing hypotheses and searching for rules when learning language. Other grammatical acquisitions cited concern negations, *wh* questions, and methods of combining simple sentences to make more complicated ones. Semantic advances beyond the two-word period include both improvements in the ability to convey meanings through the combination of words and refinements in the meanings of individual words. A discussion of children's mastery of relational words illustrates the fact that word learning is a multidetermined—and still far from perfectly understood—process.

Children's communication abilities also show dramatic improvements across childhood. Communication skills that develop during the preschool years include the ability to sustain a conversation on a single topic, to discuss the nonpresent and nonreal, to infer what is presupposed and implied from what is explicitly said, and to adapt one's speech production and comprehension to numerous properties of speakers, listeners, and social settings. Impressive as these skills are, however, research on *metacommunication* (knowledge and cognition concerning communications) suggests that children of kindergarten age and older still have some important communicative development ahead of them. They need to learn to monitor their own comprehension and to recognize the meaning and implications of feelings of uncertainty or lack of understanding. They need also to learn that the communicative quality of a message affects its communicative success. Such metacommunicative knowledge and skill relate to general changes in children's understanding of mental states or theory of mind.

A full account of children's language must include not only a description of important developmental changes but also an explanation for those changes. Attempts to explain the acquisition of word meaning have had to confront the Quinean puzzle: There are always an indefinite number of logically possible meanings for a word, yet children somehow home in quickly on the one actual meaning. Studies of *fast mapping* confirm that discovery of a word's core nature (if not its full meaning) is often a rapid process. Many researchers believe that word learning is guided by a set of *constraints* concerning what are and what are not possible meanings for words. Among the constraints that have been proposed are Whole Object (words label whole objects), the Taxonomic Assumption (words label objects from the same taxonomic category), and Mutual Exclusivity (each object has only one label). Although children's adherence to such principles is not as rigid as the term "constraint" might imply, they do seem to use tacit beliefs of various sorts to guide their hypotheses about word meaning. They also use the grammatical cues available in sentences to narrow down the possible meanings of words—a process referred to as *syntactic bootstrapping*. Finally the challenges in linking word and referent are reduced if parent and child can achieve *joint attention*, or simultaneous focus on the same object or event. Recent research indicates that young word learners are surprisingly good at discerning their conversational partner's intended focus and hence at arriving at correct word-referent mappings.

Explaining the acquisition of grammar has been the primary theoretical goal of most researchers of language development. The role of the environment in grammatical acquisition does not seem to be as direct and specific as was once believed. Children do not appear to master grammar through imitating others or through being reinforced for correct speech. Other sorts of environmental assistance may play a role; among the parental practices that have been examined are preverbal dialogues in infancy, the use of *motherese* when talking to the child, and provision of feedback in the form of expansions and recasts. The evidence suggests, however, that such practices are at best helpful; they have not been shown to be either necessary for learning to occur nor sufficient to explain how the child acquires so much grammatical knowledge so quickly.

Whatever help the environment may provide, the role of the child in his own grammatical development must be an extremely active and powerful one. Some theorists have attempted to embed the mastery of language within more general cognitive development. Piagetian-oriented approaches are most persuasive in their discussions of symbolic ability as a prerequisite for the use of words and of sensori-motor achievements as an explanation for the meanings expressed in early speech. Such approaches are least successful in their attempts to explain grammar, for they have not yet resolved the evident gap between the limited cognitive abilities of the young child and the very powerful language-learning capacities of that same child. A more influential cognitive approach at present is the MacWhinney and Bates Competition Model, the grounding for which is in information-processing theory and research. In the Competition Model, the activation strengths of competing linguistic forms (e.g., different forms of the past tense) are gradually adjusted over time through the application of general information-processing mechanisms to the available linguistic input. Still a third approach to cognition-language links is found in work on *semantic bootstrapping*, the basic idea of which is that young children use their already-developed semantic knowledge as a guide to the grammatical structure of the language they are learning.

Although the bootstrapping approach implicates general cognitive understanding, it also includes a role for innately given knowledge about the possible structure of language. More generally, a variety of considerations, both theoretical and empirical, converge on the conclusion that language acquisition has a substantial innate basis. Human children appear to be biologically equipped to acquire language of the human type; they encounter languages of rich and complex (and in part similar) grammatical structure in every human society; and they acquire such languages in an inexorable, age- and stage-related fashion that does not appear—given our current, admittedly imperfect understanding—to be explicable on experiential bases but rather looks to be strongly maturational.

9

Questions and Problems

———⟫◈⟪———

Most textbooks fail to give the reader an insider's view of the field they cover. A field looks very different to an insider—a "pro"—than it does to an outsider. Insiders continually live with its numerous questions, problems, ambiguities, and uncertainties. They become used to, although never unconcerned about, its untidy, open-ended, no-problem-ever-seems-to-get-solved character. They know how incredibly difficult it is even to think up a research study that will tell us something we really want to know. Most therefore have a healthy modesty with regard to their own such efforts, as well as a healthy skepticism with regard to the claims of others. More positively, they also have a genuine appreciation for work that manages to surmount the problems and tell us things that are really worth knowing.

The aim of this chapter is to present some of the questions and problems you would live with if you were an insider in the field of cognitive growth. By implication the aim is also to make you feel more insecure and skeptical about everything you have read in previous chapters. We can imagine two reactions that different readers might have to the content of this chapter, depending upon their backgrounds and interests. One is that finally, at long last, we are getting into the *real* issues. The authors have finished describing all the different ways that kids get smarter as they grow older and will now get into more substantive matters. As the section headings indicate, they now talk about how to assess or diagnose the child's cognitive level, about the sorts of systematic patterns (sequences, stages) it exhibits, and about how cognitive growth may be explained rather than just described. They, in short, are trying to tie it all together, provide an overview and perspective, show us What It All Means. The other reaction is that things have suddenly gotten very abstract and hard to follow. The child's cognitive development is now populated with false positives, underlying processes, cognitive entities, structures, concurrences, qualitative changes, and other intangibles. Where did the child go?

Both reactions are perfectly understandable and reasonable. To those who have the first reaction, we would suggest only that even the purely descriptive aspects of cognitive development are scientifically important, and also that—the insider's plight once again—those real issues and substantive matters are going to look very messy, very far from being resolved. To those with the second reaction, we would suggest that you either skip this chapter altogether (if that option is open to you) or else read it in a special way. The special way is to let it wash over you, trying only to get the main points. Above all try to get a sense or feeling for how cognitive growth might proceed—or more accurately, for the *alternative* conceptions of how cognitive growth might proceed. Try, in other words, to get some sort of wide-angle view of the cognitive-developmental panorama, including the outstanding questions and problems concerning it. Regardless of which of the two reactions you may have, if either, providing you with such a view is one of the main objectives of this chapter.

DIAGNOSIS

What problems and issues do psychologists face in trying to diagnose or analyze children's developing knowledge and abilities? They are many, varied, and very, very troublesome. Discussions of these problems and issues can be found in, for example, Chandler and Chapman (1991), Flavell (1971c), Flavell and Wohlwill (1969), Gold (1987), Miller (1976, 1998), Siegal (1997), Sophian (1997), and Thomas and Horton (1997).

What is involved in cognitive-developmental diagnosis can best be communicated with reference to a specific example. Transitive inference is a concrete-operational acquisition within Piaget's theoretical system. As mentioned in Chapter 5, one form of it is conceived by Piaget as consisting of this type of reasoning process: If A > B (e.g., A is longer than B) and B > C, then it has to be true that A > C—no measurement is necessary. In what follows we use transitive inference as our example, but it might be a useful exercise to think about how the points apply to other topics considered earlier in the book. Obvious candidates—for each of which questions of diagnosis were in fact addressed—include object permanence (Chapter 3), biological concepts (Chapter 4), and false belief (Chapter 6).

Developmental psychologists may ask two sorts of questions about transitive inference or any other cognitive acquisition. They both involve "diagnosis," but in somewhat different senses. One has to do with our *conceptualization* of the acquisition itself, the other with its *assessment* in children.

Conceptualization questions ask what this ability or behavior we call "transitive inference" consists of, in psychological terms. What are the cognitive processes that actually underlie acts of so-called transitive inference? What, exactly, happens inside the individual's head when, given A > B, B > C, and A ? C, she responds A > C? In short *what* develops when transitive inference develops?

Assessment questions apply once we have decided on a tentative answer to the conceptualization question. Suppose we provisionally accept someone's (e.g., Piaget's) characterization of what "transitive inference" is. The question that then arises is how can we determine (assess) whether a given child has or has not acquired transitive inference. This question *is* a question because there are always numerous possible ways of assessing any cognitive target of interest. Clearly our answer to the conceptualization question will guide selection among these possibilities, but there will still be much to decide. In the case of transitivity, the researcher would have to decide (among other decisions) what sorts of stimuli to use, which particular comparisons to present, how to word the transitivity question, and whether to require a logical explanation as well as a correct answer before crediting the child with an understanding of the concept. Other cognitive acquisitions offer a similar range of assessment options.

If children were perfectly consistent in their response to different assessment techniques, then the choice of technique would not really matter—our conclusions would be the same whatever approach we took. They are not, however. Consider the transitivity example again. If children were perfectly consistent in their performance on transitivity problems, then we would find two patterns of response. Some children would succeed on every version of the transitivity task that we might present, and other children would fail on every version. The first group of children would clearly "have" transitivity, and the second group would very probably "not have" it ("very probably" rather than "clearly" because it is always possible that some understanding exists but that it is too underdeveloped to be expressed on even the simplest-seeming task that we have yet been able to devise). In fact, however, in addition to these two extreme types we find all sorts of in-between patterns of performance: children who succeed on some versions of the task but not on others, and who thus seem sometimes to "have" the concept and other times to "not have" it. We find such heterogeneity, moreover, not just for transitivity but for all sorts of other Piagetian and non-Piagetian cognitive achievements—recall, for example, the variability in children's strategies that is depicted in Siegler's (1996) overlapping wave model (Figure 1.2).

What theoretical sense can we make of this untidy state of affairs? Will we need to distinguish several, or even many, different kinds or degrees of "having transitive inference"? If so, how should such distinctions be drawn? Perhaps the several or many we distinguish will line up nicely to form an orderly developmental sequence or progression. That is, we might theoretically define a "beginning" kind (degree? amount?) of capability for transitive inference, followed by a "more advanced" one (in what way?), and so on, until a "completely mature" (in what sense?) capability is achieved. But if we think of transitive inference as more like a developmental succession of different things than like a unitary, present or absent cognitive entity, we find ourselves confronting the conceptualization form of the diagnosis question once again. The conceptualization question, you will recall, asks what cognitive processes actually make up or underlie "transitive inferences." However, if "transitive inference" changes with age, then those cognitive processes must also change with age.

To recapitulate, we begin with a preliminary, working notion of what transitive inference is (conceptualization questions). We then try to find ways to accurately diagnose its presence/absence in the child's task performance (assessment questions). The best available diagnostic procedures suggest that, for many children, it is present sometimes and absent sometimes, depending upon the specifics of the task situation and perhaps other factors. Then we try to make developmental sense out of this lack of consistency, perhaps by hypothesizing an ontogenetic progression of different forms (degrees, or whatever) of transitive-inference-related capabilities. The existence of such a progression implies that these capabilities must change in some way from one point in that progression to another, and therefore, so also must the nature and/or organization of the cognitive processes underlying them (back to conceptualization problems again). Let us now examine this diagnostic cycle in more detail, beginning with questions of assessment.

Assessment Questions

We begin with the simplifying assumption that a child either does or does not possess the ability to make a transitive inference—with no gradations in between— and that our diagnostic goal is to find out which is the case for an individual child. There are two ways in which our diagnostic efforts might go astray. One possibility is that the child really does possess the ability but gives no evidence of it in her performance on the particular measure we have selected. An underestimation error of this sort is labeled a *false-negative* diagnostic error. Alternatively the child may not really understand transitive inference, but the testing procedures may lead to the false conclusion that she does. An overestimation error of this sort would be a *false-positive* diagnostic error.

False-negative errors can occur for a number of reasons. The child might fail to understand the task instructions, fail to attend to or comprehend the premises of the inference (i.e., the fact that A > B and B > C), or forget either the instructions or the premises at the moment when the inference normally would be made. Such failures of attention or memory may be especially likely if the information-processing demands of the task challenge the child's limited resources, hence making execution of the full problem-solving sequence effortful. The task may for some reason elicit from the child a problem-solving approach that is incompatible with transitive inference. For instance, having just learned through perception rather than inference that A > B and B > C, the child may assume that A ? C must also be solved by perception rather than inference.

The child's true ability can also be masked by motivational and emotional factors, such as lack of interest in the "game," or apprehension about the experimenter as an adult stranger. The social cues present in the assessment situation may lead the child to believe that the tester expects a certain sort of answer, and hence to respond with something other than her true belief (see Siegal, 1997, for a detailed consideration of this possibility). Children may know the correct answer but be unable to inhibit a prepotent, developmentally less mature response; recall the discussion of executive function in Chapters 5 and 6. Finally some cognitive tasks require the child to generate a complex verbal response (e.g., an explanation) in order to demonstrate the cognitive ability of interest; the child may be incapable of generating the verbal response and yet possess the ability. Every task demands from the child knowledge and skills other than, and in addition to, the target concept or ability it was designed to tap. If the child does not or cannot meet any of these additional, nontarget demands, a false-negative diagnostic error can result.

False-positive diagnostic errors can also stem from several causes. Under certain task conditions, the child may get the right answer by guessing, by direct perception of A > C, or by using some irrelevant (i.e., non-transitive-inference) solution strategy which happens to yield the A > C conclusion. One such strategy that has been identified stems from the young child's frequent tendency to think in absolute (e.g., "A is *long*") rather than relative or comparative terms (e.g., "A is *longer than* B"). The child may code the premises A > B and B > C as something like "A is long, B isn't," and "B is long, C isn't," respectively. Because in this coding, A has been thought of as "long" once but C never has, for this reason the child may tend to choose A when asked which is "longer." The answer is, of course, correct, but it was not generated by transitive inference. Recall from earlier chapters that similar false-positive alternatives have been proposed for some of the diagnostic innovations of recent years—for example, the violation-of-expectancy approach to object permanence (Chapter 3) and infant arithmetic (Chapter 4).

Researchers have thought of various ways to reduce the likelihood of false-positive errors. In the case of transitivity, it is possible to minimize perceptually based solutions by disguising the A-C relation—for example, by showing sticks A and C on a background of Muller-Lyer arrows, which creates the illusion that C is longer than A rather than vice versa. The possibility of absolute ("A is long") solutions can be ruled out by increasing the number of stimuli and comparisons. Suppose we give the child this transitive-inference problem: Given that A > B, B > C, C > D, D > E, what is the length relation between B and D? Because both B and D have been shown to be longer than one thing and shorter than another in this problem, the child cannot get the answer right by using the strategy of coding relative terms as absolutes; both B and D have had a chance to be coded as "long." Also we can reduce markedly the chances of making a false-positive diagnostic error by requiring the child to explain or justify his A > C conclusion. An answer like, "A *has* to be longer than C because it is longer than B, and even B is longer than C," could hardly emanate from a child who had no understanding of the transitivity rule. The requirement of a logical explanation is a criterion that has long been used to reduce false positives not just on transitivity but on a wide range of tasks.

But the reduction of false positives is very likely to result in an increase in false negatives. It is not hard to conceive of a child who would not fare at all well on these more stringent tests, while yet possessing at least some genuine capability for transitive inference. Indeed we know that such across-task variability in performance in fact obtains: We often find an extended period in the development of a concept during which children succeed on simplified measures of the concept but fail on more rigorous measures. Some of this variability no doubt reflects diagnostic error in one direction or the other: overestimation of ability from the use of simplified tasks that fail to tap the target concept; underestimation of ability from the use of complex tasks that obscure genuine knowledge. We suspect, however, that much of the variability reflects not diagnostic error but the nature of development, and the fact—contra the simplifying assumption with which we began this section—that for many concepts there are a number of intermediate levels of understanding between total absence and full mastery. And so our assessment efforts, which began with some conceptualization of the underlying target, lead back to issues of conceptualization. How should we conceptualize these different levels of understanding?

Conceptualization Questions

The following is one way to think about the different possible meanings and manners of "having" a concept like transitive inference. Further discussion can be found in Brown, Bransford, Ferrara, and Campione (1983), Flavell (1971c), Greeno, Riley, and Gelman (1984), various chapters in Chandler and Chapman (1991), and Sophian (1997), as well as the accompanying commentaries.

Let us imagine two children—A and B—both of whom have some understanding of transitive inference. There are various (no doubt related) ways in which A's understanding might be more advanced than B's. The knowledge may be more available to A than to B—that is, more readily called into play in situations that require transitive inference. In this case the knowledge is "in there somewhere" for both children, but B is less likely to evoke it when appropriate than is A. We discussed various reasons in the Assessment section that children might fail to reveal knowledge they possess, and there are doubtless many others as well, especially for recently acquired and hence still fragile competencies. Even if transitive inference *is* evoked, B may be less able to execute a chain of inferential reasoning than is A. Knowing what *should* be done and attempting to do it is no guarantee that the attempt will be successful, again especially in the case of newly acquired abilities. We have seen numerous examples throughout the book of divergence between attempt and outcome in children's cognitive performance (e.g., knowledge of counting principles and actual counting behavior, evocation of an appropriate mnemonic strategy and execution of that strategy).

A and B may also differ in the range of situations in which their knowledge can be applied. There may be expertise-related domain differences, with each child demonstrating the knowledge only in situations in which he or she has sufficient experience. Or there may be more general differences in range of applicability. B may be capable of transitive inference in only one or a few specific situations or types of problem, whereas A's knowledge might be applicable to any transitivity problem that comes along. Undoubtedly an important contributor to range of application is the dimension of problem complexity. Although the argument is sometimes hard to formulate in noncircular terms, it seems reasonable to believe that competencies are first expressed in relatively simple situations and only gradually extended to more complex ones. In the case of transitivity, successful solution might be limited at first to three-term problems with consistent relations (e.g., all "equals" or all "greater thans") and no countervailing perceptual illusions. Ability to solve problems without these simplifying features would come only later (which, in fact, appears to be the case—see Andrews & Halford, 1998). Again we have seen a number of examples of such a simple-to-complex progression. For example children's counting skills may be limited at first to small sets of objects, with ability to handle larger sets coming some time later. Similarly children's ability to conserve number may at first be limited to small sets.

Children may also differ in response to social support—for example, help from a parent or teacher. B may be less advanced than A in the sense of being more dependent on such support; B may require some degree of assistance to accomplish what A can do on his own. Or A and B may differ in their ability to profit from social support;

perhaps A can use such support to go well beyond his independent efforts, whereas B is unable to gain much at all from instruction. Recall that this ability to profit from instruction is at the core of Vygotsky's notion of the zone of proximal development. If we add social context to our assessment efforts, we undoubtedly will pick up differences in children's abilities that are not evident from independent problem-solving alone.

Still further differences between A and B might concern the status that the concept of transitive inference holds in the child's thinking. For child B the knowledge of transitivity might be completely implicit—a kind of procedural knowledge that guides response in certain situations but of which the child is quite unaware. For child A, in contrast, the knowledge may have become explicit—something that can be thought about, verbally justified, shared with others. This sort of implicit to explicit progression may well characterize the developmental course of a number of cognitive acquisitions (Karmiloff-Smith, 1992). Similarly for child B the A > C conclusion given A > B and B > C may be simply a best guess, something that is seen as probably but by no means definitely true. Child A may realize that the A > C judgment can be offered with certainty; indeed, he may even understand that A > C is a logically necessary conclusion given the particular premises. As we saw in Chapters 4 and 5, there is evidence that an appreciation of the logical necessity of certain outcomes increases with development.

A final possible contrast is suggested by the work of Goldin-Meadow and colleagues that we discussed briefly in Chapter 4. We have been assuming so far that both A and B can express *some* knowledge in response to a standard assessment; the differences have been in exactly how much knowledge and how readily it is expressed. What the Goldin-Meadow research program demonstrates is that not only speech but gestures can sometimes convey information about what a child knows. Furthermore, gestures and speech sometimes convey *conflicting* information about what a child knows—a phenomenon Goldin-Meadow and colleagues label *gesture-speech mismatch* (Church, 1999; Goldin-Meadow, 1997, 2000; Goldin-Meadow, Alibali, & Church, 1993). A nonconserver, for example, might refer only to the height of the liquid in her verbal response to a Piagetian conservation-of-liquid task, but at the same time cup her hands in a way that conveys some awareness of width or diameter as well. Goldin-Meadow and colleagues believe that such mismatches are a direct reflection of a knowledge state in transition; whereas earlier the child had only a single, incorrect basis for response, now she has become sensitive to other possibilities and she is struggling to reconcile them. And so still another difference between A and B might be revealed if we took gesture into account. Both may fail any standard version of a transitivity task, but one may possess some incipient, not yet verbalizable knowledge that comes through in gesture.

The studies of gesture-speech mismatch are not only of diagnostic interest. In the final section of the chapter we address the issue of cognitive change. A central question in the study of change is that of readiness—how to identify those children who are ready to make cognitive progress in some area. Gesture-speech mismatches are one index of readiness for change.

Suppose that cognitive capacities like transitive inference do in fact show the sort of developmental course just sketched. What more would we want to know? A great deal, actually, because we have not yet discovered what "transitive inference" really is. We would have some idea of the sorts of changes that transitive inference undergoes with development, but we would still need to specify exactly what it is that is changing. Is transitive inference a single cognitive entity that remains basically the same once it has entered the repertoire, albeit increasing in evocability, utilizability, and generality? Is there, to adopt a common way of talking about the issue, a single *competence* that underlies transitivity, with developmental changes coming mainly in the *performance* of that competence (Sophian, 1997)? Recall that we have seen models of this sort for various topics. In the "ancillary skills" approach to object permanence (Chapter 3), for example, the basic competence (i.e., knowledge that the object still exists) is assumed to be present quite early in infancy; development occurs as infants gradually overcome the performance limitations (e.g., inability to organize search routines) that prevent them from demonstrating that competence. Similarly, in Gelman's work on counting (Chapter 4), the basic principles that underlie counting are assumed to be in place early on, and developmental changes in counting are attributed primarily (although not totally—see Gelman, 1997) to increased skill in acting on these principles.

Alternatively perhaps there are different kinds of transitive inference, different competences, such that the most advanced form is a basically different kind of knowledge than the earliest, fledgling form. We have seen models of this sort also, including the original Piagetian six-stage theory of object permanence. And whether we posit one ability or several, what exactly goes on inside the child's head when he engages in a transitive inference? What cognitive processes intervene between the initial representation of the problem and the final generation of a response? Why are these particular processes selected, and how are they integrated and sequenced in the course of problem solution? Questions such as these are at the heart of the conceptualization part of cognitive diagnosis.

Unfortunately we possess little certain knowledge about the actual processes underlying transitive inference, or any other interesting cognitive acquisition, for that matter. It is not that we necessarily lack theories; Piaget's theory of concrete operations, for example, provides a model of how not only transitivity but a wide range of other problems are solved. But it has proved very difficult to obtain evidence that can tell us whether the processes proposed by theorists are those that actually characterize children's thinking. Here we briefly consider one approach to this problem, some research by Trabasso and colleagues (Bryant & Trabasso, 1971; Trabasso, 1975, 1977). This research suggests some surprising conclusions about how transitivity problems are solved. It will also serve to give us an example of an important information-processing methodology.

The participants in the Trabasso studies were repeatedly shown the adjacent pairs of a series of different length sticks, A > B, B > C, C > D, D > E, each stick identifiable by its color. This initial phase continued until the child had clearly memorized the relative lengths of each adjacent pair. A test phase followed, during which the child was asked to predict the relative lengths of *all* the possible A through E pairs, not just those that had been directly presented. Measures were taken not only of the solution offered but also of the time taken to reach a solution. According to the standard view of how transitive inferences are made, children arrive at an answer by logically combining the relevant premises at the time of solution. By this view, B versus E, which requires the addition of three premises (B > C, C > D, D > E), should take longer to solve than B versus D, which requires the addition of only two premises, and both should take longer than any directly learned pair, such as A versus B or C versus D. In fact just the opposite proved to be true: the farther apart the two sticks in the A . . . E series, the shorter the solution time when comparing them. Thus, children were actually faster on B versus E, which they had never seen together during training, than B versus C, which they had seen together repeatedly.

Trabasso's explanation for the response-time data focuses on the way in which participants represent the information while learning the adjacent pairs. Rather than storing information about individual pairs (A > B, B > C, etc.), children are hypothesized to construct an internal, imagelike representation of the entire ordered array: A > B > C > D > E. Once this representation is constructed, they can solve any problem by simply "reading off" the length comparison, much as though the five sticks were all lined up in order of length before their eyes. Because B and E are farther apart and more different in length than B and D, B versus E is solved more quickly than B versus D. In contrast to the logical reasoning processes stressed in Piaget's theory, transitivity by this view is a matter more of constructive memory combined with mental imagery.

Trabasso has not shown that people never use inferential rather than quasiperceptual processes when dealing with transitivity problems, or that older children do not know anything about transitive inference that younger ones do not. Personally we doubt that his model applies to every act of transitive inference at every developmental level, and the nature and development of transitive reasoning in fact remains a controversial and actively researched topic (Andrews & Halford, 1998; Goswami, 1995; Holcomb, Stromer, & Mackay, 1997; Verweij, Sijtsma, & Koops, 1999). Nevertheless Trabasso's results furnish some striking, and unexpected, evidence of how certain kinds of transitivity problems are solved. And his research provides both specific testimony to the value of response-time data (a favorite information-processing methodology) and a general model of how theories of underlying process can be evaluated empirically.

Some Conclusions regarding Diagnosis

We have said that the objectives of cognitive diagnosis include (1) determining the psychological nature of the acquisition in question; (2) determining its typical developmental course, including sequential changes in its psychological nature, its evocability, and its utilizability; (3) devising assessment procedures that can tell us what a particular child "has," or where the child stands developmentally, with respect to (1) and (2). The successful achievement of all three diagnostic objectives is crucially important for several reasons.

One reason is that we cannot determine how various cognitive entities are related without accurate diagnosis. As we discuss more fully in the next section, one major goal of cognitive-developmental research is to identify the interrelations or patterns that hold among the numerous acquisitions that constitute childhood cognitive development. One pattern of interest is that of invariant sequence: the possibility that X always emerges in development before Y, and perhaps that X and Y always emerge before Z. Another pattern of interest—one that is central to the claims of stage theories—is that of concurrence: the possibility that X, Y, and Z all emerge at the same time in development. Whether the focus is on sequences or concurrences, the conclusions that we draw are completely dependent on the accuracy of our diagnoses. If our tests for X, Y, and Z are differentially sensitive—more prone to either false-negative errors or false-positive errors in some cases than in others—then we are quite likely to misjudge the true temporal relation among the acquisitions. In addition, a better analysis of the processes that underlie X, Y, and Z—that is, a revised answer to the conceptualization question—might reveal that the relations among the various acquisitions could not be what we at first thought they were. We might decide, for example, that Y is an entirely different kind of cognitive creature than we had believed, making it quite implausible that it could be either a descendant of X or an ancestor of Z.

Questions of diagnosis are also central to another major goal of cognitive-developmental research: explaining how cognitive change comes about. When we study children's cognitive development, we hope not only to describe the various states through which the cognitive system moves but also to explain how one state changes into another. But clearly we can do so only if we have accurately diagnosed what the various states are. If our conceptualizations of what is developing are faulty or our assessments of various knowledge states are in error, then our explanations of cognitive change are unlikely to be correct.

Finally diagnosis is central to all psychological study, cognitive developmental or other. In the case of cognitive development, we absolutely must somehow penetrate to the processual heart of the acquisitions we call "transitive inference," the concept of "false belief," and so on, and also we must be able to assess with precision where individual children stand in relation to these acquisitions. Everything that we conclude about cognitive development—our very picture of what that development "is"—depends ultimately on diagnosis.

Because diagnosis is so central to everything that we do, an attempt to review diagnostic innovations and what they have told us would be essentially a review of this entire book. Nevertheless we would like to offer a few reminders of what seem to us some especially important messages that emerge from recent attempts at cognitive diagnosis.

One message is that for a number of years our assessment techniques led us to underestimate what children were capable of. As newer and more sensitive techniques have been devised, our picture of childhood competence has grown more positive. This revised picture is most evident with regard to infant development. The main innovation here has been the invention and clever exploitation of techniques (such as habituation-dishabituation) that minimize motoric and other extraneous response demands on the young infant, thus yielding a clearer picture of what babies really know. Our view of the preschool child—the poor, failure-prone "preoperational" subject of Piagetian theory—has also grown more positive. The reduction of the verbal demands that characterized many assessments has been important here, as has been a general simplification, stripping down, and movement toward child-friendly and child-natural methods of assessment.

A second message is that it is important not to overstate the implications of these findings of earlier-than-expected competence. Some competence is not full competence, and at any point in development we need a clear model not only of what children can do but also of what still remains to be developed. A 3-year-old may be more competent in a variety of domains than we used to believe, but her competence is seldom fully equivalent to that of a 12-year-old. Specifying the different senses and levels of "having" a concept is, as we saw, a central challenge for cognitive diagnosis. The point for now is simply that it is important not to confuse "first has" with "fully has" (see also Chandler, 1991, Haith, 1993, and Smith, 1991).

A third point concerns the conceptualization aspect of diagnosis—that is, the characterization of the psychological processes that underlie the overt performances that our assessment instruments reveal. Despite some recent advances, it should be clear that we still have much to learn here. It is possible that some relatively new approaches to assessment will provide insights that have not been forthcoming from traditional approaches. For example sociocultural theorists emphasize the social origins of individual thought, and the assessment methods that they have devised correspondingly focus not on the child in isolation but on the child in interaction with some more mature, and helpful, other. To the extent that thought really is created in the context of such interactions, these "dynamic" methods of assessment reveal something about how cognitive processes are assembled and organized (but see Paris & Cross, 1988, and Grigorenko & Sternberg, 1998, for critiques of this approach to diagnosis). As we saw in Chapter 1, a major goal of the information-processing approach has always been to devise methodologies that can take us beyond surface performance to get at underlying process. The response-time technique utilized by Trabasso in the research discussed earlier in this section is one example of such a method; the Siegler rule-assessment approach discussed in Chapter 5 is another example. We have seen examples of a third influential approach, the microgenetic method, at various points throughout the book, and we consider microgenetic studies again later in this chapter. Undoubtedly a main reason for the popularity of the information-processing approach is the promise that it seems to hold of finally providing some answers to questions of underlying process.

Just in case the foregoing does not seem to pose sufficient complexities and uncertainties, we add one more point. We have been assuming throughout the discussion—and will continue to assume in what follows—that it makes sense to talk of children as "having" or "not having" particular concepts or forms of knowledge. Even this minimal consensus on the conceptualization question, however, has come under fire in recent years. As we have seen, in connectionist approaches (e.g., Plunkett, 1998) children do not "have" concepts or rules; what they have are patterns of activational strength that determine response in particular situations. Similarly dynamic systems theorists (e.g., Samuelson & Smith, 2000) forswear any talk of knowledge that is permanently represented in the mind; in this approach intelligence is always an active, on-the-spot creation, with past experience and present circumstances combining to determine response. Given such fundamental disagreements about the very nature of what is developing, it is a safe prediction that issues of conceptualization will continue to engage the field for many years to come.

PATTERNS

A number of cognitive-developmental entities (concepts, skills, etc.) emerge during an individual's childhood. How might these entities be related to one another in ontogenetic time? What patterns might be discernible in the developmental mosaic?

One possibility is that one entity regularly develops prior to another—that is, a pattern of invariant *sequence*. The temporal relation in this case is one of systematic asynchrony: One thing always emerges before another. A second possibility is that the relation is one of synchrony rather than asynchrony: Two or more entities emerge at the same time in development. The pattern in this case is one of *concurrence*. Finally it is possible that during certain periods of childhood a whole group of similar or related entities emerge synchronously or concurrently. Such an ensemble of concurrent, tightly knit developments might be referred to as a major *stage* of cognitive growth. A stage would constitute a very important type of developmental pattern.

Sequences

The following discussion of cognitive-developmental sequences is largely based on Flavell (1972, 1982b). Other useful sources include Dixon (1998), Fischer (1980), Kingma and Van Den Bos (1988), Siegler (1981), and Wohlwill (1973).

Challenges of two sorts confront us when we attempt to determine whether two cognitive entities, X and Y, really develop in the sequence X-Y. One sort of challenge is diagnostic. As indicated earlier in this chapter, determining when and in what sense a child "has" a particular ability is an extremely difficult enterprise; answering the "has" question in comparable fashion for two or more different abilities is even more difficult. Suppose, in the case of X and Y, that, without our knowing it, our test x for development X had extraneous but very taxing performance demands not present in our test y for development Y. That is, test x is harder and less sensitive than test y because of heavy information-processing requirements or other task factors that have nothing intrinsically to do with the cognitive acquisition the test was designed to measure. Accordingly test x will underestimate the child's level of development of X much more than y will with respect to Y, because it will yield more false-negative type misdiagnoses. This difference in the sensitivities of the two tests could cause developments X and Y to look concurrent when X actually occurs earlier in ontogenesis than Y; it might even create the impression that Y emerges earlier than X. In either case the diagnostic uncertainties would cause us to misjudge the relation between X and Y.

The second challenge in studying sequences is a theoretical one: explaining any X-Y patterns that we may have identified. Sequences are interesting to us only if we can posit some important way in which X and Y might be related to one another. For instance the fact that sensorimotor means-end behavior (X) always develops before concrete-operational weight conservation (Y) is not very interesting, because we cannot imagine how the former could figure directly and importantly in the ontogenesis of the latter. Suppose, however, that we could be sure that X and Y usually do or always do emerge in the sequence X-Y and can also imagine an interesting developmental relationship between the two. What might that relationship be? Drawing on Flavell (1972), we suggest that there are five major types or categories of such relationships: *addition, substitution, modification, inclusion,* and *mediation*.

Addition. In most addition sequences, X and Y are alternative cognitive means to the same goal. Y does not replace X once it develops; it is simply added to the active repertoire of routes to that goal. For example (Chapter 7), children learn to use simple rehearsal strategies (X) before acquiring organizational ones (Y) in memory situations, but the former continue to be used in many of these situations after the latter are developed. Similarly (Chapter 6), Wellman (1990) has suggested that children first acquire some understanding of people's desires (a "desire psychology") and only later add to it some understanding of beliefs (a "belief-desire psychology"). The understanding of beliefs does not supplant the ability to reason on the basis of desires; it simply adds to it to provide a fuller theory of mind.

Substitution. X and Y again represent possible alternatives, but here Y more or less completely replaces or substitutes for X once it is acquired. Younger children respond to number-conservation problems by comparing row lengths and concluding that the longer row has more. When they get older they will abandon that strategy completely, substituting for it an inferential approach that will yield a conservation conclusion. Similarly the strategy of counting up from one when adding will eventually be replaced by more effective strategies, such as the min strategy or memorization of the correct response. Recall an interesting point from this research that may apply to a number of other substitution sequences as well: Early responses do not necessarily disappear immediately when more mature ones emerge; rather, various strategies may coexist for some time.

Modification. In addition and substitution sequences, X and Y are clearly two different cognitive entities. In modification, as the name suggests, there is instead some sort of developmentally progressive modification of a single entity. Y is clearly continuous with and derived from X, as woman from girl or man from boy. Three types of modifications are distinguished: *differentiation, generalization,* and *stabilization.* Initially a child may rehearse items to be remembered in only one way, for example, but in subsequent years she may differentiate several different rehearsal patterns. Likewise any given way of rehearsing may with development become progressively generalized to more and more different memory problems. Finally as any rehearsal pattern continues to be practiced, it stabilizes as a skill— becomes more readily initiated in appropriate circumstances, more skillfully and effortlessly carried out, and so on. As an additional example, sensorimotor schemes differentiate, generalize, and stabilize during infancy.

Inclusion. At some point in X's development, X becomes interconnected or coordinated with one or more other cognitive entities to form part of (become included in) a larger cognitive unit Y. For example the progressive coordination of two sensorimotor schemes to form a means-end whole constitutes an inclusion sequence: Two initially separate Xs are combined to form a larger and more complex Y. In the area of memory development, the earlier-developing ability to name objects becomes integrated into a later-developing rehearsal strategy.

Mediation. In these sequences X serves as a bridge, facilitator, or mediator with respect to the subsequent development of Y. Unlike inclusion sequences, however, X does not become an actual part or component of Y; once developed with the help of (mediation by) X, Y functions independently of X. The inversion and compensation forms of concrete-operational reversible thinking (Chapter 5, *Irreversibility versus reversibility* section) could conceivably help the child achieve conservation solutions to various conservation problems. These forms of thinking do not become integral parts of conservation concepts as, say, a means scheme becomes an integral part of a means-end whole. If we present an adult with a liquid-quantity conservation problem, she surely does not need to go through a whole train of reasoning about how height changes might compensate for width changes in order to reach a conservation conclusion.

Each of these five types of sequences illustrates something about how cognitive growth occurs. The cognitive repertoire is enriched by addition sequences: The child used to have only one approach (X) to a problem but now has two (X and Y). Substitution sequences serve to replace less (X) with more (Y) mature cognitive approaches to problems. A cognitive entity (X) develops to a higher, more mature level (Y) via a modification sequence. Inclusion sequences illustrate that developmental change often occurs neither by modifying old cognitive entities nor by adding or substituting new ones, but by coordinating or integrating existing ones to form larger wholes. Finally mediation sequences show that the development of one cognitive entity can substantially assist the development of another, distinct and independent entity.

Concurrences

The same diagnostic uncertainties that complicate the study of sequences apply as well to any attempt to identify concurrences in development. Again the difficulties in determining whether and exactly how a child "has" X and Y may cause us to miss a true concurrence or to claim a concurrence when none in fact exists.

As with sequences, concurrences are of interest because they tell us something about the nature and the origin of the cognitive entities that we are studying. In the case of concurrences, the relation of interest is one of common underlying basis: X and Y emerge together because they emanate from the same more general cognitive advance, are reflections of the same underlying rule or structure or process, are in some important sense the "same thing."

Research on theory of mind (Chapter 6) provides some examples. Recall our suggestion that a central advance in theory-of-mind development is the realization that the mind can represent objects and events either accurately or inaccurately. A number of specific developments can be plausibly linked to this very general realization: level 2 perspective taking, understanding of false belief, understanding of representational change, and mastery of the appearance-reality distinction, among others. As we saw in Chapter 6, these competencies tend to emerge at about the same time—namely, somewhere around age 4. Furthermore they are substantially correlated within children—that is, if we assess several of the abilities in the same sample we find that children tend to be consistent in their performance, either passing all or failing all (Flavell, Green, & Flavell, 1990; Gopnik & Astington, 1988). The correlations are not perfect, but then we would not expect them to be; the various competencies are only in part the "same thing," and in any case the diagnostic complexities that we have been stressing keep us from expecting a perfect relation between any two assessments. Nevertheless it is an important task for further work—not only on theory of mind but also with regard to other purported concurrences—to determine just how close is close enough when we attempt to decide whether two abilities really emerge at the same time. Most concurrences seem to be of the loose, at-about-the-same-time sort rather than tight, can't-have-one-without-the-other synchrony.

Another important question concerns the breadth or scope of concurrences in development. Few psychologists doubt that certain closely related abilities may emerge in at least rough synchrony. The claims of stage theories, however, are much stronger than this: very many interrelated abilities, all emerging at about the same time because they are all reflections of the same general stage of cognitive development. It is to the notion of stage that we turn next.

Stages

There is no shortage of discussions of stages and of issues related to stages. Among the useful sources are Bidell and Fischer (1992), Carey (1987), Case (1986, 1992), Ceci (1989), Demetriou, Efklides, and Platsidou (1993), Fischer and Silvern (1985), Flavell (1971c, 1982a, 1982b, 1992a), Flavell and Wohlwill (1969), Levin (1986), Miller (2001), and Pinard and Laurendeau (1969).

It is useful to focus on Piaget's stage of concrete operations when discussing this topic, since it has been the subject of more theoretical and experimental attention than any other. Our tentative conclusions about stages extend beyond that particular one, however. Indeed these conclusions extend beyond debates about whether development is or is not stagelike, since the issues involved are central ones in any conception of how development comes about. Most of what needs discussing in this area falls under the headings of *structures, qualitative change, abruptness,* and—once again and above all—*concurrence.*

Structures.   Piaget argued that what we actually acquire when we acquire, say, concrete operations is a unified set of cognitive *structures,* not just an accumulation of mutually isolated and independent, psychologically unconnected cognitive entities. In fact, the presence of such unified structures—*structures d'ensemble* he called them—was one of Piaget's major criteria for asserting that a given set of developments constitutes a stage.

We can ask two questions concerning cognitive-developmental structures. First, when a given body of knowledge, cognitive skills, and so on has been acquired, might cognitive structures of any sort have been acquired? Do at least some of the products of cognitive growth become interrelated in our heads, get linked into organized functional wholes, or do they tend to remain unorganized, unintegrated, and unconnected? There are good reasons to think that they do become interrelated, both in the area of concrete-operational thinking and elsewhere. This general assumption is common to a number of theoretical positions in addition to Piaget; for example the coherence and interrelatedness of beliefs within a domain is a central tenet of the theory theory approach. We doubt if a serious case could be made that the various processes and concepts inhabiting our cognitive systems do not interact with or otherwise link up with one another—do not exhibit "structure" (Flavell, 1971c, 1982b).

Piaget did not just assert that concrete-operational thinking is structured, however. Rather he argued that it possesses a definite, specific type of structure or organization. In fact he proposed quite detailed logical-mathematical models of how cognition is structured at both the concrete-operational and formal-operational stages. We did not present these models in Chapter 5, for two reasons: Their complexity defies any brief description, and they have in any case not fared well in recent years. Piaget's structural models have been the subject of intense critical scrutiny, the consensus from which seems to be that they are in varying degrees unclear, incorrect, and incomplete as theoretical descriptions of underlying mental processes. Indeed Piaget himself eventually grew dissatisfied with these models and explored other structural descriptions in his last writings (e.g., Piaget, 1985). It seems reasonable, then, to conclude that, in fact, there is considerable mental organization in the area of concrete-operational thinking, as there undoubtedly is in other areas, but that the specific formal structures Piaget proposed may not capture it very well (Flavell, 1982a, 1982b).

Qualitative Change. One is not tempted to talk about developmental stages in the case of age changes that are purely quantitative in nature. Consider the digit-span memory test mentioned in Chapter 5. It would sound silly to say that Mary was in the "three-digit stage" last year but has now entered the "four-digit stage." A stage-type characterization perhaps would not sound so silly if she had used a re-hearsal strategy to memorize things last year but then switched over to a wholly different strategy this year—for example, elaboration. A quantitative change from little apples to big apples is never called a stage change; a qualitative change from apples to oranges might be. If there were no qualitative changes in cognitive development, there could be no "stages" of cognitive development in any meaningful sense.

Are there any such qualitative changes? The answer depends on what one means by "qualitative" and on one's level of analysis or universe of discourse. We personally find it easy to think of the substitution of one memory strategy for another, or a switch from a perceptually based nonconservation answer to a conceptually based conservation one, as qualitative developmental changes; they seem like apples-to-oranges-type transformations. On the other hand, the developmental processes—whatever they are—that underlie these behavioral changes may not exhibit any real qualitative transformations, any significant discontinuities. What looks like a qualitative change at one level of analysis may not at another.

Abruptness. Cognitive development would look very stagelike if the transition from one cognitive level to another were abrupt rather than gradual. Consider as an example conservation of weight, a concrete-operational acquisition. Suppose that acquisition typically occurred very abruptly. One day, the child shows no signs of weight conservation; the next day, it is present in fully mature form. If the emergence of weight conservation and other concrete-operational accomplishments occurred in such an abrupt, metamorphosislike fashion, it would seem wholly natural to speak of stages. Indeed, even that abrupt a *quantitative* change would seem somewhat stage-like.

The truth of the matter, however, is that most important cognitive developments appear to proceed slowly and gradually rather than abruptly. As indicated in Chapter 5, concepts such as conservation and transitivity of weight may continue to mature, in the sense of becoming further consolidated and solidified, well after the point of first emergence. In Chapter 4 we saw that the same point applies to class inclusion. The development of object permanence (Chapter 3) provides another example. Clearly there are more and less mature ways of "having" weight conservation and many other cognitive-developmental products. Research evidence suggests that the period in the child's life between initial, minimal possession and fully mature, maximal command can be a matter of years.

Such evidence changes the meaning of "stage" in an interesting way. For a major stage like concrete operations, we might have expected a very brief period of change and transition, during which concrete operations emerge and mature, followed by several years of relative stasis and quiescence, during which the child is more or less stably and unchangeably concrete-operational in his thinking. If, instead, the child actually continues to perfect, generalize, and solidify his grasp of weight conservation and other stage-related achievements throughout most of middle childhood and perhaps beyond, the stage of concrete operations is all change and transition, with little or no stasis and stability. Thus the stage itself, and not the transition to it, becomes the period of continuous growth and change.

This revised conception reduces the predictability of the stage concept. Because of this continuous growth and change, one cannot predict the child's responses to concrete-operational tasks merely from the knowledge that he is in the concrete-operational stage, as one could have if being in that stage meant continuing to have essentially the same mental structure for a period of years. It is still possible, however, that the hypothesized manifestations of a stage might show the sort of interrelatedness that the notion of stage seems to imply. Suppose that all concrete-operational skills developed concurrently in an interdependent, mutually facilitative fashion. The fact that all these synchronous, closely interacting developments took a long rather than a short time to be completed would not mean that the term "stage" could not be applied meaningfully and usefully to this developmental pattern. We would simply have a more dynamic concept of stage, one that refers to an extended process of concurrent, interdependent developmental changes.

Concurrence. In fact, most developmental psychologists believe that just this kind of tightly interlocked, concurrent growth must obtain in an area of cognitive development if the term "stage" is to be usefully applied to that area. If concrete-operational entities do not really develop concurrently, for instance, they would say that the concept "concrete-operational stage" is theoretically vacuous. (For a dissenting view on this point, however, see Wohlwill, 1973, Chapter 9, and for a somewhat different interpretation of what Piaget's theory predicts, see Chapman, 1988, and Lourenco & Machado, 1996). The general reason for expecting concurrence is the same as that discussed with respect to pairs of abilities: Competencies that emanate from the same underlying cognitive basis should emerge at about the same time in development. In this case, however, the posited underlying basis is quite broad in scope—namely, a general stage of cognitive functioning—and hence the expected concurrence is also quite broad. The prediction—to state the case in terms used earlier in the book—is thus of a considerable degree of domain generality in children's cognitive functioning.

We have discussed both the complexities of diagnosing cognitive entities in isolation and the compounding of the difficulty when two entities must be assessed in comparable fashion simultaneously, as is the case with either an X-before-Y sequence or an X-and-Y-together concurrence. When concurrences of the general-stage sort are at issue, X and Y are joined by U, V, W . . . , and the problems of matching test sensitivity grow correspondingly greater. Although some researchers appear to have been quite skillful in equating the sensitivity of their tests, there really is no way one can be sure that this goal has been achieved, and therefore no way to be absolutely sure that the concurrence hypothesis is receiving a valid assessment (see Dixon, 1998, for a helpful analysis).

Despite these problems we think it is possible to make an educated guess about concurrence-nonconcurrence. Our guess is that nonconcurrence is the rule and concurrence the exception. Two types of relationship among concrete-operational entities are perhaps most commonly seen (albeit through a murky diagnostic lens). In one type, one entity regularly develops prior to another in most or all individuals tested. The pattern, therefore, is not the stage-consistent one of synchrony but rather one of systematic asynchrony, or invariant sequence. Although sequences (as we have just been stressing) may be interesting in themselves, they do not provide support for the usual interpretation of stage. In the other type of relationship, a pair of entities may develop at roughly the same age, on the average, but their levels of development are not highly correlated with one another within individuals. One may be developmentally more advanced than the other in this child; the opposite may be true in that child. Whatever concurrence there may be is therefore of the rough, group-average sort. There is little evidence that the developments are interdependent or mutually facilitative in the way that a stage characterization would suggest.

Conclusions about Stages.   As noted in Chapter 5, developmental psychologists have become increasingly skeptical in recent years about the theoretical utility of the construct of "cognitive-developmental stage." In particular Piaget's concrete-operational and formal-operational stages have been sharply criticized. The structures used to model concrete- and formal-operational thinking appear inadequate; the stage-to-stage developmental changes not quite so exclusively qualitative if you look at underlying processes; the within-stage changes more gradual, important, and extended in time than originally believed; and the same-stage developments less concurrent than Piagetian theory seemed to require. It is noteworthy that none of the relatively new theoretical positions that have emerged in the last dozen or so years (the theory theory perspective, connectionism, dynamic systems theory, modularity nativism) makes much if any use of the concept of stages of development.

Does all of this mean that the concept of stage is destined to disappear from developmental research and theorizing? Not necessarily, and in any case (our best guess here) maybe not completely. For one thing, neo-Piagetian theorists continue to develop stage models that attempt to retain the insights of Piaget's work while at the same time jettisoning some of its less promising features (such as the logical-mathematical structures) and incorporating modern emphases not considered by Piaget (such as changes in information-processing capacity). We discussed one major such attempt, the work of Robbie Case, in Chapter 1 (Case, 1998, 1999; Case & Okamoto, 1996).

Furthermore even approaches that eschew the notion of stage may retain some of the positive features of stage theories. The development-as-theory-change position (Chapters 1, 4, and 6), for example, includes a focus on the coherence of mental processes, the possibility of qualitative changes with development, and the sequential emergence of progressively more advanced competencies—all aspects of the stage approach. A major difference, of course, is that these developments are seen as occurring within a particular domain (physics, biology, etc.) rather than across the board. The domains are very broad ones, however, and thus there is still some of the generality afforded by stage conceptions. Furthermore, although we know that children's thinking does not show the cross-domain consistency required by a strong version of the general-stage approach, we still have an incomplete picture of how much consistency might actually obtain. As Wellman and Gelman (1998, p. 560) note, "Empirical studies of naïve psychology, biology, and physics have almost never attempted detailed comparisons of understandings across these domains." Perhaps one task for the next generation of research will be to probe the extent to which the domains that have emerged so clearly in the most recent generation of studies can be put back together.

COGNITIVE CHANGE

How is cognitive growth accomplished? What factors or variables play what roles in influencing the nature, rate of growth, and ultimate adult level of various forms of knowledge and cognitive ability? How, in short, can we *explain* the various changes we may have *diagnosed?*

Not surprisingly accounting for cognitive growth is at least as problematic as diagnosing forms of knowledge and identifying patterns among them. It is difficult to be sure even what is meant when we speak of "explaining" cognitive change or of specifying "causes" of development. What is it that makes some factor an explanation and not merely a further description of change? It is difficult as well to know whether different would-be explanations are really referring to distinct contributors, or whether they are perhaps simply different labels for the same idea. It is difficult to know how to go about studying the issue—how to gather evidence that would allow us to test the validity of any proposed explanation. Finally questions of diagnosis once again loom large, just as they do for any research enterprise. We cannot provide a satisfactory account of change unless we have a clear idea of where the system starts, what intermediate states it moves through, and where it ends up—in short, unless we know what it is that we are attempting to explain.

Our overview of theories in Chapter 1 touched on some of the ideas about change that are found in the major contemporary theoretical positions, and the examinations of particular topics in the ensuing chapters included some further discussions of sources and mechanisms of change. The goals of the present section are both to bring together some of this earlier material and to consider further some of the complexities and uncertainties that are involved in the study of change. We do so under three general headings: biological contributors to cognitive growth; experiential contributors and sources of influence, both social and nonsocial; and developmental principles, processes, or mechanisms that may operate to produce change. Useful further sources on this topic include Amsel and Renninger (1997), Butterworth and Bryant (1990), Carey and Gelman (1991), Demetriou and Raftopoulos (1999), de Ribaupierre (1989), McClelland and Siegler (2000), Okagaki and Sternberg (1991), Siegler (1996, 1997), and van der Maas and Hopkins (1998). Accounts of Piaget's revised equilibration theory (his conception of how children make cognitive-developmental progress) can be found in Chapman (1988) and Piaget (1985).

Biological Contributors to Cognitive Development

The idea that biological-maturational factors play a central role in shaping the nature, the timing, and the direction of cognitive development is a much more frequently discussed and seriously entertained proposition than was the case even a dozen years ago. Chapters or sections developing specific aspects of this general proposition can be found in many of the listed references, and we add further references throughout this section. Two especially valuable sources—not only for their reviews of the literature but for thoughtful, and contrasting, views of the notion of "innate" knowledge—are Elman et al. (1996) and Spelke and Newport (1998).

The general reason for the increase in nativistic theorizing is well summarized by Fischer and Bidell (1991, p. 200):

> The behavioral abilities with which human beings are genetically endowed are far richer and more complex than traditional accounts of cognitive development imply. New research seems to have revealed rich sets of perceptual and cognitive abilities in infants and young children. A key neo-nativist argument appears to be that these early abilities show the starting points from which cognitive development must emerge. As starting points, they set limits or constraints on what is possible and thereby help to channel the direction of development.

As the passage from Fischer and Bidell suggests, it is findings with regard to infant precocity that have been most responsible for the surge of nativistic theorizing in recent years. Infants have turned out to be more competent than we used to believe, and many of the competencies are evident at such early ages that it is impossible to see how they could be instilled by the environment. Furthermore the kinds of precocious competence that have been identified in recent research appear to correspond to biologically natural, species-typical domains of knowledge—that is, to precisely the sorts of knowledge that we would expect our evolutionary history to have prepared us to acquire quickly and easily. Language is the most long recognized and perhaps least disputed of these natural domains. Among the other domains for which innate structuring and innately given principles appear to be important are perception of objects (Chapters 2 and 3), perception of causality (Chapter 3), abstraction of number (Chapter 4), and theory of mind (Chapter 6).

The demonstrations of earlier-than-expected competence are not the only respect in which recent work departs from what had been established wisdom. Also unexpected has been the highly domain-specific nature of many of these early developments. We seem to be biologically prepared to do very specific kinds of information processing and very specific kinds of learning, with no apparent links between one set of processing mechanisms (e.g., those for discriminating speech sounds) and another (e.g., those for extracting numerical information). In Chapter 1 we introduced modularity nativism as one contemporary perspective that attempts to explain such specialization. By this view biology has equipped us with a number of encapsulated *modules* that, with some minimal environmental triggering, serve to process information in different domains. Other theoretical perspectives talk about these highly specialized capacities in somewhat different ways—as constraints that channel information processing in adaptive directions, for example, or as skeletal principles upon which further developments build. Common to the various conceptions, however, is an emphasis on domain specificity—these are processes that perform very specific tasks, not all-purpose learning mechanisms.

Why might biology have provided us with such specialized cognitive tools? We previewed one possible answer earlier in the reference to "our evolutionary history." The newly emergent field of *evolutionary developmental psychology* attempts to explain contemporary human cognition by reference to the adaptational challenges and selection pressures that faced our hunter/gatherer ancestors in the distant evolutionary past (Cosmides & Tooby, 1994; Geary & Bjorklund, 2000; Langer & Killen, 1998; Tomasello, 1999). A common assumption is that most of these challenges involved local or specific problems that required local solutions. Thus the challenges posed by navigating the spatial environment were different from those involved in mate selection, and both differed from those underlying the learning and use of language. One prediction, therefore, is that cognitive skills will show a high degree of domain specificity. As Cosmides and Tooby (1994, p. 90) put it, "There is no more reason to expect any two cognitive mechanisms to be alike than to expect the eye and spleen, or the pancreas and pituitary, to be alike." Another implication is that only some of the cognitive challenges of contemporary life will correspond to problems and evolved solutions from the quite different circumstances that prevailed thousands or millions of years ago (Geary, 1995). Language, for example, is a selected-for, "biologically primary ability," and thus could be expected to develop in any at all normal environment. Literacy, in contrast, emerged well after the last important evolutionary changes in our cognitive equipment, and reading is therefore a "biologically secondary ability." As such it would be expected to be more difficult to master, more dependent on specific experience, and more variable across children than is language—which, of course, is the case.

This is not to say that all biological contributors to cognitive growth are of the domain-specific sort. Development includes trans-domain as well as within-domain processes and abilities, and biology undoubtedly contributes to the former as well as to the latter. Scarr (1983) provides some interesting speculations with regard to the biological underpinnings for a set of achievements with a good deal of generality, namely, Piagetian sensorimotor development. As is not true of later cognitive acquisitions, Scarr notes, normal human beings everywhere are virtually certain to complete Piagetian sensorimotor development. As she puts it: "Do you know anyone who didn't make it to preoperational thought" (p. 211)? She speculates that the sensorimotor ontogenetic pattern evolved earlier in our primate past than those that follow it in childhood cognitive development—for example, concrete-operational thought.

The evolutionary selection pressures that led to the establishment of sensorimotor development ensured its specieswide universality in two ways: They acted on the infant and they acted on his environment, including the behavior of his caretakers. On the infant's side, selection pressures are hypothesized to have produced an organism genetically predisposed or "canalized" towards the sequential acquisition of Piagetian sensorimotor schemes rather than other imaginable cognitive attainments. This organism's evolutionary history has powerfully biased it to develop in that direction, and we would presumably have to rear it in a highly deviant, "nonhuman" way to prevent that development or deflect its basic course. On the environmental side, evolutionary selection pressures have produced a species-typical, characteristically "human" rearing environment for this genetically specialized organism. Moreover it is just the sort of environment needed to promote sensorimotor development in this particular organism. Naturally, human environments differ in many ways, and these differences undeniably contribute to individual differences in cognition, especially in later childhood and adulthood. There are also some basic commonalities across human environments, however, and these are believed to constitute the essential psychological nutriments for the acquisition of sensorimotor intelligence. Despite their diversity within and between cultures, infant worlds are "functionally equivalent," as Scarr puts it, in their capacities to support this particular process of acquisition. They all provide social and nonsocial objects, events, and experiential opportunities of the kinds needed to allow a properly designed organism to develop sensorimotor cognitive structures.

Notice that this view in no way denies the vital role of environment and experience in the process of cognitive growth. Environmental elements do not become any less essential to a particular form of development just because they are virtually certain to be available for its use. Their near-universality may make it difficult for us to detect them, but they are no less indispensable because of their low visibility. Similarly the modules-constraints-skeletal principles positions discussed earlier do not deny a role for experience; indeed, exactly the opposite is explicitly the case for many of the proponents of such positions. What biology provides is not the end point of development but rather the capacities that allow us to utilize experience in order to reach that end point.

So far we have said quite a bit about biological contributors to development without once going beneath the skin to talk about the physiological substrates and physiological processes (neurons, dendrites, synapses, parts of the brain, etc.) that underlie these contributions. An earlier edition of this book justified such reticence with the statement "We currently know nothing about the physiological events and processes underlying cognitive development." This is no longer the case. As we noted in Chapter 1, recent research in developmental cognitive neuroscience has produced an explosion of findings with respect to brain development and brain-behavior relations, much of it made possible by the development of new techniques for measuring brain activity. Here we briefly consider two lines of argument concerning possible physiological bases for cognitive change, both of which were touched on earlier in the book. Among the sources for more detailed treatments are Fox, Leavitt, and Warhol (1999); Johnson (1998, 1999a, 1999b); Nelson (1999); and Nelson and Bloom (1997). Valuable discussion of the psychological implications of the new knowledge about the brain—including cautions with respect to popular-press versions of the "new brain science"—can be found in Bransford, Brown, and Cocking (1999) and Breur (1999).

As we saw in Chapter 3, Adele Diamond (1991a, 1991b, 1999, 2000) has argued that many of the cognitive advances of infancy are made possible by maturational changes in the infant's brain. The advance on which we focused in Chapter 3 was Piagetian object permanence, but Diamond cites a variety of other examples as well. The maturational changes that she emphasizes involve the frontal cortex: changes in the supplementary motor area, in dorsolateral prefrontal cortex, and in connections and communication among regions of the cortex. For our purposes the specific biological bases are less important than the chain of reasoning and evidence that leads to the conclusion that a particular maturational change underlies a particular behavioral development. Consider again the object permanence task. Successful response to object permanence tasks requires not only the knowledge that hidden objects still exist (Piaget's interest) but also the ability to organize behaviors into search sequences and to inhibit prepotent but nonoptimal responses (such as the reach for A in an A-not-B paradigm). It is these latter developments, Diamond believes, that must wait upon frontal lobe development in the last half of the first year—which is why infants' ability to act adaptively in hidden-object situations lags so far beyond their first demonstrations of knowledge.

Several kinds of evidence converge on this conclusion. There is, to begin with, an impressive degree of temporal synchrony between developments in the behavioral and biological realms; maturational changes in frontal cortex coincide nicely with the emerging achievements that such changes are meant to explain. In itself, of course, such synchrony is a necessary but far from sufficient basis for inferring a causal relation, since many things are undergoing more or less simultaneous change at any point in a child's development. The synchrony argument gains

strength, however, from the fact that similar biology-behavior parallels can be identified in other species at times that correspond to major maturational changes for the
species in question. In rhesus monkeys, for example, changes in frontal cortex occur
several months earlier than in human infants, and improvements on search
and delayed-response tasks are also evident several months earlier. Research with
other species, moreover, offers kinds of evidence not available with humans.
Experimental interruption of normal frontal lobe functioning—either permanently
through surgical lesions or temporarily through techniques such as drug administra-
tion—produces deficits in the ability to inhibit behavior and to solve search and
delayed-response tasks. The effects, moreover, are quite specific—not across-the-
board deficits but impairment of precisely those functions that are thought to be
governed by the brain areas in question. In intact and normally functioning brains,
increases in both electrical and metabolic activity are evident in the frontal lobe regions when search and delayed-response tasks are performed. Finally adult humans
who have sustained lesions to the frontal lobes show behavioral deficits that are in
some ways parallel to those of young infants. They have difficulty, for example, in
inhibiting dominant responses and in maintaining memory for objects or locations
over time.

The second posited neurological basis for cognitive change was briefly discussed in Chapter 1. It involves a process called *synaptogenesis*. Synapses are
junctions between neurons across which information can be transmitted, and synaptogenesis is the process by which such connections are established. The growth of
synapses shows an interesting developmental course: The number of synapses in
many regions of the brain peaks during infancy and then gradually declines across
childhood. Thus, infants and toddlers actually have more synapses (up to 50 to 60
percent more in some regions of the brain) than do adults. Much of development,
then, seems to consist of a pruning back of synapses following the initial phase of
overproduction (Huttenlocher, 1999).

Greenough and colleagues (Greenough & Black, 1999; Greenough, Black, &
Wallace, 1987) have argued that experience plays an important role in determining
which synapses survive and which are pruned back. They present a variety of kinds
of evidence that indicates that neural connections are most likely to survive if experience gives them a chance to be utilized; conversely, in the absence of relevant experience, connections may wither away. This sort of selective survival of synapses is seen
as being especially important for what Greenough and colleagues label *experience-
expectant* processes. The term experience-expectant refers to developments that are
essentially species-wide because the necessary experiences are available in any normal, expectable environment that a member of the species might encounter (in contrast, *experience-dependent* processes depend on individual learning and the
formation of new synaptic connections rather than the survival of preexisting ones).
For example early visual input of various sorts is necessary for normal visual development in a variety of species; such input, however, is ensured in any normal,
species-typical environment. Because the necessary experience is available, the
synaptic connections that are activated by such input will be maintained and development of the visual system will proceed normally. Note the similarity between this
position and Scarr's (1983) more macrolevel discussion of the evolutionary basis
for sensorimotor development. In both cases biology and experience are assumed to
act together to produce the normal course of development for the species. And in
both cases experience does not create or strongly mold this developmental course;

rather we develop as we do because we are biologically predisposed to utilize any reasonably normal set of experiences in species-typical and adaptive ways.

Environmental-Experiential Contributors to Cognitive Development

There are many ways to conceptualize and to cut up the environmental sources for cognitive growth. Perhaps the most general cut is the division between social and nonsocial: what children acquire from their interactions with other people, versus what they acquire from their dealings with the inanimate physical world. Within the realm of social experience we can draw a distinction among different social agents: parents, teachers, siblings, peers. Social experiences can also be divided into those that are explicitly instructional (such as schooling) and those whose cognitive benefits are more incidental and happenstantial. Whether the experience is social or nonsocial, we can ask about the child's own contribution; to what extent is development a matter of self-generated discovery or construction, as opposed to a direct taking in of information from the environment? We can ask about specific modalities and specific types of experiences—what do we acquire from vision, hearing, touch, movement, language? Many theorists have addressed a number of these dimensions, and the field as a whole offers a variety of ideas with respect to each of them.

Suppose that we have identified a putative environmental contributor to cognitive growth—some factor A that we believe helps to engender development X. How can we determine whether A does in fact play a role in the development of X? Two common strategies are to see how X fares in children who have been experimentally provided with A, and to study the development of X in children who for some reason have gone without A. Such investigations are often called *enrichment* and *deprivation* studies, respectively. Piagetian training studies are enrichment studies; see Beilin (1978), Field (1987), Halford (1982), and Kuhn (1974) for more information on this extensive body of research. An investigator interested in explaining Piagetian acquisitions might hypothesize that a certain A is the usual developmental bridge to a certain X in everyday human ontogenesis. She might believe, for example, that children gradually acquire conservation of number in the natural environment by gradually learning, through practice coupled with informational feedback, to attend to number-relevant information and disregard number-irrelevant information, such as length of row. She then does a training study to test her hypothesis. Children who do not yet conserve number are provided with such practice and feedback to see if it leads them to give conservation instead of nonconservation responses. In effect the investigator attempts to simulate or mimic development in the laboratory in order to explain how it proceeds in everyday life, much as other psychologists try to simulate human problem solving on the computer in hopes of explaining how it proceeds in human minds.

In neither case, however, is it possible for the researcher to conclude that nature has been faithfully imitated—that what happened in the training experience or in the computer is the same as what normally happens in real-life conservation development or problem solving. The same outcomes may have been achieved in both nature and its attempted simulation (although it is sometimes hard to be sure even of this). This is no guarantee, however, that the same processes were responsible for those outcomes. In the developmental case, it is unfortunately true that enrichment studies are just logically incapable of proving that a certain kind of experiential or milieu factor is a *nec-*

essary contributor to any development. In real life some or all children may acquire conservation of number with the aid of a wholly different factor, via some entirely different "developmental route." The investigator's enrichment study cannot rule out this possibility, no matter how effective her training regimen proved to be in that study. At most such studies can suggest how the development of something *could* proceed; they do not tell us how it actually *does* proceed.

What about deprivation studies? Unlike the case with enrichment experiments, it would be highly unethical to do a deprivation experiment on children. One can, however, study the effects of deprivations that occur naturally. But there are also problems in interpreting deprivation studies. In particular it may be difficult to determine precisely of what the child in question has and has not been deprived. Deprivation studies can nevertheless be very useful in determining whether particular kinds of experience are really necessary for particular sorts of development.

In a general sense, the message that emerges from deprivation studies is the same as the message suggested by Piagetian training studies. Both kinds of study suggest that human beings are flexible and versatile learners who can utilize a variety of experiences and follow a number of developmental routes in moving toward the same eventual end point. In the case of training studies, an astonishing diversity of experimentally provided experiences have proved to be beneficial in helping children to master conservation and other concrete-operational concepts. If we assume that laboratory demonstrations of this sort have any real-life applicability, the conclusion must be that no single kind of experience underlies such acquisitions for all children; rather children are capable of extracting the same knowledge from a diverse range of inputs.

In the case of deprivation studies, cognitive growth has often been found to proceed remarkably well despite major limitations in the ability to utilize certain kinds of experience. For example, research by Furth (1971) and others on deaf children has shown that many aspects of cognitive development are surprisingly similar in deaf and hearing children, despite the fact that the former group are deprived of auditory input in general and (in the case of many deaf children) linguistic input in particular. Recent studies of theory of mind add to this conclusion; although deaf children of hearing parents tend to be slowed down in theory of mind development (as we noted in Chapter 6), those with deaf parents, and thus with exposure to sign language within the home, show no apparent lags (Remmel et al., in press). Research by Landau and colleagues (1991; Landau, Spelke, & Gleitman, 1984) has demonstrated an impressive degree of spatial knowledge in children who have been blind since birth, and hence lacking in the most obvious channel for information about the spatial world. And several case study reports (Décarie, 1969; Jordan, 1972; Kopp & Shaperman, 1973) of children with severe motoric handicaps (e.g., children born with defects of the limbs because their mothers had taken the drug thalidomide during pregnancy) suggest that the ability to manipulate objects with hands or feet is not a necessary condition for normal cognitive development.

Of course a demonstration that development can proceed in the absence of some factor does not mean that the factor is unimportant in the normal, nondeprived case. But it does mean that children are adaptive creatures who can often make do with whatever acquisitional machinery they possess and with whatever environmental content comes their way. If the usual, typical developmental route is blocked, children may find an unusual, atypical one that somehow gets them to at least approximately the same cognitive destination.

We should add some qualifications to these optimistic, Rousseauesque notions of developmental versatility and resiliency. Even if adult-level competence is eventually attained, the rate of development toward this competence may be slowed, and slower-than-average development can pose a number of problems for both child and parent. Furthermore children do not always prove versatile and resilient in the face of organismic or environmental handicaps. Many aspects of intellectual development show marked individual differences in the quality of children's performance, and limitations in relevant experience are undoubtedly one reason that some children do relatively poorly. Many writers of books on cognitive growth would emphasize both individual differences and their origins more than we have done. Nevertheless available knowledge on this important issue is still rather limited: We have much to learn about exactly what sorts of experience at what points in development for what sorts of children nurture what kinds of cognitive acquisitions. The importance of this last variable has often been overlooked. Some kinds of development appear to be much more dependent on specific and variably available experiences than do others. Such developments are more "experience-dependent" in Greenough's terms, more "biologically secondary" in the language of evolutionary psychology. Recall our earlier example. The ability to read and write and the ability to speak and understand oral language are both enormously significant cognitive accomplishments. The development of the latter seems much more "biological-evolutionary" than the former, however, and is much more certain to result from exposure to a normal human environment. Some forms of cognitive development clearly exhibit much more versatility and resiliency than others.

Many of the points made in this section can be illustrated through a brief consideration of a popular current approach to studying the experiential bases for cognitive change: the Vygotsky-inspired sociocultural or contextual approach. More than is true for most approaches to the study of cognitive development, issues of change are central to the sociocultural approach. This centrality is evident in the guiding metaphor for the approach: the child as apprentice (Rogoff, 1990). According to sociocultural theorists, children are embedded in a social context from birth, and cognitive growth occurs through a process of guided participation in which others, especially parents, provide various kinds of help tailored to the child's current level of ability (thus working within Vygotsky's "zone of proximal development"). Cognitive development is therefore not an individual but a joint construction, in which children are guided toward culturally embedded skills and bodies of knowledge, rather than having to somehow discover such knowledge on their own.

Undoubtedly part of the reason for the popularity of the sociocultural approach lies in the fact that it seems to redress limitations in some of the other major approaches to children's thinking. Although Piagetian theory does talk about the contribution of social experience, the dominant image that one takes away from Piaget's writings is of the autonomous child who self-constructs knowledge through his own active commerce with the environment. A focus on the child in isolation could also be argued to be characteristic of much of what is said in both the information-processing and IQ or psychometric perspectives on intelligence. The sociocultural child, in contrast, is rooted in a social world from birth. Furthermore sociocultural theorists have offered a number of interesting ideas about what kinds of social experiences are important at what points in development; they have thus at least begun to address the need for specificity with regard to environmental influences that we stressed earlier. And although theorizing so far outstrips research, workers in this tradition have provided some compelling demonstrations of how social interaction can mediate individual development. Examples discussed earlier in the book include Freund's (1990) research on maternal guidance of preschoolers' problem solving (Chapter 1), Saxe's (1991) studies of both familial and cultural contributions to numerical understanding (Chapter 4), and work by various researchers on the social origins of autobiographical memory (Chapter 7). A good idea of the achievements of the sociocultural approach to date can be gained from books and chapters by Cole (1997), Cox and Lightfoot (1997), Nelson (1997), Rogoff (1990, 1998), and Wertsch (1998).

What about possible cautions? Is cognitive development really as intrinsically social, as culturally embedded, and as dependent on guidance from others as sociocultural theorists maintain? It may be, but this claim is a long way from established fact. Our own guess (which, we should acknowledge, is a more negative assessment than many commentators would offer) is that some aspects of cognitive functioning are in fact socially created in the ways that sociocultural theorists emphasize, but that others are not—or at least not as strongly or as uniformly as some proponents of the approach seem to imply. This guess reflects a theme of this section: Different kinds of knowledge have different kinds of dependence on environmental input. Some forms of knowledge may be dependent on specific sorts of experience, may be in a real sense created by that experience, and may vary across children because the relevant experiences vary across children. Other forms of knowledge may have a much stronger biological basis, may require only very general experience to "prime" their development, and may be common across children because the necessary experiences are common across all human environments. It is true that one of the common elements across "expectable" human environments is the presence of other people and of certain kinds of interaction between children and the more mature members of the culture. Social experience may be involved in a very general sense in any human cognitive acquisition. Nevertheless we are doubtful that the apprentice model will prove to be the best way to explain (to give a partial list) the infant's understanding of objects, the toddler's mastery of grammatical rules, the preschooler's appreciation of the appearance-reality distinction, or the grade schooler's mastery of Piagetian concepts.

Processes or Mechanisms of Cognitive Development

One approach to the problem of explaining cognitive development is to identify processes or mechanisms that seem to be operative in many or all cases in which cognitive growth occurs. Many such mechanisms have been proposed; Siegler (1991a) lists 20 processes that have been put forth as explanations for cognitive change, and this list was undoubtedly far from exhaustive even at the time it was compiled. Clearly one challenge here is to get clear about similarities and overlap among various proposed mechanisms.

Another challenge, once again, is to figure out how to study the question—how to obtain evidence that would tell us whether a proposed mechanism is really operating when cognitive change occurs. Enrichment or training studies are again one possible source of evidence. Just as we can attempt to simulate some environmental contributor experimentally, so can we attempt to create a learning situation in which some mechanism of change will be revealed. Another possible approach is Siegler's *microgenetic method* (Siegler & Crowley, 1991; Siegler & Jenkins, 1989).

In a microgenetic study, the researcher records children's behavior as they work repeatedly and intensively within some problem domain—perhaps dozens of hours of observation spread across several weeks. The attempt is to capsulize the time frame for cognitive change—to observe within a relatively short period processes that might ordinarily be spread across a much longer time frame. In contrast to a training study, the typical microgenetic study is relatively nondirective; the researcher's goal is not to teach new knowledge but rather to create situations in which natural processes of knowledge acquisition can be observed. The microgenetic method was the source for many of Siegler's conclusions concerning children's arithmetical strategies that we discussed earlier in the book. Productive applications of microgenetic techniques by other researchers to other content areas include Coyle and Bjorklund (1996); Kuhn, Garcia-Mila, Zohar, and Anderson (1995); and Thornton (1999). Reviews and critical evaluations of the approach can be found in Kuhn (1995), Miller and Coyle (1999), and Pressley (1992).

A rough distinction can be drawn between two general categories of change mechanisms. Some proposed mechanisms concern what we might call the on-line processing of information—that is, the processes that operate when children take in information and adapt to environmental challenges. Piaget's assimilation-accommodation model falls in this category. Another example is the construct of encoding that is stressed in some of Siegler's balance-scale research (e.g., Siegler, 1976). As Siegler uses the term, encoding refers to identifying the features of objects and events and using the features to form internal representations. As we saw in Chapter 5, encoding proved to be important in children's response to the balance scale. It was only when Rule I users began to encode information about distance from the fulcrum that they were able to benefit from feedback concerning the effects of distance and begin to formulate rules that took both of the relevant dimensions into account.

Other change mechanisms have to do less with the immediate processing of information than with changes in the general characteristics of the cognitive system that make developmental advances possible. Here, too, we have seen a number of examples. One such mechanism that is stressed in both information-processing and neo-Piagetian theories is increased information-processing capacity. As children develop, the amount of information that they can hold in working memory increases, and this increase permits forms of mental activity that were not possible as long as the system was more limited. Increased capacity is especially important in Case's (1992; Case & Okamoto, 1996) neo-Piagetian theory, in which stage to stage changes are explained largely in terms of the new operations that increased capacity allows. A closely related mechanism is increased processing speed. Research by Hale (1990) and by Kail (1991, 2000) has shown that the speed with which information is processed increases steadily across childhood. An increase in speed is of benefit in itself, in that more can be taken in and more can be done within any period of time. Older children, for example, can move through a line of reasoning more quickly than can younger children. In addition, as we saw in Chapter 7, the increase in speed is one basis for the increase in capacity. Finally the ability to inhibit prepotent responses may be a third general mechanism of this sort. Our discussions in Chapter 3 and earlier in this chapter emphasized the role of inhibition in infant development—in particular, Diamond's work on object concept. The same general argument, however, has been advanced for older children as well (Dempster & Corkhill, 1999; Harnishfeger & Bjorklund, 1993): Mature problem solving often depends on the capacity to inhibit dominant but less mature responses, and as children develop they become more and more capable of such inhibition.

Two points can be made about the change mechanisms just discussed. First, these are factors that have their own developmental histories. That is, capacity, speed, and inhibition all contribute to developmental change, but they are also all processes that undergo development themselves: Older children are better at all of these things than are younger children. This sort of dual role as outcome and as determinant—as both the "what" and the "how" of development—may be true of a number of mechanisms of change (Flavell, 1984). It applies, for example, to encoding: Encoding previously unnoticed information helps children to form new concepts and to solve new problems, but skill at encoding information itself improves as children develop. Similarly the ability to manipulate symbols is an important outcome of infant development, but once present, symbolic ability contributes enormously to future cognitive change. Many other processes that have been proposed as mechanisms of change (e.g., strategy construction, reasoning by analogy, generalization) show this same dual character: As they develop themselves, they contribute to other developments.

The second point concerns why it is that mechanisms of change undergo change themselves. The reasons are almost certainly both biological and environmental. In the case of processing speed, there is considerable evidence to suggest that some sort of "hard wired" maturational change underlies the general increase in speed that comes with development. Similarly improvements in inhibition during infancy have been linked to maturational changes in areas of the frontal cortex. Yet it is also clear that experience can contribute to such changes. Practice in executing an operation, for example, can lead to greater efficiency, which in turn can mean both greater speed and more capacity left over for other operations. Practice can also affect the ability to inhibit. A conclusion that nature and nurture are both important is generally a safe one, and such a conclusion is certainly valid here.

Our discussion to this point may have given the impression that there are many different mechanisms that contribute to cognitive growth. If so this impression was intended: There *do* seem to be multiple bases for cognitive change. Some of these bases are of the on-line processing sort; others of the general-system sort. Some may be highly domain-specific (e.g., techniques for extracting information about language); others may be more domain-general. Some may have both domain-specific and domain-general aspects. For example the increase in information-processing capacity with age is a quite general change that cuts across a number of aspects of children's development. Yet content-specific expertise can also affect capacity, and children may have greater functional capacity for some domains than for others.

Despite the apparent plethora of change mechanisms, it is still reasonable to ask about possible commonalities. Perhaps the various mechanisms are not really as distinct as they at first seem. Perhaps instead they are specific manifestations of some more general principle—some overarching process of development that subsumes the individual mechanisms and serves as the ultimate explanation for why development proceeds as it does.

The best-known general principle of this sort is Piaget's construct of equilibration. For Piaget equilibration—or the biological tendency of self-regulation—performed exactly this sort of role as general coordinator and director of development. A very brief synopsis of this complicated notion is as follows (again, see Chapman, 1988, for more details, including a description of how Piaget's thinking about equilibration changed over time). The natural direction of development, according to Piaget, is toward states of equilibrium—that is, states of balance among different elements of the cognitive system, balance between the processes of assimilation and accommodation, and balance between the cognitive system and the outer world. A state of equilibrium implies a synchronized, smoothly running, "comfortable" cognitive system, one that yields ready and consistent answers to the problems with which it is faced. In contrast a state of disequilibrium, or cognitive conflict, implies some imbalance, some lack of fit, some uncertainty in the solutions that the cognitive structures yield. Such states are assumed to be motivating; the child will attempt to resolve the disequilibrium and to arrive at a better level of understanding (recall our discussion of Cognitive Motivation in Chapter 3).

The conservation of number problem (Chapter 4) provides an example. Initially the nonconserver tends to focus only on the length of the row of objects, a strategy that yields the conclusion that the longer row contains more. The child's thinking about the problem is in equilibrium, albeit at an immature, nonconservation level. Eventually, however, the child begins to notice that the longer row has also become less dense, a fact that by itself would incline him to conclude that this row contains fewer objects. If the child finds both of these opposing conclusions plausible at the same psychological moment, then his cognitive system has moved from a state of equilibrium to one of disequilibrium for this particular problem. The child can resolve the disequilibrium and achieve a new, more intellectually advanced equilibrium state by considering the length and density changes simultaneously and recognizing that one change compensates for or cancels out the other, hence leaving the number unchanged. A developmental advance has been made by means of a process of equilibration composed of these major steps: (1) cognitive equilibrium at a lower developmental level; (2) cognitive disequilibrium or conflict, induced by awareness of contradictory, discrepant, "nonassimilable" data not previously attended to; (3) cognitive equilibrium (or reequilibration) at a higher developmental level, caused by reconceptualizing the problem in such a way as to harmonize what had earlier been seen as conflicting. Piaget argued that all significant cognitive-developmental advances are made through this kind of equilibration process.

Piaget's equilibration model has been subject to a number of criticisms (Bryant, 1990; Chapman, 1992; Flavell, 1971a; Zimmerman & Blom, 1983). Even if the model makes sense for some cognitive acquisitions, it is by no means clear that every cognitive advance can be explained in terms of a cognitive conflict-reequilibration sequence. Nor is it clear, even if we grant that equilibration is occurring, that we have really fully explained everything. Rather parts of the equilibration process (How does the child come to perceive a conflict? Why does he resolve it in the way that he does?) could be argued to be themselves in need of explanation. At the least the model seems incomplete; it provides a general framework for conceptualizing cognitive change, but it leaves much still to be accounted for.

Are there any models of the change process that rival equilibration theory in their intended explanatory scope? Some are beginning to appear. Interestingly many seem to incorporate aspects (albeit selectively) of the equilibration model, suggesting that Piaget's attempts may indeed serve as a framework within which more satisfactory theories can be developed. In the theory theory approach, for example (e.g., Wellman & Gelman, 1998), change is viewed not as the accretion of isolated bits of knowledge but, à la Piaget, as a more general reworking of the overall system—ultimately, as the replacement of one general theory by a more advanced new theory. Furthermore contradiction and conflict are central to the change process. Children revise their theories, just as do scientists, when the press of counterevidence becomes too great—that is, when the existing theory, even in modified form, can no longer incorporate all the evidence to which the child has become sensitive.

Dynamic systems approaches to change (e.g., Lewis, 2000; van Geert, 1998) also show similarities to equilibration theory. Indeed the similarities are probably most marked in this case, and are in fact often noted by proponents of the approach. Thus dynamic systems theorists, like Piaget, view the child as an active, self-regulating, self-organizing system. Behavior is always a dual function of the immediate state of the organism and the immediate state of the environment, and change occurs through countless organism-environment interactions. In addition there is a natural direction to the change, as the dynamics of the self-organizing system assure increased complexity and increased organization over time.

Finally one element of the equilibration model is competition among opposed bases for response. It is as the child becomes aware of previously unrealized possibilities (e.g., not only length but also density as a possible determinant of number) that an initial phase of equilibrium gives way to disequilibrium and eventually reequilibration at a higher level. Siegler (1996) has suggested that competition may be a common element across a variety of different conceptions of change. As he points out, a number of change mechanisms seem to involve selection among competing possibilities, with more adaptive approaches gradually winning out over less adaptive ones. Such a competition model applies, for example, to his own work on strategy choice in the domain of arithmetical problem solving. It applies to the MacWhinney and Bates Competition Model of language acquisition (see Chapter 8). It applies, at a neurological level, to synaptogenesis and the selective survival of only some synapses. And, as just noted, it can be argued to apply to Piaget's equilibration theory, in which the cognitive conflict engendered by competing ways of thinking forces a reworking of the cognitive system.

Competition and selection are also central, of course, to a well known theory from outside the domain of psychology. Conceptions of the process of change are another way in which many contemporary psychologists draw from evolutionary theory. Just as evolution involves a survival of the fittest among species, so may cognitive development involve a survival of the fittest among cognitive processes. These similarities are not surprising, because they follow from the similar tasks of evolution and development: to produce adaptive change over time.

SUMMARY

Psychologists who work in the area of cognitive development see it as replete with difficult questions and problems. Many of these can be subsumed under the headings of *diagnosis, patterns,* and *cognitive change.*

Questions and problems in the area of diagnosis can be grouped into two closely related types: those concerned with our *conceptualization* of the underlying nature of the cognitive abilities that we study, and those concerned with our *assessment* of those abilities in children. A useful cognitive-developmental acquisition to illustrate these points is transitive inference concerning length relations—for example, if A > B and B > C, then A > C can be inferred.

Assessments of transitive inference or any other cognitive acquisition can err in two ways. A *false-negative* error consists of falsely concluding that a particular child has not yet acquired a capacity. Even though the child does really possess this capacity, he or she fails to show it in test performance because of information-processing, linguistic, motivational, emotional, or other problems. If the child fails to respond appropriately to any of these nontarget demands, a false-negative diagnostic error can result. Conversely a false-positive error consists in falsely concluding that a child does possess the target capacity. For example the child may conclude that A > C simply because A had been called "longer than" something else (i.e., B) whereas C had not; the child therefore reaches the correct conclusion, but not by means of transitive inference. It is often possible to design a cognitive task in such a way that the probability of making a false-positive diagnostic error is reduced. Unfortunately, these very same changes may increase the risk of false-negative errors.

Such facts suggest that there may be developmental changes in how the child "has" cognitive entities like transitive reasoning, and this possibility leads us to questions of conceptualization. How can we characterize the difference in the way that two children "have" transitive inference? A variety of possibilities were suggested. One child may have a more advanced grasp of the concept in the sense of being able to evoke the knowledge more readily in appropriate situations. Given that the knowledge has been evoked, one child may be able to execute the problem-solving strategy more effectively than another. The range of situations in which the knowledge can be applied may increase with development, expanding from simple and limited to maximally general. Finally with development the knowledge may change from implicit to explicit, and may come to be held not just as probably true but as certainly and maybe even necessarily true.

The delineation of these various possibilities still leaves some basic questions of conceptualization unanswered. Is transitive inference a single ability or "competence," with variations among children or across development in such "performance" dimensions as evocability and utilizability? Or are there perhaps different kinds of transitive inference, different forms of competence at different developmental levels? And what exactly takes place in the child's head—what cognitive processes are activated in what order—when the child solves a transitive-inference problem? Some research by Trabasso was described both as an example of how to study these questions and as an illustration that these processes may sometimes be quite different from those previously assumed.

Good diagnosis is essential for determining the patterns that hold among cognitive entities, as well as for studying processes of cognitive change. More basically, diagnosis is ultimately at the root of all psychological research and hence of any conclusions that we might draw about children's cognitive development. One conclusion that emerges from a consideration of recent diagnostic innovations is that traditional assessment techniques have often led us to underestimate children's abilities, especially during the infant and preschool periods. The caution is added, however, that these early competencies are typically not full competencies, and that it remains important to trace changes in knowledge beyond its first emergence.

The patterns that hold among cognitive-developmental entities are of interest because they tell us something about the causal-functional relations among those entities. Three possible types of patterns are *sequence, concurrences,* and *stages.* Five types of X-Y developmental sequences can be distinguished, where X and Y represent cognitive entities: Y develops after X and constitutes an additional, alternative cognitive means to the same goal (*addition* sequence). Later-developing Y replaces earlier-developing X as an approach to a given problem (*substitution*). Y is derived from X by *differentiation, generalization,* or *stabilization* (*modification*). X becomes a component part of a larger cognitive unit Y (*inclusion*). X serves as a developmental facilitator of, or bridge to, Y (*mediation*).

The relation of interest in the study of developmental concurrences is one of common origin: X and Y emerge at the same time because they stem from the same underlying cognitive advance. For example a number of contemporaneous achievements in the domain of theory of mind can be linked to a general understanding of the mental representational process. Here and in general, however, concurrences are typically loose rather than tight.

One implication of the notion of stage is that many related abilities emerge more or less in concurrence. Other concepts relevant to an evaluation of stage theories are *structures, qualitative change,* and *abruptness*. Tentative conclusions were offered with regard to each of these criteria. Cognitive structures develop, but Piaget's structural models may not accurately characterize them. Many of the major cognitive-developmental changes appear to be qualitative rather quantitative, at least at some level of analysis. Cognitive growth is gradual—perhaps very gradual—rather than abrupt. Although diagnostic problems make it difficult to tell for sure, it does not appear that cognitive acquisitions normally develop in the tightly knit, concurrent fashion that Piaget's theory seems to predict. Thus the existing evidence suggests that cognitive growth is not as strongly and clearly a stage-like process as Piaget's theory claims it is. It should be added, however, that a number of developmental psychologists, especially neo-Piagetians, still advocate some form of stage theory of cognitive development.

How is cognitive growth to be explained? Not entirely by environmental factors, according to much recent research and theorizing directed to the biological bases of cognitive development. Common to much of this work is an emphasis on infant precocity: on skills that are present so early that it is difficult to see how they could be acquired from experience. Many of these early competencies appear to be domain-specific and to correspond to biologically natural, evolutionary prepared domains of development (e.g., language). Scarr has proposed a more domain-general form of evolutionary shaping; she suggests that the human infant is strongly predisposed to acquire sensorimotor intelligence, and that the normal human caretaking environment has evolved to support exactly this sort of development.

Although most such proposals have not attempted to specify physiological bases, much progress in this area has been made recently. Two examples were discussed: studies of frontal lobe maturation as a basis for the ability to inhibit dominant responses that interfere with mature problem solving (e.g., on object permanence tasks), and the selective survival of synaptic connections as a function of the availability of relevant experience.

A variety of sources of environmental influence may contribute to children's cognitive development. The results of *enrichment* and *deprivation* studies are often used to make inferences about environmental-experiential contributions. Piagetian training experiments are instances of enrichment studies, whereas investigations of individuals born with sensory or motor handicaps, or reared in psychologically impoverished circumstances, would be examples of deprivation studies. An enrichment study can show that experience A is capable of facilitating the development of cognitive skill X, but it cannot show that A is necessary to X's acquisition, nor even that it normally plays a formative role in the real-world, extralaboratory ontogenesis of X. In contrast a deprivation study is potentially capable of showing that A is or is not necessary to X's real-world ontogenesis. Several deprivation studies illustrate how *versatile* and *resilient* a developing child can be; both these studies and Piagetian training studies suggest that there may be multiple routes to the same developmental end point. Developmental versatility is not always in evidence, however, and the extent to which it is found may vary across different sorts of development. Some developments may be more dependent on specific kinds of experience, and hence more variable across environments and across children, than are others. It is suggested that this point may be important in evaluating claims from the sociocultural/contextual approach regarding the role of social experience in cognitive development.

One way to explain cognitive growth is to specify the processes or mechanisms that are operative when growth occurs. Two general categories of such explanations can be identified. Some proposed mechanisms focus on how information is processed and incorporated into the cognitive system; Piaget's assimilation-accommodation model is an example in this category. Other mechanisms concern changes in general characteristics of the cognitive system that facilitate cognitive growth. Examples in this category include increases in information-processing capacity, speed of processing, and the ability to inhibit responses. Mechanisms of this sort undergo development themselves at the same time they affect other developments—something that is probably true of change mechanisms in general. Both biological and environmental factors contribute to these changes.

Current evidence suggests that a variety of mechanisms operate to produce cognitive growth. Nevertheless the search for a single, overarching principle continues. The best-known such principle is Piaget's construct of *equilibration*. According to the equilibration model, development takes place in three basic steps. Initially, the child's cognitive system with respect to some problem is in equilibrium at a lower developmental level. Subsequently the child detects something that conflicts with his present system, something that the system cannot assimilate or accommodate to, and therefore something which puts it in a state of disequilibrium. Finally equilibrium is reestablished at a higher developmental level by modifying the cognitive system so that what was formerly perceived as discordant is now readily assimilable. Two criticisms of this model were offered: (1) it may not apply to every instance of cognitive change; (2) it is not sufficiently specific to provide a complete explanation of how change occurs. It was also suggested, however, that more viable models may incorporate aspects of equilibration theory, something that was argued to be true of both the theory theory and dynamic systems approaches. More generally Siegler has proposed that competition may be a common element of the change process: that development occurs through a process of competition among cognitive processes (strategies, rules, etc.) and the selective survival of only the most adaptive processes.

References

ACKIL, J. K., & ZARAGOZA, M. S. (1995). Developmental differences in eyewitness suggestibility and memory for source. *Journal of Experimental Child Psychology, 60,* 57–83.

ACREDOLO, L. P., & GOODWYN, S. (1990). Development of communicative gesturing. In R. Vasta (Ed.), *Annals of child development* (Vol. 7). Greenwich, CT: JAI Press.

ADAMS, A., & BULLOCK, D. (1986). Apprenticeship in word use: Social convergence processes in learning categorically related nouns. In S. Kuczaj II & M. Barrett (Eds.), *The development of word meaning.* New York: Springer Verlag.

ADAMS, R. J. (1995). Further exploration of human neonatal chromatic-achromatic distinction. *Journal of Experimental Child Psychology, 60,* 344–360.

ADAMS, S., KUEBLI, J., BOYLE, P., & FIVUSH, R. (1995). Gender differences in parent-child conversations about past emotions: A longitudinal investigation. *Sex Roles, 33,* 309–323.

ADOLPH, K. E. (1997). Learning in the development of infant locomtion. *Monographs of the Society for Research in Child Development, 62* (3, Serial No. 251).

AGUIAR, A., & BAILLARGEON, R. (1998). Eight-and-a-half-month-old infants' reasoning about containment events. *Child Development, 69,* 635–653.

AGUIAR, A., & BAILLARGEON, R. (1999). 2.5-month-old infants' reasoning about when objects should and should not be occluded. *Cognitive Psychology, 39,* 116–157.

AHMED, A., & RUFFMAN, T. (1998). Why do infants make A not B errors in a search task, yet show memory for the location of hidden objects in a nonsearch task? *Developmental Psychology, 34,* 441–453.

AKHTAR, N, & TOMASELLO, M. (1996). Twenty-four-month-old children learn words for absent objects and actions. *British Journal of Developmental Psychology, 14,* 79–93.

AKHTAR, N, & TOMASELLO, M. (1998). Intersubjectivity in early language learning and use. In S. Braten (Ed.), *Intersubjective communication and emotion in early ontegeny.* Cambridge: Cambridge University Press.

ALDRIDGE, M. A., BRAGA, E. S., WALTON, G. E., & BOWER, T. G. R. (1999). The intermodal representation of speech in newborns. *Developmental Science, 2,* 42–46.

ALEXANDER, J. M., & SCHWANENFLUGEL, P. J. (1994). Strategy regulation: The role of intelligence, metacognitive attributes, and knowledge base. *Developmental Psychology, 30,* 709–723.

AMSEL, E., & RENNINGER, K. A. (Eds.). (1997). *Change and development.* Mahwah, NJ: Erlbam.

ANDERSON, J. R. (1980). *Cognitive psychology and its implications.* San Francisco: W. H. Freeman.

ANDREWS, G. & HALFORD, G. S. (1998). Children's ability to make transitive inferences: The importance of premise integration and structural complexity. *Cognitive Development, 13,* 479–513.

ANGLIN, J. M. (1977). *Word, object, and conceptual development.* New York: W. W. Norton.

ANGLIN, J. M. (1993). Vocabulary development: A morphological analysis. *Monographs of the Society for Research in Child Development, 58* (10, Serial No. 238).

ANISFELD, M. (1991). Neonatal imitation. *Developmental Review, 11,* 60–97.

ANISFELD, M. (1996). Only tongue protrusion modeling is matched by neonates. *Developmental Review, 16,* 149–161.

ANTELL, S. E., & KEATING, D. P. (1983). Perception of numerical invariance in neonates. *Child Development, 54,* 695–701.

ASHER, S. R. (1979). Referential communication. In G. J. Whitehurst & B. J. Zimmerman (Eds.), *The functions of language and communication.* New York: Academic Press.

ASHER, S. R., & COIE, J. D. (Eds.). (1990). *Peer rejection in childhood.* Cambridge: Cambridge University Press.

ASHMEAD, D. H., & PERLMUTTER, M. (1980). Infant memory in everyday life. In M. Perlmutter (Ed.), *New directions for child development: No. 10. Children's memory.* San Francisco: Jossey-Bass.

ASLIN, R. N. (1987). Visual and auditory development in infancy. In J. D. Osofsky (Ed.), *Handbook of infant development* (2nd ed.). New York: Wiley.

ASLIN, R. N. (1988). Anatomical constraints on oculomotor development: Implications for infant perception. In A. Yonas (Ed.), *Minnesota symposia on child psychology: Vol. 20. Perceptual development in infancy.* Hillsdale, NJ: Erlbaum.

ASLIN, R. N., JUSCZYK, P. W., & PISONI, D. B. (1998). Speech and auditory processing during infancy: Constraints on and precursors to language. In W. Damon (Series Ed.) & D. Kuhn & R. S. Siegler (Vol. Eds.), *Handbook of child psychology: Vol. 2. Cognition, perception, and language* (5th ed.). New York: Wiley.

ASTINGTON, J. W. (1993). *The child's discovery of the mind.* Cambridge, MA: Harvard University Press.

ASTINGTON, J. W. (Ed.). (2000). *Minds in the making.* Malden, MA: Blackwell.

ASTINGTON, J. W., & GOPNIK, A. (1991). Theoretical explanations of children's understanding of the mind. *British Journal of Developmental Psychology, 9,* 7–32.

ATKINSON, J. (1998). The "where and what" or "who and how" of visual development. In F. Simion & G. Butterworth (Eds.), *The development of sensory, motor and cognitive capacities in early infancy: From perception to cognition.* Hove, UK: Psychology Press.

ATKINSON, R. C., & SHIFFRIN, R. M. (1968). Human memory: A proposed system and its control processes. In K. W. Spence & J. T. Spence (Eds.), *The psychology of learning and motivation* (Vol. 2). New York: Academic Press.

ATRAN, S. (1998). Folk biology and the anthropology of science: Cognitive universals and cultural particulars. *Behavioral and Brain Sciences, 21,* 547–609.

AU, T. K., & MARKMAN, E. M. (1987). Acquiring word meanings via linguistic contrast. *Cognitive Development, 2,* 217–236.

AVIS, J., & HARRIS, P. L. (1991). Belief-desire reasoning among Baka children: Evidence for a universal conception of mind. *Child Development, 62,* 460–467.

AZMITIA, M., & HESSER, J. (1993). Why siblings are important agents of cognitive development: A comparison of siblings and peers. *Child Development, 64,* 430–444.

BACKSCHEIDER, A.G., SHATZ, M., & GELMAN, S. A. (1993). Preschoolers' ability to distinguish living kinds as a function of regrowth. *Child Development, 64,* 1242–1257.

BAHRICK, L. E., NETTO, D., & HERNANDEZ-REIF, M. (1998). Intermodal perception of adult and child faces and voices by infants. *Child Development, 69,* 1263–1275.

BAHRICK, L. E., & PICKENS, J. N. (1995). Infant memory for object motion across a period of three months: Implications for a four-phase attention function. *Journal of Experimental Child Psychology, 59,* 343–371.

BAI, D. L., & BERTENTHAL, B. I. (1992). Locomotor status and the development of spatial search skills. *Child Development, 63,* 215–226.

BAILLARGEON, R. (1986). Representing the existence and the location of hidden objects: Object permanence in 6- and 8-month-old infants. *Cognition, 23,* 21–41.

BAILLARGEON, R. (1987a). Object permanence in 3.5- and 4.5-month-old infants. *Developmental Psychology, 23,* 655–664.

BAILLARGEON, R. (1987b). Young infants' reasoning about the physical and spatial properties of a hidden object. *Cognitive Development, 2,* 179–200.

BAILLARGEON, R. (1993). The object concept revisited: New directions in the investigation of infants' physical knowledge. In C. E. Granrud (Ed.), *Visual perception and cognition in infancy.* Hillsdale, NJ: Erlbaum.

BAILLARGEON, R. (1994). How do infants learn about the physical world? *Current Directions in Psychological Science, 3,* 133–140.

BAILLARGEON, R. (1995). A model of physical reasoning in infancy. In C. Rovee-Collier & L. P. Lipsitt (Eds.), *Advances in infancy research* (Vol. 9). Norwood, NJ: Ablex.

BAILLARGEON, R. (1998). Infants' understanding of the physical world. In M. Sabourin, F. Craik, & M. Robert (Eds.), *Advances in psychological science: Vol. 2. Biological and cognitive aspects*. Hove, UK: Erlbaum.

BAILLARGEON, R. (1999). Young infants' expectations about hidden objects: A reply to three challenges. *Developmental Science, 2*, 115–132.

BAILLARGEON, R., DeVos, J., & GRABER, M. (1989). Location memory in 8-month-old infants in a non-search AB task: Further evidence. *Cognitive Development, 4*, 345–367.

BAILLARGEON, R., & GRABER, M. (1988). Evidence of location memory in eight-month-old infants in a nonsearch AB task. *Developmental Psychology, 24*, 502–511.

BAKER, L. (1982). An evaluation of the role of metacognitive deficits in learning disabilities. *Topics in Learning and Learning Disabilities, 2*, 27–35.

BALDWIN, D. A. (1991). Infants' contribution to the achievement of joint reference. *Child Development, 62*, 875–890.

BALDWIN, D. A. (1993). Early referential understanding: Infants' ability to recognize referential acts for what they are. *Developmental Psychology, 29*, 832–843.

BALDWIN, D. A., & MOSES, L. J. (1994). Early understanding of referential intent and attentional focus: Evidence from language and emotion. In C. Lewis & P. Mitchell (Eds.), *Children's early understanding of mind: Origins and development*. Hillsdale, NJ: Erlbaum.

BALTES, P. B., LINDENBERGER, U., & STAUDINGER, U. M. (1998). Life-span theory in developmental psychology. In W. Damon (Series Ed.) & R. M. Lerner (Vol. Ed.), *Handbook of child psychology: Vol. 1. Theoretical models of human development*. New York: Wiley.

BANERJEE, M. (1997). Peeling the onion: A multi-layered view of children's emotional development. In S. Hala (Ed.). *The development of social cognition*. East Sussex, England: Psychology Press.

BANERJEE, M., & WELLMAN, H. M. (1990, May). *Children's understanding of emotions: A belief-desire perspective*. Paper presented at the meeting of the Jean Piaget Society, Philadelphia, PA.

BANKS, M. S., & GINSBURG, A. P. (1985). Infant visual preferences: A review and new theoretical treatment. In H. W. Reese (Ed.), *Advances in child development and behavior* (Vol. 19). Orlando, FL: Academic Press.

BANKS, M. S., & SALAPATEK, P. (1981). Infant pattern vision: A new approach based on the contrast sensitivity function. *Journal of Experimental Child Psychology, 31*, 1–45.

BARON-COHEN, S. (1995). *Mindblindness: An essay on autism and theory of mind*. Cambridge, MA: M.I.T. Press.

BARONI, M. R., & AXIA, G. (1989). Children's meta-pragmatic abilities and the identification of polite and impolite requests. *First Language, 9*, 285–297.

BARR, R., DOWDEN, A., & HAYNE, H. (1996). Developmental changes in deferred imitation by 6- to 24-month-old infants. *Infant Behavior and Development, 19*, 159–170.

BARRERA, M. E., & MAURER, D. (1981). Recognition of mother's photographed face by the three-month-old infant. *Child Development, 52*, 714–716.

BARRETT, M. (1982). The holophrastic hypothesis: Conceptual and empirical issues. *Cognition, 11*, 47–76.

BARTLETT, E. J. (1976). Sizing things up: The acquisition of the meaning of dimensional adjectives. *Journal of Child Language, 3*, 205–219.

BARTSCH, K. (1990, May). *Children's talk about beliefs and desires: Evidence of a developing theory of mind*. Paper presented at the Symposium of the Jean Piaget Society, Philadelphia.

BARTSCH, K., & ESTES, D. (1996). Individual differences in children's developing theory of mind and implications for metacognition. *Learning and Individual Differences, 8*, 281–304.

BARTSCH, K., & LONDON, K. (2000). Children's use of mental state information in selecting persuasive arguments. *Developmental Psychology, 36*, 352–365.

BARTSCH, K., & WELLMAN, H. M. (1995). *Children talk about the mind*. New York: Oxford University Press.

BATES, E. (1976). *Language and context: The acquisition of pragmatics*. New York: Academic Press.

BATES, E., BRETHERTON, I., & SNYDER, L. (1988). *From first words to grammar: Individual differences and dissociable mechanisms*. Cambridge: Cambridge University Press.

BATES, E., CARLSON-LUDEN, V., & BRETHERTON, I. (1980). Perceptual aspects of tool using in infancy. *Infant Behavior and Development, 3*, 127–140.

BATES, E., & MacWHINNEY, B. (1987). Competition, variation, and language learning. In B.

MacWhinney (Ed.), *Mechanisms of language acquisition*. Hillsdale, NJ: Erlbaum.

BATES, E., & SNYDER, L. (1985). The cognitive hypothesis in language development. In I. Uzgiris & J. McV. Hunt (Eds.), *Research with scales of psychological development in infancy*. Champaign-Urbana, IL: University of Illinois Press.

BAUER, P. J. (1997). The development of memory in early childhood. In N. Cowan (Ed.), *The development of memory in childhood*. Hove, UK: Psychology Press.

BAUER, P. J., HERTSGAARD, L. A., & DOW, G. A. (1994). After 8 months have passed: Long-term recall of events by 1- to 2-year-old children. *Memory, 2,* 353–382.

BAUER, P. J., & MANDLER, J. M. (1989). One thing follows another: Effects of temporal structure on 1- to 2-year-olds' recall of events. *Developmental Psychology, 25,* 197–206.

BAUER, P. J., & MANDLER, J. M. (1990). Remembering what happened next: Very young children's recall of event sequences. In R. Fivush & J. A. Hudson (Eds.), *Knowing and remembering in young children*. Cambridge: Cambridge University Press.

BAUER, P. J., & SHORE, C. M. (1987). Making a memorable event: Effects of familiarity and organization on young children's recall of action sequences. *Cognitive Development, 2,* 327–338.

BAUER, P. J., & THAL, D. J. (1990). Scripts or scraps: Reconsidering the development of sequential understanding. *Journal of Experimental Child Psychology, 50,* 287–304.

BAUER, P. J., WENNER, J. A., DROPIK, P. L., & WEWERKA, S. S. (2000) Parameters of remembering and forgetting in the transition from infancy to early childhood. *Monographs of the Society for Research in Child Development, 65* (4, Serial No. 263).

BEAL, C. R. (1985). Development of knowledge about the use of cues to aid prospective retrieval. *Child Development, 56,* 631–642.

BEAL, C. R. (1988). Children's knowledge about representations of intended meaning. In J. W. Astington, P. L. Harris, & D. R. Olson (Eds.), *Developing theories of mind*. Cambridge: Cambridge University Press.

BEAL, C. R., & BELGRAD, S. L. (1990). The development of message evaluation skills in young children. *Child Development, 61,* 705–712.

BEAL, C. R., & FLAVELL, J. H. (1982). The effect of increasing the salience of message

ambiguities on kindergartners' evaluations of communicative success and message adequacy. *Developmental Psychology, 18,* 43–48.

BEAL, C. R., & FLAVELL, J. H. (1984). Development of the ability to distinguish communicative intention and literal message meaning. *Child Development, 55,* 920–928.

BEARISON, D. J. (1969). Role of measurement operations in the acquisition of conservation. *Developmental Psychology, 1,* 653–660.

BECKER, J. A. (1986). Bossy and nice requests: Children's production and interpretation. *Merrill-Palmer Quarterly, 32,* 393–413.

BECKER, J. A. (1988). The success of parents' indirect techniques for teaching their preschoolers pragmatic skills. *First Language, 8,* 173–182.

BECKER, J. A. (1994a). Pragmatic socialization: Parental input to preschoolers. *Discourse Processes, 17,* 131–148.

BECKER, J. A. (1994b). "Sneak-shoes," "sworders" and "nose-beards": A case study of lexical innovation. *First Language, 14,* 195–211.

BEDARD, J., & CHI, M. T. H. (1992). Expertise. *Current Directions in Psychological Science, 1,* 135–139.

BEEGHLY, M., BRETHERTON, I., & MERVIS, C. B. (1986). Mothers' internal state language to toddlers. *British Journal of Developmental Psychology, 4,* 247–261.

BEHL-CHADHA, G. (1996). Basic-level and superordinate-like categorical representations in early infancy. *Cognition, 60,* 105–141.

BEILIN, H. (1978). Inducing conservation through training. In G. Steiner (Ed.), *Psychology of the 20th century: Vol.7. Piaget and beyond*. Zurich: Kindler.

BEILIN, H. (1992). Piaget's enduring contribution to developmental psychology. *Developmental Psychology, 28,* 191–204.

BEILIN, H., & FIREMAN, G. (2000). The foundation of Piaget's theories: Mental and physical action. In H. W. Reese (Ed.), *Advances in child development and behavior* (Vol. 27). San Diego: Academic Press.

BEILIN, H., & PUFALL, P. B. (Eds.). (1992). *Piaget's theory: Prospects and possibilities*. Hillsdale, NJ: Erlbaum.

BERKO, J. (1958). The child's learning of English morphology. *Word, 14,* 150–177.

BERNDT, T. J., & PERRY, T. B. (1990). Distinctive features and effects of early adolescent friendships. In R. Montmeyer, S. R. Adams, & T. P. Gullota (Eds.), *From childhood to adolescence: A transition period?* Newbury Park, CA: Sage.

BERTENTHAL, B. I., & CAMPOS, J. J. (1990). A systems approach to the organizing effects of self-produced locomotion during infancy. In C. Rovee-Collier & L. P. Lipsitt (Eds.), *Advances in infancy research* (Vol. 6). Norwood, NJ: Ablex Publishing Co.

BERTENTHAL. B. I., CAMPOS, J. J., & KERMOIAN, R. (1994). An epigenetic perspective on the development of self-produced locomotion and its consequences. *Current Directions in Psychological Science, 3,* 140–145.

BERTENTHAL, B. I., & CLIFTON, R. K. (1998). Perception and action. In W. Damon (Series Ed.) & D. Kuhn & R. S. Siegler (Vol. Eds.), *Handbook of child psychology: Vol. 2. Cognition, perception, and action* (5th ed.). New York: Wiley.

BERTONCINI, J. R., BIJELJAC-BABIC, S. E., BLUMSTEIN, S. E., & MEHLER, J. (1987). Discrimination in neonates of very short CV's. *Journal of the Acoustic Society of America, 82,* 31–37.

BEST, D. L., & ORNSTEIN, P. A. (1986). Children's generation and communication of mnemonic organizational strategies. *Developmental Psychology, 22,* 845–853.

BEVER, T. G. (Ed.). (1982). *Regressions in mental development: Basic phenomena and theories.* Hillsdale, NJ: Erlbaum.

BIBACE, R., & WALSH, M. E. (1981). Children's conceptions of illness. In R. Bibace & M. E. Walsh (Eds.), *New directions for child development: No. 14. Children's conceptions of health, illness, and bodily functions.* San Francisco: Jossey Bass.

BIDELL, T., & FISCHER, K. (1992). Beyond the stage debate: Action, structure, and variability in Piagetian theory and research. In R. J. Sternberg & C. Berg (Eds.), *Intellectual development.* Cambridge, Eng.: Cambridge University Press.

BIGLER, R. S., & LIBEN, L. S. (1992). Cognitive mechanisms in children's gender stereotyping: Theoretical and educational implications of a cognitive-based intervention. *Child Development, 63,* 1351–1363.

BIGLER, R. S., & LIBEN, L. S. (1993). A cognitive-developmental approach to racial stereotyping and reconstructive memory in Euro-American children. *Child Development, 64,* 1507–1518.

BIRNHOLZ, J. C., & BENACERRAF, B. R. (1983). The development of human fetal hearing. *Science, 222,* 516–518.

BJORKLUND, D. F. (1987). How age changes in knowledge base contribute to the development of children's memory: An interpretive review. *Developmental Review, 7,* 93–130.

BJORKLUND, D. F. (2000a). *Children's thinking.* (3rd ed). Belmont, CA; Wadsworth.

BJORKLUND, D. F. (Ed.). (2000b). *False-memory creation in children: Theory, research, and implications.* Mahwah, NJ: Erlbaum.

BJORKLUND, D. F., & GREEN, B. L. (1992). The adaptive nature of cognitive immaturity. *American Psychologist, 47,* 46–54.

BJORKLUND, D. F., & HARNISFEGER, K. K. (1987). Developmental differences in the mental effort requirements for the use of an organizational strategy in free recall. *Journal of Experimental Child Psychology, 44,* 109–125.

BJORKLUND, D. F., & HARNISHFEGER, K. K. (1990). Children's strategies: Their definition and origins. In D. F. Bjorklund (Ed.), *Children's strategies: Contemporary views of cognitive development.* Hillsdale, NJ: Erlbaum.

BJORKLUND, D. F., MILLER, P. H., COYLE, T. R., & SLAWINSKI, J. L. (1997). Instructing children to use memory strategies: Evidence of utilization deficiencies in memory training studies. *Developmental Review, 17,* 411–442.

BJORKLUND, D. F., & ZEMAN, B. R. (1982). Children's organization and metamemory awareness in their recall of familiar information. *Child Development, 53,* 799–810.

BLEVINS-KNABE, B., & MUSUN-MILLER, L. (1996). Number use at home by children and their parents and its relationship to early mathematics performance. *Early Development and Parenting, 5,* 35–45.

BLEWITT, P. (1982). Word meaning acquisition in young children. A review of theory and research. In H. W. Reese (Ed.), *Advances in child development and behavior* (Vol. 17). New York: Academic Press.

BLOOM, L. (1970). *Language development: Form and function in emerging grammars.* Cambridge, MA: MIT Press.

BLOOM, L. (1973). *One word at a time: The use of single word utterances before syntax.* The Hague: Mouton.

BLOOM, L. (1993). *The transition from infancy to language: Acquiring the power of expression.* Cambridge, Eng.: Cambridge University Press.

BLOOM, L. (1998). Language acquisition in its developmental context. In W. Damon (Series Ed.) & D. Kuhn & R. S. Siegler (Vol. Eds.),

Handbook of child psychology: Vol. 2. Cognition, perception, and language (5th ed.). New York: Wiley.

BLOOM, L., & CAPATIDES, J. B. (1987). Sources of meaning in the acquisition of complex syntax: The sample case of causality. *Journal of Experimental Child Psychology, 43,* 112–128.

BLOOM, P. (1996). Controversies in language acquisition: Word learning and the part of speech. In R. Gelman & T. K. Au (Eds.), *Perceptual and cognitive development.* San Diego: Academic Press.

BLOOM, P. (2000). *How children learn the meanings of words.* Cambridge, MA: MIT Press.

BLOOM, P., & MARKSON, L. (1998). Intention and analogy in children's naming of pictorial representations. *Psychological Science, 9,* 200–204.

BLÖTE, A. W., RESING, W. C. M., MAZER, P., & VAN NOORT, D. A. (1999). Young children's organizational strategies on a same-different task: A microgenetic study and a training study. Journal of *Experimental Child Psychology, 74,* 21–43.

BOGARTZ, R. S., SHINSKEY, J. L., & SPEAKER, C. J. (1997). Interpreting infant looking: The event set x event set design. *Developmental Psychology, 33,* 408–422.

BOHANNON, J. N., & BONVILLIAN, J. D. (1997). Theoretical approaches to language acquisition. In J. B. Gleason (Ed.), *The development of language* (4th ed.). Boston: Allyn and Bacon.

BOHANNON, J. N., PADGETT, R. J., NELSON, K. E., & MARK, M. (1996). Useful evidence on negative evidence. *Developmental Psychology, 32,* 551–555.

BOHANNON, J. N., & STANOWICZ, L. (1988). The issue of negative evidence: Adult responses to children's language errors. *Developmental Psychology, 24,* 684–689.

BONITATIBUS, G. (1988a). Comprehension monitoring and the apprehension of literal meaning. *Child Development, 59,* 60–70.

BONITATIBUS, G. (1988b). What is said and what is meant in referential communication. In J. W. Astington, P. L. Harris, & D. R. Olson (Eds.), *Developing theories of mind.* Cambridge: Cambridge University Press.

BONVILLIAN, J. D., & FOLVEN, R. J. (1993). Sign language acquisition: Developmental aspects. In M. Marschark & M. D. Clark (Eds.), *Psychological perspectives on deafness.* Hillsdale, NJ: Erlbaum.

BORKOWSKI, J. G., & TURNER, L. A. (1990). Transituational characteristics of metacogni-

tion. In W. Schneider & F. E. Weinert (Eds.), *Interactions among aptitude, strategies, and knowledge in cognitive performance.* Hillsdale, NJ: Erlbaum.

BORNSTEIN, M. H. (1981). Psychological studies of color perception in human infants: Habituation, discrimination and categorization, recognition, and conceptualization. In L. P. Lipsitt (Ed.), *Advances in infancy research* (Vol. 1). Norwood, NJ: Ablex.

BORNSTEIN, M. H., & ARTERBERRY, M. E. (1999). Perceptual development. In M. H. Bornstein & M. E. Lamb (Eds.), *Developmental psychology: An advanced textbook* (4th ed.). Mahwah, NJ: Erlbaum.

BORNSTEIN, M. H., & SIGMAN, M. D. (1986). Continuity in mental development from infancy. *Child Development, 57,* 251–274.

BOWER, T. G. R. (1966). The visual world of infants. *Scientific American, 215,* 90–92.

BOWER, T. G. R. (1974). *Development in infancy.* San Francisco: W. H. Freeman.

BOWERMAN, M. (1978). The acquisition of word meaning: An investigation into some current conflicts. In N. Waterson & C. Snow (Eds.), *The development of communication.* New York: Wiley.

BOWERMAN, M. (1989). Learning a semantic system: What role do cognitive predispositions play? In M. Rice & R. Schiefelbusch (Eds.), *The teachability of language.* Baltimore: Brookes.

BOWERMAN, M. (1996). Learning how to structure space for language: A cross-linguistic perspective. In P. Bloom, M. Peterson, L. Nadel, & M. Garrett (Eds.), *Language and space.* Cambridge, MA: MIT Press.

BOWLBY, J. (1969). *Attachment and loss: Vol. 1. Attachment.* New York: Basic Books.

BOYSSON-BARDIES, B. (1999). *How language comes to children.* Cambridge, MA: MIT Press.

BOYSSON-BARDIES, B., HALLE, P., SAGART, L., & DURAND, C. (1989). A crosslinguistic investigation of vowel formants in babbling. *Journal of Child Language, 16,* 1–17.

BRAINE, M. D. S., & RUMAIN, B. (1983). Logical reasoning. In J. H. Flavell & E. M. Markman (Eds.), P. H. Mussen (Series Ed.), *Handbook of child psychology: Vol. 3. Cognitive development.* New York: Wiley.

BRAINERD, C. J., & POOLE, D. A. (1997). Long-term survival of children's false memories: A review. *Learning and Individual Differences, 9,* 125–152.

BRAINERD, C. J., & REYNA, V. F. (1989). Output-interference theory of dual-task deficits in memory development. *Journal of Experimental Child Psychology, 47,* 1–18.

BRAINERD, C. J., & REYNA, V. F. (1993). Domains of fuzzy trace theory. In M. L. Howe & R. Pasnak (Eds.), *Emerging themes in cognitive development: Vol. 1, Foundations.* New York: Springer-Verlag.

BRAINERD, C. J., & REYNA, V. F. (in press). Fuzzy-trace theory: Dual processes in memory, reasoning, and cognitive neuroscience. In H. W. Reese (Ed.), *Advances in child development and behavior* (Vol. 28). San Diego: Academic Press.

BRANSFORD, J. D., BROWN, A. L., & COCKING, R. (Eds.). (1999). *How people learn.* Washington, DC: National Academy Press.

BRANSFORD, J. D., & FRANKS, J. J. (1971). The abstraction of linguistic ideas. *Cognitive Psychology, 2,* 331–350.

BRETHERTON, I. (1988). How to do things with one word: The ontogenesis of intentional message making in infancy. In M. D. Smith & J. L. Locke (Eds.), *The emergent lexicon: The child's development of a linguistic vocabulary.* San Diego, CA: Academic Press.

BRETHERTON, I. (1990). Open communication and internal working models: Their role in the development of attachment relationships. In R. A. Thompson (Ed.), *Nebraska symposium on motivation: Vol. 38. Socioemotional development.* Lincoln, NE: University of Nebraska Press.

BRETHERTON, I. (1991). Pouring new wine into old bottles: The Social Self as internal working model. In M. R. Gunnar & L. A. Sroufe (Eds.), *Minnesota symposia on child psychology:* Vol. 23, *Self processes and development.* Hillsdale, NJ: Erlbaum.

BRETHERTON, I. (1993). From dialogue to internal working models: The co-construction of self in relationships. In C. A. Nelson (Ed.), *Minnesota symposia on child psychology:* Vol. 26. *Memory and affect in development.* Hillsdale, NJ: Erlbaum.

BRETHERTON, I., & BEEGHLY, M. (1982). Talking about internal states: The acquisition of an explicit theory of mind. *Developmental Psychology, 18,* 906–921.

BRETHERTON, I., MCNEW, S., & BEEGHLY-SMITH, M. (1981). Early person knowledge as expressed in gestural and verbal communication: When do infants acquire a "theory of mind"? In M. Lamb & L. Sherrod (Eds.), *Social cognition in infancy.* Hillsdale, NJ: Erlbaum.

BRETHERTON, I., & MUNHOLLAND, K. A. (1999). Internal working models in attachment relationships: A construct revisited. In J. Cassidy & P. R. Shaver (Eds.), *Handbook of attachment.* New York: Guilford.

BREUR, J. T. (1999). *The myth of the first three years.* New York: The Free Press.

BRIARS, D., & SIEGLER, R. S. (1984). A featural analysis of preschoolers' counting knowledge. *Developmental Psychology, 20,* 607–618.

BRIGGS, J. L. (1970). *Never in anger: Portrait of an Eskimo family.* Cambridge, MA: Harvard University Press.

BRONFENBRENNER, U., & MORRIS, P. A. (1998). The ecology of developmental processes. In W. Damon (Series Ed.) & R. M. Lerner (Vol. Ed.), *Handbook of child psychology: Vol. 1. Theoretical models of human development* (5th ed.). New York: Wiley.

BROWN, A. L. (1989). Analogical learning and transfer: What develops? In S. Vosniadou & A. Ortony (Eds.), *Similarity and analogical reasoning.* Cambridge: Cambridge University Press.

BROWN, A. L., BRANSFORD, J. D., FERRARA, R. A., & CAMPIONE, J. C. (1983). Learning, remembering, and understanding. In J. H. Flavell & E. M. Markman (Eds.), P. H. Mussen (Series Ed.), *Handbook of child psychology: Vol. 3. Cognitive development.* New York: Wiley.

BROWN, A. L., & CAMPIONE, J. C. (1990). Communities of learning and thinking, or a context by any other name. In D. Kuhn (Ed.), *Developmental perspectives on teaching and learning thinking skills.* Basel: Karger.

BROWN, A. L., & DELOACHE, J. S. (1978). Skills, plans, and self-regulation. In R. S. Siegler (Ed.), *Children's thinking: What develops?* Hillsdale, NJ: Erlbaum.

BROWN, A. L., & PALINCSAR, A. S. (1985), *Reciprocal teaching of comprehension strategies: A natural history of a program for enhancing learning* (Tech. Rep. No. 334). Urbana: University of Illinois, Center for the Study of Reading.

BROWN, K. W., & GOTTFRIED, A. W. (1986). Development of cross-modal transfer in early infancy. In L. P. Lipsitt & C. K. Rovee-Collier (Eds.), *Advances in infancy research* (Vol. 4). Norwood, NJ: Ablex.

BROWN, R. (1958). How shall a thing be called? *Psychological Review, 65,* 14–21.

BROWN, R. (1973). *A first language: The early stages.* Cambridge, MA: Harvard University Press.

BROWN, R., CAZDEN, C. B., & BELLUGI, U. (1969). The child's grammar from I to III. In J. P. Hill (Ed.), *Minnesota symposia on child psychology* (Vol. 2). Minneapolis: University of Minnesota Press.

BROWN, R., & HANLON, C. (1970). Derivational complexity and order of acquisition. In J. R. Hayes (Ed.), *Cognition and the development of language.* New York: Wiley.

BRUCK, M., & CECI, S. J. (1999). The suggestibility of children's memory. *Annual Review of Psychology, 50,* 419–439.

BRUNER, J. S. (1975). The ontogeny of speech acts. *Journal of Child Language, 2,* 1–19.

BRUNER, J. S. (1990). *Acts of meaning,* Cambridge, MA: Harvard University Press.

BRYANT, P. E. (1990). Empirical evidence for causes of development. In G. Butterworth & P. E. Bryant (Eds.), *Causes of development.* Hillsdale, NJ: Erlbaum.

BRYANT, P. E., & TRABASSO, T. (1971). Transitive inferences and memory in young children. *Nature, 232,* 456–458.

BUGENTAL, D. B., & JOHNSTON, C. (2000). Parental and child cognitions in the context of the family. *Annual Review of Psychology, 51,* 315–344.

BULLOCK, M., & LÜTKENHAUS, P. (1990). Who am I? Self-understanding in toddlers. *Merrill-Palmer Quarterly, 36,* 217–238.

BULLOCK, M., & ZIEGLER, A. (1999). Scientific reasoning: Developmental and individual differences. In F. E. Weinert & W. Schneider (Eds.), *Individual development from 3 to 12: Findings from the Munich longitudinal study.* New York: Cambridge University Press.

BUSHNELL, E. W. (1982). Visual-tactual knowledge in 8-, 9-, and 11-month-old infants. *Infant Behavior and Development, 5,* 63–75.

BUSHNELL, E. W. (1994). A dual-processing approach to cross-modal matching: Implications for development. In D. J. Lewkowicz & R. Lickliter (Eds.), *The development of intersensory perception: Comparative perspectives.* Hillsdale, NJ: Erlbaum.

BUSHNELL, I. W. R., SAI, F. & MULLIN, J. T. (1989). Neonatal recognition of the mother's face. *British Journal of Developmental Psychology, 7,* 3–15.

BUTTERWORTH, G. (1977). Object disappearance and error in Piaget's Stage IV task. *Journal of Experimental Child Psychology, 23,* 391–401.

BUTTERWORTH, G., & BRYANT, P. E. (Eds.). (1990). *Causes of development.* Hillsdale, NJ: Erlbaum.

BYRNE, R. W., & WHITEN, A. (1988). Toward the next generation in data quality: A new survey of primate tactical deception. *Behavioral and Brain Science, 11,* 267–283.

BYRNES, J. P. (1988a). Formal operations: A systematic reformulation. *Developmental Review, 8,* 1–22.

BYRNES, J. P. (1988b). What's left is closer to right. A response to Keating. *Developmental Review, 8,* 385–392.

CAIN, K. M., HEYMAN, G. D., & WALKER, M. E. (1997). Preschoolers' ability to make dispositional predictions within and across domains. *Social Development, 6,* 53–75.

CALL, J., & TOMASELLO, M. (1999). A nonverbal false belief task: The performance of children and great apes. *Child Development, 70,* 381–395.

CAMPOS, J. J., BERTENTHAL, B. I., & KERMOIAN, R. (1992). Early experience and emotional development: The emergence of wariness of heights. *Psychological Science, 3,* 61–64.

CAMPOS, J. J., HIATT, S., RAMSAY, D., HENDERSON, C., & SVEJDA, M. (1978). The emergence of fear on the visual cliff. In M. Lewis & L. A. Rosenblum (Eds.), *The origins of affect.* New York: Plenum.

CANFIELD, R. L., & SMITH, R. G. (1996). Number-based expectations and sequential enumeration by 5-month-old infants. *Developmental Psychology, 32,* 269–279.

CAREY, S. (1977). Less may never mean more. In R. Campbell & P. Smith (Eds.), *Recent advances in the psychology of language.* New York: Plenum.

CAREY, S. (1978). The child as word learner. In M. Halle, J. Bresnan, & G. A. Miller (Eds.), *Linguistic theory and psychological reality.* Cambridge, MA: MIT Press.

CAREY, S. (1985a). *Conceptual change in childhood.* Cambridge, MA: MIT Press.

CAREY, S. (1985b). Are children fundamentally different thinkers and learners than adults? In S. F. Chipman, J. W. Segal, & R. Glaser (Eds.), *Thinking and learning skills* (Vol. 2). Hillsdale, NJ: Erlbaum.

CAREY, S. (1987). Theory change in childhood. In B. Inhelder, D. de Caprona, & A. Cornu-Wells (Eds.), *Piaget today.* Hillsdale, NJ: Erlbaum.

CAREY, S. (1991). Knowledge acquisition: Enrichment or conceptual change? In S. Carey & R. Gelman (Eds.), *The epigenesis of mind: Essays in biology and cognition.* Hillsdale, NJ: Erlbaum.

CAREY, S. (1999). Sources of conceptual change. In E. K. Scholnick, K. Nelson, S. A. Gelman, & P. H. Miller (Eds.), *Conceptual development: Piaget's legacy.* Mahwah, NJ: Erlbaum.

CAREY, S., & BARTLETT, E. (1978). Acquiring a single new word. *Papers and reports on child language development* (Department of Linguistics, Stanford University), *15,* 17–29.

CAREY, S., & GELMAN, R. (Eds.). (1991). *The epigenesis of mind: Essays on biology and cognition.* Hillsdale, NJ: Erlbaum.

CARLSON, S. M., & MOSES, L. J. (in press). Individual differences in inhibitory control and children's theory of mind. *Child Development.*

CARLSON, S. M., MOSES, L. J., & HIX, H. R. (1998). The role of inhibitory processes in young children's difficulties with deception and false belief. *Child Development, 69,* 672–691.

CARPENDALE, J. I., & CHANDLER, M. J. (1996). On the distinction between false belief understanding and subscribing to an interpretive theory of mind. *Child Development, 67,* 1686–1706.

CARPENTER, M., NAGELL, K., & TOMASELLO, M. (1998). Social cognition, joint attention, and communicative competence from 9 to 15 months of age. *Monographs of the Society for Research in Child Development, 63* (4, Serial No. 255).

CARR, M., KURTZ, B. E., SCHNEIDER, W., TURNER, L. A., & BORKOWSKI, J. G. (1989). Strategy acquisition and transfer among American and German children: Environmental influences on metacognitive development. *Developmental Psychology, 25,* 765–771.

CARRAHER, T. N., CARRAHER, D. W., & SCHLIEMANN, A. D. (1985). Mathematics in the streets and in schools. *British Journal of Developmental Psychology, 3,* 21–29.

CARVER, L. J., & BAUER, P. J. (1999). When the event is more than the sum of its parts: Individual differences in 9-month-olds' long-term ordered recall. *Memory, 2,* 147–174.

CASASOLA, M., & COHEN, L. B. (2000). Infants' association of linguistic labels with causal actions. *Developmental Psychology, 34,* 503–511.

CASE, R. (1986). The new stage theories in intellectual development: Why we need them; what they assert. In M. Perlmutter (Ed.), *Minnesota symposia on child psychology: Vol. 19. Perspectives on intellectual development.* Hillsdale, NJ: Erlbaum.

CASE, R. (1992). *The mind's staircase: Exploring the conceptual underpinnings of children's thought and knowledge.* Hillsdale, NJ: Erlbaum.

CASE, R. (1998). The development of conceptual structures. In W. Damon (Series Ed.) & D. Kuhn & R. S. Siegler (Vol. Eds.), *Handbook of child psychology: Vol. 2, Cognition, perception, and language* (5th ed.). New York: Wiley.

CASE, R. (1999). Conceptual development in the child and in the field: A personal view of the Piagetian legacy. In E. K. Scholnick, K. Nelson, S. A. Gelman, & P. H. Miller (Eds.), *Conceptual development: Piaget's legacy.* Mahwah, NJ: Erlbaum.

CASE, R., MARINI, Z., MCKEOUGH, A., DENNIS, S., & GOLDBERG, J. (1986). Horizontal structure in middle childhood: Cross domain parallels in the course of cognitive growth. In I. Levin (Ed.), *Stage and structure: Reopening the debate.* Norwood, NJ: Ablex.

CASE, R., & OKAMOTO, Y. (1996). The role of central conceptual structures in the development of children's thought. *Monographs of the Society for Research in Child Development, 61* (1–2, Serial No. 246).

CASSEL, W. S., ROEBERS, C. E. M., & BJORKLUND, D. F. (1996). Developmental patterns of eyewitness responses to increasingly suggestive questions. *Journal of Experimental Child Psychology, 61,* 116–133.

CECI, S. J. (1989). On domain specificity . . . More or less general and specific constraints on cognitive development. *Merrill-Palmer Quarterly, 35,* 131–142.

CECI, S. J. (1996). *On intelligence: A bioecological treatise on intellectual development* (expanded ed.). Cambridge, MA: Harvard University Press.

CECI, S. J., & BRUCK, M. (1995). *Jeopardy in the courtroom: A scientific analysis of children's testimony.* Washington, DC: American Psychological Association.

CECI, S. J., & BRUCK, M. (1998). Children's testimony. In W. Damon (Series Ed.) & I. E. Sigel & K. A. Renninger (Vol. Eds.), *Handbook of child psychology: Vol. 4. Child psychology in practice (5th ed.).* New York: Wiley.

CECI, S. J., ROSS, D. F., & TOGLIA, M. P. (1987). Age differences in suggestibility: Narrowing the uncertainties. In S. J. Ceci, M. P. Toglia, & D. F. Ross (Eds.), *Children's eyewitness memory*. New York: Springer-Verlag.

CHANDLER, M. (1991). Alternative readings of the competence-performance relation. In M. Chandler & M. Chapman (Eds.). *Criteria for competence: Controversies in the conceptualization and assessment of children's abilities*. Hillsdale, NJ: Erlbaum.

CHANDLER, M., & BOYES, M. (1982). Social-cognitive development. In B. Wolman (Ed.), *Handbook of developmental psychology*. Englewood Cliffs, NJ: Prentice-Hall.

CHANDLER, M., & CHAPMAN, M. (Eds.). (1991). *Criteria for competence: Controversies in the conceptualization and assessment of children's abilities*. Hillsdale, NJ: Erlbaum.

CHANDLER, M., FRITZ, A. S., & HALA, S. M. (1989). Small scale deceit: Deception as a marker of two-, three-, and four-year-olds' early theories of mind. *Child Development, 60,* 1263–1277.

CHANDLER, M., & HELM, D. (1984). Developmental changes in the contributions of shared experience to social role-taking competence. *International Journal of Behavioral Development, 7,* 145–156.

CHANDLER, M., & LALONDE, C. E. (1996). Shifting to an interpretive theory of mind: 5- to 7-year-olds' changing conceptions of mental life. In A. Sameroff & M. Haith (Eds.), *The 5 to 7 year shift: The age of reason and responsibility*. Chicago: University of Chicago Press.

CHAPMAN, M. (1988). *Constructive evolution: Origins and development of Piaget's thought*. Cambridge: Cambridge University Press.

CHAPMAN, M. (1992). Equilibration and the dialectics of organization. In H. Beilin & P. B. Pufall (Eds.), *Piaget's theory: Prospects and possibilities*. Hillsdale, NJ: Erlbaum.

CHARLESWORTH, W. R. (1966, September). *Development of the object concept: A methodological study*. Paper presented at the meeting of the American Psychological Association, New York.

CHAVAJAY, P., & ROGOFF, B. (1999). Cultural variation in management of attention by children and their caregivers. *Developmental Psychology, 35,* 1079–1090.

CHEN, Z., & KLAHR, D. (1999). All other things being equal: Children's acquisition of the control of variables strategy. *Child Development, 70,* 1098–1120.

CHEN, Z., SANCHEZ, R. P., & CAMPBELL, T. (1997). From beyond to within their grasp: The rudiments of analogical problem solving in 10- and 13-month-olds. *Developmental Psychology, 33,* 780–801.

CHEN, Z., & SIEGLER, R. S. (2000). Across the great divide: Bridging the gap between understanding of toddlers' and older children's thinking. *Monographs of the Society for Research in Child Development, 65* (2, Serial No. 261).

CHI, M. T. H. (1978). Knowledge structures and memory development. In R. S. Siegler (Ed.), *Children's thinking: What develops?* Hillsdale, N. J.: Erlbaum.

CHI, M. T. H. (1985). Interactive roles of knowledge and strategies in the development of organized sorting and recall. In S. F. Chipman, J. W. Segal, & R. Glaser (Eds.), *Thinking and learning skills: Vol. 2. Research and open questions*. Hillsdale, NJ: Erlbaum.

CHI, M. T. H., & GLASER, R. (1980). The measurement of expertise: Analysis of the development of knowledge and skill as a basis for assessing achievement. In E. L. Baker & E. S. Quellmalz (Eds.), *Educational testing and evaluation: Design, analysis and policy*. Beverly Hills, CA: Sage Publications.

CHI, M. T. H., HUTCHINSON, J. E., & ROBIN, A. F. (1989). How inferences about novel domain-related concepts can be constrained by structured knowledge. *Merrill-Palmer Quarterly, 35,* 27–62.

CHI, M. T. H., & KOESKE, R. D. (1983). Network representation of a child's dinosaur knowledge. *Developmental Psychology, 19,* 29–39.

CHOI, S. (1997). Language-specific input and early semantic development: Evidence from children learning Korean. In D. I. Slobin (Ed.). *The cross-linguistic study of language acquisition. Vol. 5: Expanding the contexts*. Mahwah, NJ: Erlbaum.

CHOI, S. (2000). Caregiver input in English and Korean: Use of nouns and verbs in book-reading and toy-play contexts. *Journal of Child Language, 27,* 69–96.

CHOI, S., & GOPNIK, A. (1995). Early acquisition of verbs in Korean: A cross-linguistic study. *Journal of Child Language, 22,* 497–529.

CHOMSKY, N. (1972). *Language and mind* (enlarged ed.). San Diego, CA: Harcourt Brace Jovanovich.

CHOMSKY, N. (1981). *Lectures on government and binding*. Dordrecht, Netherlands: Foris.

CHOMSKY, N. (1988). *Language and problems of knowledge: The Managua lectures*. Cambridge, MA: MIT Press.

CHURCH, R. B. (1999). Using gesture and speech to capture transitions in learning. *Cognitive Development, 14,* 313–342.

CHURCHLAND, P. M. (1984). *Matter and consciousness.* Cambridge, MA: Bradford Books/MIT Press.

CLARK, E. V. (1983). Meanings and concepts. In J. H. Flavell & E. M. Markman (Eds.), P. H. Mussen (Series Ed.), *Handbook of child psychology: Vol. 3. Cognitive development.* New York: Wiley.

CLARK, E. V. (1987). The principle of contrast: A constraint on language acquisition. In B. MacWhinney (Ed.), *Mechanisms of language acquisition.* Hillsdale, NJ: Erlbaum.

CLARK, E. V. (1988). On the logic of contrast. *Journal of Child Language, 15,* 317–335.

CLARK, E. V. (1993). *The lexicon in acquisition.* New York: Cambridge University Press.

CLARK, E. V. (1995). Later lexical development and word learning. In P. Fletcher & B. MacWhinney (Eds.), *The handbook of child language.* Cambridge, MA: Blackwell.

CLARK, E. V., & CHOUINARD, M. M. (in press). Enonces enfantins, formules adultes dans l'acquisition de language. *Language.*

CLARK, H. H., & CLARK, E. V. (1977). *Psychology and language: An introduction to psycholinguistics.* San Diego, CA: Harcourt Brace Jovanovich.

CLEARFIELD, M. W., & MIX, K. S. (1999). Number versus contour length in infants' discrimination of small visual sets. *Psychological Science, 10,* 408–411.

CLEMENTS, W. A., & PERNER, J. (1994). Implicit understanding of belief. *Cognitive Development, 9,* 377–395.

CLIFTON, R. K., PERRIS, E., & BULLINGER, A. (1991). Infants' perception of auditory space. *Developmental Psychology, 27,* 187–197.

COHEN, L. B. (1998). An information-processing approach to infant perception and cognition. In F. Simion & G. Butterworth (Eds.), *The development of sensory, motor and cognitive capacities in early infancy: From perception to cognition.* Hove, UK: Psychology Press.

COHEN, L. B., & AMSEL, G. (1998). Precursors to infants' perception of the causality of a simple event. *Infant Behavior and Development, 21,* 713–731.

COHEN, L. B., AMSEL, G., REDFORD, M. A., & CASASOLA, M. (1998). The development of infant causal perception. In A. Slater (Ed.), *Perceptual development: Visual, auditory, and speech perception in infancy.* Hove, UK: Psychology Press.

COHEN, L. B., RUNDELL, L. J., SPELLMAN, B. A., & CASHON, C. H. (1999). Infants' perception of causal chains. *Psychological Science, 10,* 412–418.

COHEN, L. B., & STRAUSS, M. S. (1979). Concept acquisition in the human infant. *Child Development, 50,* 419–424.

COIE, J. D., & DODGE, K. A. (1998). Aggression and antisocial behavior. In W. Damon (Series Ed.) & N. Eisenberg (Vol. Ed.), *Handbook of child psychology: Vol. 3. Social, emotional, and personality development* (5th ed.). New York: Wiley.

COLE, M. (1996). *Culural psychology: A once and future discipline.* Cambridge, MA: Harvard University Press.

COLE, M. (1997). Cultural mechanisms of cognitive development. In E. Amsel & K. A. Renninger (Eds.), *Change and development.* Mahwah, NJ: Erlbaum.

COLE, M. (1999). Culture in development. In M. Bornstein & M. Lamb (Eds.), *Developmental psychology: An advanced textbook* (4th ed.). Mahwah, NJ: Erlbaum.

COLE, M., & COLE, S. (1989). *The development of children.* New York: W. H. Freeman.

COLE, M., & SCRIBNER, S. (1977). Cross-cultural studies of memory and cognition. In R. V. Kail & J. W. Hagen (Eds.), *Perspectives on the development of memory and cognition.* Hillsdale, NJ: Erlbaum.

COLEY, J. D. (2000). On the importance of comparative research: The case of folkbiology. *Child Development, 71,* 82–90.

COOPER, R. G. (1984). Early number development: Discovering number space with addition and subtraction. In C. Sophian (Ed.), *Origins of cognitive skills.* Hillsdale, NJ: Erlbaum.

COOPER, R. P., & ASLIN, R. N. (1989). The language environment of the young infant: Implications for early perceptual development. *Canadian Journal of Psychology, 43,* 247–265.

COOPER, R. P., & ASLIN, R. N. (1990). Preference for infant-directed speech in the first month after birth. *Child Development, 61,* 1584–1595.

COSMIDES, L., & TOOBY, J. (1994). Origins of domain specificity: The evolution of functional organization. In L. A. Hirschfield & S. A. Gelman (Eds.), *Mapping the mind: Domain specificity in cognition and culture.* New York: Cambridge University Press.

COURAGE, M. L., & ADAMS, R. J. (1990). Visual acuity assessment from birth to three years using the acuity card procedures: Cross-sectional and longitudinal samples. *Optometry and Vision Science, 67,* 713–718.

COWAN, N. (1997). The development of working memory. In N. Cowan (Ed.), *The development of memory in childhood.* Hove, UK: Psychology Press.

COWAN, R., DOWKER, A., CHRISTAKIS, A., & BAILEY, S. (1996). Even more precisely assessing children's understanding of the order-irrelevance principle. *Journal of Experimental Child Psychology, 62,* 84–101.

COX, B. D., & LIGHTFOOT, C. (Eds.). (1997). *Sociogenetic perspectives on internalization.* Mahwah, NJ: Erlbaum.

COYLE, T. R. (in press). Factor analysis of variability measures in eight independent samples of children and adults. *Journal of Experimental Child Psychology.*

COYLE, T. R., & BJORKLUND, D. F. (1996). The development of strategic memory: A modified microgenetic assessment of utilization deficiencies. *Cognitive Development, 11,* 295– 314.

COYLE, T. R., & BJORKLUND, D. F. (1997). Age differences in, and consequences of, multiple- and variable-strategy use on a multitrial sort-recall task. *Developmental Psychology, 33,* 372–380.

CRATON, L. G. (1996). The development of perceptual completion abilities: Infants' perception of stationary, partially occluded objects. *Child Development, 67,* 890–904.

CULTICE, J. C., SOMERVILLE, S. C., & WELLMAN, H. M. (1983). Preschooler's memory monitoring: Feeling-of-knowing judgments. *Child Development, 54,* 1480–1486.

CUSTER, W. L. (1996). A comparison of young children's understanding of contradictory references in pretense, memory, and belief. *Child Development, 67,* 678–688.

DAMON, W. (1981). Exploring children's social cognition on two fronts. In J.H. Flavell & L. Ross (Eds.), *Social cognitive development: Frontiers and possible futures.* Cambridge: Cambridge University Press.

DANNEMILLER, J. L., & STEPHENS, B. R. (1988). A critical test of infant pattern preference models. *Child Development, 59* 210–216.

DAVIS, P. J. (1999). Gender differences in autobiographical memory for childhood emotional experiences. *Journal of Personality and Social Psychology,76,* 498–510.

DEAK, G. O. (2000). Hunting the fox of word learning: Why "constraints" fail to capture it. *Developmental Review, 20,* 29–80.

DÉCARIE, T. G. (1969). A study of the mental and emotional development of the thalido-mide child. In B. M. Foss (Ed.), *Determinants of infant behavior* (Vol. 4). London: Methuen.

DECASPER, A. J., & FIFER, W. P. (1980). Of human bonding: Newborns prefer their mother's voice. *Science, 208,* 1174–1176.

DECASPER, A. J., & SPENCE, M. J. (1986). Prenatal maternal speech influences newborn's perception of speech sounds. *Infant Behavior and Development, 9,* 133–150.

DE HAAN, M., & NELSON, C. A. (1998). Discrimination and categorisation of facial expressions of emotion during infancy. In A. Slater (Ed.), *Perceptual development: Visual, auditory, and speech perception in infancy.* Hove, UK: Psychology Press.

DELOACHE, J. S. (1987). Rapid change in the symbolic functioning of very young children. *Science, 238,* 1556–1557.

DE LOACHE, J. S. (1996). Shrinking trolls and expanding minds: Early symbolic development. *Psychological Science Agenda.* May/June, 8–9.

DELOACHE, J. S., CASSIDY, D. J., & BROWN, A. L. (1985). Precursors of mnemonic strategies in very young children's memory. *Child Development, 56,* 125–137.

DELOACHE, J. S., MILLER, K. F., & PIERROUTSAKOS, S. L. (1998). Reasoning and problem solving. In W. Damon (Series Ed.) & D. Kuhn & R. S. Siegler (Vol. Eds.), *Handbook of child psychology: Vol. 2. Cognition, perception, and language* (5th ed.). New York: Wiley.

DELOACHE, J. S., MILLER, K. F., & ROSENGREN, K. (1997). The credible shrinking room: Very young children's performance in symbolic and non-symbolic tasks. *Psychological Science, 8,* 308–313.

DELOACHE, J. S., PIERROUTSAKOS, S. L., UTTAL, D. H., ROSENGREN, K. S., & GOTTLIEB, A. (1998). Grasping the nature of pictures. *Psychological Science, 9,* 205–210.

DELOACHE, J. S., & SMITH, C. M. (1999). Early symbolic representation. In I. E. Sigel (Ed.), *Development of mental representation: Theories and applications.* Mahwah, NJ: Earlbaum.

DELOACHE, J. S., & TODD, C. M. (1988). Young children's use of spatial categorization as a mnemonic strategy. *Journal of Experimental Child Psychology, 46,* 1–20.

DEMARIE-DREBLOW, D. (1991). Relation between knowledge and memory: A reminder that correlation does not imply causality. *Child Development, 62,* 484–498.

DeMarie-Dreblow, D., & Miller, P. H. (1988). The development of children's strategies for selective attention: Evidence for a transitional period. *Child Development, 59,* 1504–1513.

DeMarie-Dreblow, D., Miller, P. H., Cunningham, W. R., & Wielgos, C. (1999, April) *Path analysis tests of four theoretical models of children's memory development.* Poster session presented at the meeting of the Society for Reserch in Child Development, Albuquerque, NM.

Demetriou, A., Efklides, A., & Platsidou, M. (1993). The architecture and dynamics of developing mind: Experiential structuralism as a frame for unifying cognitive developmental theories. *Monographs of the Society for Research in Child Development, 58* (5–6, Serial No. 234).

Demetriou, A., & Raftopoulos, A. (1999). Modeling the developing mind: From structure to change. *Developmental Review, 19,* 319–368.

Dempster, F. N. (1981). Memory span: Sources of individual and developmental differences, *Psychological Bulletin, 89,* 63–100.

Dempster, F. N., & Corkhill, A. J. (1999). Interference and inhibition in cognition and behavior: Unifying themes for educational psychology. *Educational Psychology Review, 11,* 1–88.

de Ribaupierre, A. (Ed.). (1989). *Transition mechanisms in child development: The longitudinal perspective.* Cambridge: Cambridge University Press.

de Villiers, J. G., & de Villiers, P. A. (1973). A cross-sectional study of the acquisition of grammatical morphemes. *Journal of Psycholinguistic Research, 2,* 267–278.

de Villiers, J. G., & de Villiers, P.A. (1999). Language development. In M. H. Bornstein & M. E. Lamb (Eds.), *Developmental psychology: An advanced textbook* (4th ed.). Mahwah, NJ: Erlbaum.

de Villiers, P. A., & de Villiers, J. G. (1978). *Language acquisition.* Cambridge, MA: Harvard University Press.

de Villiers, P. A., & de Villiers, J. G. (1979). *Early language.* Cambridge, MA: Harvard University Press.

Diamond, A. (1985). Development of the ability to use recall to guide action, as indicated by infants' performance on A$\bar{\text{B}}$. *Child Development, 56,* 868–883.

Diamond, A. (1991a). Frontal lobe involvement in cognitive changes during the first year of life. In K. R. Gibson & A. C. Petersen (Eds.), *Brain maturation and cognitive development: Comparative and cross-cultural perspectives.* Hawthorne, NY: Aldine de Gruyter.

Diamond, A. (1991b). Neuropsychological insights into the meaning of object concept development. In S. Carey & R. Gelman (Eds.), *The epigenesis of mind: Essays on biology and cognition.* Hillsdale, NJ: Erlbaum.

Diamond, A. (1999). Development of cognitive functions is linked to the prefrontal cortex. In N. A. Fox, L. A. Leavitt, & J. G. Warhol (Eds.), *The role of early experience in infant development.* Pompton Plains, NJ: Johnson and Johnson Pediatric Institute.

Diamond, A. (2000). Close interrelation of motor development and cognitive development and of the cerebellum and prefrontal cortex. *Child Development, 71,* 44–56.

Diamond, A., Cruttenden, L., & Neiderman, D. (1994). A$\bar{\text{B}}$ with multiple wells: 1. Why are multiple wells sometimes easier than two wells? 2. Memory or memory + inhibition? *Developmental Psychology, 30,* 192–205.

Dickson, W. P. (Ed.). (1981). *Children's oral communication skills.* New York: Academic Press.

DiLalla, L. F., & Watson, M. W. (1988). Differentiation of fantasy and reality: Preschoolers' reactions to interruptions in their play. *Developmental Psychology, 24,* 286–291.

Dixon, J. A. (1998). Developmental ordering, scale types, and strong inference. *Developmental Psychology, 34,* 131–145.

Dobson, V., & Teller, D. Y. (1978). Visual acuity in human infants: A review and comparison of behavioral and electrophysiological studies. *Vision Research, 18,* 1469–1483.

Dodge, K. A. (1986). A social information processing model of social competence in children. In M. Perlmutter (Ed.), *Minnesota symposia on child psychology: Vol. 18. Cognitive perspectives on children's social and behavioral development.* Hillsdale, NJ: Erlbaum.

Dodge, K. A. (1991). Emotion and social information processing. In J. Garber & K. A. Dodge (Eds.), *The development of emotion regulation and dysregulation.* Cambridge: Cambridge University Press.

Dodge, K. A., Murphy, R. M., & Buchsbaum, K. (1984). The assessment of intention-cue detection skills in children: Implications for developmental psychopathology. *Child Development, 55,* 163–173.

DONALDSON, M., & WALES, R. J. (1970). On the acquisition of some relational terms. In J. R. Hayes (Ed.), *Cognition and the development of language.* New York: Wiley.

DONLAN, C. (Ed.). (1998). *The development of mathematical skills.* Philadelphia: Psychology Press.

DROMI, E. (1987). *Early lexical development.* Cambridge, MA: Cambridge University Press.

DUBE, E. F. (1982). Literacy, cultural familiarity, and "intelligence" as determinants of story recall. In U. Neisser (Ed.), *Memory observed: Remembering in natural contexts.* San Francisco: W. H. Freeman.

DUNCAN, J. (1986). Disorganization of behavior after frontal lobe damage. *Cognitive Neuropsychology, 3,* 271–290.

DUNN, J. (1999). Mindreading and social relationships. In M. Bennett (Ed.), *Developmental psychology: Achievements and prospects.* Philadelphia: Psychology Press.

DUNN, J., BRETHERTON, I., & MUNN, P. (1987). Conversations about feeling states between mothers and their young children. *Developmental Psychology, 23,* 132–139.

DUNN, J., BROWN, J., & BEARDSALL, L. (1991). Family talk about feeling states and children's later understanding of others' emotions. *Developmental Psychology, 27,* 448–455.

DUNN, J., & KENDRICK, C. (1982a). *Siblings: Love, envy, and understanding.* Cambridge, MA: Harvard University Press.

DUNN, J., & KENDRICK, C. (1982b). The speech of two- and three-year-olds to infant siblings: "Baby talk" and the context of communication. *Journal of Child Language, 9,* 579–595.

DUNN, J., & MUNN, P. (1985). Becoming a family member: Family conflict and the development of social understanding in the second year. *Child Development, 56,* 480–492.

DWECK, C. S. (1975). The role of expectations and attributions in the alleviation of learned helplessness. *Journal of Personality and Social Psychology, 31,* 674–685.

DWECK, C. S. (1991). Self-theories and goals: Their role in motivation, personality and development. In R. Dienstbier (Ed.), *Nebraska symposium on motivation* (Vol. 38). Lincoln, NE: University of Nebraska Press.

DWECK, C. S. (1999). *Self theories: Their role in motivation, personality, and development.* Philadelphia: Psychology Press.

DWECK, C. S., & REPPUCCI, N. D. (1973). Learned helplessness and reinforcement responsibility in children. *Journal of Personality and Social Psychology, 25,* 109–116.

EATON, W. O., & RITCHOT, K. F. M. (1995). Physical maturation and information-processing speed in middle childhood. *Developmental Psychology, 31,* 967–972.

ECCLES, J. S., WIGFIELD, A., & SCHIEFELE, U. (1998). Motivation to succeed. In W. Damon (Series Ed.) & N. Eisenberg (Vol. Ed.), *Handbook of child psychology: Vol. 3. Social, emotional, and personality development* (5th ed.). New York: Wiley.

EDER, R. A. (1989). The emergent personologist: The structure and content of 3½-, 5½-, and 7½-year-olds' concepts of themselves and other persons. *Child Development, 60,* 1218–1228.

EDER, R. A. (1990). Uncovering young children's psychological selves: Individual and developmental differences. *Child Development, 61,* 849–863.

EIMAS, P. D., SIQUELAND, E. R., JUSCZYK, P., & VIGORITO, J. (1971). Speech perception in infants. *Science, 171,* 303–306.

EISENBERG, N., LOSOYA, S., & GUTHRIE, I. K. (1997). Social cognition and prosocial development. In S. Hala (Ed.), *The development of social cognition.* Hove, UK: Psychology Press.

EIZENMAN, D. R., & BERTENTHAL, B. I. (1998). Infants' perception of object unity in translating and rotating displays. *Developmental Psychology, 34,* 426–434.

ELDER, G. H., JR. (1998). The life course and human development. In W. Damon (Series Ed.), & R. M. Lerner (Vol. Ed.), *Handbook of child psychology: Vol. 1. Theoretical models of human development.* New York: Wiley.

ELLIS, S., KLAHR, D., & SIEGLER, R. S. (1993, March). *Effects of feedback and collaboration on changes in children's use of mathematical rules.* Paper presented at the meeting of the Society for Research in Child Development, New Orleans.

ELLIS, S., & SIEGLER, R. S. (1994). Development of problem solving. In R. J. Sternberg (Ed.), *Handbook of perception and cognition: Vol. 12. Thinking and problem solving.* New York: Academic Press.

ELLIS, S., & SIEGLER, R. S. (1997). Planning and strategy choice, or why don't children plan when they should? In S. L. Friedman & E. K. Scholnick (Eds.), *Why, how, and when do we plan: The developmental psychology of planning.* Hillsdale, NJ: Erlbaum.

ELMAN, J. L., BATES, E. A., JOHNSON, M. H., KARMILOFF-SMITH, A., PARISI, D., & PLUN-

KETT, K. (1996). *Rethinking innateness: A connectionist perspective on development.* Cambridge, MA: MIT Press.

ERVIN, S. M. (1964). Imitation and structural change in children's language. In E. H. Lenneberg (Ed.), *New directions in the study of language.* Cambridge, MA: MIT Press.

FABRICIUS, W. V. (1997). Review of memory performance and competencies: Issues in growth and development. *Merrill Palmer Quarterly, 44,* 114–119.

FABRICIUS, W. V., & CAVALIER, L. (1989). The role of causal theories about memory in young children's memory strategy choice. *Child Development, 60,* 298–308.

FABRICIUS, W. V., & HAGEN, J. W. (1984). The use of causal attributions about recall performance to assess metamemory and predict strategic memory behavior in young children. *Developmental Psychology, 20,* 975–987.

FABRICIUS, W. V., & IMBENS-BAILEY, A. L. (2000). False belief about false beliefs. In P. Mitchel & K. Riggs (Eds). *Children's reasoning and the mind.* Mahwah, NJ: Erlbaum.

FABRICIUS, W. V., & SCHICK, K. (1995, April). *Strategy construction and choice in 18- to 36-month-olds: Flexibility in early spatial problem solving.* Paper presented at the meeting of the Society for Research in Child Development, Indianapolis, IN.

FABRICIUS, W. V., & SCHWANENFLUGEL, P. J. (1994). The older child's theory of mind. In A. Demetriou & A. Efklides (Eds.), *Intelligence, mind, and reasoning: Structure and development.* Amsterdam, the Netherlands: Elsevier.

FABRICIUS, W. V., SCHWANENFLUGEL, P. J., KYLLONEN, P. C., BARCLAY, C. R., & DENTON, S. M. (1989). Developing theories of the mind: Children's and adults' concepts of mental activities. *Child Development, 60,* 1278–1290.

FAGAN, J. F., III (1973). Infants' delayed recognition memory and forgetting. *Journal of Experimental Child Psychology, 16,* 424–450.

FAGAN, J. F., III (1976). Infants' recognition of invariant features of faces. *Child Development, 47,* 627–638.

FANTZ, R. L. (1961). The origin of form perception. *Scientific American, 204,* 66–72.

FARRANT, K., & REESE, E. (2000). Maternal style and children's participation in reminiscing: Stepping stones in children's autobiographical memory development. *Journal of Cognition and Development, 1,* 193–225.

FARRAR, M. J. (1990). Discourse and the acquisition of grammatical morphemes. *Journal of Child Language, 17,* 607–624.

FARRAR, M. J. (1992). Negative evidence and grammatical morpheme acquisition. *Developmental Psychology, 28,* 90–98.

FARRAR, M. J., & BOYER-PENNINGTON, M. E. (1999). Remembering specific episodes of a scripted event. *Journal of Experimental Child Psychology, 73,* 266–288.

FARRAR, M. J., FASIG, L. G., & WELCH-ROSS, M. (1997). Attachment and emotion in autobiographical memory development. *Journal of Experimental Child Psychology, 67,* 389–408.

FARRAR, M. J., & GOODMAN, G. S. (1990). Developmental differences in the relation between scripts and episodic memory: Do they exist? In R. Fivush & J. Hudson (Eds.) *Knowing and remembering in young children.* Cambridge: Cambridge University Press.

FARRAR, M. J., & GOODMAN, G. S. (1992). Developmental changes in event memory. *Child Development, 63,* 173–187.

FARRAR, M. J., RANEY, G. B., & BOYER, M. E. (1992). Knowledge, concepts and inferences in childhood. *Child Development, 63,* 673–691.

FEINFIELD, K. A., LEE, P. P., FLAVELL, E. R., GREEN, F. L., & FLAVELL, J. H. (1999). Young children's understanding of intention. *Cognitive Development, 14,* 463–472.

FENSON, L., DALE, P. S., REZNICK, J. S., BATES, E., THAL, D. J., & PETHICK, S. J. (1994). Variability in early communicative development. *Monographs of the Society for Research in Child Development, 59* (5, Serial No. 242).

FENSON, L., DALE, P. S., REZNICK, J. S., THAL, D. J., BATES. E., HARTUNG, J. P., PETHICK, S. J., & REILLY, J. S. (1993). *MacArthur Communicative Development Inventories: User's guide and technical manual.* San Diego, CA: Singular Publishing Group.

FERNALD, A. (1985). Four-month-old infants prefer to listen to "motherese." *Infant Behavior and Development, 8,* 181–195.

FERNALD, A., & MORIKAWA, H. (1993). Common themes and cultural variations in Japanese and American mothers' speech to infants. *Child Development, 64,* 637–656.

FERNALD, A., & SIMON, T. (1984). Expanded imitation contours in mothers' speech to newborns. *Developmental Psychology, 20,* 104–113.

FERRARI, M., & STERNBERG, R. J. (1998). The development of mental abilities and styles. In

W. Damon (Series Ed.) & D. Kuhn & R. S. Siegler (Vol. Eds.), *Handbook of child psychology: Vol. 2. Cognition, perception, and language* (5th ed.), New York: Wiley.

FIELD, D. (1987). A review of preschool conservation training: An analysis of analyses. *Developmental Review, 7,* 210–241.

FIELD, T., HEALY, B., GOLDSTEIN, S., & GUTHERTZ, M. (1990). Behavior-state matching and synchrony in mother-infant interactions of nondepressed versus depressed dyads. *Developmental Psychology, 26,* 7–14.

FISCHER, K. W. (1980). A theory of cognitive development: The control and construction of hierarchies of skills. *Psychological Review, 87,* 477–531.

FISCHER, K. W., & BIDELL, T. (1991). Constraining nativist inferences about cognitive capacities. In S. Carey & R. Gelman (Eds.), *The epigenesis of mind: Essays on biology and cognition.* Hillsdale, NJ: Erlbaum.

FISCHER, K. W., & BIDELL, T. R. (1998). Dynamic development of psychological structures in action and thought. In W. Damon (Series Ed.) & R. M. Lerner (Vol. Ed.), *Handbook of child psychology: Vol. 1. Theoretical models of human development* (5th ed.). New York: Wiley.

FISCHER, K. W., & SILVERN, L. (1985). Stages and individual differences in cognitive development. *Annual Review of Psychology, 36,* 613–648.

FISHER, C. (2000). From form to meaning: A role for structural alignment in the acquisition of language. In H. W. Reese (Ed.), *Advances in child development and behavior* (Vol. 27). San Diego, CA: Academic Press.

FIVUSH, R. (1990, August). *Self, gender, and emotion in parent-child conversations about the past.* Paper presented at the meeting of the American Psychological Association, Boston, MA.

FIVUSH, R. (1997). Event memory in early childhood. In N. Cowan (Ed.), *Development of memory in childhood.* Hove East Sussex, UK: Psychology Press.

FIVUSH, R., & HAMOND, N. R. (1989). Time and again: Effects of repetition and retention interval on 2-year-olds' event recall. *Journal of Experimental Child Psychology, 47,* 259–273.

FIVUSH, R., & HAMOND, N. R. (1990). Autobiographical memory across the preschool years: Toward reconceptualizing childhood amnesia. In R. Fivush & J. A. Hudson (Eds.), *Knowing and remembering in young children.* Cambridge: Cambridge University Press.

FIVUSH, R., & SLACKMAN, E. A. (1986). The acquisition and development of scripts. In K. Nelson (Ed.), *Event knowledge.* Hillsdale, NJ: Erlbaum.

FLANNAGAN, D., BAKER-WARD, L., & GRAHAM, L. (1995). Talk about preschool: Patterns of topic discussion and elaboration related to gender and ethnicity. *Sex Roles, 32,* 1–15.

FLAVELL, J. H. (1963). *The developmental psychology of Jean Piaget.* Princeton, NJ: Van Nostrand.

FLAVELL, J. H. (1970a). Concept development. In P. H. Mussen (Ed.), *Carmichael's manual of child psychology* (3rd ed., Vol. 1). New York: Wiley.

FLAVELL, J. H. (1970b). Developmental studies of mediated memory. In H. W. Reese & L. P. Lipsitt (Eds.), *Advances in child development and behavior* (Vol. 5). New York: Academic Press.

FLAVELL, J. H. (1971a). Comments on Beilin's "The development of physical concepts." In T. Mischel (Ed.), *Cognitive development and epistemology.* New York: Academic Press.

FLAVELL, J. H. (1971b). First discussant's comments: What is memory development the development of? *Human Development, 14,* 272–278.

FLAVELL, J. H. (1971c). Stage-related properties of cognitive development. *Cognitive Psychology, 2,* 421–453.

FLAVELL, J. H. (1972). An analysis of cognitive-developmental sequences. *Genetic Psychology Monographs, 86,* 279–350.

FLAVELL, J. H. (1974). The development of inferences about others. In T. Mischel (Ed.), *Understanding other persons.* Oxford: Blackwell, Basil, and Mott.

FLAVELL, J. H. (1976, July). *The development of metacommunication.* Paper presented at the Twenty-First Annual Congress of Psychology, Paris.

FLAVELL, J. H. (1977). *Cognitive development.* Englewood Cliffs, NJ: Prentice-Hall.

FLAVELL, J. H. (1978). Metacognitive development. In J. M. Scandura & C. J. Brainerd (Eds.), *Structural/process theories of complex human behavior.* Alphen a. d. Rijn, The Netherlands: Sijthoff and Noordhoff.

FLAVELL, J. H. (1981a). Cognitive monitoring. In W. P. Dickson (Ed.), *Children's oral communication skills.* New York: Academic Press.

FLAVELL, J. H. (1981b). Monitoring social cognitive enterprises: Something else that may develop in the area of social cognition. In J. H. Flavell & L. Ross (Eds.), *Social cognitive de-*

velopment: Frontiers and possible futures. Cambridge: Cambridge University Press.

FLAVELL, J. H. (1982a). On cognitive development. *Child Development, 53,* 1–10.

FLAVELL, J. H. (1982b). Structures, stages, and sequences in cognitive development. In W. A. Collins (Ed.), *Minnesota symposia on child psychology* (Vol. 15). Hillside, NJ: Erlbaum.

FLAVELL, J. H. (1984). Discussion. In R. J. Sternberg (Ed.), *Mechanisms of cognitive development.* New York: W. H. Freeman & Co.

FLAVELL, J. H. (1988). The development of children's knowledge about the mind: From cognitive connections to mental representations. In J. W. Astington, P. L. Harris, & D. R. Olson (Eds.), *Developing theories of mind.* Cambridge: Cambridge University Press.

FLAVELL, J. H. (1992a). Cognitive development: Past, present, and future. *Developmental Psychology, 28,* 998–1005.

FLAVELL, J. H. (1992b). Perspectives on perspective taking. In H. Beilin & P. Pufall (Eds.), *Piaget's theory: Prospects and possibilities.* Hillsdale, NJ: Erlbaum.

FLAVELL, J. H. (1996). Piaget's legacy. *Psychological Science, 7,* 200–203.

FLAVELL, J. H. (1999). Cognitive development: Children's knowledge about the mind. *Annual Review of Psychology, 50,* 21–45.

FLAVELL, J. H. (2000). Development of children's knowledge about the mental world. *International Journal of Behavioral Development, 24,* 15–23.

FLAVELL, J. H., BEACH, D. H., & CHINSKY, J. M. (1966). Spontaneous verbal rehearsal in a memory task as a function of age. *Child Development, 37,* 283–299.

FLAVELL, J. H., BOTKIN, P. T., FRY, C. L., WRIGHT, J. W., & JARVIS, P. E. (1968). *The development of role-taking and communication skills in children.* New York: Wiley. (Reprinted by Robert E. Krieger Publishing Company, Huntington, New York, 1975).

FLAVELL, J. H., FLAVELL, E. R., & GREEN, F. L. (1983). Development of the appearance-reality distinction. *Cognitive Psychology, 15,* 95–120.

FLAVELL, J. H., FLAVELL, E. R., GREEN, F. L., & MOSES, L. J. (1990). Young children's understanding of fact beliefs versus value beliefs. *Child Development, 61,* 915–928.

FLAVELL, J. H., FRIEDRICHS, A.G., & HOYT, J. D. (1970). Developmental changes in mem-

orization processes. *Cognitive Psychology, 1,* 324–340.

FLAVELL, J. H., GREEN, F. L., & FLAVELL, E. R. (1986). Development of knowledge about the appearance-reality distinction. *Monographs of the Society for Research in Child Development, 51* (1, Serial No. 212).

FLAVELL, J. H., GREEN, F. L., & FLAVELL, E. R. (1990). Developmental changes in young children's knowledge about the mind. *Cognitive Development, 5,* 1–27.

FLAVELL, J. H., GREEN, F. L., & FLAVELL, E. R. (1995a). The development of children's knowledge about attentional focus. *Developmental Psychology, 31,* 706–712.

FLAVELL, J. H., GREEN, F. L., & FLAVELL, E. R. (1995b). Young children's knowledge about thinking. *Monographs of the Society for Research in Child Development, 60* (1, Serial No. 243).

FLAVELL, J. H., GREEN, F. L., & FLAVELL, E. R. (1998). The mind has a mind of its own: Developing knowledge about mental uncontrollability. *Cognitive Development, 13,* 127–138.

FLAVELL, J. H., GREEN, F. L., & FLAVELL, E. R. (2000). Development of children's awareness of their own thoughts. *Journal of Cognition and Development, 1,* 97–112.

FLAVELL, J. H., GREEN, F. L., FLAVELL, E. R., & LIN, N. T. (1999). Development of children's knowledge about unconsciousness. *Child Development, 70,* 396–412.

FLAVELL, J. H., & MILLER, P. H. (1998) Social cognition. In W. Damon (Series Ed.) & D. Kuhn & R. S. Siegler (Vol. Eds.), *Handbook of child psychology: Vol. 2. Cognition, perception, and language* (5th ed.). New York: Wiley.

FLAVELL, J. H., MUMME, D. L., GREEN, F. L., & FLAVELL, E. R. (1992). Young children's understanding of moral and other beliefs. *Child Development, 63,* 960–977.

FLAVELL, J. H., & O'DONNELL, A. K. (in press). Development of intuitions about mental experiences. *Enfance.*

FLAVELL, J. H., & ROSS, L. (1981). Concluding remarks. In J. H. Flavell & L. Ross (Eds.), *Social cognitive development: Frontiers and possible futures.* Cambridge: Cambridge University Press.

FLAVELL, J. H., SHIPSTEAD, S. G., & CROFT, K. (1978). Young children's knowledge about visual perception: Hiding objects from others. *Child Development, 49,* 1208–1211.

FLAVELL, J. H., SPEER, J. R., GREEN, F. L., & AUGUST, D. L. (1981). The development of comprehension monitoring and knowledge about communication. *Monographs of the Society for Research in Child Development, 46* (Serial No. 192).

FLAVELL, J. H., & WELLMAN, H. M. (1977). Metamemory, In R. V. Kail & J. W. Hagen (Eds.), *Perspectives on the development of memory and cognition.* Hillsdale, NJ: Erlbaum.

FLAVELL, J. H., & WOHLWILL, J. F. (1969). Formal and functional aspects of cognitive development. In D. Elkind & J. H. Flavell (Eds.), *Studies in cognitive development: Essays in honor of Jean Piaget.* New York: Oxford University Press.

FLAVELL, J. H., ZHANG, X-D., ZOU, H., DONG, Q., & QI. S. (1983). A comparison between the development of the appearance-reality distinction in the People's Republic of China and the United States. *Cognitive Psychology, 15,* 459–466.

FLIELLER, A. (1999). Comparison of the development of formal thought in adolescent cohorts aged 10 to 15 years (1967–1999 and 1972–1993). *Developmental Psychology, 35,* 1048–1058.

FODOR, J. A. (1983). *The modularity of mind.* Cambridge, MA: MIT/Bradford Books.

FORGUSON, L. (1989). *Common sense.* London: Routledge.

FORREST, D. L., & WALLER, T. G. (1979, March). *Cognitive and metacognitive aspects of reading.* Paper presented at the meeting of the Society for Research in Child Development, San Francisco.

FOX, N. A., & FITZGERALD, H. E. (1990). Autonomic function in infancy. *Merrill-Palmer Quarterly, 36,* 27–52.

FOX, N. A., LEAVITT, L. A., & WARHOL, J. G. (EDS.). (1999). *The role of early experience in infant development.* Pompton Plains, NJ: Johnson & Johnson Pediatric Institute.

FRANCIS, D. (1978). *Trial run.* New York: Harper & Row.

FREEMAN, K., MCKIE, S., & BAUER, P. (1994, March). *Analogical reasoning in 2-year-olds.* Paper presented at the Conference on Human Development, Pittsburgh, PA.

FREUD, S. (1953). Three essays on the theory of sexuality. In L. Strachey (Ed. and Trans.), *The standard edition of the complete psychological works of Sigmund Freud* (Vol. 7). London: Hogarth Press. (Original work published 1905)

FREUND, L. S. (1990). Maternal regulation of children's problem-solving behavior and its impact on children's performance. *Child Development, 61,* 113–126.

FRIEDMAN, S. L., & E. K. SCHOLNICK (Eds.). (1997). *Why, how, and when do we plan; The developmental psychology of planning.* Hillsdale, NJ: Erlbaum.

FRIEND, M., & DAVIS, T. L. (1993). Appearance-reality distinction: Children's understanding of the physical and affective domains. *Developmental Psychology, 29,* 907–914.

FRYE, D. (1999). Development of intention: The relation of executive function to theory of mind. In P. D. Zelazo, J. W. Astington, & D. R. Olson (Eds), *Developing theories of intention: Social understanding and self.* Mahwah, NJ: Erlbaum.

FURMAN, L. N., & WALDEN, T. A. (1990). Effect of script knowledge on preschool children's communicative interactions. *Developmental Psychology, 26,* 227–233.

FURROW, D., NELSON, K., & BENEDICT, H. (1979). Mothers' speech to children and syntactic development: Some simple relationships. *Journal of Child Language, 6,* 423–442.

FURTH, H. G. (1971). Linguistic deficiency and thinking: Research with deaf subjects 1964–1969. *Psychological Bulletin, 76,* 58–72.

FUSON, K. C. (1988). *Children's counting and concepts of number.* New York: Springer-Verlag.

GALLISTEL, C. R., & GELMAN, R. (1992). Preverbal and verbal counting and computation. *Cognition, 44,* 43–74.

GALLUP, G. G. (1977). Self-recognition in primates: A comparative approach to the bidirectional properties of consciousness. *American Psychologist, 32,* 329–338.

GARNER, R. (1990). Children's use of strategies in reading. In D. F. Bjorklund (Ed.), *Children's strategies: Contemporary views of cognitive development.* Hillsdale, NJ: Erlbaum.

GARTON, A. F., & PRATT, C. (1990). Children's pragmatic judgements of direct and indirect requests. *First Language, 10,* 51–59.

GAUVAIN, M. (1998). Cognitive development in social and cultural context. *Current Directions in Psychological Science, 7,* 188–192.

GAUVAIN, M., & GREENE, J. K. (1994). What do young children know about objects? *Cognitive Development, 9,* 311–330.

GEARY, D. C. (1994). *Children's mathematical development: Research and practical applications.* Washington, DC: American Psychological Association.

GEARY, D. C. (1995). Reflections of evolution and culture in children's cognition: Implications for mathematical development and instruction. *American Psychologist, 50,* 24–37.

GEARY, D. C., & BJORKLUND, D. F. (2000). Evolutionary developmental psychology. *Child Development, 71,* 57–65.

GEARY, D. C., BOW-THOMAS, C., FAN, L., & SIEGLER, R. S. (1993). Even before formal instruction, Chinese children outperform American children in mental addition. *Cognitive Development, 8,* 517–529.

GELMAN, R. (1972). Logical capacity of very young children: Number invariance rules. *Child Development, 43,* 75–90.

GELMAN, R. (1982). Basic numerical abilities. In R. J. Sternberg (Ed.), *Advances in the psychology of human intelligence* (Vol. 1). Hillsdale, NJ: Erlbaum.

GELMAN, R. (1990). First principles organize attention to and learning about relevant data: Number and the animate-inanimate distinction. *Cognitive Science, 14,* 79–106.

GELMAN, R. (1991). Epigenetic foundations of knowledge structures: Initial and transcedent constructions. In S. Carey & R. Gelman (Eds.), *The epigenesis of mind: Essays on biology and cognition.* Hillsdale, NJ: Erlbaum.

GELMAN, R. (1997). Constructing and using conceptual competence. *Cognitive Development, 12,* 305–313.

GELMAN, R., & BAILLARGEON, R. (1983). A review of Piagetian concepts. In P. H. Mussen (Series Ed.) & J. H. Flavell & E. M. Markman (Vol. Eds.), *Handbook of child psychology: Vol. 3. Cognitive development.* New York: Wiley.

GELMAN, R., DURGIN, F., & KAUFMAN, L. (1995). Distinguishing between animates and inanimates: Not by motion alone. In D. Sperber, D. Premack, & A. J. Premack (Eds.), *Causal cognition: A multidisciplinary debate.* New York: Oxford University Press.

GELMAN, R., & GALLISTEL, C. R. (1978). *The child's understanding of number.* Cambridge, MA: Harvard University Press.

GELMAN, R., & MECK, E. (1992). Early principles aid early but not later conceptions of number. In J. Bideaud & C. Meljae (Eds.), *Pathways to number.* Hillsdale, NJ: Erlbaum.

GELMAN, R., SPELKE, E. S., & MECK, E. (1983). What preschoolers know about animate and inanimate objects. In D. R. Rogers & J. A. Sloboda (Eds.), *The acquisition of symbolic skills.* New York: Plenum.

GELMAN, R., & WILLIAMS, E. M. (1998). Enabling constraints for cognitive development and learning: Domain specificity and cognitive development. In W. Damon (Series Ed.) & D. Kuhn & R. S. Siegler (Vol. Eds.), *Handbook of child psychology: Vol. 2. Cognition, perception, and language* (5th ed.). New York: Wiley.

GELMAN, S. A. (1988). The development of induction within natural kind and artifact categories. *Cognitive Psychology, 20,* 65–95.

GELMAN, S. A. (2000). The role of essentialism in children's concepts. In H. W. Reese (Ed.), *Advances in child development and behavior* (Vol. 27). San Diego, CA: Academic Press.

GELMAN, S. A., & COLEY, J. D. (1990). The importance of knowing a dodo is a bird: Categories and inferences in 2½-year-old children. *Developmental Psychology, 26,* 796–804.

GELMAN, S. A., & DIESENDRUCK, G. (1999). A reconsideration of concepts: On the compatibility of psychological essentialism and context sensitivity. In E. K. Scholnick, K. Nelson, S. A. Gelman, & P. H. Miller (Eds.), *Conceptual development: Piaget's legacy.* Mahwah, NJ: Erlbaum.

GELMAN, S. A., & GOTTFRIED, G. M. (1996). Children's causal explanations of animate and inanimate motion. *Child Development, 67,* 1970–1987.

GELMAN, S. A., & HEYMAN, G. D. (1997, April). *Thinking about the origins of human dispositions.* Paper presented at the meeting of the Society for Research in Child Development, Washington, DC.

GELMAN, S. A., & KREMER, K. E. (1991). Understanding natural cause: Children's explanations of how objects and their properties originate. *Child Development, 62,* 396–414.

GELMAN, S. A., & MARKMAN, E. M. (1986). Categories and induction in young children. *Cognition, 23,* 183–209.

GELMAN, S. A., & MARKMAN, E. M. (1987). Young children's inductions from natural kinds: The role of categories and appearances. *Child Development, 58,* 1532–1541.

GELMAN, S. A., & O'REILLY, A. W. (1988). Children's inductive inferences within superordinate categories: The role of language and category structure. *Child Development, 59,* 876–887.

GELMAN, S. A., & WELLMAN, H. M. (1991). Insides and essences: Early understandings of the non-obvious. *Cognition, 38,* 213–244.

GENTNER, D., & RATTERMAN, M. J. (1991). Language and the career of similarity. In S. A. Gelman & J. P. Byrnes (Eds.), *Perspectives on thought and language: Interrelations in development.* Cambridge: Cambridge University Press.

GENTNER, D., RATTERMANN, M. J., MARKMAN, A., & KOTOVSKY, L. (1995). Two forces in the development of relational similarity. In T. J. Simon & G. S. Halford (Eds.), *Developing cognitive competence: New approaches to process modeling.* Hillsdale, NJ: Erlbaum.

GERBER, E. (1975). *The cultural patterning of emotions in Samoa.* Unpublished doctoral dissertation, University of California, San Diego.

GHATALA, E. S. (1984). Developmental changes in incidental memory as a function of meaningfulness and encoding condition. *Developmental Psychology, 20,* 208–211.

GIBSON, E. J. (1969). *Principles of perceptual learning and development.* New York: Appleton-Century-Crofts.

GIBSON, E. J. (1988). Levels of description and constraints on perceptual development. In A. Yonas (Ed.), *Minnesota symposia on child psychology: Vol. 20. Perceptual development in infancy.* Hillsdale, NJ: Erlbaum.

GIBSON, E. J., & PICK, A. (2000). *An ecological approach to perceptual learning and development.* New York: Oxford University Press.

GIBSON, E. J., & SPELKE, E. S. (1983). The development of perception. In J. H. Flavell & E. M. Markman (Eds.), P. H. Mussen (Series Ed.), *Handbook of child psychology: Vol. 3. Cognitive development.* New York: Wiley.

GIBSON, E. J., & WALK, R. D. (1960). The "visual cliff." *Scientific American, 202,* 64–71.

GIBSON, E. J., & WALKER, A. S. (1984). Development of knowledge of visual-tactual affordances of substance. *Child Development, 55,* 453–460.

GIBSON, J. J. (1979). Foreword: A note on E. J. G. by J. J. G. In A. D. Pick (Ed.), *Perception and its development: A tribute to Eleanor J. Gibson.* Hillsdale, NJ: Erlbaum.

GINSBURG, H. P., KLEIN, A., & STARKEY, P. (1998). The development of children's mathematical thinking: Connecting research with practice. In W. Damon (Series Ed.) & I. E. Sigel & K. A. Renninger (Vol. Eds.), *Handbook of child psychology: Vol. 4. Child psychology in practice* (5th ed.). New York: Wiley.

GINSBURG, H. P., & OPPER, S. (1988). *Piaget's theory of intellectual development: An introduction* (3rd ed.). Englewood Cliffs, NJ: Prentice-Hall.

GLASER, R., & CHI, M. T. H. (1988). Overview. In M. T. H. Chi, R. Glaser, & M. J. Farr (Eds.), *The nature of expertise.* Hillsdale, NJ: Erlbaum.

GLEASON, T. R., SEBANC, A. M., & HARTUP, W. W. (2000). Imaginary companions of preschool children. *Developmental Psychology, 36,* 419–428.

GLEITMAN, L. R. (1990). The structural sources of word meaning. *Language Acquisition, 1,* 3–55.

GLEITMAN, L. R., & GILLETTE, J. (1999). The role of syntax in verb learning. In W. C. Ritchie & T. K. Bhatia (Eds.), *Handbook of child language acquisition.* San Diego, CA: Academic Press.

GLEITMAN, L. R., & WANNER, E. (1988). Current issues in language learning. In M. H. Bornstein & M. E. Lamb (Eds.), *Developmental psychology: An advanced textbook.* Hillsdale, NJ: Erlbaum.

GLUCKSBERG, S., KRAUSS, R. M., & HIGGINS, E. T. (1975). The development of communication skills in children. In F. Horowitz (Ed.), *Review of child development research* (Vol. 4). Chicago: University of Chicago Press.

GNEPP, J., & HESS, D. L. R. (1986). Children's understanding of verbal and facial display rules. *Developmental Psychology, 22,* 103–108.

GOBBO, C., & CHI, M. T. H. (1986). How knowledge is structured and used by expert and novice children. *Cognitive Development, 1,* 221–237.

GOLD, M. E. (1967). Language identification in the limit. *Information and Control, 10,* 447–474.

GOLD, R. (1987). *The description of cognitive development: Three Piagetian themes.* Oxford: Clarendon Press.

GOLDFIELD, B. (1987). The contributions of child and caregiver to referential and expressive language. *Applied Psycholinguistics, 8,* 267–280.

GOLDFIELD, B. E., & SNOW, C. E. (1997). Individual differences: Implications for the study of language development. In J. B. Gleason (Ed.), *The development of language* (4th ed.). Boston: Allyn and Bacon.

GOLDIN-MEADOW, S. (1979). Structure in a manual communication system developed without a conventional language model: Language without a helping hand. In H. Whitaker &

H. A. Whitaker (Eds.), *Studies in neurolinguistics* (Vol. 4). New York: Academic Press.

GOLDIN-MEADOW, S. (1997). When gestures and words speak differently. *Current Directions in Psychological Science, 6,* 138–143.

GOLDIN-MEADOW, S. (2000). Beyond words: The importance of gesture to researchers and learners. *Child Development, 71,* 231–239.

GOLDIN-MEADOW, S., ALIBALI, M. W., & CHURCH, R. (1993). Transitions in concept acquisition: Using the hand to read the mind. *Psychological Review, 100,* 279–297.

GOLINKOFF, R. M. (1983). The preverbal negotiation of failed messages: Insights into the transition period. In R. M. Golinkoff (Ed.), *The transition from prelinguistic to linguistic communication.* Hillsdale, NJ: Erlbaum.

GOLINKOFF, R. M., HIRSH-PASEK, K., MERVIS, C. B., & FRAWLEY, W. B. (1995). Lexical principles can be extended to the acquisition of verbs. In M. Tomasello & W. E. Merriman (Eds.), *Beyond names for things: Young children's acquisition of verbs.* Hillsdale, NJ: Erlbaum.

GOODMAN, G. S. (1984). Children's testimony in historical perspective. *Journal of Social Issues, 40,* 9–31.

GOODMAN, G. S., & AMAN, C. (1990). Children's use of anatomically detailed dolls to recount an event. *Child Development, 61,* 1859–1871.

GOODMAN, G. S., AMAN, C., & HIRSCHMAN, J. (1987). Child sexual and physical abuse: Children's testimony. In S. J. Ceci, M. P. Toglia, & D. F. Ross (Eds.), *Children's eyewitness memory.* New York: Springer-Verlag.

GOODMAN, G. S., & QUAS, J. A. (1997). Trauma and memory: Individual differences in children's recounting of a stressful experience. In N. L. Stein, P. A. Ornstein, B. Tversky, & C. Brainerd (Eds.), *Memory for everyday and emotional events.* Mahwah, NJ: Erlbaum.

GOODMAN, G. S., RUDY, L., BOTTOMS, B. L., & AMAN, C. (1990). Children's concerns and memory: Issues of ecological validity in the study of children's eyewitness testimony. In R. Fivush & J. A. Hudson (Eds.), *Knowing and remembering in young children.* Cambridge: Cambridge University Press.

GOODNOW, J. J., & COLLINS, W. A. (1990). *Development according to parents: The nature, sources, and consequences of parents' ideas.* Hove & London: Erlbaum.

GOPNIK, A. (1984). The acquisition of *gone* and the development of the object concept. *Journal of Child Language, 11,* 273–292.

GOPNIK, A. (1988). Three types of early word: The emergence of social words, names and cognitive-relational words in the one-word stage and their relation to cognitive development. *First Language, 8,* 49–70.

GOPNIK, A. (1998). Wanting to get it right: Commentary on Lillard and Joseph. *Child Development, 69,* 994–995.

GOPNIK, A., & ASTINGTON, J. W. (1988). Children's understanding of representational change and its relation to the understanding of false belief and the appearance-reality distinction. *Child Development, 59,* 26–37.

GOPNIK, A., & MELTZOFF, A. N. (1986). Relations between semantic and cognitive development in the one-word stage: The specificity hypothesis. *Child Development, 57,* 1040–1053.

GOPNIK, A., & MELTZOFF, A. N. (1997). *Words, thoughts, and theories.* Cambridge, MA: MIT Press.

GOPNIK, A., & SOBEL, D. (2000). Detecting blickets: How young children use information about novel causal powers in categorization and induction. *Child Development, 71,* 1205–1222.

GORDON, F. R., & FLAVELL, J. H. (1977). The development of intuitions about cognitive cueing. *Child Development, 48,* 1027–1033.

GOSWAMI, U. (1995). Transitive relational mappings in three-and four-year-olds: The analogy of Goldilocks and the three bears. *Child Development, 66,* 877–892.

GOSWAMI, U. (1996). Analogical reasoning and cognitive development. In H. Reese (Ed.), *Advances in child development and behavior* (Vol. 26). New York: Academic Press.

GOTTFRIED, G. M., GELMAN, S. A., & SCHULTZ, J. (1999). Children's understanding of the brain: From early essentialism to biological theory. *Cognitive Development, 14,* 147–174.

GOTTLIEB, G., WAHLSTEN, D., & LICKLITER, R. (1998). The significance of biology for human development: A developmental psychobiological systems view. In W. Damon (Series Ed.) & R. M. Lerner (Vol. Ed.), *Handbook of child psychology: Vol 1. Theoretical models of human development* (5th ed.). New York: Wiley.

GRANOTT, N. (May, 1991). *From macro to micro and back: On the analysis of microdevelopment.* Paper presented at the meeting of the Jean Piaget Society, Philadelphia.

GRATCH, G. (1972). A study of the relative dominance of vision and touch in six-month-old infants. *Child Development, 43,* 615–623.

GRATCH, G., & LANDERS, W. F. (1971). Stage IV of Piaget's theory of infants' object concepts: A longitudinal study. *Child Development, 42,* 359–372.

GRAY, W. M. (1990). Formal operational thought. In W. F. Overton (Ed.), *Reasoning, necessity, and logic: Developmental perspectives.* Hillsdale, NJ: Erlbaum.

GRECO, C., HAYNE, H., & ROVEE-COLLIER, C. (1990). Roles of function, reminding, and variability in categorization by 3-month-olds. *Journal of Experimental Psychology: Learning, Memory, and Cognition, 16,* 617–633.

GREENO, J. G., RILEY, M. S., & GELMAN, R. (1984). Conceptual competence and children's counting. *Cognitive Psychology, 16,* 94–134.

GREENOUGH, W. T., & BLACK, J. E. (1999). Experience, neural plasticity, and psychological development. In N. A. Fox, L. A. Leavitt, & J. G. Warhol (Eds.), *The role of early experience in infant development.* Pompton Plains, NJ: Johnson and Johnson Pediatric Institute.

GREENOUGH, W. T., BLACK, J. E., & WALLACE, C. S. (1987). Experience and brain development. *Child Development, 58,* 539–559.

GRIGORENKO, E. L., & STERNBERG, R. J. (1998). Dynamic testing. *Psychological Bulletin, 124,* 75–111.

GUERRA, N. G., & SLABY, R. G. (1990). Cognitive mediators of aggression in adolescent offenders: 2. Intervention. *Developmental Psychology, 26,* 269–277.

GUTTENTAG, R. E. (1984). The mental effort requirement of cumulative rehearsal: A developmental study. *Journal of Experimental Child Psychology, 37,* 92–106.

GUTTENTAG, R. E. (1997). Memory development and processing resources. In N. Cowan (Ed.), *The development of memory in childhood.* Hove East Sussex, UK: Psychology Press.

HAGEN, J. W., JONGEWARD, R. H., & KAIL, R. V. (1975). Cognitive perspectives on the development of memory. In H. W. Reese (Ed.), *Advances in child development and behavior* (Vol. 10). New York: Academic Press.

HAINLINE, L. (1998). The development of basic visual abilities. In A. Slater (Ed.), *Perceptual development: Visual, auditory, and speech perception in infancy.* Hove, UK: Psychology Press.

HAITH, M. M. (1980). *Rules that babies look by.* Hillsdale, NJ: Erlbaum.

HAITH, M. M. (1990). Progress in the understanding of sensory and perceptual processes in early infancy. *Merrill-Palmer Quarterly, 36,* 1–26.

HAITH, M. M. (1993). Preparing for the 21st century: Some goals and challenges for studies of infant sensory and perceptual development. *Developmental Review, 13,* 354–371.

HAITH, M. M. (1998). Who put the cog in infant cognition? *Infant Behavior and Development, 21,* 161–179.

HAITH, M. M., & BENSON, J. B. (1998). Infant cognition. In W. Damon (Series Ed.) & D. Kuhn & R. S. Siegler (Vol. Eds.), *Handbook of child psychology: Vol. 2. Cognition, perception, and language* (5th ed.). New York: Wiley.

HALA, S. (Ed.). (1997). *The development of social cognition.* Hove, UK: Psychology Press.

HALA, S., CHANDLER, M. J, & FRITZ, A. S. (1991). Fledgling theories of mind: Deception as a marker of three-year-olds' understanding of false belief. *Child Development, 62,* 83–97.

HALE, S. (1990). A global developmental trend in cognitive processing speed. *Child Development, 61,* 653–663.

HALFORD, G. S. (1982). *The development of thought.* Hillsdale, NJ: Erlbaum.

HALFORD, G. S. (1989). Reflections on 25 years of Piagetian cognitive developmental psychology, 1963–1988. *Human Development, 32,* 325–357.

HALFORD, G. S. (1993). *Children's understanding: The development of mental models.* Hillsdale, NJ: Erlbaum.

HALFORD, G. S. (1999). The properties of representations used in higher cognitive processes: Developmental implications. In I. E. Sigel (Ed.), *Development of mental representations: Theories and applications.* Mahwah, NJ: Erlbaum.

HALFORD, G. S., MAYBERY, M. T., & BAIN, J. D. (1988). Set-size effects in primary memory: An age-related capacity limitation? *Memory and Cognition, 16,* 480–487.

HAMOND, N. R., & FIVUSH, R. (1991). Memories of Mickey Mouse: Young children recount their trip to Disneyworld. *Cognitive Development, 6,* 433–448.

HAN, J .J., LEITCHMAN, M. D., & WANG, Q. (1998). Autobiographical memory in Korean, Chinese, and American Children. *Developmental Psychology, 34,* 701–713.

HARDING, C. (1984). Acting with intention: A framework for examining the development of the intention to communicate. In L. Feagans, C. Garvey, & R. Golinkoff (Eds.), *The origins and growth of communication.* Norwood, NJ: Ablex Publishing Co.

HARLEY, K., & REESE, E. (1999). Origins of autobiographical memory. *Developmental Psychology, 35,* 1338–1348.

HARNISHFEGER, K. K. (1995). The development of cognitive inhibition: Theories, definitions, and research evidence. In F. Dempster & C. Brainerd (Eds.), *New perspectives on interference and inhibition in cognition.* New York: Academic Press.

HARNISHFEGER, K. K., & BJORKLUND, D. F. (1993). The ontogeny of inhibition mechanisms: A renewed approach to cognitive development. In M. L. Howe & M. R. Pasnak (Eds.), *Emerging themes in cognitive development: Vol. 1. Foundations.* New York: Springer-Verlag.

HARRIS, M., JONES, D., & GRANT, J. (1983). The nonverbal context of mothers' speech to infants. *First Language, 4,* 21–30.

HARRIS, P. L. (1983). Infant cognition. In M. M. Haith & J. J. Campos (Eds.)., P. H. Mussen (Series Ed.), *Handbook of child psychology: Vol. 2. Infancy and developmental psychobiology.* New York: Wiley.

HARRIS, P. L. (1989a). *Children and emotion.* Oxford: Basil Blackwell.

HARRIS, P. L. (1989b). Object permanence in infancy. In A. Slater & G. Bremner (Eds.), *Infant development.* Hillsdale, NJ: Erlbaum.

HARRIS, P. L. (1992). From simulation to folk psychology: The case for development. *Mind and Language, 7,* 120–144.

HARRIS, P. L. (1994). Understanding pretense. In C. Lewis & P. Mitchell (Eds.), *Children's early understanding of mind: Origins and development.* Hillsdale, NJ: Erlbaum.

HARRIS, P. L. (1999). Acquiring the art of conversation: Children's developing conception of their conversation partner. In M. Bennett (Ed.), *Developmental psychology: Achievements and prospects.* Philadelphia: Psychology Press.

HARRIS, P. L. (2000). *Children and imagination.* Malden, MA: Blackwell.

HARRIS, P. L., BROWN, E., MARRIOTT, C., WHITTALL, S., & HARMER, S. (1991). Monsters, ghosts and witches: Testing the limits of the fantasy-reality distinction in young children. *British Journal of Developmental Psychology, 9,* 105–123.

HARRIS, P. L., DONNELLY, K., GUZ, G. R., & PITT-WATSON, R. (1986). Children's understanding of the distinction between real and apparent emotion. *Child Development, 57,* 895–909.

HART, D., & FEGLEY, S. (1994). Social imitation and the emergence of a mental model of self. In S. Parker, M. Boccia, & R. Mitchell (Eds.). *Self-awareness in animals and humans: Developmental perspectives.* New York: Cambridge University Press.

HARTER, S. (1982). Children's understanding of multiple emotions: A cognitive-developmental approach. In W. F. Overton, (Ed.), *The relationship between social and cognitive development.* Hillsdale, NJ: Erlbaum.

HARTER, S. (1988). Developmental processes in the construction of the self. In T. D. Yawkey & J. E. Johnson (Eds.). *Integrative processes and socialization: Early to middle childhood.* Hillsdale, NJ: Erlbaum.

HARTER, S. (1998). The development of self-representations. In W. Damon (Series Ed.) & N. Eisenberg (Vol. Ed.), *Handbook of child psychology (5th ed.): Vol. 3, Social, emotional, and personality development.* New York, Wiley.

HARTER, S. (1999). *The construction of the self: A developmental perspective.* New York: Guilford Press.

HARTER, S. & BUDDIN, B. (1987). Children's understanding of the simultaneity of two emotions: A five-stage developmental acquisition sequence. *Developmental Psychology, 23,* 388–399.

HARTNETT, P., & GELMAN, R. (1998). Early understanding of numbers: Paths or barriers to the construction of new understanding? *Learning and Instruction, 8,* 341–374.

HASSELHORN, M. (1992). Task dependency and the role of category typicality and metamemory in the development of an organizational strategy. *Child Development, 63,* 202–214.

HASSELHORN, M. (1995). Beyond production deficiency and utilization inefficiency: Mechanisms of the emergence of strategic categorization in episodic memory tasks. In F. E. Weinert & W. Schneider (Eds.), *Memory performance and competencies: Issues in growth and development.* Mahwah, NJ: Erlbaum.

HAYES, C. (1951). *The ape in our house.* New York: Harper.

HAYNE, H. (1996). Categorization in infancy. In C. Rovee-Collier & L. P. Lipsitt (Eds.), *Advances in infancy research* (Vol. 10). Norwood, NJ: Ablex.

HAYNE, H., ROVEE-COLLIER, C., & PERRIS, E. E. (1987). Categorization and memory retrieval by three-month-olds. *Child Development, 58,* 750–767.

HEILBECK, T. H., & MARKMAN, E. M. (1987). Word learning in children: An examination of fast mapping. *Child Development, 58,* 1021–1034.

HEYMAN, G. D., & GELMAN, S. A. (1998). Young children use motive information to make trait inferences. *Developmental Psychology, 34,* 310–321.

HEYMAN, G. D., & GELMAN, S. A. (1999). The use of trait labels in making psychological inferences. *Child Development, 70,* 604–619.

HICKEY, F. L., & PEDUZZI, J. D. (1987). Structure and development of the visual system. In P. Salapatek & L. Cohen (Eds.), *Handbook of infant perception: Vol. 1. From sensation to perception.* Orlando, FL: Academic Press.

HICKLING, A. K., WELLMAN, H. M., & GOTT-FRIED, G. M. (1997). Preschoolers' understanding of others' mental attitudes towards pretend happenings. *British Journal of Developmental Psychology, 15,* 339–354.

HIRSH-PASEK, K., & GOLINKOFF, R. (1996). *The origins of grammar.* Cambridge, MA: MIT Press.

HITCH, G. J., & TOWSE, J. (1995). Working memory: What develops? In F. E. Weinert & W. Schneider (Eds.), *Memory performance and competencies: Issues in growth and development.* Hillsdale, NJ: Erlbaum.

HOBSON, R. P. (1991). Against the theory of "theory of mind." *British Journal of Developmental Psychology, 9,* 33–51.

HOCHBERG, J. E. (1962). Nativism and empiricism in perception. In L. Postman (Ed.), *Psychology in the making.* New York: Knopf.

HOCK, H. S., PARK, C. L., & BJORKLUND, D. F. (1998). Temporal organization in children's strategy formation. *Journal of Experimental Child Psychology, 70,* 187–206.

HOEK, D., INGRAM, D., & GIBSON, D. (1986). An examination of the possible causes of children's early word extensions. *Journal of Child Language, 13,* 477–494.

HOFFMAN, M. L. (1981). Perspectives on the difference between understanding people and understanding things. The role of affect. In J. H. Flavell & L. Ross (Eds.), *Social cognitive development: Frontiers and possible futures.* Cambridge: Cambridge University Press.

HOFSTADTER, M. C., & REZNICK, J. S. (1996). Response modality affects human infant delayed-response performance. *Child Development, 67,* 646–658.

HOFSTEN, C. VON (1980). Predictive reaching for moving objects by human infants. *Journal of Experimental Child Psychology, 30,* 369–382.

HOFSTEN, C. VON, & SPELKE, E. S. (1985). Object perception and object-directed reaching in infancy. *Journal of Experimental Psychology: General, 114,* 198–212.

HOLCOMB, W. L., STROMER, R., & MACKAY, H. A. (1997). Transitivity and emergent sequence performances in young children. *Journal of Experimental Child Psychology, 65,* 96–124.

HOLLICH, G. J., HIRSH-PASEK, K., & GOLINKOFF, R. M. (2000). Breaking the language barrier: An emergentist coalition model of word learning. *Monographs of the Society for Research in Child Development, 65* (3, Serial No. 262).

HOOD, L., & BLOOM, L. (1979). What, when, and how about why: A longitudinal study of early expressions of causality. *Monographs of the Society for Research in Child Development, 44* (6, Serial No. 181).

HOWE, M. L. (2000). *The fate of early memories.* Washington, DC: APA.

HOWE, M. L., & COURAGE, M. L. (1997). The emergence and early development of autobiographical memory. *Psychological Review, 104,* 499–523.

HOWE, M. L., & RABINOWITZ, F. M. (1989). On the uninterpretability of dual-task performance. *Journal of Experimental Child Psychology, 47,* 32–38.

HUDSON, J. A. (1986). Memories are made of this: General event knowledge and development of autobiographic memory. In K. Nelson (Ed.), *Event knowledge: Structure and function in development.* Hillsdale, NJ: Erbaum.

HUDSON, J. A. (1990). The emergence of autobiographical memory in mother-child conversations. In R. Fivush & J. A. Hudson (Eds.), *Knowing and remembering in young children.* NY: Cambridge University Press.

HUDSON, J. A., & FIVUSH, R. (1991). As time goes by: Sixth grade children recall a kindergarten experience. *Applied Cognitive Psychology, 5,* 346–360.

HUDSON, J. A., & SHEFFIELD, E. G. (1999). The role of reminders in young children's memory development. In L. Balter & C. S. Tamis-Lemonda (Eds.), *Child psychology: A hand-*

book of contemporary issues. Philadelphia: Psychology Press.

HUGHES, C. (1998). Finding your marbles: Does preschoolers' strategic behavior predict later understanding of mind? *Developmental Psychology, 34,* 1326–1339.

HUTTENLOCHER, J., NEWCOMBE, N., & VASILYEVA, M. (1999). Spatial scaling in young children. *Psychological Science, 10,* 393–397.

HUTTENLOCHER, J., & SMILEY, P. (1990). Emerging notions of persons. In N. L. Stein, B. Leventhal, & T. Trabasso (Eds.), *Psychological and biological approaches to emotions.* Hillsdale, NJ: Erlbaum.

HUTTENLOCHER, P. R. (1999). Synaptogenesis in human cerebral cortex and the concept of critical periods. In N. A. Fox, L. A. Leavitt, & J. G. Warhol (Eds.), *The role of early experience in infant development.* Pompton Plains, NJ: Johnson and Johnson Pediatric Institute.

INAGAKI, K. (1997). Emerging distinctions between naïve biology and naïve psychology. In H. M.Wellman & K. Inagaki (Eds.), *New directions for child development: No. 75. The emergence of core domains of thought: Children's reasoning about physical, psychological, and biological phenomena.* San Francisco: Jossey Bass.

INAGAKI, K., & HATANO, G. (1987). Young children's spontaneous personification as analogy. *Child Development, 58,* 1013–1020.

INAGAKI, K., & HATANO, G (1996). Young children's recognition of commonalities between animals and plants. *Child Development, 67,* 2823–2840.

INAGAKI, K., & SUGIYAMA, K. (1988). Attributing human characteristics: Developmental changes in over- and underattribution. *Cognitive Development, 3,* 55–70.

INGRAM, D. (1989). *First language acquisition.* Cambridge: Cambridge University Press.

INHELDER, B., & PIAGET, J. (1958). *The growth of logical thinking from childhood to adolescence.* New York: Basic Books.

INHELDER, B., & PIAGET, J. (1964). *The early growth of logic in the child.* New York: Harper & Row.

JAMES, W. (1890). *The principles of psychology* (Vol. 1). New York: Henry Hold.

JENKINS, J. M., & ASTINGTON, J. W. (1996). Cognitive factors and family structure associated with theory of mind development in young children. *Developmental Psychology, 32,* 70–78.

JENKINS, J. M., & ASTINGTON, J. W. (2000). Theory of mind and social behavior: Causal models tested in a longitudinal study. *Merrill-Palmer Quarterly, 46,* 203–220.

JOHNSON, C. N. (1990). If you had my brain, where would I be? Children's understanding of the brain and identity. *Child Development, 61,* 962–972.

JOHNSON, J., & NEWPORT, E. (1989). Critical period effects in second language learning: The influence of maturational state on the acquisition of English as a second language. *Cognitive Psychology, 21,* 60–99.

JOHNSON, K. E., & MERVIS, C. B. (1994). Microgenetic analysis of first steps in children's acquisition of expertise on shorebirds. *Developmental Psychology, 30,* 418–435.

JOHNSON, K. E., & MERVIS, C. B. (1998). Impact of intuitive theories on feature recruitment throughout the continuum of expertise. *Memory & Cognition, 26,* 383–401.

JOHNSON, K. E., SCOTT, P., & MERVIS, C. B. (1997). Development of children's understanding of basic-subordinate inclusion relations. *Developmental Psychology, 33,* 745–763.

JOHNSON, M. H. (1998). The neural basis of cognitive development. In W. Damon (Series Ed.) & D. Kuhn & R. S. Siegler (Vol. Eds.), *Handbook of child psychology: Vol. 2. Cognition, perception, and language* (5th ed.). New York: Wiley.

JOHNSON, M. H. (1999a). Developmental cognitive neuroscience. In M. Bennett (Ed.), *Developmental psychology: Achievements and prospects.* Philadelphia: Psychology Press.

JOHNSON, M. H. (1999b). Developmental neuroscience. In M. H. Bornstein & M. E. Lamb (Eds.), *Developmental psychology: An advanced textbook.* Mahwah, NJ: Erlbaum.

JOHNSON, M. H. (2000). Functional brain development in infants: Elements of an interactive specialization framework. *Child Development, 71,* 75–81.

JOHNSON, M. H., DZIURAWIEC, S., ELLIS, H., & MORTON, J. (1991). Newborns' preferential tracking of facelike stimuli and its subsequent decline. *Cognition, 40,* 1–19.

JOHNSON, M. H., & MORTON, J. (1991). *Biology and cognitive development: The case of face recognition.* Cambridge, MA: Blackwell.

JOHNSON, S. P. (1998). Object perception and object knowledge in young infants: A view from studies of visual development. In A. Slater (Ed.), *Perceptual development: Visual, auditory, and speech perception in infancy.* Hove, UK: Psychology Press.

JOHNSON, S. P., & ASLIN, R. N. (1995). Perception of object unity in 2-month-old infants. *Developmental Psychology, 31,* 739–745.

JOHNSTON, J., & SLOBIN, D. I. (1979). The development of locative expressions in English, Italian, Serbo-Croatian, and Turkish. *Journal of Child Language, 6,* 531–547.

JOHNSTON, J. R. (1985). Cognitive prerequisites: The evidence from children learning English. In D. I. Slobin (Ed.), *The crosslinguistic study of language acquisition: Vol. 2. Theoretical issues.* Hillsdale, NJ: Erlbaum.

JONES, E. E. (1990). *Interpersonal perception.* New York: W. H. Freeman.

JONES, S. S. (1996). Imitation or exploration? Young infants' matching of adults' oral gestures. *Child Development, 67,* 1952–1969.

JORDAN, N. (1972). Is there an Achilles heel in Piaget's theorizing? *Human Development, 15,* 379–382.

JOSEPH, R. M. (1998). Intention and knowledge in preschoolers' conception of pretend. *Child Development, 69,* 966–980.

JOSHI, M. S., & MACLEAN, M. (1994). Indian and English children's understanding of the distinction between real and apparent emotion. *Child Development, 65,* 1372–1384.

JOYNER, M. H., & KURTZ-COSTES, B. (1997). Metamemory development. In N. Cowan (Ed.), *The development of memory in childhood.* Hove East Sussex, UK: Psychology Press.

JUSCZYK, P. W. (1997). *The discovery of spoken language.* Cambridge: MIT Press.

JUSCZYK, P. W., HOUSTON, D. M., & GOODMAN, M. (1998). Speech perception during the first year. In A. Slater (Ed.), *Perceptual development: Visual, auditory, and speech perception in infancy.* Hove, UK: Psychology Press.

JUSTICE, E. M. (1989). Preschoolers' knowledge and use of behaviors varying in strategic effectiveness. *Merrill-Palmer Quarterly, 35,* 363–377.

JUSTICE, E. M., BAKER-WARD, L., GUPTA, S., & JANNINGS, R. (1997). Means to the goal of remembering: Developmental changes in awareness of strategy use-performance relations. *Journal of Experimental Child Psychology, 76,* 293–314.

KAIL, R. V. (1991). Development of processing speed in childhood and adolescence. In H. W. Reese (Ed.), *Advances in child development*

and behavior (Vol. 23), San Diego, CA: Academic Press.

KAIL, R. V. (1997). Phonological skill and articulation time independently contribute to the development of memory span. *Journal of Experimental Child Psychology, 67,* 57–68.

KAIL, R. V. (2000). Speed of information processing: Developmental change and links to intelligence. *Journal of School Psychology, 38,* 51–61.

KAIL, R. V., & SALTHOUSE, T. A. (1994). Processing speed as a mental capacity. *Acta Psychologica, 86,* 199–225.

KAISER, M. K., McCLOSKEY, M., & PROFFITT, D. R. (1986). Development of intuitive theories of motion: Curvilinear motion in the absence of external forces. *Developmental Psychology, 22,* 67–71.

KAISER, M. K., PROFFITT, D. R., & McCLOSKEY, M. (1985). The development of beliefs about falling objects. *Perception and Psychophysics, 38,* 533–539.

KALISH, C. W. (1997). Preschoolers' understanding of mental and bodily reactions to contamination: What you don't know can hurt you, but cannot sadden you. *Developmental Psychology, 33,* 79–91.

KALISH, C. W. (1998). Natural and artifactual kinds: Are children realists or relativists about categories? *Developmental Psychology, 34,* 376–391.

KALISH, C. W. (1996). Causes and symptoms in preschoolers' conceptions of illness. *Child Development, 67,* 1647–1670.

KALISH, C. W., & GELMAN, S. A. (1992). On wooden pillows: Multiple classification and children's category-based inductions. *Child Development, 63,* 1536–1557.

KARMILOFF-SMITH, A. (1992). *Beyond modularity: A developmental perspective on cognitive science.* Cambridge, MA: MIT Press.

KARMILOFF-SMITH, A., GRANT, J., BERTHOUD, I., DAVIES, M., HOULIN, P., & UDWIN, O. (1997). Language and Williams Syndrome: How intact is "intact"? *Child Development, 68,* 246–262.

KARZON, R. G. (1985). Discrimination of polysyllabic sequences by one- to four-month-old infants. *Journal of Experimental Child Psychology, 39,* 326–342.

KAVANAUGH, R. D., & HARRIS, P. L., (1999). Pretense and counterfactual thought in young children. In L. Balter & C. S. Tamis-LeMonda (Eds.), *Child psychology: A handbook of contemporary issues.* Philadelphia: Psychology Press.

KAY, D. A., & ANGLIN, J. (1982). Overextension and underextension in the child's expressive and receptive speech. *Journal of Child Language, 9,* 83–98.

KEARINS, J. M. (1981). Visual spatial memory in Australian aboriginal children of desert regions. *Cognitive Psychology, 13,* 434–460.

KEATING, D. P. (1988). Byrnes' reformulation of Piaget's formal operations: Is what's left what's right? Commentary. *Developmental Review, 8,* 376–384.

KEATING, D. P. (1990). Adolescent thinking. In S. S. Feldman & G. R. Elliot (Eds.), *At the threshold: The developing adolescent.* Cambridge, MA: Harvard University Press.

KEENEY, T. J., CANNIZZO, S. R., & FLAVELL, J. H. (1967). Spontaneous and induced verbal rehearsal in a recall task. *Child Development, 38,* 953–966.

KEIL, F. C. (1979). *Semantic and conceptual development.* Cambridge, MA: Harvard University Press.

KEIL, F. C. (1981). Constraints on knowledge and cognitive development. *Psychological Review, 88,* 197–227.

KEIL, F. C. (1989). *Concepts, kinds, and cognitive development.* Cambridge, MA: MIT Press.

KEIL, F. C. (1991). The emergence of theoretical beliefs as constraints on concepts. In S. Carey & R. Gelman (Eds.), *The epigenesis of mind: Essays on biology and cognition.* Hillsdale, NJ: Erlbaum.

KEIL, F. C. (1992). The origins of an autonomous biology. In M. R. Gunnar & M. Maratsos (Eds.), *Minnesota symposia on child psychology: Vol. 25. Modularity and constraints in language and cognition.* Hillsdale, NJ: Erlbaum.

KEIL, F. C., & BATTERMAN, N. (1984). A characteristic-to-defining shift in the development of word meaning. *Journal of Verbal Learning and Verbal Behavior, 23,* 221–236.

KEIL, F. C., LEVIN, D. T., RICHMAN, B. A., & GUTHEIL, G. (1999). Mechanism and explanation in the development of biological thought: The case of disease. In D. Medin & S. Atran (Eds.), *Folkbiology.* Cambridge, MA: MIT Press.

KELLMAN, P. J., & ARTERBERRY, M. E. (1998). *The cradle of knowledge: Development of perception in infancy.* Cambridge: MIT Press.

KELLMAN, P. J., & BANKS, M. S. (1998). Infant visual perception. In W. Damon (Series Ed.) & D. Kuhn & R. S. Siegler (Vol. Eds.), *Handbook of child psychology: Vol. 2. Cognition, perception, and language* (5th ed.). New York: Wiley.

KELLMAN, P. J., & SPELKE, E. S. (1983). Perception of partly occluded objects in infancy. *Cognitive Psychology, 15,* 483–524.

KEMLER NELSON, D. G., HIRSH-PASEK, K., JUSCZYK, P., & CASSIDY, K. W. (1989). How the prosodic cues in motherese might assist language learning. *Journal of Child Language, 16,* 55–68.

KERMOIAN, R., & CAMPOS, J. J. (1988). Locomotor experience: A facilitator of spatial cognitive development. *Child Development, 59,* 908–917.

KESTENBAUM, R., & GELMAN, S. A. (1995). Preschool children's identification and understanding of mixed emotions. *Cognitive Development, 10,* 443–458.

KESTENBAUM, R., TERMINE, N., & SPELKE, E. S. (1987). Perception of objects and object boundaries by three-month-old infants. *British Journal of Developmental Psychology, 5,* 367–383.

KIM, I. K., & SPELKE, E. S. (1999). Perception and understanding of effects of gravity and inertia on object motion. *Developmental Science, 2,* 339–362.

KINGMA, J., & VAN DEN BOS, K. P. (1988). Unidimensional scales: New methods to analyze the sequences in concept development. *Genetic, Social, and General Psychology Monographs, 114,* 479–508.

KISTER, M. C., & PATTERSON, C. J. (1980). Children's conceptions of the causes of illness: Understanding of contagion and use of immanent justice. *Child Development, 51,* 839–846.

KLACZYNSKI, P. A., & NARASIMHAM, G. (1998). Development of scientific reasoning biases: Cognitive versus ego-protective explanations. *Developmental Psychology, 34,* 175–187.

KLAHR, D. (2000). *Exploring science: The cognition and development of discovery processes.* Cambridge, MA: MIT Press /Bradford.

KLAHR, D., & MACWHINNEY, B. (1998). Information processing. In W. Damon (Series Ed.) & D. Kuhn & R. S. Siegler (Vol. Eds.), *Handbook of child psychology: Vol. 2. Cognition, perception, and language* (5th ed.). New York: Wiley.

KOHLBERG, L. (1969). Stage and sequence: The cognitive-developmental approach to socialization. In A. A. Goslin (Ed.), *Handbook of socialization theory and research.* Skokie, IL: Rand McNally.

KOPP, C. B., & SHAPERMAN, J. (1973). Cognitive development in the absence of object manipulation during infancy. *Developmental Psychology, 9,* 430.

KOSLOWSKI, B. (1996). *Theory and evidence: The develoment of scientific reasoning.* Cambridge, MA: Bradford.

KOTOVSKY, L., & BAILLARGEON, R. (1994). Calibration-based reasoning about collision events in 11-month-old infants. *Cognition, 51,* 107–129.

KOTOVSKY, L., & BAILLARGEON, R. (1998). The development of calibration-based reasoning about collision events in 11-month-old infants. *Cognition, 67,* 311–351.

KRAUSS, R. M., & GLUCKSBERG, S. (1969). The development of communication: Competence as a function of age. *Child Development, 40,* 255–266.

KREITLER, S., & KREITLER, H. (1987). Conceptions and processes of planning: The developmental perspective. In S. L. Friedman, E. K. Scholnick, & R. R. Cocking (Eds.), *Blueprints for thinking: The role of planning in cognitive development.* New York: Cambridge University Press.

KREUTZER, M. A., LEONARD, C., & FLAVELL, J. H. (1975). An interview study of children's knowledge about memory. *Monographs of the Society for Research in Child Development, 40* (1, Serial No 159).

KUCZAJ, S. A., II. (1977). The acquisition of regular and irregular past tense forms. *Journal of Verbal Learning and Verbal Behavior, 16,* 589–600.

KUCZAJ, S. A., II. (1981). Factors influencing children's hypothetical reference. *Journal of Child Language, 8,* 131–137.

KUCZAJ, S. A., II. (1999). The world of words: Thoughts on the development of a lexicon. In M. Barrett (Ed.), *The development of language* (pp. 133–159). Hove, UK: Psychology Press.

KUEBLI, J., & FIVUSH, R. (1994). Children's representation and recall of event alternatives. *Journal of Experimental Child Psychology, 58,* 25–45.

KUHL, P. K. (1987). Perception of speech and sound in early infancy. In P. Salapatek & L. Cohen (Eds.), *Handbook of infant perception: Vol. 2. From perception to cognition.* Orlando, FL: Academic Press.

KUHL, P. K., & MELTZOFF, A. N. (1982). The bimodal perception of speech in infancy. *Science, 218,* 1138–1141.

KUHL, P. K., & MELTZOFF, A. N. (1984). The intermodal representation of speech in infants.

Infant Behavior and Development, 7, 361–381.

KUHL, P. K., & MELTZOFF, A. N. (1988). Speech as an intermodal object of perception. In A. Yonas (Ed.), *Minnesota symposia on child psychology: Vol. 20. Perceptual development in infancy.* Hillsdale, NJ: Erlbaum.

KUHL, P. K., & MILLER, J. D. (1975). Speech perception by the chinchilla: Voiced-voiceless distinction in alveolar plosive consonants. *Science, 190,* 69–72.

KUHL, P. K., & PADDEN, D. M. (1983). Enhanced discriminability at the phonetic boundaries for the place features in macaques. *Journal of the Acoustical Society of America, 73,* 1003–1010.

KUHN, D. (1974). Inducing development experimentally: Comments on a research paradigm. *Developmental Psychology, 10,* 590–600.

KUHN, D. (1995). Microgenetic study of change: What has it told us? *Psychological Science, 6,* 135–139.

KUHN, D. (1999). Metacognitive development. In L. Balter & C. S. Tamis-Monda (Eds.). *Child psychology: A handbook of contemporary issues.* Philadelphia: Psychology Press.

KUHN, D. (2000). Why development does (and doesn't) occur: Evidence from the domain of inductive reasoning. In J. McClelland & R. Siegler (Eds.), *Mechanisms of cognitive development: Behavioral and neural perspectives.* Mahwah, NJ: Erlbaum.

KUHN, D., AMSEL, E., & O'LOUGHLIN, M. (1988). *The development of scientific thinking skills.* San Diego, CA: Academic Press.

KUHN, D., GARCIA-MILA, M., ZOHAR, A., & ANDERSEN, C. (1995). Strategies of knowledge acquisition. *Monographs of the Society for Research in Child Development, 60* (Serial No. 245).

KUHN, D., & PEARSALL, S. (1998). Relations between metastrategic knowledge and strategic performance. *Cognitive Development, 13,* 227–247.

KUHN, D., & PEARSALL, S. (2000). Developmental origins of scientific thinking. *Journal of Cognition and Development, 1,* 113–129.

KURTZ, B. E. (1990). Cultural influences on children's cognitive and metacognitive development. In W. Schneider & F. E. Weinert (Eds.), *Interactions among aptitude, strategies, and knowledge in cognitive performance.* Hillsdale, NJ: Erlbaum.

KURTZ, B. E., & BORKOWSKI, J. G. (1984). Children's metacognition: Exploring relations among knowledge, process, and motivational variables. *Journal of Experimental Child Psychology, 37,* 335–354.

KURTZ, B. E., SCHNEIDER, W., CARR, M., BORKOWSKI, J. G., & RELLINGER, E. (1990). Strategy instruction and attributional beliefs in West Germany and the United States: Do teachers foster metacognitive development? *Contemporary Educational Psychology, 15,* 268–283.

KURTZ-COSTES, B., SCHNEIDER, W., & RUPP, S. (1995). Is there evidence for intraindividual consistency in performance across memory tasks? New evidence on an old question. In F. E. Weinert & W. Schneider (Eds.), *Memory performance and competencies: Issues in growth and development.* Hillsdale, NJ: Erlbaum.

LACHMAN, R., LACHMAN, J. L., & BUTTERFIELD, E. C. (1979). *Cognitive psychology and information processing: An introduction.* Hillsdale, NJ: Erlbaum.

LAKOFF, R. (1977). What you can do with words: Politeness, pragmatics, and performatives. In A. Rogers, B. Wall, & J. Murphy (Eds.), *Proceedings of the Texas conference on performatives, presuppositions, and implicatures.* Arlington, VA: Center for Applied Linguistics.

LALONDE, C. E., & CHANDLER, M. J. (1995). False belief understanding goes to school: On the social-emotional consequences on coming early or late to a first theory of mind. *Cognition and Emotion, 9,* 167–186.

LANDAU, B. (1991). Spatial representation of objects in the young blind child. *Cognition, 38,* 145–178.

LANDAU, B., SPELKE, E. S., & GLEITMAN, H. (1984). Spatial knowledge in a young blind child. *Cognition, 16,* 225–260.

LANDRY, M. O., & LYONS-RUTH, K. (1980). Recursive structure in cognitive perspective taking. *Child Development, 51,* 386–394.

LANGER, J. (1998). Phylogenetic and ontogenetic origins of cognition: Classification. In J. Langer & M. Killen (Eds.), *Piaget, evolution, and development.* Mahwah, NJ: Erlbaum

LANGER, J., & KILLEN, M. (Eds.). (1998). *Piaget, evolution, and development.* Mahwah, NJ: Erlbaum.

LANGER, J., RIVERA, S., SCHLESINGER, M., & WAKELEY, A. (in press). Cognitive development in the first two years. In J. Valsiner & K. Connolly (Eds.), *Handbook of developmental psychology.* London: Sage.

LANGLOIS, J. H., RITTER, J. M., ROGGMANN, L. A., & VAUGHN, L. S. (1991). Facial diversity and infant preferences for attractive faces. *Developmental Psychology, 27,* 79–84.

LECANUET, J-P. (1998). Faetal responses to auditory and speech stimuli. In A. Slater (Ed.), *Perceptual development: Visual, auditory, and speech perception in infancy.* Hove, UK: Psychology Press.

LEGERSTEE, M. (1991). The role of person and object in eliciting early imitation. *Journal of Experimental Child Psychology, 51,* 423–433.

LEGERSTEE, M. (1992). A review of the animate-inanimate distinction in infancy: Implications for models of social and cognitive knowing. *Early Development and Parenting, 1,* 59–67.

LEGERSTEE, M., ANDERSON, D., & SCHAFFER, A. (1998). Five- and eight-month-old infants recognize their faces and voices as familiar and social stimuli. *Child Development, 69,* 37–50.

LEMPERS, J. D., FLAVELL, E. R., & FLAVELL, J. H. (1977). The development in very young children of tacit knowledge concerning visual perception. *Genetic Psychology Monographs, 95,* 3–53.

LENNEBERG, E. H. (1967). *Biological foundations of language.* New York: John Wiley.

LENNEBERG, E. H., REBELSKY, F. G., & NICHOLS, I. A. (1965). The vocalization of infants born to deaf and hearing parents. *Human Development, 8,* 23–37.

LERNER, R. M. (1998). Theories of human development: Contemporary perspectives. In W. Damon (Series Ed.) & R. M. Lerner (Vol. Ed.), *Handbook of child psychology: Vol. 1. Theoretical models of human development* (5th ed.). New York: Wiley.

LESLIE, A. M. (1984). Spatiotemporal continuity and the perception of causality in infants. *Perception, 13,* 287–305.

LESLIE, A. M. (1986). Getting development off the ground: Modularity and the infant's perception of causality. In P. van Geert (Ed.), *Theory building in developmental psychology.* Amsterdam: Elsevier Science Publishers.

LESLIE, A. M. (1987). Pretense and representation: The origins of "theory of mind." *Psychological Review, 94,* 412–426.

LESLIE, A. M. (1988). The necessity of illusion: Perception and thought in infancy. In L. Weiskrantz (Ed.), *Thought without language.* Oxford: Clarendon Press.

LESLIE, A. M. (1994). ToMM, ToBy, and agency: Core architecture and domain specificity. In

L. A. Hirschfeld & S. A. Gelman (Eds.), *Mapping the mind: Domain specificity in cognition and culture.* Cambridge, England: Cambridge University Press.

LESLIE, A. M. (1995). A theory of agency. In D. Sperber, D. Premack, & A. J. Premack (Eds.), *Causal cognition.* Oxford: Clarendon Press.

LESLIE, A. M., & KEEBLE, S. (1987). Do six-month-old infants perceive causality? *Cognition, 25,* 265–288.

LESLIE, A. M., & ROTH, D. (1993), What autism teaches us about metarepresentation. In S. Baron-Cohen, H. Tager-Flusberg, & D. J. Cohen (Eds.), *Understanding other minds: Perspectives from autism.* Oxford, England: Oxford University Press.

LEVIN, I. (Ed.). (1986). *Stage and structure: Reopening the debate.* Norwood, NJ: Ablex.

LEVIN, I., SIEGLER, R. S., & DRUYAN, S. (1990). Misconceptions about motion: Development and training effects. *Child Development, 61,* 1544–1557.

LEVI-STRAUSS, C. (1967). *Savage thought.* Chicago: Chicago University Press.

LEWIS, C. (1994). Episodes, events, and narratives in the child's understanding of mind. In C. Lewis & P. Mitchell (Eds.), *Children's early understanding of mind: Origins and development.* Hillsdale, NJ: Erlbaum.

LEWIS, C., & MITCHELL, P. (Eds.). (1994). *Children's early understanding of mind: Origins and development.* Hillsdale, NJ: Erlbaum.

LEWIS, C. C. (1995). *Educating hearts and minds.* New York: Cambridge University Press.

LEWIS, M. (1989). Cultural differences in children's knowledge of emotional scripts. In C. Saarni & P. L. Harris (Eds.), *Children's understanding of emotion.* Cambridge University Press.

LEWIS, M. (1999). Social cognition and the self. In P. Rochat (Ed.), *Early social cognition.* Mahweh, NJ: Erlbaum.

LEWIS, M., & BROOKS-GUNN, J. (1979). *Social cognition and the acquisition of self.* New York: Plenum Press.

LEWIS, M., SULLIVAN, M. W., STANGER, C., & WEISS, M. (1989). Self development and self-conscious emotions. *Child Development, 60,* 146–156.

LEWIS, M. D. (2000). The promise of dynamic systems approaches for an integrated account of human development. *Child Development, 71,* 36–43.

LEWKOWICZ, D. J., & LICKLITER, R. (Eds.). (1994). *The development of intersensory perception: Comparative perspectives.* Hillsdale, NJ: Erlbaum.

LIBEN, L. S. (1999). Developing an understanding of external spatial representations. In I. E. Sigel (Ed.), *Development of mental representation: Theories and applications.* Mahwah, NJ: Erlbaum.

LIBEN, L. S., & DOWNS, R. M. (1991). The role of graphic representations in understanding the world. In R. M. Downs, L. S. Liben, & D. S. Palermo (Eds.), *Visions of aesthetics, the environment, and development: The legacy of Joachim Wohlwill.* Hillsdale, NJ: Erlbaum.

LICKLITER, R., & BAHRICK, L. E. (2000). The development of infant intersensory perception: Advantages of a comparative convergent-operations approach. *Psychological Bulletin, 126,* 260–280.

LILLARD, A. S. (1993). Young children's conceptualization of pretense: Action or mental representational state? *Child Development, 64,* 372–386.

LILLARD, A. S. (1994). Making sense of pretense. In C. Lewis & P. Mitchell (Eds.), *Children's early understanding of mind: Origins and development.* Hillsdale, NJ: Erlbaum.

LILLARD, A. S. (1996). Body or mind: Children's categorization of pretense. *Child Development, 67,* 1717–1734.

LILLARD, A. S. (1998a). Ethnopsychologies: Cultural variations in theories of mind. *Psychological Bulletin, 123,* 3–32.

LILLARD, A. S. (1998b). Wanting to be it: Children's understanding of intentions underlying pretense. *Child Development, 69,* 981–993.

LILLARD, A. S., & FLAVELL, J. H. (1990). Young children's preference for mental state versus behavioral descriptions of human action. *Child Development, 61,* 731–741.

LILLARD, A. S., & SOBEL, D. (1999). Lion Kings or Puppies: Children's understanding of pretense. *Developmental Science, 2,* 75–80.

LIVESLEY, W. J., & BROMLEY, D. B. (1973). *Person perception in childhood and adolescence.* London: Wiley.

LLOYD, P., CAMAIONI, L., & ERCOLANI, P. (1995). Assessing referential skills in the primary school years: A comparative study. *British Journal of Developmental Psychology, 13,* 13–29.

LLOYD, P., MANN, S, & PEERS, I. (1998). The growth of speaker and listener skills from five to eleven years. *First Language, 18,* 81–103.

LOCKE, J. L. (1983). *Phonological acquisition and change.* New York: Academic Press.

LOCKE, J. L. (1997). A theory of neurolinguistic development. *Brain and Language, 58,* 265–326.

LOCKE, J. L., & PEARSON, D. M. (1990). Linguistic significance of babbling: Evidence from a tracheostomized infant. *Journal of Child Language, 17,* 1–16.

LOCKMAN, J. J. (2000). A perception-action perspective on tool use development. *Child Development, 71,* 137–144.

LOURENCO, O., & MACHADO, A. (1996). In defense of Piaget's theory: A reply to 10 common criticisms. *Psychological Review,103,* 143–164.

LOVETT, S. B., & FLAVELL, J. H. (1990). Understanding and remembering: Children's knowledge about the differential effects of strategy and task variables on comprehension and memorization. *Child Development, 61,* 1842–1858.

LOVETT, S. B., & PILLOW, B. H. (1995). Development of the ability to distinguish between comprehension and memory: Evidence from strategy-selection tasks. *Journal of Educational Psychology, 87,* 523–536.

LOVETT, S. B., & PILLOW, B. H. (1996). Development of the ability to distinguish between comprehension and memory: Evidence from goal-state evaluation tasks. *Journal of Educational Psychology, 88,* 546–562.

LUTZ, C. (1983). Parental goals, ethnopsychology, and the development of emotional meaning. *Ethos, 11,* 246–262.

LYNCH, M. P., EILERS, R. E., OLLER, K. D., & URBANO, R. C. (1990). Innateness, experience, and music perception. *Psychological Science, 1,* 272–276.

MACK, N. K. (1990). Learning fractions with understanding: Building on informal knowledge. *Journal for Research in Mathematics Education, 21,* 16–32.

MACWHINNEY, B. (1987). The competition model. In B. MacWhinney (Ed.), *Mechanisms of language acquisition.* Hillsdale, NJ: Erlbaum.

MACWHINNEY, B. (1989). Competition and connectionism. In B. MacWhinney & E. Bates (Eds.), *The crosslinguistic study of sentence processing.* Cambridge: Cambridge University Press.

MACWHINNEY, B. (1995). *The CHILDES project: Tools for analyzing talk.* Hillsdale, NJ: Erlbaum.

MACWHINNEY, B. (1999a). The CHILDES system. In W. C. Ritchie & T. K. Bhatia (Eds.), *Handbook of child language acquisition.* San Diego: Academic Press.

MACWHINNEY, B. (Ed.). (1999b). *The emergence of language.* Mahwah, NJ: Erlbaum.

MACWHINNEY, B. J., LEINBACH, J., TARABAN, R., & MCDONALD, J. L. (1989). Language learning: Cues or rules? *Journal of Memory and Language, 28,* 255–277.

MADOLE, K. L., & OAKES, L.M. (1999). Making sense of infant categorization: Stable processes and changing representations. *Developmental Review, 19,* 263–296.

MAGUIRE, M., & DUNN, J. (1997). Friendships in early childhood and social understanding. *International Journal of Behavioral Development, 21,* 669–686.

MAIN, M., & GOLDWIN, R. (1998). Adult attachment rating and classification systems. In M. Main (Ed.), *Assessing attachment through discourse, drawings, and reunion situations.* New York: Cambridge University Press.

MANDLER, J. M. (1983). Representation. In J. H. Flavell & E. M. Markman (Eds.), P. H. Mussen (Series Ed.), *Handbook of child psychology: Vol. 3. Cognitive development.* New York: Wiley.

MANDLER, J. M. (1988). How to build a baby: On the development of an accessible representational system. *Cognitive Development, 3,* 113–136.

MANDLER, J. M. (1990). Recall of events by preverbal infants. In A. Diamond (Ed.), *The development and neural bases of higher cognitive functions.* New York: The New York Academy of Sciences.

MANDLER, J. M. (1992a). The foundations of conceptual thought in infancy. *Cognitive Development, 7,* 273–285.

MANDLER, J. M. (1992b). How to build a baby: II. Conceptual primitives. *Psychological Review, 99,* 587–604.

MANDLER, J. M. (1998). Representation. In W. Damon (Series Ed.) & D. Kuhn & R. S. Siegler (Vol. Eds.), *Handbook of child psychology: Vol. 2. Cognition, perception, and language* (5th ed.). New York: Wiley.

MANDLER, J. M. (2000). Perceptual and conceptual processes in infancy. *Journal of Cognition and Development, 1,* 3–36.

MANDLER, J. M., & BAUER, P. J. (1988). The cradle of categorization: Is the basic level basic? *Cognitive Development, 3,* 247–264.

MANDLER, J. M., & BAUER, P. J., & MCDONOUGH, L. (1991). Separating the sheep from the goats: Differentiating global categories. *Cognitive Psychology, 23,* 263–298.

MANDLER, J. M., & McDONOUGH, L. (1993). Concept formation in infancy. *Cognitive Development, 8,* 291–318.

MANDLER, J. M., & McDONOUGH, L. (1995). Long-term recall of event sequences in infancy. *Journal of Experimental Child Psychology, 59,* 457–474.

MANDLER, J. M., & McDONOUGH, L. (1996). Drinking and driving don't mix: Inductive generalization in infancy. *Cognition, 59,* 307–335.

MANDLER, J. M., & McDONOUGH, L. (1998). Studies in inductive inference in infancy. *Cognitive Psychology, 37,* 60–96.

MARATSOS, M. (1976). *Language development: The acquisition of language structure.* Morristown, NJ: General Learning Press.

MARATSOS, M. (1998). The acquisition of grammar. In W. Damon (Series Ed.) & D. Kuhn & R. S. Siegler (Vol. Eds.), *Handbook of child psychology: Vol. 2. Cognition, perception, and language* (5th ed.). New York: Wiley.

MARCOS, H., & BERNICOT, J. (1997). How do young children reformulate assertions? A comparison with requests. *Journal of Pragmatics, 27,* 781–798.

MARCOVITCH, S., & ZELAZZO, P. D. (1999). The A-Not-B error: Results from a logistic meta-analysis. *Child Development, 70,* 1297–1313.

MARCUS, G. F., PINKER, S., ULLMAN, M., HOLLANDER, M., ROSEN, T. J., & XU, F. (1992). Overregularization in language acquisition. *Monographs of the Society for Research in Child Development, 57* (4, Serial No. 228).

MARESCHAL, D., PLUNKETT, K., & HARRIS, P. (1999). A computational and neuropsychological account of object-oriented behaviours in infancy. *Developmental Science, 2,* 306–317.

MARKMAN, E. M. (1978). Empirical versus logical solutions to part-whole comparison problems concerning classes and collections. *Child Development, 49,* 168–177.

MARKMAN, E. M. (1979). Review of Siegler's *Children's thinking: What develops? Contemporary Psychology, 24,* 963–964.

MARKMAN, E. M. (1989). *Categorization and naming in children: Problems of induction.* Cambridge, MA: MIT Press.

MARKMAN, E. M. (1991). The whole object, taxonomic, and mutual exclusivity assumptions as initial constraints on word meanings. In J. P. Byrnes & S. A. Gelman (Eds.), *Perspectives on language and cognition: Interrelations in development.* Cambridge: Cambridge University Press.

MARKOVITS, H., & BOUFFARD-BOUCHARD, T. (1992). The belief-bias effect in reasoning: The development and activation of competence. *British Journal of Developmental Psychology, 10,* 269–284.

MARKUS, H. R., & KITAYAMA, S. (1991). Culture and the self: Implications for cognition, emotion, and motivation. *Psychological Review, 98,* 224–253.

MASANGKAY, Z. S., McCLUSKEY, K. A., McINTYRE, C. W., SIMS-KNIGHT, J., VAUGHN, B. E., & FLAVELL, J. H. (1974). The early development of inferences about the visual percepts of others. *Child Development, 45,* 237–246.

MASATAKA, N. (1996). Perception of motherese in a signed language by 6-month-old deaf infants. *Developmental Psychology, 32,* 874–879.

MASATAKA, N. (1998). Perception of motherese in Japanese sign language by 6-month-old hearing infants. *Developmental Psychology, 34,* 241–246.

MASSEY, C. M., & GELMAN, R. (1988). Preschooler's ability to decide whether a photographed unfamiliar object can move itself. *Developmental Psychology, 24,* 307–317.

MAURER, D., STAGER, C. L., & MONDLOCH, C. J. (1999). Cross-modal transfer of shape is difficult to demonstrate in one-month-olds. *Child Development, 70,* 1047–1057.

MAZZONI, G. (1998). Memory suggestibility and metacognition in child eyewitness testimony: The roles of source monitoring and self-efficacy. *European Journal of Psychology of Education, 13,* 43–60.

McCABE, A. E. (1989). Differential language learning styles in young children: The importance of context. *Developmental Review, 9,* 1–20.

McCLELLAND, J., & SIEGLER, R. S. (Eds.). (2000). *Mechanisms of cognitive development: Neural and behavioral perspectives.* Mahwah, NJ: Erlbaum.

McDANIEL, D., McKEE, C., & CAIRNS, H. S. (Eds.). (1996). *Methods for assessing children's syntax.* Cambridge, MA: MIT Press.

McDEVITT, T., & FORD, M. (1987). Processes in young children's communicative functioning and development. In M. E. Ford & D. H. Ford (Eds.), *Humans as self-constructing living systems: Putting the framework to work.* Hillsdale, NJ: Erlbaum.

McDONOUGH, L., & MANDLER, J. M. (1994). Very long-term recall in infants: Infantile amnesia reconsidered. *Memory, 2,* 339–352.

McPHERSON, S. L., & THOMAS, J. R. (1989). Relation of knowledge and performance in boys' tennis: Age and expertise. *Journal of Experimental Child Psychology, 48,* 190–211.

MEDIN, D. L. (1989). Concepts and conceptual structure. *American Psychologist, 44,* 1469–1481.

MEDIN, D. L., & ATRAN, S. (Eds.). (1999). *Folkbiology.* Cambridge, MA: MIT Press.

MEERUM TERWOGT, M., & HARRIS, P. L. (1993). Understanding of emotion. In M. Bennett (Ed.), *The development of social cognition: The child as psychologist.* New York: Guilford Press.

MEHLER, J., BERTONCINI, J., BARRIERE, M., & JASSIK-GERSCHENFELD, D. (1978). Infant recognition of mother's voice. *Perception, 7,* 491–497.

MEIER, R. (1981). Icons and morphemes: Models of the acquisition of verb agreement in ASL. *Papers and Reports on Child Language Development, 20,* 92–99.

MEIER, R. P., & NEWPORT, E. L. (1990). Out of the hands of babes: On a possible sign advantage in language acquisition. *Language, 66,* 1–23.

MELTZOFF, A. N. (1988). Infant imitation and memory: Nine-month-old infants in immediate and deferred tests. *Child Development, 59,* 217–225.

MELTZOFF, A. N. (1990). Foundations for developing a concept of self: The role of imitation in relating self to other and the value of social mirroring, social modeling, and self practice in infancy. In D. Cicchetti & M. Beeghly (Eds.), *The self in transition: Infancy to childhood.* Chicago: University of Chicago Press.

MELTZOFF, A. N. (1995). Understanding the intentions of others: Re-enactment of intended acts by 18-month-old children. *Developmental Psychology, 31,* 838–850.

MELTZOFF, A. N., & BORTON, R. W. (1979). Intermodal matching by human neonates. *Nature, 282,* 403–404.

MELTZOFF, A. N., GOPNIK, A., & REPACHOLI, B. M. (1999). Toddlers' understanding of intentions, desires and emotions: Explorations of the dark ages. In P. D. Zelazo, J. W. Astington, & D. R. Olson (Eds.), *Developing theories of intention.* Mahwah, NJ: Erlbaum.

MELTZOFF, A. N., & MOORE, M. K. (1977). Imitation of facial and manual gestures by human neonates. *Science, 198,* 75–78.

MELTZOFF, A. N., & MOORE, M. K. (1983a). Newborn infants imitate adult facial gestures. *Child Development, 54,* 702–709.

MELTZOFF, A. N., & MOORE, M. K. (1983b). The origins of imitation in infancy: Paradigm, phenomena, and theories. In L. P. Lipsitt & C. Rovee-Collier (Eds.), *Advances in infancy research* (Vol. 2). Norwood, NJ: Ablex.

MELTZOFF, A. N., & MOORE, M. K. (1989). Imitation in newborn infants: Exploring the range of gestures imitated and the underlying mechanisms. *Developmental Psychology, 25,* 954–962.

MELTZOFF, A. N., & MOORE, M. K. (1994). Imitation, memory, and the representation of persons. *Infant Behavior and Development, 17,* 83–99.

MELTZOFF, A. N., & MOORE, M. K. (1998). Object representation, identity, and the paradox of early permanence: Steps toward a new framework. *Infant Behavior and Development, 21,* 201–235.

MELTZOFF, A. N., & MOORE, M. K. (1999). A new foundation for cognitive development in infancy: The birth of the representational infant. In E. K. Scholnick, K. Nelson, S. A. Gelman, & P. H. Miller (Eds.), *Conceptual development: Piaget's legacy.* Mahwah, NJ: Erlbaum.

MENIG-PETERSON, C. L. (1975). The modification of communicative behavior in preschool-aged children as a function of the listener's perspective. *Child Development, 46,* 1015–1018.

MENN, L., & RATNER, N. B. (Eds.). (2000). *Methods for studying language production.* Mahwah, NJ: Erlbaum.

MERRIMAN, W. E., & BOWMAN, L. L. (1989). The mutual exclusivity bias in children's word learning. *Monographs of the Society for Research in Child Development, 54* (Serial No. 220).

MERVIS, C. B. (1987). Child-basic object categories and early lexical development. In U. Neisser (Ed.), *Concepts and conceptual development: Ecological and intellectual bases of categorizations.* Cambridge: Cambridge University Press.

MERVIS, C. B., & BERTRAND, J. (1994). Acquisition of the Novel Name-Nameless Category (N3C) principle. *Child Development, 65,* 1646–1662.

MERVIS, C. B., & ROSCH, E. (1981). Categorization of natural objects. *Annual review of psychology, 32,* 89–115. Palo Alto, CA: Annual Reviews Inc.

MESSER, D. J. (1983). The redundancy between adult speech and nonverbal interaction: A contribution to acquisition? In R. M. Golinkoff (Ed.), *The transition from prelinguistic to linguistic communication.* Hillsdale, NJ: Erlbaum.

MILLER, J. G. (1986). Early cross-cultural commonalities in social explanation. *Developmental Psychology, 22,* 514–520.

MILLER, J. G. (1987). Cultural influences on the development of conceptual differentiation in person description. *British Journal of Developmental Psychology, 5,* 309–319.

MILLER, K. F. (1989). Measurement as a tool for thought: The role of measuring procedures in children's understanding of quantitative invariance. *Developmental Psychology, 25,* 589–600.

MILLER, K. F., & STIGLER, J. W. (1987). Counting in Chinese: Cultural variation in a basic cognitive skill. *Cognitive Development, 2,* 279–305.

MILLER, P. H. (1985). Children's reasoning about the causes of human behavior. *Journal of Experimental Child Psychology, 39,* 343–362.

MILLER, P. H. (1990). The development of strategies of selective attention. In D. F. Bjorklund (Ed.), *Children's strategies: Contemporary views of cognitive development.* Hillsdale, NJ: Erlbaum.

MILLER, P. H. (2000). How best to utilize a deficiency: Commentary on Waters' "Memory strategy development." *Child Development, 71,* 1013–1017.

MILLER, P. H. (2001). *Theories of developmental psychology* (4th ed.). New York: Worth.

MILLER, P. H., & ALOISE, P. A. (1989). Young children's understanding of the psychological causes of behavior: A review. *Child Development, 60,* 257–285.

MILLER, P. H., & ALOISE-YOUNG, P. A. (1996). Preschoolers' strategic behavior and performance on a same-different task. *Journal of Experimental Child Psychology, 60,* 284–303.

MILLER, P. H., & BIGI, L. (1979). The development of children's understanding of attention. *Merrill-Palmer Quarterly, 25,* 235–250.

MILLER, P. H., & COYLE, T. R. (1999). Developmental change: Lessons from microgenesis. In E. K. Scholnick, K. Nelson, S. A. Gelman, & P. H. Miller (Eds.)., *Conceptual development: Piaget's legacy.* Mahwah, NJ: Erlbaum.

MILLER, P. H., & DeMARIE-DREBLOW, D. (1990). Social-cognitive correlates of children's understanding of displaced aggression. *Journal of Experimental Child Psychology, 49,* 488–504.

MILLER, P. H., HAYNES, V. F., DeMARIE-DREBLOW, D., & WOODY-RAMSEY, J. (1986) Children's strategies for gathering information in three tasks. *Child Development, 57,* 1429–1439.

MILLER, P. H., KESSEL, F. S., & FLAVELL, J. H. (1970). Thinking about people thinking about people thinking about . . . : A study of social cognitive development. *Child Development, 41,* 613–623.

MILLER, P. H., & SEIER, W. L. (1994). Strategy utilization deficiencies in children: When, where, and why. In H. W. Reese (Ed.), *Advances in child development and behavior* (Vol. 25). New York: Academic Press.

MILLER, P. H., SEIER, W. S., BARRON, K. A., & PROBERT, J. S. (1994). What causes a memory strategy utilization deficiency? *Cognitive Development, 9,* 77–101.

MILLER, P. H., SEIER, W. S., & PROBERT, J. S., & ALOISE, P. A. (1991). Age differences in the capacity demands of a strategy among spontaneously strategic children. *Journal of Experimental Child Psychology, 52,* 149–165.

MILLER, P. H., & SHANNON, K. (1984). Young children's understanding of the effect of noise and interest level on learning. *Genetic Psychology Monographs, 110,* 71–90.

MILLER, P. H., & WEISS, M. C. (1981). Children's attention allocation, understanding of attention, and performance on the incidental learning task. *Child Development, 57,* 1183–1190.

MILLER, P. H., WOODY-RAMSEY, J., & ALOISE, P. A. (1991). The role of strategy effortfulness in strategy effectiveness. *Developmental Psychology, 27,* 738–745.

MILLER, P. H., & ZALENSKI, R. (1982). Preschoolers' knowledge about attention. *Developmental Psychology, 18,* 871–875.

MILLER, P. J., FUNG, H., & MINTZ, J. (1996). Self-construction through narrative practices: A Chinese and American comparison of early socialization. *Ethos, 24,* 237–279.

MILLER, S. A. (1973). Contradiction, surprise, and cognitive change: The effects of disconfirmation of belief on conservers and nonconservers. *Journal of Experimental Child Psychology, 15,* 47–62.

MILLER, S. A. (1976). Nonverbal assessment of Piagetian concepts. *Psychological Bulletin, 83,* 405–430.

MILLER, S. A. (1986a). Certainty and necessity in the understanding of Piagetian concepts. *Developmental Psychology, 22*, 3–18.

MILLER, S. A. (1986b). Parents' beliefs about their children's cognitive abilities. *Developmental Psychology, 22*, 276–284.

MILLER, S. A. (1988). Parents' beliefs about children's cognitive development. *Child Development, 59*, 259–285.

Miller, S. A. (1998). *Developmental research methods* (2nd ed.). Englewood Cliffs, NJ: Prentice Hall.

MILLER, S. A. (2000). Children's understanding of preexisting differences in knowledge and belief. *Developmental Review, 20*, 227–282.

MILLER, S. A., CUSTER, W., & NASSAU, G. (in press). Children's understanding of the necessity of logically necessary truths. *Cognitive Development.*

MILLER, S. A., & DAVIS, T. L. (1992). Beliefs about children: A comparative study of mothers, teachers, peers, and self. *Child Development, 63*, 1251–1265.

MILLER, S. A., & LIPPS, L. (1973). Extinction of conservation and transitivity of weight. *Journal of Experiment Child Psychology, 16*, 388–402.

MILLER, S. A., SCHWARTZ, L. C., & STEWART, C. (1973). An attempt to extinguish conservation of weight in college students. *Developmental Psychology, 8*, 316.

MISCHEL, W., & PEAKE, P. K. (1982). Beyond *deja vu* in the search for cross-situational consistency. *Psychological Review, 89*, 730–755.

MISTRY, J. (1997). The development of remembering in cultural context. In N. Cowan (Ed.), *The development of memory in childhood*. Hove East Sussex, UK: Psychology Press.

MITCHELL, P. (1994). Realism and early conception of mind: A synthesis of phylogenetic and ontogenetic issues. In C. Lewis & P. Mitchell (Eds.), *Children's early understanding of mind: Origins and development*. Hillsdale, NJ: Erlbaum.

MITCHELL, P. (1997). *Introduction to theory of mind: Children, autism and apes*. London: Arnold.

MITCHELL, P., MUNNO, A., & RUSSELL, J. (1991). Children's understanding of the communicative value of discrepant verbal messages. *Cognitive Development, 6*, 279–299.

MITCHELL, P., ROBINSON, E. J., NYE, R. M., & ISAACS, J. E. (1997). When speech conflicts with seeing: Young children's understanding of informational priority. *Journal of Experimental Child Psychology, 64*, 276–294.

MODGIL, S., & MODGIL, C. (1976). *Piagetian research: Compilation and commentary* (Vol. 2). Windsor, England: NFER Publishing Co.

MOLFESE, D. L., & MOLFESE, V. J. (1979). Hemispheric and stimulus differences as reflected in the cortical responses of newborn infants to speech stimuli. *Developmental Psychology, 15*, 505–511.

MONDLOCH, C. J., LEWIS, T. L., BUDREAU, D. R., MAURER, D., DANNEMILLER, J. L., STEPHENS, B. R., & KLEINER-GATHERCOAL, K. A. (1999). Face perception during early infancy. *Psychological Science, 10*, 419–422.

MONTANGERO, J., & MAURICE-NAVILLE, D. (1997). *Piaget on the advance of knowledge*. Mahwah, NJ: Erlbaum.

MONTGOMERY, D. E. (1992). Young children's theory of knowing: The development of a folk epistemology. *Developmental Review, 12*, 410–430.

MONTGOMERY, D. E. (1993). Young children's understanding of interpretive diversity between different-aged listeners. *Developmental Psychology, 29*, 337–345.

MONTGOMERY, D. E. (1994). Situational features influencing young children's mentalistic explanations of action. *Cognitive Development, 9*, 425–454.

MONTGOMERY, D. E., & MILLER, S. A. (1997). Young children's attributions of knowledge when speaker intent and listener access conflict. *British Journal of Developmental Psychology, 14*, 159–175.

MOON, C., COOPER, R. P., & FIFER, W. P. (1993). Two-day-old infants prefer their native language. *Infant Behavior and Development, 16*, 495–500.

MOORE, C. (1996). Theories of mind in infancy. *British Journal of Developmental Psychology, 14*, 19–40.

MOORE, C. (1999). Intentional relations and triadic interactions. In P. D. Zelazo, J. W. Astington, & D. R. Olson (Eds.), *Developing theories of intention*. Mahwah, NJ: Erlbaum.

MOORE, C., & CORKUM, V. (1994). Social understanding at the end of the first year of life. *Developmental Review, 14*, 349–372.

MOORE, M. K., & MELTZOFF, A. N. (1999). New findings on object permanence: A developmental difference between two types of occlusion. *British Journal of Developmental Psychology, 17*, 623–644.

MORRIS, A. K., & SLOUTSKY, V. M. (1998). Understanding of logical necessity: Developmental antecedents and cognitive consequence. *Child Development, 69,* 721–741.

MORRISON, F. J., GRIFFITH, E. M., & ALBERTS, D. M. (1997). Nature-nurture in the classroom: Entrance age, school readiness, and learning in children. *Developmental Psychology, 33,* 254–262.

MORRISON, F. J., SMITH, L., & DOW-EHRENSBERGER, M. (1995). Education and cognitive development: A natural experiment. *Developmental Psychology, 31,* 789–799.

MORRONGIELLO, B. A. (1988). Infants' localization of sounds along two spatial dimensions: Horizontal and vertical axes. *Infant Behavior and Development, 11,* 127–143.

MORRONGIELLO, B. A., FENWICK, K. D., & CHANCE, G. (1990). Sound localization acuity in very young infants: An observer-based testing procedure. *Developmental Psychology, 26,* 75–84.

MOSES, L. J. (1993) Young children's understanding of belief constraints on intention. *Cognitive Development, 8,* 1–25.

MOSES, L. J., BALDWIN, D. A., ROSICKY, J. G., & TIDBALL, G. (in press). Evidence for referential understanding in the emotions domain at 12 and 18 months. *Child Development.*

MOSHMAN, D. (1998). Cognitive development beyond childhood. In W. Damon (Series Ed.) & D. Kuhn & R. S. Siegler (Vol. Eds.), *Handbook of child psychology: Vol. 2. Cognition, perception, and language* (5th ed.). New York: Wiley.

MOSIER, C. E., & ROGOFF, B. (1994). Infants' instrumental use of their mothers to achieve their goals. *Child Development, 65,* 70–79.

MUIR, D., & CLIFTON, R. K. (1985). Infants' orientation to the location of sound sources. In G. Gottlieb & N. A. Krasnegor (Eds.), *Measurement of audition and vision in the first year of postnatal life.* Norwood, NJ: Albex.

MULLEN, M. K., & YI, S. (1995). The cultural context of talk about the past: Implications for the development of autobiographical memory. *Cognitive Development, 10,* 407–419.

MULLER, U., & OVERTON, W. F. (1998). How to grow a baby: A reevaluation of image-schema and Piagetian action approaches to representation. *Human Development, 41,* 71–111.

MULLER, U., SOKOL, B., & OVERTON, W. F. (1998). Reframing a constructivist model of the development of mental representation: The role of higher-order operations. *Developmental Review, 18,* 155–201.

MUNAKATA, Y. (1998). Infant perseveration and implications for object permanence theories: A PDP model of the AB̄ task. *Developmental Science, 1,* 161–184.

MUNAKATA, Y., MCCLELLAND, J. L., JOHNSON, M H., & SIEGLER, R. S. (1997). Rethinking infant knowledge: Toward an adaptive process account of successes and failures in object permanence tasks. *Psychological Review, 104,* 686–713.

MURPHY, C., & MESSER, D. (1977). Mothers, infants, and pointing: A study of gesture. In H. R. Schaffer (Ed.), *Studies in mother-infant interaction.* London: Academic Press.

NAIGLES, L. G. (1990). Children use syntax to learn verb meanings. *Journal of Child Language, 17,* 357–374.

NEEDHAM, A., & MODI, A. (2000). Infants' use of prior experiences with objects in object segregation: Implications for object recognition in infancy. In H. W. Reese (Ed.), *Advances in child development and behavior* (Vol. 27). San Diego, CA: Academic Press.

NEISSER, U. (1993). The self perceived. In U. Neisser (Ed.), *The perceived self: Ecological and interpersonal sources of self knowledge.* New York: Cambridge University Press.

NELSON, C. A. (1997). The neurobiological basis of early memory development. In N. Cowan (Ed.), *The development of memory in childhood.* Hove East Sussex, UK: Psychology Press.

NELSON, C. A. (1999). Neural plasticity and human development. *Current Directions in Psychological Science, 8,* 42–45.

NELSON, C. A., & BLOOM, F. E. (1997). Child development and neuroscience. *Child Development, 68,* 970–987.

NELSON, K. (1973). Structure and strategy in learning to talk. *Monographs of the Society for Research in Child Development, 38* (Serial No. 149).

NELSON, K. (1981). Individual differences in language development: Implications for development and language. *Developmental Psychology, 17,* 170–187.

NELSON, K. (1986). *Event knowledge: Structure and function in development.* Hillsdale, NJ: Erlbaum.

NELSON, K. (1988). Constraints on word learning? *Cognitive Development, 3,* 221–246.

NELSON, K. (1990). Comment on Behrend's "Constraints and Cognitive Development." *Cognitive Development, 5,* 331–339.

NELSON, K. (1996). *Language in cognitive development: The emergence of the mediated mind.* New York: Cambridge University Press.

Nelson, K. (1997). Cognitive change as collaborative construction. In E. Amsel & K. A. Renninger (Eds.), *Change and development.* Mahwah, NJ: Erlbaum.

NELSON, K. (1999). The developmental psychology of language and thought. In M. Bennett (Ed.), *Developmental psychology: Achievements and prospects.* Philadelphia: Psychology Press.

NELSON, K., & HUDSON, J. (1988). Scripts and memory: Functional relationships in development. In F. E. Weinert & M. Perlmutter (Eds.), *Memory development: Universal changes and individual differences.* Hillsdale, NJ: Erlbaum & Associates.

NEVILLE, H. J. (1995). *Brain plasticity and the acquisition of skill.* Paper presented at the Cognitive Neuroscience and Education Conference, Eugene, OR.

NEWCOMBE, N., DRUMMEY, A. B., FOX, N. A., LIE, E., & OTTINGER-ALBERTS, W. (2000). Remembering early childhood: How much, how, and why (or why not). *Current Directions in Psychological Science, 9,* 55–58.

NEWCOMBE, N., & FOX, N. A. (1994). Infantile amnesia: Through a glass darkly. *Child Development, 65,* 31–40.

NEWCOMBE, N., & HUTTENLOCHER, J. (1998). Making space: An interactionist account of development in the spatial domain. *Psychological Science Agenda, 11,* 6–7.

NEWPORT, E. (1988). Constraints on learning and their role in language acquisition: Studies of the acquisition of American Sign Language. *Language Sciences, 10,* 147–172.

NEWPORT, E. (1990). Maturational constraints on language learning. *Cognitive Science, 14,* 11–28.

NEWPORT, E., GLEITMAN, L., & GLEITMAN, H. (1977). Mother I'd rather do it myself: Some effects and non-effects of motherese. In C. E. Snow & C. Ferguson (Eds.), *Talking to children: Language input and acquisition.* Cambridge: Cambridge University Press.

NICHOLS, S., & STICH, S. (2000). A cognitive theory of pretense. *Cognition, 74,* 115–147.

NINIO, A., & SNOW, C. E. (1996). *Pragmatic development.* Boulder, CO: Westview.

NINIO, A., & SNOW, C. E. (1999). The development of pragmatics: Learning to use language appropriately. In W. C. Ritchie & T. K. Bhatia (Eds.), *Handbook of child language acquisition.* San Diego, CA: Academic Press.

NISBETT, R., & ROSS, L. (1980). *Human inference: Strategies and shortcomings of social judgment.* Englewood Cliffs, N. J.: Prentice-Hall.

NUNES, T., & BRYANT, P. (1996). *Children doing mathematics.* Cambridge, MA: Blackwell.

NUNES, T., CARRAHER, D. W., & SCHLIEMANN, A. D. (1993). *Street mathematics and school mathematics.* New York: Cambridge University Press.

OAKES, L. M., & COHEN, L. B. (1990). Infant perception of a causal event. *Cognitive Development, 5,* 193–207.

OAKES, L. M., & MADOLE, K. L. (2000). The future of infant categorization research: A process-oriented approach. *Child Development, 71,* 119–126.

O'BRYAN, K. G., & BOERSMA, F. J. (1971). Eye movements, perceptual activity, and conservation development. *Journal of Experimental Child Psychology, 12,* 157–169.

OKAGAKI, L., & STERNBERG, R. J. (Eds.). (1991). *Directors of development: Influences on the development of children's thinking.* Hillsdale, NJ: Erlbaum.

OLIVER, A., JOHNSON, M. H., KARMILOFF-SMITH, & PENNINGTON, B. (2000). Deviations in the emergence of representations: A neuroconstructivist framework for analysing developmental disorders. *Developmental Science, 3,* 1–23.

OLLER, D. K., & EILERS, R. E. (1988). The role of audition in infant babbling. *Child Development, 59,* 441–449.

OLSHO, L. W., SCHOON, C., SAKAI, R., TURPIN, R., & SPERDUTO, V. (1982). Auditory frequency discrimination in infancy. *Developmental Psychology, 18,* 721–726.

O'NEILL, D. K. (1996). Two-year-olds' sensitivity to a parent's knowledge state when making requests. *Child Development, 51,* 659–677.

O'NEILL, D. K., ASTINGTON, J., & FLAVELL, J. H. (1992). Young children's understanding of the role that sensory experiences play in knowledge acquisition. *Child Development, 63,* 474–490.

O'NEILL, D. K., & GOPNIK, A. (1991). Young children's ability to identify the sources of their beliefs. *Developmental Psychology, 27,* 390–397.

ORNSTEIN, P. A., MERRITT, K. A., BAKER-WARD, L., FURTADO, E., GORDON, B. N., & PRINCIPE, G. (1998). Children's knowledge, expectation, and long-term retention. *Applied Cognitive Psychology, 12,* 387–405.

OSHERSON, D. N., & MARKMAN, E. M. (1975). Language and the ability to evaluate contradictions and tautologies. *Cognition, 2,* 213–226.

OVERTON, W. F. (Ed.) (1990). *Reasoning, necessity, and logic: Developmental perspectives.* Hillsdale, NJ: Erlbaum.

PALEY, V. G. (1984). *Boys and girls.* Chicago: University of Chicago Press.

PALINCSAR, A. S., & BROWN, A. L. (1984). Reciprocal teaching of comprehension-fostering and comprehension-monitoring activities. *Cognition and Instruction, 1,* 117–175.

PALINCSAR, A. S., BROWN, A. L., & CAMPIONE, J. C. (1993). First-grade dialogues for knowledge acquisiton and use. In E. A. Forman, N. Minick, & C. A. Stone (Eds.), *Contexts for learning: Sociocultural dynamics in children's development.* New York: Oxford University Press.

PAN, B. A., & SNOW, C. E. (1999). The development of conversational and discourse skills. In M. Barrett (Ed.), *The development of language.* Hove, UK: Psychology Press.

PARIS, S. G. (1975). Integration and inference in children's comprehension and memory. In F. Restle, R. Shiffrin, J. Castellan, H. Lindman, & D. Pisoni (Eds.), *Cognitive theory* (Vol. 1). Hillsdale, N. J.: Erlbaum.

PARIS, S. G. (1988). Models and metaphors of learning strategies. In C. E. Weinstein, E. T. Goetz, & P. A. Alexander (Eds.), *Learning and study strategies: Issues in assessment, instruction, and evaluation.* San Diego, CA: Academic Press.

PARIS, S. G., & CROSS, D. R. (1988). The zone of proximal development: Virtues and pitfalls of a metaphorical representation of children's learning. *The Genetic Epistemologist, 16,* 27–37.

PARIS, S. G., & MAHONEY, G. J. (1974). Cognitive integration in children's memory for sentences and pictures. *Child Development, 45,* 633–642.

PASCALIS, O., DE SCHONEN, S., MORTON, J., & DERUELLE, C. (1995). Mother's face recognition by neonates: A replication and an extension. *Infant Behavior and Development, 18,* 79–95.

PASCUAL-LEONE, J. (1970). A mathematical model for the transition rule in Piaget's developmental stages. *Acta Psychologica, 32,* 301–345.

PASCUAL-LEONE, J., & JOHNSON, J. (1999). A dialectical constructivist view of representation: Role of mental attention, executives, and symbols. In I. E. Sigel (Ed.), *Development of mental representation: Theories and applications.* Mahwah, NJ: Erlbaum.

PECHEUX, M., LEPECQ, J., & SALZARULO, P. (1988). Oral activity and exploration in 1–2-month-old infants. *British Journal of Developmental Psychology, 6,* 245–256.

PERNER, J. (1991). *Understanding the representational mind.* Cambridge, MA: Bradford Books/MIT Press.

PERNER, J. (1999). Theory of mind. In M. Bennett (Ed.), *Developmental psychology: Achievements and prospects.* Philadelphia: Psychology Press.

PERNER, J., BAKER, S., & HUTTON, D. (1994). Prelief: The conceptual origins of belief and pretense. In C. Lewis & P. Mitchell (Eds.), *Children's early understanding of mind: Origins and development.* Hillsdale, NJ: Erlbaum.

PERNER, J., & DAVIES, G. (1991). Understanding the mind as an active information processor: Do young children have a "copy theory of mind"? *Cognition, 39,* 51–69.

PERNER, J., & LANG, B. (1999). Development of theory of mind and executive control. *Trends in Cognitive Science, 3,* 337–344.

PERNER, J., & LEEKAM, S. R. (1986). Belief and quantity: Three-year-olds' adaptation to listener's knowledge. *Journal of Child Language, 13,* 305–315.

PERNER, J., RUFFMAN, T., & LEEKAM, S. R. (1994). Theory of mind is contagious: You catch it from your sibs. *Child Development, 65,* 1228–1238.

PERNER, J., STUMMER, S., & LANG, B. (1999). Executive functions and theory of mind: Cognitive complexity or functional dependence? In P. D. Zelazo, J. W. Astington, & D. R. Olson (Eds.), *Developing theories of intention.* Mahwah, NJ: Erlbaum.

PERNER, J., & WIMMER, H. (1985). "John *thinks* that Mary *thinks* that . . ." Attribution of second-order beliefs by 5- to 10-year-old children. *Journal of Experimental Child Psychology, 39,* 437–471.

PERRIS, E. E., MYERS, N. A., & CLIFTON, R. K. (1990). Long-term memory for a single infancy experience. *Child Development, 61,* 1796–1807.

PETERSON, C. C., & SIEGAL, M. (1997). Psychological, physical, and biological thinking in normal, autistic, and deaf children. In H. M. Wellman & K. Inagaki (Eds.), *The emergence of core domains of thought: Chil-*

dren's reasoning about physical, psychological, and biological phenomena, San Francisco: Jossey-Bass

PETITTO, L. A. (1992). Modularity and constraints in early lexical acquisition: Evidence from children's early language and gesture. In M. R. Gunnar (Ed.), *Minnesota symposia on child psychology: Vol. 25. Modularity and constraints in language and cognition.* Hilldsale, NJ: Erlbaum.

PETITTO, L. A. (1993). On the ontogenetic requirements for early language acquisition. In B. de Boysson-Bardies, S. de Schonen, P. Jusczyk, P. MacNeilage, & J. Morton (Eds.), *Developmental neurocognition: Speech and face processing in the first year of life.* Dordrecht, The Netherlands: Kluwer.

PETITTO, L. A., & MARANTETTE, P. F. (1991). Babbling in the manual mode: Evidence for the ontogeny of language. *Science, 251,* 1493–1496.

PIAGET, J. (1929). *The child's conception of the world.* New York: Harcourt, Brace.

PIAGET, J. (1932). *The moral judgment of the child.* New York: Harcourt Brace.

PIAGET, J. (1952). *The origins of intelligence in children.* New York: International Universities Press.

PIAGET, J. (1954). *The construction of reality in the child.* New York: Basic Books.

PIAGET, J. (1962). *Play, dreams, and imitation in childhood.* New York: Norton.

PIAGET, J. (1970). Piaget's theory. In P. H. Mussen (Ed.), *Carmichael's manual of child psychology* (Vol. 1). New York: Wiley.

PIAGET, J. (1985). *The equilibration of cognitive structures.* Chicago: University of Chicago Press.

PIAGET, J., & SZEMINSKA, A. (1952). *The child's conception of number.* New York: Humanities Press.

PIATELLI-PALMARINI, M. (Ed.). (1980). *Learning and language.* Cambridge, MA: Harvard University Press.

PILLEMER, D. B., & WHITE, S. H. (1989). Childhood events recalled by children and adults. In H. W. Reese (Ed.), *Advances in child development and behavior* (Vol. 21). New York: Academic Press.

PILLOW, B. H. (1988). The development of children's beliefs about the mental world. *Merrill-Palmer Quarterly, 34,* 1–32.

PILLOW, B. H. (1989). The development of beliefs about selective attention. *Merrill-Palmer Quarterly, 35,* 421–443.

PILLOW, B. H. (1991). Children's understanding of biased social cognition. *Developmental Psychology, 27,* 539–551.

PILLOW, B. H. (1995). Two trends in the development of conceptual perspective-taking: An elaboration of the passive-active hypothesis. *International Journal of Behavioral Development, 18,* 649–676.

PILLOW, B. H., & HENRICHON, A. J. (1996). There's more to the picture than meets the eye: Young children's difficulty understanding biased interpretation. *Child Development, 67,* 802–819.

PINARD, A., & LAURENDEAU, M. (1969). "Stage" in Piaget's cognitive-developmental theory: Exegesis of a concept. In D. Elkind & J. H. Flavell (Eds.), *Studies in cognitive development: Essays in honor of Jean Piaget.* New York: Oxford University Press.

PINE, J. M. (1994). Environmental correlates of variation in lexical style: Interactional style and the structure of the input. *Applied Psycholinguistics, 15,* 355–370.

PINKER, S. (1984). *Language learnability and language development.* Cambridge, MA: Harvard University Press.

PINKER, S. (1987). The bootstrapping problem in language acquisition. In B. MacWhinney (Ed.), *Mechanisms of language acquisition.* Hillsdale, NJ: Erlbaum..

PINKER, S. (1989). *Learnability and cognition: The acquisition of argument structure.* Cambridge, MA: MIT Press.

PINKER, S. (1991). Rules of language. *Science, 253,* 530–535.

PINKER, S. (1994). *The language instinct: How the mind creates language.* New York: William Morrow.

PINKER, S. (1997). *How the mind works.* New York: Norton.

PLOMIN, R. (1999). Behavior genetics. In M. Bennett (Ed.), *Developmental psychology: Achievements and prospects.* Philadelphia: Psychology Press.

PLUNKETT, K. (Ed.). (1998). *Language acquisition and connectionism.* Philadelphia: Psychology Press.

POOLE, D. A., & WHITE, L. T. (1995). Tell me again and again: Stability and change in the repeated testimonies of children and adults. In M. S. Zaragoza, J. R. Graham, C. N. Gordon, R. Hirschman, & Y. S. Ben Porath (Eds.), *Memory and testimony in the child witness.* Newbury Park, CA: Sage.

POULIN-DUBOIS, D. (1999). Infants' distinction between animate and inanimate objects: The origins of naive psychology. In P. Rochat (Ed.), *Early social cognition.* Mahwah, NJ: Erlbaum.

POULIN-DUBOIS, D., & SHULTZ, T. R. (1988). The development of the understanding of human behavior: From agency to intentionality. In J. W. Astington, P. L. Harris, & D. R. Olson (Eds.), *Developing theories of mind.* Cambridge: Cambridge University Press.

POULSON, C. L., NUNES, L. R. D., & WARREN, S. F. (1989). Imitation in infancy: A critical review. In H. W. Reese (Ed.), *Advances in child development and behavior* (Vol. 22). San Diego, CA: Academic Press.

POVINELLI, D. J., & EDDY, T. J. (1996). What young chimpanzees know about seeing. *Monographs of the Society for Research in Child Development, 61,* (3, Serial No. 247).

PREMACK, D., & WOODRUFF, G. (1978). Does the chimpanzee have a theory of mind? *Behavioral and Brain Sciences, 1,* 515–526.

PRESSLEY, M. (1992). How *not* to study strategy discovery. *American Psychologist, 47,* 1240–1241.

PRESSLEY, M., BORKOWSKI, J. J., & SCHNEIDER, W. (1987). Cognitive strategies: Good strategy users coordinate metacognition and knowledge. In R. Vasta & G. Whitehurst (Eds.), *Annals of child development* (Vol. 5). Greenwich, CT: JAI Press.

PRESSLEY, M., CARIGLIA-BULL, T., DEANE, S., & SCHNEIDER, W. (1987). Short-term memory, verbal competence, and age as predictors of imagery instructional effectiveness. *Journal of Experimental Child Psychology, 43,* 194–211.

PRESSLEY, M., LEVIN, J. R., & BRYANT, S. L. (1983). Memory strategy instruction during adolescence: When is explicit instruction needed? In M. Pressley & J. R. Levin (Eds.), *Cognitive strategy research: Psychological foundations.* New York: Springer-Verlag.

PRIEL, B., & DE SCHONEN, S. (1986). Self-recognition: A study of a population without mirrors. *Journal of Experimental Child Psychology, 41,* 237–250.

QIN, J., QUAS, J. A., REDLICH, A. D., & GOODMAN, G. S. (1997). Children's eyewitness testimony: Memory development in the legal context. In N. Cowan (Ed.), *The development of memory in childhood.* Hove, UK: Psychology Press.

QUINE, W. V. O. (1960). *Word and object.* Cambridge, MA: MIT Press.

QUINN, P. C. (1999). Development of recognition and categorization of objects and their spatial relations in young infants. In L. Balter & C. S. Tamis-Monda (Eds.). *Child psychology: A handbook of contemporary issues.* Philadelphia: Psychology Press.

QUINN, P. C., & EIMAS, P. D. (1996). Perceptual cues that permit categorical differentiation of animal species by infants. *Journal of Experimental Child Psychology, 63,* 189–211.

QUINN, P. C., & EIMAS, P. D. (2000). The emergence of category representations during infancy: Are separate perceptual and conceptual processes involved? *Journal of Cognition and Development, 1,* 55–61.

RABINOWITZ, F. M., HOWE, M. L., & LAWRENCE, J. A. (1989). Class inclusion and working memory. *Journal of Experimental Child Psychology, 48,* 379–409.

REAUX, J. E., THEALL, L. A., & POVINELLI, D. J. (1999). A longitudinal investigation of chimpanzees' understanding of visual perception. *Child Development, 70,* 275–290.

REDDY, V. (1991). Playing with others' expectations: Teasing and mucking about in the first year. In A. Whiten (Ed.), *Natural theories of mind: Evolution, development and simulation of everyday mindreading.* Oxford: Basil Blackwell Ltd.

REDDY, V. (1999). Prelinguistic communication. In M. Barrett (Ed.), *The development of language* (pp. 25–50). Hove, UK: Psychology Press.

REESE, E., & FIVUSH, R. (1993). Parental styles for talking about the past. *Developmental Psychology, 29,* 596–606.

REESE, E., HADEN, C. A., & FIVUSH, R. (1993). Mother-child conversations about the past; Relationships of style and memory over time. *Cognitive Development, 8,* 403–430.

REILLY, J., KLIMA, E. S., & BELLUGI, U. (1990). Once more with feeling: Affect and language in atypical populations. *Development and Psychopathology, 2,* 367–391.

REISSLAND, N. (1988). Neonatal imitation in the first hour of life: Observation in rural Nepal. *Developmental Psychology, 24,* 464–469.

REMMEL, E., BETTGER, J. G., & WEINBERG, A. M. (in press). Theory of mind in deaf children. In M. D. Clark, M. Marschark, & M. Karchmer (Eds.), *Context, cognition, and deafness.* Washington, DC: Gallaudet University Press.

RENNINGER, K. A. (1998). Developmental psychology and instruction: Issues from and for practice. In W. Damon (Series Ed.) & I. E. Siegel & K. A. Renninger (Vol. Eds.), *Handbook of child psychology: Vol. 4.*

Child psychology in practice. New York: Wiley.

REPACHOLI, B. M., & GOPNIK, A. (1997). Early reasoning about desires: Evidence from 14- and 18-month-olds. *Developmental Psychology, 33,* 12–21.

RESCORLA, L. (1980). Overextension in early language development. *Journal of Child Language, 7,* 321–336.

REVELLE, G. L., WELLMAN, H. M., & KARABENICK, J. D. (1985). Comprehension monitoring in preschool children. *Child Development, 56,* 654–663.

RHOLES, W. S., NEWMAN, L. S., & RUBLE, D. N. (1990). Understanding self and others: Developmental and motivational aspects of perceiving persons in terms of invariant dispositions. In E. Higgins & R. Sorrentino (Eds.), *Handbook of motivation and cognition: Foundations of social behavior* (Vol. 2). New York: Guilford.

RHOLES, W. S., & RUBLE, D. N. (1984). Children's understanding of dispositional characteristics of others. *Child Development, 33,* 550–560.

RICE, M. L., & WOODSMALL, L. (1988). Lessons from television: Children's word learning when viewing. *Child Development, 59,* 420–429.

RICHARDS, D. S., FRENTZEN, B. GERHARDT, K. J., McCANN, M. E., & ABRAMS, R. M. (1992). Sound levels in the human uterus. *Obstetrics and Gynecology, 80,* 186–190.

RICHARDS, J. E., & RADER, N. (1983). Affective, behavioral, and avoidance responses on the visual cliff: Effect of crawling onset age, crawling experience, and testing age. *Psychophysiology, 20,* 633–642.

RIESS, J. A., & CUNNINGHAM, J. G. (1989, April). *From three to five: Understanding infant facial expressions and multiple emotions in events.* Paper presented at the meeting of the Society for Research in Child Development. Kansas City, MO.

RITCHIE, W. C., & BHATIA, T. K. (Eds.). (1999). *Handbook of child language acquisition.* Orlando, FL: Academic Press.

RITTLE-JOHNSON, B., & SIEGLER, R. S. (1998). The relation between conceptual and procedural knowledge in learning mathematics: A review. In C. Donlan (Ed.), *The development of mathematical skills.* Hove, UK: Psychology Press.

RIVERA, S. M., WAKELEY, A., & LANGER, J. (1999). The drawbridge phenomenon: Representational reasoning or perceptual preference? *Developmental Psychology, 35,* 427–435.

ROBINSON, E. J. (1981). Conversational tactics and the advancement of the child's understanding about referential communication. In W. P. Robinson (Ed.), *Communication in development.* London: Academic Press.

ROBINSON, E. J., CHAMPION, H., & MITCHELL, P. (1999). Children's ability to infer utterance veracity from speaker informedness. *Developmental Psychology, 35,* 535–546.

ROBINSON, E. J., & ROBINSON, W. P. (1981). Egocentrism in verbal referential communication. In M. Cox (Ed.), *Are young children egocentric?* London: Concord Books.

ROCHAT, P. (Ed.) (1999). *Early social cognition.* Mahwah, NJ: Erlbaum.

ROCHAT, P., QUERIDO, J. G., & STRIANO, T. (1999). Emerging sensitivity to the timing and structure of protoconversation in early infancy. *Developmental Psychology, 35,* 950–957.

ROCHAT, P., & STRIANO, T. (1999). Emerging self-exploration by 2-month-old infants. *Developmental Science, 2,* 206–218.

ROGOFF, B. (1990). *Apprenticeship in thinking.* New York: Oxford University Press.

ROGOFF, B. (1998). Cognition as a collaborative process. In W. Damon (Series Ed.) & D. Kuhn & R. S. Siegler (Vol. Eds.), *Handbook of child psychology: Vol. 2. Cognition, perception, and language* (5th ed.). New York: Wiley.

ROGOFF, B., MISTRY, J., GONCU, A, & MOSIER, C. (1993). Guided participation in cultural activity by toddlers and caregivers. *Monographs of the Society for Research in Child Development, 58* (8, Serial No. 236).

ROSCH, E., MERVIS, C. B., GRAY, W. D., JOHNSON, D. M., & BOYES-BRAEM, P. (1976). Basic objects in natural categories. *Cognitive Psychology, 8,* 382–439.

ROSE, S. A. (1990). Cross-modal transfer in human infants: What is being transferred? In A. Diamond (Ed.), *The development and neural bases of higher cognitive functions.* New York: The New York Academy of Sciences.

ROSE, S. A. (1994). From hand to eye: Findings and issues in infant cross-modal transfer. In D. J. Lewkowicz & R. Lickliter (Eds.), *The development of intersensory perception: Comparative perspectives.* Hillsdale, NJ: Erlbaum.

ROSE, S. A., & RUFF, H. A. (1987). Cross-modal abilities in human infants. In J. S. Osofsky (Ed.), *Handbook of infant development* (2nd ed.). New York: Wiley.

ROSENGREN, K. S., GELMAN, S. A., KALISH, C. W., & McCORMICK, M. (1991). As time goes by: Children's early understanding of growth in animals. *Child Development, 62,* 1302–1320.

ROSENSHINE, B., & MEISTER, C. (1994). Reciprocal teaching: A review of research. *Review of Educational Research, 64,* 479–530.

ROVEE-COLLIER, C. K. (1999). The development of infant memory. *Current Directions in Psychological Science, 8,* 80–85.

ROVEE-COLLIER, C. K., & GERHARDSTEIN, P. (1997). The development of infant memory. In N. Cowan (Ed.), *The development of memory.* Hove, UK: Psychology Press.

ROVEE-COLLIER, C. K., & HAYNE, H. (1987). Reactivation of infant memory: Implications for cognitive development. In H. W. Reese (Ed.), *Advances in child development and behavior* (Vol. 20). New York: Academic Press.

ROVEE-COLLIER, C. K., SULLIVAN, M. W., ENRIGHT, M., LUCAS, D., & FAGEN, J. W. (1980). Reactivation of infant memory. *Science, 208,* 1159–1161.

RUBIN, K. H., BUKOWSKI, W., & PARKER, J. G. (1998). Peer interactions, relationships, and groups. In W. Damon (Series Ed.) & N. Eisenberg (Vol. Ed.), *Handbook of child psychology: Vol. 3. Social, emotional, and personality development* (5th ed.). New York: Wiley.

RUBLE, D. N. (1987). The acquisition of social knowledge: A self-socialization perspective. In N. Eisenberg (Ed.), *Contemporary topics in developmental psychology.* New York: Wiley.

RUBLE, D. N., & DWECK, C. (1995). Self-conceptions, person conception, and their development. In N. Eisenberg (Ed.), *Review of personaltiy and social psychology: Development and social psychology: The interface* (Vol. 15). Thousand Oaks, CA: Sage.

RUDY, L., & GOODMAN, G. S. (1991). Effects of participation on children's reports: Implications for eyewitness testimony. *Developmental Psychology, 27,* 527–538.

RUFFMAN, T. K., OLSON, D. R., & ASTINGTON, J. W. (1991). Children's understanding of visual ambiguity. *British Journal of Developmental Psychology, 9,* 89–103.

RUFFMAN, T. K., PERNER, J., OLSON, D. R., & DOHERTY, M. (1993). Reflecting on scientific thinking: Children's understanding of the hypothesis-evidence relation. *Child Development, 64,* 1617–1636.

RUSSELL, J., JARROLD, C., & POTEL, D. (1994). What makes strategic deception difficult for children, the deception or the strategy? *British Journal of Developmental Psychology, 12,* 301–314.

RUSSELL, J., MAUTHNER, N., SHARPE, S., & TIDSWELL, T. (1991). The "windows task" as a measure of strategic deception in preschoolers and autistic subjects. *British Journal of Developmental Psychology, 9,* 331–359.

SAARNI, C. (1988). Children's understanding of the interpersonal consequences of dissemblances of nonverbal emotional-expressive behavior. *Journal of Nonverbal Behavior, 12,* 275–294.

SAARNI, C. (1989, April). Cognitive capabilities involved in the socialization of emotion: Development in middle childhood. In T. Trabasso (Chair), *The social-cognitive basis of emotional understanding.* Symposium conducted at the meeting of the Society for Research in Child Development, Kansas City, MO.

SAARNI, C., MUMME, D. L., & CAMPOS, J. J. (1998). Emotional development: Action, communication, and understanding. In W. Damon (Series Ed.) & N. Eisenberg (Vol. Ed.), *Handbook of child psychology: Vol. 3. Social, emotional, and personality development* (5th ed.). New York: Wiley.

SABBAGH, M. A., & TAYLOR, M. (2000). Neural correlates of theory of mind reasoning: An event-related potential study. *Psychological Science, 11,* 46–50.

SACHS, J. (1997). Communication development in infancy. In J. B. Gleason (Ed.), *The development of language* (4th ed.). Boston: Allyn and Bacon.

SACHS, J., & DEVIN, J. (1976). Young children's use of age appropriate speech styles in social interaction and role-playing. *Journal of Child Language, 3,* 81–98.

SACKS, O. (1985). *The man who mistook his wife for a hat.* New York: Summit Books.

SAMARAPUNGAVAN, A., VOSNIADOU, S., & BREWER, W. F. (1996). Mental models of the earth, sun, and moon: Indian children's cosmologies. *Cognitive Development, 11,* 491–521.

SAMUELSON, L. K., & SMITH, L. B. (2000). Grounding development in cognitive processes. *Child Development, 71,* 98–106.

SAVAGE-RUMBAUGH, E. S., & McDONALD, K. (1988). Deception and social manipulation in symbol-using apes. In R. W. Byrne & A. Whiten (Eds.), *Machiavellian intelligence: Social expertise and the evolution of intellect in monkeys, apes, and humans.* Oxford: Oxford University Press.

SAXE, G. B. (1981). Body parts as numerals: A developmental analysis of numeration among the Oksapmin in Papua New Guinea. *Child Development, 52,* 306–316.

SAXE, G. B. (1982). Developing forms of arithmetical thought among the Oksapmin of Papua New Guinea. *Developmental Psychology, 18,* 583–594.

SAXE, G. B. (1991). *Culture and cognitive development: Studies in mathematical understanding.* Hillsdale, NJ: Erlbaum.

SAXE, G. B. (1999). Sources of concepts: A cultural-developmental perspective. In E. K. Scholnick, K. Nelson, S. A. Gelman, & P. H. Miller (Eds.), *Conceptual development: Piaget's legacy.* Mahwah, NJ: Erlbaum.

SAXE, G. B., GUBERMAN, S. R., & GEARHART, M. (1987). Social processes in early number development. *Monographs of the Society for Research in Child Development, 52* (Serial No. 216).

SAXTON, M. (1997). The Contrast Theory of negative input. *Journal of Child Language, 24,* 139–161.

SAYWITZ, K., GOODMAN, G., NICHOLS, G., & MOAN, S. (1991). Children's memory of a physical examination involving genital touch: Implications for reports of child sexual abuse. *Journal of Consulting and Clinical Psychology, 5,* 682–691.

SCAIFE, M., & BRUNER, J. (1975). The capacity for joint visual attention in the infant. *Nature, 253,* 265–266.

SCARR, S. (1983). An evolutionary perspective on infant intelligence: Species patterns and individual variations. In M. Lewis (Ed.), *Origins of intelligence: Infancy and early childhood* (3rd ed.). New York: Plenum.

SCHACTER, D. L., MOSCOVITCH, M., TULVING, E., MCLACHLAN, D. R., & FREEDMAN, M. (1986). Mnemonic precedence in amnesic patients: An analogue of the AB̄ error in infants? *Child Development, 57,* 816–823.

SCHAFER, G., & PLUNKETT, K. (1998). Rapid word learning by fifteen-month-olds under tightly controlled conditions. *Child Development, 69,* 309–320.

SCHAUBLE, L. (1990). Belief revision in children: The role of prior knowledge and strategies for generating evidence. *Journal of Experimental Child Psychology, 49,* 31–57.

SCHAUBLE, L. (1996). The development of scientific reasoning in knowledge-rich contexts. *Developmental Psychology, 32,* 102–119.

SCHIEFFELIN, B., & OCHS, E. (1983). A cultural perspective on the transition from prelinguistic to linguistic communication. In R. M. Golinkoff (Ed.), *The transition from prelinguistic to linguistic communication.* Hillsdale, NJ: Erlbaum.

SCHLESINGER, M., & LANGER, J. (1999). Infants' developing expectations of possible and impossible tool-use events between ages 8 and 12 months. *Developmental Science, 2,* 195–205.

SCHNEIDER, D. J., HASTORF, A. H., & ELLSWORTH, P. C. (1979). *Person perception* (2nd ed.). Reading, MA: Addison-Wesley.

SCHNEIDER, W. (1999). The development of metamemory in children. In D. Gopher & A. Koriat (Eds.), *Attention and performance XVII. Cognitive regulation of performance: Interaction of theory and application.* Cambridge, MA: MIT Press.

SCHNEIDER, W., & BJORKLUND, D. (1998). Memory. In W. Damon (Series Ed.) & D. Kuhn & R. S. Siegler (Vol. Eds.), *Handbook of child psychology: Vol. 2. Cognition, perception, and language* (5th ed.). New York: Wiley.

SCHNEIDER, W., KORKEL, J., & WEINERT, F. E. (1987). The effects of intelligence, self-concept, and attributional style on metamemory and memory behavior. *International Journal of Behavioral Development, 10,* 281–299.

SCHNEIDER, W., KORKEL, J., & WEINERT, F. E. (1989). Domain-specific knowledge and memory performance: A comparison of high- and low-aptitude children. *Journal of Educational Psychology, 81,* 306–312.

SCHNEIDER, W., & PRESSLEY, M. (1997). *Memory development: Between two and twenty* (2nd ed.). Mahwah, NJ: Erlbaum.

SCHNEIDER, W., SCHLAGMÜLLER, M., & VISE, M. (1998). The impact of metamemory and domain-specific knowledge on memory performance. *European Journal of Psychology of Education, 13,* 91–103.

SCHNEIDER, W., & SODIAN, B. (1988). Metamemory-memory relationships in preschool children: Evidence from a memory-for-location task. *Journal of Experimental Child Psychology, 45,* 209–233.

SCHNEIDER, W., & WEINERT, F. E. (1989). Memory development: Universal changes and individual differences. In A. de Ribaupierre (Ed.), *Transitional mechanisms in child development: The longitudinal perspective.* Cambridge: Cambridge University Press.

SCHNEIDER, W., & WEINERT, F. E. (1995). Memory development during early and middle childhood: Findings from the Munich longitudinal study (LOGIC). In F. E. Weinert & W. Schneider (Eds.), *Memory performance and competencies: Issues in growth and development.* Hillsdale, NJ: Erlbaum.

SCHOLNICK, E. K. (1999). Representing logic. In I. E. Sigel (Ed.), *Development of mental representation: Theories and application.* Mahwah, NJ: Erlbaum.

SCHOLNICK, E. K., NELSON, K., GELMAN, S. A., & MILLER, P. H. (Eds.). (1999). *Conceptual development: Piaget's legacy.* Mahwah, NJ: Erlbaum.

SCHWANENFLUGEL, P. J., HENDERSON, R. L., & FABRICIUS, W. V. (1998). Developing organization of mental verbs and theory of mind in middle childhood. Evidence from extension. *Developmental Psychology, 34,* 512–524.

SCHWARTZ, S. R. (Ed.). (1977). *Naming, necessity, and natural kinds.* Ithaca, NY: Cornell University Press.

SCOLLON, R. (1976). *Conversations with a one year old.* Honolulu: University Press of Hawaii.

SECHENOV, I. M. (1935). Elements of thought. In *Selected works.* Moscow/Leningrad: Izd. Akad. Nauk SSSR.

SERA, M. D., & CONNOLLY, L. M. (1990). *Low planes, big worms, and other pairs of terms.* Unpublished manuscript.

SHANTZ, C. U. (1983). Social cognition. In P. H. Mussen (Series Ed.) & J. H. Flavell & E. M. Markman (Vol. Eds.), *Handbook of child psychology: Vol. 3. Cognitive development.* New York: Wiley.

SHATZ, M., & GELMAN, R. (1973). The development of communication skills: Modifications in the speech of young children as a function of listener. *Monographs of the Society for Research in Child Development, 38,* (5, Serial No. 152).

SHATZ, M., WELLMAN, H. M., & SILBER, S. (1983). The acquisition of mental verbs: A systematic investigation of the first reference to mental state. *Cognition, 14,* 301–321.

SHORE, C. M. (1995). *Individual differences in language development.* Thousand Oaks, CA: Sage.

SHULTZ, T. R. (1980). Development of the concept of intention. In W. A. Collins (Ed.), *Minnesota symposia on child psychology: Vol. 13. Development of cognition, affect, and social relations.* Hillsdale NJ: Erlbaum.

SHULTZ, T. R. (1991). Modelling embedded intention. In D. Frye & C. Moore (Eds.), *Children's theories of mind.* Hillsdale, NJ: Erlbaum.

SHULTZ, T. R., SCHMIDT, W. C., BUCKINGHAM, D., & MARESCHAL, D. (1995). Modeling cognitive development with a generative connectionist algorithm. In T. Simon & G. Halford (Eds.), *Developing cognitive competence: New approaches to process modeling.* Hillsdale, NJ: Erlbaum.

SHWE, H. I., & MARKMAN, E. M. (1997). Young children's appreciation of the mental impact of their communicative signals. *Developmental Psychology, 33,* 630–636.

SHWEDER, R. A. (1980). Scientific thought and social cognition. In W. A. Collins (Ed.), *Minnesota symposia on child psychology* (Vol. 13). Hillsdale, NJ: Erlbaum.

SHWEDER, R. A., GOODNOW, J., HATANO, G., LEVINE, R. A., MARKUS, H., & MILLER, P. (1998). The cultural psychology of development: One mind, many mentalities. In W. Damon (Series Ed.) & R. M. Lerner (Vol. Ed.), *Handbook of child psychology: Vol. 1. Theoretical models of human development* (5th ed.). New York: Wiley.

SIEGAL, M. (1997). *Knowing children: Experiments in conversation and cognition* (2nd ed.). Hove, UK: Psychology Press.

SIEGAL, M., & SHARE, D. L. (1990). Contamination sensitivity in young children. *Developmental Psychology, 26,* 455–458.

SIEGLER, R. S. (1976). Three aspects of cognitive development. *Cognitive Psychology, 8,* 481–520.

SIEGLER, R. S. (1978). The origins of scientific reasoning. In R. S. Siegler (Ed.), *Children's thinking: What develops?* Hillsdale, NJ: Erlbaum.

SIEGLER, R. S. (1981). Developmental sequences within and between concepts. *Monographs of the Society for Research in Child Development, 46* (2, Serial No. 189).

SIEGLER, R. S. (1983). Information processing approaches to cognitive development. In W. Kessen (Ed.), P. H. Mussen (Series Ed.), *Handbook of child psychology: Vol. 1. History, theory, and methods.* New York: Wiley.

SIEGLER, R. S. (1988). Individual differences in strategy choices: Good students, not-so-good students, and perfectionists. *Child Development, 59,* 833–851.

SIEGLER, R. S. (1989). How domain-general and domain-specific knowledge interact to produce strategy choices. *Merrill-Palmer Quarterly, 35,* 1–26.

SIEGLER, R. S. (1991a). *Children's thinking* (2nd ed.). Englewood Cliffs, NJ: Prentice-Hall.

SIEGLER, R. S. (1991b). In young children's counting, procedures precede principles *Educational Psychology Review, 3,* 127–135.

SIEGLER, R. S. (1996). *Emerging minds: The process of change in children's thinking.* New York: Oxford University Press.

SIEGLER, R. S. (1997). Concepts and methods for studying cognitive change. In E. Amsel & K. A. Renninger (Eds.), *Change and development.* Mahwah, NJ: Erlbaum.

SIEGLER, R. S. (1998). *Children's thinking* (3rd ed.). Englewood Cliffs, NJ: Prentice-Hall.

SIEGLER, R. S., & CROWLEY, K. (1991). The microgenetic method: A direct means for studying cognitive development. *American Psychologist, 46,* 606–620.

SIEGLER, R. S., & JENKINS, E. (1989). *How children discover new strategies.* Hillsdale, NJ: Erlbaum.

SIEGLER, R. S., & SHIPLEY, C. (1995). Variation, selection, and cognitive change. In T. Simon & G. Halford (Eds.), *Developing cognitive competence: New approaches to process modeling.* Hillsdale, NJ: Erlbaum.

SIGEL, I. E. (Ed.) (1999). *Development of mental representation: Theories and applications.* Mahwah, NJ: Erlbaum.

SIGNORELLA, M. L., & LIBEN, L. S. (1984). Recall and reconstruction of gender-related pictures: Effects of attitude, task difficulty, and age. *Child Development, 55,* 393–405.

SIMION, F., VALENZA, E., & UMILTA, C. (1998). Mechanisms underlying face preference at birth. In F. Simion & G. Butterworth (Eds.), *The development of sensory, motor and cognitive capacities in early infancy: From perception to cognition.* Hove, UK: Psychology Press.

SIMON, H. A. (1995). The information-processing theory of mind. *American Psychologist, 50,* 507–508.

SIMON, T. J. (1997). Reconceptualizing the origins of number knowledge: A "non-numerical" account. *Cognitive Development, 12,* 349–372.

SIMON, T. J., HESPOS, S. J., & ROCHAT, P. (1995). Do infants understand simple arithmetic? A replication of Wynn (1992). *Cognitive Development, 10,* 253–269.

SKEEN, J. A., & ROGOFF, B. (1987). Children's difficulties in deliberate memory for spatial relationships: Misapplications of verbal mnemonic strategies? *Cognitive Development, 2,* 1–19.

SKINNER, E. A. (1990). Age differences in the dimensions of perceived control during middle childhood: Implications for developmental conceptualizations and research. *Child Development, 61,* 1882–1890.

SKINNER, E. A. (1991). Development and perceived control: A dynamic model of action in context. In M. R. Gunnar & L. A. Sroufe (Eds.). *Minnesota symposia on child psychology: Vol. 23. Self processes and development.* Hillsdale, NJ: Erlbaum.

SLATER, A. (1995). Individual differences in infancy and later IQ. *Journal of Child Psychology and Psychiatry and Allied Disciplines, 36,* 69–112.

SLATER, A. (Ed.). (1998). *Perceptual development: Visual, auditory, and speech perception in infancy.* Hove, UK: Psychology Press.

SLATER, A., JOHNSON, S. P., BROWN, E., & BADENOCH, M. (1996). Newborn infants' perception of partly occluded objects. *Infant Behavior and Development, 19,* 145–148.

SLATER, A., MATTOCK, A., & BROWN, E. (1990). Size constancy at birth: Newborn infants' responses to retinal and real size. *Journal of Experimental Child Psychology, 49,* 314–322.

SLATER, A., MORISON, V., SOMERS, M., MATTOCK, A., BROWN, B., & TAYLOR, D. (1990). Newborn and older infants' perception of partly occluded objects. *Infant Behavior and Development, 13,* 33–49.

SLAUGHTER, V., & GOPNIK, A. (1996). Conceptual coherence in the child's theory of mind: Training children to understand belief. *Child Development, 67,* 2967–2988.

SLOBIN, D. I. (1970). Universals of grammatical development in children. In G. B. Flores d'Arcais & W. J. M. Levelt (Eds.), *Advances in psycholinguistics.* Amsterdam: North-Holland Publishing.

SLOBIN, D. I. (Ed.). (1985). *The crosslinguistic study of language acquisition: Vol. 2. Theoretical issues.* Hillsdale, NJ: Erlbaum.

SMITH, C. L. (1979). Children's understanding of natural language hierarchies. *Journal of Experimental Child Psychology, 27,* 437–458.

SMITH, L. (1991). Age, ability, and intellectual development. In M. Chandler & M. Chapman (Eds.), *Criteria for competence: Controversies in the conceptualization and assessment of children's abilities.* Hillsdale, NJ: Erlbaum.

SMITH, L. B., THELEN, E., TITZER, R., & McLIN, D. (1999). Knowing in the context of acting: The task dynamics of the A-not-B error. *Psychological Review, 106,* 235–260.

SMITH, M. D. (1988). The meaning of reference in emergent lexicons. In M. D. Smith & J. L.

Locke (Eds.), *The emergent lexicon: The child's development of a linguistic vocabulary.* San Diego, CA: Academic Press.

SODIAN, B. (1988). Children's attributions of knowledge to the listener in a referential communication task. *Child Development, 59,* 378–385.

SODIAN, B., TAYLOR, C., HARRIS, P. L., & PERNER, J. (1991). Early deception and the child's theory of mind: False trails and genuine markers. *Child Development, 62,* 753–766.

SODIAN, B., ZAITCHIK, D., & CAREY, S. (1991). Young children's differentiation of hypothetical beliefs from evidence. *Child Development, 62, 753–766.*

SOKOLOFF, J. L., & SNOW, C. E. (1994). The changing role of negative evidence in theories of language development. In C. Gallaway & B. J. Richards (Eds.), *Input and interaction in language acquisition.* Cambridge: Cambridge University Press.

SOLOMON, G. E. A., & CASSIMATIS, N. L. (1999). On facts and conceptual systems: Young children's integration of their understanding of germs and contagion. *Developmental Psychology, 35,* 113–126.

SOLOMON, G. E. A., JOHNSON, S. C., ZAITCHIK, D., & CAREY, S. (1996). Like father, like son: Young children's understanding of how and why offspring resemble their parents. *Child Development, 67,* 151–171.

SOPHIAN, C. (1995). *Children's numbers.* Madison, WI: Brown & Benchmark.

SOPHIAN, C. (1997). Beyond competence: The significance of performance for conceptual development. *Cognitive Development, 12,* 281–303.

SOPHIAN, C. (1998). A developmental perspective on children's counting. In C. Donlan (Ed.), *The development of mathematical skills.* Hove, UK: Psychology Press.

SOPHIAN, C. (2000). Perceptions of proportionality in young children: Matching spatial ratios. *Cognition, 75,* 145–170.

SPELKE, E. S. (1982). Perceptual knowledge of objects in infancy. In J. Mehler, E. C. F. Walker, & M. Garrett (Eds.), *Perspectives on mental representation.* Hillsdale, NJ: Erlbaum.

SPELKE, E. S. (1985). Perception of unity, persistence, and identity: Thoughts on infants' conceptions of objects. In J. Mehler & R. Fox (Eds.), *Neonate cognition.* Hillsdale, NJ: Erlbaum.

SPELKE, E. S. (1987). The development of intermodal perception. In P. Salapatek & L.

Cohen (Eds.), *Handbook of infant perception: Vol. 2, From perception to cognition.* Orlando, FL: Academic Press.

SPELKE, E. S. (1988). Where perceiving ends and thinking begins: The apprehension of objects in infancy. In A. Yonas (Ed.), *Minnesota symposia on child psychology: Vol. 20. Perceptual development in infancy.* Hillsdale, NJ: Erlbaum.

SPELKE, E. S. (1990). Principles of object perception. *Cognitive Science, 14,* 29–56.

SPELKE, E. S. (1991). Physical knowledge in infancy: Reflections on Piaget's theory. In S. Carey & R. Gelman (Eds.), *The epigenesis of mind: Essays in biology and cognition.* Hillsdale, NJ: Erlbaum.

SPELKE, E. S. (1998). Nativism, empiricism, and the origins of knowledge. *Infant Behavior and Development, 21,* 181–200.

SPELKE, E. S., BREINLINGER, K., MACOMBER, J., & JACOBSON, K. (1992). Origins of knowledge. *Psychological Review, 99,* 605–632.

SPELKE, E. S., & COURTELYOU, A. (1981). Perceptual aspects of social learning: Looking and listening in infancy. In M. E. Lamb & L. R. Sherrod (Eds.), *Infant social cognition: Empirical and theoretical considerations.* Hillsdale, NJ: Erlbaum.

SPELKE, E. S., HOFSTEN, C. VON, & KESTENBAUM, R. (1989). Object perception in infancy: Interaction of spatial and kinetic information for object boundaries. *Developmental Psychology, 25,* 185–196.

SPELKE, E. S., & NEWPORT, E. L. (1998). Nativism, empiricism, and the development of knowledge. In W. Damon (Series Ed.) & D. Kuhn & R. S. Siegler (Vol. Eds.), *Handbook of child psychology: Vol. 2. Cognition, perception, and language* (5th ed.). New York: Wiley.

SPELKE, E. S., & OWSLEY, C. J. (1979). Intermodal exploration and knowledge in infancy. *Infant Behavior and Development, 2,* 13–24.

SPELKE, E. S., PHILLIPS, A., & WOODWARD, A. L. (1995). Infant's knowledge of object motion and human action. In D. Sperber, D. Premack, & A. J. Premack (Eds.), *Causal cognition: A multidisciplinary debate.* Oxford, England: Clarendon Press.

SPELKE, E. S., & VAN DE WALLE, G. A. (1993). Perceiving and reasoning about objects: Insights from infants. In N. Eilan, W. Brewer, & R. McCarthy (Eds.), *Spatial representation.* Oxford: Basil Blackwell.

SPELKE, E. S., VISHTON, P., & HOFSTEN, C. VON (1995). Object perception, object-directed action, and physical knowledge in infancy. In M. S. Gazzaniga (Ed.), *The cognitive neurosciences*. Cambridge, MA: MIT Press.

SPRINGER, K. (1992). Children's awareness of the biological implications of kinship. *Child Development, 63,* 950–959.

SPRINGER, K. (1996). Young children's understanding of a biological basis for parent-offspring relations. *Child Development, 67,* 2841–2856.

SPRINGER, K., & BELK, A. (1994). The role of physical contact and association in early contamination sensitivity. *Developmental Psychology, 30,* 864–868.

SPRINGER, K., & KEIL, F. C. (1989). On the development of biologically specific beliefs: The case of inheritance. *Child Development, 60,* 637–648.

SPRINGER, K., & KEIL, F. C. (1991). Early differentiation of causal mechanisms appropriate to biological and nonbiological kinds. *Child Development, 62,* 767–781.

STARKEY, P., SPELKE, E. S., & GELMAN, R. (1990). Numerical abstraction by human infants. *Cognition, 36,* 97–127.

STEELE, H., STEELE, M., & FOHAGY, P. (1996). Associations among attachment classifications of mothers, fathers, and their infants. *Child Development, 67,* 541–555.

STEIN, N. L., & TRABASSO, T. (1989). Children's understanding of changing emotional states. In C. Saarni & P. L. Harris (Eds.), *Children's understanding of emotion*. Cambridge: Cambridge University Press.

STERNBERG, R. J. (1999). Looking back and looking forward on intelligence: Toward a theory of successful intelligence. In M. Bennett (Ed.), *Developmental psychology: Achievements and prospects*. Philadelphia: Psychology Press.

STEVENSON, H., LEE, S., & STIGLER, J. (1986). Achievement in mathematics. In H. Stevenson, H. Azuma, & K. Hakuta (Eds.), *Child development and education in Japan*. New York: W. H. Freeman.

STIPEK, D. J., & DANIELS, D. H. (1990). Children's use of dispositional attributions in predicting the performance and behavior of classmates. *Journal of Applied Developmental Psychology, 11,* 13–18.

STIPEK, D. J., & MACIVER, D. (1989). Developmental change in children's assessment of intellectual competence. *Child Development, 60,* 521–538.

STONE, V. E., BARON-COHEN, S., & KNIGHT, R. T. (1998). Frontal lobe contributes to theory of mind. *Journal of Cognitive Neuroscience, 10,* 640–656.

STRAUSS, M. S., & CURTIS, L. E. (1981). Infant perception of numerosity. *Child Development, 52,* 1146–1152.

STRERI, A., & SPELKE, E. S. (1988). Haptic perception of objects in infancy. *Cognitive Psychology, 20,* 1–23.

STRERI, A., & SPELKE, E. S. (1989). Effects of motion and figural goodness on haptic object perception in infancy. *Child Development, 60,* 1111–1125.

STRIANO, T., & ROCHAT, P. (in press). Emergence of selective social referencing in infancy. *Infancy.*

SVEJDA, M., & SCHMID, D. (1979, March). *The role of self-produced locomotion on the onset of fear of heights on the visual cliff*. Paper presented at the meeting of the Society for Research in Child Development, San Francisco.

TAGER-FLUSBERG, H. (1997). Morphology and syntax in the preschool years. In J. B. Gleason (Ed.), *The development of language* (4th ed.). Boston: Allyn and Bacon.

TAYLOR, M. (1988). The development of children's ability to distinguish what they know from what they see. *Child Development, 59,* 703–718.

TAYLOR, M. (1996). A theory of mind perspective on social cognitive development. In R. Gelman, & T. Au (Eds.) & E. C. Carterette & M. P. Friedman (Gen. Eds.), *Handbook of perception and cognition: Vol. 13. Perceptual and cognitive development*. New York: Academic Press.

TAYLOR, M. (1999). *Imaginary companions and the children who create them*. New York: Oxford University Press.

TAYLOR, M., ESBENSEN, B. M., & BENNETT, R. T. (1994). Children's understanding of knowledge acquisition: The tendency for children to report they have always known what they have just learned. *Child Development, 65,* 1581–1604.

TAYLOR, M. G. (1996). The development of children's beliefs about social and biological aspects of gender differences. *Child Development, 67,* 1555–1571.

TAYLOR, S. E. (1989). *Positive illusions*. New York: Basic Books.

TELLER, D. Y., & BORNSTEIN, M. H. (1987). Infant color vision and color perception. In P. Salapatek & L. Cohen (Eds.), *Handbook of infant perception: Vol. 1. From sensation to perception*. Orlando, FL: Academic Press.

TENNEY, Y. J. (1975) The child's conception of organization and recall. *Journal of Experimental Child Psychology, 19,* 100–114.

THELEN, E., FISHER, D. M., & RIDLEY-JOHNSON, R. (1984). The relationship between physical growth and a newborn reflex. *Infant Behavior and Development, 7,* 479–493.

THELEN, E., & SMITH, L. B. (1994). A dynamic systems approach to the development of cognition and action. Cambridge, MA: MIT Press.

THELEN, E., & SMITH, L. B. (1998). Dynamic systems theory. In W. Damon (Series Ed.) & R. M. Lerner (Vol. Ed.), *Handbook of child psychology: Vol. 1. Theoretical models of human development* (5th ed.). New York: Wiley.

THOMAS, H., & HORTON, J. J. (1997). Competency criteria and the class inclusion task: Modeling judgments and justifications. *Developmental Psychology, 33,* 1060–1073.

THOMPSON, J. R., & CHAPMAN, R. (1977). Who is "Daddy" revisited: The status of two-year-olds' over-extended words in use and comprehension. *Journal of Child Language, 4,* 359–375.

THOMPSON, R. A. (1998). Early sociopersonality development. In W. Damon (Series Ed.) & N. Eisenberg (Vol. Ed.), *Handbook of child psychology: Vol. 3. Social, emotional, and personality development* (5th ed.). New York: Wiley.

THORNTON, S. (1999). Creating the conditions for cognitive change: The interaction between task structures and specific strategies. *Child Development, 70,* 588–603.

TOMASELLO, M. (Ed.). (1998). *The new psychology of language.* Mahwah, NJ: Erlbaum.

TOMASELLO, M. (1999). *The cultural origins of human cognition.* Cambridge, MA: Harvard University Press.

TOMASELLO, M. (2000). Do young children have adult syntactic competence? *Cognition, 74,* 209–253.

TOMASELLO, M., & BARTON, M. (1994). Acquiring words in non-ostensive contexts. *Developmental Psychology, 30,* 639–650.

TOMASELLO, M., & BROOKS, P. J. (1999). Early syntactic development: A Construction Grammar approach. In M. Barrett (Ed.), *The development of language.* Hove, UK: Psychology Press.

TOMASELLO, M., & FARRAR, M. J. (1986). Joint attention and early language. *Child Development, 57,* 1454–1463.

TOMASELLO, M., KRUGER, A. C., & RATNER, H. H. (1993). Cultural learning. *Behavioral and Brain Sciences, 16,* 495–552.

TRABASSO, T. (1975). Representation, memory, and reasoning: How do we make transitive inferences? In A. D. Pick (Ed.), *Minnesota symposia on child psychology* (Vol. 9). Minneapolis: University of Minnesota Press.

TRABASSO, T. (1977). The role of memory as a system in making transitive inferences. In R. V. Kail & J. W. Hagen (Eds.), *Perspectives on the development of memory and cognition.* Hillsdale, NJ: Erlbaum.

TREHUB, S. E. (1976). The discrimination of foreign speech contrasts by infants and adults. *Child Development, 47,* 466–472.

TREHUB, S. E., & SCHNEIDER, B. A. (1983). Recent advances in the behavioral study of infant audition. In S. E. Gerber & G. T. Mencher (Eds.), *Development of auditory behavior.* New York: Grune & Stratton.

TREHUB, S. E., THORPE, L. A., & COHEN, A. J. (1991, April). *Infants' auditory processing of numerical information.* Paper presented at the meeting of the Society for Research in Child Development, Seattle.

TREIBER, F., & WILCOX, S. (1984). Discrimination of number by infants. *Infant Behavior and Development, 7,* 93–100.

TURIEL, E. (1998). The development of morality. In W. Damon (Series Ed.) & N. Eisenberg (Vol. Ed.), *Handbook of child psychology: Vol. 3. Social, emotional, and personality development* (5th ed.). New York: Wiley.

TVERSKY, A., & KAHNEMAN, D. (1973). Availability: A heuristic for judging frequency and probability. *Cognitive Psychology, 5,* 207–232.

TVERSKY, B. (1985). Development of taxonomic organization of named and pictured categories. *Developmental Psychology, 21,* 1111–1119.

UCCELLI, P., HEMPHILL, L., PAN, B. A., & SNOW, C. (1999). Telling two kinds of stories: Sources of narrative skill. In L. Balter & C. S. Tamis-LeMonda (Eds.), *Child psychology: A handbook of contemporary issues.* Philadelphia: Psychology Press.

ULLER, C., CAREY, S., HUNTLEY-FENNER, G., & KLATT, L. (1999). What representations might underlie infant numerical knowledge? *Cognitive Development, 14,* 1–36.

UZGIRIS, I. C., & HUNT, J. McV. (1975). *Assessment in infancy: Ordinal scales of psychological development.* Champaign: University of Illinois Press.

UZGIRIS, I. C., & HUNT, J. McV. (1987). *Infant performance and experience: New findings with the ordinal scales.* Champaign: University of Illinois Press.

VALIAN, V. (1999). Input and language acquisition. In W. C. Ritchie & T. K. Bhatia (Eds.), *Handbook of child language acquisition.* San Diego: Academic Press.

VAN DER MAAS, H. L. J., & HOPKINS, B. (1998). Developmental transitions: So what's new? *British Journal of Developmental Psychology, 16,* 1–13.

VAN GEERT, P. (1998). A dynamic systems model of basic developmental mechanisms: Piaget, Vygotsky, and beyond. *Psychological Review, 105,* 634–677.

VAN LOOSBROEK, E., & SMITSMAN, A. W. (1990). Visual perception of numerosity in infancy. *Developmental Psychology, 26,* 916–922.

VARNHAGEN, C., MORRISON, F. J., & EVERALL, R. (1994). Age and schooling effects in story recall and production. *Developmental Psychology, 30,* 969–979.

VERWEIJ, A. C., SIJTSMA, K., & KOOPS, W. (1999). An ordinal scale for transitive reasoning by means of a deductive strategy. *International Journal of Behavioral Development, 23,* 241–264.

VIHMAN, M. M. (1996). *Phonological development.* Cambridge, MA: Blackwell.

VINDEN, P. G. (1996). Junin Quechua children's understanding of mind. *Child Development, 67,* 1707–1716.

VOSNIADOU, S., & BREWER, W. (1992). Mental models of the earth; A study of conceptual change in childhood. *Cognitive Psychology, 24,* 535–585.

VYGOTSKY, L. (1978). *Mind in society.* Cambridge, MA: Harvard University Press.

WAKELEY, A., RIVERA, S., & LANGER, J. (2000). Can young infants add and subtract? *Child Development, 71,* 1525–1534

WALK, R. D., & GIBSON, E. J. (1961). A comparative and analytic study of visual depth perception. *Psychological Monographs, 75,* 8.

WALKER, A. S. (1982). Intermodal perception of expressive behaviors by human infants. *Journal of Experimental Child Psychology, 33,* 514–535.

WALKER, L. J., & HENNIG, K. H. (1997). Moral development in the broader context of personality. In S. Hala (Ed.), *The development of social cognition.* Hove, UK: Psychology Press.

WALKER-ANDREWS, A. S., BAHRICK, L. E., RAGLIONI, S. S., & DIAZ, I. (1991). Infants' bimodal perception of gender. *Ecological Psychology, 3,* 55–75.

WALTON, G. E., BOWER, N. J., & BOWER, T. G. (1992). Recognition of familiar faces by newborns. *Infant Behavior and Development, 15,* 265–269.

WARREN, A. R., & McCLOSKEY, L. A. (1997). Language acquisition in social contexts. In J. B. Gleason (Ed.), *The development of language* (4th ed.). Boston: Allyn and Bacon.

WARREN-LEUBECKER, A., & BOHANNON, J. N. (1983). The effects of verbal feedback and listener type on the speech of preschool children. *Journal of Experimental Child Psychology, 35,* 540–548.

WATSON, A. C., NIXON, C. L., WILSON, A., & CAPAGE, L. (1999). Social interaction skills and theory of mind in young children. *Developmental Psychology, 35,* 386–391.

WAXMAN, S. R. (1989). Linking language and conceptual development: Linguistic cues and the construction of conceptual hierarchies. *Genetic Epistemology, 17,* 13–20.

WAXMAN, S. R. (1990). Linguistic biases and the establishment of conceptual hierarchies: Evidence from preschool children. *Cognitive Development, 5,* 123–150.

WAXMAN, S. R. (1994). The development of an appreciation of specific linkages between linguistic and conceptual organization. *Lingua, 92,* 229–257.

WEINERT, F. E., & SCHNEIDER, W. (Eds.). (1999). *The Munich longitudinal study on the genesis of individual competencies (LOGIC).* Cambridge: Cambridge University Press.

WEINERT, F. E., SCHNEIDER, W., & KNOPF, M. (1988). Individual differences in memory development across the life-span. In P. B. Baltes, D. L. Featherman, & R. M. Lerner (Eds.), *Life-span development and behavior* (Vol. 8). Hillsdale, NJ: Erlbaum.

WELCH-ROSS, M. K. (1997). Mother-child participation in conversation about the past: Relationships to preschoolers' theory of mind. *Developmental Psychology, 33,* 618–629.

WELCH-ROSS, M. K. (1999). Preschoolers' understanding of mind: Implications for suggestibility. *Cognitive Development, 14,* 101–131.

WELCH-ROSS, M. K. (2000). A mental state-reasoning model of suggestibility and memory source-monitoring. In K. Roberts & M. Blades (Eds.), *Children's source monitoring.* Mahwah, NJ: Erlbaum.

WELCH-ROSS, M. K., DIECIDUE, K., & MILLER, S. A. (1997). Young children's understanding of conflicting mental representation predicts suggestibility. *Developmental Psychology, 33,* 43–53.

WELCH-ROSS, M. K., & MILLER, P. H. (2000). Relations between children's theory of mind and a selective attention strategy. *Journal of Cognition and Development, 1,* 281–303.

WELLMAN, H. M. (1979). *A child's theory of mind.* Paper presented at the conference, The growth of insight in the child, Madison, Wisconsin.

WELLMAN, H. M. (1985a). The child's theory of mind: The development of conceptions of cognition. In S. R. Yussen (Ed.), *The growth of reflection in children.* San Diego, CA: Academic Press.

WELLMAN, H. M. (1985b). The origins of metacognition. In D. Forrest, G. Mackinnon, & T. Walker (Eds.), *Metacognition, cognition, and human performance.* New York: Academic Press.

WELLMAN, H. M. (1990). *The child's theory of mind.* Cambridge, MA: Bradford Books/MIT Press.

WELLMAN, H. M. (1993). Early understanding of mind: The normal case. In S. Baron-Cohen, H. Tager-Flusberg, & D. Cohen (Eds.), *Understanding other minds: Perspectives from autism.* Oxford: Oxford University Press.

WELLMAN, H. M. (1998). Culture, variation, and levels of analysis in our folk psychologies. *Psychological Bulletin, 123,* 33–36.

WELLMAN, H. M., CROSS, D., & BARTSCH, K. (1986). Infant search and object permanence: A meta-analysis of the A-not-B error. *Monographs of the Society for Research in Child Development, 51* (3, Serial No. 214).

WELLMAN, H. M., CROSS, D., & WATSON, J. K. (in press). A meta-analysis of theory of mind development: The truth about false belief. *Child Development.*

WELLMAN, H. M., & ESTES, D. (1986). Early understanding of mental entities: A re-examination of childhood realism. *Child Development, 57,* 910–923.

WELLMAN, H. M., & GELMAN, S. A. (1988). Children's understanding of the nonobvious. In R. J. Sternberg (Ed.), *Advances in the psychology of human intelligence* (Vol. 4). Hillsdale, NJ: Erlbaum.

WELLMAN, H. M., & GELMAN, S. A. (1992). Cognitive development: Foundational theories of core domains. *Annual Review of Psychology, 43,* 337–375.

WELLMAN, H. M., & GELMAN, S. A. (1998). Knowledge acquisition in foundational domains. In W. Damon (Series Ed.) & D. Kuhn & R. S. Siegler (Vol. Eds.), *Handbook of child psychology: Vol. 2. Cognition, perception, and language* (5th ed). New York: Wiley.

WELLMAN, H. M., & HICKLING, A. K. (1994). The mind's "I": Children's conception of the mind as an active agent. *Child Development, 65,* 1564–1580.

WELLMAN, H. M., & LEMPERS, J. D. (1977). The naturalistic communication abilities of two-year-olds. *Child Development, 48,* 1052–1057.

WENTWORTH, N., BENSON, J. B., & HAITH, M. M. (2000). The development of infants' reaches for stationary and moving targets. *Child Development, 71,* 576–601.

WERKER, J. F. (1989). Becoming a native listener. *American Scientist, 77,* 54–59.

WERKER, J. F., & McLEOD, P. J. (1989). Infant preference for both male and female infant-directed talk: A developmental study of attentional and affective responsiveness. *Canadian Journal of Psychology, 43,* 230–246.

WERKER, J. F., SHI, R., DESJARDINS, R., PEGG, J. E., POLKA, L., & PATTERSON, M. (1998). Three methods for testing infant speech perception. In A. Slater (Ed.), *Perceptual development: Visual, auditory, and speech perception in infancy.* Hove, UK: Psychology Press.

WERKER, J. F., & TEES, R. C. (1983). Developmental changes across childhood in the perception of non-native speech sounds. *Canadian Journal of Psychology, 37,* 278–286.

WERKER, J. F., & TEES, R. C. (1999). Influences on infant speech processing: Toward a new synthesis. *Annual Review of Psychology, 50,* 509–535.

WERTHEIMER, M. (1961). Psychomotor coordination of auditory-visual space at birth. *Science, 134,* 1692.

WERTSCH, J. (1998). *Mind as action.* New York: Oxford University Press.

WETHERBY, A. M., & PRIZANT, B. M. (1989). The expression of communicative intent: Assessment guidelines. *Seminars in Speech and Language, 10,* 77–91.

WEXLER, K. (1982). A principle theory for language acquisition. In E. Wanner & L. R. Gleitman (Eds.), *Language acquisition: The state of the art.* Cambridge: Cambridge University Press.

WEXLER, K., & CULICOVER, P. (1980). *Formal principles of language acquisition.* Cambridge, MA: MIT Press.

WHITCOMB, D. (1992). *When the child is a victim* 2nd ed.). Washington, DC: National Institute of Justice.

WILCOX, M. J., & WEBSTER, E. J. (1980). Early discourse behavior: An analysis of children's responses to listener feedback. *Child Development, 51,* 1120–1125.

WILLATTS, P. (1989). Development of problem-solving in infancy. In A. Slater & G. Bremner (Eds.), *Infant development.* Hillsdale, NJ: Erlbaum.

WIMMER, H., HOGREFE, A., & PERNER, J. (1988). Children's understanding of informational access as source of knowledge. *Child Development, 59,* 386–396.

WIMMER, H., & PERNER, J. (1983). Beliefs about beliefs: Representation and constraining function of wrong beliefs in young children's understanding of deception. *Cognition, 13,* 103–128.

WIMMER, H., & WEICHBOLD, V. (1994). Children's theory of mind: Fodor's heuristics or understanding informational causation. *Cognition, 53,* 45–57.

WINER, G. A. (1980). Class-inclusion reasoning in children: A review of the empirical literature. *Child Development, 51,* 309–328.

WINER, G. A., & COTTRELL, J. E. (1991, August). *Developmental changes in understanding perception.* Paper presented at the meeting of the American Psychological Association, San Francisco.

WINER, G. A., COTTRELL, J. E., KAREFILAKI, K. D., & CHRONISTER, M. (1996). Conditions affecting beliefs about visual perception among children and adults. *Journal of Experimental Child Psychology, 61,* 93–115.

WOHLWILL, J. F. (1973). *The study of behavioral development.* New York: Academic Press.

WOOD, D. (1980). Teaching the young child: Some relationships between social interaction, language, and thought. In D. Olson (Ed.), *The social foundations of language and thought.* New York: Norton.

WOODWARD, A. L., & MARKMAN, E. M. (1991). Constraints on learning as default assumptions: Comments on Merriman and Bowman's "The mutual exclusivity bias in children's word learning." *Developmental Review, 11,* 137–163.

WOODWARD, A. L., & MARKMAN, E. M. (1998). Early word learning. In W. Damon (Series Ed.) & D. Kuhn & R. S. Siegler (Vol. Eds.), *Handbook of child psychology: Vol. 2. Cognition, perception, and language* (5th ed.). New York: Wiley.

WOODWARD, A. L., & SOMMERVILLE, J. A. (2000). Twelve-month-old infants interpret action in context. *Psychological Science, 11,* 73–77.

WOODY-RAMSEY, J., & MILLER, P. H. (2000). *Children's individual differences in capacity: Effects on strategy production and utilization.* Under review.

WOOLLEY, J. D. (1995). The fictional mind: Young children's understanding of imagination, pretense, and dreams. *Developmental Review, 15,* 172–211.

WOOLLEY, J. D., & WELLMAN, H. M. (1990). Young children's understanding of realities, nonrealities, and appearances. *Child Development, 61,* 946–961.

WYNN, K. (1990). Children's understanding of counting. *Cognition, 36,* 155–193.

WYNN, K. (1992). Addition and subtraction by human infants. *Nature, 358,* 749–750.

WYNN, K. (1995). Origins of numerical knowledge. *Mathematical Cognition, 1,* 36–60.

WYNN, K. (1996). Infants' individuation and enumeration of sequential actions. *Psychological Science, 7,* 164–169.

WYNN, K. (1998a). An evolved capacity for number. In D. C. Dellarosa & C. Allen (Eds.), *The evolution of mind.* New York: Oxford University Press.

WYNN, K. (1998b). Numerical competence in infants. In C. Donlan (Ed.), *The development of mathematical skills: Studies in developmental psychology.* Hove, UK: Psychology Press.

XU, F., & SPELKE, E. S. (2000). Large number discrimination in 6-month-old infants. *Cognition, 74,* B1–B15.

YONAS, A. (1981). Infants' responses to optical information for collision. In R. N. Aslin, J. R. Alberts, & M. R. Peterson (Eds.), *Development of perception: Psychobiological perspectives: Vol. 2, The visual system.* New York: Academic Press.

YONAS, A., & GRANRUD, C. E. (1985). Development of visual space perception in young infants. In J. Mehler & R. Fox (Eds.), *Neonate cognition.* Hillsdale, NJ: Erlbaum.

YONAS, A., & OWSLEY, C. (1987). Development of visual space perception. In P. Salapatek & L. B. Cohen (Eds.), *Handbook of infant perception: Vol. 2. From perception to cognition.* Orlando, FL: Academic Press.

YOUNGBLADE, L. M., & DUNN, J. (1995). Individual differences in young children's pretend play with mother and sibling: Links to relationships and understanding of other people's feelings and beliefs. *Child Development, 66,* 1472–1492.

YOUNGER, B. A., & COHEN, L. B. (1986). Developmental change in infants' perception of correlations among attributes. *Child Development, 57,* 803–815.

YUILL, N. (1992). Children's conception of personality traits: A critical review and analysis. *Human Development, 35,* 265–279.

YUILL, N. (1997) Children's understanding of traits. In S. Hala (Ed.). *The development of social cognition.* Hove, UK: Psychology Press.

YUSSEN, S. R., & BIRD, J. E. (1979). The development of metacognitive awareness in memory, communication, and attention. *Journal of Experimental Child Psychology, 28,* 300–313.

ZAHN-WAXLER, C., RADKE-YARROW, M., WAGNER, E., & CHAPMAN, M. (1992). Development of concern for others. *Developmental Psychology, 28,* 126–136.

ZARAGOZA, M. S. (1987). Memory, suggestibility, and eyewitness testimony in children and adults. In S. J. Ceci, M. P. Toglia, & D. F. Ross (Eds.). *Children's eyewitness testimony.* New York: Springer-Verlag.

ZARAGOZA, M. S., & WILSON, M. (1989, April). Suggestibility in the child witness. In G. S. Goodman (Chair), *Do children provide accurate eyewitness reports?: Research and social policy implications.* Symposium conducted at the meeting of the Society for Research in Child Development, Kansas City, MO.

ZELAZO, P. D. (1999). Language, levels of consciousness, and the development of intentional action. In P. D. Zelazo, J. W. Astington, & D. R. Olson (Eds), *Developing theories of intention: Social understanding and self.* Mahwah, NJ: Erlbaum.

ZELAZO, P. D., ASTINGTON, J. W., & OLSON, D. R. (Eds.). (1999). *Developing theories of intention.* Mahwah, NJ: Erlbaum.

ZELAZO, P. D., & SHULTZ, T. R. (1989). Concepts of potency and resistance in causal prediction. *Child Development, 60,* 1307–1315.

ZIMMERMAN, B. J., & BLOM, D. E. (1983). Toward an empirical test of cognitive conflict in learning. *Developmental Review, 3,* 18–38.

ZUKOW, P. G., REILLY, J., & GREENFIELD, P. M. (1982). Making the absent present: Facilitating the transition from sensorimotor to linguistic communications. In K. E. Nelson (Ed.), *Children's language* (Vol. 3). Hillsdale, NJ: Erlbaum

Name Index

Subject Index